MORE MONEY THAN GOD

ALSO BY SEBASTIAN MALLABY

The World's Banker: A Story of Failed States, Financial Crises,
and the Wealth and Poverty of Nations

After Apartheid: The Future of South Africa

MORE MONEY THAN GOD

HEDGE FUNDS AND THE
MAKING OF A NEW ELITE

SEBASTIAN MALLABY

A Council on Foreign Relations Book

THE PENGUIN PRESS

New York   2010

THE PENGUIN PRESS
Published by the Penguin Group
Penguin Group (USA) Inc., 375 Hudson Street, New York, New York 10014, U.S.A. • Penguin Group (Canada),
90 Eglinton Avenue East, Suite 700, Toronto, Ontario, Canada M4P 2Y3 (a division of Pearson Penguin Canada Inc.) •
Penguin Books Ltd, 80 Strand, London WC2R 0RL, England • Penguin Ireland, 25 St. Stephen's Green, Dublin 2,
Ireland (a division of Penguin Books Ltd) • Penguin Books Australia Ltd, 250 Camberwell Road, Camberwell,
Victoria 3124, Australia (a division of Pearson Australia Group Pty Ltd) • Penguin Books India Pvt Ltd, 11 Community
Centre, Panchsheel Park, New Delhi – 110 017, India • Penguin Group (NZ), 67 Apollo Drive, Rosedale, North Shore
0632, New Zealand (a division of Pearson New Zealand Ltd) • Penguin Books (South Africa) (Pty) Ltd,
24 Sturdee Avenue, Rosebank, Johannesburg 2196, South Africa

Penguin Books Ltd, Registered Offices:
80 Strand, London WC2R 0RL, England

First Published in 2010 by The Penguin Press,
a member of Penguin Group (USA) Inc.

The Council on Foreign Relations (CFR) is an independent, nonpartisan membership organization, think tank, and publisher dedicated to being a resource for its members, government officials, business executives, journalists, educators and students, civic and religious leaders, and other interested citizens in order to help them better understand the world and the foreign policy choices facing the United States and other countries. Founded in 1921, CFR carries out its mission by maintaining a diverse membership, with special programs to promote interest and develop expertise in the next generation of foreign policy leaders; convening meetings at its headquarters in New York and in Washington, DC, and other cities where senior government officials, members of Congress, global leaders, and prominent thinkers come together with CFR members to discuss and debate major international issues; supporting a Studies Program that fosters independent research, enabling CFR scholars to produce articles, reports, and books and hold roundtables that analyze foreign policy issues and make concrete policy recommendations; publishing *Foreign Affairs*, the preeminent journal on international affairs and U.S. foreign policy; sponsoring Independent Task Forces that produce reports with both findings and policy prescriptions on the most important foreign policy topics; and providing up-to-date information and analysis about world events and American foreign policy on its website, www.cfr.org.

The Council on Foreign Relations takes no institutional position on policy issues and has no affiliation with the U.S. government. All statements of fact and expressions of opinion contained in its publications are the sole responsibility of the author or authors.

Photograph credits appear on page 483.

Library of Congress Cataloging-in-Publication Data

Mallaby, Sebastian.
More money than god : hedge funds and the making of a new elite / Sebastian Mallaby.
p. cm.
Includes bibliographical references and index.
ISBN 978-1-59420-255-1
1. Hedge funds.   2. Investment advisors.   I. Title.
HG4530.M249 2010
332.64'524—dc22
2009053253

Printed in the United States of America
1   3   5   7   9   10   8   6   4   2

DESIGNED BY MEIGHAN CAVANAUGH

To my parents, Christopher and Pascale

CONTENTS

INTRODUCTION:
THE ALPHA GAME

The first hedge-fund manager, Alfred Winslow Jones, did not go to business school. He did not possess a PhD in quantitative finance. He did not spend his formative years at Morgan Stanley, Goldman Sachs, or any other incubator for masters of the universe. Instead, he took a job on a tramp steamer, studied at the Marxist Workers School in Berlin, and ran secret missions for a clandestine anti-Nazi group called the Leninist Organization. He married, divorced, and married again, honeymooning on the front lines of the civil war in Spain, traveling and drinking with Dorothy Parker and Ernest Hemingway. It was only at the advanced age of forty-eight that Jones raked together $100,000 to set up a "hedged fund," generating extraordinary profits through the 1950s and 1960s. Almost by accident, Jones improvised an investment structure that has endured to this day. It will thrive for years to come, despite a cacophony of naysayers.

Half a century after Jones created his hedge fund, a young man named Clifford Asness followed in his footsteps. Asness did attend a business school. He did acquire a PhD in quantitative finance. He did work for Goldman Sachs, and he was a master of the universe. Whereas Jones had launched his venture in his mature, starched-collar years, Asness rushed into the business at the grand old age of thirty-one, beating all records for a new start-up by raising an eye-popping $1 billion. Whereas Jones had been discreet about his methods and the riches that they brought, Asness was refreshingly open, tearing up his schedule to do TV interviews and confessing to the *New York Times* that "it doesn't suck" to be worth millions.[1] By the eve of the subprime mortgage crash in 2007, Asness's firm, AQR Capital Management, was running a remarkable $38 billion and Asness himself personified the new globe-changing finance. He was irreverent, impatient, and scarcely even bothered to pretend to be grown up. He had a collection of plastic superheroes in his office.[2]

Asness freely recognized his debt to Jones's improvisation. His hedge funds, like just about all hedge funds, embraced four features that Jones had combined to spectacular effect. To begin with, there was a performance fee: Jones kept one fifth of the fund's investment profits for himself and his team, a formula that sharpened the incentives of his lieutenants. Next, Jones made a conscious effort to avoid regulatory red tape, preserving the flexibility to shape-shift from one investment method to the next as market opportunities mutated. But most important, from Asness's perspective, were two ideas that had framed Jones's investment portfolio. Jones had balanced purchases of promising shares with "short selling" of unpromising ones, meaning that he borrowed and sold them, betting that they would fall in value. By being "long" some stocks and "short" others, he insulated his fund at least partially from general market swings; and having hedged out market risk in this fashion, he felt safe in magnifying, or "leveraging," his bets with borrowed money. As we will see in the next chapter, this combination of hedging and leverage had a magical effect on Jones's portfolio of stocks. But its true genius was the one that Asness emphasized later: The same combination could be applied to bonds, futures, swaps, and options—and indeed to any mixture of these instruments. More by luck than by design, Jones had invented a platform for strategies more complex than he himself could dream of.

No definition of hedge funds is perfect, and not all the adventures recounted in this book involve hedging and leverage. When George Soros and Stan Druckenmiller broke the British pound, or when John Paulson shorted the mortgage bubble in the United States, there was no particular need to hedge—as we shall see later. When an intrepid commodities player negotiated the purchase of the Russian government's entire stock of non-gold precious metals, leverage mattered less than the security around the armored train that was to bring the palladium from Siberia. But even when hedge funds are not using leverage and not actually hedging, the platform created by A. W. Jones has proved exceptionally congenial. The freedom to go long and short in any financial instrument in any country allows hedge funds to seize opportunities wherever they exist. The ability to leverage allows hedge funds to size each bet to maximum effect. Performance fees create a powerful incentive to coin money.

Ah yes, that money! At his death in 1913, J. Pierpont Morgan had accumulated a fortune of $1.4 billion in today's dollars, earning the nickname "Jupiter" because of his godlike power over Wall Street. But in the bubbly first years of this century, the top hedge-fund managers amassed more money than God in a couple of years of trading. They earned more—vastly more—than the captains of Wall Street's mightiest investment banks and eclipsed even private-equity barons. In 2006 Goldman Sachs awarded its chief executive, Lloyd C. Blankfein, an unprecedented $54 million, but the *bottom guy* on *Alpha* magazine's list of the top twenty-five hedge-fund earners reportedly took home $240 million. That same year, the leading private-equity partnership, Blackstone Group, rewarded its boss, Stephen Schwarzman, with just under $400 million. But the top three hedge-fund moguls each were said to have earned more than $1 billion.[3] The compensation formula devised by Jones conjured up hundreds of fast fortunes, not to mention hundreds of fast cars in the suburbs of Connecticut. Reporting from the epicenter of this gold rush, the *Stamford Advocate* observed that six local hedge-fund managers had pocketed a combined $2.15 billion in 2006. The total personal income of all the people in Connecticut came to $150 billion.

In the 1990s magazines drooled over the extravagance of dot-com millionaires, but now the spotlight was on hedge funds. Ken Griffin, the creator of Citadel Investment Group, bought himself a $50 million Bombardier Express private jet and had it fitted with a crib for his two-year-old. Louis Bacon, the founder of Moore Capital, acquired an island in the

Great Peconic Bay, put transmitters on the local mud turtles to monitor their mating habits, and hosted traditional English pheasant shoots. Steven Cohen, the boss of SAC Capital, equipped his estate with a basketball court, an indoor pool, a skating rink, a two-hole golf course, an organic vegetable plot, paintings by van Gogh and Pollock, a sculpture by Keith Haring, and a movie theater decorated with the pattern of the stars on his wedding night sixteen years earlier. The hedge-fund titans were the new Rockefellers, the new Carnegies, the new Vanderbilts. They were the new American elite—the latest act in the carnival of creativity and greed that powers the nation forward.

And what an elite this was. Hedge funds are the vehicles for loners and contrarians, for individualists whose ambitions are too big to fit into established financial institutions. Cliff Asness is a case in point. He had been a rising star at Goldman Sachs, but he opted for the freedom and rewards of running his own shop; a man who collects plastic superheroes is not going to remain a salaried antihero for long, at least not if he can help it. Jim Simons of Renaissance Technologies, the mathematician who emerged in the 2000s as the highest earner in the industry, would not have lasted at a mainstream bank: He took orders from nobody, seldom wore socks, and got fired from the Pentagon's code-cracking center after denouncing his bosses' Vietnam policy. Ken Griffin of Citadel, the second highest earner in 2006, started out trading convertible bonds from his dorm room at Harvard; he was the boy genius made good, the financial version of the entreprenerds who forged tech companies such as Google. The earliest pioneers of the industry were cut from equally bright cloth. Julian Robertson staffed his hedge fund with college athletes half his age; then he flew them out to various retreats in the Rockies and raced them up the mountains. Michael Steinhardt was capable of reducing underlings to sobs. "All I want to do is kill myself," one said. "Can I watch?" Steinhardt responded.[4]

Like the Rockefellers and Carnegies before them, the new moguls made their mark on the world beyond business and finance. George Soros was the most ambitious in his reach: His charities fostered independent voices in the emerging ex-communist nations; they pushed for the decriminalization of drugs; they funded a rethink of laissez-faire economics. Paul

Tudor Jones, the founder of Tudor Investment Corporation, created Robin Hood, one of the first "venture philanthropies" to fight poverty in New York City: It identified innovative charities, set demanding benchmarks for progress, and paid for performance. Bruce Kovner emerged as a godfather of the neoconservative movement, chairing the American Enterprise Institute in Washington, D.C.; Michael Steinhardt bankrolled efforts to create a new secular Judaism. But of course it was in finance that these egos made the most impact. The story of hedge funds is the story of the frontiers of finance: of innovation and increasing leverage, of spectacular triumphs and humiliating falls, and of the debates spawned by these dramas.

For much of their history, hedge funds have skirmished with the academic view of markets. Of course, academia is a broad church, teaming with energetic skeptics. But from the mid 1960s to the mid 1980s, the prevailing view was that the market is efficient, prices follow a random walk, and hedge funds succeed mainly by being lucky. There is a powerful logic to this account. If it were possible to know with any confidence that the price of a particular bond or equity is likely to move up, smart investors would have pounced and it would have moved up already. Pouncing investors ensure that all relevant information is already in prices, though the next move of a stock will be determined by something unexpected. It follows that professional money managers who try to foresee price moves will generally fail in their mission. As this critique anticipates, plenty of hedge funds have no real "edge"—if you strip away the marketing hype and occasional flashes of dumb luck, there is no distinctive investment insight that allows them to beat the market consistently. But for the successful funds that dominate the industry, the efficient-market indictment is wrong. These hedge funds could drop their *h* and be called edge funds.

Where does this edge come from? Sometimes it consists simply of picking the best stocks. Despite everything that the finance literature asserts, A. W. Jones, Julian Robertson, and many Robertson protégés clearly did add value in this way, as we shall see presently. But frequently the edge consists of exploiting kinks in the efficient-market theory that its proponents conceded at the start, even though they failed to emphasize them.

The theorists stipulated, for example, that prices would be efficient only if liquidity was perfect—a seller who offers a stock at the efficient price should always be able to find a buyer, since otherwise he will be forced to offer a discount, rendering the price lower than the efficient level. But in the 1970s and 1980s, a big pension fund that wanted to dump a large block of shares could not actually find a buyer unless it offered a discount. Michael Steinhardt made his fortune by milking these discounts in a systematic way. An unassuming footnote in the efficient-market view became the basis for a hedge-fund legend.

The nature of hedge funds' true edge is often obscured by their bosses' pronouncements. The titans sometimes seem like mystic geniuses: They rack up glorious returns but cannot explain how they did it.[5] Perhaps the most extreme version of this problem is presented by the young Paul Tudor Jones. To this day, Jones maintains that he anticipated the 1987 crash because his red-suspendered, twentysomething colleague, Peter Borish, had mapped the 1980s market against the charts leading up to 1929; seeing that the two lines looked the same, Jones realized that the break was coming. But this explanation of Jones's brilliant market timing is inadequate, to say the least. For one thing, Borish admitted to massaging the data to make the two lines fit.[6] For another, he predicted that the crash would hit in the spring of 1988; if Jones had really followed Borish's counsel, he would have been wiped out when the crash arrived the previous October. In short, Jones succeeded for reasons that we will explore later, not for the reasons that he cites. The lesson is that genius does not always understand itself—a lesson, incidentally, that is not confined to finance. "Out of all the research that we've done with top players, we haven't found a single player who is consistent in knowing and explaining exactly what he does," the legendary tennis coach Vic Braden once complained. "They give different answers at different times, or they have answers that simply are not meaningful."[7]

Starting in the 1980s, financial academics came around to the view that markets were not so efficient after all. Sometimes their conversions were deliciously perfect. A young economist named Scott Irwin procured an especially detailed price series for commodity markets from a small firm in Indianapolis, and after painstaking analysis he proclaimed that prices moved in trends—the changes were not random. Little did he know that, almost twenty years earlier, a pioneering hedge fund called Commodities Corporation had analyzed the same data, reached the same conclusion, and programmed a computer to trade on it. Meanwhile, other researchers acknowledged that markets were not perfectly liquid, as Steinhardt had discovered long before, and that investors were not perfectly rational, a truism to hedge-fund traders. The crash of 1987 underlined these doubts: When the market's valuation of corporate America changed by a fifth in a single trading day, it was hard to believe that the valuation deserved much deference. "If the efficient markets hypothesis was a publicly traded security, its price would be enormously volatile," the Harvard economists Andrei Shleifer and Lawrence Summers wrote mockingly in 1990. "But the stock in the efficient markets hypothesis—at least as it has traditionally been formulated—crashed along with the rest of the market on October 19, 1987."[8]

The acknowledgment of the limits to market efficiency had a profound effect on hedge funds. Before, the prevailing line from the academy had been that hedge funds would fail. After, lines of academics were queuing up to join them. If markets were inefficient, there was money to be made, and the finance professors saw no reason why they should not be the ones to profit. Cliff Asness was fairly typical of the new wave. At the University of Chicago's Graduate School of Business, his thesis adviser was Eugene Fama, one of the fathers of the efficient-market hypothesis. But by 1988, when Asness arrived in Chicago, Fama was leading the revisionist charge: Along with a younger colleague, Kenneth French, Fama discovered non-random patterns in markets that could be lucrative for traders. After contributing to this literature, Asness headed off to Wall Street and soon opened his hedge fund. In similar fashion, the Nobel laureates Myron Scholes and Robert Merton, whose formula for pricing options grew out of the efficient-markets school, signed up with the hedge fund Long-Term Capital Management. Andrei Shleifer, the Harvard economist who had compared the efficient-market theory to a crashing stock, helped to create an investment company called LSV with two fellow finance professors.

His coauthor, Lawrence Summers, made the most of a gap between stints
as president of Harvard and economic adviser to President Obama to sign
on with D. E. Shaw, a quantitative hedge fund.[9]

Yet the biggest effect of the new inefficient-market consensus was not
that academics flocked to hedge funds. It was that institutional investors
acquired a license to entrust vast amounts of capital to them. Again, the
years after the 1987 crash were an inflection point. Before, most money
in hedge funds had come from rich individuals, who presumably had not
heard academia's message that it was impossible to beat the market. After,
most money in hedge funds came from endowments, which had been told
by their learned consultants that the market could be beaten—and which
wanted in on the action. The new wave was led by David Swensen, the
boss of the Yale endowment, who focused on two things. If there were systematic patterns in markets of the sort that Fama, French, and Asness had
identified, then hedge funds could milk these in a systematic way: There
were strategies that could be expected to do well, and they could be identified prospectively. Further, the profits from these strategies would be more
than just good on their own terms. They would reduce an endowment's
overall risk through the magic of diversification. The funds that Swensen
invested in were certainly diverse: In 2002, a swashbuckling West Coast
fund named Farallon swooped into Indonesia and bought the country's
largest bank, undeterred by the fact that a currency collapse, a political
revolution, and Islamist extremism had scared most westerners out of the
country. Following Swensen's example, endowments poured money into
hedge funds from the 1990s on, seeking the uncorrelated returns that
endowment gurus called "alpha."

The new inefficient-market view also imbued hedge funds with a
social function. This was the last thing they had sought: They had gotten
into the alpha game with one purpose above all, and that was to make
money. But if alpha existed because markets were inefficient, it followed
that savings were being allocated in an irrational manner. The research of
Fama and French, for example, showed that unglamorous "value" stocks
were underpriced relative to overhyped "growth" stocks. This meant that
capital was being provided too expensively to solid, workhorse firms and

too cheaply to their flashier rivals: Opportunities for growth were being squandered. Similarly, the discounts in block trading showed that prices could be capricious in small ways, raising risks to investors, who in turn raised the premium that they charged to users of their capital. It was the function of hedge funds to correct inefficiencies like these. By buying value stocks and shorting growth stocks, Cliff Asness was doing his part to reduce the unhealthy bias against solid, workhorse firms. By buying Ford's stock when it dipped illogically after a large-block sale, Michael Steinhardt was ensuring that the grandma who owned a piece of Ford could always count on getting a fair price for it. By computerizing Steinhardt's art, statistical arbitrageurs such as Jim Simons and David Shaw were taking his mission to the next level. The more markets could be rendered efficient, the more capital would flow to its most productive uses. The less prices got out of line, the less risk there would presumably be of financial bubbles—and so of sharp, destabilizing corrections. By flattening out the kinks in market behavior, hedge funds were contributing to what economists called the "Great Moderation."

But hedge funds also raised an unsettling question. If markets were prone to wild bubbles and crashes, might not the wildest players render the turbulence still crazier? In 1994, the Federal Reserve announced a tiny one-quarter-of-a-percentage-point rise in short-term interest rates, and the bond market went into a mad spin; leveraged hedge funds had been wrong-footed by the move, and they began dumping positions furiously. Foreshadowing future financial panics, the turmoil spread from the United States to Japan, Europe, and the emerging world; several hedge funds sank, and for a few hours it even looked as though the storied firm of Bankers Trust might be dragged down with them. As if this were not warning enough, the world was treated to another hedge-fund failure four years later, when Long-Term Capital Management and its crew of Nobel laureates went bust; terrified that a chaotic bankruptcy would topple Lehman Brothers and other dominoes besides, panicked regulators rushed in to oversee LTCM's burial. Meanwhile, hedge funds wreaked havoc with exchange-rate policies in Europe and Asia. After the East Asian crisis, Malaysia's prime minister, Mahathir Mohamad, lamented that "all these countries have spent years trying to build up their economies and a moron like Soros comes along with a lot of money to speculate and ruins things."[10]

And so, by the start of the twenty-first century, there were two competing views of hedge funds. Sometimes the funds were celebrated as the stabilizing heroes who muscled inefficient prices into line. Sometimes they were vilified as the weak links whose own instability or wanton aggression threatened the global economy. The heart of the matter was the leverage embraced by A. W. Jones—or rather, a vastly expanded version of it. Leverage gave hedge funds the ammunition to trade in greater volume, and so to render prices more efficient and stable. But leverage also made hedge funds vulnerable to shocks: If their trades moved against them, they could burn through thin cushions of capital at lightning speed, obliging them to dump positions fast—*destabilizing* prices.[11] After the bond-market meltdown of 1994 and the Long-Term Capital failure in 1998, the two competing views of hedge funds wrestled to a stalemate. In the United States and Britain, hedge funds' stabilizing impact received the most emphasis; elsewhere, the risk of destabilizing panics got most of the attention. Funnily enough, the countries that liked hedge funds the best were also the ones that hosted them.

Then came the crisis of 2007–2009, and every judgment about finance was thrown into question. Whereas the market disruptions of the 1990s could be viewed as a tolerable price to pay for the benefits of sophisticated and leveraged finance, the convulsion of 2007–2009 triggered the sharpest recession since the 1930s. Inevitably, hedge funds were caught up in the panic. In July 2007, a credit hedge fund called Sowood blew up, and the following month a dozen or so quantitative hedge funds tried to cut their positions all at once, triggering wild swings in the equity market and billions of dollars of losses. The following year was more brutal by far. The collapse of Lehman Brothers left some hedge funds with money trapped inside the bankrupt shell, and the turmoil that followed inflicted losses on most others. Hedge funds needed access to leverage, but nobody lent to anyone in the weeks after the Lehman shock. Hedge funds built their strategies on short selling, but governments imposed clumsy restrictions on shorting amid the post-Lehman panic. Hedge funds were reliant upon the patience of their investors, who could yank their money out on short notice. But patience ended abruptly when markets went into a tailspin. Investors demanded their capital back, and some funds withheld it by imposing "gates." Surely now it was obvious that the risks posed by hedge funds outweighed the benefits? Far from bringing about the Great Moderation, they had helped to trigger the Great Cataclysm.

This conclusion, though tempting, is almost certainly mistaken. The cataclysm has indeed shown that the financial system is broken, but it has not actually shown that hedge funds are the problem. It has demonstrated, to begin with, that central banks may have to steer economies in a new way: Rather than targeting consumer-price inflation and turning a blind eye to asset-price inflation, they must try to let the air out of bubbles—a lesson first suggested, incidentally, by the hedge-fund blowup of 1994. If the Fed had curbed leverage and raised interest rates in the mid 2000s, there would have been less craziness up and down the chain. American households would not have increased their borrowing from 66 percent of GDP in 1997 to 100 percent a decade later. Housing finance companies would not have sold so many mortgages regardless of borrowers' ability to repay. Fannie Mae and Freddie Mac, the two government-chartered home lenders, would almost certainly not have collapsed into the arms of the government. Banks like Citigroup and broker-dealers like Merrill Lynch would not have gorged so greedily on mortgage-backed securities that ultimately went bad, squandering their capital. The Fed allowed this binge of borrowing because it was focused resolutely on consumer-price inflation, and because it believed it could ignore bubbles safely. The carnage of 2007–2009 demonstrated how wrong that was. Presented with an opportunity to borrow at near zero cost, people borrowed unsustainably.

The crisis has also shown that financial firms are riddled with dysfunctional incentives. The clearest problem is "too big to fail"—Wall Street behemoths load up on risk because they expect taxpayers to bail them out, and other market players are happy to abet this recklessness because they also believe in the government backstop. But this too-big-to-fail problem exists primarily at institutions that the government has actually rescued: commercial banks such as Citigroup; former investment banks such as

Goldman Sachs and Morgan Stanley; insurers such as AIG; the money-market funds that received an emergency government guarantee at the height of the crisis. By contrast, hedge funds made it through the mayhem without receiving any direct taxpayer assistance: There is no precedent that says that the government stands behind them. Even when Long-Term Capital collapsed in 1998, the Fed oversaw its burial but provided no money to cover its losses. At some point in the future, a supersized hedge fund may prove to be too big to fail, which is why the largest and most leveraged should be subject to regulation. But the great majority of hedge funds are too small to threaten the broader financial system. They are safe to fail, even if they are not fail-safe.[12]

The other skewed incentive in finance involves traders' pay packages. When traders take enormous risks, they earn fortunes if the bets pay off. But if the bets go wrong, they don't endure symmetrical punishment—the performance fees and bonuses dry up, but they do not go negative. Again, this heads-I-win-tails-you-lose problem is sharper at banks than at hedge funds. Hedge funds tend to have "high-water marks": If they lose money one year, they take reduced or even no performance fees until they earn back their losses. Hedge-fund bosses mostly have their own money in their funds, so they are speculating with capital that is at least partly their own—a powerful incentive to avoid losses. By contrast, bank traders generally face fewer such restraints; they are simply risking other people's money. Perhaps it is no surprise that the typical hedge fund is far more cautious in its use of leverage than the typical bank. The average hedge fund borrows only one or two times its investors' capital, and even those that are considered highly leveraged generally borrow less than ten times. Meanwhile investment banks such as Goldman Sachs or Lehman Brothers were leveraged thirty to one before the crisis, and commercial banks like Citi were even higher by some measures.[13]

The very structure of hedge funds promotes a paranoid discipline. Banks tend to be establishment institutions with comfortable bosses; hedge funds tend to be scrappy upstarts with bosses who think nothing of staying up all night to see a deal close. Banks collect savings from households with the help of government deposit insurance; hedge funds have to demonstrate that they can manage risk before they can raise money from clients. Banks know that if they face a liquidity crisis they have access to the central bank's emergency lending, so they are willing to rely heavily on short-term loans; hedge funds have no such safety net, so they are increasingly reluctant to depend on short-term lending. Banks take the view that everything is going wonderfully so long as borrowers repay; hedge funds mark their portfolios to market, meaning that slight blips in the risk that borrowers will hit trouble in the future can affect the hedge funds' bottom line immediately.[14] Banks' investment judgment is often warped by their pursuit of underwriting or advisory fees; hedge funds live and die by their investment performance, so they are less distracted and conflicted. For all these reasons, a proper definition of hedge funds should stress their independence. So-called hedge funds that are the subsidiaries of large banks lack the paranoia and focus that give true hedge funds their special character.

As I finished writing this book, in early 2010, regulators seemed poised to clamp down on the financial industry. To a large extent, their instincts were right: At their peak, financial companies hogged more human capital than they deserved, and they took risks that cost societies dearly. But Wall Street's critics should pause before they sweep hedge funds into their net. Who, in the final analysis, will manage risk better? Commercial banks and investment banks, which either blew up or were bailed out by the government? Mutual-fund companies, which peddled money-market products that the government was forced to backstop? And which sort of future do the critics favor: one in which risk is concentrated inside giant banks for which taxpayers are on the hook, or one in which risk is dispersed across smaller hedge funds that expect no lifelines from the government? The crisis has compounded the moral hazard at the heart of finance: Banks that have been rescued can expect to be rescued all over again the next time they blow up; because of that expectation, they have weak incentives to avoid excessive risks, making blowup all too likely. Capitalism works only when institutions are forced to absorb the consequences of the risks that they take on. When banks can pocket the upside while spreading the cost of their failures, failure is almost certain.

If they are serious about learning from the 2007–2009 crisis, policy makers need to restrain financial supermarkets with confused and overlapping objectives, encouraging focused boutiques that live or die according to the soundness of their risk management. They need to shift capital out of institutions underwritten by taxpayers and into ones that stand on their own feet. They need to shrink institutions that are too big to fail and favor ones that are small enough to go under. The story of A. W. Jones and his successors shows that a partial alternative to banking supermarkets already exists. To a surprising and unrecognized degree, the future of finance lies in the history of hedge funds.

1

BIG DADDY

t the dawn of America's second gilded age, and on the eve of the twenty-first century's first financial crash, the managers of a few dozen hedge funds emerged as the unofficial kings of capitalism. Globalization was generating unheralded prosperity; and the prosperity was generating deep pools of wealth; and the wealth was being parked in quiet funds, whose managers profited mightily. Just in the three years from 2003 to 2006, the volume of money in the top one hundred hedge funds doubled to $1 trillion[1]—enough to buy all shares listed on the Shanghai Stock Exchange or an entire year's worth of output from the Canadian economy. Nobody doubted that this hedge-fund phenomenon was new, unprecedented, and symbolic of the era. "Running a few hundred million dollars for a hedge fund—and taking tens of millions for yourself—has become the going Wall Street dream," one magazine writer declared.[2] "Hedge funds are the ultimate in today's stock market—the logical extension of the current gun-slinging, go-go cult of success," according to another.[3]

But hedge funds are not new, and not unprecedented; and whereas the first line just quoted comes from a *New York* magazine article published in 2004, the second comes from a remarkably similar essay, also in *New York* magazine, published four decades earlier. The 2004 article gushed that hedge-fund managers are the type who can "call the direction of the market correctly 22 days in a row." The 1968 version invoked "the hedge fund guy who made 20 percent on his money in a week, for *seven* weeks in a row." The 2004 essay complained of hedge funds that "in addition to being arrogant and insular, they're also clandestine." The 1968 version said peevishly that "most people involved in hedge funds are reluctant to talk about their success." If hedge-fund managers had emerged as the It Boys of the new century—if they had supplanted the leveraged-buyout barons of the 1980s and the dot-com wizards of the 1990s—it was worth remembering that they were also the hot stars of an earlier era. A hedge-fund manager "can be away from the market and still know where its rhythm and his are meshing," according to a famous account of the 1960s boom. *"If you really know what's going on, you don't even have to know what's going on to know what's going on . . .* You can ignore the headlines, because you anticipated them months ago."[4]

The largest legend of the first hedge-fund era was Alfred Winslow Jones, the founding father whom we have encountered already. He was described in *New York* magazine's 1968 essay as the "big daddy" of the industry, but he was an unlikely Wall Street patriarch; like many of the hedge-fund titans of a future age, he changed the nature of finance while standing somewhat aloof from it. In 1949, when Jones invented his "hedged fund," the profession of money management was dominated by starchy, conservative types, known tellingly as "trustees"—their job was merely to conserve capital, not to seek to grow it. The leading money-management companies had names like Fidelity and Prudential, and they behaved that way too: A good trustee was, in the words of the writer John Brooks, "a model of unassailable probity and sobriety; his white hair neatly but not too neatly combed; his blue Yankee eyes untwinkling."[5] But Jones was cut from different cloth. By the time he turned his hand to finance, he had experimented restlessly with multiple careers. He kept the company of writers and artists, not all of them sober. And although he was to become the father of hypercapitalist hedge funds, he had spent a good portion of his youth flirting with Marxism.

Jones was born in the ninth hour of the ninth day of the ninth month of 1900—a fact with which he would bore his family years later.[6] He was the son of an expatriate American who ran the Australian operations of General Electric; according to Jones family lore, they owned the first car in Australia. A formal photograph from the time shows the three-year-old Alfred wearing a white sailor cap with a white jacket; on one side of him sits his father in a stiff, winged collar, on the other side is his mother in an elaborate feathered hat. After the family returned to GE's company headquarters in Schenectady, New York, Alfred went to school there and followed in the family tradition by attending Harvard. But when he graduated in 1923, he was at a loss for what to do; none of the obvious career paths for a gifted scion of the Ivy League appealed to him. The Jazz Age was beginning its ascent; F. Scott Fitzgerald was conjuring the dissolute antiheroes of *The Great Gatsby*; slim, tall, with soft features and thick hair, Jones would have fitted into Fitzgerald's world with little difficulty. But Jones had other ideas about his life. Having inherited the wanderlust of his father, he signed on as a purser on a tramp steamer and spent a year touring the world. He took a job as an export buyer and another as a statistician for an investment counselor. And then, after drifting aimlessly some more, he took the foreign-service exam and joined the State Department.[7]

Jones was immediately posted to Berlin, arriving as America's vice-consul in December 1930. Germany's economy was in free fall: Output had shrunk 8 percent that year, and unemployment stood at 4.5 million. In the elections three months earlier, the little-known National Socialist Party had capitalized on popular fury, winning 107 seats in the Reichstag.[8] Jones's work brought him face to face with Germany's troubles: He wrote two studies on the conditions of Germany's workers, one dealing with their access to food and a second with housing. But his engagement with Germany became intense when he met Anna Block, a socialite and left-wing anti-Nazi activist. The daughter of a Jewish banking family, Anna was attractive, flirtatious, and resourceful: For a while she escaped Nazi detection by operating out of the maternity wing of a Berlin hospital; and years later, when she was involved in the Paris underground, she bet that she could bluff her way into the finest London hotel, equipped only with a cardboard box as her luggage. When Jones met Anna in 1931, she was working for a group called the Leninist Organization and bent on finding a third husband. Captivated by Anna's heady mix of socialist engagement and bourgeois charm, Jones became the servant of her purposes, political and personal.[9]

Jones married Anna in secret, but the union was soon discovered by his embassy colleagues. The breach forced his resignation from the State Department in May 1932, just a year and a half after joining. But his involvement with Germany did not end there. He returned to Berlin in the fall of 1932, operating under the pseudonym "Richard Frost" and working secretly for the Leninist Organization.[10] The next year he represented the group in London, assuming the cover name "H. B. Wood" and seeking to persuade the British Labour Party, which was tinged with pacifism, to wake up to the need for military action against Hitler. The British authorities grew suspicious of Jones's activities, all the more so when they discovered that he had attended the Marxist Workers School in Berlin, which was organized by the German Communist Party. "It is understood that Mr. Jones expressed an interest in communism while connected with the Foreign Service," a State Department official wrote in response to an urgent query from London.[11]

The German resistance to Hitler proved more romantic than practical. The same could also have been said of Jones's relationship with Anna. The couple divorced after a few months, and Jones left London for New York in 1934, enrolling as a graduate student in sociology at Columbia University and marrying Mary Elizabeth Carter, a middle-class plantation girl from Virginia.[12] But if Jones's life seemed to be shifting into conventional channels, the shift was not complete. He maintained his connections to the German Left through the 1930s and early 1940s and may have been involved in U.S. intelligence operations.[13] After his marriage to Mary, he set off in 1937 for a honeymoon in war-torn Spain.[14] The newlyweds hitchhiked to the front lines with the writer Dorothy Parker. They encountered Ernest Hemingway, who treated them to a bottle of Scotch whiskey.

———

THE DISINTEGRATION OF EUROPE THAT JONES HAD WIT-
nessed, first in Germany and then in Spain, was an extreme version of the
turmoil in his own country. The America of *The Great Gatsby* had given
way to the America of John Steinbeck's *The Grapes of Wrath*; the Jazz Age
had given way to the Depression. On Wall Street, the crash of October
1929 was followed by a series of collapses in the early 1930s. Investors fled
the market in droves, and the bustling brokerages fell quiet; it was said
that you could walk the famous canyons near the stock exchange and
hear only the rattle of backgammon dice through the open windows.[15]
But what is striking about Jones, given his youthful adventures with the
undercover Left, is that he emerged from this turmoil more levelheaded
than before. He grappled ambitiously with the biggest questions of his
age, but his conclusions tended to be moderate.

Jones's politics emerged from his writings as a sociologist and journalist. In the late 1930s, as the Nazi menace spread across Europe, Jones
plunged into the research for his doctoral thesis, motivated by a desire
to understand whether the same calamity could befall his own country.[16]
His thesis topic reflected the preoccupation of the political Left with class
structure. He was bent on teasing out the links between Americans' economic conditions and their attitudes toward property; his purpose was "to
help find out to what extent, in our basic ideas, we are a united people, and
to what extent we are a house divided."[17] In late 1938 and early 1939, Jones
decamped with Mary to a hotbed of industrial conflict, Akron, Ohio, and
organized a team of assistants to conduct 1,700 field interviews. Subject-
ing his interview results to a series of statistical tests, he concluded that
acute economic divisions did not actually carry over into polarized world-
views. It was a repudiation of the socialist assumptions of his youth and a
testimony to the vitality of American democracy.

Jones's thesis, which appeared as a book titled *Life, Liberty and Property*
in 1941, became a standard sociology textbook. Meanwhile it served to
launch Jones on yet another career—this time as a journalist. *Fortune*
magazine published the thesis in condensed form and also offered Jones a

job; he signed on happily, even though he found writing a hard process. In an essay published in 1942, Jones gave warning that Roosevelt's economic statism would need to be dismantled once the war ended.[18] His respect for the market, which confirmed his retreat from socialism toward the political center, was mixed with continued interest in redistributive programs. "The ideal," he wrote in *Fortune,* was a sort of left-right blend: *"As conservative as possible in protecting the free market and as radical as necessary in securing the welfare of the people."*

In 1948 a writing assignment for *Fortune* gave Jones the opportunity to turn his mind to finance, a subject he had largely ignored since his stint with an investment counselor two decades earlier. The resulting essay, which appeared in March 1949 under the title "Fashions in Forecasting," anticipated many of the hedge funds that came after him. The essay started out by attacking the "standard, old-fashioned method of predicting the course of the stock market," which was to examine freight-car loadings, commodity prices, and other economic data to determine how stocks ought to be priced. This approach to market valuation failed to capture much of what was going on: Jones cited moments when stocks had shifted sharply in the absence of changed economic data. Having dismissed fundamental analysis, Jones turned his attention to what he believed was a more profitable premise: the notion that stock prices were driven by predictable patterns in investor psychology. Money might be an abstraction, a series of numerical symbols, but it was also a medium through which greed and fear and jealousy expressed themselves; it was a barometer of crowd psychology.[19] Perhaps it was natural that a sociologist should find this hypothesis attractive.

Jones believed that investor emotions created trends in stock prices. A rise in the stock market generates investor optimism, which in turn generates a further rise in the market, which generates further optimism, and so on; and this feedback loop drives stock prices up, creating a trend that can be followed profitably. The trick is to bail out at the moment when the psychology turns around—when the feedback loop has driven prices to an unsustainable level, and greed turns to fear, and there is a reversal of the pendulum. The forecasters whom Jones profiled in *Fortune* offered fresh methods for catching these tipping points. Some believed that if the Dow Jones index was rising while most individual stocks were falling, the rally was about to peter out. Others argued that if stock prices were rising but trading volume was falling, the bull market was running out of buyers and the tide would soon reverse. All shared the view that stock charts held the secret to financial success, because the patterns in the charts repeated themselves.

In his deference to chart-watching forecasters, Jones seemed oddly ignorant of academic economics. In 1933 and 1944, Alfred Cowles, one of the fathers of statistical economics, had published two studies reviewing thousands of investment recommendations issued by financial practitioners. The first of these two articles was titled "Can Stock Market Forecasters Forecast?" The three-word abstract answered the question: "It is doubtful." Jones cited Cowles's work selectively in *Fortune*, mentioning in passing that the master had found evidence of trends in monthly prices. He neglected to mention that Cowles had found no trends when he examined prices reported at three-week intervals, nor did he say that Cowles had concluded that any appearance of patterns in markets was too faint and unreliable to be traded upon profitably.[20] Yet despite Jones's superficial reading of Cowles, there was at least one point on which the two saw eye to eye: Both believed that successful market forecasters could not sustain their performance. The very act of forecasting a trend was likely to destroy it. Suppose, for example, that a financial seer could tell when an upward trend was going to be sustained for several days until the market hit a certain level. Money would follow this advice, pushing up prices to the predicted level straight away and cutting the trend off in its infancy. In this way, the forecasters would speed up the workings of the market while working themselves out of a job. As Jones concluded in his *Fortune* piece, the price trends would cease. The market would be left to "fluctuate in a relatively gentle, orderly way to accommodate itself to fundamental economic changes only."

To an extent that he could not possibly have foreseen, Jones was anticipating the history of hedge funds. Over the succeeding decades, wave upon wave of financial innovators spotted opportunities to profit from

markets, and many of them found that once their insight had been understood by a sufficient number of investors, the profit opportunity faded
because the markets had grown more efficient. In the 1950s and 1960s,
Jones himself was destined to impose a new efficiency upon markets. But
the nature of that change was not at all what he expected.

BY THE TIME THE *FORTUNE* ESSAY APPEARED IN MARCH
1949, Jones had launched the world's first hedge fund. It was not that
he had suddenly turned passionate about finance; on the contrary, he was
more preoccupied with his political migration from liberalism to socialism and back, and with the pleasures of gardening at his new country
home in Connecticut.[21] But, now in his late forties, with two children and
expensive New York tastes, he decided that he needed money.[22] His efforts
to earn more in journalism had fizzled: He had left the staff of *Fortune*
hoping to launch a new magazine, but two blueprints had failed to attract
financial backing. Stymied in these publishing ventures, Jones moved to
plan B. He raised $60,000 from four friends and put up $40,000 of his
own to try his hand at investing.

Jones's investment record over the next twenty years was one of the
most remarkable in history. By 1968 he had racked up a cumulative return
of just under 5,000 percent, meaning that the investor who had given him
$10,000 in 1949 was now worth a tidy $480,000.[23] He left his competitors in the dust: For instance, in the five years to 1965 he returned 325
percent, dwarfing the 225 percent return on the hottest mutual fund for
that period. In the ten years to 1965 Jones earned almost two times as
much as his nearest competitor.[24] By some measures, Jones's performance
in these years rivaled even that of Warren Buffett.[25]

Jones's investment venture started out in a shabby one-and-a-half-room
office on Broad Street. He rented space from an insurance business owned
by one of his investors, Winslow Carlton, a dapper man who favored blue
shirts with white collars and tightly knotted ties and who drove a magnificent Packard convertible. Some mornings in those early years, Carlton
would have his resplendent vehicle brought out of its garage, and he would

drive over to Jones's apartment at 30 Sutton Place, and the two of them would proceed down the East Side with the roof off, trading predictions about the market. Jones kept a Royal typewriter on his desk and a dictionary mounted on a stand. There was a stock-exchange ticker with a glass dome over it, an electromechanical calculating machine that you cranked by hand, and a couch on which Jones liked to nap after his lunches. [26]

Jones set out to see whether he could translate the chart watchers' advice into investment profits. But it was the structure of his fund that was truly innovative. The standard practice for professional investors was to load up with stocks when the market was expected to go up and to hold a lot of cash when it was expected to topple. But Jones improved on these options. When the charts signaled a bull market, he did not merely put 100 percent of his fund into stocks; he borrowed in order to be, say, 150 percent "long"—meaning that he owned stocks worth one and a half times the value of his capital. When the charts signaled trouble, on the other hand, Jones did not merely retreat to cash. He reduced his exposure by selling stocks "short"—borrowing them from other investors and selling them in the expectation that their price would fall, at which point they could be repurchased at a profit.

Both leverage and short selling had been used in the 1920s, mostly by operators speculating with their own money.[27] But the trauma of 1929 had given both techniques a bad name, and they were considered too racy for professionals entrusted with other people's savings. Jones's innovation was to see how these methods could be combined without any raciness at all—he used "speculative means for conservative ends," as he said frequently. By selling a portion of his fund short as a routine precaution, even when the charts weren't signaling a fall, Jones could insure his portfolio against market risk. That freed him to load up on promising stocks without worrying about a collapse in the Dow Jones index: "You could buy more good stocks without taking as much risk as someone who merely bought," as Jones put it.[28] Whereas traditional investors had to sell hot companies like Xerox or Polaroid if the market looked wobbly, a hedged fund could profit from smart stock picking even at times when the market seemed overvalued.

In a prospectus distributed privately to his outside partners in 1961,

Jones explained the magic of hedging with an example.[29] Suppose there are two investors, each endowed with $100,000. Suppose that each is equally skilled in stock selection and is optimistic about the market. The first investor, operating on conventional fund-management principles, puts $80,000 into the best stocks he can find while keeping the balance of $20,000 in safe bonds. The second investor, operating on Jones's principles, borrows $100,000 to give himself a war chest totaling $200,000, then buys $130,000 worth of good stocks and shorts $70,000 worth of bad ones. This gives the second investor superior diversification in his long positions: Having $130,000 to play with, he can buy a broader range of stocks. It also gives him less exposure to the market: His $70,000 worth of shorts offsets $70,000 worth of longs, so his "net exposure" to the market is $60,000, whereas the first investor has a net exposure of $80,000. In this way, the hedge-fund investor incurs less stock-selection risk (because of diversification) and less market risk (because of hedging).

It gets better. Consider the effect on Jones's profits. Suppose the stock market index rises by 20 percent, and, because they are good at stock selection, the investors in Jones's example see their longs beat the market by ten points, yielding a rise of 30 percent. The short bets of the hedged investor also turn out well: If the index rises by 20 percent, his shorts rise by just 10 percent because he has successfully chosen companies that perform less well than the average. The two investors' performance will look like this:

TRADITIONAL INVESTOR	HEDGED INVESTOR
30% gain on $80,000 worth of stocks	30% gain on $130,000 worth of stocks
	10% loss on $70,000 worth of shorts
Gain: $24,000	Net gain: $39,000–$7,000 = $32,000

The result appears to defy a basic rule of investing, which is that you can only earn higher returns by assuming higher risk. The hedged investor earns a third more, even though he has assumed less market risk and less stock-selection risk.

Now consider a down market: The magic works even better. If the market falls by 20 percent, and if the stocks selected by the two investors beat the market average by the same ten-point margin, the returns come out like this:

TRADITIONAL INVESTOR	HEDGED INVESTOR
10% loss on $80,000 worth of stocks	10% loss on $130,000 worth of stocks
	30% gain on $70,000 worth of shorts
Loss: $8,000	Net gain: $21,000–$13,000 = $8,000

In sum, the hedged fund does better in a bull market *despite* the lesser risk it has assumed; and the hedged fund does better in a bear market *because of* the lesser risk it has assumed. Of course, the calculations work only if the investors pick good stocks; a poor stock picker could have his incompetence magnified under Jones's arrangement. Still, given the advantages of the hedged format, the question was why other fund managers failed to emulate it.

The answer began with short selling, which, as Jones observed in his report to investors, was "a little known procedure that scares away users for no good reason."[30] A stigma had attached to short selling ever since the crash and was to survive years into the future; amid the panic of 2008, regulators slapped restrictions on the practice. But as Jones patiently explained, the successful short seller performs a socially useful contrarian function: By selling stocks that rise higher than seems justified, he can dampen bubbles as they emerge; by repurchasing the same stocks later as they fall, he can provide a soft landing. Far from fueling wild speculation, short sellers could moderate the market's gyrations. It was a point that hedge-fund managers were to make repeatedly in future years. The stigma nonetheless persisted.

But there were other reasons why rival investors had not deployed the Jones method. Up to a point, shorting bad stocks is no more difficult than buying good ones: It involves the same intellectual process, only inverted. Instead of seeking out stocks with fast earnings growth, you look for slow earnings growth; instead of identifying companies with strong management, you look for companies led by charlatans. In other ways, however, shorting is harder. Because of the prejudice against it, shorting faces tougher tax and regulatory treatment; and whereas the investor who buys a stock can potentially make infinite profits, the short seller can only earn 100 percent—and that is if the stock falls to zero.[31] Moreover, shorting only works as part of a hedging strategy once a further refinement is brought in. It was here that Jones was way ahead of his contemporaries.

The refinement begins with the fact that some stocks bounce up and down more than others: They have different volatilities. Buying $1,000 worth of an inert stock and shorting $1,000 worth of a volatile one does not provide a real hedge: If the market average rises by 20 percent, the inert stock might rise by only ten points while the fast mover might shoot up by thirty. So Jones measured the volatility of all stocks—he called it the "velocity"—and compared it with the volatility of Standard & Poor's 500 Index.[32] For example, he examined the significant price swings in Sears Roebuck since 1948 and determined that these were 80 percent as big as the swings in the market average: He therefore assigned Sears a "relative velocity" of 80. On the other hand, some stocks were more volatile than the broad market: General Dynamics had a relative velocity of 196. Clearly, buying and selling the same number of Sears and General Dynamics stocks would not provide a hedge. If the Jones fund sold short 100 shares of volatile General Dynamics at $50, for example, it would need to hold 245 shares in stodgy Sears Roebuck at $50 to keep the fund's market exposure neutral.

In his report to his investors, Jones explained the point this way:

WE BUY	WE SELL SHORT
245 shares in Sears Roebuck at $50 = $12,250	100 shares in GD at $50 = $5,000
$12,250 x Sears's velocity, 0.80 = $9,800	$5,000 x GD's velocity, 1.96 = $9,800

Jones pointed out that the velocity of a stock did not determine whether it was a good investment. A slow-moving stock might be expected to do well; a volatile one might be expected to do poorly. But to understand a stock's effect on a portfolio, the size of a holding had to be adjusted for its volatility.

Jones's next innovation was to distinguish between the money that his fund made through stock picking and the money that it made through its exposure to the market. Years later, this distinction became commonplace: Investors called skill-driven stock-picking returns "alpha" and passive market exposure "beta."[33] But Jones tracked the different sources of his profits from the start, revealing the facility with statistics he had honed amid Akron's industrial tensions. Each evening, sometimes with the help of his children, he would look up the closing prices of his stocks in the *World Telegraph* or the *Sun* and note them in pencil in a dog-eared leather book.[34] Then he would construct chains of reasoning like this one:[35]

Our long stocks, worth $130,000, should have gone up by $1,300 to keep pace with the 1% rise in the market. But they actually went up by $2,500, and the difference, attributable to good stock selection, is $1,200 or 1.2% on our fund's $100,000 of equity.

Our short stocks, worth $70,000, should have gone up also by 1%, which would have shown us a loss of $700. But the actual loss was only $400, and the difference, attributable to good short stock selection, is a gain of $300 or 0.3%.

Being net long by the amount of $60,000, the market rise of 1% helped us along by 1% of $60,000, or $600, or 0.6%.

Our total gain comes to $2,100, or 2.1% of equity. 1.5 percentage points of the return were attributable to stock selection. The remaining 0.6 percentage points stemmed from exposure to the market.

Jones's calculations were impressive on two levels. In the precomputer age, figuring the volatility of stocks was a laborious business, and Jones and his small staff performed these measurements for about two thousand firms at two-year intervals. But, more than Jones's patience, it was the conceptual sophistication that stood out. In a rough-and-ready way, his techniques anticipated the breakthroughs in financial academia of the 1950s and 1960s.

IN 1952, THREE YEARS AFTER JONES HAD LAUNCHED HIS fund, modern portfolio theory was born with the publication of a short paper titled "Portfolio Selection." The author was a twenty-five-year-old graduate student named Harry Markowitz, and his chief insights were twofold: The art of investment is not merely to maximize return but to maximize risk-adjusted return, and the amount of risk that an investor takes depends not just on the stocks he owns but on the correlations among them. Jones's investment method crudely anticipated these points. By paying attention to the velocity of his stocks, Jones was effectively controlling risk, just as Markowitz advocated. Moreover, by balancing the volatility of his long and short positions, Jones was anticipating Markowitz's insight that the risk of a portfolio depends on the relationship among its components.[36]

Jones's approach was more practical than that of Markowitz. For years the 1952 paper was ignored on Wall Street because it was impossible to implement: Working out the correlations among a thousand stocks required almost half a million calculations, and the requisite computer power was not yet available. In the mid-1950s Markowitz attempted to estimate correlations for just twenty-five stocks, but he found that even this demanded more computer memory than the Yale economics department could provide for him. And so it fell to another future Nobel laureate, William Sharpe, to develop a variation that would render Markowitz's work useful: In a paper titled "A Simplified Model for Portfolio Analysis," Sharpe replaced the hopeless injunction to calculate the multiple relationships among stocks with the simpler idea of calculating a single correlation between each stock and the market index. This was precisely what Jones's velocity calculations were designed to do. By the time Sharpe published his paper in 1963, Jones had been implementing its advice for more than a decade.

Jones also anticipated the work of James Tobin, another Nobel Prize–winning father of modern portfolio theory. In 1958 Tobin proposed what came to be known as the separation theorem, which held that an investor's choice of stocks should be separate from the question of his risk appetite. Most investment advisers in the 1950s assumed that certain types of stocks suited certain types of investor: A widow should not own a go-go stock such as Xerox, whereas a successful business executive should have no interest in a stodgy utility such as AT&T. Tobin's insight was to see why this was wrong: An investor's choice of stocks could be separated from the amount of risk he wanted. If an investor was risk averse, he should buy the best stocks available but commit only part of his savings. If an investor was risk hungry, he should buy exactly the same stocks but borrow money to buy more of them. Yet nine years before Tobin published his groundbreaking article, Jones was onto the same point. His fund made one judgment about which companies to own and a second about how much risk to take, adjusting the risk as it saw fit by using the device of leverage.[37]

In the 1950s and into the 1960s, almost nobody understood Jones's investment methods; in his secrecy as in much else, Jones anticipated the future of the hedge-fund industry. His clandestine activities in Europe had taught him how to stay under the radar, and he had multiple reasons to approach finance in the same fashion.[38] To begin with, Jones wanted to protect his investment methods from competitors: Brokers who visited the A. W. Jones offices on Broad Street were cross-examined vigorously about the stocks they were touting, but they left the place with no idea what the Jones men were thinking. Equally, Jones wanted to avoid drawing attention to the tax loopholes devised for him by Richard Valentine, an attorney at the firm of Seward & Kissel. Valentine was a creative genius who could be cartoonishly absentminded in his personal dealings: He once phoned a colleague's home and launched into a lengthy exposition of his latest tax idea, oblivious to the fact that he was talking to his colleague's five-year-old.[39] It was Valentine who realized that if managers took a share of a hedge fund's investment profits rather than a flat management fee, they could be taxed at the capital-gains rate: Given the personal tax rates of the times, that could mean handing 25 percent to Uncle Sam rather than 91 percent.[40] Jones duly charged his investors 20 percent of the upside, claiming that he had been inspired to do so by Mediterranean history rather than tax law: He told people that his profit share was modeled after Phoenician merchants, who kept a fifth of the profits from successful voyages, distributing the rest to their investors. Dignified by this impressive cover story, Jones's performance fee (termed a "performance reallocation" in order to distinguish it from an ordinary bonus that would attract normal income tax) was happily embraced by successive generations of hedge funds.

Jones's reasons for secrecy went beyond a desire to stave off competitors and reduce tax: He was anxious to escape regulation. He declined to register under the Securities Act of 1933, the Investment Company Act of 1940, and the Investment Advisors Act of 1940, arguing that none of these laws applied to him, principally because his funds were "private." Not registering under these laws was essential: They restricted investment funds from borrowing or selling short, the two central components of Jones's hedging strategy, and also imposed fee restrictions. To sustain the idea that his funds were private, Jones never advertised them publicly;

he marketed them by word of mouth, which sometimes mean
between mouthfuls at his dinner table. Much of his capital came fro
network of intellectual friends, including Louis Fischer, a biographer
Lenin, and Sam Stayman, the inventor of the bridge convention "Stayman
over no-trump."[41] Jones also took care not to allow too many investors into
his fund. In 1961 he set up a second partnership rather than allow his first
one to cross the permissible threshold of one hundred members.[42]

This stealth allowed Jones and his later imitators to escape regulatory
oversight. But it came at a price. There is nothing like secrecy to pique
the public's curiosity, and by the mid-1960s, hedge funds had begun to
attract the sort of breathless commentary that later grew commonplace.
They were "Wall Street's last bastions of secrecy, mystery, exclusivity, and
privilege," according to the writer John Brooks; they were "the parlor
cars of the new gravy train."[43] Perhaps the threat of deadening regulation
made Jones's clandestine style inevitable. But thanks to the pattern that he
established in those early years, hedge funds have been forever mysterious,
shadowy, and resented.

EVEN AS HE ANTICIPATED THE INSIGHTS OF MODERN
portfolio theory, Jones paid a price for ignoring Alfred Cowles's writings.
The verdict that trends in market prices are too faint to be profitable
proved all too correct, at least in Jones's case: His efforts to call the overall
direction of the market failed as often as they succeeded. In 1953, 1956,
and again in 1957, Jones lost money on his market calls, leveraging himself
up when the market did poorly and vice versa. In 1960 Cowles published
an update to his earlier research: He reversed his earlier finding of faint
trends in monthly prices, concluding that they did not exist after all.[44]
Oblivious, Jones carried on trying to time the market, but with no better
results. In early 1962, he was net long 140 percent of his capital, where-
upon the market fell. Then he turned bearish, but the market turned up.
At one particularly excruciating moment in August 1965, Jones had a net
exposure of *minus* 18 percent, meaning that his short positions exceeded
his longs to the tune of 18 percent of his funds' capital. Perfectly on cue,

the market embarked on a hot rally. Future hedge-fund managers were to prove that trend surfing can be profitable, and future academics were to revise Cowles's findings. But Jones never turned a profit by following the charts, even though chartism had provided the premise for his hedged fund.[45]

Jones's statistical methods revealed precisely how much money he was losing from bad calls on the market.[46] But his funds still performed marvelously. The reason lay in a discovery that he had stumbled upon almost accidentally. He had begun with theories about trends created by investor sentiment, which turned out to be blind alleys. He had invented the hedged strategy, which was conceptually brilliant but not in itself a source of profits. Next, having designed a hedged portfolio, he needed to choose stocks to put inside it. Through skill and a coincidence of temperament, Jones devised a way of assembling stock pickers who beat the pants off Wall Street.

Jones knew he could not be a great stock picker himself. He was an investment novice, and the details of company balance sheets had never captured his imagination. Instead, he created a system to get the best out of others. Starting in the early 1950s, he invited brokers to run "model portfolios" for his fund: Each man would select his favorite shorts and longs, and phone in changes as though he were running real money. Jones used these paper portfolios as a source of stock-picking ideas. His statistical methods, which separated the fruits of stock selection from the effect of market moves, allowed him to pinpoint each manager's results precisely. Jones then compensated the brokers according to how well their suggestions worked. It was a marvelous technique for getting brokers to phone in hot ideas before they gave them to others.[47]

This system gave Jones an edge over his competitors. In the 1950s, Wall Street was a sleepy, unsophisticated place. At the universities and business schools, practically nobody took courses in finance; the investment course at Harvard was dubbed "Darkness at Noon," because the university administrators allocated it the unpopular lunchtime slot in order to save classroom space for more popular subjects. The trustees at the old investment institutions were compensated by the volume of assets under management rather than by a performance fee, and they reached decisions by committee. Jones's method broke the mold. It was each stock picker for himself; it substituted individualism for collectivism and adrenaline for complacency. Even in the 1960s, when Jones's enterprise had grown big enough to have half a dozen stock pickers on its payroll, he continued to cultivate a Darwinian system. He convened remarkably few investment meetings because he found committees intolerably tedious.[48] Instead, he allotted each in-house manager a segment of the partners' capital, laid down the desired market exposure, and left him to invest the money. At the end of each year, the managers who performed best were also the best rewarded.

You could see the results in the way the Jones men operated. In the Wall Street of the 1950s and 1960s, information did not reach everyone at once: There were no blast e-mails from brokers, no instant analysis from cable TV squawkers. In this environment, the investment team with the most hustle could beat out sleepier rivals; and the Jones men hustled hardest. The model portfolio managers rushed to call in hot ideas, and the in-house segment managers worked the phones, scrambling for the gossip and insights that would put them ahead of their competitors. Even in the 1960s, when Wall Street finally shrugged off its postcrash stupor, it was surprising how easily sheer diligence could set a man apart. Alan Dresher, one of the Jones stock pickers, had the idea of going over to the Securities and Exchange Commission offices to read company filings the moment they came out. The extraordinary thing was that he was all alone. The rest of the Street was waiting for the filings to arrive in a bundle from the post office.

The linking of compensation to results was the key to Jones's formula. When a broker passed a stock tip to a normal mutual fund, there was no certain connection between the quality of the tip and what the broker would be paid for it. For one thing, the mutual funds lacked Jones's system for tracking how stock recommendations turned out. For another, mutual-fund companies paid out thousands of dollars to salesmen who brought in investors' capital, leaving little money over to reward excellent research. Jones, on the other hand, was meticulous in paying for good

research ideas, and he paid handsomely.[49] A young broker could see his
salary double if the recommendations in his model portfolio generated
profits.[50] Meanwhile the funds' performance fees were divvied up among
Jones's in-house money managers according to whose segment did best,
and Jones devised two further ways of sharpening incentives. Each year
successful segment managers were given extra capital to manage, which
increased their chances of generating profits in the coming year and so
earning a large bonus; unsuccessful managers received less capital to
play with. And in another innovation that anticipated the hedge funds
of later times, Jones required his partners to have their own capital in
the funds, so that their wealth as well as their income was riding on their
performance.[51]

Without realizing the significance of what he was doing, Jones had created the competitive multimanager structure that has been used to great
effect by later generations of hedge funds. As we shall see in chapter three,
the same structure was reinvented in the 1970s by a firm in Princeton,
New Jersey, and later dozens of hedge funds came to use it. But in the
1950s and 1960s, the combination of Darwinist individualism and top-
down risk control was almost unique to Jones, and this gave him a powerful advantage. The market may be efficient, in the sense that information
is reflected in prices to the extent that existing institutional arrangements
allow. But Jones blew up those institutional arrangements, scrapping staid
committee meetings and paying people to perform. Thus did he create the
edge that brought in serious money.

AT THE START OF 1964, ALFRED JONES INVITED A YOUNG
analyst to lunch at his Manhattan club. Now in his sixties, he had achieved
the material comfort he had sought fifteen years earlier; his family had
graduated from its Dodge station wagon to a Citroën DS and finally to a
monstrous Mercedes. Jones peered at the young analyst and asked, "When
you go to pee in a restaurant urinal, do you wash your hands before or
after you pee?"

The analyst was a bit surprised. "Afterwards, sir," he ventured.

"That's the wrong answer," Jones retorted. "You're a conventional thinker and not rational."[52]

Jones was trying to be funny. He was recycling a version of a joke that was doing the rounds, but he had mangled it hopelessly. The analyst, a future Wall Street grandee named Barton Biggs, took instantly against Jones, and although he accepted the opportunity to run a model portfolio for his fund, he never grew to like him. Jones seemed aloof, conceited, and ignorant about stocks. He was reaping the fruits of young analysts' hard work while himself appearing in the office sporadically.

Perhaps not surprisingly, the man who had spent his early adulthood among clandestine anti-Hitler activists never had much passion for investing. He disdained the monomaniacal market types with no interests beyond finance: "Too many men don't want to do something *after* they make money. They just go on and make a lot more money," he complained to one interviewer.[53] Jones cultivated literary infatuations: He was enthralled by the theory that Edward de Vere, the seventeenth Earl of Oxford, was the true author of Shakespeare's plays, and he named his poodle Edward. He carved a tunnel through the weeping willows at his country house and nursed his lawn tennis court as though it were a sickly infant. He founded a philanthropy devoted to what he called "the humiliated poor" and set to work on a book that he intended as a sequel to Michael Harrington's famous poverty study, *The Other America*. Dorothy Parker was now too drunk to be invited over much, but Alfred and Mary entertained a cosmopolitan cast of intellectuals and United Nations diplomats, and dinner conversation was less likely to be about finance than about Russian hegemony in Yugoslavia.[54] It was not surprising that committed Wall Streeters resented him.

Soon after Jones's lunch with Biggs, the resentments burst out into the open. One of Jones's in-house money managers left to set up a rival hedged fund called City Associates.[55] From the point of view of the defector, the choice was rational: The hedged concept was easy to copy, and there was no need to share the loot with a dilettante overseer. Jones had his lawyers harass his departing partner but the old man took the blow in stride; and at the end of 1964 he spent his Christmas vacation on a

Himalayan tiger shoot hosted by Indian friends from the United Nations. There were elephant-back outings, a big bonfire and fine food, and incongruous sessions in which the Hindu hosts sang Christmas carols. But while Jones was away, more trouble was brewing. Barton Biggs, the audience for Jones's urinal joke, persuaded Jones's longest-serving fund manager to quit and start up a rival fund. On his way out the door, the defector took some of Jones's clients with him.[56]

Sooner or later, every great investor's edge is destined to unravel. His techniques are understood and copied by rivals; he can no longer claim to be more efficient than the market. Jones's extraordinary profits had fostered jealousies among the partners about how the money should be shared, and after the first two defections, others inevitably followed. At the start of 1968, there were said to be forty imitator firms; by 1969 estimates ranged from two hundred to five hundred; and many of the leading lights were run by people who had worked for Jones or served him as brokers.[57] *The Economist* claimed that this new investment industry had about $11 billion under management, or five times the figure of two years earlier.[58] The expression "hedge fund," a corrupted version of Jones's "hedged fund," entered the Wall Street lexicon.[59] Every sideburned gunslinger was determined to work for one.

The early effect of this unraveling was paradoxical. As the first imitator funds sprang up, word got about the Street, and Jones came to be seen as the founder of a hot new movement. A flattering profile appeared in *Fortune* in 1966: "There are reasons to believe that the best professional manager of investors' money these days is a quiet-spoken, seldom-photographed man named Alfred Winslow Jones," the article began, though somehow *Fortune* had obtained a large photo of Jones, showing him with a thick thatch of white hair and large dark-framed glasses.[60] Investors fell over one another to get money into the Jones funds, ambitious young analysts came looking for jobs, and for a while the party continued.[61] Jones himself was said to be earning "something in the millions," and the Jones defectors were raking in the money too: One City Associates partner acquired a penthouse, a helicopter, a wine cellar, and bodyguards; his office was

staffed by curvaceous women who allegedly were secretaries.⁶² It all added
to the gossip and the envy and fun. Hedge funds embodied the spirit of
the age; and as *New York* magazine proclaimed in 1968, A. W. Jones was
their big daddy.

The boom attracted the attention of regulators—much as other hedge-
fund booms did later. In 1968, the New York Stock Exchange and the
American Stock Exchange began to consider restrictions on their members' dealings with hedge funds. In January 1969, the Securities and
Exchange Commission sent out a questionnaire to two hundred hedge
funds, demanding to know "who they are, how they came into being,
the way in which they are organized"—and especially "what impact their
trading may have on the market."⁶³ Commission officials made no secret
of the fact that they wanted hedge funds to register under one of the federal acts, but some of the complaints about the new upstarts seemed a bit
curious. It was said that hedge funds accounted for half the short interest
in certain stocks; nobody explained why this short selling, which presumably prevented indifferent companies from attaining unsustainable
market valuations, might be pernicious. It was noted that hedge funds
turned over their portfolios more aggressively than mutual funds, but
somehow this boost to market liquidity was portrayed as a bad thing.
There was a tall story about an A. W. Jones manager who bought a large
block in a go-go company one morning and sold it after lunch. Nobody
could explain how this alleged crime harmed anyone. However much they
might be envied and adored, hedge funds were also the object of not-
quite-rational resentment.

In the three years starting in the summer of 1966, Jones's investors
pocketed returns, after subtracting fees, of 26 percent, 22 percent, and
47 percent.⁶⁴ But this Indian summer concealed trouble. The Jones funds
were losing their distinctive edge: Their stock pickers were defecting to
set up rival firms, and Jones's hedging principles no longer seemed so relevant. The hedge[d]-fund model deserved to drop its *d*: Caught up in the
bull market, the Jones men came to regard shorting as a sucker's game and
lost interest in protecting the fund against a fall in the S&P 500. Instead,

they pushed the boundaries of leverage: Each segment manager was out to buy as many go-go stocks as possible. Even the velocity calculations fell by the wayside. The Jones men did not like being told to buy less of a hot stock merely because it might be volatile. Because the stock market was roaring, and because Jones himself was increasingly absent, the stock pickers did what they wanted.[65] This was the sixties; they were young; the market belonged to their generation.

For most of his financial life, Jones had been lucky. He had opened his hedged fund just as the trauma of the crash was beginning to wear off: In 1950 only one in twenty-five American adults owned stocks; by the end of the 1950s, one in eight did.[66] As retail brokerages sprang up on every high street, the S&P 500 index rose from 15 at the time of Jones's launch to a peak of 108 in late 1968, and meanwhile the financial culture changed: The trustee bankers were eclipsed by go-go types for whom the crash was ancient history. The new generation believed that financial turmoil would never rear its head again. The Fed was watching over the economy, the SEC was watching over the market, and Keynesian budget policies had repealed the tyranny of the business cycle. This state of blissful optimism found its apotheosis in the Great Winfield, the semifictional investor immortalized by Jerry Goodman, the financial writer and broadcaster who became famous under the pseudonym "Adam Smith." The Great Winfield entrusts his money to twentysomething managers with no memories and no fear—whose chief virtue is inexperience. "Show me a portfolio, I'll tell you the generation," he says. "You can tell the swinger stocks because they frighten all the other [older] generations."[67]

Jones had caught the go-go era early. A portion of his wealth, though certainly not all, was the result of riding a long bull market. But the multimanager structure that empowered go-go segment managers was not designed to save Jones from a sudden reversal—a problem that multimanager hedge funds were to discover later. On the contrary: The more the market rose, the more Jones's performance-tracking system rewarded aggressive segment managers who took the most risk. There was no mechanism for getting out before disaster struck; and in May 1969 the stock market started to fall hard, shedding a quarter of its value over the next year. When Jones reported his results for the year ending in May 1970, he was obliged to tell his clients that he had done even worse than the market. He had lost 35 percent of their money.[68]

The following September, Jones marked his seventieth birthday. It was a time of celebration for his family: Jones's daughter-in-law was expecting his first grandchild, and his daughter's wedding engagement was announced at the birthday party. A marquee was put up on the lawn of his beloved country house, up the hill from the grass tennis court that he nurtured like an infant. The band played dance music, and the young men traded guesses about who Miss Jones's betrothed might be. But the patriarch was out of sorts. He fretted that his segment managers would resent the extravagance of the occasion: "I hate the boys seeing me spending money like a drunken sailor," he kept saying.[69] After two decades of eminence, Jones's investment edge was gone. The markets had finally caught up with him.

‖‖‖‖‖‖‖‖‖‖‖‖‖‖‖‖‖‖‖

2

‖‖‖‖‖‖‖‖‖‖‖‖‖‖‖‖‖‖‖

THE BLOCK TRADER

The years from 1969 to 1973 marked a watershed for the American economy. The nation had brimmed with confidence for the previous two decades: Jobs were plentiful, wages rose, and finance was almost quaintly stable. The dollar didn't fluctuate because it was pegged firmly to gold; interest rates moved within a narrow range and were capped by regulation. But starting in the late 1960s, inflation tore this world apart. Having stayed below 2 percent in the first half of the decade, it hit 5.5 percent in the spring of 1969, forcing the Federal Reserve to jam on the monetary brakes and squeeze the life out of the stock market. The bear market that followed was only the first shock. In 1971 the Nixon administration was forced to acknowledge that inflation had eroded the real value of the dollar, and it responded by abandoning the gold standard. Suddenly money could be worth one thing today, another tomorrow; and the realization inevitably fueled further inflationary pressure. Another round of monetary tightening soon followed, and the market crashed again in 1973–74. Go-go was gone-gone. The 1960s were over.

The turbulence put an end to the first hedge-fund era. Between the close of 1968 and September 30, 1970, the 28 largest hedge funds lost two thirds of their capital.[1] Their claim to be hedged turned out to be a bald-faced lie; they had racked up hot performance numbers by borrowing hard and riding the bull market. By January 1970, there were said to be only 150 hedge funds, down from between 200 and 500 one year before; and the crash of 1973–74 wiped out most of the rest of them.[2] The Securities and Exchange Commission gave up on its campaign to regulate a sector that was now too small to bother with, and in 1977 *Institutional Investor* magazine ran an article asking where all the hedge funds had gone.[3] As late as 1984, a survey by a firm called Tremont Partners identified only 68 of them. The A. W. Jones partnership withered from the $100 million plus it had managed in the late 1960s to $35 million in 1973 and a mere $25 million a decade after that.[4] It proved hard to keep going in hard times. Performance fees dried up in an era of nonperformance.

Adversity did not rule out success, however; and the first winner amid the new uncertainty was Steinhardt, Fine, Berkowitz & Company. The firm's dominant partner, Michael Steinhardt, became a legend in the story of hedge funds, partly because of his success as a trader but also because of his personality. He had been brought up by a single mother in hardscrabble Brooklyn, and his father was confrontational, short-tempered, and addicted to gambling—traits that the younger Steinhardt later brought to his own trading. At sixteen he was admitted to the University of Pennsylvania, from which he graduated at nineteen; and by the mid 1960s, when Steinhardt was still only about twenty-five, he had become, in his own estimation, the "hottest analyst on Wall Street."[5] He was short, barrel-chested, and prone to terrifying outbursts. When the volcano stirred within him, his face and then his temples would turn red. He would let forth a blood-curdling torrent of abuse that left his colleagues shaking.

Steinhardt quit the brokerage business in 1967, launching a hedge fund with two equally young friends named Jerrold Fine and Howard Berkowitz. The bull market was still very much alive, and at first Steinhardt, Fine, Berkowitz seemed typical of the outfits that sprang up in imitation of the A. W. Jones partnerships. The three founders equipped their offices with a pool table, proclaimed the intellectual superiority of youth, and ignored the advice of their lawyer, who said that Steinhardt, Fine, Berkowitz sounded too much like a Jewish delicatessen.[6] In their first full year in business, the trio loaded up on the story stocks of the era.

They owned King Resources, whose charming chief executive claimed to have discovered new oil and gas reserves. They owned National Student Marketing because they believed in the youth market. They owned technology companies whose names featured "Data" or "-onics." It was a time when investors loved anything that had the scent of growth, and at the end of their first full year they were up 84 percent after subtracting fees. "My God, I am rich," Jerry Fine recalls thinking.[7] Indeed, he and his two friends had each become millionaires.

The following year, the bull market ended. Other go-go funds blew up; Fred Mates, the top-performing mutual-fund manager of 1968, found himself working as a bartender. But almost alone among the gunslingers, Steinhardt, Fine, and Berkowitz had sensed that the long postwar expansion had finally overreached and that a time of uncertainty was beginning. Fifteen years earlier, the famous value investor, Benjamin Graham, had made the fateful decision not to buy shares in the Xerox maker, Haloid, saying he saw no reason to buy stocks on the basis of their future growth; Haloid had sextupled in the next two years, and the cult of the growth stock had since gone unquestioned. But in 1969, Steinhardt, Fine, and Berkowitz concluded that this cult had gone too far; it was one thing to pay a premium for a company with bright prospects, another to pay so much that uninterrupted, supersonic growth was extrapolated into the hereafter.

At the start of 1969, Steinhardt and his friends shorted enough of the story stocks to balance their long positions; unlike most hedge funds, they were actually hedging. When the S&P 500 index fell by 9 percent that year, the firm preserved all but a sliver of its capital; the following year, when the S&P 500 dropped by another 9 percent, the troika actually made money.[8] Having survived 1969–70, the firm went on the offensive; it turned bullish in 1971, catching the bounce from the bear market. When *Fortune* published its list of the top twenty-eight hedge funds that year, Steinhardt, Fine, Berkowitz was the only one to have actually expanded during the shakeout. The partnership had racked up a return of 361 percent since opening for business in July 1967, a performance that was thirty-six times better than that of the stock market index over that period.[9]

In 1972, the young troika turned pessimistic again. This time the sources of their doubt went beyond the cult of growth investing. The edifice of America's postwar confidence seemed to be cracking: The Nixon administration was covering up the truth about its failures in Vietnam; it was covering up inflation with an impractical wage-and-price-control program; and meanwhile, America's finest companies were covering up the truth about themselves with accounting shenanigans. Jerry Fine and Howard Berkowitz, who led the firm's analytical effort, were finding red flags in the footnotes of annual reports on a regular basis, and no less a figure than Leonard Spacek, chairman emeritus of Arthur Andersen and the most respected accountant of the era, had exclaimed that "financial statements are a roulette wheel." "The research reports that were released in the early seventies were so simplistic that we looked at them as nonsense," Howard Berkowitz recalled. "Deferred this, different tax rate that, capital gains that they put as operating earnings," said Jerry Fine of the company reports of the period.[10] In short, the stock market was trading at levels that reflected broad political and financial delusions. So whereas in 1969 the young troika shorted enough stocks to protect themselves from a downturn, they went further in 1972. They positioned their portfolio so that their short positions greatly outweighed their longs, and they waited for the crash to happen.

At first, it did not happen. The market sailed along for the rest of 1972, and the fund was down 2 percent in the year to September, at a time when the S&P 500 index rose 9 percent. But then the payoff came: The S&P fell 2 percent in the year to September 1973 and a shocking 41 percent the following year, and Steinhardt, Fine, Berkowitz racked up gains of 12 percent and then 28 percent after fees, an extraordinary performance in a bear market. The young partners were raking in the money while just about every other portfolio manager was losing his proverbial shirt; their results looked great, but they were not universally popular. As the stock market careened downward, desperate sellers called up the troika's trading desk, knowing that the firm had borrowed shares to sell them short, urging that now would be the time to buy shares back to cover their positions. Michael Steinhardt, who ran the firm's trading, generally gave these supplicants the cold shoulder, and the troika watched their short positions generate ever bigger profits as the market rout continued. In this climate, the old prejudice against short selling came back with a vengeance: Steinhardt, Fine, and Berkowitz were resented as arrogant, greedy, and even un-American; betting against American companies was portrayed as one step away from treason.[11] Thinking back on that period, Steinhardt recalls the vilification this way: "That was, for me, the height of professional satisfaction."[12]

THE SUCCESS OF STEINHARDT, FINE, BERKOWITZ DEM-onstrated the capacity for contrarianism that marked later hedge funds. A. W. Jones had invented the hedge-fund structure to control market exposure. His go-go imitators had turned it into a way of maximizing market exposure. But the troika made it into something else—a vehicle for betting against conventional wisdom. Indeed, aggressive contrarianism became a sort of company credo, especially for Michael Steinhardt.

Some contrarians balance a faith in their opinions with a reluctance to offend, but Steinhardt positively enjoyed baiting people. He loved taking guests to see the exotic animals on his upstate New York farm, especially the Falkland flightless steamer duck, which would viciously bite anyone who approached too closely. He loved calling up a broker and placing a juicy order for a nonexistent stock, leaving the poor man scrambling to identify the company so that he could collect the commission. For a while in the 1980s, Steinhardt allowed he might need help: He permitted a psychiatrist to roam around his premises offering "organizational therapy." The psychiatrist conducted interviews with staff members and noted the prevalence of expressions such as "battered children," "random violence," and "rage disorder." But the therapy was cut short when Steinhardt lost his temper with the man and threw him out of the office.

If Steinhardt didn't mind offending people, he loved offending the consensus. During the liberal 1970s he was a Republican, and during the Reaganite 1980s he leaned toward the Democrats. In the early 1990s he bankrolled the centrist Democratic Leadership Council, which helped to put Bill Clinton in the White House; as soon as Clinton was installed, Steinhardt turned against the movement.[13] In his relationship with Judaism, he followed his own course: He declared he had no faith in God but gave millions to Jewish causes. And when it came to investing, Steinhardt's contrarian instincts reached full flower. He trawled Wall Street for unconventional ideas and backed them on a scale that would terrify a normal mortal.

John LeFrere, an analyst hired by Steinhardt in the 1970s, recalls his first weeks on the job; he visited IBM and returned convinced that its profits were headed upward. At the partnership's Monday-morning meeting, LeFrere recommended buying IBM stock ahead of that Friday's quarterly results, but Steinhardt pushed back. The boss had been watching IBM splutter about aimlessly on the stock ticker, and he had a black feeling in his gut that the stock was going nowhere.

"Mike, I think you're wrong," LeFrere said. It took courage to contradict Steinhardt, but LeFrere had a strong build and figured he could bench him.

"I hate the pig," said Steinhardt.

"Mike, I don't care how it looks on the tape. The results are going to be good and the stock's going up."

Steinhardt's contrarian radar flickered. "How much you want to buy then?"

"How about ten thousand?" LeFrere ventured, calculating that, with IBM trading at $365, owning three and a half million dollars' worth of one stock was about the maximum conceivable.

Steinhardt hit a button and ordered his trader to buy 25,000 IBM immediately.

"Mike, I said ten thousand," LeFrere said anxiously.

"How convinced are you of your fuckin' opinion?" Steinhardt barked.

"I'm very convinced."

"You better be right," Steinhardt said grimly. He hit the button again and bought another 25,000.

That exchange left Steinhardt with some $18 million worth of IBM, representing perhaps a quarter of his capital. It was a hefty concentration of risk in one stock, five times the size that LeFrere had recommended. But when IBM's results came out at the end of the week, the stock shot up 20 points, yielding an instant profit of $1 million. LeFrere had survived his rite of passage.[14]

If there was one quality that Steinhardt valued in people, it was the balls to take a position. At first, the partnership's big bets were based on straightforward intellectual confidence, bolstered by a 1960s faith in youth: Each member of the young troika had studied at Wharton; each knew himself to be extremely smart; each had no problem sorting through the footnotes in company reports and shorting the life out of a firm that appeared to be concealing something. But soon this high-octane analysis was blended with a dash of eccentricity. In 1970, Steinhardt recruited Frank "Tony" Cilluffo, a mathematically gifted autodidact with limited formal education.

Cilluffo hailed from the wild fringes of Wall Street. He had grown up in Brooklyn, dropped out of City College without a degree, and spent much of his youth devising a mathematical system to predict the outcome of horse races. He had found his way to Arthur Lipper and Company, a brokerage firm known for servicing a notorious con man named Bernie Cornfeld, and he was an avid student of Kondratiev wave theory. The theory held that capitalist economies move in long cycles, with the upswings occurring during periods of technological innovation and abundant investment and the downswings occurring as new investments dry up and old ones lose value. Nikolai Kondratiev, the theory's Russian inventor, founded the Institute of Conjuncture in Moscow in 1920; he identified upswings between 1789 and 1814, 1849 and 1873, and 1896 and 1920. Cilluffo was convinced that the pattern of twenty-four-year advances would repeat itself again, meaning that the economy would hit the rocks in 1973, twenty-four years after the start of the postwar bull market. It was not exactly clear why cycles of innovation should echo themselves so precisely across different centuries and circumstances: Kondratiev's conjuncture was based mainly on conjecture. But Cilluffo was undeterred;

the more the theory was pooh-poohed by the mainstream, the more he seemed to like it. This suited Steinhardt fine. The boss wanted people with contrarian views, and he didn't mind how they arrived at them.[15]

Steinhardt recruited Cilluffo to work with him on the trading desk. The two of them sat in a room strewn with the residue of unfinished lunches, chain-smoking relentlessly. Cilluffo calculated that it took eight minutes and thirteen seconds to smoke a Dunhill, and he got through four packs of them per day; Steinhardt smoked a milder brand, but he would light up two cigarettes at once when the markets got difficult. Both men approached trading with a spiritual intensity; but whereas intensity drove Steinhardt to volcanic eruptions of temper, Cilluffo's main symptom was a superstitious eating habit. During times when the partnership was making money, he would order precisely the same lunch day after day, switching only when the markets turned; he ordered two toasted English muffins with jam for one two-year stretch, following that up with a long run of cream-cheese-and-olive sandwiches.[16] Meanwhile, he would gulp down gallons of coffee and invoke Kondratiev's teachings, declaring with unwavering conviction that a particular stock that was then trading at $80 would hit $10 by next summer. Not all his colleagues knew how to respond. "He was either brilliant or crazy," one of them recalls. "You can't do four packs of Dunhills a day and eight cups of coffee without waking up at three in the morning and seeing pink elephants flying around." But Steinhardt had great faith in Cilluffo. As he wrote later in his memoir, Tony "truly had a direct line to God (if indeed there was one)."[17]

Whether by luck or some mysterious power, the Kondratiev prediction of a turndown in 1973 proved uncannily accurate. The bear market that began that year completed the crack-up of the postwar economic order; for the rest of that decade markets were in a funk and the economy was plagued by stagflation, an ugly new term for an ugly new condition. The number of Americans owning stock actually fell by seven million over the course of the decade, and in the summer of 1979 a *BusinessWeek* cover proclaimed "The Death of Equities." But throughout this difficult period, Steinhardt's contrarian style paid off. Having returned 12 percent and then 28 percent by holding short positions in the 1973–74 bear market, the partnership turned bullish in time to return 54 percent after fees in the strong market of 1975; and for the next three years, returns continued to be solid.

By the fall of 1978, when Steinhardt took his leave from Wall Street for a sabbatical year, his group's eleven-year record was one of the most remarkable of all time. A dollar invested in 1967 would have been worth $12 by 1978, whereas a dollar invested in the broad market would have been worth only $1.70. After subtracting fees, the partnership compounded at an average annual rate of 24.3 percent in this period, a performance virtually identical to that of A. W. Jones in its heyday. And unlike A. W. Jones, Steinhardt and his friends were fighting the headwind of a lousy economic climate.

FOR BELIEVERS IN EFFICIENT MARKETS, STEINHARDT'S success presents a puzzle. Did he triumph because he had a real investment "edge," or was he merely fortunate? The law of probabilities predicts that if two hundred people flip eleven coins, five will have the luck to get heads nine out of eleven times. Perhaps it is not surprising that of the two hundred-plus hedge funds founded in the late 1960s, at least one called the market right for nine of the next eleven years—the two misses coming in 1969 and 1972, when Steinhardt, Fine, Berkowitz was down by just a fraction.

Steinhardt's attempts to explain the partnership's success sometimes fuel the suspicion that luck played a part in it. "The stock market is an inexact phenomenon," he confesses. "Laypersons' opinions often seem as worthy as professionals', and shoeshine men and brokers compete for genius."[18] Unable to articulate a precise investment philosophy, Steinhardt falls back on vague talk about instinct. He deployed "an often inchoate judgment," he believes—a sixth sense that grew out of the experience of making investment judgments daily. Steinhardt had been fascinated by finance since his thirteenth birthday, when his absentee father presented him with stock certificates as a bar mitzvah gift, and he believes that constant immersion in the market creates an "intuition [that] should be lauded and worshipped."[19] The idea that experience builds judgment may sound plausible, but it falls short of a testable truth. And it is weakened by the fact that Steinhardt made his biggest errors late in his career, at times when experience should presumably have protected him.

Steinhardt also believes that sheer "intensity" favored him. "I had an overriding need to win every day," he says. "If I was not winning, I suffered as though a major tragedy had occurred." It is true that not winning could be tragic for Steinhardt's colleagues; the boss's tantrums would blaze over the firm's "hoot-and-holler" intercom system, which broadcast Steinhardt's voice to every corner of the office, compounding the humiliation for his victim. It is also true that, even when Steinhardt *was* winning, the intensity (read: temper) remained; one time, when a stock favored by a Steinhardt analyst netted a fantastic profit for the firm, the boss yelled at the poor man for recommending it a bit early.[20] Perhaps this way of doing business gave Steinhardt an edge: There was an emotional penalty for failure that drove his team forward. But again, this is not a testable theory. The opposite hypothesis—that Steinhardt's temper inhibited the sharing of ideas and drove good colleagues away—seems at least as compelling.[21]

If Steinhardt's explanations of his own success are not always satisfying, those offered by his former colleagues don't completely fill the gap, either. Howard Berkowitz and Jerry Fine believe that the quality of their stock analysis was simply better than that of other firms: Hence, the partnership made money. "Why did we do well? We cared a lot. We worked very hard. It meant everything to us," Fine says simply.[22] There is almost certainly much truth in this: As we will see later in our story, stock-picking prowess has driven the success of other celebrated funds, even though academic studies have doubted that this sort of skill really exists in practice.[23] But superior stock picking remains a less complete explanation for success in the case of Steinhardt, Fine, Berkowitz than in the case of A. W. Jones. The Jones funds could beat the market because they had created a novel system to pay for performance; but by the time Steinhardt, Fine, Berkowitz got going in the late 1960s, there were dozens of hedge funds. Besides, pension funds, endowments, and other institutions that had been half asleep in Jones's day were now altogether more professional.

————

IN SHORT, THE SUCCESS OF STEINHARDT, FINE, BERKO-
witz is difficult to explain, including for the former partners. But it does
not follow that their success was merely lucky. When you sift through
the story of the partnership, two factors stand out. Each helps to account
for success in a way that is consistent with the commonsense rendition of
efficient-market teaching: The market is difficult to beat—except when
you come up with an approach that others haven't yet exploited.

The first example of innovation at Steinhardt, Fine, Berkowitz concerns Tony Cilluffo. His enthusiasm for Kondratiev may have been weird,
but he brought another passion to the firm that was evidently sensible.
Starting in the 1960s, Cilluffo had begun tracking monetary data, hoping it might anticipate shifts in the stock market. A decade or so later, this
sort of exercise was common on Wall Street: Everybody recognized that
fast monetary growth predicted inflation and therefore would compel the
Federal Reserve to force up interest rates; when that happened, investors would move their money into bank deposits or bonds, preferring to
collect interest rather than incur the risk of staying in the stock market.
As money shifted out of stocks, the market inevitably would fall; and
stocks in companies that were sensitive to interest rates—home builders,
equipment suppliers—would fall the hardest. But during the 1960s, Wall
Street's equity investors could not be bothered with this sort of analysis.
They had learned their trade during the first half of the decade, a time
when the inflation rate never exceeded 2 percent. Monetary conditions
and the Federal Reserve's response were marginal to their thinking.[24]
An eccentric autodidact from out of the mainstream, Cilluffo was the
exception.

By the time he joined Steinhardt, Fine, Berkowitz in 1970, Cilluffo
had already devised a crude monetary model. He tracked the large banks
that formed the Federal Reserve System, and the moment they switched
from reporting spare lending capacity to reporting that they had hit the
limit of what could be supported by their capital reserves, Cilluffo's radar

bleeped: Banks had maxed out on their lending, so monetary growth was set to slow, so economic growth would head down and stocks would be in trouble. Cilluffo examined historical patterns and found that stocks began falling two months after the crossover point in the bank data. The relationship also worked in the opposite direction. If banks switched from reporting no lending capacity to reporting free reserves, the stock market would turn up imminently.[25]

Cilluffo had grasped the rules of investing in the high-inflation, post–gold standard world—even before that world had emerged fully. His approach gave Steinhardt, Fine, Berkowitz an edge in anticipating the hairpin bends in the stock market. Cilluffo anticipated both the collapse of 1973–74 and the sharp recovery that followed; in each case he reinforced the conclusions of colleagues who formed their view of the market using traditional stock analysis. If Cilluffo deserves a significant part of the credit for the fund's positioning in 1973–75, it follows that he deserves a significant part of the credit for the whole decade. The firm's performance in those three years accounted for the bulk of its profits during the 1970s.

Cilluffo's colleagues were only dimly aware of his insights because he was bad at explaining them. They knew, for example, that the wiry guy on the trading desk hated Kaufman & Broad, the nation's biggest home builder, and they knew that the firm was short 100,000 shares; they did not necessarily know that Cilluffo hated Kaufman because home builders are vulnerable to rising interest rates and the monetary data screamed that rates were heading upward. But Steinhardt saw to it that Cilluffo was empowered to test his views: He adored this guy's conviction, and he didn't care if others were baffled by his reasoning. The short position on Kaufman earned Steinhardt, Fine, Berkowitz over $2 million. And so, wittingly or otherwise, Cilluffo's colleagues were the beneficiaries of his innovation: the application of monetary analysis to stock markets.[26]

THE SECOND INNOVATION AT STEINHARDT, FINE, BERKO-
witz began with another change in the financial climate. Just as the

partnership anticipated how stock-market investing would adapt to inflation, so it anticipated how the profession would respond to shifting patterns in the custodianship of money.

Until the 1960s, the stock market was dominated by individual investors. Pension funds, insurance funds, and mutual funds—the institutional
managers of savings—were not yet significant. In 1950, for example, only
about ten million American workers were covered by a company pension, and because most of these plans were in their infancy, they had
relatively few assets. By 1970, however, the number of workers with company pensions had more than tripled; pension-fund assets now stood at
an eye-popping $130 billion and were growing at $14 billion annually.[27]
Meanwhile, individuals sold their direct stock holdings and entrusted the
proceeds to a new breed of money men. By the late 1960s mutual funds
managed more than $50 billion, up from $2 billion in 1950. Investing was
no longer the province of amateurs, advised by gentleman-brokers. It had
become a professional business.[28]

This transformed Wall Street. It was now harder to beat the market
simply by knowing about stocks, since the chances were that six other professional investors had the same information you did. But the profession-
alization of investment created a new opportunity just as it clouded the
old one. That opportunity came in the activity of trading, which would
come to play a central role in the story of hedge funds.

Before the big institutions came along, equity trading was dominated
by "specialists" on the floor of the New York Stock Exchange. When an
individual wanted to sell 50 shares in Ford, his broker called the New
York Stock Exchange market maker who specialized in that stock; having a feel for the deal flow, the specialist would buy the shares at a price
slightly below what he could sell them for a bit later. But this simple system broke down with the rise of the pension funds and mutual funds;
suddenly, these institutions wanted to trade Ford in 100,000-share blocks,
and the specialists lacked the capital to swallow that much. And so an
opportunity arose. A few enterprising brokers, led by Oppenheimer and
Goldman Sachs, began to make markets themselves. Rather than taking

block trades to the specialists, they began to handle them in-house, some-times finding buyers among their clients and sometimes buying the stock with their own capital. In 1965 block trading of this sort accounted for less than 5 percent of the transactions on the New York Stock Exchange. By 1970 that share had tripled.[29]

The new block-trading game was glorious. The big savings institutions needed somebody to make a market for large blocks of stock, and they were prepared to pay for this service. Indeed, they were prepared to pay handsomely because they had little choice: If they tried to unload 100,000 shares in Ford little by little, the price would move against them as they sold; and if the news of their selling leaked midway, the value of their shares would plummet. From the point of view of the savings institutions, therefore, it was better to give Goldman Sachs or Oppenheimer the whole 100,000-share block, even if that meant accepting a substantial discount to the market. But from the point of view of the brokers, the markdown could mean rapid profits. If they could find a buyer for the discounted shares, they could collect a hefty commission for arranging the trade. Alternatively, if they used their own capital to take the discounted stock onto their own books, they stood a good chance of selling it later at a profit.

The trick for the brokers was to know buyers with the guts to play in size, and that was where Steinhardt, Fine, Berkowitz came into the picture. The firm treated the trading function in an unusual manner. At most investment houses of the time, trading was a dull, back-office task, not something that a brilliant analyst would get involved in.[30] But at Stein-hardt, Fine, Berkowitz, the trading desk was manned by Steinhardt him-self; and when Goldman Sachs and Oppenheimer called to offer blocks of stock, Steinhardt was happy to oblige, provided that the discount was sufficiently enticing. The more Steinhardt dealt with the block traders, the more they were happy to call him. The brokers needed someone on a trad-ing desk who could make a big decision fast. Unlike the junior traders at most money-management firms, Steinhardt had the seniority to risk mil-lions on his own authority. Perhaps because he had inherited the gambling gene from his father, Steinhardt was positively thrilled to take these risks. "Trading went from being a mechanical, insignificant, clerklike function in the fifties and sixties to a function of great significance in the seventies and eighties," Steinhardt said later. [31]

All new markets are inefficient at first, and the inefficiency means profits for early adapters. The brokers whom Steinhardt dealt with were shooting from the hip. There were few trading guidelines to govern what sort of discount made sense for a given size of block; the bosses who would later step in with trading rules and risk controls were still fumbling in uncharted territory. In this state of nature, making money could be as easy as taking candy from a baby, to use a phrase that Steinhardt loved: Once he was offered 700,000 heavily discounted shares in Penn Central, the bankrupt railroad firm; he bought and resold them straightaway, realizing more than half a million dollars in the space of eight minutes.[32] Around 1970, Salomon Brothers resolved to become the third major block-trading house, alongside Goldman and Oppenheimer. To establish itself as a big player, it was willing to absorb large lots of stock at wafer-thin discounts, allowing Steinhardt to buy deeply discounted blocks elsewhere and off-load them on Salomon for a fat profit.[33]

Regulatory oddities created still other opportunities. Until the Securities and Exchange Commission stepped in toward the end of the 1970s, some parts of the block-trading business were transparent while others were shrouded in shadows. If you traded with Goldman or Salomon, firms that were members of the stock exchange, the price and size of the transaction would be reported on the ticker tape that was watched by every investor; if you got a discount, everybody knew about it. But if you traded in the so-called third market with brokers that were not members of the stock exchange, no transaction was reported. Steinhardt specialized in picking up unreported bargains in the third market, then unloading them quickly before anybody realized what was happening.

The more Steinhardt traded, the more money he found he could make. The third-market transactions, for example, worked only because of Steinhardt's reputation as a big swinger. Brokers who needed to off-load shares quickly and discreetly turned to him instinctively because he was the one fund manager with the guts to buy half a million shares on the strength of a brief phone call. Equally, Steinhardt was able to resell those shares because of who he was. His partnership was a huge generator of commissions for brokers, so the traders at Oppenheimer, Salomon, and Goldman could be counted upon to help him.

"I would say [to the broker], 'I got this block in the third a few hours ago. I bought it down one point. Do you want to work with me?'" Steinhardt recalls. "Down one point" meant that Steinhardt had received a discount on each share of $1.

"How many shares?" the broker would ask.

"Four hundred thousand."

"What do you want for them?"

"Why don't we do two hundred thousand, up an eighth," Steinhardt would say.

"Up an eighth!?" The broker would do a double take. Steinhardt was suggesting that they sell the discounted shares to an unsuspecting third party for 12.5 cents *more* than the price on the tape.

"Yeah, well, we need to attract some buyers. Let's put it up an eighth and it will look like a positive trade."[34]

Often enough, this bluff would work. Nobody knew that a huge block had been sold earlier at a discount on the opaque third market, so investors could be persuaded to buy at a premium. Even after paying the broker's commission, Steinhardt would clear a handsome profit.

Whatever the academic skepticism about stock pickers' ability to beat the market, it was not at all mysterious that block traders should outperform it. Block traders had figured out a new approach: They weren't engaged in the overcrowded business of analyzing company data and picking the stocks that would do well; instead, they aimed to make money by supplying something that other investors needed—liquidity. The new institutional custodians of savings were looking to trade large blocks of stocks quickly and discreetly, and they were willing to pay the guy who made that possible. Steinhardt's genius was to extract good fees for providing liquidity, as when he secured a hefty discount on a block of third-market stock; and at the same time to pay little or nothing to those who provided liquidity to him, as when he managed to off-load third-market stock at 12.5 cents above the market.

Though he did not express the point this way, Steinhardt had put his finger on a weakness in efficient-market theory. The theory holds that the market price embodies all relevant information about a stock; that is why beating the market is next to impossible. In the medium to long term, that theory may be roughly true. But in the short term, information is often not the chief driver of prices. Instead, stock prices bounce around because of minute-to-minute changes in investor appetites. An insurance company needs to sell a large block of stocks to pay storm-damage claims: The selling pressure drives down prices. A pension fund needs to buy a large block to employ a fresh inflow of cash from workers: The buying pressure drives up prices. In efficient-market models, these temporary price shocks are ignored; liquidity is assumed to be perfect.[35] The real world is different.

This wrinkle in efficient-market models becomes especially pronounced when the demand for large transactions jumps and market structures have yet to adapt—as happened in the late 1960s and into the 1970s and 1980s. For some years after block trading started up, major sales could push a stock sharply away from the "efficient" price—the one that reflected analysts' best assessment of all known earnings-related information. These short-run dislocations created opportunities for alert traders to seize bargains, and Steinhardt seized them aggressively.[36] Moreover, the great beauty of Steinhardt's method was that it was hard to copy. Once Wall Street had understood the mechanics of the A. W. Jones model, two hundred imitators had sprung up. But Steinhardt's block-trading business was protected by "network effects," which created barriers to entry. Steinhardt got the big calls from the block-trading brokers because he had a reputation for getting the big calls. He could trade his way out of big purchases because he had the network of broker relationships that came with being a big trader. Would-be rivals faced a frustrating catch-22 as they scrambled to catch up with him.

There was one less beautiful feature of the Steinhardt edge. It pushed the bounds of what was legal.

BEFORE WE GET TO THE SHADY STUFF, THINK BACK TO
the question of liquidity. When a large block of stock comes on the market, would-be buyers can't tell whether the seller knows something special.
Maybe the seller has been tipped off that the company is about to revise its
earnings down. Maybe he knows that another big institution is about to
dump shares in the same company. Because buyers don't know what they
don't know, they hesitate before bidding for 400,000 shares. Fearing that
they may be at an informational disadvantage, they demand a discount in
exchange for the provision of liquidity.

How could Steinhardt make money in such circumstances? Again,
Steinhardt's scale was important: He did so much block trading, and
generated so many commissions for brokers, that he could expect special information from them.[37] Theoretically, brokers were not supposed to
identify their clients; if a seller came to the market with 400,000 shares,
the seller's identity was secret. The brokers were not meant to let on, for
example, that the seller was a plodding insurance fund and therefore that
it was probably selling for liquidity reasons—in which case its block discount would represent a bargain. But, as the brokers' prized customer,
Steinhardt could expect some creative bending of the rules.[38] If the seller
was a smart hedge fund rather than an insurer, the broker might avoid
inviting Steinhardt to be the buyer, since the hedge fund might be selling on the basis of bearish information. Or if the sale represented the
first sell order in a big series, the broker might issue a discreet warning.[39]
"The idea was not to try to hurt anybody. You wanted to do business with
them," said John Lattanzio, a Goldman Sachs block trader, recalling the
clubby atmosphere of the 1970s.[40] "You'd say, 'Don't buy the first hundred, there's four hundred behind it,'" added Will Weinstein, the head
trader at Oppenheimer, explaining that the big block traders were looking
to do "things that were not collusive but were just honest attempts to protect each other."[41] How Weinstein could view this as anything other than
collusion is a mystery.

Sometimes the collusion was more elaborate. A broker might call to say that a big institution was about to unload 500,000 shares of such and such, so perhaps Steinhardt should get short ahead of time, before the selling hit the market. Then, when the big order came through and the shares started to move down, Steinhardt would cover his short by buying the tail end of the order at the newly depressed price, pocketing some easy money. From the broker's point of view, the tip-off to Steinhardt positioned his hedge fund to act as a buyer for the last tranche of the big sale: This helped the sale to go through without the price's falling as much as it might have, making the broker look like a genius in the eyes of the seller.[42] But the catch was that Steinhardt's shorting had moved the market down before the transaction had begun: The block sale went through at something near the market price because the market had been lowered in preparation. This rigging was a clear violation of the rules. The seller had hired the broker to get the best price for his shares, but the broker had sold him out to Steinhardt.

From the safe distance of three decades, Steinhardt is remarkably frank about this. "I was being told things that other accounts were not being told," Steinhardt says, describing the mechanics of his collusion with brokers. "I got information I shouldn't have. It created a lot of opportunities for us. Were they risky? Yes. Was I willing to do it? Yes. Were they talked about much? Not particularly."[43]

IT'S IMPOSSIBLE TO QUANTIFY THE CONTRIBUTION OF block trading to Steinhardt, Fine, Berkowitz. Steinhardt himself says that it "represented a meaningful portion of the noise, but not the profits," though the more you listen to his descriptions of trading, the more you suspect he may be lowballing its significance.[44] Certainly, the focus on trading represented the partnership's most distinctive edge; and it is surely no coincidence that, of the three extremely gifted founding partners, it was Steinhardt who went on to become a legend. During twenty-eight years in the markets, Steinhardt suffered losses in just four. The probability of that happening is one in eleven thousand.[45] At some point the coin-tossing niggles become irrelevant.

But there is another question about Steinhardt's trading. If his collusion had been known at the time, might the Securities and Exchange Commission have revived its interest in regulating hedge funds—and might the story of the industry have been substantially different? Collusion between hedge funds and big brokers was sometimes suspected, to be sure; but it was never proved. During the 1970s, the Securities and Exchange Commission came after Steinhardt once: It alleged that in January 1970 his partnership had purchased a large block of stock in Seaboard Corporation, apparently as a favor to a broker who wanted to boost its price ahead of a public offering; the SEC maintained that Steinhardt had acted on the understanding that it would be compensated for any losses. But in 1976 Steinhardt settled the case without admitting wrongdoing.[46] The suspicion of collusive market behavior remained just that—a suspicion.

Even so, it is not clear that Steinhardt's admission would have tipped the balance in favor of a regulatory clampdown, still less that it should have. To the extent that Steinhardt was acting on privileged information, regulators were already empowered to go after him—as they did in the Seaboard incident. Besides, part of Steinhardt's success reflected regulatory oddities that were not of his own making. In 1975 and again in 1978, the regulators acknowledged their own failings and sought to put them right: They set about bringing Steinhardt's beloved third market out of the shadows, first insisting that all stock transactions be printed on a new "consolidated tape," then stipulating that bids and offers for stocks be similarly reported.[47] The intention was to spread trading information evenly to all market players, eroding the unfair edge of Wall Street's inner circle.

Yet the main reason to hold back the outrage is more basic: Taken as a whole, Steinhardt's activities were good for the economy. The search for the smoking gun of "market disruption," on which the Securities and Exchange Commission embarked in 1969, had ended in failure because no disruption could be identified. Equally, the success of Steinhardt, Fine, Berkowitz over the ensuing years did not disrupt markets. It stabilized them.

Two themes in the young troika's success were unambiguously good for the stability of the financial system. The partnership's contrarian-ism made a small contribution toward dampening disruptive swings in stock prices: The troika sold during the bubble of 1972; it went long at the end of 1974, when the postcrash market was desperately in need of buyers. Likewise, by pioneering the application of monetary analysis to stock markets, the partnership brought new sophistication to the pricing of assets. If the bubble-to-bust cycles of 1968–70 and 1972–74 reflected Wall Street's naïveté about inflation, Tony Cilluffo's analytical techniques made such bubbles less likely in the future.

And then there was the matter of that block trading. Steinhardt's col-lusion with the big brokers sometimes damaged outsider investors, who might have gotten better prices for their stock if the insiders hadn't fixed the market. The outsider investors included mutual funds and pension funds, so the ultimate losers were ordinary Americans—while the win-ners were the millionaires who invested with Steinhardt. But this reverse Robin Hood story is not the whole picture. The block-trading business grew up because the outsider investors needed liquidity to shift big chunks of stock; by providing the outsiders with an opportunity to trade, Stein-hardt was helping them. It was not as though the institutional investors enjoyed the benefits of wonderfully efficient markets, only to have an evil hedge fund corrupt them. Rather, institutional investors faced lousy mar-kets that were highly inefficient in the short run. Steinhardt's contribution was to offer liquidity that they were free to use or to ignore, and the fact that they chose to use it was revealing. In all probability, the service Stein-hardt provided outweighed the effects of his wrongdoing.

If that sounds too charitable, fast-forward to 1987. The stock-market crash in October of that year provided a lesson in what life might be like without Steinhardt and his trading counterparts. In the wake of Black Monday, the big block-trading desks pulled back from the busi-ness, and the result was a furious outcry. The *New York Times* reported in December that blocks of 25,000 shares now disrupted prices as much as 100,000-share blocks had done before the crash; the market had grown horribly unstable.[48] The mere rumor that an institution might be selling a block of Ford or IBM was enough to drive the share price down; because the block traders had irresponsibly pulled back, innocent companies were being damaged. In a twist that put the debates of the 1960s and 1970s in a whole new light, the SEC promised to investigate the troubling lack of block trading. The only thing worse than fast-trading hedge funds was a sudden dearth of them.

Steinhardt traded the markets as though he were fighting a war, and the effort exhausted him. In the fall of 1978, he took a sabbatical from his firm, declaring that his aim was to shrink his waistline and expand his head: to find meaning in life beyond wealth accumulation. Some said he might be leaving for good, but others had their doubts; "there's as much chance of Michael giving up Wall Street for a year as there is of Vladimir Horowitz giving up the piano permanently," one friend insisted.[49] As it turned out, Steinhardt managed to stay away from trading until the fall of the following year. Then he stormed back, broke up with his partners, and marched into the 1980s.

PAUL SAMUELSON'S SECRET

In famous congressional testimony in 1967, the great economist Paul Samuelson delivered his verdict on the money-management indus- try. Citing a recent dissertation by a PhD candidate at Yale, he sug- gested that randomly chosen stock portfolios tended to beat professionally managed mutual funds. When the House banking committee chairman sounded incredulous, the professor stood his ground. "When I say 'ran- dom,' I want you to think of dice or think of random numbers or a dart," he emphasized.[1] Three years later, Samuelson became the third econo- mist to win the Nobel Prize, but the recognition did not mellow him one bit. "Most portfolio decision makers should go out of business—take up plumbing, teach Greek, or help produce the annual GNP by serving as corporate executives," he wrote in 1974. "Even if this advice to drop dead is good advice, it obviously is not counsel that will be eagerly followed."[2]

Samuelson's pronouncements did not sound much like an endorse- ment of hedge funds. But his condemnation of professional investors left room for exceptions. Even if most fund managers might contribute more to society as plumbers, Samuelson believed that a giant with genu- inely fresh insights could beat the market.[3] "People differ in their heights, pulchritude, and acidity," he wrote. "Why not in their P.Q. or perfor- mance quotient?"[4] Of course, these exceptional investors would not rent themselves out cheaply "to the Ford Foundation or to the local bank trust department. They have too high an I.Q. for that." The giants were more likely to form small partnerships that would capture the gains for themselves: They were more likely to start hedge funds. Samuelson never lacked for confidence—by the age of twenty-five, he had published more papers than he was years old—and he naturally believed he could pick out the rare exceptions from the ranks of should-have-been plumbers. In 1970 he became a founding backer of an investment start-up called Commodities Corporation, diversifying his portfolio around the same time with an investment in Warren Buffett.[5]

Commodities Corporation was among the first boutiques created by hard-core "quants"—the breed of computer-wielding modelers sometimes known as "rocket scientists."[6] The company's premise, as proclaimed on the first page of its prospectus, was to harness "large scale econometric analysis, impossible prior to the introduction of computers."[7] The founding traders at Commodities Corporation included Paul Cootner, a colleague of Samuelson's at the Massachusetts Institute of Technology, who was ironically famous in academia for his contribution to efficient-market theory.[8] Along with several other economics PhDs, the firm later hired a programmer who had worked on the Apollo project—he was literally a rocket scientist.[9] The venture was legally structured as a corporation rather than a partnership, but it was in other ways a typical hedge fund.[10] It went both long and short. It used leverage. Its astronomical profits were shared between its managers and a small number of investors. Samuelson paid $125,000 for his stake in Commodities Corporation and agreed to become an active board member.

Samuelson's involvement was principally a bet on F. Helmut Weymar, the driven, anguished, and mildly megalomaniacal president of the company.[11] Weymar had recently completed a PhD dissertation that proposed a method of anticipating the price of cocoa: It crunched historical data to determine the extent to which economic growth boosted chocolate consumption and hence cocoa demand, the extent to which drought or humidity in West Africa impacted supply, and so on. Weymar had studied at the Massachusetts Institute of Technology, where he had known both Samuelson and Cootner. But although Weymar looked to his teachers for help in refining his mathematical and computing skills, he was unimpressed by their efficient-market theories. "I thought random walk was bullshit," he said later. "The whole idea that an individual can't make serious money with a competitive edge over the rest of the market is wacko."[12]

Weymar was tall and bespectacled, with high cheekbones and a distinguished Northern European air inherited from his German parents. He had moved cities frequently during his childhood, and the experience had left him with an independent streak and a determination to make so much money that he would be beholden to nobody. Even as a graduate student, he had built an ambitious mathematical model of the frozen-orange-juice industry, and when the model suggested that the price of orange-juice concentrate would double, he borrowed $20,000 to buy a large consignment from a warehouse. The model turned out to be accurate, and the price duly shot up. The only hitch was that local supermarkets were leery of buying wholesale orange juice from a student. Weymar had to sell the juice back to the warehouse, which raked off a fifth of his profit.[13]

After completing his PhD on the cocoa market, Weymar went to work for the food company Nabisco, where he soon persuaded his bosses to trade on his forecasts. The idea was that as cocoa prices fell relative to his model's prediction, Nabisco would buy to cover its chocolate-making needs; if the market rose higher than the model expected, Nabisco would pause its procurement. As soon as Weymar's program began trading, cocoa prices fell way below what the model predicted, so Weymar started to buy cocoa futures by the truckload. Then the price fell even more, which meant that Weymar had registered a loss; but following the rules of his program, Weymar carried on buying anyway. Nabisco's chief financial officer started to worry, and Weymar had to fend him off with a smoke screen of quantitative jargon; meanwhile, he found himself sitting on enough beans to cover two years of Nabisco's production. "You sure you know what you are doing?" Weymar's boss demanded more than once; and Weymar projected as much confidence as he could while inwardly sweating bullets. But just as Weymar's nerves were breaking, the African crops failed and cocoa prices almost doubled. Weymar sold back part of his stockpile at a vast profit. "This wasn't a period of maximum modesty or self-doubt in my life," he confessed later.[14]

Emboldened by that success, Weymar resolved to start up his own enterprise. He began plotting with Frank Vannerson, another freshly minted economics PhD who had joined him at Nabisco's forecasting unit. The two made an unlikely pair. Weymar brimmed with sunny confidence, while Vannerson was bearded and subdued; one colleague imagined him as a medieval friar with leather sandals and a hooded robe; another suggested he gave off the vibes of a friendly psychotherapist.[15] But Weymar and Vannerson were close friends, and Vannerson's PhD thesis on the wheat market complemented Weymar's expertise in cocoa. Weymar pulled in other coconspirators, and they coalesced around a plan. After raising start-up capital of $2.5 million, the founders opened up shop in Princeton, New Jersey, near where Weymar and Vannerson were living. Their farmhouse headquarters were surrounded by flowering trees and acres of lawn. On his first day at the office, Weymar wore a suit. Vannerson showed up with a polo shirt, khakis, and his dog, Peanuts.[16]

Weymar's office was kitted out with a huge walnut executive desk and a big red leather chair; the combination suited him perfectly. But Vannerson's informal and egalitarian style quickly came to dominate the firm; if there was a company meeting at Commodities Corporation, Agnes, the cook, was invited. The community in the old farmhouse included a German shepherd dog named Cocoa that had lost one leg to a collision with a car. Weymar's small band of employees, comprising seven professionals and six support staff, sometimes pitched horseshoes at lunch and played softball after the markets closed. The informal atmosphere signaled the firm's distance from the hustle of New York: Commodities Corporation was not about salesmanship and relationships and *looking* like a market insider; it was about beating the market with computer models, math, and superior information. The founders exchanged trading theories at regular seminars, filling a blackboard with formulas. It was a long way from the stock-jockey ethos at A. W. Jones or from the pizza-strewn chaos of Michael Steinhardt's trading room.

Weymar had assembled a team that was heavy on fundamental analysis. He wanted econometricians who built models that predicted where prices ought to be, on the theory that profits would ensue when reality caught up with the forecasts. Weymar traded cocoa; Vannerson took responsibility for wheat; Paul Cootner, the MIT professor, arrived at the firm armed with an econometric model of the pork-belly market. Kenneth Meinken, an econometrician who had taught at Rutgers University, signed on to trade soybeans and feed grains. By recruiting specialists in different commodities, Weymar hoped to diversify the firm's exposure to any one market.

Weymar fed his cocoa model with a vast array of data. To anticipate the supply of cocoa before the West African growing countries reported officially on their harvests, he examined the correlation between weather and cocoa yields in the Ivory Coast and Ghana. By tracking rain and humidity patterns, he could predict the cocoa harvest, and hence cocoa supply, and hence, ultimately, prices. The start-up group also included Hans Kilian, a German who toured the African countryside in a Land Rover, surveying cocoa trees and recording the number, length, and condition of the pods. A cocoa tree is as tall as an apple tree and contains about twenty-five pods, so the pod counter complained of a stiff neck. His Land Rover frequently broke down. He battled to get his hands on the large amounts of Ghanaian currency needed to pay local workers who helped with the counting. But the effort provided a way of confirming or correcting the supply projections derived from weather patterns. Weymar had devised a sophisticated model for pricing cocoa, and now he had sophisticated data to feed into it.

SOPHISTICATION DID NOT GUARANTEE SUCCESS, HOW-ever. Shortly after Commodities Corporation got under way, U.S. cornfields were hit by a fungal disease known as the corn blight. Some plant experts predicted that the blight would reappear the following year, and on a bigger scale; corn futures started to move up in expectation of impending scarcity. Faced with a thicket of semiscientific rumor that was scaring the market, Weymar and his colleagues saw a chance to get an edge. They retained a plant pathologist at Rutgers University who advised the state of New Jersey, increasing his research budget and covering his expenses as he journeyed around the country attending scientific conferences. After some weeks of investigation, the Rutgers pathologist concluded that the blight fright was overdone: The plethora of scare stories reflected nothing more infectious than the alarmist bias of the media. Weymar and his colleagues jumped. The pathologist's conclusion meant that corn prices would be coming down, so the traders started to pile in, building vast short positions in anticipation of the time when the alarmism would prove to be unfounded. Then one Friday night, alongside its regular coverage of Vietnam, CBS News ran a special report on the corn blight. It featured the Illinois state plant pathologist, a man representing a state with a lot more corn than New Jersey. And the man from the corn state was predicting a catastrophic corn harvest.

Weymar and his colleagues didn't sleep much that weekend. They had built a vast short position in the corn market, betting their firm on the advice of a pathologist who was now being contradicted by a senior colleague. When the markets finally opened on Monday, corn futures jumped so steeply that trading was immediately suspended: Commodity exchanges place a limit on allowable daily movements to dampen extreme swings in prices. There was no chance whatever to get out of the market; prices hit their limit after a smattering of contracts had changed hands, and Weymar and his friends were trapped in their positions. It wasn't until Tuesday that the Commodities Corporation traders managed to dump their short positions, and by then the damage had been done: The firm's start-up capital of $2.5 million now stood at $900,000. Weymar's young company was crashing before his eyes. It was not much consolation that the pathologist from Rutgers eventually turned out to be right. There was no corn blight, and Commodities Corporation had closed out its short positions at the absolute top of the market.

The corn debacle of 1971 brought Commodities Corporation to within a hairbreadth of closure. The relationships among the founding traders frayed; Weymar wondered how nervous he should be about the shotgun that an angry cofounder kept in his office to shoot rabbits and pheasants. Several of the firm's founding board members wanted to withdraw their capital: Despite their quantitative sophistication and impressive PhDs, Weymar and his team appeared to lack that high "performance quotient" that Samuelson was after. But Weymar was determined, and he had come back from adversity before. Once, as a student, he had lost all his money on a series of bad bets and had taken himself off to the bleachers at a Red Sox game to drink too many beers and think his way to a recovery. This time he was in Princeton, and the booze-and-baseball therapy was less conveniently to hand, but he was no more ready to give in. He pictured himself as the romantic hero in one of the great novels he had been raised on; he responded to his setback with a sort of fascinated masochism, wallowing in the angst and introspection that accompany adversity. He had no intention of abandoning his young company, with the late-afternoon softball and the flowering trees. If Cocoa the watchdog could soldier on despite losing a leg, a cocoa trader could soldier on despite losing a large chunk of his capital.

The board of Commodities Corporation met in July 1971 and agreed to give Weymar a last chance: The firm would be closed if it lost another $100,000.[17] In the bloodletting that followed, four of the original seven founding professionals, including Cootner, left the firm. But the recovery came soon, and it laid the foundations for one of the most successful trading operations of the era.

AFTER THE 1971 DEBACLE, WEYMAR SET ABOUT RETHINK-ing his theory of the market. He had begun with an economist's faith in model building and data: Prices reflected the fundamental forces of supply and demand, so if you could anticipate those things you were on your way to riches. But experience had taught him some humility. An exaggerated faith in data could turn out to be a curse, breeding the sort of hubris that leads you into trading positions too big to be sustainable.

If Commodities Corporation had bet against the corn blight on a more modest scale, it might not have been scared out of its positions by an item on the evening news. The result would have been a profit rather than a near-death experience.

Weymar's rethink began with a new approach to risk taking. The most dangerous people in the world, he now liked to say, were very smart traders who had never gotten their teeth kicked in.[18] In moments of self-awareness, he probably acknowledged that the wildest trader at the company might be none other than himself; a colleague once suggested that putting Weymar in charge of risk controls was like putting Evel Knievel in charge of road safety.[19] In the first year of its existence, Commodities Corporation had operated a risk-control system designed by Paul Cootner; it was mathematically elegant but too complex to enforce effectively. Under Cootner's system, the firm's trading capital sat in one big pot. The traders could dip into it freely, but the firm charged them penal interest rates on the money if they added to large and volatile positions. In theory, a trader had to be brimming with confidence to double up a bet in a turbulent market. But the corn blight proved that brimming confidence was alarmingly abundant in a company of strong egos, and the clerical staff was so far behind in tracking traders' exposure that there was effectively no risk control of any nature. Now that Cootner's system had proved defective and Cootner himself was gone, Weymar set about creating a practical replacement.[20]

The upshot was a risk-control system that survives, more or less, in the contemporary hedge funds whose origins are entwined with Commodities Corporation.[21] Its basics resembled the segment-manager system used at A. W. Jones: Each trader was treated as an independent profit center and was allocated a pot of capital whose size reflected previous performance.[22] But the system also forced traders to control bets, something that scarcely mattered in the relatively stable world of stock-market investing, but that was crucial in commodities. Under the rules that governed equities, an investor could only borrow up to half the value of the stocks he bought; there was no way he could leverage himself more than two to one, even if he was crazy enough to want to do so. But commodity futures were a whole different world. Traders could borrow most of the value of their positions, putting down only a small "margin" of hard cash; because their leverage was higher, one ill-conceived bet could wipe out a large chunk of their capital. The new Commodities Corporation system capped the risk that a trader could take in any one position; and if a trader racked up big losses, more controls kicked in. Anyone who blew half of his initial capital had to sell all his positions and take a month off. He was required to write a memo to the management explaining his miscalculations.[23]

The new risk-control system was connected to another rethink that followed the corn debacle: Weymar and his colleagues developed fresh respect for trends in prices. Of course, efficient-market theory holds that such trends do not exist: The random-walk consensus was so dominant that, through the 1970s and much of the 1980s, it was hard to get alternative views published in academic journals.[24] But Frank Vannerson had gotten his hands on a trove of historical commodity price data that had been gathered and formatted by Dunn & Hargitt, a firm in Indiana. Before leaving Nabisco, Vannerson had spent a year working on the Dunn & Hargitt data, analyzing daily prices for fifteen commodities; and by the time Commodities Corporation opened its doors in March 1970, he had satisfied himself that price trends really did exist, no matter what academics might assert to the contrary.[25] Moreover, Vannerson had devised a computer program that could trade on that finding. He called his brainchild the Technical Computer System, or TCS. It was one of the first in a long line of automated trading systems spawned by the hedge-fund industry.[26]

Weymar was initially skeptical of Vannerson's project.[27] His trend-following concept seemed disarmingly simple: Buy things that have just gone up on the theory that they will continue to go up; short things that have just gone down on the theory that they will continue to go down. Even though Vannerson's program took a step beyond that—it tried to distinguish upticks that might signify a lasting trend from upticks that signified nothing—Weymar still doubted that anyone could make serious money from something apparently so trivial. But by the summer of 1971, Weymar had reversed himself. The humiliation of the corn episode was one reason:

The great virtue of an automated trading system was that risk controls had to be programmed into the computer from the start, and there was no danger of overconfident traders exceeding their allowed limits. But the TCS had proved itself to be superior at calling the market too. Weymar's cocoa model, which had worked so well at Nabisco, had misjudged the direction of the market expensively during Commodities Corporation's first year. But Vannerson's trend-following model, which watched patterns in the market rather than the fundamentals of chocolate consumption or rainfall, had made money consistently from the day the firm opened.

After the debacle of the corn blight, Weymar began to allocate more capital to the Technical Computer System, and the human traders developed a fresh respect for the program's decisions. Indeed, the new risk-control system gave them little choice: It prohibited traders from committing more than a tenth of their capital in betting against a trend, and the trends used in implementing the controls were the ones identified by Vannerson's program. Even Paul Samuelson was won over to the new approach. He stumped up a fresh chunk of capital to be invested by the TCS, even though trend following had little standing within academia and none within his own research.

IN 1974 A YOUNG RECRUIT NAMED MICHAEL MARCUS joined the team at Commodities Corporation. He was far removed from Weymar's original conception of the model trader. He was not an econometrician specialized in one commodity; indeed, he lacked even a degree in economics. He had no use for computers and little use for math; he had dropped out of a PhD program in psychology, and was one of the first Commodities Corporation traders to be hired without a doctorate.[28] Marcus's arrival raised some eyebrows, but the skeptics were soon silenced as he started to earn triple-digit returns on his capital. Over a ten-year period at Commodities Corporation, Marcus increased the value of his trading account by 2,500 percent. There were years when his profits exceeded those of all the other traders put together.

Marcus was intense, quiet, and fearsomely controlled, a trait that found expression in his approach to his own body. He believed that most foods contained poisons, and he monitored his intake; he once purified himself with a diet of raw vegetables and fruits, becoming so emaciated that he hired a dietician-cum-driver to coax him back to equilibrium. He splashed his winnings on elaborate parties and exotic travel; at one point he owned about ten homes, some of which he later sold without spending a single night in them. He chartered a jet and had a bus converted into a traveling dwelling, stocked with an entourage of admirers. He took kick-boxing lessons with an international champion.[29]

Whatever the extremes of his lifestyle, Marcus's intensity did wonders for his trading. In keeping with the founding vision for Commodities Corporation, he studied the economic fundamentals that might drive markets. He would arrive in the office each morning with an oversized briefcase packed full of market reports; there were no Post-its back then, but Marcus used sticky tape to attach careful handwritten notes to key pages from his reading. He pored over newsletters and scanned data about the basic drivers of supply and demand, searching for shifts that would push prices. He thought through scenarios that might threaten his portfolio. If corn went up, would wheat follow? And if the weather turned colder, which crops would be first affected? But in keeping with Frank Vannerson's trend following, Marcus did not restrict himself to watching the fundamental drivers of prices. He was a keen student of price charts, which he regarded as a window into the psychology of investors, and he focused especially on the interaction between charts and fundamentals. For example, if the fundamentals delivered bad news but the charts showed the market continuing to trend up, it meant that investors had already digested the possibility of setbacks. Nothing was going to spoil their mood. There was nowhere to go but upward.

Marcus's respect for trends reflected his experience. He had spent time on the floor of the cotton exchange early in his career and had watched traders respond to the tempo of their colleagues. Sometimes they would work one another up into a crescendo of shouting, and sometimes they would fall back, exhausted. If the price of a commodity headed up past its high point of the previous day, there was a decent chance that it would keep riding upward on a wave of excitement; so Marcus would take a large position at those crossover moments, protecting himself with a stop-loss order that would kick him out of the market if the trade went against him. Either the market took off and ran or Marcus was out: It was like mounting a surfboard, ready for the wave; if your timing was off, you just plopped back into the water. Like the storied hedge-fund traders who emulated this method later, Marcus reckoned that he caught the wave on less than half of his attempts. But his winning rides earned profits of twenty or thirty times the small losses he took when he got stopped out of his position.

As Marcus developed his investing style, he absorbed lessons from his colleagues and vice versa, so that the Princeton set converged upon a common culture. As the traders watched the price charts, looking for waves that could be profitably surfed, they recognized recurring patterns. Market bottoms tended to be rounded, because a bumper harvest not only drives the price down but causes excess produce to be held in storage; this inventory overhang keeps prices low for an extended period. By contrast, market tops tend to be spike shaped: If there is a sudden shortage in a crop, consumption has to fall sharply and prices shoot up; but if the next harvest is good, the shortage goes away and prices quickly shoot down again. The details of these patterns varied from one commodity to the next. Pork bellies and eggs, for example, were notorious for their spike bottoms. There were limits to how long these commodities could be stored, so a glut got dumped on the market rather than being held in inventory.

The Commodities Corporation traders also developed views on investor psychology. People form opinions at their own pace and in their own way; the notion that new information could be instantly processed was one of those ivory-tower assumptions that had little to do with reality. This gradual absorption of information by investors explained why markets moved in trends, as new developments were gradually digested. But market psychology was more subtle than that; there were times when investors' reactions accelerated. Human being do not simply make forward-looking judgments about markets, the Commodities Corporation traders recognized; they react to recent experiences. For example, losses might trigger an anxious bout of selling; gains might set off waves of euphoric buying. This realization led to an insight about congestion points—the places on the charts where prices bounced within a narrow range before speeding off in one direction or the other. When a commodity broke out of its usual price band, investors who had bet wrong would experience a sharp loss; panicking, they would close their positions in a rush, hastening the market's escape from its old price range. The patterns reminded the traders of travelers in a train station crowding around a door. They took a long time to pass through the bottleneck in either direction, but once they were through they usually accelerated.

The triumph of Michael Marcus's trading style rendered Weymar's initial concept for his firm inoperative. Later in the story of hedge funds, the hardcore quants would have their day; but so long as trend surfing delivered marvelous profits, it made little sense to focus obsessively on econometric modeling. The original Weymar data crunching seemed relatively thankless: There were so many variables that drove prices, it was virtually impossible to get all of them right; moreover, even if you were right you could go broke waiting for the rest of the market to catch up with you.[30] Marcus's performance also upended Weymar's initial belief in specialized traders. If the profits came from financial surfing, then the game was to spot the commodities that generated strong waves; there was no point wasting time studying sugar or wheat, for example, if these markets were going through a tranquil period. Having worked on the floor of the cotton exchange, Marcus knew what it was like to specialize. He preached the gospel of generalization with the zeal of the converted.[31]

Marcus's determination not to specialize made him a natural pioneer in the new field of currency trading. Following Nixon's abandonment of the dollar-gold link, Chicago's Mercantile Exchange began trading futures in seven free-floating currencies in May 1972. Marcus quickly saw an opportunity to apply his surfing skills to a new beach; investor psychology could be counted upon to generate the same waves in currency markets as existed in commodities. By the mid- to late 1970s, about a third of Marcus's trading was in currencies, and by the end of the decade, two thirds was.[32] Marcus's colleagues at Commodities Corporation began to trade currencies as well, as did many of the independent traders whom the firm seeded. A new kind of hedge-fund player—the "macro" traders who became the scourge of central bankers in the 1980s and beyond—was starting to stir in the incongruous setting of a Princeton farmhouse.

Marcus was a libertarian, and his political outlook turned out to be useful in the climate of the 1970s.[33] In some eras, markets appear destabilizing while governments are heroes, but in the stagflationary 1970s the libertarian view that big government screws up was frequently vindicated. At the start of the decade, Nixon imposed price controls that turned out to be the functional equivalent of the misguided currency controls of later years: They made for bad public policy because they proved not to be sustainable, and they created a bonanza for speculators. By fixing plywood, for example, at $110 per thousand square feet, the Nixon administration was putting up traffic cones in the path of an invading tank: The United States was in the midst of a construction boom, and demand for plywood was booming; builders were willing to buy planks for much more than the price mandated by the government. Pretty soon, plywood warehouses were shipping supplies to Canada and back again to get around Nixon's controls, or they were performing "added-value services" such as shaving a sliver off their planks and then charging $150 per thousand square feet for them. Meanwhile, builders who could not get all the wood they needed were starting to buy it in the futures market, where prices were not regulated. Confident that artificial scarcity in the physical market would drive the futures up and up, Marcus bought plywood futures by the truckload. Their value virtually doubled.[34]

When Nixon's price controls were abandoned at the start of 1973, Marcus made even more money. As any libertarian could see, incompetent government was debasing the currency by inflating the money supply, so a trader was likely to get rich simply by leveraging himself up and holding huge positions in grains and beans and metals. In 1974 alone, the coffee price went up by a quarter, rice went up by two thirds, and white sugar doubled; anyone who bought these commodities on margin was multiplying his money.[35] Then food commodities turned around and embarked on an equally tradable downward trend: Sugar lost 67 percent of its peak value, cotton and rubber lost 40 percent, and cocoa fell more than 25 percent.[36] When the Carter administration tried to stimulate the economy, the boost to inflation caused the dollar to drop by a third against the yen and the deutsche mark, and the big moves gave surfers of the new currency-futures markets ample opportunity.[37]

In early 1975, Marcus spied an opportunity that anticipated the victories against exchange-rate pegs for which later hedge funds became notorious. In his search for dumb government policies that violated good market sense, he fixed on an intervention as enticing as Nixon's price controls: Saudi Arabia had pegged its currency to the dollar. It didn't take a genius to notice that the peg was in trouble. As Saudi Arabia's export revenues ballooned along with the oil price, its economy was flooded with money, creating upward pressure on the exchange rate. Of course, revaluation was not certain: Saudi Arabia could decide to live with the capital inflows, even though they stoked inflation. But, following the logic of currency speculators who later attacked exchange-rate pegs everywhere from Britain to Thailand, Marcus saw that, whether or not revaluation happened, devaluation was inconceivable. This made betting on the Saudi currency a hugely attractive one-way gamble: There could be no guarantee of winning, but there was a near guarantee of not losing. So Marcus took huge positions in the riyal, leveraging himself up with borrowed money and sleeping perfectly soundly. In March 1975, Saudi Arabia abandoned its dollar link and revalued. Marcus made another killing.[38]

BY THE END OF THE 1970S, THE SUCCESS OF COMMODIT- ies Corporation had become prodigious. The corn-blight fiasco was a faded memory; trend surfing, Michael Marcus style, was delivering returns of 50 percent plus for many of the firm's traders. The company's capital swelled from under $1 million at its low point to some $30 million; the farmhouse acquired an extra wing and a new building was commissioned. Weymar hired new traders, and each trader hired researchers to keep track of the charts; new administrative staff arrived at a rate the old-timers found absurd, especially since the overhead came out of their trading profits. But the profits were large enough to paper over the problem. In 1980 alone, they came to an astronomical $42 million, so that even after shelling out $13 million in bonuses to 140 employees, Weymar's quiet firm outearned fifty-eight of the Fortune 500 companies. Weymar flew his employees and their families first class to a company retreat in Bermuda. The traders hijacked the occasion to lambaste Weymar for his free-spending ways, but they of all people recognized that Commodities Corporation was a phenomenon.[39]

The phenomenon was first and foremost a triumph of flexibility. In moving beyond econometric analysis to focus on trends, Weymar had demonstrated a pragmatism that crops up repeatedly in the history of hedge funds—and indeed in business history generally. Innovation is often ascribed to big theories fomented in universities and research parks: Thus Stanford's engineering school stands at the center of Silicon Valley's creativity, and the National Institutes of Health underpin innovation in the pharmaceutical industry. But the truth is that innovation frequently depends less on grand academic breakthroughs than on humble trial and error—on a willingness to go with what works, and never mind the theory that may underlie it. Even in finance, a field in which research findings can be translated directly into business plans, trial and error turns out to be key. A. W. Jones started out expecting that chart following would allow him to call the broad market; this turned out to be a blind alley, but he succeeded by improvising a new system of incentives for stock pickers. Steinhardt, Fine, and Berkowitz started out as equity analysts. But their success owed much to block trading plus an eccentric focus on monetary policy.

Much like Michael Steinhardt's troika, Commodities Corporation benefited from an approach that fit the 1970s. Financial markets are mechanisms for matching people who want to avoid risk with people who get paid to take it on: There is a transfer from insurance seeker to insurance seller. In the 1960s not many people sought insurance against commodity price fluctuations. Government set minimum prices for agricultural products, while surpluses prevented prices from rising; traders at the Chicago Board of Trade whiled away the hours on the steps of the soybean pit by reading newspapers. But in the inflationary 1970s, the new volatility in food prices created a rush for insurance: Food companies used the futures market to hedge the risk of high prices; food growers used the futures market to hedge the risk of low prices.[40] Similarly, the new volatility in exchange rates created a rush for currency hedging; multinational firms woke up to the fact that the dollar's rise or fall could upend their performance. During the first half of the 1970s, turnover on the Chicago Board of Trade rose rapidly. The traders in the pits had no time to waste on newspapers.

This rush of insurance seekers into the market was bound to profit the insurance sellers—that is to say, the speculators. The farmers and the food companies were buying and selling futures because they needed to shed risk, not because they had a sophisticated view on the direction of prices; speculators who did have such a view were bound to have the upper hand in trading with them. Moreover, the speculators earned especially good profits because they faced relatively little competition. The exchanges imposed limits on the number of contracts a speculator could buy, thereby limiting the supply of "insurance" and boosting its value artificially. Commodities Corporation pocketed the higher insurance premiums created by this artificial scarcity, then figured out another way to win as well. It got around the exchanges' restrictions by arranging off-exchange trades with wholesalers.[41]

The big jump in insurance seeking explains part of the success of Commodities Corporation. But the most important factor by far was the firm's conversion to trend following. By developing his Technical Computer System and demonstrating how wrong the random walkers were, Frank Vannerson gave Commodities Corporation the confidence to hire trend followers such as Michael Marcus and to turn to his combination of fundamental analysis and charts into a sort of company credo.[42] Years later, financial academia caught up with Vannerson's discovery. In 1986 a paper in the prestigious *Journal of Finance* found that trend following in the currency markets could earn sizable profits, and in 1988 another study found the same for commodities as well as currency futures.[43] There was an amusing symmetry to some of this research. Scott Irwin, one of the authors of the 1988 paper, had been prompted to begin his investigations by an encounter with Dennis Dunn, whose firm, Dunn & Hargitt, had provided Vannerson with the data to build the Technical Computer System. Examining the same price series that Vannerson had worked on almost two decades before, Irwin came to the same conclusion.[44]

IN 1977 MICHAEL MARCUS PLACED AN AD IN THE FINAN-cial press for an assistant trader. It was answered by an unlikely character who had dropped out of a Harvard PhD program and was now working part-time as a cab driver. When the candidate presented himself, it was love at first sight. Marcus picked up the phone and called Weymar. "Helmut," he said eagerly, "I have in my office the next president of Commodities Corp."[45]

The candidate was Bruce Kovner, and Weymar could see why Marcus was enthusiastic. The young man was tall, imposing, with a big head topped by a thick crop of hair; he exuded confidence and natural ease, and his intellectual range was striking. He had been part of a circle of political scientists at Harvard that included James Q. Wilson and Daniel Patrick Moynihan; he had devoted himself for a while to the full-time study of music; he had worked on a number of political campaigns; and he had contributed freelance articles to *Commentary* magazine on subjects from music to the purposes of economic growth. Trading was just another thing that he had learned along the way. Prompted by a conversation with a friend, he had studied the futures markets, borrowed $3,000 against a MasterCard, and turned it into $22,000. Marcus and Weymar tested the would-be trading assistant by mentioning a couple of financial texts, but Kovner had read more than they had, starting with historical classics such as Charles Mackay's *Extraordinary Popular Delusions and the Madness of Crowds* and extending to contemporary newsletters. "I really value richness in intellect, and Bruce was rich up the kazoo," Weymar recalls.[46] Kovner was hired in short order, not as an assistant but as a trader.[47]

Kovner's encounter with Marcus and Weymar launched one of the most illustrious careers in hedge-fund history. Over the next decade, Kovner racked up gains averaging some 80 percent per year; he launched his own hedge fund, Caxton Corporation; and he emerged as a colorful figure in the arts and politics. He became a godfather of the conservative movement through his chairmanship of the American Enterprise Institute and his backing of the *New York Sun*. He chaired the Juilliard School of music and sponsored an artist who produced an illustrated edition of the Bible, the Pennyroyal Caxton, complete with an engraving of Kovner in the image of King Solomon. When Kovner needed a bachelor pad following a divorce, he converted Manhattan's International Center of Photography into a private residence. The mansion has a vault for Kovner's collection of rare books and a study that doubles as a radiation-proof bomb shelter.

Michael Marcus, who had once studied psychology, noticed something about Kovner early on: He had a physical and psychological strength that set him apart from his colleagues. Kovner knew how to let go of distractions; he did not overthink his trades and had no trouble sleeping. Other traders might make money faster, but they would lose it faster too; Kovner was consistent, and he had a sort of nerveless temperament. One time Kovner took a hit on a silver position, suffering the sort of loss that would have left most traders vomiting in the bathroom. He showed up that same day at an administrative meeting as though nothing untoward had happened.[48]

Unlike many traders, Kovner combined a feel for the markets with organizational talent. He hired several assistants to track numbers and compose charts, never paying any of them more than was absolutely necessary. He could get the best out of ordinary people: He employed an ex-librarian to monitor the relationship between interest rates and gold futures; whenever the relationship showed an unusual blip, the librarian had instructions to bet on normalcy's return, a formula that generated handsome profits. Meanwhile, Kovner was adept at extracting financial concessions from Weymar, frequently raising the hackles of colleagues. Rather than paying for his assistants out of his own profits, Kovner would sometimes get the company's central budget to cough up; rather than setting aside his own capital allocation to trade on their ideas, Kovner would persuade Weymar to allocate them extra money.[49] In the judgment of Irwin Rosenblum, the chief financial officer, Bruce Kovner amassed a larger fortune at Commodities Corporation than anyone else at the company.[50]

Kovner combined fundamental analysis with attention to the charts, confirming the shift away from the model-driven research with which Weymar had started.[51] As with Michael Marcus, the charts sometimes came first: Indeed, Kovner once argued that the most profitable opportunities arise when you have *no* fundamental information.[52] If a market is behaving normally, ticking up and down within a narrow band, a sudden breakout in the absence of any discernible reason is an opportunity to jump: It means that some insider somewhere knows information that the market has yet to understand, and if you follow that insider you will get in there before the information becomes public. One time Kovner and Marcus were betting against the dollar when it inexplicably strengthened. Assuming that insiders had caught wind of important news, the traders immediately bailed out, and that weekend President Carter announced a dollar support program. If the duo had waited for the official announcement—if they had traded on the fundamental data in the way that Weymar sought to do at first—they would have been annihilated.[53]

In 1981 Kovner and an associate, Roy Lennox, hit on a strategy that later became a hedge-fund staple. They searched for currencies that cost a lot less in the future than in the present and bought them at the bargain forward rate. Most traders assumed that there was nothing to be gained from this behavior: If the forward rate was lower, that was because the currency was likely to depreciate. But Kovner and Lennox saw that this was wrong. A low forward rate usually reflected high interest rates: If Spanish banks were paying 7 percent interest to depositors, the peseta would be worth 7 percent more in the immediate "spot" market than in the one-year forwards—effectively, the discount in the forward market was compensating buyers for missing the chance to collect interest. Far from being a signal that a currency was likely to depreciate, a forward-market discount was a sign that a currency might rise, since the high interest rate was likely to drive inflation down and suck capital into the country. For the next decade or so, Kovner and Lennox bought currency forwards that were trading at a big discount and sold currency forwards that were trading at small ones. This "carry trade" raked in glorious profits until rivals caught on to it.[54]

Kovner's success forms a kind of epilogue to the heyday of Commodities Corporation. As word of the firm's profits reached sharp ears on Wall Street, Weymar found himself facing a challenge. New York brokers approached his top traders, seeking to place their clients' capital directly with the stars; they were effectively pressing the likes of Marcus and Kovner to begin hedge funds within the structure of Weymar's company. Weymar at first resisted, but the traders had the upper hand; the boss had loaded up Commodities Corporation with such vast administrative overhead that traders were already tempted to go independent, and now Wall Street was offering them an alternative source of trading funds—plus a fat fee for accepting them.[55] After some internal argument, the traders got their way, and pretty soon Kovner was managing millions of dollars of Wall Street cash. His army of trading assistants expanded to the point that he was running a state within a state. By the time Kovner broke off to start Caxton Corporation in 1983, he was already an independent hedge-fund mogul in everything but name. He was secretive, leveraged, and enviably successful.

Meanwhile, a pair of younger futures traders was rising in his wake. Paul Tudor Jones and Louis Bacon, whom we will encounter later in this story, both received seed capital from Commodities Corporation; and in the early 1980s the two would arrive by helicopter from Manhattan to attend traders' dinners in Princeton. Jones and Bacon both learned from Commodities Corporation, sharing ideas on trends and chart patterns and adopting its risk-control procedures; Bacon eventually hired Elaine Crocker, a senior administrative officer at Commodities Corporation, to be the president of his hedge fund, Moore Capital. But Bacon was too independent a figure to fit into Weymar's company, and Jones turned down a job offer; he was happy to take seed money from Commodities Corporation, but he did not want to join it.[56] The difficulty of bringing in star performers combined with Weymar's big spending to create a crisis at the firm; and in 1984 an internal revolt forced Weymar to promise lower overhead and a return to "the simple life."[57] Though it soldiered on after that, Commodities Corporation never recaptured its old verve. The center of gravity shifted: from Weymar to a younger set, from the idyll in Princeton to a new generation of New York hedge funds.

4

THE ALCHEMIST

The London School of Economics was abuzz in 1949, when a young Hungarian named George Soros arrived there. The trauma of World War II was fresh; victims of Nazism, exiles from communism, and young leaders from Britain's disintegrating empire found refuge together in London. There was a search for grand theories, for an understanding of how Europe had destroyed itself and how it could be rebuilt; the Labour government was refashioning Britain with its new welfare state, and Marshall aid was speeding reconstruction on the continent. In the LSE's lecture halls, impassioned Marxists rubbed shoulders with the libertarian Friedrich Hayek; Keynesians and anti-Keynesians debated one another. It was in this era, as a historian of the school wrote, that "the myth of LSE was born."[1]

Soros had already endured much by the time he arrived at the university. Born to a well-to-do Jewish family in Budapest, he had survived the Nazi occupation by separating from his family, assuming a Christian identity, and hiding with various of his father's acquaintances. He had seen corpses in the streets of his city, mangled figures with bound hands and crushed heads, and he had helped his family survive by hawking jewelry to black-market dealers. In 1947, when he was barely seventeen, Soros had left Hungary for a better future in London, bidding good-bye to his parents, whom he expected not to see again. He took jobs as a dishwasher, a house painter, a busboy; a headwaiter told him that, provided he worked hard, he might one day end up as his assistant. The summer before Soros began his studies at LSE, he at last found a job he liked. He was a lifeguard at a swimming pool with not many swimmers. He read Adam Smith, Thomas Hobbes, and Niccolò Machiavelli.

The LSE luminary who inspired Soros the most was Karl Popper, a philosopher who had fled his native Austria to escape Nazism—and who, in an entirely unintended way, stamped his ideas on the young man who was to become the most famous of all hedge-fund managers. Popper's central contention was that human beings cannot know the truth; the best they can do is to grope at it through trial and error. This notion had an obvious appeal to someone of Soros's background. It suggested that all political dogmas were flawed: The Nazism and communism inflicted upon Hungary by outside powers each claimed an intellectual certainty to which neither was entitled. Popper's masterwork, *The Open Society and Its Enemies,* created in Soros a lifelong desire to make his own contribution to philosophy. It pointed him toward a distinctive way of thinking about finance and inspired the name of the philanthropy he was to found, the Open Society Institute.

Soros left LSE with mediocre grades and spent a while in dead-end jobs, at one point selling handbags in northern Wales. He escaped this version of his destiny by writing to all the investment banks in the City of London, inquiring about entry-level positions. Spurned by the establishment because of his lack of social ties, he eventually landed a job with a brokerage run by Hungarian émigrés; after learning the financial ropes, he found his way to New York in 1956, figuring he could stomach Wall Street for five years, long enough to put aside the savings he needed to support a life as an independent philosopher.[2] But he soon found he was too good at the investing game to quit. By 1967 he was the head of research at Arnhold and S. Bleichroeder, a venerable Wall Street brokerage specializing in European stocks. And after getting to know the A. W. Jones segment managers by pitching ideas to them, he launched his own $4 million long/short stock-picking vehicle in 1969. He called it the Double Eagle Fund, and he managed it under the Bleichroeder umbrella.[3]

By now Soros had melded Karl Popper's ideas with his own knowledge of finance, arriving at a synthesis that he called "reflexivity." As Popper's writings suggested, the details of a listed company were too complex for the human mind to understand, so investors relied on guesses and shortcuts that approximated reality. But Soros was also conscious that those short-cuts had the power to change reality as well, since bullish guesses would drive a stock price up, allowing the company to raise capital cheaply and boosting its performance. Because of this feedback loop, certainty was doubly elusive: To begin with, people are incapable of perceiving reality clearly; but on top of that, reality itself is affected by these unclear percep-tions, which themselves shift constantly. Soros had arrived at a conclu-sion that was at odds with the efficient-market view. Academic finance assumes, as a starting point, that rational investors can arrive at an objec-tive valuation of a stock and that when all information is priced in, the market can be said to have attained an efficient equilibrium. To a disciple of Popper, this premise ignored the most elementary limits to cognition.[4]

Even as his financial career took off in the 1960s, Soros continued to hide away in the study of his weekend home, struggling to express his philosophy on paper. His ideas affected the way that he invested too, despite later suggestions that Soros superimposed the theory of reflexivity on his investment success as an after-the-fact rationalization. In an invest-ment note written in 1970, Soros explained the workings of real-estate investment trusts in explicitly reflexive terms. "The conventional method of security analysis is to try to predict the future course of earnings," he began; but in the case of these investment trusts, future earnings would themselves depend on investors' perceptions about them. If investors were bullish, they would pay a premium for a share in a successful trust, inject-ing it with cheap capital. The cheap capital would boost earnings, which would in turn reinforce the appearance of success, persuading other inves-tors to buy into the trust at an even greater premium. The trick, Soros insisted, was to focus neither on the course of earnings nor on the psychol-ogy that drove investors' appetite. Rather, Soros homed in on the feedback loop between the two, predicting that each would drive the other forward until the trusts were so completely overvalued that a crash was inevitable.

Sure enough, the real-estate investment trusts followed the boom-bust sequence that Soros expected. His fund made a fortune as they went up and another as they crashed downward.[5]

In 1973, Soros left Bleichroeder to set up his own company. He rented an office a block away from his co-op on Central Park West, bringing along his partner from Bleichroeder, an irascible, workaholic analyst named Jim Rogers. Interviewed years later in his Manhattan home, Rogers conducted the discussion while wincing and gasping on an exercise bike that was rigged up with a laptop and phone for maximum multitasking.[6] Together with Rogers, Soros continued to look for moments when an unstable equilibrium might reverse. He saw, for example, that financial deregulation was changing the game in banking, transforming a dull sector of the stock market into a sexy one: He made a fortune from bank stocks. He spotted that the Arab-Israeli war of 1973 changed the game for the defense industry, since Soviet weaponry used by Egypt had performed well, demonstrating that the United States faced a greater challenge than previously imagined. Soros predicted that the Pentagon would soon persuade Congress to authorize some catch-up investments. He plunged into defense stocks.[7]

When Soros sensed a game-changing moment, he was not afraid to bet the store on it. After he decided military spending would go up, he became the largest outside shareholder in the defense contractor Lockheed. He was willing to take the plunge without waiting for conclusive evidence that he was right. If he found an investment idea attractive on cursory examination, he figured that others would be seduced too; and since he believed that perfect cognition was impossible, there was no point in sweating the details. On a skiing vacation once in Switzerland, he bought the *Financial Times* at the bottom of the chairlift, read on the way up about the British government's plan to bail out Rolls-Royce, and called his broker from the top of the mountain with an order to buy British government bonds.[8] Let specialists obsess about minutiae. Soros's motto was "Invest first, investigate later."[9]

By the start of 1981, Soros had achieved success beyond his wildest imaginings. His hedge fund, renamed the Soros Fund in 1973 and the Quantum Fund in 1978, had accumulated assets of $381 million, multiplying its initial capital almost a hundredfold despite the tough equity markets of the 1970s. The teenager who had eked out a precarious living in London, sometimes relying on charities for support, had accumulated a personal fortune worth $100 million and was himself becoming a philanthropist. In June 1981, a reverential magazine profile in *Institutional Investor* called Soros "the world's greatest money manager." Rivals expressed their admiration by echoing Ilie Nastase's tribute to Bjorn Borg: "We're playing tennis and he's playing something else."[10]

Soros was not above celebrating his own brilliance. "I stood back and looked at myself with awe: I saw a perfectly honed machine," he wrote, with no apparent irony.[11] "I fancied myself as some kind of god or an economic reformer like Keynes (each with his General Theory)," he confessed on another occasion. "Or, even better, a scientist like Einstein (reflexivity sounds like relativity)."[12] But the tragedy was that he was not happy. Success as an investor required a visceral as well as intellectual focus on markets, which could be so intense as to be physical. If there was trouble stirring in his portfolio, Soros would first know about it when his back seized up; believing that markets could turn against him at any time, Soros would defer to these physical signals and sell out his positions. The business of investing consumed all the time and energy he had. He thought of himself as a boxer in training who had to sacrifice all personal life for the sake of victory. He compared himself to a sick person with a parasitic fund swelling inexorably inside his body.[13]

Even as he built success upon success, Soros began to rethink his priorities. In 1980 he parted company with Jim Rogers, whom he blamed for driving younger employees out of the firm, frustrating Soros's hopes of spreading his workload; and he began to look for new partners to whom he could delegate responsibility.[14] The distraction of the search caused his investment performance to crater. After gaining more than 100 percent in 1980, the Quantum Fund was down 23 percent the following year, its first-ever loss, and Soros was hit by a wave of redemptions that halved his capital from $400 million to $200 million.[15] By September 1981 a humiliated Soros had entrusted the remaining money to other investors. Like Michael Steinhardt three years earlier, he took a break from the markets.

WHEN SOROS RETURNED TO FULL-TIME INVESTING IN
1984, it was with a new sense of balance. Before, he had been paranoid
that if he ceased to be paranoid his performance would suffer. But during his midlife crisis, a psychoanalyst had helped him to slay some of
his demons. He recognized his success and permitted himself to relax,
knowing that doing so might kill the golden goose, but also knowing that
not doing so would render the success pointless. His visceral identification with his fund ended; it was as though something physical had been
excised from his body. He compared this change to a painful operation
he had endured to extract a hard ball of calcium from his salivary gland.
Once the stone was removed and exposed to the air, it crumbled to powder. "That is what happened to my hang-ups," Soros recalled. "Somehow,
they dissolved when they were brought to light."[16]

Soros replaced the signals from his aching back with a more cerebral
process. Starting in August 1985, he kept a diary of his investment thinking, hoping that the discipline of recording his thoughts would sharpen
his judgments. The resulting "real-time experiment" is dense, repetitive,
and filled with complex ruminations about scenarios that never in the end
materialize. But because it is free of the biases that afflict retrospective
explanations of success, it is a true portrait of the speculator at work. Moreover, Soros's journal happened to capture one of his greatest triumphs—a
bet against the dollar that he described as "the killing of a lifetime."

Soros had come out of the stock-picking culture of Wall Street. But
his preoccupation with reflexive feedback loops led him to think broadly
about opportunities. Like Michael Marcus of Commodities Corporation,
who abandoned his seat on the floor of the cotton exchange to become a
generalist trader, Soros saw no point in knowing everything about a few
stocks in the hope of anticipating small moves; the game was to know a
little about a lot of things, so that you could spot the places where the big
wave might be coming. By the 1980s, the post–Bretton Woods system of
floating currencies had emerged as a natural playground. The value of the

dollar was based on traders' perceptions, which Soros naturally believed were flawed. And since these perceptions could reverse at any time, the dollar could move dramatically.

This was not the conventional view of the way currency markets functioned. In the 1970s and into the 1980s, most economists believed that currency markets, like equity markets, tended toward an efficient equilibrium.[17] If the dollar was overvalued, U.S. exports would be hurt and imports would be boosted. The resulting trade deficit would mean that foreigners did not need as many dollars to buy American goods as Americans needed other currencies to buy foreign goods; the relatively low demand for the dollar would drive its value down, cutting the trade deficit until the system reached equilibrium. In the traditional view, moreover, speculators were in no position to disrupt this process. If they anticipated the currency's future path correctly, they merely accelerated its arrival at the equilibrium point. If they judged wrong, they would slow its correction—but the delay would not persist because the speculators would lose money.

Soros could see that equilibrium theory failed to explain how currencies actually behaved in practice. Between 1982 and 1985, for example, the United States had run a growing trade deficit, implying a weak demand for dollars; but over this period, the dollar had strengthened. The reason was that speculative flows of capital had pushed the dollar up; and these speculative flows tended to be self-reinforcing. When hot capital flowed into the United States, the dollar rose; the rising dollar drew in yet more speculators, driving the exchange rate *away* from equilibrium.[18] If speculators were the real force determining exchange rates, it followed that currencies would exhibit a perpetual boom-bust sequence. In the first stage of the sequence, speculators would develop a prevailing bias, and this bias would reinforce itself, driving the exchange rate further and further from the level needed to achieve trade equilibrium. The more out of line the exchange rate got, the more the speculators would feel themselves confirmed, and the more the imbalance in trade would keep growing. Eventually, the pressure of enormous trade imbalances would overwhelm the speculators' bias. A reversal would occur, the speculators would swivel 180 degrees, and a new trend would take off in the opposite direction.[19]

In the summer of 1985, the challenge that preoccupied Soros was how to judge the timing of the dollar's reversal. When he began keeping his diary, on August 16, he suspected that the moment might be close at hand. President Reagan had reshuffled his administration at the start of his second term, and the new team appeared determined to bring the dollar down in order to reduce the U.S. trade deficit. The fundamentals, insofar as they were relevant, pointed the same way. Interest rates were falling, making it unrewarding for speculators to hold dollars. If the combination of political action and low interest rates could persuade even a few speculators to abandon the greenback, the upward trend in the currency could suddenly reverse. In the mature phase of a cycle, all the speculators who want to ride the dollar have already climbed aboard. There are hardly any buyers left, so it takes only a few sellers to make the market perform a U-turn.

Soros agonized about whether the turn was imminent. If U.S. growth accelerated, interest rates would rise, making a dollar reversal less likely. On the other hand, if banks entered a cycle of credit contraction, in which falling collateral values and reduced lending fed back on themselves, the trouble in the banking sector could slow the economy sharply and push interest rates downward. "Who am I to judge?" Soros wondered; but then he added, "The only competitive edge I have is the theory of reflexivity." The theory led him to weight the risk of a self-reinforcing banking mess especially heavily and so inclined him to bet against the dollar; besides, certain technical indicators pointed in the same direction.[20] Having digested arguments from the quasi science of economics, the quasi philosophy of reflexivity, and the quasi psychology of the charts, Soros arrived at an investment conclusion. It was time to short the dollar.

Despite his inner doubts, Soros plunged decisively. As of August 16, Quantum owned $720 million worth of the main currencies against which the dollar would fall—yen, German marks, and sterling—an exposure that exceeded all the equity in the fund by a margin of $73 million. His appetite for risk was startling: "As a general rule, I try not to exceed 100 percent of the Fund's equity capital in any one market," he remarked breezily in his diary, "but I tend to adjust my definition of what constitutes a market to suit my current thinking."[21] The idea that a hedge fund should actually be hedged had been casually discarded.

Three weeks later, on September 9, Soros's second diary entry reported that his experiment had begun badly. The dollar had been buoyed by a batch of bullish U.S. economic indicators, and the currency bet had cost Quantum $20 million. Soros embarked on another bout of soul-searching. He continued to focus on the weak banking system, and the charts whispered that his luck might turn: The German mark appeared to be following a pattern that suggested a sharp rise might be coming. Then Soros brought a further dimension into his analysis. Putting himself in the shoes of the monetary authorities, he argued that interest rates were likely to stay low, even if the economy proved stronger than expected. The Federal Reserve would be reluctant to raise interest rates because of its responsibility as the regulator of the banks; the last thing that wobbly lenders need is more expensive capital. Moreover, the Fed would have room not to raise interest rates because Reagan's reshuffled administration was determined to rein in the budget deficit, relieving inflationary pressure. Weighing his options that September, Soros resolved to stick with his losing bet against the dollar, but to abandon half of it if the market moved further against him.

Soros's investment decisions were often balanced on a knife edge. The truth is that markets are at least somewhat efficient, so most information is already in the price; the art of speculation is to develop one insight that others have overlooked and then trade big on that small advantage. Soros would often pick through the evidence, formulate a thesis, but then turn on a dime; a stray remark from a lunch guest could tip the balance of the argument, and Soros would leap up and instruct a trader to get out of his positions.[22] Soros's decision to hold on to his dollar shorts in that second week of September was one of those close calls. If he had blinked after his initial loss, his life story would have turned out differently.[23]

But Soros did not blink. Less than two weeks after his second diary entry, on September 22, 1985, Treasury secretary James Baker assembled his counterparts from France, West Germany, Japan, and Britain at the Plaza Hotel in New York. Together the five powers promised coordinated intervention in currency markets to push the dollar downward. The news of the Plaza accord delivered Soros an overnight profit of $30 million. The yen rose more than 7 percent against the dollar the next day, its largest one-day jump in history.

Soros had been somewhat lucky. He had seen clearly ahead of time that the Reagan administration wanted to manage the dollar down, but he had no idea how this intention would play out and no foreknowledge of the Plaza meeting.[24] What happened after Plaza, however, was nothing to do with luck—and everything to do with Soros's emergence as a legend. Rather than cashing in his bet against the dollar and resting on his laurels, Soros piled on harder. The turn in the dollar had finally come. Everything he knew about reflexive feedback loops argued that the dollar's initial fall was merely the beginning.

The Plaza Hotel meeting ended on a Sunday in New York, but it was already Monday morning in Asia. Soros immediately called brokers in Hong Kong with orders to buy additional yen for his portfolio. The next day, when his firm's own traders began taking profits in the small subportfolios they ran, Soros succumbed to a rare moment of fury. He charged out of his office, yelling at the traders to stop selling yen and telling them that he would assume their positions.[25] The traders had wanted to throw their arms around success before it ran away.[26] But as far as Soros was concerned, the top governments of the world had telegraphed that the dollar was headed down. Plaza had given the signal, so why shouldn't he hog more yen positions?

Over the next days, Soros continued buying. By the Friday after the Plaza meeting, he had added $209 million to his holdings of yen and German marks and had established an extra $107 million worth of short positions in the dollar.[27] If there was a risk in this posture, it was that the Plaza communiqué would turn out to be a paper tiger; the declaration was suspiciously thin on actionable detail, and it depended on the uncertain commitment of governments to follow up with concrete measures. But more than any other New York fund manager, Soros had a web of political contacts in Washington, Tokyo, and Europe, and his network encouraged him to believe that Plaza was serious.[28] By early December he had loaded up on another $500 million worth of yen and German marks, while adding almost $300 million to his short position in the dollar.[29] "I have assumed maximum market exposure in all directions," Soros recorded in his diary.[30]

In December 1985 Soros concluded the first phase of his real-time experiment. He looked back on a period that had begun with a hypothesis that the dollar was ripe for reversal and that had culminated with the theory's confirmation. His repeated conjectures about a collapse in the banking system had turned out to be a red herring; "the outstanding feature of my predictions is that I keep on expecting developments that do not materialize," he admitted.[31] But the errors had been dwarfed by one central success. Soros had understood that nothing more substantial than slippery perceptions had driven up the dollar, and therefore that a trigger could set off a sudden reversal. Because he had grasped the system's instability, he had understood the Plaza accord's meaning faster than others. Plaza was the trigger, and it didn't even matter that the details of the new policy had yet to be filled in. A political jolt had kick-started a new trend, which would now feed on itself and become self-sustaining.

The rewards from the Plaza trade were astonishing. In the four months from August, Soros's fund jumped by 35 percent, yielding a profit of $230 million. Convinced that the act of writing his diary had contributed to his performance, Soros joked that his profit represented the highest honorarium ever received by an author.[32] When the diary was published two years later, as part of Soros's book *The Alchemy of Finance*, reviewers mocked its dense prose. But as one commentator said, financial alchemy certainly beat boiling up mercury with egg yolks.[33]

THE PUBLICATION OF *THE ALCHEMY OF FINANCE* IN MAY 1987 confirmed Soros's status as a celebrity. The diary struck a chord with several of the younger stars in the hedge-fund firmament, who saw in it an honest picture of a speculator wrestling anxiously with multiple imponderables. Paul Tudor Jones, the whiz-kid cotton trader who had received seed capital from Commodities Corporation and later built the wildly successful Tudor Investment Corporation, made *Alchemy* required reading among his employees.[34] In a foreword to *Alchemy*, Jones declared that, having published, Soros should now beware; and he invoked a scene from the World War II movie *Patton*, in which the great American general savors victory over Field Marshal Erwin Rommel. Patton has prepared for battle by reading Rommel's tactical writings, and in a climactic moment in the movie, he peers out from his command post and delivers Jones's favorite line: "Rommel, you magnificent bastard. I read your *book*!"[35]

Soros was having too much fun to fret about such warnings. At last he was becoming the kind of public intellectual he had admired at the LSE; and his expensively tailored figure, topped off with large glasses and a thick tangle of hair, began popping up on magazine covers. His Central European accent added to the exotic aura that surrounded him. Soros, said the profiles, had been a student of global investing years before most fund managers had discovered Tokyo on the map; he embraced futures, options, and forward currency contracts; he went long and short with equal facility. From his eerily quiet trading floor in Manhattan, he ruled over the markets of the world, hobnobbing with global financiers in five languages.[36] *The Economist* called him "the world's most intriguing investor," and a cover story in *Fortune* suggested he might rank ahead of Warren Buffett as "the most prescient investor of his generation."[37] But just as the flattering profile of Soros in *Institutional Investor* in 1981 had presaged that year's humiliating 23 percent loss, so the adulation of 1987 presaged a calamity.

The *Fortune* cover story appeared on September 28, 1987, and its title posed the question of the moment. "Are stocks too high?" the magazine

THE ALCHEMIST 95

asked; after the long bull market that had begun at the start of the decade, the stocks in Standard & Poor's index of four hundred industrial companies sold at an average of three times book value, the highest level since World War II. *Fortune* introduced Soros as its first expert witness on the stock market's level, and it explained that Soros was sanguine. The fact that trend followers had driven the market upward did not mean that the crash was coming soon: "Just because the market is overvalued does not mean it is not sustainable," Soros declared delphically. For evidence to support his view, Soros pointed to Japan, where stocks had soared even higher above traditional valuations. Eventually a crash would come. But it would hit Tokyo before Wall Street.

Soros was not alone in being bullish. The following week Salomon Brothers issued a research note promising that the bull market would continue into 1988, and the week after that, Byron Wien, a well-known Morgan Stanley strategist and Soros friend, predicted "a new high before this cycle is over." It was the era of the leveraged buyout, and debt-fueled takeovers were driving stock prices steadily higher; the lives of corporate raiders were the stuff of drooling magazine features. The mood of the moment was captured by a hitherto unknown financier named P. David Herrlinger, who announced a $6.8 billion offer for Dayton Hudson Corporation. Herrlinger appeared on his front lawn to tell reporters that his offer might or might not be a hoax—"It's no more of a hoax than anything else," he said—and the news of the apparent takeover sent Dayton Hudson stock into the stratosphere. But a hoax is what it was, and Herrlinger was soon removed to a hospital.[38]

The buyout mania neatly fitted Soros's ideas on reflexivity. The takeovers were feeding on themselves: As each acquisition was announced, the stock of every company in the sector jumped, and the prospects of returning acquired companies to the stock market at a profit grew rosier. The avalanche of loans to finance deals kept on coming; the spiral drove prices further and further from any approximation of fundamental value, just as the Soros theory predicted. Of course, sooner or later the takeover deals would collapse under the weight of their own debt, and the trend would reverse itself. But there seemed no strong evidence that the reversal would come soon. Soros continued to pursue his new avocation as Wall Street's philosopher-in-chief, holding court to journalists and appearing on television shows.

On October 5 Soros invited one of his new fans over to his office. The guest was Stanley Druckenmiller, the hottest mutual-fund manager on the Street, who had read *Alchemy* and expressed an interest in a meeting. Soros held forth grandly and offered Druckenmiller a job.[39] He wanted a successor who could run Quantum, leaving him more time for philosophy and philanthropy. Money management was wearing on him.

Druckenmiller refused to be lured so easily, but the two struck up a close relationship. Druckenmiller was as tall and broad shouldered as Soros was compact; he was as plainspoken as Soros was complex; he was as unflashy and middle American as Soros was exotic and middle European. But the two got along well. Soros, then in his late fifties, would pontificate; Druckenmiller, still in his midthirties, had his ego sufficiently in check to listen. And although they shared many views about the market, their funds were positioned differently. Druckenmiller had decided that a market break was coming, and he was short Wall Street; Quantum was short Japan but long the U.S. market. Indeed, Soros had recently added to his team of stock pickers, and Quantum was racking up eye-popping returns by loading up on the hot takeover stocks—the "garbitrage" stocks, as the wags of Wall Street called them. By riding the market wave, Soros's team was up some 60 percent by the end of September. Everything was going wonderfully.

On October 14 Soros published an article in the *Financial Times* reaffirming his view that the crash would arrive in Tokyo. That Wednesday morning, he headed off to Harvard's Kennedy School to give a talk on boom-bust theory. After delivering his lecture, he emerged to find that Wall Street had sold off. The newswires were reporting that Congress might raise taxes associated with corporate mergers, a move that could silence one engine of the bull market.[40] The Dow Jones Industrial Average dropped 3.8 percent that day, a move that should have caught Soros's attention. He knew that the market was far from equilibrium; he knew

that booms can be quickly followed by sharp busts. As he ruefully confessed later, "That's when I should have been in the office and getting the
hell out of the market."[41]

On Thursday stocks continued to head down; and on Friday they dove
precipitously. After the markets closed that day, Soros received a visit from
his new confidant. The three-day sell-off had convinced Druckenmiller
that the Dow had given up enough ground; according to his charts, prices
had fallen to a point from which they would probably bounce upward.
That Friday afternoon, Druckenmiller had switched from a short to a long
position.[42]

Soros listened to his friend and spread a raft of charts in front of him.
These had been prepared by Paul Tudor Jones, the other admirer of
Alchemy, whom Soros also spoke with frequently. Druckenmiller examined
the patterns and sensed a panic rising in his gut. Jones's charts appeared
to show that he had committed a disastrous error. The lines on the paper
illustrated the stock market's historical tendency to accelerate downward
whenever an upward sloping parabolic curve had been broken, and they
suggested a parallel between the market of 1987 and the market of 1929.
Maybe a collapse was coming.[43]

The next morning Druckenmiller visited Jack Dreyfus, the patriarch
of the Dreyfus family of mutual funds, where Druckenmiller was working. Dreyfus had instructed his secretary to keep charts not just of the
broad market indices but of individual stocks. "We went over all these
individual charts and I knew I was cooked," Druckenmiller recalled later.
"What I saw wasn't a bunch of stocks that were necessarily down a lot.
They had just broken out," he said, meaning that they had broken out
of a congestion point and would now accelerate downward. "Stock after
stock after stock had just made a clean break right there. . . . Clearly I had
misread the situation."[44] By focusing on the broad market, Druckenmiller
had missed the alarming action in individual shares—and there is an old
saying among chart watchers that soldiers lead generals. Druckenmiller
was scared to death for the rest of the weekend. On Monday he bailed
out of his positions as quickly as he could, and by late morning he had

flipped 180 degrees. After a harrowing few hours, he was again short the market.

That day, October 19, went down in history as Black Monday. The Dow Jones index lost 22.6 percent of its value, the largest drop since the venerable index had been launched ninety-one years earlier. By flipping his position so rapidly, Druckenmiller escaped the worst of the chaos, but the same was not true of Soros. He did his best to bail out of the market, but he was running more money than Druckenmiller; and the garbitrage stocks that had been riding high just days earlier were hard to unload in a panic. Around lunchtime, when Druckenmiller had completed his reversal but Soros was still desperately selling, the market descended into pandemonium. "People didn't believe their stocks could go down that fast," one Wall Streeter recalled later. She steadied herself by looking out of her window at a hot dog stand. So long as hot dogs were selling, the world could not be ending.[45]

On Monday evening Soros reassessed the situation. Wall Street had hit him hard, but his short position in Japan had paid off as the Nikkei stock index fell, cushioning his losses. There were rumors that the extraordinary collapse in New York had been caused by a newfangled instrument known as "portfolio insurance," which promised investors protection against a market fall. The insurance worked by selling futures as the market weakened, putting a floor under an investor's potential loss; but when thousands of insurance policies triggered futures selling in a weak market, the result was a meltdown unprecedented in history. If this account was right, there was an obvious message for Soros. A market collapse triggered by program trading rather than by fundamental factors was more likely to be corrected soon. Perhaps a rebound was coming.

On Tuesday morning, sure enough, the market rallied. Soros seized the opportunity to pile back into the market. But his Japanese positions were hit by extraordinary bad luck. He had established his short position on the Nikkei index by selling futures in Hong Kong, where the market was more liquid. But when stocks collapsed on Black Monday, the masters of the Hong Kong futures exchange decided to staunch losses by closing it down, and when Wall Street began to rally on Tuesday, portending a rally the next day in Japan, Soros could not get out of his short position. On Wednesday the Nikkei leaped 9.3 percent, its biggest one-day gain since 1949. Soros could do nothing.[46]

A few minutes before the markets closed in New York that Wednesday, Soros spoke again with Druckenmiller. The Dow had by now rallied strongly for two days, and Druckenmiller thought another turn was coming. He had studied the history of crashes, and he had seen a pattern: A sharp fall in the market was usually followed by a wild two-day rally, but then the market would collapse back to its low again.[47] That Wednesday afternoon, Druckenmiller told Soros that he was short the market.

Soros was not persuaded. He had consulted other confidants, and was convinced that Black Monday had been a freak. It was a bad dream caused by portfolio insurance.[48]

Druckenmiller was an early riser and he woke up on Thursday morning nervous as a goat.[49] The market had closed strongly the previous evening, and Soros might prove right that the historical pattern would not hold because of the anomaly of portfolio insurance. But when he checked in on the action in London, he saw that stocks were getting killed. If New York took its cue from London, Druckenmiller's short positions would come good and Soros would be in trouble.

Around 8:00 A.M., Druckenmiller got a call from the futures desk at Salomon Brothers.

"There's an elephant in the marketplace and the futures could open under two hundred," the broker informed him. This was a bombshell. The futures had closed at 258 the night before; an instant fall to 200, under the pressure of this elephant trader's selling, would represent a drop of almost a quarter. Druckenmiller figured that he might as well position himself for this drama in case it really did occur. He placed an order with the broker to close his short positions if the futures contracts fell to 195. At that rock-bottom level, Druckenmiller would be happy to take profits.

The market opened, and the elephant crashed down upon it. The futures fell to 200 and below, and Druckenmiller's orders with Salomon were all filled, yielding a 25 percent return on a position he had held only since the previous evening. By about ten o'clock in the morning, the elephant's selling had been completed and the market stabilized, and Druckenmiller reckoned it was time for yet another flip in his position. Remembering the conversation of the previous afternoon, Druckenmiller picked up the phone and called Soros.

"George, I just wanted you to know I was negative last night but I think maybe this is the bottom," he told him. "Some crazy person just sold the hell out of this thing. Like, really recklessly."

Soros sounded calm, detached. "Right now I'm licking my wounds," he said. "I'll come back and fight another day."[50]

It was not until that weekend that Druckenmiller realized what had happened. He picked up the newest edition of *Barron's* and read that the elephant in the market had been none other than Soros.[51]

The full story, which *Barron's* reported partially, was connected to the trouble in Japan. After its huge leap on Wednesday, Tokyo had risen again on Thursday. Soros wanted out of his short position in the futures market, but there was no way he could sell until the Hong Kong authorities reopened the exchange; meanwhile, he was bleeding money. Coming on top of the losses in the New York market on Monday, Quantum risked the sudden evaporation of confidence that can destroy any leveraged fund. Once your lenders sense you are in trouble, they start calling in their loans; the calls force you to sell stocks into a weak market, setting off a death spiral.[52] When Soros saw the London market fall early on Thursday, portending another sell-off in New York, he decided it was time to jump for the sidelines. He had been too slow to get out of the market on Monday, and he did not want to let that happen twice in a week.

"I don't understand what's going on," he said. "We've just got to move to cash. There'll be another day to play." Then he gave the order to his trader, Joe Orofino, to get out of the market by selling S&P futures on the Chicago Mercantile Exchange; and Orofino placed the sell order with brokers at Shearson Lehman Hutton. Quantum's entire $1 billion position was to be dumped, and quickly. But it was impossible to sell that size of position without moving the market. Traders in the futures pit began to sell frantically as soon as the Soros fire sale started, and investors such as Druckenmiller understood that they could allow the market to crash through the floor before taking profits on short positions. "When they saw an order like that they made the market very, very low," Soros later recalled, ruefully. [53]

Soros's decision to go to cash that day was perhaps the worst call of his career, costing his fund about $200 million.[54] It capped a cataclysmic run: In roughly a week, Quantum had gone from being up 60 percent for the year to being some 10 percent down; $840 million had vanished.[55] The episode demonstrated a weakness in hedge funds that would haunt the industry in later years: The larger the funds grew, the harder it became to jump in and out of markets without disrupting prices and damaging themselves in the process. If Quantum had been smaller, Soros might have bailed out on Monday as swiftly as Druckenmiller had; and he could have sold his position on Thursday without causing prices to crater. Soros's trading style assumed the ability to turn on a dime, and when that assumption proved wrong, Soros was in trouble.

THE SCALE OF THE CRASH DESTROYED THE CONFIDENCE of many money managers. Proud figures retreated into the fetal position: "I was so depressed that fall that I did not want to go on," Michael Steinhardt recalled later; "my confidence was shaken. I felt alone."[56] Soros experienced only a mild echo of those sentiments. He was tired of running Quantum, as he had confided to Druckenmiller even before the crash; the option of quitting was always somewhere in his consciousness. But his nerve was not in doubt, not in 1987 nor, indeed, at any time, and within the community of Soros fans, the manner of his recovery after the crash ranks among his greatest accomplishments. A week or two after Black Monday, Soros spotted an opportunity to short the dollar, and he put on a gutsy, leveraged position as though nothing untoward had happened. The dollar duly fell, and the gamble paid off. Quantum ended 1987 up 13 percent, despite having languished in the red only two months earlier.

In the wake of Black Monday, there had been inevitable sniggers. An anonymous source chortled to the *Times* of London, "It took 20 years to make George Soros a genius; four days to make him a jerk."[57] An item in

Forbes recalled Soros's unfortunate bullishness in the *Fortune* cover story of just weeks earlier. "If George Soros, the rich, immensely conceited and famous Hungarian-born money manager, appears beside a gushing head-line on the cover of a business magazine, sell your stocks," it sneered.[58] The reports of Quantum's setback quickly spread to eastern Europe, where there were fears that it would put an end to Soros's philanthropy in the region; Soros flew to Hungary to reassure the prime minister that his giv-ing would continue. But by the end of 1987, the rumors of Soros's finan-cial death had been shown up as premature. *Financial World* listed Soros as the second-highest earner on Wall Street. The top dog was none other than Paul Tudor Jones, chartist and Patton aficionado.

The Lazarus act of 1987, coming on top of the killing during the Plaza accord two years earlier, cemented Soros's status as an investment folk hero. But it had a wider influence as well, for Soros's example did much to create what came to be known as the "macro" hedge fund, at least in its modern incarnation. From 1924 until his death in 1946, John Maynard Keynes invested the endowment, the College Chest, of King's College, Cambridge, in the global markets, and although the term "hedge fund" did not yet exist, he employed many of the devices that modern macro managers would recognize. He speculated in currencies, bonds, and equi-ties, and he did it on a global scale; he went both long and short, and he magnified returns with leverage. After World War II, stable inflation, regulated interest rates, and immobile currencies caused Keynes's tradi-tion of macro investing to die out—ironically Keynes himself had helped to negotiate the fixing of exchange rates at the Bretton Woods conference. After the Bretton Woods system unraveled in the 1970s, macro investing began to stir again. But at first it did so tentatively.

Two streams of investors helped to revive it. Equity types such as Michael Steinhardt realized that shifts in interest rates could drive the stock market, as we have seen; starting in the 1980s, they took the logical next step and bet directly on interest-rate movements by speculating in bonds, first in the United States and later internationally.[59] Meanwhile, commodity investors such as Michael Marcus and Bruce Kovner started out trading cotton, gold, and so on; but as commodity markets created new contracts on currencies and interest rates, they began to surf these instruments. Until the publication of Soros's *Alchemy*, however, the equity and commodity traditions remained separate. The equity investors came from a culture dominated by fundamental analysis. The commodity traders came from a culture dominated by charts and trend following. But Soros's example had something for both tribes. The real-time experiment in *Alchemy* combined fundamental analysis with a belief in trends; it combined the language of economists with the instincts of a chart watcher. In this way, Soros managed to communicate with both halves of the hedge-fund house, reminding each that there was wisdom in the other.[60] Within a few years, commodity people like Paul Tudor Jones and equity people like Stan Druckenmiller were regarded simply as "macro" investors.[61]

FOR YEARS AFTER THE CRASH, THE EVENTS OF BLACK Monday were picked over for some deeper meaning. Modern financial engineering, which later blurred with hedge funds in the public mind, was blamed for the debacle. The engineers had created a destabilizing feed-back loop: A fall in the market triggered insurance-based selling, which in turn triggered a further fall in the market and another insurance-based sell-off. Mark Rubinstein, a Berkeley economics professor and coinventor of portfolio insurance, descended into what he would later recognize as a clinical depression. He fretted that the weakening of American markets might tempt the Soviet Union to attack, making him personally responsible for a nuclear conflict.[62]

Not for the first time, financial innovation was being blamed too eagerly. Soros had believed that portfolio insurance created Black Monday; but markets had crashed periodically throughout history, and foreign markets, in which there was far less portfolio insurance, also suffered precipitous falls. Even in the United States, the postmortems on the crash found that of the $39 billion worth of stock sold on October 19 via the futures and the cash markets, only about $6 billion worth of sales were triggered by portfolio insurers. Low-tech villains were just as important. Many investors had standing orders with brokers to sell if their positions fell, and these old-fashioned stop-loss policies may have accounted for at least as much selling as portfolio insurance. Besides, fears of a crash had been widespread in the run-up to the event, so there were psychological explanations for the mayhem too. A story in the *Atlantic Monthly* at the time was headlined "The 1929 Parallel," and the *Wall Street Journal* ran a piece on the morning of Black Monday superimposing a graph of the market's recent decline on a graph of the market of the 1920s.[63] The tools of finance were, in the end, just tools. People bought portfolio insurance or put in stop-loss orders because of the skittish atmosphere of the moment.[64]

Whatever the role of portfolio insurance, the larger lesson of the crash was different. Wall Street's gyrations administered a crippling blow to the efficient-market theories that Soros had long criticized. Over the course of a week, the value of corporate America had bounced around like a pachinko ball; there was nothing efficient about this, nor was there any sign of equilibrium. "The theory of reflexivity can explain such bubbles, while the efficient market hypothesis cannot," Soros wrote later, and broadly, he was right.[65] It was surely no coincidence that efficient-market thinking had originated on American university campuses in the 1950s and 1960s—the most stable enclaves within the most stable country in the most stable era in memory. Soros, who had survived the Holocaust, the war, and penury in London, had a different view of life; and after the wild ride of Black Monday, the academic consensus began to come around to him. The crash had been a humiliation for Soros in investing terms. But in intellectual terms it was a vindication.

The recasting of the academic consensus had three parts to it. The efficient-market hypothesis had always been based on a precarious assumption: that price changes conformed to a "normal" probability distribution—the one represented by the familiar bell curve, in which numbers at and near the median crop up frequently while numbers in the tails of the distribution are rare to the point of vanishing. Even in the early 1960s, a maverick mathematician named Benoit Mandelbrot argued that the tails of the distribution might be fatter than the normal bell curve assumed; and Eugene Fama, the father of efficient-market theory, who got to know Mandelbrot at the time, conducted tests on stock-price changes that confirmed Mandelbrot's assertion. If price changes had been normally distributed, jumps greater than five standard deviations should have shown up in daily price data about once every seven thousand years. Instead, they cropped up about once every three to four years.

Having made this discovery, Fama and his colleagues buried it. The trouble with Mandelbrot's insight was that it was too awkward to live with; it rendered the statistical tools of financial economics useless, since the modeling of abnormal distributions was a problem largely unsolved in mathematics. Paul Cootner, the efficient-market theorist and cofounder of Commodities Corporation, complained that "Mandelbrot, like Prime Minister Churchill before him, promises us not utopia but blood, sweat, toil and tears. If he is right, almost all of our statistical tools are obsolete— least squares, spectral analysis, workable maximum-likelihood solutions, all our established sample theory, closed distribution functions. Almost without exception, past econometric work is meaningless."[66] To prevent itself from toppling into this intellectual abyss, the economics profession kept its eyes trained the other way, especially since the mathematics of normal distributions was generating stunning breakthroughs. In 1973 a trio of economists produced a revolutionary method for valuing options, and a thrilling new financial industry was born. Mandelbrot's objections were brushed off. "The normal distribution is a good working approximation," Fama now contended.[67]

The crash of 1987 forced the economics profession to reexamine that assertion. In terms of the normal probability distribution, a plunge of the size that befell the S&P 500 futures contracts on October 19 had a probability of one in 10^{160}—that is, a "1" with 160 zeroes after it. To put that probability into perspective, it meant that an event such as the crash would not be anticipated to occur even if the stock market were to remain open for twenty billion years, the upper end of the expected duration of the universe, or even if it were to be reopened for further sessions of twenty billion years following each of twenty successive big bangs. Mandelbrot, who had abandoned financial economics after the brush-off in the early 1970s, returned to the subject with a vengeance. His Soros-like thinking on "chaos theory," which emphasized that small pieces of information could generate large price moves because of complex feedback loops, acquired a cult following among money managers.

As well as challenging the statistical foundation of financial economists' thinking, Black Monday forced a reconsideration of their institutional assumptions. Efficient-market theory assumed investors always had the means to act: If they knew that a share of IBM was worth $90 rather than the prevailing price of $100, they would sell it short until the weight of their trading moved the price down by $10. This assuming away of institutional frictions involved a number of heroic leaps. You had to presume that the knowledgeable speculators could find enough IBM stocks to borrow in order to be able to sell them short. And you had to gloss over the fact that, in real life, the "knowledge" that IBM was worth $90 would be less than certain. Speculation always involved risk, and there was only so much risk that speculators could shoulder. They could not necessarily be counted upon to move prices to their efficient level.

Before the 1987 crash, these quibbles seemed insignificant. To be sure, the great mass of ordinary investors might lack the means and confidence to act, but efficient-market theory pinned its hopes on the exceptional minority. It would take only a small handful of investors armed with information and capital to pounce on mispricings and correct them.[68] But Black Monday demonstrated that sophisticated investors would not always succeed in correcting prices. In the chaos of the market meltdown, brokers' phone lines were jammed with calls from panicking sellers; it was hard to get through and place an order. Any leveraged investor feared that his credit lines might be canceled; access to borrowing, assumed to be straightforward in efficient-market models, was in reality uncertain. And, most important, the sheer weight of selling made it too risky to go against the trend. When the whole world is selling, it doesn't matter whether sophisticated hedge funds believe that prices have fallen too far. Buying is crazy.

At a minimum, it seemed, the efficient-market hypothesis did not apply to moments of crisis. But the crash raised a further question too: If markets were efficient, why had the equity bubble inflated in the first place? Again, the answer seemed to lie partly in the institutional obstacles faced by speculators. In the summer of 1987, investors could see plainly that stocks were selling for higher multiples of corporate earnings than they had historically; but if the market was determined to value them that way, it would cost money to buck it. Hedge fund managers knew better than anyone that borrowing stocks to short is difficult and that the few skilled operators who do this have limited war chests. Because of these institutional realities, the overvaluation might well last. The efficient-market assumption of wise speculators pushing prices into line was, at a minimum, exaggerated.

The third post-1987 assault on efficient-market theory was perhaps the closest to Soros's own complaint about it. This line of attack went after the protagonist at the center of economists' models, the impeccably rational figure known as *Homo economicus*. When investors could revise their valuation of corporate America by as much as a quarter in a single day, something other than rational analysis was in play; *homo* was not fully *economicus*. Economists were suddenly open to ideas that might explain the extent of the divergence. In 1988 Richard Thaler of the University of Chicago began to publish regular features in the *Journal of Economic Perspectives* that pointed out instances in which human choices appeared to violate economists' expectations of rational beings. To Soros, who had obsessed about the limits to cognition since his student days in London, it was another victory.

The triple attack on efficient-market theory—statistical, institutional, and psychological—was in some ways a vindication for the hedge-fund industry. It helped to explain how Michael Steinhardt's block trading or Helmut Weymar's commodity speculators could have done so well, and it showed that market practitioners had often been ahead of academic theorists. The realization that market efficiency is imperfect encouraged a wave of finance professors to launch their own hedge funds, and it persuaded sophisticated endowments to pour money into their coffers, triggering the industry's headlong growth after 1987. But there was a darker side to this revolution in ideas. If markets were not always efficient and rational, their effects on society might be pernicious too: Boom-bust sequences could distort and destabilize the economy, damaging ordinary workers and households. And if markets could be demons, surely fast-trading hedge funds must be demons on steroids? This suspicion, however exaggerated, haunted hedge funds repeatedly as they entered their golden era of expansion.

5

TOP CAT

In the late spring of 1984, Columbia Business School played host to a clash of the financial titans. It invited Michael Jensen, one of the deans of academic finance, to make the case for the efficient-market view; and it invited Warren Buffett to challenge him. Knowing that he faced a New York audience stacked with professional investors, Jensen bravely rehearsed the random walkers' argument. If stock pickers remain in business, it is only because befuddled laymen have a "psychic demand for answers" about where to invest—and never mind the fact that the answers are worthless. The few money managers who appear to defy the random-walk hypothesis are merely lucky, Jensen assured his listeners. Sure, some beat the market for five years straight. But if you asked a million people to flip coins, some would flip five heads in a row. There is no skill in coin flipping—and investment is no different.[1]

Then Warren Buffett delivered a rejoinder that could serve as a hedge-fund manifesto. He began by playing along with Jensen's argument, inviting his audience to imagine a national coin-flipping contest. At the start of the competition, everyone in America would flip a coin, and those who turned up tails would withdraw from the contest. At the end of ten rounds, 220,000 flippers would be left—and, human nature being what it is, the survivors would start to get a little cocky. At parties they would occasionally admit to attractive members of the opposite sex what their technique was and what marvelous insights they brought to the field of flipping. At the end of twenty rounds, the 215 remaining contestants would start to wax insufferable, publishing fatuous books on the art and science of coin flipping. But then some business-school professor would point out that if 225,000,000 orangutans engaged in a coin-flip-a-thon, the results would be the same. There would be 215 egotistical orangutans with twenty straight winning flips.

Having made Jensen's argument better than Jensen, Buffett proceeded to cut holes in it. If the 215 winning orangutans were distributed randomly about the country, their success could be dismissed as luck. But if 40 of the 215 winners hailed from the same zoo, wouldn't something else explain their coin flipping? Phenomena that appear statistically random can appear altogether different when you consider their distribution, Buffett was saying. If you found that a rare cancer was common in a particular village, you would not put that down to chance. You would analyze the water.

Buffett then argued that stock-picking success is not randomly distributed. On the contrary, clusters of excellence spring from certain "villages," defined not by geography but by their approach to investment. To demonstrate his point, Buffett laid out the records of nine money managers from the value-investing tradition started by Ben Graham, Buffett's mentor. Three had worked at the Graham-Newman Corporation in the mid-1950s; the others had been converted to the Graham approach by Buffett or his associates. Buffett insisted that he had not cherry-picked his examples; he was reporting the results of *all* Graham-Newman alumni for whom there were records and all the fund managers whom he had won over to the value-investing method. Without any exception, and without copying one another's stock choices, each of Ben Graham's heirs had beaten the market.[2] Could this be simple fortune?

Buffett's general point was indisputable. When investment managers are viewed merely as sets of performance numbers, the handful of success stories can be dismissed as products of chance—the equivalent of ten-heads-in-a-row coin flippers. But if investment managers are understood as belonging to distinct intellectual "villages" or styles, their success may be concentrated in a way that is not random. The story of hedge funds features several of these high-performance clusters, and the most famous of them all was created by a booming North Carolina native. His name was Julian Robertson.[3]

MASTERS OF THE MARKET CAN SOMETIMES BE ALOOF. They have no use for the sorts of flattery and tolerance that lubricate human affairs. There are just facts; you make money or you don't; social skills won't change the bottom line on your portfolio. Visiting the legendary macro trader Louis Bacon in his office one day, a fellow hedge-fund manager found an Oz-like figure hidden behind banks of screens. When Bacon later bought a private island, there seemed little to be gained. He was already as isolated as he could be.[4]

Julian Hart Robertson came out of a different tradition. He was a charmer in a southern way, a networker in a New York way; and far from being coldly in control, his mood could swing alarmingly. Tall, confident, and athletic of build, he was a guy's guy, a jock's jock, and he hired in his own image. To thrive at Robertson's Tiger Management, you almost needed the physique; otherwise you would be hard-pressed to survive the Tiger retreats, which involved vertical hikes and outward-bound contests in Idaho's Sawtooth Mountains. The Tigers would fly out west on Robertson's private plane and be taken to a hilltop. They would split up into teams, each equipped with logs the size of telephone poles, some rope, and two paddles. Then they would heave the equipment down to a nearby lake, lash the logs together, and race out to a buoy—with the twist that not all of the team could fit on the raft, so some had to plunge into the icy water. Even away from these adventure holidays, the testosterone quotient at Tiger remained exceptional. The firm retained a private trainer, and if an analyst showed signs of shirking his workouts, the trainer would come up to him. "You're going to a business dinner in fifteen minutes?" he would ask. "Do you have time to run two miles and shower before that?"

Like Soros and Steinhardt, Robertson was inspired to set up his hedge fund by A. W. Jones's example. While working at Kidder Peabody in the 1970s, Robertson had befriended Bob Burch, A. W. Jones's son-in-law. Occasionally, the friends would take the old patriarch to lunch, and Robertson would quiz Jones on the mechanics of his partnership. Robertson was also close to a fellow southerner named Alex Porter, who had moved to New York in the 1960s, bunked in Robertson's apartment, and gone on to become an A. W. Jones segment manager. Robertson's sister was a *Fortune* magazine journalist who had written about the Jones-style funds, and through her Robertson got to know Carol Loomis, the *Fortune* writer who had first explained the hedged investment structure. A few years after Robertson launched Tiger, Bob Burch entrusted him with $5 million, a fifth of the Jones money that remained.[5] It was a wise decision.

Robertson launched Tiger in 1980, at the relatively advanced age of forty-eight. During his first winter the heating in his tiny office broke and he caught a cold and lost his voice, so that he squeaked out buy and sell orders. He brought along a carefree partner named Thorpe McKenzie, but there was no doubt who was in control: "When we disagreed, I caved," McKenzie recalled later.[6] Throughout his reign at Tiger, Robertson kept a close hold on the responsibility for buying and selling, rather than delegating to segment managers beneath him; but in most other ways he was faithful to the Jones model.[7] He picked stocks, long and short, hedging out part of the risk in the market.[8] He dismissed commentary about the market's overall direction as "gibberish" and promised his clients that he would prosper through stock selection.[9] As the fund grew, Robertson picked stocks internationally, not just in the United States; and he played in commodities, currencies, and bonds, so that the original Jones method acquired a macro-investing overlay. He sometimes hedged his market exposure with futures or options, a method unavailable to Jones; but he emphasized that these speculative instruments were being used for conservative ends, echoing Jones's language.[10]

Between its inception in May 1980 and its peak in August 1998, Tiger earned an average of 31.7 percent per year after subtracting fees, trouncing the 12.7 percent annual return on the S&P 500 index.[11] The fact that stock picking succeeded in this period was an affront to the efficient-market hypothesis. It was understandable that A. W. Jones could prosper in an earlier era, when rivals at bureaucratic trust banks made investment decisions by committee. It was understandable that Michael Steinhardt could make money by being inside the charmed circle of block traders; that the quants and trend surfers at Commodities Corporation were ahead of their rivals; and perhaps even that George Soros, autodidact and seer, had a feel for turning points in markets. But Robertson made no claim to have discovered institutional weaknesses in markets, a fancy quantitative strategy, or some philosophical vision. He once summed up his approach to investing in a letter to Robert Karr, Tiger's man in Tokyo, and the sheer blandness of his message underlined the mystery of his success. A Tiger should manage the portfolio aggressively, removing good companies to make room for better ones; he should avoid risking more than 5 percent of capital on one bet; and he should keep swinging through bad times until his luck returned to him.[12] The simple truth was that the big jock and his lieutenants—a handful at the outset, perhaps a dozen later on—just analyzed companies, currencies, and commodities and bet on their prospects. This was exactly what the efficient marketers believed to be impossible.

Efforts to explain away this anomaly are mostly unsatisfying. Like the Jones funds, Tiger was undoubtedly launched at a propitious time, at the start of an equity bull market. The 401(k) retirement plan was invented in 1981, the year after Robertson opened for business; by the time Tiger closed its doors, 401(k) pensions were ubiquitous and their owners had stashed 75 percent of their assets in equities. For long stretches of this period, the market rode skyward on the back of corporate mergers and buyouts: Between 1981 and 1988, for example, almost 1,550 American companies went private, and every transaction made remaining public stocks scarcer and more valuable. It was a good time to be an equity investor.

Robertson certainly made the most of this bonanza. He was instinctively in tune with the merger boom: His aim as a stock picker was to look through the price of a company as announced by the market and to discern its true value; this process often led him to buy stocks that were also attractive to takeover artists. In 1985, for example, Tiger bought Empire

Airlines at $9 a share and was taken out by a corporate acquirer that bid $15. It bought Aviall, a distributor of aviation parts, at $12.50 a share; it was taken out at $25.[13] At the end of that year, Tiger was up an astonishing 51.4 percent after subtracting fees, and Robertson broke the news to his investors with a note of mock warning. "Bluntly," his letter to them advised, "if you are not planning on buying emeralds or diamonds, don't show your wife this letter."

Yet it would be wrong to presume that Robertson generated his record simply by riding the bull market upward. Because of the shorts in his portfolio, his fund was not set up to rise as fast as the market, but he nearly always beat it.[14] Some Tiger alumni suggest that he achieved this by focusing on small companies. According to this theory, the market price of a big corporation such as United Airlines is likely to be efficient because Wall Street analysts pore over its books; lesser firms escape scrutiny. It's true that Tiger did seek out small companies that lazier investors missed; but it made money on big ones too—including, spectacularly, on that very same United Airlines. But the deeper objection to the small-stock theory is that its logic is debatable. The fact that small stocks are underanalyzed does not tell you there are easy profits to be had from them. To be sure, the majority of investors may never have heard of a particular provincial retailer or third-tier bank, but they are not the ones holding the stock. When Tiger bought shares in those companies, it was buying from people who knew enough to own the shares themselves—and who also knew enough to want to become sellers.[15]

Tiger's success in stock picking undoubtedly owed something to its freedom to go short, an option denied to the majority of fund managers. Nearly all the Jones-style hedge funds had been washed out in the early 1970s, so the competition among short sellers was modest. Even better for Robertson, Wall Street analysis was congenitally bullish: On one reckoning, brokers at the major houses issued ten buys for every sell recommendation in the early 1980s.[16] No analyst wanted to put a sell recommendation in writing for fear of losing his relationship with the companies he covered, especially since the investment bankers at his firm coveted advisory fees from those same companies. So Robertson would call up the analysts and sweet-talk them into divulging their best short ideas over the telephone. "I know you all consider these companies to be your children, but just call me with your least favorite child," Robertson would coax them.[17]

Robertson was temperamentally a skeptic, and short selling came naturally to him. In a typical letter to his investors in July 1983, he complained of bullishness gone wild. "The media, public and analysts, virtually everybody, are so bullish that they could be described as 'eating grass,' " Robertson declared. "When this happens it may be best to crawl in a log and slurp some honey." When the market hit a weak patch, Robertson's skepticism paid off. In 1984, for example, the S&P 500 index rose just 6.3 percent while Tiger returned 20.2 percent; more than half of Robertson's returns came from his short investments.[18] The following year a portfolio manager named Patrick Duff began to suspect that a hotel chain called Prime Motor Inns was in a rather worse position than its accounts suggested. Duff did nothing about it, because he was working for a conventional pension fund at the time; but when he joined Tiger in 1989, he persuaded Robertson to short the company. Within a year, Prime Motor Inns fell from $28 to $1, demonstrating how profitable short selling could be. Robertson had an arrow in his quiver that conventional funds lacked. "It's me and the patsies," he once told an associate.[19]

But Tiger's defiance of efficient-market presumptions cannot be explained entirely by short selling. In most years Robertson would have beaten the market even without the profits from his shorts, suggesting that he had an edge precisely where the theory said no edge was possible: in traditional stock buying. Moreover, Robertson's record, like Buffett's record, was not an isolated phenomenon. Just as Buffett was part of an investment "village"—the cluster of superstars who had been schooled in Ben Graham's value-investing style—so Robertson was a village headman. On one count in 2008, thirty-six former Tiger employees had set up "Tiger cub" funds, which collectively managed $100 billion; and Robertson had seeded a further twenty-nine funds after restructuring his firm in 2000.[20] These Robertson protégés did well: A test of Tiger cubs' performance, presented in the first appendix to this book, shows that they beat not only the market but also other hedge funds. Moreover, the test covers the years 2000 to 2008, a period in which the profusion of long/short equity hedge funds had long since ended whatever easy profits might have existed in short selling during the 1980s.

If Robertson's achievement had stood by itself, it might have been possible to dismiss him as a lucky coin flipper. But the success of Tiger's numerous offshoots puts paid to that thesis. Whatever the source of Robertson's investment edge, it was profitable—and transferable.

THE REAL EXPLANATION FOR ROBERTSON'S SUCCESS begins with an updated version of an A. W. Jones innovation. Jones had revolutionized money management by paying for performance. He rewarded his segment managers in proportion to their returns; he created incentives for outside analysts to bring him good ideas, tracking the profits that they generated and handing out commissions accordingly. Likewise, Robertson put rocket fuel in the veins of his employees, but he did it in a different way. It was not just about money.

There was something about Robertson that made you want to please him. He would zero in on people with his Carolina charm, flattering and drawling until they purred like sleepy kittens. "Pah-wah-ful, Bob," he might address a young subordinate. "Ah find mah-self utterly pah-ra-lyzed without your pah-wah-ful assistance." The rich pleasure of basking in Robertson's attention was spiked with the knowledge that his mood might turn. "Why, you petty tin-pot dictator," he might say, and his voice would be ice cold. "You Latin American dictator." Robertson would assemble his lieutenants each Friday around a long table to listen to the fruits of their week's work, and the emotional payoffs were extreme. "That is the be-yest idea Ah ever saw," he might exclaim after listening to a square-shouldered twentysomething analyst deliver a stock pitch, and the young hunk would be whooping and high-fiving himself inside his swollen head for the rest of the meeting. "That is the dumbest idea Ah ever heard," Robertson might also say, in which case six-foot-plus of Wall Street alpha male would shrivel pitifully.[21]

Working for Tiger was not merely a job. It was like joining a special-forces unit. The commander made you bigger, brighter, tougher than you were before; he made you believe that you could beat the market, year after year, because you were part of a team that would outthink and out-hustle every rival. For the first dozen years or so of Tiger's history, the commander operated from a desk out in the open, next to his young men; they watched him schmooze and holler down the phone, sucking infor-mation out of his vast network.[22] Robertson's two assistants operated a pair of giant Rolodexes, almost the size of wagon wheels, and if a Tiger analyst pitched an investment to the boss, Robertson would soon be test-ing the idea on three old friends who worked in that same company. The analyst might say, "I think it's time to short Boeing." Robertson might respond, "I know the guy who used to run Boeing's international market-ing." The assistants would work the wagon wheels, the former marketing chief would crackle on the speakerphone, and Robertson would tell his twentysomething analyst to defend his short recommendation.[23]

For a young man with the wits to thrive in this environment, the sky was the limit. So long as you were doing well, you basked in the attention of the boss: He would call you "big tiger" and show you off to his exalted buddies. Robertson introduced one young analyst to Jerry Reinsdorf, the owner of the Chicago Bulls, saying, "This man is *my* Michael Jordan." He introduced a lieutenant who loved golf to Jack Nicklaus and Ely Callaway. He took one prized employee to the White House to visit Bill Clinton: "Bill, this is Lou," Robertson said. "He can do anything in the world. He is unbelievable." But as always with Robertson, the risks could be as great as the rewards. Eighteen months after his introduction to Clinton, that same Lou was gone. He had gone from White House to shit house in record time, as he put it to a colleague.[24]

Robertson drew people in by sheer force of personality. He met the singer Paul Simon and persuaded him to invest in Tiger on the strength of a shared passion for baseball.[25] The writer Tom Wolfe was a Tiger investor too, and Robertson knew how to use these stars to recruit others. In 1986 he set his sights on hiring a Goldman Sachs analyst named Michael Bills, never mind the fact that Goldman's big pooh-bahs were promising the young man a great Goldman future. Robertson gave Bills the full charm treatment, and he wheeled in Lew Lehrman, the financier, philanthropist, and history buff who had campaigned for the New York governorship in 1982, wearing his trademark red suspenders. In all his long experience, Lehrman earnestly told Bills, he had never encountered an investor to compare with Julian Robertson—not anyone, not ever. Then Robertson brought out his trump: Tom Wolfe called Bills to talk about the young man's father. Bills senior had served as a military pilot, and there was no better tribute to military pilots than Wolfe's book *The Right Stuff.* Pretty soon Wolfe and Bills were sharing their profound feelings about flying and honor and courage. By the end of that twenty-minute call, Goldman Sachs had lost its man. Bills signed on with Tiger.

Tiger's roster of investors was crammed with captains of industry and finance, and Robertson never hesitated to call on them for insights. His letters to his partners frequently encouraged them to call in ideas, "or, particularly in the case of ladies, intuition." In the early 1980s Tiger tripled its money in a stock called Mentor, which a Tiger investor had recommended. In the early 1990s the fund's best stock picks included General Instrument Corporation and Equitable Life Insurance; in both cases Tiger friends who were connected to those firms had urged Robertson to buy them. Around the same time, Robertson began to buy stock in Citicorp, mainly because the bank seemed poised to recover strongly after clearing out its real-estate losses, but also because a Tiger friend was willing to vouch for John Reid, Citi's chief executive. Robertson was not engaging in insider trading: His contacts were offering broad guidance, not secrets on upcoming earnings announcements that could have an immediate impact on stocks. But he was consciously building his network and cashing in on it brilliantly.[26]

To those who watched Robertson up close in his heyday, there was no doubt about his talent. He could drop in on a meeting with a chief executive and demonstrate a grasp of company detail that rivaled that of the analyst who tracked it.[27] He could listen to a presentation on a firm he knew nothing about and immediately pounce on the detail that would make or break it. He could play golf with the chief executive, see the man nudge his ball into a better position when it landed in the rough, and write himself a mental note never to buy stock in the man's company. Jim

Chanos, a celebrated short seller who ran money for the three hedge-fund titans of the 1980s—Robertson, Soros, and Steinhardt—remembers Robertson as the most intellectually engaging of the bunch. "If I had had to give my own money to any of them, I would have given it to Robertson," Chanos recalls. "I knew that he knew stocks better than anyone."[28]

ROBERTSON'S PERSONALITY, HIS ABILITY TO GET THE best out of people, constituted his clearest advantage. But this sort of edge could be tricky to define, and people who knew Robertson less well than Chanos could be forgiven for missing it. An *Institutional Investor* profile from May 1986 set out to describe what the magazine billed as "the red-hot world of Julian Robertson," but it made the special sauce seem bland. "It's not that Robertson does anything dramatically different from other money managers; it's just that he does it so well," the profiler pleaded.[29] Meanwhile, Robertson's supposed knack for judging managers could sometimes misfire: Writing off a company because its boss cheated at golf fell short of scientific method. But although Robertson's approach was neither formal nor original, he was right more than he was wrong—and that is the definition of success in money management. No system, human or computerized, is correct all the time. The mathematicians who build state-of-the-art quantitative systems are delighted when they call the market right on six out of ten occasions.

The same six-out-of-ten rule applied to another hallmark of the Tiger style: long-termism. Wall Street analysts typically feed clients the twelve- to eighteen-month view, and hedge funds frequently do well either by being more short-term or more long-term. Robertson was firmly in the long-term camp. His ideal investment—a *fah-bulous* investment, as Robertson would say—was something that might plausibly double in three years. If Robertson believed he had found such an investment, he was willing to hang on, gritting his teeth through the hard times until the world caught up with his analysis. In 1983 Robertson decided that oil prices would come down, and he took big short positions in oil and oil-service stocks. The bet hurt for a while, but it was right: Three years on,

crude had halved in value. In 1984, Robertson shorted generic pharmaceutical makers, believing that there could be no durable profit margin
in nonbranded products. Again, the bet lost money, but Robertson kept
faith. Two years later, he celebrated the collapse of Zenith Labs, whose
stock crashed 45 percent in the space of one quarter.[30]

Tenacity, like character judgment, is not the sort of edge that pays off
every time—and sometimes when it did, luck was the crucial factor. In
1987 a young lieutenant named John Griffin persuaded Robertson to short
a small appliance maker whose manufacturing was based in China. The
company proceeded to rack up terrific Christmas sales, and the stock shot
up from $20 to $25. Griffin and Robertson stuck with their convictions,
but the news did not improve: The company powered its way into the
spring, and the stock hit $35. In 1988 Griffin went off to business school
at Stanford but begged his commander to keep faith with the trade: It
would come good! He was convinced of it! Robertson indulged Griffin,
even though the stock had by now doubled to $40—meaning that the bet
had so far cost Tiger 100 percent of its original stake. One day at Stanford,
Griffin got a fax from the big man. There were no words on the paper. It
just said, "$50!"

Months passed. And then, in April 1989, one hundred thousand
demonstrators marched into Tiananmen Square in China's capital. The
demonstrations gathered momentum; the protesters pressed political
reform; a full-blown revolution seemed possible. Not surprisingly, American companies with factories in China saw their stocks fall off a cliff.
Tiger's short was no exception.

Griffin ran excitedly to a pay phone. At last he was redeemed! He was
ecstatic to speak to his mentor.

"Julian, I told you it would work! You stayed with it! You believed in
me! It worked! I KNEW it would work!"

Seated on the other side of the American continent, Robertson listened
to this outburst. "Now, John, now, John," he answered in his honeysuckle
drawl. "The way *Ah* see it, is that it took a revolution of a *bihl-lion* people
for your darn short to work out."

If this story shows how Robertson's tenacity could hurt in the absence of sheer luck, it also shows his genius. A young hotshot like Griffin, who would later run his own multibillion-dollar hedge fund, had left Tiger for business school. But psychologically he had not left at all; he was still running to get the big man on the phone, desperate for redemption. Even a quarter century later, the bond remained intense; in a speech in 2007, Griffin described the enduring sense that Robertson was watching over him, judging his decisions. "All money managers wish they had a little birdie on their shoulder who might whisper the correct market move from time to time," Griffin declared. "Well, my little birdie has a deep southern drawl and a bald head. Sometimes I hear him chirp: 'Big guy, don't do that.'"[31]

Under Robertson's tutelage, young men like Griffin hustled harder than they might have elsewhere, and in the pre-Internet era, hustle counted hugely. The search engines and terminals that later made data ubiquitous had not yet been born; so if a Tiger analyst wanted to know how Ford's sales were shaping up, he would sit on the phone until he had talked to Ford's customers, competitors, and suppliers; to the car dealers, part makers, and Detroit rivals; to anyone, indeed, who might have a useful angle. One analyst who was considering a possible stake in Avon Products developed her own edge by becoming an Avon representative. Another was contemplating a short in a Korean carmaker whose engines were said to malfunction, so he bought two of its cars and hired a mechanic to test them.[32] When Mexico defaulted at the start of 1995, most New York investors worried that American banks might take a hit. But Tiger's analyst flew to Mexico and found that Citicorp was not exposed and, further, that Mexicans were eager to do business with Citi now that their own banks had been weakened. As panicky New Yorkers hammered Citi's stock, Tiger snapped up more at bargain prices.

Robertson's gregarious personality marked him off from other hedge-fund titans, and it gave him an edge. It allowed him to set up a contest between the workaday masses and his own special-force unit. It was him against the patsies.[33]

———

AS THE TAKEOVER BONANZA OF THE 1980S GAVE WAY TO
the globalization bonanza of the 1990s, Robertson went global also. He
was not a natural cosmopolitan, unlike George Soros. But travel suited
his swashbuckling style, and he took to it vigorously. He flew to Hong
Kong in the company of the buyout tycoon Teddy Forstmann. He zipped
through Europe at high speed, reporting that the American embassy in
Paris was "very, very liveable."[34] He lamented the low ratio of women to
men on Brazil's beaches but marveled at the sophistication of São Paulo's
business leaders. Everywhere he went, Robertson met new people and discovered new ways to have fun. He would pitch up in a city, stroll into the
first couple of meetings, and charm his hosts into setting him up with the
top people in their Rolodexes.

Robertson's trips were managed by a "camp counselor" who helped
him find his way around, and usually the counselor was John Griffin.
Smart, indefatigable, an Ironman triathlete, Griffin was the ideal Robertson lieutenant. The two men pitched up at company meetings all over the
world, then broke off to play high-voltage tennis before cross-examining
another batch of companies.[35] After a lunch at the Union Bank of Switzerland in Zurich, at which Griffin gobbled up a large dollop of chocolate
mousse as well as a pastry, Robertson and his camp counselor raced back
to the hotel to grab a rental car. As he reported later to his investors, the
two men "turned the music up to full blast and took off for Austria with
a brief stop in Lichtenstein. Purpose—skiing."[36]

In early November 1989, when Griffin was on leave at business school
at Stanford, the fax machine that he had installed in his room sputtered
out a message from the chief: "Big guy, the Berlin Wall is coming down
soon. This is gonna be a VERY big deal." A few days later, the wall duly
fell, and two days after that Tiger began to load up on German securities.
Robertson knew next to nothing about Germany; but Griffin had studied
the German market during a summer stint in London, and Robertson
was not going to let an absence of experience get in the way of a historic
opportunity. Tiger bought Deutsche Bank, which stood to profit from a

unification boom. It bought Veba, a large utility that owned power plants along the West German–East German border and could be expected to capture the emerging eastern market. It bought Felten & Guilleaume, the firm that made the power cables that would carry the electricity into the new territories. Sure enough, Germany's stock market went on a euphoric tear, and Tiger's stake in Felten & Guilleaume soon doubled.[37]

The following summer, Robertson and Griffin rode into Germany. They went to East Berlin, where they discovered that nobody had heard of hedge funds or Julian Robertson. They also discovered that Germany was not quite what Robertson had thought. Sitting in the waiting room on his first company visit, Robertson touched the table and held up a dust-blackened finger. "These people have a long way to go," he said a bit suspiciously. The meetings continued, with Robertson asking Wall Street questions and the Germans doing their best to be genial, and all the while Robertson was grappling with the gap between what he could see in the numbers and what came out of the mouths of these people. By American standards, and relative to the factories and other assets that they owned, German stocks were ludicrously cheap. If the Germans could manage these assets as American managers would, they would generate huge returns for shareholders; and if the incumbent managers were too sluggish to do that, surely a wave of Wall Street–style takeovers would quickly solve the problem?[38] But the more Robertson toured Germany, the less enthusiastic he became. He would sit in a manager's office and ask about his company's return on equity, but the managers cared more about their sales than their profits; they were running the company for the sake of the employees rather than for the shareholders. At the chemical company Bayer for example, Robertson was treated to a lavish lunch by the company's top management.

"It must be great to be the chief executive if you can eat like this," Robertson said, not mentioning that he would have preferred that the company save money.

"Oh no," his hosts replied. "We serve this meal to all employees."

"My! The planes here fly so close," Robertson said, looking out the window.

"Yes, that is the company flying club," came back the answer. "Anyone who wants can train for their pilot's license."[39]

After the lunch ended, Robertson delivered his verdict to Griffin: "These people just don't get it." German managers could not care less about return on equity. By 1994, Robertson had come full circle on his view of the Germans. The nation's industry was nothing more, he wrote, than a "giant flab bag of inefficiency."[40]

Robertson's adventure in Germany, his transition from bull to disaffected bear, contained a warning for Tiger. In branching out in all directions, the fund was lurching into areas that it barely knew. Expansion generated new opportunities—including opportunities to be wrong, and perhaps one day to lose some serious money.

AT THE END OF 1990, ROBERTSON SAT FOR ANOTHER MAG-azine profile. The essay opened as though lifting the veil on a secret. "The public manifestations of Julian Robertson are . . . sparse," it began. "An SEC filing here. A paragraph in the financial press there. Fame has not come to Julian Robertson. Fortune, yes. But not fame." Of course, these observations were self-canceling, since there is no better way to attract attention than to be described as a secret, especially when the article proceeded to broadcast Robertson's performance record. Money from wealthy individuals, and increasingly from endowments, began to flood into Tiger's coffers. The year after the article appeared, Tiger became the third hedge fund to manage more than $1 billion.

Throughout the 1980s, Robertson had proclaimed that small was beautiful, arguing that it gave him a significant edge over lumbering competitors. But in the 1990s he threw caution to the wind: A bigger staff, a bigger office, a bigger list of exalted investors—it all seemed too appealing. In the race to accumulate assets, Robertson became fearsomely competitive. He passed the $1 billion milestone behind Soros and Steinhardt, but by the end of 1993 he was running a formidable $7 billion, more than Steinhardt and only slightly less than Soros. Even being number two was not quite good enough, and Robertson envied Soros's ability to capture the limelight.

There had been many years when Tiger had posted better performance than Quantum, and Robertson was so obsessed with the comparison that he could recite his victories by heart. In 1981 "we beat him to death; [in 1982] he beat us; [in 1983] we beat him to death; [in 1984] we beat him to death again," he had once informed an interviewer.[41] But somehow it was Soros who garnered the most attention and the most assets.

Robertson's competitive expansion involved risks, however. It forced him to diversify beyond his core strengths: There were too few opportunities in the U.S. equity markets to sustain a fund worth several billion dollars. Small-cap stocks, in particular, became virtually off limits: An analyst might identify a promising small company and figure that its value could double over three years, but if there was only $20 million worth of shares available to buy, it was hardly worth bothering with.[42] Robertson's charge into foreign equity markets was one response to this problem. But in going abroad, Robertson was betting that his American instincts would work in different cultural settings. The German experience showed that companies that appeared undervalued by American metrics might actually be fairly valued given the German indifference to profits; and meanwhile, Robertson encountered the mirror image of the German problem in Japan. With impeccable logic, Tiger had shorted Japanese bank stocks: The big banks were mismanaged, they lent at interest rates that brought in negligible profits, they were laden down with bad loans and yet traded at huge multiples. In 1992 Robertson assured his investors that Tokyo's bizarre valuations presented a rich opportunity for Tiger.[43] But three years later Robertson's Japan analyst was forced to write a memo asking why bank stocks refused to collapse. "I don't know the answer to that question," he admitted candidly.[44]

Tiger's expansion also pushed Robertson to take more risks in macro trading. He had dabbled in currencies from early on: Just over a quarter of his huge gain in 1985 came from a bet against the dollar—a smaller version of the Plaza accord play made famous by George Soros.[45] Meanwhile, Tiger also did well on a version of the "carry trade" that Bruce Kovner had been milking since his time at Commodities Corporation. Robertson bought Australian and New Zealand bonds with interest rates ranging from 16 percent to 24 percent, borrowing much of the money to do so in countries whose interest rates were less than 10 percent and locking in the difference. But as Tiger expanded in the early 1990s, Robertson resolved to redouble his commitment to the currency markets. In 1991 he hired David Gerstenhaber, a Japanese-speaking currency specialist from Morgan Stanley. A currency trader named Barry Bausano arrived at Tiger soon after.

The trouble was that Robertson was not equipped to thrive as a macro trader. Jim Chanos, the short seller who worked with both Soros and Robertson, vouched for Robertson's superior grasp of stocks; but no macro trader would have said the same about Robertson's grasp of interest rates or currencies.[46] Indeed, the value-investing mind-set almost disqualified Robertson from mastering macro. Value investors generally buy stocks using little or no leverage, and they hold them for the long term; if the investment moves against them, they typically buy more, because a stock that was a bargain at $25 is even more of a bargain at $20. But macro investors take leveraged positions, which make such trend bucking impossibly risky; they have to be ready to jump out of the market if a bet moves against them. Similarly, value investors pride themselves on rock-solid convictions. They have torn apart a company balance sheet and figured out what it is worth; they *know* they have found value. Macro investors have no method of generating comparable conviction. There is no reliable way to determine the objective "value" of a currency.

The macro traders who worked for Robertson in the 1990s struggled to adapt to his style of investing. They quickly found that the boss could not abide charts, which he had been known to describe as "hocus-pocus, mumbojumbo bullshit." They also found that their risk-control instincts rankled with him. If a trade went against them, the macro men reckoned they were late on it or simply wrong; it would be wiser to get out than to stick around and play the hero. But Robertson reacted in the opposite way. He had conviction; he would stay the course; he was going to reach the mountaintop eventually. One time the macro men feared that the markets would turn against their European bond position in the short term, and they advised Robertson to protect Tiger from losses by putting on a temporary hedge.

"Hedge?" Robertson retorted angrily. "*Hey-edge?* Why, that just means that if I'm right I'm going to make less money."

"Well, that's right," the macro men answered him.

"Why would I want to do that? Why? Why? That's just dirt under my fingernails."

That was the end of that attempt at risk management.

THROUGH THE 1980S AND EARLY 1990S, ROBERTSON'S strengths dwarfed his potential weaknesses. His special-forces unit parachuted into markets around the world; and although it could stumble, as the exaggerated hopes for Germany had shown, it was more often successful. Robertson frequently took a macro conviction and expressed it in stocks. After the Plaza accord it was clear that the dollar would be in for a weak spell; Robertson identified the U.S. firms that would benefit from strong exports and rode them to great profits. After U.S. real estate collapsed in 1990, Robertson correctly saw which banks to short; and the moment that the bad property debts were gone, Robertson went long financials. Meanwhile, Tiger's march into bonds and currencies, though dangerous, paid off spectacularly for a while. From the start of 1988 to the end of 1992, Tiger beat the S&P 500 index for five straight years; and the next year Robertson surpassed himself. He returned 64 percent to his investors after subtracting fees, and *BusinessWeek* estimated that his personal earnings for the year had come to $1 billion.

And yet around this time, something subtle shifted. Robertson spent more time away, and not always because he was traveling on business. In a ten-week period at the start of 1993, he spent five long weekends skiing in Sun Valley, one long weekend hunting sailfish in Costa Rica, three days at the Augusta National Golf Club, and a full fortnight in Kenya. He remodeled Tiger's premises, setting himself up in an elegant corner office that distanced him from his lieutenants. He hired a psychiatrist, a natty man named Aaron Stern, to help manage his people and his own mood swings, putting a new buffer between himself and his analysts. As Robertson became less of an everyday presence, his intensity and passion grated more. For days on end the lieutenants would not see their commander, and then he would descend on them, demanding facts and figures and the fresh scoop on the stocks that they were following. "If you bleed easily, you won't be happy here," the psychiatrist would warn people; and he was right. Many of the analysts who joined Tiger were out within a year or so.

But Robertson also lost people whom he wanted to keep. At the annual Tiger party in the fall of 1992, Robertson had introduced his macro men: "Meet David and Barry, who earned $1 billion last year." A reference like that made it easy for the duo to raise capital on their own, and in the spring of 1993 they quit to set up their own hedge fund. Soon the macro team's secession turned out to be the start of a series.[47] Tiger had grown so successful that the lieutenants felt they ought to be running their own shows, particularly since Robertson refused to share control; he had toyed with the idea of creating subportfolios that lieutenants could run, but he never ceded real authority. Besides, quitting was becoming seductively easy. Wealthy investors were increasingly on the lookout for the next generation of stars, and a Tiger analyst could go out on his own and quickly raise a fortune. Within two months of opening their doors, Gerstenhaber and Bausano were running $200 million in their Argonaut fund, many times more than the $8.5 million with which Tiger had started back in 1980.

As the Tiger family expanded, Robertson tried to preserve the special-force culture with trips out west to the mountains. The Tigers flew out there in Robertson's plane, primed to do battle with the elements. One winter, they strapped skins under their skis and hiked up a mountainside with sixty-pound packs, sleeping in tents at temperatures below zero. On another occasion they were taken to a forest and divided into teams, each equipped with a few bikes and a list of objects to collect before their rivals got to them. After their exertions, the Tigers would convene around the campfire and Robertson sometimes arranged for two analysts who had been quarreling to share the same tent. But these contrived efforts at team building frequently backfired, and the tensions in the Tiger family bubbled through the cracks in the camaraderie. The evening campfire gatherings created the expectation of a grand discussion on the future of Tiger: Would Robertson allow some of the men to run their own portfolios? What was the succession plan at Tiger? But Robertson had no intention of ceding control. He had not organized these retreats to discuss his own retreat, and he reacted angrily.

On one of those trips out to the mountains, a guide led a group of Tigers to three ropes slung across a ravine, a sheer fall of several hundred feet beneath them. The rain was driving and the wind was blowing hard, but the young men proceeded anyway. One by one, they fixed a pair of safety lines from their climbing harnesses onto the makeshift rope bridge and stepped out over the nothingness. As each man neared the center of the crossing, the point farthest from the ropes' moorings, the whole construction wiggled in the wind, and the spirit of Julian Robertson, fearless investor, adventurer, and commander of men, shone down upon him. Then an analyst named Tom McCauley slipped on the wet rope. He fell perhaps ten feet before the safety line saved him.

The Tigers looked on at their comrade, dangling from the rope with a long chute of emptiness beneath him. McCauley had taken the fall in true Tiger fashion; he was laughing and bouncing on the safety line, using the whole apparatus like an outsized baby jumper. Then one of the onlookers gave a start. Rather than having two safety lines holding him, McCauley had just one; and the carabiner on the end of that line was coming open. Some of the Tigers shouted; others went plain numb; and some found themselves musing surreally about the fluffy white outfit that McCauley had on—he looked like the Pillsbury doughboy.

"Hey, Tom, stop bouncing," somebody shouted.

"There's an issue with your carabiner."

"REALLY, STOP BOUNCING."

There were a few long seconds while the guide shimmied out onto the rope and locked McCauley's carabiner shut. But that moment when Tiger's reach exceeded its grasp stuck in the group's memory.[48]

ROCK-AND-ROLL
COWBOY

The late 1980s marked a turning point for hedge funds. After the bear market of the early 1970s, the industry had almost been wiped out; the few dozen funds that existed operated mostly under the radar, and the amount of capital they managed was insignificant. But after the 1987 crash, something profound changed. By one count in 1990, six hundred hedge funds had sprouted from the desert, and by 1992 there were over a thousand.[1] Financial commentators began to refer knowingly to the "Big Three"—Soros, Robertson, and Steinhardt—and 1993 was celebrated as "the year of the hedge fund."[2] Behind the Big Three, a pack of younger rivals was expanding fast, and the connections among the leading stars reinforced the sense of a new movement. Julian Robertson was related by marriage to the young trader Louis Bacon. Michael Steinhardt had gone into business briefly with Bruce Kovner of Caxton. The hedge-fund moguls went hunting and fishing on one another's estates, sat on some of the same charitable boards, and gathered annually in the Bahamian resort of Lyford Cay. Their very presence in one room signaled the birth of a new force on Wall Street.

The most colorful of the younger titans was Paul Tudor Jones II, the Patton aficionado and Soros friend whom we have already encountered. He was born in 1954 to a Memphis family with deep ties to cotton: His grandfather had prospered as a cotton merchant, and his uncle, Billy Dunavant, was a proud baron of the industry. After studying undergraduate economics at the University of Virginia, Jones landed an apprenticeship with a cotton trader in New Orleans, then moved after two years to the New York Cotton Exchange. Rubbing shoulders with the floor traders, it was hard to believe that markets reflected all available information in some kind of efficient way. The key drivers of prices in the commodity pits were not the economic data but the wild guys screaming in your face—the cotton cowboys who downed martinis at lunchtime and then wheeled into battle, determined to gun the market up or down, depending on how things felt to them. To be sure, the cowboys responded to new information—announcements about growth and unemployment and so on. But if you aimed to survive as a floor trader, it was less important to understand the news than to foresee the pit's reaction to it. The story is told of a floor operator who made $10 million in a spasm of trading following the release of a government inflation report. When the pandemonium had subsided he walked out of the ring and asked, "By the way, what was the number?"[3]

Jones left the floor of the cotton exchange in 1983 and set about building his own firm, Tudor Investment Corporation. Still not thirty, he was young to head out on his own; but he had a helping hand from Commodities Corporation, which invested $35,000 in his fund and put him in touch with a community of veterans who validated his view of the markets. Quickly, Jones emerged as a prodigy with a distinctive style. He approached trading as a game of psychology and high-speed bluff, a kind of poker that combined sly subtlety with crazed bravado. It was not enough to look at your own cards and decide what you might bet; you had to sense what other traders were up to—whether they felt greedy or afraid, whether they were poised to go all in or were dangerously extended. You might hear bullish news for sugar, but then you had to ask yourself how others would react. If the big traders had already bought their fill, the news would scarcely budge the price; but if they were waiting to rush in, the market would take off like a rocket.[4] The more you watched your rival traders, the more you knew how they would play; and eventually you could get inside their heads, luring them along when they were in the mood to buy, spooking them out of the market when they were feeling fearful. If you sensed that the big traders were nervous, you could yell that you were selling and know that they'd sell too. Then you could pivot right around and buy the hell out of the market.[5]

In this game of wits and bluff, loud flamboyance could be helpful. Jones happily described himself as "a cowboy in the purest sense," and he approached the markets with the violent passion of the boxer he had been in college.[6] He would scream huge orders down the phone to his brokers on various exchange floors, frequently reversing his instructions in the course of one call, knowing that the crazier he sounded the more he would keep rivals off balance. He would vary his methods to suit his purpose: Sometimes he would place small orders with multiple brokers in an attempt to stay under the radar; sometimes he would ambush the market, guns blazing, knowing that the shock appearance of a big buyer could send other traders scrambling to buy also. Perhaps because Jones wielded notoriety as a trading weapon, he was willing to publicize this style. In 1986 and 1987 he allowed a documentary film team to follow him around, capturing his trading tantrums.[7]

In one early sequence of the film, Jones is sitting calmly at his desk just before the market opens. He's wearing a white shirt, a conservative tie, and a signet ring; it's a preppy look, almost an accountant's look, rounded off by large glasses and brown hair combed into a tidy parting.

"Eight minutes to go," Jones drawls lazily, his Memphis childhood resonant in his voice.

"I'm getting ready," he continues, his voice picking up the pace a bit.

"Getting a little drums along the Mohawk," he says, louder, jiggling his legs with nervous energy.

And then the accountant suddenly explodes. "Doing a little tom-tomming on the market!" he roars, leaping up like a warrior possessed, pumping his fists and waving at the speakerphone.

"Offer three thousand at seventy!" he yells at the speaker, waving his hands around as though ordering the execution of a captured enemy. He sits down for a second and then springs up again. "Danny, don't offer that! Sell five forty market! Sell five forty market!"

The broker's voice echoes through the speakerphone, confirming the order. Jones punches the air urgently. "Yeah! March! Go!" he yells, and squadrons of traders fan out across the pit to do his bidding.

A little while into the documentary, Jones puts on a multimillion-dollar bet and then embarks on a strange ritual. He takes off his preppy shoes and switches into sneakers.

"These tennis shoes, the future of this country hangs on them," he says gravely to the camera. "They've been good for a point rally in bonds and about a thirty-dollar rally in stocks every time I put them on," he continues, sitting back in his leather office chair in his button-down shirt and conservative tie and the incongruous shiny white footwear.

"I wait till I get the max and then I put these suckers on," he says, trying hard to thicken his young voice, like a prep schooler imitating an action hero. "I bought these at a charity auction. They are Bruce Willis's. The man is a stud."

Then, on top of one of his trading screens, Jones erects an inflatable Godzilla.

WHAT WAS THE INTELLECTUAL PROCESS BEHIND THESE bizarre antics? The answer is subtle, because Jones's explanations of his own success were not always convincing.[8] They began with his twenty-something chief economist, Peter Borish, who compensated for youth by wearing old-fashioned suspenders and was fond of expounding on the eerie parallels between the 1980s and the 1920s. Borish had plotted the stock charts of the two periods one on top of the other, and—surprise!—they both rose in a vertiginous line, convincing Borish and his boss that a spectacular 1929-scale crash was coming. In one remarkably candid interview, Borish admitted to fudging his results; he had juggled with the starting points for the two lines until he got the fit he wanted.[9] On this quasi-quantitative foundation, Jones built up a house of anecdote. Wall Street's exorbitant pay packets signaled that a correction must be due. Banks' capital was thinly stretched. A van Gogh painting had just sold for ten times its preauction estimate. In the 1987 documentary, Jones looks calmly into the camera and predicts a bloodcurdling collapse. "It's going to be total rock and roll," he says, and his eyes look positively gleeful.

Jones may have been happy for the world to think that Borish had invented some kind of crystal ball; it could only help to strike fear into his rivals. Given his performance in the mid-1980s, the rivals might well have believed anything he said: In 1985 Jones had returned 136 percent, and in 1986 he was on his way to returning 99 percent. But the truth was that Borish's examination of the 1920s was incidental to Jones's success, even though a crash did come in October 1987. Most players on Wall Street expected the market to break sooner or later; the hard thing was to put a date on it. Borish predicted that the crash would arrive in the spring of 1988—in other words, his forecast was no better than the others that littered the investment business.[10]

Jones's other efforts to explain his own success were scarcely more credible. Like Tony Cilluffo, the eccentric autodidact who had powered Steinhardt's 1970s success, Jones was taken with Kondratiev wave theory, which held that the world moves in predictable twenty-four-year cycles. Kondratiev's teachings had helped Cilluffo to anticipate the crash of 1973, which presumably meant that the next cataclysm was not due until 1997; yet in 1987 Jones nonetheless believed that the theory reinforced the case that "total rock and roll" was imminent. Jones was even more enamored of Elliott wave analysis, as expounded by an investment guru named Robert Prechter. The guru asserted with great confidence that stocks would experience one last upward explosion before plunging at least 90 percent: It would be the greatest crash since the bursting of the South Sea bubble in England in 1720. Jones told one interviewer, apparently in all sincerity, "I attribute a lot of my own success to the Elliott Wave approach."[11] But Prechter's predictions of disaster were wildly overblown, and even Jones agreed that Prechter had no way of pinpointing when the crash would happen.[12]

The truth was that Jones's trading profits came from agile short-term moves, not from understanding multidecade supercycles whose existence was dubious. Like the traders at Commodities Corporation, Jones was adept at riding market waves; he would get up on his surfboard when a swell seemed to be coming, ready to jump off quickly if the market turned against him. "When you take an initial position, you have no idea if you are right," he once confessed, undermining the notion that any long-range analysis could explain his success. Rather, as he explained in his more candid moments, his method was "to write a script for the market," setting out how it might behave; and then to test the hypothesis repeatedly with low-risk bets, hoping to catch the moment when his script became reality.[13] Years later, Jones described the mental gymnastics that went into writing these scripts. "Every evening I would close my eyes in a quiet place in my apartment. I would picture myself in the pit. I would visualize the opening and walk myself through the day and imagine the different emotional states that the market would go through. I used to repeat that exercise every day. Then when you get there, you are ready for it. You have been there before. You are in a mental state to take advantage of emotional extremes because you have already lived through them."[14]

The crash of 1987 demonstrated the power of this sort of preparation. The moment the S&P 500 started to head down on Friday, October 16, Jones sensed that the expected market break might at last be coming. It didn't matter that Borish's crude comparison with the 1920s had suggested that the crash was several months off; Jones never took that stuff too literally. What did matter was that Jones visualized the possiblity of a crash; he understood that once the market started falling, the chances of a really monster fall were significant. Investors had been anticipating a day of reckoning for months; their confidence could crack decisively. Portfolio insurance added to the danger of a downward lurch: Falling stocks would trigger selling by portfolio insurers, which would cause stocks to fall more. Because of the way the market was positioned, betting on its decline was irresistible. If the early fall on Friday petered out into nothing, Jones might lose modestly by going short; he would simply close his position and await the next opportunity. But if investor skittishness and portfolio insurance caused the market to crater, the payoff could be enormous. The balance of risk and reward was overwhelmingly attractive.[15]

By Friday evening, Jones had sold armfuls of S&P 500 futures. He took off for his hunting lodge in a remote part of Virginia, together with Louis Bacon, the fellow trader and Commodities Corporation seedling, and some friends from Europe. When the weekend was over, there were too many guests to fit on the private plane that was returning to New York. Jones, ever chivalrous, offered the last seats to his friends. He would stay back in Virginia.

"No," somebody said. "We know you've got a big position."[16]

Jones got on the plane, and on the morning of Black Monday he was at his desk in Manhattan. If his guests had been less generous, he would have missed the largest one-day equity collapse in his lifetime. Stocks fell sharply in the morning, then went into a bloodcurdling dive, and Jones rode the cascade all the way down to the bottom. Frantic investors flooded brokers with phone calls, desperate to sell out of the market, and the only people who weren't panicking were the ones who just turned numb in the face of the destruction. Some years later, Jones likened Wall Street's reaction to the crash to his own crash with a boat. "I remember the time I got run over by a boat, and my backside was chewed up by the propeller. My first thought was, 'Dammit, I just ruined my Sunday afternoon because I have to get stitched up.' Because I was in shock, I didn't even realize how badly cut up I was until I saw the faces of my friends."[17] The crash of 1987 paralyzed some people's reactions in a similar fashion. But Jones had written a script for the market. He was mentally prepared for mayhem.

Even as he rode the market down, Jones seized a second chance to profit. He had been thinking about how the Fed would respond to the collapse, writing a script for the markets as he always did, and he had reasoned that the authorities would seek to calm everybody's nerves by pumping cash into the banks to make borrowing cheaper. Here, Jones figured, might be another asymmetrical bet: If the Fed did as he expected, the bond market would soar; but if the Fed did nothing, there was no reason to expect the market to go downward. When the bond market ticked up late on Black Monday, Jones took that as a signal that his script was coming true. He bought the largest bond position that he had ever owned, and soon it turned out to be his most profitable one.

Jones's double coup on Black Monday reportedly netted his Tudor Investment Corporation between $80 million and $100 million, contributing to the 200 percent return that he racked up that year. Not long afterward, Jones revealed a side of his personality that contrasted with the cowboy antics. He launched a charity, the Robin Hood Foundation, which tapped into the new hedge-fund wealth, channeling millions of dollars to New York's poorest neighborhoods.

JONES'S TRIUMPH ON BLACK MONDAY WAS NOT AN ISO-lated fluke. The late 1980s were a good time for others who came out of the Commodities Corporation tradition. The Big Three—Soros, Stein-hardt, and Robertson—all lost heavily in the 1987 crash, but Bruce Kovner and Louis Bacon both fared well, though they made less money than Jones did. The Big Three and the junior three shared the expectation of a market reversal; they had discussed the prospect frequently among themselves, and Jones had even tried to persuade Julian Robertson to run a portfolio of stock shorts for him.[18] But it was one thing to expect trouble and another to respond like lightning when it actually arrived: This is where the Commodities Corporation trio proved nimbler than the older group, which had come out of the equity tradition. A stock picker like Julian Robertson was wedded to his stocks: His Tigers had researched each of them exhaustively, and it hurt to unload them. But Jones, Kovner and Bacon had none of that baggage. Their hallmark was flexibility, and they could turn on a dime.[19] They didn't care about individual stocks. They traded the whole market.

After the stock market crash, Kovner and Bacon both piled into bonds, profiting from the same script that Jones had followed.[20] The next year and for the rest of the decade, they continued to thrive. Kovner reaped glori-ous rewards in currencies, building on the carry trade that he had devel-oped at Commodities Corporation; in 1989 and 1990, he was reportedly the highest earner on Wall Street, thanks not least to bets on oil futures. Meanwhile, Louis Bacon did so well trading a small account as a broker at Shearson Lehman Hutton that he split off to found his own hedge fund, Moore Capital, in 1989. That year he was up 86 percent, and the follow-ing year he was up 29 percent, having correctly foreseen the effect of Iraq's invasion of Kuwait on the equity and oil markets. The seed money Bacon had received from Commodities Corporation was now dwarfed by other cash. Paul Jones, who was unable to absorb all the money that was pressed on him, advised his clients to invest instead with Bacon.

Meanwhile, Jones himself scored big in Tokyo. Like all the Wall Street cognoscenti, he had seen in the late 1980s that a bubble was forming. The Japanese authorities had cut interest rates aggressively after the Plaza accord, seeking to offset the effect of the strong yen on their economy. The resulting flood of cheap capital had driven up the cost of Japanese assets, and plenty of foreign assets too: Japanese money became the key buyer for everything from California golf courses to impressionist paintings. In 1987, the Japanese phone company Nippon Telegraph and Telephone was floated on the Tokyo stock market at the fantastical price-earnings ratio of 250. The market was overvalued on any sane measure, and yet it continued to head upward.

As with all bubbles, the challenge with Japan was not so much to see that it would crash but to anticipate the moment. Shorting the Tokyo market aggressively in the wake of NTT's flotation would have been tantamount to suicide: Over the next two years, the Nikkei stock index gained an astonishing 63 percent, proof that there are few things more costly than tilting against a bubble. Jones of all people was not about to tilt early; so long as the bulls had momentum on their side, he was too much of a trend follower to risk betting against them.[21] And so he bided his time, watching for the moment when the trend might turn. Then at the start of 1990, the Tokyo market fell nearly 4 percent in a matter of days. At last Jones had the signal that he had been waiting for.

At a discussion organized by *Barron's* in mid-January 1990, Jones rattled off the reasons why Tokyo was primed for a sharp fall.[22] He began with the standard stock analyst's observation: The market was trading at huge multiples to its earnings. But as with Wall Street in 1987, he focused with particular passion on the way that market players were positioned.[23] In the Wall Street case, portfolio insurance had created a mechanism that would exacerbate a fall, creating an asymmetrical bet for speculators. In the Tokyo case, Japan's financial culture created a similar asymmetry: Japanese savers expected their fund managers to show returns of 8 percent per year, and because of the importance attached to this hurdle, fund managers would respond to a reversal in the equity market by rushing defensively into bonds, where they could lock in 8 percent returns on a risk-free basis.[24]

It made all the difference, Jones argued, that the Tokyo market had suffered its 4 percent correction at the beginning of the year. If the market had fallen in December after rising strongly in the previous months, fund managers who were still above the 8 percent hurdle might not have minded—particularly since holding bonds for the last couple of weeks of the year would have yielded too little income to bother with. But a fall in January was different. Fund managers were not sitting on a cushion created by earlier equity returns; and there were fifty weeks still left in the year, enough for the managers to secure their 8 percent target by taking refuge in the bond market. If the fund managers behaved in the defensive manner that Jones expected, the resulting stampede out of equities could push the stock market off a precipice.

Jones's script for Japan soon played out in reality. The Nikkei 225 index fell 7 percent in February and 13 percent in March; and by the end of the year it had lost two fifths of its value, crippling what had previously been the world's biggest stock market. But Jones did not merely get the big call right. With almost uncanny accuracy, he anticipated Tokyo's fluctuations on the way to its final destination. Based on his knowledge of the patterns in previous bear markets, he predicted in January that the Nikkei's fall would be followed by a weak rally; and when the Nikkei stabilized in the spring, he duly switched from a heavy short position to a mild long one.[25] The maneuver underlined the difference between the flexible style of a commodities trader and the dogged persistence of a value investor such as Julian Robertson, who never traded in and out of his position. Sure enough, the Nikkei rose 8 percent in May and Jones profited again, even though he was firmly convinced that the rally was temporary.

That month, May 1990, Jones sat for another interview with *Barron's*. The magazine congratulated him on his January prediction that Tokyo was riding for a fall, and Jones modestly recalled that he had predicted a Japanese crash prematurely in 1988 and 1989—though the very essence of his skill was that he could predict such things without actually making losing bets on them. Then Jones reiterated his forecast that the market would experience rallies on the way down, diving precipitously each time after a bounce proved disappointing. His logic was that investors who had not sold out during the first leg of the crash would be desperately hoping to make their money back; but each time they experienced a rally that was too feeble to recover their losses, more of them would give up and sell out of the market. For the moment, Jones said, he was lightly long Japan, but he planned to be short again by late summer. Sure enough, Jones's timing proved excellent: Tokyo's market fell steeply from July through early October.[26] That year, 1990, Jones estimated that he returned 80 percent to 90 percent on his portfolio, largely on the strength of his trading in Tokyo.

Jones's real achievement was not just to predict that Japan would fall, nor even how it would experience brief rallies on the way down. It was to spot a situation in which the odds were so good that they warranted a bet, even in the absence of predictive certainty. In October 1987 and again in January 1990, Wall Street and the Tokyo market could have recovered, in which case Jones would have bailed out of his short positions with a small loss. But Jones could see that a decline was more likely than a market rise; and, crucially, that a decline, if it happened, would be far more dramatic than any conceivable rally. He was like a gambler playing a roulette game that has been doctored in two ways: There are two extra red numbers on the wheel, giving red a somewhat-better-than-even chance of winning; and the croupier is paying out five to one if red comes up, creating a mouthwatering skew in the reward-to-risk ratio. Jones had no way of being certain that his bets would win. But he knew that it was time to shove his chips onto the table.

MANY OF JONES'S TRADING SUCCESSES OWED SOMETHING to this formula. From his time on the floor of the cotton exchange, he had understood the importance of watching how other players were positioned. If you knew whether the big guys were sitting on cash stockpiles or were already fully invested, you could tell which way a market might break out—you could sense the mix of risk and reward in any situation. Pit traders knew how their rivals were positioned because they watched them yelling out their bids, and once Jones migrated off the floor he ad-libbed various tricks to reproduce that same feel for the markets. He would call up brokers who represented big institutional clients, check in with the trading companies that used the commodity markets to hedge physical positions, and speak frequently with fellow hedge-fund managers. He tracked the data that showed whether investors were buying more call options (signaling that they expected stocks might rise) or put options (signaling they feared that stocks might crater); he consulted reports on the balance between cash and stocks in pension and insurance portfolios. But it was not enough simply to know what other investors were holding. You needed to know what they wanted to hold—what their objectives were, how they would react in different situations. If you knew that Japanese fund managers were obsessed with clearing that 8 percent hurdle, you knew that they might switch to bonds if the market fell in January.

Jones's method was an extension of the psychological insights that were common at Commodities Corporation. He understood that behavioral quirks colored the markets, tinting the pure randomness imagined by efficient-market theorists. But Jones was attuned to a different sort of bias too. If investors could buy and sell irrationally for psychological reasons, they could do much the same thing for institutional ones. Sometimes psychological and institutional factors combined. Cotton farmers, for example, invariably clung to part of their harvest for weeks after it had been picked, hoping that prices would turn higher. But at the end of the year their psychological bias against selling ran into an institutional factor: They had to unload crops or they would suffer adverse tax consequences. As a result, Jones recognized a pattern: Each year the cotton market would be hit by a wave of sell orders in December; and each year the market would recover its lost ground in January.[27] Similar distortions lurked in other commodity markets too. It took nearly a year for a calf to gestate inside its mother's belly, so the supply of cattle responded only sluggishly to rising prices; as a result, supply could take months to catch up with demand, and upward trends in cattle futures tended to be durable. Or, to take an example from the equity market, stocks in the Dow Industrials index tended to do well on the closing Friday of each quarter, because that was when arbitrage traders bought back stocks that they had sold short to hedge expiring futures contracts.

Jones's focus on institutional distortions helps to explain how he could beat the market. It allowed him to buy and sell in situations where he knew he was getting a good price because the person on the other side of the trade was a forced seller. The efficient-market theorists had demonstrated that it was hard for an investor to foresee the future movement of a stock or a commodity because all relevant information is reflected in today's price. But Jones sidestepped the theory by getting something better than the going price—from farmers who had no choice but to dump cotton at the end of the year, or from arbitrage traders who were forced to buy back stocks on the last Friday of each quarter. Jones's success, in this sense, resembled Steinhardt's: In the 1970s and 1980s, Steinhardt could buy blocks of equities at a discount because institutional sellers needed to unload in size and were willing to pay for the privilege. This sort of trading did not require Jones or Steinhardt to predict the future course of prices with godlike prescience. It merely required them to provide liquidity when it was needed.

There was a further element in Jones's success, and it goes back to the swashbuckling style that he displayed in the 1987 documentary. If Jones's method was to look for the trigger that might set off a sudden market move, he was also willing on occasion to become that trigger himself—to jump-start a reversal in the market with a massive trade, so initiating a stampede that would make his script become reality. Again, this technique homed in on a weakness in efficient-market thinking. The theory presumes that if, say, Ford's stock was too low, a handful of smart investors could buy Ford shares until they forced the price up to its efficient level. But in reality there is a limit to smart investors' firepower; they may lack sufficient cash to keep buying Ford until it hits its rational level. When a whole market is out of kilter, the smart investors are especially likely to fall short. They might know that Japan's equity bubble—or the dot-com bubble or the mortgage bubble—makes no sense, but they cannot borrow enough to bet against it with the force that would deflate it. This is why there is a limit to the power of contrarians. It is why markets swing in trends and why finance is prone to bubbles.

This insight—christened "the limits to arbitrage" by the economists Andrei Shleifer and Robert Vishny—points to an opportunity that Jones could sense intuitively. Markets can move away from fundamental value because speculators lack the muscle to challenge the consensus; a trend can keep going far beyond the point at which it ceases to be rational. But if you are a trader with more ammunition and courage than the rest, you can ambush the market and jolt it out of its sleepwalk. And because you will have started a new trend, you will be the first to profit from it.

Jolting the market was something of a Jones specialty. He had seen the cowboys in the cotton pit wrong-foot their rivals, but he was perhaps the first trader to deploy this tactic across multiple markets. Most "upstairs traders" tried to conceal their positions by placing orders discreetly through multiple brokers, but Jones saw that sometimes it could pay to be as loud as possible.[28]

In one sequence in the documentary, Jones reacts with skepticism to an OPEC agreement to cut oil production. In theory, a production cut will push prices higher, so the OPEC announcement starts an upward trend in oil prices. But Jones knows that OPEC countries seldom muster the collective discipline to abide by lower quotas, so he figures that the upward trend has no basis in reality. His challenge is to break the market's baseless momentum and profit from its reversal.

At first Jones proceeds with stealth. He calls in multiple small sell orders, hoping to disguise his intentions so that the upward trend won't be disturbed while he is building his short position. But once those quiet trades are done, Jones switches to his wild cowboy style. Now he wants the market to know that some big swinger is selling. He wants to scare the daylights out of it.

"Offer a thousand!" he yells at his broker. "No, offer fifteen hundred! Show 'em size! Tell him that there's more behind it! Do it! Do it! There's more behind it!"

Having rattled the market, Jones calls a friend at an oil-trading firm to gauge whether his macho sales have broken oil's momentum. He is doing what a pit trader would do—feeling the mood of his adversaries. The two talk for some minutes, then Jones hangs up.

"He said, '*Those guys*, they've sold the hell out of it,' " Jones reports, with evident delight. "The people he works with don't know that it was . . ." and here Jones winks conspiratorially and points melodramatically at his own chest. "That's even better. I hope they think it's some wild-as-shit Arab who knows the whole agreement is getting ready to fall apart."[29] Sure enough, the Jones ambush succeeded and the oil rally was reversed. Rather than await the trigger that would make his script for oil come true, Jones had succeeded in creating it.

In the spring of 1987, Jones decided it was silver's moment. Gold had already staged a rally, and silver usually followed; besides, there were rumors that output at key mines might be disrupted. Early on a March morning, Jones executed a pincer movement worthy of his hero, General George S. Patton: He bought a gutsy position in silver futures, buying up contracts from floor traders and leaving them all short; then he bought physical silver from four dealers. Soon the dealers were doing precisely what Jones expected them to do. Because they understood that gold had already rallied and silver was positioned to follow, the dealers didn't want to be caught with depleted inventories; they immediately phoned the silver exchange with purchase orders to replace what they had sold to Jones some minutes earlier. When their phone calls reached the exchange, the dealers were in for a surprise: The traders who would usually have had silver futures to offload had already sold out to Tudor. The traders, for their part, followed Jones's script too. When the dealers called them with urgent buy orders, they assumed that the rumors of a supply disruption must have come true, and they rushed to buy back some of the contracts that they had sold to Jones earlier. Before very long, pandemonium broke out; the speculators and dealers whom Jones had left short were scrambling to protect themselves from spiking prices, driving those prices up further as they did so. By sensing when the market was poised for a rally and having the guts to give it a kick start, Jones made off with a handsome profit.[30]

These maneuvers did not mean that Jones had boundless power over markets. "I can go into any market at just the right moment, by giving it a little gas on the upside, I can create the illusion of a bull market," he once confessed. "But, unless the market is really sound, the second I stop buying, the price is going to come right down."[31] Yet although Jones was trying to emphasize the limits to his power over prices, it was more the admission than the qualification that stood out: The fact that Jones could move the market, if only for a short time, was in itself remarkable. Jones was like a boy atop a mountain after a fresh snowfall; if a great mass of powder was ready to tumble down the slope, he could throw a well-aimed stone and set off an avalanche of money. Of course, as Jones insisted, he could no more move a market against fundamental economic forces than a boy on a mountain can cause snow to fall uphill. But the ability to start an avalanche is a formidable thing. If he could judge a market's potential for a move, Jones could set off a chain reaction at a time of his choosing—and be the first to win from it.

Jones's power to cause avalanches reflected his willingness to risk enormous trades, but his reputation was also significant. When people saw the wild cowboy coming, they assumed that he would make the market move; their assumption was self-fulfilling. The more Jones gained in size and notoriety, the more his power grew—even in the deepest and most liquid markets. In the late 1980s, for example, Treasury bond futures changed hands routinely in $50 million lots, but Jones would sometimes send a broker into the pit with an order twice that size, triggering a panicked reaction from traders who wanted to be on the right side of the stampeding elephant.[32] James Elkins, one of the biggest traders of S&P 500 stock-index futures in the early 1990s, recalls the effect that Jones could have. "Whenever he entered the market, the whole pit would run scared. My size could be bigger than his size, but his reputation was such that when he entered, it would throw the whole thing off whack. The reactions were dramatic."[33]

From his earliest days in the cotton pit, Jones had understood that the market is influenced by psychology; he was anticipating the academic findings on behavioral finance that surfaced from the late 1980s. Meanwhile,

Jones also saw that markets have institutional quirks; here he anticipated an academic literature on tax-driven buying and selling, which created numerous kinks in the efficient-market hypothesis. But Jones's most distinctive strength lay not in his awareness of the markets but in the fact that he was *self*-aware. He understood how his own trading could change the calculations of others, setting off profitable chain reactions.

The more hedge funds grew in size and stature, the greater the consequence of Jones's insight. For as billions of dollars flowed into the war chests of the most famous hedge titans, it was no longer just oil traders or silver traders who needed to beware. Starting in the 1990s, hedge funds became large enough to move markets of all kinds. They could even overpower governments.

7

WHITE WEDNESDAY

I n the autumn of 1988, Stan Druckenmiller agreed to join Soros Fund Management. His friends had advised him against entrusting his future to Soros, and Druckenmiller half expected the relationship to break down within a year or so.[1] Soros had been dangling offers, saying that Druckenmiller was a genius who would take over his fund. But his record suggested that he would have trouble ceding real authority, and Druckenmiller wondered how far to rely on Soros's assurances. The day before he started the new job, Druckenmiller went out to see the great man at his weekend home in Southampton. There on the front lawn he encountered Soros's son, Robert. "Congratulations," he was told, "you're my father's ninth permanent successor."[2]

Soros and Druckenmiller were stylistic opposites. If Soros's hobby was to write philosophical books, Druckenmiller's was to watch the Pittsburgh Steelers butt heads at Three Rivers Stadium. But as investors the two men were an ideal fit. Like Soros, Druckenmiller came out of a stock-picking background. Like Soros, he was not really attached to it.

Druckenmiller began his career as an equity analyst at the Pittsburgh National Bank, but his rapid progression prevented him from mastering the tools that most stock experts take for granted. Promoted to the position of research director at the grand old age of twenty-five, he never spent long enough in the trenches to develop an edge in analyzing corporate balance sheets.[3] Instead, his forte lay in combining different disciplines. To a solid sense of equities he added a strong feel for currencies and interest rates, picked up from the PhD course in economics that he had begun before deciding that the ivory tower was not to his liking. As one admiring colleague put it, Druckenmiller understood the stock market better than economists and understood economics better than the stock pickers; it was a profitable mixture. By following equities and speaking regularly with company executives, Druckenmiller got advance warning of economic trends, which informed his view of bonds and currencies. By following economies, he got advance warning of the climate for stocks. If a currency was heading downward, export stocks would be a buy. If interest rates were rising, it was time to short real-estate developers.

To his sense of companies and economies Druckenmiller added a third skill: technical analysis. His first boss in Pittsburgh had been a student of charts, and although most stock pickers disdained this pattern recognition as voodoo, Druckenmiller soon found it could be useful. It was one thing to do the fundamental analysis that told you that a stock or bond was overvalued; it was another to know when the market would correct, and the charts hinted at the answers. Technical analysis taught Druckenmiller to be alert to market waves, to combine the trading agility of Paul Tudor Jones with the stock-picking strengths of Julian Robertson. He survived the crash of 1987 and profited richly in the days after. The same could not be said for any of the managers who came out of a pure equity background—not even Soros.

After four years at the bank in Pittsburgh, Druckenmiller gave a presentation in New York. At the end of the meeting he was accosted by an impressed member of the audience.

"You're at a bank! What the hell are you doing at a bank?"

After chatting with Druckenmiller for a few minutes, the man asked: "Why don't you start your own firm?"

Druckenmiller didn't have enough capital behind him, but the man persisted: "I'll pay you ten thousand dollars a month just to speak to you."[4]

And so in February 1981, at the age of twenty-eight, Druckenmiller launched Duquesne Capital Management and began to hone his style as a macro trader of the new school, blending views on companies and economies with a sense of the charts to create a freewheeling portfolio. Four years later he attracted the attention of the mutual-fund company Dreyfus, which invited him to manage several funds while also running Duquesne; one Druckenmiller fund shot up 40 percent within three months, turning the young manager into a Wall Street celebrity. In 1987, when the publication of *The Alchemy of Finance* revealed Soros's blend of fundamental and technical trading, Druckenmiller saw that the master had a style that resembled his approach. The two men met over lunch at Soros's office and experienced an instant meeting of the minds. By the end of that first encounter, Soros had made his first attempt at hiring Druckenmiller.

When Druckenmiller eventually accepted, Robert Soros's derisive welcome on the lawn seemed at first to be well founded. Quantum's incumbent analysts, who included some earlier "permanent successors," clashed with the new pretender to the throne, never mind the fact that he was built like the pro footballers he loved to watch on Sundays. To make matters worse, Soros seemed to regard Druckenmiller as an S&P 500 specialist, even though he had traded bonds and currencies as well as equities. One evening in August 1989, Druckenmiller flew to Pittsburgh, where he still maintained Duquesne, and discovered that his bond position at Quantum had been sold out behind his back. He called up Soros and exploded down the phone. There was no way he could succeed with a boss who second-guessed him.[5]

"I feel cramped by your presence," Druckenmiller was yelling at Soros. "I'm intimidated and I feel dissatisfied because I don't think I'm doing as well as I could.

"I want to leave," he said finally.

That outburst might have ended Druckenmiller's tenure at Quantum. But instead it provoked one of the best Soros gambles ever.

"Don't leave," Soros responded. "I'll leave."

Showing a coolness that was all the more remarkable given that he owned much of the money in Quantum, Soros moved his family to

London. "I'm going to Europe," he told Druckenmiller as he went. "Now we'll find out whether I've just been in your hair too much or whether you really are inept."[6]

The next few months gave Soros ample reason to feel pleased with his gamble. The Berlin wall came down, and the move to London gave him the freedom that he craved to focus on philanthropy in eastern Europe. Meanwhile, the collapse of the wall created the sort of market turbulence that Druckenmiller relished, and his returns entered an astonishing period. He was up 31.5 percent in 1989, followed by 29.6 percent, 53.4 percent, 68.8 percent, and 63.2 percent in the next four years; he was like Bob Dylan in the midsixties, producing one hit album after the next, as a colleague put it.[7] Assets in Quantum leaped from $1.8 billion to $5 billion, and Soros Fund Management opened new funds alongside its flagship, so that by the end of 1993 its total assets under management had soared to $8.3 billion.[8]

Soros had the sense to recognize his good fortune. He learned a lesson from Druckenmiller's early outburst and took care not to undermine him; he had wanted a permanent successor, and he had been lucky to find a talent like this one. Throughout the 1990s, Soros behaved as the younger man's coach; he prodded his protégé with questions and advice, but he left him to pull the trigger. To satisfy the craving to make his own bets, Soros retained a pot of capital that he traded on the side, but Druckenmiller was firmly in control of the much larger Quantum fund.[9] If journalists continued to attribute Quantum's success to Soros, that was partly because Soros did little to discourage their error—and partly because Druckenmiller detested the limelight as intensely as Soros enjoyed it.[10]

From the moment Soros moved to London, Druckenmiller's approach was an extension of the coach's. He had absorbed the teachings in *Alchemy* and had spoken to Soros continually for two years; he had learned everything there was to learn about his methods. Following Soros's practice, Druckenmiller invested Quantum's capital in a long/short equity portfolio, then used borrowed capital to trade S&P 500 futures, as well as bonds and currencies. Following Soros's practice too, Druckenmiller stayed in touch with company executives, reckoning that on-the-ground stories from firms could provide early warning of trends in the economy. And following Soros's practice, Druckenmiller seized opportunities with both hands. If there was one thing that the disciple had learned from the master, it was to pile on with all you've got when the right moment presents itself.[11]

Soon after Soros decamped with his family to London, the collapse of the Berlin wall created such a moment. Joyful East Germans flooded into the freer and richer West, expecting jobs and social benefits; the associated costs seemed certain to force the German government to run large budget deficits. Other things equal, budget deficits fuel inflation, eroding a currency's value; based on this logic, traders dumped deutsche marks after the wall came down, and the currency dipped against the dollar. But Druckenmiller took a different view. He recalled the passage in *Alchemy* on Reagan's early budget deficits: Rather than weakening the dollar, those deficits had indirectly strengthened it.[12] The reason was that Reagan's loose budgets were offset by tight policy from the Fed; high interest rates encouraged investors to hold money in dollars, *strengthening* the currency. Druckenmiller saw that Germany would follow the same pattern. Loose budgets would drive Germany's hawkish central bankers to raise interest rates, and the deutsche mark would rally. And so, after the wall fell, Druckenmiller went headlong into the German currency, buying a $2 billion position in the space of a few days. Over the course of the next year, the mark rose by a quarter against the dollar.[13]

The beauty of this trade was that it built on a version of Paul Tudor Jones's insight: If you understand the other players in a market, you can identify trades with hugely attractive risk-to-reward ratios. Jones's early specialty was to see how private traders were positioned; but Druckenmiller was onto a bigger and more attractive game—understanding *governments*. Central banks, in particular, could be a gift to a trader. Their intentions were often evident—the Bundesbank, for example, made no secret of its determination to fight inflation—and their actions could move markets. In November 1989, it was enough for Druckenmiller to see that the Bundesbank would raise interest rates. This fact alone would be sufficient to create a trend that he could ride profitably.[14]

The Deutsche mark trade fueled Quantum's 29.8 percent return in 1990; but it was merely a dress rehearsal. Two years later, Druckenmiller staged the greatest coup of his career, shattering the European monetary order and establishing hedge funds as a rising force in global finance.

GERMAN UNIFICATION DID NOT MERELY CAUSE THE Bundesbank to act in a deliciously predictable manner. It exposed the central bank's conflicted role as the anchor of the deutsche mark and simultaneously of Europe's exchange-rate mechanism. This system had been set up in 1979 to dampen currency fluctuations within Europe, allowing companies to invest and trade without worrying that wild exchange-rate swings would upend their business models. For more than a decade, the mechanism worked well, stabilizing currencies without going to the extreme of unifying them. Participating currencies were allowed to move against one another within narrow bands; and if that flexibility was not enough, a country could negotiate devaluation with its European partners. These rules afforded national governments some room to use interest rates to manage their economic cycles. The system balanced the objectives of exchange-rate stability on the one hand and interest-rate flexibility on the other.

German unification strained this compromise. It created inflationary pressure within Germany, pushing the Bundesbank to raise interest rates. But the German rate hikes came at a time when other European economies were experiencing a recession that cried out for lower interest rates. High interest rates in Germany coupled with relatively low rates elsewhere caused money to flow into deutsche marks; as a result, the weaker European currencies, notably the Italian lira and the British pound, traded near the bottom of the band permitted by the exchange-rate mechanism—and threatened to break out of it. This presented Europe's governments with two options. Germany could cut its rates in order to attract less capital, while the Italians and British did the opposite. Or central banks could intervene in the currency markets, selling marks and buying lire and pounds. If both interest-rate adjustment and currency intervention failed, Italy and Britain would be forced into devaluation.

In the summer of 1992, Druckenmiller began to ponder these tensions. He was particularly focused on Britain, where a young Quantum portfolio manager, Scott Bessent, had studied the volatile housing sector and shorted several of the stocks in it. Bessent pointed out to Druckenmiller that interest rates on British mortgages were generally not fixed; when the Bank of England raised rates, families felt the pinch immediately in their home payments. Because of this transmission mechanism, high German interest rates would put Britain in an especially tight bind. If the Bank of England raised rates to protect the pound's position within the exchange-rate mechanism, the instant hit to mortgage payers would dent consumption at a time when Britain was already in recession.

Druckenmiller saw an opening for one of those bets that could scarcely go against him. There was a significant chance that the British authorities would balk at higher rates and allow sterling to devalue. On the other hand, there was virtually no chance that sterling would rise against the deutsche mark; with Britain's economy in the doldrums, the Bank of England would certainly not raise rates more than it had to. Seizing on this asymmetrical bet, Druckenmiller loaded up on deutsche marks and sold pounds, investing $1.5 billion in this position by the end of August.[15]

Thus far the sterling trade had employed three Druckenmiller skills. It involved, first, an appreciation for equity research as a source of insights into economic trends; like Soros, but unlike the Commodities Corporation trio, Druckenmiller focused on companies as an important harbinger of an economy's performance. It involved, second, an understanding of currencies and interest rates; like Soros, but unlike Julian Robertson, Druckenmiller was an equity trader who was equally at home trading other instruments. And it involved, finally, an eye for the institutional factors that created bets with good risk-to-reward ratios: Just as Paul Jones had seen the asymmetrical bet created by the expectation that Japanese fund managers should clear a hurdle of 8 percent per year, so Druckenmiller grasped the significance of Britain's floating mortgage rates. But the next stage of the sterling bet drew upon a different talent. It required Drucken-miller to understand the financial politics of Europe, starting with the pressures that swirled around the Bundesbank.

Ever since the hyperinflation that had fueled Hitler's rise, the Germans had prized monetary stability. In the United States, the Federal Reserve's statutory mandate requires it to target both low inflation and full employ-ment; in Germany, the Bundesbank's mission was exclusively to fight inflation. For this reason, it was clear that the Germans' first instinct would be to refuse to cut interest rates so long as the costs of reunification were causing budget deficits; and if Germany hung tough, the pressure on sterling would grow ever greater. But there was at least a chance that, for political reasons, the Bundesbank would soften its stance. Europe's leaders had recently signed the Maastricht Treaty, which envisaged the eventual creation of a single European currency, the euro. Germany's government supported this project. It would have to think twice before fighting infla-tion with such zeal that Europe's monetary order splintered.

When Druckenmiller made his first bets against sterling, it was not obvious how the Bundesbank would weigh its traditional anti-inflation stance against its responsibility toward Europe. But German intentions soon became clearer. On September 4 and 5, European Community finance ministers and central-bank officials met in the pretty English town of Bath. Desperate to create space for lower British interest rates, and egged on by Italian and French counterparts who were also battling recession, the British finance minister, Norman Lamont, pressed repeat-edly for an easing of German monetary policy. He banged his fist on the table and shouted at Helmut Schlesinger, the Bundesbank president: "Twelve finance ministers are all sitting here demanding that you lower your interest rates. Why don't you do it?"

Schlesinger was so shaken that his first instinct was to walk out. He prized the independence of the Bundesbank, to which he had devoted his career; he resented political pressure, especially from a foreigner. When Schlesinger eventually recovered his composure, he ventured that, although he didn't plan to cut interest rates, he saw no reason to raise rates, either. Lamont seized upon this statement and presented it to the media as a concession, even though nobody expected interest rates to rise anyway.[16]

In a pattern that was to repeat itself over the next few days, Lamont's overreach infuriated Schlesinger. The Bundesbank president felt compelled to correct the impression that he had compromised his institution's independence. On September 8, after a central bankers' gathering in Basel, Schlesinger declared publicly that he could make no guarantees about the future course of interest rates. Far from conceding that Germany would modify its monetary policy to make life easier for its neighbors, he warned that he had little confidence in the fixed relationships among European currencies. As if to underline the point, Schlesinger alluded particularly to the unsoundness of the Italian lira.

Seated in the audience as Schlesinger made his remarks was none other than George Soros. To make sure he had heard the Bundesbank president correctly, Soros approached him after the speech was done. To gauge the German commitment to European harmony, Soros asked Schlesinger what he thought of the ECU, the notional European currency that preceded the euro. Schlesinger replied that he liked the concept of a European currency but didn't like "ECU" as a name. He would have preferred to call it the mark.

Schlesinger's answer was as clear as Soros could have wished for.[17] The Bundesbank was open to the idea of monetary union, but not at any price; its first priority was to preserve the proud tradition of the inflation-proof deutsche mark, and if other economies could not stomach the austerity that this implied, well, then they should devalue. Soros suspected that Schlesinger would be perfectly content to see his hard line on inflation sabotage the plans for European monetary union, since that union would involve the creation of a European central bank, which would supplant the Bundesbank.[18] All bureaucracies are motivated by self-preservation, Soros reflected; and Schlesinger, a career Bundesbank official, was surely the personification of this tendency. In a state of some excitement, Soros called Druckenmiller in New York and told him that the lira was heading for a fall. Druckenmiller quickly added a bet against the Italian currency to his existing bet against sterling.[19]

When Soros returned to New York, he called Robert Johnson, a currency expert who was in the process of moving from Bankers Trust to Soros Fund Management. Soros was convinced that the lira was going down, but now he was looking beyond that. Perhaps the rules of Europe's game were changing.

"What do you think about sterling?" Soros asked.

"I think I better come and see you," Johnson answered. He did not want to keep talking on the phone because Bankers Trust recorded its traders' conversations.

Johnson took a cab to the run-down Soros offices at 888 Seventh Avenue. There was duct tape on the carpet and a couple of screens by Druckenmiller's desk. Johnson, Soros, and Druckenmiller sat around a small conference table.

Soros asked Johnson to describe the risks in betting against sterling.

"Well, sterling is liquid, so you can always exit losing positions," Johnson responded. "The most you could lose is half a percent or so."

"What could you gain on the trade?" Druckenmiller asked.

"If this thing busts out, you'd probably make fifteen or twenty percent," Johnson answered.

"How likely is that to happen?" Druckenmiller pressed.

"On a three-month time frame," Johnson responded, "about ninety percent."

By now Druckenmiller and Soros were looking at each other. They could hardly stay sitting in their chairs.[20]

"How much would you do in your own fund?" Soros asked, referring to a portfolio that Johnson ran for Bankers Trust.

Johnson indicated that he would leverage himself up to take advantage of this trade. He might do three to five times capital.

"Oh my God," Druckenmiller said quickly. His eyes had widened and his huge frame was taut. You could almost hear the big inhale that a basketball player takes before he springs for the basket.

"Well, they only have twenty-two billion pounds' worth of reserves," Johnson continued, a sum equivalent to some $44 billion. Quantum could only sell sterling so long as someone was willing to buy it. Given Schlesinger's comments, there were few private buyers left; the main buyers were the Bank of England and other central banks that were trying to support sterling. Once the Bank of England ran out of reserves, it would be impossible to place further bets against sterling. So $44 billion might be the limit.

"Maybe we can get fifteen of that," Druckenmiller said. He was suggesting that he might multiply his existing sterling bet fully ten times over.[21]

"How long do you think they can hold out?" Soros asked.

Not more than a few months, Johnson estimated.

Then Druckenmiller got Scott Bessent on the conference phone to ask his opinion. Bessent went even further than Johnson. The British government had no stomach for higher interest rates. Given a choice between an even deeper recession and devaluing the pound, the government would choose devaluation.[22] The British might let sterling go sooner than anyone expected.

Johnson left the meeting with a sense of premonition. He could feel the coiled energy of the two men. When the right moment came, they would destroy the British currency.[23]

THE NEXT FEW DAYS MARKED A WATERSHED IN THE RELA-tionship between governments and markets. A financial tidal wave broke across Europe, demonstrating how huddles of traders in midtown Manhattan could have consequences globally. Druckenmiller and Soros were the central players in this drama, but they were not the only ones. Other hedge funds that traded currencies, including the Commodities Corporation trio, joined in the attacks on Europe's weaker currencies; so did the trading desks of banks and the treasury departments of multinational companies. Through the 1970s and 1980s, nobody had imagined that these private players could overwhelm powerful central banks—the Plaza accord of 1985 had confirmed governments' influence over exchange rates. But since the mid-1980s, cross-border flows of money had roughly tripled.[24] Hedge funds and other players now commanded large war chests, and the balance of power had shifted. In August 1992, the administration of George H. W. Bush orchestrated the concerted purchasing of dollars by eighteen central banks. But by now so much private capital was sloshing through the currency markets that the central banks' efforts failed to budge the dollar.[25]

In early September, the consequences of central banks' new nakedness cascaded across Europe. In conversations like the one among Druckenmiller, Soros, and Johnson, traders convinced one another that recession-battered economies pegged to the deutsche mark were now hopelessly vulnerable. On Tuesday, September 8, the day that Schlesinger declared he could make no promises on German interest rates, a wave of speculative selling overpowered the Finnish central bank, forcing the government to abandon its peg to the ECU; the Finnish markka fell nearly 15 percent that day, handing traders instant profits and whetting their appetite for the next victim. On Wednesday there was a run against Sweden, which managed to attract capital back into the country by raising overnight interest rates to the extraordinary level of 75 percent; then the electronic herd stampeded the Italian lira. Italian interest rates stood at 15 percent, which ordinarily would have been enough to keep capital in the country, but the vast growth of currency markets had changed the game: Italy's currency presented an asymmetrical bet; the trend cried out to technical traders to get on their surfboards; and smart speculators sensed that the wave of money crashing down on Italy's authorities would overwhelm their best efforts to respond to it. By Friday, September 11, the lira had broken through the bottom of the band permitted by the exchange-rate mechanism. Over the weekend that followed, Italy negotiated the formal devaluation of its currency.

The lira's collapse was especially sobering. Finland had not been formally part of Europe's exchange-rate mechanism, and so could not expect the help of other European central banks when the speculators came after it. But Italy was a different case: Its devaluation represented the first time that a member of the exchange-rate mechanism had been so bloodied by the markets.[26] Italy's membership in the mechanism entitled it to support from the mighty Bundesbank, which bought DM 24 billion ($15.4 billion) worth of lire in the week before devaluation, an unprecedented intervention.[27] But speculative selling of the lira overwhelmed the Bundesbank's efforts, and traders bagged another payout.

Even after the lira's fall, European officials struggled to come to terms with the new order. On Saturday, September 12, while the Italians negotiated devaluation with visiting German officials, Norman Lamont, the British finance minister, kept to his schedule as though nothing were amiss; that evening he honored a national musical ritual by attending the Last Night of the Proms and singing "Rule Britannia" with great gusto.[28] After learning of the fate of the lira, Lamont assembled his Treasury advisers the next morning for a breakfast of croissants; but he and his team still did not believe that they were facing an immediate crisis. Indeed, one British press account of the breakfast described Lamont as "cock-a-hoop." As part of the deal on lira devaluation, the Bundesbank was promising an interest-rate cut of a quarter of 1 percent. That might actually boost sterling.

Given the assumptions of the times, Lamont's cheerfulness was not surprising. Financial analysts and journalists were arguing that Italy and Britain were not comparable cases: The first was the most shambolic rich country in Europe; the second was governed by a Conservative Party that had transformed Britain's economic performance. The Bank of England had successfully fended off market pressure on sterling since August, and on September 3 it had improvised a new weapon against the electronic herd: Just as hedge funds attack currencies using borrowed money, so Britain announced it was borrowing 10 billion ECUs (£7.25 billion, or $14 billion) to expand its ability to defend sterling. The day of that announcement, the pound had experienced a sharp rise; currency traders believed that the government now had the firepower to fight off the speculators.[29] To Soros and Druckenmiller, this was faintly amusing: The amount that Britain had borrowed to buy sterling was equal to the amount that the Quantum Fund alone aspired to sell.[30] But in early September 1992, nobody outside the Soros offices could conceive that a single hedge fund, employing fewer than fifty people, might muster a war chest comparable to a government's.

When the markets opened on Monday, September 14, Lamont's optimism appeared vindicated. The Bank of England spent $700 million to support the currency; coming on top of the German interest-rate cut, that relatively modest intervention was enough to lift sterling slightly. But to an extent that Lamont and his advisers failed to grasp, Monday's trading sealed Britain's fate. Sterling's small rise confirmed the speculators' premise. Bets against currencies anchored by shaky pegs could be leveraged aggressively, because the worst that could happen was that they would move against you *slightly*.

Sure enough, the pound took a beating the next day. Spain's finance minister telephoned Lamont to ask him how things were. "Awful," Lamont answered.[31]

That evening Lamont convened a meeting with his Treasury team and Robin Leigh-Pemberton, the governor of the Bank of England. They agreed to support sterling aggressively the next morning; if that did not work, they would consider raising interest rates. As the meeting wound down, Leigh-Pemberton read out a message from his press office. Helmut Schlesinger had given an interview to the *Wall Street Journal* and a German financial newspaper, *Handelsblatt*. According to a news agency report on his remarks, the Bundesbank governor believed that a broad realignment of Europe's currencies would have been better than a narrow adjustment of the lira.

Lamont was stunned. Schlesinger's remark was tantamount to calling for sterling to devalue. Already his public statements after the Bath meeting had triggered the assault on the lira. Now the German was attacking Britain. Lamont asked Leigh-Pemberton to call Schlesinger immediately, overruling Leigh-Pemberton's concern that the punctilious Bundesbanker did not like to have his dinner interrupted.

After completing the phone call, Leigh-Pemberton reported that Schlesinger had granted the interview on the condition that he could check quotations attributed to him, but he had not yet found the time to do that.

Lamont protested that this was a dangerously leisurely response. Schlesinger's purported comments were already on newswires; traders in New York and Asia would react overnight; Schlesinger needed to issue a denial quickly. Leigh-Pemberton placed more calls to Germany, but to no avail. The Bundesbank press office explained that the Schlesinger quotations were "unauthorized," since they had not yet been approved; Schlesinger said he would check the article and issue an appropriate statement when he reached his office in the morning. Lamont seethed, but there was little he could do. Germany's monetary master was in no hurry to adapt to a world of twenty-four-hour trading.

That night, Lamont went to bed knowing that the next day would be difficult. But he could not imagine how difficult. As he recounts in his memoir, the thought that Britain would be forced out of Europe's monetary system the next day "simply did not cross my mind."[32]

DRUCKENMILLER READ SCHLESINGER'S COMMENTS ON Tuesday afternoon in New York. He didn't care whether they were "authorized" or not: He reacted immediately.[33] Schlesinger had made it obvious that he was perfectly happy to see the pound ejected from the exchange-rate mechanism. The Bundesbank was not going to indulge weak neighbors with further interest-rate cuts. Given the recessionary forces in Britain, sterling's devaluation was now all but inevitable.

Druckenmiller walked into Soros's office and told him it was time to move. He had held his $1.5 billion bet against the pound since August and had started to do more since the conversation with Robert Johnson. Now a trigger had arrived, and Druckenmiller announced that he would build on the position steadily.

Soros listened and looked puzzled. "That doesn't make sense," he objected.

"What do you mean?" Druckenmiller asked.

Well, Soros responded, if the news story was accurate and there was almost no downside, why just build steadily? Why not jump straight to $15 billion? "Go for the jugular," Soros advised him.

Druckenmiller could see that Soros was right: Indeed, this was the man's genius. Druckenmiller had done the analysis, understood the politics, and seen the trigger for the trade; but Soros was the one who sensed that this was the moment to go nuclear. When you knew you were right, there was no such thing as betting too much. You piled on as hard as possible.[34]

For the rest of that Tuesday, Druckenmiller and Soros sold sterling to anyone prepared to buy from them. Normally they left it to their traders to execute orders, but this time they got on the phones themselves, searching for banks that would agree to take the other side of their orders.[35] Under the rules of the exchange-rate mechanism, the Bank of England was obliged to accept offers to sell sterling for DM 2.7780, the lowest level permissible in the band, but this requirement only held during the trading day in London. With the Bank of England closed for business, it was a scramble to find buyers, particularly once word got around that Soros and Druckenmiller were selling crazily. Banks that got vast sell orders from Quantum would alert their own currency traders, who would soon start selling too, and as their calls rippled out around the world, everybody understood that an avalanche was starting.[36] Pretty soon the pound was knocked out of its permitted band, and it became almost impossible to find buyers of the currency.[37]

Late that day, Louis Bacon called Stan Druckenmiller. The two talked about how the drama might play out, and Bacon said he was still finding ways to dump sterling.

"Really?" Druckenmiller blurted out. He told Bacon to wait, and a few seconds later Soros joined the call.

"Where did you get the market?" Soros demanded furiously.[38]

SOROS AND DRUCKENMILLER EVENTUALLY WENT HOME, leaving their traders to search for opportunities to sell more sterling. Asleep in his New York apartment, Robert Johnson was beeped by Quantum's head trader; he slipped out of bed and quietly returned the call, anxious not to alert his wife to the conversation since she was an official at the New

York Fed. Around two the next morning, Druckenmiller returned to the office. He wanted to be at his desk when London trading reopened and the Bank of England would be forced to resume purchases of sterling.

Scott Bessent, the portfolio manager who had been based in London, arrived shortly after Druckenmiller. He could see the hulking outline of the boss standing in his dark office. Druckenmiller was taking off his coat, and the nighttime Manhattan skyline stretched out behind him. The only light in his office came from the telephone: Soros was on the line, and Druckenmiller had hit the speaker button. A disembodied eastern European accent filled the dark room. Soros was urging Druckenmiller to leverage himself up and redouble his selling.[39]

When the markets opened in London, the expectation of Bank of England support restored sterling to its band, but it was flat on the bottom of it. Acting on the plan that Lamont had authorized the previous evening, the Bank of England intervened twice before 8:30 A.M., each time buying £300 million. But the buying had absolutely no effect. Druckenmiller was manning his cockpit on the other side of the Atlantic, clamoring to sell sterling by the *billion*, and his clamor was driving legions of imitators to sell also. The Bank of England carried on intervening, not realizing how completely it was outgunned. By 8:40 A.M. it had purchased a total of £1 billion, but sterling still refused to budge. Ten minutes later, Lamont told Prime Minister John Major that intervention was failing. Britain would have to raise interest rates in order to protect sterling.

To Lamont's frustration, Major refused to authorize a rate hike. He had been responsible for taking Britain into the exchange-rate mechanism. He feared that his credibility would collapse if the policy was seen to be failing; he might face a leadership challenge from a member of his own cabinet. Major pleaded that new economic data would come out later that day. He told Lamont to hang tough in the hope that the markets would subside eventually.

By now central bankers the world over were on high alert. Another call went out to Robert Johnson's apartment, this time from the New York Fed; Johnson's wife spent the remainder of the night monitoring the crisis, unaware that her husband had helped cause it. The Bank of

England continued to buy pounds because it was obliged to do so by the rules of the exchange-rate mechanism. But it no longer aspired to lift the currency off its floor; it was merely providing liquidity to Druckenmiller and his cohorts.[40] Every hour that went by, hedge funds and banks sold more sterling to the Bank of England, which was being forced to load up on a currency that seemed sure to be devalued soon. Britain was presiding over a vast financial transfer from its long-suffering taxpayers to a global army of traders. At 10:30 A.M. Lamont called John Major again to urge a rise in interest rates.

While Lamont was calling the prime minister, British officials did their best to project confidence. Eddie George, the number two at the Bank of England, went ahead with a long-scheduled meeting with David Smick, a financial consultant who fed political intelligence to Druckenmiller and Soros. Smick showed up at the Bank of England's exquisite building on Threadneedle Street to find George in apparently fine form, decked out in a checkered shirt and striped tie in the manner of a London banker. "We have it all under control," George said cheerily; in the extreme case, which was unlikely, to be sure, the Bank of England would raise interest rates by a full percentage point to see off the speculators. Smick wondered whether George understood the weight of the money that was crashing on Britain. The avalanche had begun. It might be too late to stop it.

Smick summoned up his nerve and asked George straight out: "Aren't you worried that you may have slipped too far behind the curve on this thing?"

George's look betrayed mild annoyance. He was about to respond when the telephone rang. After a minute of intense conversation, he hung up.

"I've learned we've just raised interest rates by two hundred basis points," he said softly—a full two percentage points. Then he rose and shook Smick's hand and left the room running.[41]

Lamont's plea to the prime minister had succeeded this time, and the announcement of the dramatic rate hike had been set for 11:00 A.M. A few minutes before the appointed hour, Lamont walked over to his outer office at the Treasury to watch the Reuters screen. But when the announcement came, the pound did not respond at all. The line on the screen remained totally flat. Lamont felt like a surgeon who looks at a heart monitor and realizes that his patient has expired. All that remained was to unplug the system.[42]

Lamont had no time to negotiate a realignment of sterling within Europe's exchange-rate mechanism. A realignment would involve lengthy coordination with other European governments; but with every minute that ticked by, the vast transfer of wealth from taxpayers to traders continued. Italy had been lucky to get into trouble on Friday, just before the respite of the weekend. But now Britain found itself on the edge of the same cliff, and unfortunately it was Wednesday. Lamont's only recourse was to quit the European exchange-rate mechanism unilaterally. But this would require the prime minister's approval.

The prime minister was not immediately available. Lamont had his staff call Major's office repeatedly to stress the urgency of a meeting, but no audience was granted. Eventually Lamont led a team of advisers over to Admiralty House, the fine Georgian building that was serving temporarily as the prime ministerial residence; there they cooled their heels for at least another quarter of an hour before Major would see them. Lamont calculated that the nation was losing hundreds of millions of pounds every few minutes, but his boss looked annoyingly relaxed. He began the meeting by wondering aloud whether there was room for further financial diplomacy with Germany, then added that several other government ministers would shortly be joining the meeting to add their various perspectives. A meandering discussion ensued. Could Britain withdraw from the exchange-rate mechanism without offending its European partners? If it did withdraw, would there be calls for ministers' resignations? It became clear that Major's objective was to share responsibility for the crisis with the other people in the room—"We were there to put our hands in the blood," one minister later commented.[43] It was a shrewd maneuver, and from Major's perspective it served to neutralize potential rivals to his throne. Meanwhile, Druckenmiller and Soros were adding to their positions.

The Admiralty House meeting broke up without the decision to quit the exchange-rate mechanism that Lamont had wanted. Instead, Major insisted on another interest-rate hike—this time of three percentage points, effective the next day—as a last-ditch effort to save sterling. Again Lamont watched the news break on the Reuters screen. Again there was no effect on sterling's value. At their desks on the other side of the Atlantic, Druckenmiller and Soros saw the rate hikes as an act of desperation by a dying man. They were a signal that the end was nigh—and that it was time for one last push to sell the life out of the British currency.[44]

Lamont proceeded to warn his fellow finance ministers in Europe of sterling's plight. His Italian counterpart, Piero Barucci, suggested that rather than quitting the exchange-rate mechanism, Lamont suspend markets to give himself time to negotiate a realignment. Lamont had to point out that it is not in the power of a modern finance minister to suspend currency markets that trade continuously and globally.

That evening, Lamont called a press conference in the Treasury's central courtyard. At 7:30 P.M., facing a massive battery of TV cameras from all over the world, he announced Britain's exit from the exchange-rate mechanism. The markets had won, and the government had at last recognized it.

DURING THE FIRST HALF OF SEPTEMBER, THE BANK OF England spent $27 billion worth of reserves in its efforts to defend sterling, and much of that sum was drained away during the last day of the crisis.[45] After the pound left the exchange-rate mechanism, it fell about 14 percent against the deutsche mark, so British taxpayers could be said to have lost around $3.8 billion on their purchases of sterling.[46] An army of banks and hedge funds were on the other side of that trade, but hedge funds led the charge, and Quantum was easily the biggest. By the time sterling broke, Druckenmiller and Soros had succeeded in selling about $10 billion of sterling short—less than the $15 billion they had aspired to dump, but still a monumental position.[47] Of the almost $4 billion loss to British taxpayers, an estimated $300 million flowed to Bruce Kovner, the senior member of the Commodities Corporation trio, and $250 million to Paul Jones; the top seven currency desks at U.S. banks were said to have bagged $800 million among them.[48] But Soros Fund Management's profit on the sterling bet came to over $1 billion.[49]

Soros's startling payout was unknown in the immediate aftermath of the pound's devaluation. But in October, Gianni Agnelli, the Italian industrial magnate, let slip to journalists that his investment in Quantum would earn him more that year than his takings from Fiat, his car company. The next day, Saturday, October 24, Britain's *Daily Mail* newspaper ran a photo of a smiling Soros, drink in hand, and a headline proclaiming, "I Made a Billion as the Pound Crashed." When Soros opened his front door that morning, he was met by a throng of reporters, and over the next months the press drooled over his winnings. Soros was said to have enlarged his personal fortune by $650 million in 1992, and one magazine observed that it took Soros five minutes to earn what the median American family could expect for a full year of labor.[50] A few years earlier, people had reacted with horrified fascination to the $550 million earned by Michael Milken, the champion of junk bonds; but now Milken had been surpassed. Soros became known as the man who broke the Bank of England, and hedge funds began to displace the 1980s buyout kings as the objects of popular envy.

The full profits of the Soros funds were considerably larger than outsiders imagined. Just as Paul Jones had coupled his shorting of the equity market during the crash of 1987 with a profitable bet on bonds, so Druckenmiller built out from his sterling coup. As the pound came under pressure, Britain's equity and government-bond markets were hit too; traders reasoned that the flight of capital from Britain would damage other asset prices. But Druckenmiller took a different view. Britain's ejection from the exchange-rate mechanism would free the government to cut interest rates, which would drive government bonds up; and a weaker currency and lower interest rates would be good for equities. As he sold sterling on Tuesday and Wednesday, Druckenmiller was buying British government bonds and equities. Sure enough, Druckenmiller's bets paid off. Over the next two months, both markets were up steeply.

Britain was not the sole focus of Druckenmiller's attention. In the wake of sterling's fall, speculators mounted an attack on the French franc, but this time Druckenmiller believed that the central bank would win out against the markets. Unlike British homeowners, French families were not exposed to floating mortgage rates, and the French state had myriad ways of subsidizing its people: As a result, it would be easier for the French to fight off speculators with temporary interest-rate hikes than it had been for the British. Acting on this theory, Druckenmiller bought armfuls of French bonds, which soared in 1993, helping to explain why Quantum's extraordinary 69 percent return in the year of the sterling bet was followed by a 63 percent return the year after. But Quantum's greatest post-sterling coup was also the most discreet. Thanks to Robert Johnson, who had by now joined the fund full-time, Quantum shorted the Swedish krona before its devaluation in November 1992, again pocketing upward of $1 billion. Having learned a lesson from the publicity following the sterling trade, Soros and Druckenmiller made sure that nobody spoke publicly about their killing in Sweden.[51]

The triumph of macro trading proved, if further proof was possibly needed, that the efficient-market hypothesis missed a large part of the story. If markets were dominated by rational investors seeking maximum profits, then efficiency might possibly prevail; but if markets were driven by players with other agendas, there was no reason to expect efficient pricing. Macro trading exploited a prime example of this insight: Governments and central banks were clearly not trying to maximize profits. At the height of the sterling crisis, John Major effectively bought sterling from Stan Druckenmiller at a price both knew to be absurd. Major did this for a reason that appears nowhere in financial texts: He wanted to force political rivals to share responsibility for devaluation.

Druckenmiller's coup also served to show that currency pegs were vulnerable in a world of deep and liquid markets. During the 1950s and 1960s, the system of fixed currencies worked well because regulations restricted the flow of capital across borders; but now that these controls were gone, it was time for governments to accept the limits to their power over money. They could either use interest rates to manage the value of their currency, so dampening exchange-rate swings, or they could use them to manage their economic ups and downs, so dampening recessions.

Attempts to have it both ways via "flexible pegs" such as the exchange-rate mechanism were likely to backfire: The contrast between the United States and Europe illustrated the point vividly. When the Bush administration had tried and failed to lift the dollar in August, no calamity had ensued; the dollar was floating anyway, so there was no sudden break in its fortunes. But the currency pegs of Finland, Italy, Britain, and Sweden were a different matter; they presented speculators with targets that were too appealing to pass up, exposing their economies to wrenching dislocations. In committing to the exchange-rate mechanism, European governments had made a promise that they lacked the ability to keep. They had bottled up currency movements until a power greater than themselves had blown the cork into their faces.

The implications of a world featuring Druckenmiller and other macro investors were not immediately absorbed by policy makers. As happens after every financial crisis, the first instinct was to vilify the markets rather than to learn the awkward lessons that they teach: in this case, that currency pegs were dangerous. The week after the pound's devaluation, when the French franc came under pressure, French finance minister Michel Sapin suggested that troublemaking traders should be guillotined, as during the French revolution.[52] The following summer, after the exchange rate mechanism suffered another round of disruptions, French premier Edouard Balladur argued that governments had an economic and moral responsibility to curb speculators. In Belgium, foreign affairs minister Willy Claes chimed in that Anglo-Saxon financiers were plotting to divide Europe.[53]

In characteristic fashion, Soros accepted much of the attack on his profession. On the one hand, he had proved himself more ruthless than any other market player: Whereas bank trading desks had to live with regulators, and therefore were reluctant to assail governments too violently, Soros had no such inhibitions.[54] On the other hand, Soros was intellectually disposed to see markets as wild things, constantly at risk of boom and bust, constantly destabilizing. Shortly after the pound's devaluation, Soros saw Jean-Claude Trichet, the governor of the French central bank, and told him that, out of concern for the destabilizing effects of his own trading, he would not attack the franc.[55] The claim to selflessness was a bit

much, since Quantum had correctly calculated that the franc would hold
and was about to make a killing on this prophecy. Nevertheless, Soros's
overture dramatized the mood that followed sterling's fall. The greatest
speculator of them all was unwilling to defend speculation.[56]

Druckenmiller did not share Soros's misgivings. The British press
had dubbed the day of sterling's humiliation "Black Wednesday." But
Druckenmiller thought "White Wednesday" would have been more appo-
site. Britain had been freed from the yoke of the Bundesbank's high interest rates—freed to pursue the recession-fighting policies it needed. The
London stock market's reaction to the devaluation made Druckenmiller's
point: The FTSE index jumped by almost a fifth in the two months that
followed. To be sure, Druckenmiller's trading had upended the economic
policy of the British government, but this was not necessarily bad. The
high interest rates accompanying German unification had created a situation in which sterling needed to exit the exchange-rate mechanism. Britain's rulers had failed to recognize this truth until Druckenmiller had
recognized it for them. The fact that John Major had transferred $1 bil-
lion plus of taxpayers' money to the Soros funds was not entirely Druckenmiller's fault. If somebody had fleeced the country blind, it was the
prime minister, not the speculator.

The Soros-Druckenmiller divide anticipated a debate within economics. In the years before the sterling trade, economists argued that currency
crises were triggered by bad economic policy: The villain was not speculation but government mismanagement. But during the 1990s, the academic consensus shifted—from Druckenmiller's view to Soros's. The new
view emphasized that traders might attack currencies that were decently
managed, and that the attacks might prove self-fulfilling. The spectacular collapse of sterling created a tipping point in this debate. Druckenmiller was correct in saying that Britain had invited the crisis by imposing
untenably high interest rates. But once his own trading had demonstrated
the power of speculators over governments, the risk that speculators might
abuse that power became obvious. Whereas before traders might only
have attacked currencies that were doomed by economic fundamentals,
now they might feel empowered to have a go at stable ones. When French

politicians complained that hedge funds were amassing dangerous and excessive power, their concerns were not totally baseless.

Whatever this danger, little was done to reduce it. Clamping down on speculators—guillotining them, as the French finance minister had urged—would have involved taming the waves of cross-border money on which the speculators surfed: It would have involved a return to Bretton Woods and the reimposition of capital controls. Most policy makers viewed this option with horror. If free trade in goods and services was beneficial, surely free flows of capital were good for the same reason; just as trade allowed car manufacturing to be concentrated in the countries that did it best, so cross-border capital flows funneled scarce savings to places that would invest them most productively. Moreover, capital controls might be impractical as well as intellectually suspect. In the week after the sterling crisis, Spain and Ireland tried to dampen speculative attacks on their currencies by restricting banks' freedom to trade them. The controls were quickly circumvented.

If capital controls were off the table, there was one remaining way to prevent speculative attacks on national currencies—abolish them. "Speculation can be very harmful," Soros told an interviewer in the wake of sterling's bust; a single European currency "would put speculators like me out of business, but I would be delighted to make that sacrifice."[57] Europe eventually unified its currencies in 1999, but not everybody learned. Emerging economies in Asia and Latin America stuck with the policy of pegging, creating immense opportunities for hedge funds later in the decade.

||||||||||||||||||||||

8

||||||||||||||||||||||||

HURRICANE
GREENSPAN

In December 1993, Michael Steinhardt escaped to his vacation home in Anguilla. His staff called in with regular updates, and one afternoon the news was particularly pleasing. Steinhardt's funds were up more than $100 million in a single day. "I can't believe I'm making this much money and I'm sitting on the beach," Steinhardt marveled. It was an extraordinary moment, but his lieutenants counseled him to take it in stride: "Michael, this is how things are meant to be," one of them assured him. After all, Steinhardt Partners was running about $4.5 billion in capital; it had built up a staff of more than a hundred employees; in 1991 and 1992, it had returned 47 percent and 48 percent after subtracting fees, and in 1993 it was heading for a similar performance.[1] Magazines were reporting on Steinhardt's purchase of a Picasso drawing for almost $1 million, and the portly figure of the investor, with glistening head and bristling mustache, was surrounded at New York parties by supplicants desperate to entrust their money to him. Perhaps this was indeed the way that things were meant to be. Steinhardt could scarcely imagine that he was about to face humiliation.

Steinhardt had returned from his sabbatical in 1979, set up his own firm, and resumed his combination of stock picking and block trading. But he also began to make money in bonds, and by the early 1990s he was pioneering an early version of what later came to be known as the shadow banking system.[2] Like Druckenmiller's currency trading, the strategy involved taking advantage of the policies of a central bank—though this time it was the U.S. Federal Reserve that proved obliging. In 1990 and 1991, the U.S. economy was in recession following the savings and loans crisis, and the Fed was trying to stimulate it by keeping short-term interest rates low. This created a situation in which Steinhardt could borrow short-term money exceedingly cheaply, then load up on longer-term bonds that yielded considerably more, pocketing the difference. The risk in this trade was that if longer-term interest rates spiked up, the value of Steinhardt's bonds would crater. But the sluggish economy kept the demand for capital low, meaning that the price of capital—the interest rate—was unlikely to head upward. Sure enough, longer-term interest rates *fell* at the start of the 1990s, handing Steinhardt a capital gain on his bonds on top of the profits from the gap between short- and long-term interest rates.

Just as John Major had enriched Stan Druckenmiller because he wanted to neutralize political rivals, so the Fed rewarded Steinhardt because it was trying to assist the battered banking system. By increasing the gap between short- and long-term rates, the Fed was making it more lucrative for banks to engage in their normal business, which is to borrow short and lend long; it was sharpening banks' incentive to push money into the economy.

Steinhardt was effectively crashing this party. The Fed wanted to help banks, so Steinhardt turned himself into a shadowbank: He borrowed short and lent long, just like any bank would do. The difference was that Steinhardt bypassed the tedious business of hiring armies of tellers to collect customer deposits and flotillas of credit officers to lend the deposits on to companies. Instead, he borrowed from brokerages such as Goldman Sachs and Salomon Brothers, then lent by buying bonds. And because he had none of the infrastructure of the banks, he could charge in and out of their business as the Fed's policies shifted.

Steinhardt's shadowbank enjoyed a further advantage. Real banks faced regulatory controls on how much they could lend: For every $100 worth of customer deposits that they turned into loans, they had to set aside about $10 in capital to ensure that, even if their loans went sour, they could still repay depositors. But Steinhardt had no depositors and hence no "capital adequacy" rule: He could borrow whatever his brokers were prepared to lend to him.[3] And the brokers were prepared to lend an astronomical amount. For every $100 that Steinhardt borrowed to buy U.S. government bonds, he could often get away with setting aside as little as $1 in capital.[4]

In 1993 Steinhardt and his fellow speculators took the bond strategy to Europe. With the crises of the exchange-rate mechanism over, Europe was headed for monetary union, and the process was forcing interest rates across the continent to converge on one another. Countries such as Spain and Italy, which had a weak record on inflation and therefore had to compensate investors with high interest rates, were now subjected to strict inflation-fighting rules; their interest rates began to fall toward those of Germany. Steinhardt and other traders bought truckloads of Spanish and Italian bonds, realizing a capital gain as interest rates came down. Again, they were jumping on an opportunity that governments had practically invited them to take. European statesmen had made no secret of their plans for monetary union, nor about the resulting convergence in interest rates.

Because they were set up to seize such opportunities in a way that most rivals were not, hedge funds profited hugely in the early 1990s. Senior investment bankers quit Goldman Sachs and Salomon Brothers to get in on the new game, and one Wall Street law firm claimed to be midwifing new hedge-fund partnerships at a rate of two per month.[5] The Helmsley Building at the foot of Park Avenue, known previously for its ornate Art Deco lobby and worked-brass elevators, became notorious as a hedge-fund hotel: In unmarked suites on the upper floors, small bands of traders opened shop, investing money every which way on behalf of rich clients. The number of hedge funds leaped from a bit over one thousand in 1992 to perhaps three thousand the next year, and their fees expanded almost as quickly.[6] At the dawn of the industry, A. W. Jones had charged no management fee, asking only for a 20 percent share of the investment profits. The second generation of hedge funds, such as Michael Steinhardt's, had demanded a 1 percent management fee plus the 20 percent profit share. Now, in the intoxicating boom of the early 1990s, hot new funds demanded "2 and 20." "Perhaps never before in history have so few made so much money so fast," an article in *Forbes* marveled.[7]

The fast money was not without controversy. Steinhardt's energetic shadowbanking, which was mirrored by most of the other major funds, caused him to buy up vast amounts of newly issued government bonds, at one point resulting in an effective takeover of the market. In the April 1991 Treasury bond auction, Steinhardt and Bruce Kovner between them bid for $6.5 billion of the $12 billion worth of paper that was due to be issued; then they lent these bonds to short sellers and bought them back again, ending up with $16 billion of bonds—considerably more, in other words, than 100 percent of the market.[8] As the bonds shot up in value, the short sellers tried to get out; but they couldn't buy back the paper because Steinhardt and Kovner had cornered the market, and they were not selling. The victims of this short squeeze included Goldman Sachs, Salomon Brothers, and Bear Stearns; it was hardly a case of the sharks eating the innocents. But, inevitably, someone sued. After three years of fighting in the courts, Steinhardt and Kovner settled without admitting guilt. Steinhardt agreed to pay $40 million in compensation to the short sellers, and Kovner paid $36 million.[9] As if one brush with the law were not enough, the duo was also sued over irregularities in the May Treasury auction. Again they agreed to settlements that involved payments to the plaintiffs.[10]

The allegations of market manipulation should not have been the only public concern about the shadowbanks, however. To an extent that was generally not realized at the time, hedge funds were changing monetary policy. As they responded to the Fed's low short-term rates by aggressively buying longer-dated Treasuries, the link between short-term and long-term interest rates grew tighter. A cut in the Fed's rate, which in the old world might have taken weeks to feed through into lower long-term rates, now fed through a lot faster. In some ways this could be a good thing: If the Fed wanted to stimulate the economy, it was helpful that hedge funds chased long bond rates downward. But the new world could be dangerous too. The bond market might respond to the Fed quickly, but the real economy was bound to lag. If the Fed held interest rates down until Main Street began to feel the benefits, Wall Street was likely to inflate a giant bond bubble.

Moreover, such bubbles threatened to be newly scary. A world in which hedge funds could corner a Treasury auction was a new kind of world: a world built on breathtaking leverage. The American system was pyramiding debt upon debt: The government was borrowing from hedge funds, which in turn borrowed from brokers, which in turn borrowed from some other indebted somebody. If one player in this chain collapsed, the rest could lose their access to those borrowed funds. That could force them to dump assets fast. A bubble could burst instantly.

At the start of 1994, this prospect was not on anybody's mind, least of all Michael Steinhardt's. In January he authorized one of his lieutenants to buy a staggering position in Canadian bonds, adding to the bets he already had in the United States, Japan, and Europe. Then, together with his wife and friends, he headed off to China on another vacation.

ON JANUARY 21, 1994, FEDERAL RESERVE CHAIRMAN Alan Greenspan made his way over to the White House. Fueled by low interest rates, the economy had first recovered and then grown smoothly for thirty-four consecutive months, but now Greenspan was visiting President Clinton and his entourage to deliver an unwelcome message. Even though inflation was quiescent, it was time to preempt its resurgence with a small rate hike. By acting early, Greenspan hoped to avoid the overheating that would force him to slam on the brakes later. He aimed to pilot the economy toward a "soft landing."

"Wait a minute!" Vice President Gore objected. In the past, a small rate hike had signaled the beginning of a long series: In 1988–89, the Fed's short-term rate had gone from 6.5 percent to nearly 10 percent in a dozen small increments. If the markets expected the same this time, long rates might shoot upward in anticipation of more tightening to come.

The bond market would crash. The hard landing that Greenspan said he wanted to avoid might become a reality.[11]

Gore was raising the sort of question that Greenspan loved to answer. The Fed chairman had spent much of his career as an economic consultant in New York; more than most Washington figures, and perhaps more than the British mandarins who had lost the battle over sterling, he understood the markets. The possibility that a rate hike might cause a nasty Wall Street backlash was one he had certainly considered, but he was focused above all on the reaction in the stock market. Having entered record territory in 1993, the S&P 500 index appeared ripe for a correction. The bond market seemed to be of secondary importance.

Greenspan assured Gore that long-term interest rates were governed mainly by inflation expectations. If the Fed raised short rates, it would signal that the authorities were going to be vigilant on price pressures. The result would be lower inflation expectations, which in turn ought to mean lower long-term interest rates. The rate hike that Greenspan proposed should be bullish for the bond market.

A fortnight after that exchange with the vice president, on February 4, 1994, Greenspan presided over the next meeting of the Fed's interest-rate committee. He proposed to head off inflation with a gentle rate hike of twenty-five basis points, from 3 percent to 3.25 percent; more than that risked triggering a backlash from the traditionally volatile stock market.[12] In comments that would later seem a touch too confident, Greenspan instructed his colleagues on the ways of investors. "I've been around a long time watching markets behave and I will tell you that if we do 50 basis points today, we have a very high probability of cracking these markets," he cautioned. "I think that would be a very unwise procedure."[13]

Greenspan's sense of the stock market was right. After the Fed announced its quarter-point rate hike, the S&P 500 index dipped, precisely the sort of gentle correction that the Fed chairman had wanted. But Greenspan's assurances about the bond market proved mistaken. He had told Gore that a hike in short-term rates would calm inflation fears, which logically would allow long-term rates to ease. Instead, the

Fed's twenty-five-basis-point tightening produced a swift increase of the same magnitude in the ten-year Treasury rate. Something mysterious was stirring.[14]

In the era before shadowbanking, Greenspan's reassurances might have proved justified. But the new shadowbanks were not as focused on inflation as the Fed chairman expected. The way the shadowbankers saw things, the first Fed hike in half a decade created uncertainty, and uncertainty meant risk; and because even a small fall in the bond market could wipe out the thin capital base of leveraged hedge funds, the mere *possibility* of a fall forced them to reduce risk by selling part of their holdings. The new logic of leverage changed the central-banking game. In response to the rate hike, the shadowbanks dumped bonds and forced long-term interest rates up—the opposite of what Greenspan had expected.

A week after the Fed's action, on Friday, February 11, there was another shock to the bond market. Trade talks between the Clinton administration and Japan broke down, with the American side seeking revenge by signaling that a stronger yen would be in order. Within a week, the yen had jumped 7 percent against the dollar, wrong-footing several hedge funds. Stan Druckenmiller had an $8 billion bet against the yen, a position almost as massive as his wager against sterling; in the space of two days, he lost $650 million.[15] According to the traditional central-banking logic, this should have had no impact on inflation expectations and bonds, but the sheer scale of hedge-fund leverage ensured a vicious chain reaction. Losses from the yen shock forced hedge funds to dump assets and raise capital; and since hedge funds held a lot of bonds, the bond market was knocked backward. Over the course of the next two weeks, the ten-year Treasury yield jumped more than a quarter of a percent.[16] A world in which hedge funds traded everything was a world of unpredictable connections.

The next victim was Europe. In February the central banks of Germany, Britain, France, and Belgium had pushed short-term rates downward, signaling that they saw no inflation risk and hence little reason for long rates to move upward. But in the aftermath of the yen shock, traders' logic asserted itself once again. Europe's long-term interest rates spiked up: In the space of a fortnight, the yield on the German government's ten-year bonds rose by thirty-seven basis points, Italy's rose by fifty-eight basis points, and Spain's rose by sixty-two.[17] Hedge funds and banks' proprietary trading desks had lost money on U.S. Treasuries and the yen. They were responding by dumping European bonds, never mind the continent's economic fundamentals.

Once hedge funds began to flee Europe, the stampede built on its own momentum. Brokers that had been willing to lend freely to the shadow-bankers suddenly reversed themselves now that their trades were going wrong: Rather than accepting $1 million of collateral, or "margin," to back every $100 million of bonds, the brokers demanded $3 million or $5 million to protect themselves from the danger that a hedge fund might prove unable to repay them. To meet the brokers' margin calls, hedge funds had to liquidate holdings on a grand scale: If you are leveraged one hundred to one, and if your broker demands an extra $4 million in margin, you have to sell $400 million worth of bonds—quickly. As hedge funds liquidated bond positions, the selling pressure drove their remaining holdings down, triggering yet further margin calls from brokers. The scary pyramiding of debt, which had fueled the bond bubble in good times, now accelerated its implosion.

Some two weeks after the yen shock, on March 1, yet more bad news buffeted the markets. New data suggested that U.S. inflation was more of a threat than had been feared; in keeping with the Greenspan view, the yield on ten-year Treasury bonds jumped by fifteen basis points. But although economic logic explained the reaction in the United States, no such logic could explain what happened next: Bond markets in Japan and Europe cratered. Far from being spooked by an expected surge in inflation, Japan was grappling with the threat of *deflation*, and yet ten-year Japanese interest rates jumped by seventeen basis points on March 2. As brokers issued yet more margin calls to hedge funds, the logic of leverage transmitted the trouble to Europe. In order to raise capital, hedge funds off-loaded an estimated $60 billion worth of European bond holdings, and long-term interest rates spiked upward.[18]

The frenzy of selling created sharp losses across Wall Street. Paul Tudor

Jones, whose great strength was to sense how other traders were positioned, failed to spot the danger in Europe, and in the spring of 1994 his fund was down sharply. The same went for the other members of the Commodities Corporation trio, Bruce Kovner and Louis Bacon. David Gerstenhaber, the macro trader whom Julian Robertson had hired in 1991, was by now running his own hot fund; he blew up spectacularly. Proprietary trading desks did badly too; in 1994, Goldman Sachs experienced its worst year in a decade. The insurance industry was reckoned to have lost as much money on its bond holdings as it had paid out for damages following the recent Hurricane Andrew; "I'm starting to call this Hurricane Greenspan," quipped one insurance analyst.[19] For a few hours on March 2, no less a firm than Bankers Trust teetered on the brink of bankruptcy. Trading was suspended on the New York Stock Exchange, and New York Fed president William McDonough phoned top bankers up and down Wall Street in an attempt to rally confidence. Ultimately, Bankers Trust survived. The storm of deleveraging had pushed a Wall Street powerhouse to the edge, but it had not pushed it over—at least not this time.

The greatest casualty of the bloodbath was none other than Michael Steinhardt. He had returned from his vacation in China to find that the U.S. bond market had sold off, and he had suffered modest losses. His biggest bets were in Japan, Canada, and especially Europe, where he had accumulated an astonishing $30 billion bond portfolio; he consoled himself that the Fed's tightening in the United States would not hit foreign markets too severely. But then the logic of deleveraging kicked in, and every bond market was whipsawed. For Steinhardt's vast and leveraged portfolio, each basis-point move upward in European interest rates entailed a $10 million loss; and by the end of February, he had bled a stunning $900 million.[20] He was down almost 20 percent, and his troubles were not yet over.

Steinhardt had not merely misjudged the markets' direction; he had misjudged their liquidity. The supposed beauty of macro trading, remember, was that bond and currency markets could absorb huge quantities of capital—far more than individual stocks could. In the boom years of the early 1990s, hedge funds and other foreign traders had encountered no difficulty in establishing vast positions in European bonds: They had bought up about half of Germany's government and government-guaranteed bonds, for example. But they had been able to accumulate these positions without moving the price adversely for a simple reason: They were building their holdings gradually, and if a particular bond proved difficult to buy, they had no problem waiting a few days for another opportunity. But when a shock hit the markets and brokers issued margin calls, hedge funds had to sell out in a rush—and at exactly the same time as others were rushing to sell also. Everybody scrambled to sell to everybody else. The liquidity was gone. Nobody was buying.

In the old days of equity block trading, Steinhardt had known the brokers personally; he could rely on them even in a serious crisis. He was, after all, a major client; they wanted to keep his business. But Europe's bond markets were a different game. Steinhardt was dealing with brokers based a continent away—anonymous voices in a different time zone. The European bond brokers didn't know Steinhardt and he didn't know them. When the liquidity crunch came, they were not willing to help Steinhardt get out of his positions.

Seated at his bow-shaped desk, staring at seven blinking computer screens, Steinhardt witnessed the implosion of his fund. He had a desperate sensation of not being able to catch his breath; it was as though he were drowning.[21] He ate little and slept less; known for his explosive blowups, he now took to conferring in whispers with his top lieutenants behind closed doors as his traders fought to get out of their positions. The traders seemed to think that if they waited, there would be a better opportunity to sell. But prices kept falling like stones. Everybody was looking for a bid, but the market seemed to consist exclusively of sellers.

John Lattanzio, a veteran Steinhardt lieutenant, marched over to the firm's bond trading desk.

"Just sell 'em!" Lattanzio barked. This was no time to wait for a good price. "Just sell 'em!"

"I can't," the trader answered flatly.[22]

Seeing no other way forward, Steinhardt resolved to dump his bonds at any price—even if that meant offering up the sort of discounts that he

used to extract from block sellers of equities. At the end of a four-day selling burst in early March, his traders had dumped $1 billion in European
bonds.[23] Meanwhile, the battle to escape Japan and Canada continued.
The Canadian central bank would periodically call up nervously to ask
whether Steinhardt's traders were done selling.

Steinhardt had fallen into a trap that would come to be well known
in the new leveraged markets. He had failed to sense when a trade had
become *crowded*. In a world in which a broker's margin call could force
leveraged funds into fire sales, the key was to beware markets in which
leveraged players were concentrated. Looking back on 1994, Steinhardt
conceded his own naïveté. "The trade in European bonds was crowded,
a fact that totally passed me by," he confessed. When the dust settled at
the end of March, Steinhardt's funds were down 30 percent. About $1.3
billion of capital had been vaporized.[24]

STEINHARDT'S HUMILIATION WAS QUICKLY FOLLOWED
by another hedge-fund collapse, this one centering on a hubristic outfit
called Askin Capital Management. Its eponymous manager, David Askin,
had launched his business in the glory days of 1993, creating a $2.5 billion
portfolio of mortgage securities. Askin had little experience of actually
managing money—he was a financial analyst and salesman. But his pitch
was that as the former head of mortgage research at the investment bank
Drexel Burnham Lambert, he could make money from mortgages in any
financial climate.

Askin claimed to have an edge in analyzing the likelihood that a mortgage might be paid off early. Mortgages with a high risk of prepayment
logically were worth less than mortgages that were likely to keep paying out, since prepayment would deprive investors of the income stream
that they had counted on.[25] Further, Wall Street was busy slicing mortgages into all kinds of exotic instruments. The interest payments and the
principal payment on a mortgage were cut into two separate "strips": If
homeowners prepaid mortgages rapidly, the interest-only strips (known
as IOs) would lose and the principal-only strips (POs) would gain; if

Before starting the first "hedged fund" in 1949, Alfred Winslow Jones flirted with Marxism and worked as an undercover operative against the Nazis. He pioneered the combination of short selling and leverage, spawning a shoal of early imitators. In 1963 he took his family on a tiger shoot in the Indian Himalayas.

Michael Steinhardt turned the trading desk at his hedge fund from a dull backwater into a dynamic profit center, sometimes resorting to techniques that pushed the bounds of legality. After flourishing through the 1970s and 1980s, he lost a third of his investors' wealth in the market storm of 1994—a foretaste of the financial crises that came later.

During the 1970s, Helmut Weymar (top left) led the wildly successful Commodities Corporation, which attracted investment from Nobel laureate Paul Samuelson, even though Samuelson had argued that markets were too efficient to be beaten. Among Weymar's early partners was Paul Cootner (top right), another academic proponent of market efficiency; Frank Vannerson (bottom left), the creator of one of the first computerized trend-following trading systems; and Michael Marcus (bottom right), libertarian, New Age faddist, and gifted trend surfer whose style anticipated that of the macro traders of the next decades.

George Soros set up his first hedge fund in 1969, combining traditional stock analysis with an eclectic appetite for price charts and Karl Popper's philosophy. He made a killing from currency trades, but his parallel life as a philanthropist-statesman created a complex two-sided persona that damaged his performance.

Stan Druckenmiller became Soros's chief investment trigger puller, leading the Quantum Fund's spectacular attacks on the British pound and the Thai baht. He rode the dot-com bubble to huge profits and sold out of the market weeks before the crash. But then he jumped back in at exactly the wrong time, losing almost $3 billion.

Julian Robertson's Tiger fund defied the academic finding that stock-pickers cannot beat markets, racking up legendary returns through the 1980s and 1990s and incubating an army of Tiger cubs that carry on his tradition. On the eve of Russia's default, Tiger came close to buying the entire stock of palladium, rhodium, and silver owned by the Russian government.

Paul Tudor Jones donned Bruce Willis's old sneakers when he geared up for a major trade and named a trading system after Madonna. He predicted "total rock-and-roll" on Wall Street, and made a fortune when the market collapsed in October 1987. In 2008 he foresaw that the failure of Lehman Brothers would lead to a generalized meltdown, but he allowed others at his firm to lose heavily in emerging markets.

Bruce Kovner began his career at Commodities Corporation and pioneered the currency play known as the carry trade. He went on to build Caxton Associates and emerged as a godfather of the neoconservative movement.

Together with Paul Tudor Jones and Bruce Kovner, Louis Bacon was the third macro investor who carried on the trading style pioneered at Commodities Corporation. He speculated in commodities and currencies, successfully anticipating the market consequences of the first Iraq War.

David Swensen invested the capital of the Yale endowment in hedge funds, leading imitators at other universities to follow. In 2005 his investment picks were credited with having generated $7.8 billion of the $14 billion in Yale's endowment, making him the university's greatest benefactor.

Tom Steyer's Farallon Capital Management was the first hedge fund to attract money from Yale. One of several funds spun out of Robert Rubin's arbitrage group at Goldman Sachs, Farallon pioneered the "event-driven" investment style. Between 1990 and 1997, there was not a single month in which Farallon lost money.

Jim Simons hired mathematicians, code breakers, and translation experts to create the most successful hedge fund ever. The statistical programs that drove his Medallion fund made profits every year from 1990 on, faring especially well in moments of turbulence. In the 2008 crisis, Medallion was up 160 percent. Simons himself earned over $1 billion annually.

David Shaw applied computer science to markets, starting his eponymous hedge fund in a rented space above a communist book shop in Greenwich Village. Having narrowly escaped collapse in the 1998 financial crisis, Shaw's team of quants went on to manage $27 billion of clients' capital.

Jim Chanos and David Einhorn profited from bets against financial firms as the credit bubble began to implode in 2007. After the collapse of Lehman Brothers, governments clamped down on short selling.

Ken Griffin's Citadel bought the assets of other collapsing funds in 2006 and 2007, demonstrating that a hedge fund could swoop in to stabilize the financial system in moments of turmoil. In 2008, Citadel itself came close to collapse. But unlike many banks, it survived without the help of taxpayers.

prepayments lagged, the opposite would happen. Askin dabbled in IOs and POs, inverse IOs and inverse POs, and even in a creature known as the "forward inverse IO." For a firm that nailed prepayment risks, the opportunities were endless.

Askin's pitch won over a roster of respected names, and his investors included firms such as the insurance giant AIG and charities such as the Rockefeller Foundation.[26] But not for the last time in the story of hedge funds, the sales pitch was fraudulent. Askin claimed that his funds were "market neutral"—they would make money regardless of whether the bond market was up or down—but the truth was that he had little idea how his clever investments might perform in a crisis.[27] He claimed to use sophisticated modeling to analyze prepayment risks, saying that his proprietary software was stored on his own computer. But no such model existed.[28]

When the Fed raised interest rates in February, Askin's funds began to fall in value. The surge in long-term interest rates raised the cost of mortgages and removed the incentive for homeowners to refinance; prepayments of existing mortgages declined, so that their duration stretched out like chewing gum. Despite his claims to market neutrality, Askin turned out to be acutely exposed to this duration change; indeed, for any given rise in long-term interest rates, his portfolio fell five times more than an ordinary bond would. At first Askin covered up this discovery by misreporting his results. But a revolt within his firm forced him to come clean, and on Friday, March 25, he admitted that his funds had fallen 20 percent in February.[29] Moreover, the assassination of a Mexican presidential candidate on March 23 had ratcheted up the panic in the bond market: Investors responded to the killing by dumping Mexican bonds, then dumping all emerging-market bonds, then dumping rich-world bonds as they fought to rebalance their portfolios. For Askin, this was the last straw. The renewed surge in interest rates guaranteed that his March results would be awful.

On the morning of Monday, March 28, the brokers began to issue margin calls to Askin. Bear Stearns demanded $20 million in additional capital; Kidder Peabody wanted $41 million; and by that afternoon Bear had upped its request to $50 million. The next day Salomon Brothers, Lehman Brothers, and a host of other creditors piled on, and soon it became clear that Askin would have to sell huge portions of his port-folio to satisfy his creditors. A team of Kidder mortgage traders showed up uninvited at Askin's premises, demanding to inspect his books; they worked through the night, aiming to come up with a fair price for a chunk of Askin's funds, but they soon confronted a problem. If Askin had owned his portfolio outright, Kidder could have made a bid, providing Askin with the cash to stave off his other creditors. But Askin's holdings had been pledged as collateral to dozens of creditors, whose claims could not be unscrambled easily. Here was yet another lesson about leverage that was to haunt hedge funds in future years. Not only can it cause a fund to crash. It can complicate its burial.

On Wednesday, March 30, the sharks continued to circle. The brokers issued ever bigger margin calls, desperate to get their hands on Askin's cash before other creditors got to it. A Swiss investment-management firm called Unigestion, which owned one of Askin's subfunds, ordered Askin to liquidate its positions; Askin contacted eighteen dealers, but most of the bids were so low as to be worthless. Two of Askin's positions, consist-ing of those mind-boggling "forward inverse IOs," failed to attract any bids at all. In another premonition of future troubles, the sheer complexity of these instruments made them impossible to sell. Nobody on the Street knew how to value them.[30]

At 3:45 P.M. on that Wednesday, Bear Stearns offered to buy a chunk of Askin's portfolio for a paltry $5 million. As though trying to kill its victim with one swift bite, Bear demanded that Askin answer yes or no within fifteen minutes. Askin prevaricated, asked for an extra fifteen min-utes, and ultimately refused: He was not going to make life easier for the predators by taking his shirt off for them. The brokers now gave up hope of a negotiated asset sale and began to take possession of whatever collateral they held, hedging their new holdings by dumping Treasuries. The bond market reeled again as the remains of Askin's fund were dismembered.

The panic in the bond market, which had swept from the United States to foreign markets and from Treasuries to mortgage bonds, now reached the top echelons of government. On the morning of March 31, 1994, as Askin's brokers were selling the life out of the Treasury market,

Bill Clinton interrupted his California vacation. The president had been schooled by his advisers to view the bond market with a special awe; the previous year he had raised taxes on the theory that a smaller federal budget deficit would reduce the government's demand for capital, which would in turn send bond rates lower. Clinton didn't love this argument— his first reaction had been to denounce the undue power of "a bunch of fucking bond traders."[31] But his advisers had pressed hard; and as the Clinton tax hike was followed by a fall in market interest rates amid the bond bubble of 1993, the advisers appeared to have been vindicated. The collapse of the bond market in early 1994 came as a rude shock. Interest rates were shooting up again, and Clintonomics didn't look so brilliant.

Clinton phoned Robert Rubin, the ex–Goldman Sachs chief who served as the top economic adviser in the White House. Rubin more than anyone had persuaded Clinton to believe that his tax hike would be rewarded by the bond market. Now the president demanded to know what was going on.

For about half an hour, Rubin labored to explain why long-term interest rates were soaring. Trends in growth or inflation could not provide the answer, he confessed. The bond market was behaving in new ways; Wall Street had been changing faster than anyone had noticed. The Fed had raised interest rates just twice—by twenty-five basis points in early February and then by the same amount in March—and yet bonds were falling off a cliff; it was the steepest decline in more than a decade. Nobody seemed to understand exactly what was going on: not the Federal Reserve chairman, not hedge-fund gurus such as Michael Steinhardt, and not even Rubin.

The president finished his telephone conversation and walked out to face the gaggle of reporters that was always shadowing him. "No one believes that there's a serious problem with the underlying American economy," he pleaded. "Some of these corrective things will happen from time to time, but there's no reason for people to overreact."[32]

SEEN WITH THE BENEFIT OF HINDSIGHT, THE PRESIdent's plea encapsulated the response to financial panics that has been standard for a generation. The bond market had confounded Clinton's gurus, as well it might have done: Events as disparate as Japanese trade negotiations and Mexican assassinations had been linked in terrifying ways by the tentacles of leverage. But the best the president could do in the face of this extraordinary chain reaction was to plead for calm, and to do so in a way that misconceived the challenge posed by hedge funds. "There's no reason for people to overreact," the president said; but the truth was that, in the new leveraged world, overreaction was inevitable. The whole point of leverage, the very definition of the term, is that investors feel ripples from the economy in a magnified way. They are forced to keep their fingers on a hair trigger. Overreaction becomes mandatory.

Rubin was correct when he said that Wall Street had changed radically. As leverage multiplied investors' buying power, the sheer size of the bond market had been transformed. In 1981, according to Securities Data Company, new public issues of bonds and notes (excluding Treasury securities) totaled $96 billion. By 1993 those offerings had multiplied thirteenfold to $1.27 trillion.[33] The market was growing steadily more complex as well as larger: Askin had exaggerated his analytic powers, but other Wall Street firms were hiring physicists and equipping them with supercomputers as they designed ever more fanciful securities. Small wonder that government's power to influence and even understand the markets was waning. Just as the deepening of currency markets had destroyed the ability of central banks to intervene successfully, as Britain had discovered in 1992, so the deepening of bond markets had weakened governments' ability to anticipate shifts in long-term interest rates, let alone control them.

The policy makers' response to this new world could have proceeded along two tracks, and the first concerned monetary policy. The Fed chairman conceded that the bond market's reaction to the supposedly gentle rate hike had been a shock: Some three weeks into the mayhem, on February 28, the Fed's interest-rate committee had convened by conference call, and Greenspan had said as much.[34] Alan Blinder, the Princeton professor who became the Fed's deputy chairman in June, lamented the bond market's capricious behavior, denouncing the exaggerated power of "twenty-seven-year-olds in yellow suspenders."[35] The Fed's leaders recognized that they were up against a new phenomenon. What conclusions should they have drawn from this?

The Fed could have chosen to redefine its inflation-fighting mandate. It had traditionally set interest rates with a view to keeping consumer prices stable. But the question raised by the bond market collapse of 1994 concerned the stability of asset prices. If the bond market heads into record territory, as it had in 1993, shouldn't this be taken as a signal that credit is too cheap—and that it is time to raise interest rates in order to deflate a bubble? Because the Fed had been targeting inflation rather than the bond market, it had allowed the bubble to expand. But then Steinhardt had blown up; Askin had blown up; more than $600 billion had been knocked off the value of U.S. securities, and another $900 billion or so of wealth had been destroyed in foreign bond markets—surely an earlier hike in interest rates could have reduced this carnage? Over the course of the next decade, Greenspan wrestled with this question, ultimately deciding that using monetary policy to deflate bubbles was a bad idea. Bubbles were hard to identify until after they popped, the Fed chairman maintained, and it was easier to clean up after them than to prick them preemptively. Besides, the central bank would have to hike interest rates truly aggressively to dampen asset prices, and the cost in terms of growth forgone would exceed the benefits of calmer markets. For several years, this judgment seemed right. But in the wake of the huge credit bubble in the mid-2000s, the clean-up-afterward approach proved disastrously costly. The case for considering asset bubbles when setting monetary policy, and for requiring financiers to restrain leverage when markets appeared frothy, was belatedly vindicated.

The second response-that-might-have-been concerned regulatory policy. The deleveraging of 1994 had shown the risks that hedge funds and leverage more generally posed to the financial system. Storied investment banks were entrusting billions of dollars to cowboys, some housed within hedge funds and some seated at the banks' own proprietary trading desks: What happened if the cowboys blew up and brought the banks down with them? Askin's implosion had shown how an obscure and relatively small hedge fund could leave its three main brokers—Kidder Peabody, Bear

Stearns, and Donaldson, Lufkin & Jenrette—with a $500 million loss among them. If a small hedge fund could inflict that sort of damage, what might a big one do? Surely Askin was a warning.

As the bond market melted down, plenty of regulators posed this sort of question. On March 7 and March 8, hedge funds' impact on markets was topic A at a gathering of the top central bankers in Basel. In Washington a government committee called the President's Working Group on Financial Markets began to study the dangers of hedge funds and of leverage more generally.[36] Representative Henry González, the chairman of the House Financial Services Committee, growled that "hedge funds deserve extra scrutiny."[37] All signs pointed toward a government crackdown. "Hedge funds are rogue elephants: overleveraged, undersupervised, and disruptive to the markets," *BusinessWeek* thundered, citing a recent market commentary titled "The Hedge Fund Crisis."[38]

In the midst of this febrile atmosphere, González announced that his committee would hold hearings on hedge funds. The *Washington Post* confidently reported that these would "light a fire" under the regulators.[39] But unbeknownst to the public, a counterattack was taking shape. Robert Johnson, the Soros economist who had helped to shape the sterling coup, had once worked on the Senate banking committee, and his research assistant from that time was now González's staff director. After Johnson had heard González call for a clampdown on hedge funds, he had sensed a moment to push back: González and other lawmakers were bad-mouthing the industry without understanding what it did; it was time to call their bluff—to force them to say concretely what they would do to make hedge funds safer. So Johnson had called up his former researcher and urged him to organize the hearings. Far from lighting a fire under the regulators, Johnson was betting that the hearings would cool the temperature in Washington.[40]

Having made his pitch to lawmakers, Johnson set to work on Soros. Unless he made some effort to educate lawmakers about hedge funds, Johnson told his boss, a regulatory backlash was certain. Ordinary Americans were suspicious of hedge funds because they did not understand their role; they worried that "when they went to bed at night, this jack in the box could come out of the ceiling panel and eat their net worth, and his name is George Soros." "You have to demystify that," Johnson counseled. Given a better communication strategy, there was no reason why professional investors should be hated. After all, Warren Buffett was a folk hero.

On April 13, when the House hearings convened, a bevy of regulatory chiefs testified before the first panel. It soon became clear that the regulators had no concrete ideas on how to stop imploding hedge funds from damaging their creditors; and in the absence of an action plan, they resorted to plan B—assert that no action is needed. Eugene Ludwig, the comptroller of the currency, insisted that hedge funds barely threatened the banking system: Only eight national banks lent money to hedge funds, most of these loans were secured by collateral, and Ludwig's office had full-time examiners on site at the eight banks in question. Fed governor John LaWare gave González's committee the same line: The Fed's bank supervisors were not losing sleep over the risks posed by hedge funds. When Representative Melvin Watt asked what would happen if a big hedge fund blew up, the panelists assured him that banks and brokers would be fine. They would not be so foolish as to endanger themselves by lending excessively to hedge funds.

When the second session of the hearing convened, the sole witness was George Soros. Johnson's calculation proved exactly right: Having called the hearing, the House staff had been forced to prepare questions for Soros; and this process had taught them that they lacked any firm ground for treating him aggressively. From the moment the hearing opened, the new tone was on display. González invited Representative Tom Lantos to introduce his fellow Hungarian American and teach House members how to pronounce his name: "Shurush," González ventured, and he sounded tickled at his own progress. Soros launched into a lecture on reflexivity, seizing the occasion to advertise his book, and then gently explained why hedge funds were not the right target for regulation. Leverage could be destabilizing for markets, Soros conceded; but restrictions on leverage should be applied not just to hedge funds but to a range of financial actors, starting with the big brokerages. Of course, if this advice had been taken, leverage across the whole financial system might have been reined in, and the financial history of the next decade might have turned out differently. But, in their fixation with the novel threat posed by hedge funds, the lawmakers failed to heed Soros's warning. A few befuddled committee members were still struggling to understand what hedge funds actually were. "Nowadays, the term is applied so indiscriminately," Soros lamented. "There is as little in common between my type of hedge funds and the hedge fund that was recently liquidated, as between the hedgehog and the people who cut the hedges in the summer," he said, referring to Askin's implosion.[41]

And so the search for a regulatory response fizzled. Clinton administration officials, including the future Treasury secretaries Robert Rubin and Lawrence Summers, engaged in the debates on regulatory options for hedge funds but did not push for action. The New York Fed governor, William McDonough, had manned the phones to save Bankers Trust on that hectic day in March; he did nothing thereafter to rein in the leverage that had fueled the panic. The postmortem of Askin's failure demonstrated that, despite all those assurances to Representative Watt, the brokerage departments of the investment banks had indeed lent to Askin carelessly. But, in perhaps the clearest error that related specifically to hedge funds, little was done to prod the banks to be cautious. The upshot was that when Long-Term Capital Management failed four years later, the crisis that ensued made 1994 look trivial.

FOR MICHAEL STEINHARDT'S FAMILY OF FUNDS, THE losses of 1994 were terminal. Steinhardt had flirted with the idea of retirement for years: "I don't feel what I do is profoundly virtuous," he had told *Institutional Investor* as far back as 1987. "The idea of making wealthy people wealthier is not something that strikes to the inner parts of my soul." After the humiliation of the bond-market meltdown, Steinhardt resolved to make his exit.[42]

To those who worked for Steinhardt at the time, it was clear that his nerve had been shattered. He was frightened to take risks, and his temper went from bad to horrible.[43] He would fire an employee at lunchtime and invite him to return the following day; he would scream at people with his intercom switched on, so that his bloodcurdling curses were relayed to every corner of the office. Steinhardt hung on through 1995, turning in a surprisingly good 27 percent return and recouping $700 million of his losses.[44] His honor thus restored, he announced his long-rumored retirement.

Steinhardt's departure was a watershed moment in the history of hedge funds: After twenty-seven years as a wizard of the trading screens, one of the Big Three was exiting the business. A dollar invested with Steinhardt in 1967 would have been worth $480 on the day he closed the firm, twenty-six times more than the $18 it would have been worth if it had been invested in the S&P 500 index. The debacle of 1994 had cost Steinhardt's funds an astonishing $1.5 billion, but he had earned more than twice that much between 1991 and 1993, and his returns over the rest of his career had been excellent.[45] "I've made my investors and myself more money than I ever conceived of as a kid," Steinhardt reflected. His retirement would give him more time to dance with Martha, the elegant blue crane on his country estate that had taken to courting him with a graceful gavotte. There was life beyond Wall Street.

For those who remained behind, the question was what 1994 implied for the hedge-fund industry. Even if regulators were inclined to be soft, clients might take a different view: By September 1994, investors had pulled roughly $900 million out of hedge funds, and the withdrawals were still coming.[46] Financial magazines pointed out indignantly that hedge funds were not actually hedged, and *Forbes* magazine proclaimed, not for the first time, "The hedge fund party is over."[47] Macro hedge funds, which had disastrously overestimated the liquidity in currencies and bonds, returned money to their clients rather than waiting to be asked to do so. Paul Tudor Jones handed back a third of his capital to investors, while Bruce Kovner decided in June 1995 to give back two thirds; both cited the difficulty of maneuvering in and out of markets with too much capital. A month after Kovner's announcement, Soros wrote a letter to Quantum's investors, blaming recent disappointments on the same problem of size.

Macro investing was now contemptuously dubbed "leveraged directional speculating."[48]

In the early 1970s a similar backlash had buried hedge funds for a generation. But by the mid-1990s the industry was more resilient than before: With the exception of Steinhardt, famous funds were forced to shrink but carried on in business. An ecosystem of smaller players had evolved a rich range of investment styles, some of which performed robustly in a crisis. There were funds that bet on company mergers, funds that lent to companies in bankruptcies, funds based on computer models that arbitraged the gaps between similar financial instruments. One survey found that the average decline for a hedge fund in the first quarter of 1994 was a surprisingly modest 2.2 percent—less than the 3.3 percent decline for the average equity mutual fund.[49] Another found that hedge funds had beaten the S&P 500 stock index over the past five years and had also been considerably less volatile.[50] University endowments and other sophisticated investors were waking up to the fact that hedge-fund returns could diversify the risks from holding stocks and bonds. They could work wonders for a large portfolio.

And so, in the aftermath of the bond-market crisis of 1994, there were two verdicts on hedge funds. Regulators were forced to confront worrisome questions about the industry; but lacking a good theory of how to tame it, they ultimately chose to look the other way. Meanwhile, institutional investors reached a critical verdict: Notwithstanding the turmoil of 1994, hedge funds promised risk-adjusted returns that were simply irresistible. In a sense, the two verdicts were one. Because markets are not perfectly efficient, hedge funds and other creatures of the markets raise difficult issues: They are part of an unstable game that can wreak havoc on the world economy. But by the same token, the inefficiency of the markets allowed hedge funds to do well. Investors would line up to get into them.

||||||||||||||||||||||

9

||||||||||||||||||||||

SOROS VERSUS SOROS

To create the mining city of Noril'sk, Stalin resorted to slavery. His secret police arrested hundreds of engineers on fabricated charges and hauled them off to the Siberian Arctic, where there were no trees or plants or vegetation. Perhaps two hundred thousand *zeks*, or political prisoners, died in the process of building the city and its mine; years later the annual melting of the snow continued to flush out the skulls and bones of Stalin's victims. By the mid-1990s, some 260,000 inhabitants huddled in this bleak setting, fighting temperatures that fell to −40 degrees Celsius and choking on the sulfurous smog that billowed from Dickensian smelters. The sun vanished during the five months of the polar night. "Time somehow passes," one resident told a visitor, "but we remain."[1]

Geographically and psychologically, it was hard to imagine a setting more remote from the fast-paced trading rooms of Manhattan. But in 1990 Paul Tudor Jones and a few other hedge funders vacationed at a fishing camp on the nearby Ponoi River.[2] The visitors reveled in the Arctic wilderness, pitting their wits against powerful salmon; and with the instinct that wealthy people sometimes develop, they resolved that since they liked the camp so much the right thing was to buy it. When they got to negotiating the fishing rights with the provincial government, they

heard a story that caught their attention. At a meeting in Helsinki that
was ostensibly about fishing, one of the Russian officials had mentioned
Noril'sk, lamenting that the creaking Soviet infrastructure at the mine
was on the verge of collapsing. Thorpe McKenzie, the former partner of
Julian Robertson's at Tiger who was negotiating on behalf of the hedge-
fund fishermen, pricked up his ears. Noril'sk's mine contained more than
half the world's palladium. A breakdown in production would have global
consequences.[3]

McKenzie returned to the Ponoi River annually for the next few years;
he hosted Russian officials at his fishing camp and pumped them for information about the mine and its prospects. He researched the structure of
the palladium market and found that the metal had three principal uses:
dentistry, for which demand was more or less stable; catalytic converters
for automobiles, for which demand was growing thanks to environmental regulation; and cell phones, a new market that looked to have some
promise. Aside from Noril'sk, the other major suppliers of palladium were
in Africa, which faced its own infrastructure challenges. Having sized
up the situation, McKenzie concluded that demand for palladium would
outgrow the uncertain sources of supply. He bought some of the metal
for his own account and passed the word along to Julian Robertson. By
1994 Tiger had bought $40 million worth of palladium, and a young
Tiger commodities specialist named Dwight Anderson was dispatched to
investigate.

Anderson was one of those turbocharged young men whom Robertson
hired, and an appetite for adventure came in useful on this mission. He
flew to Moscow, which was then just emerging as a go-go town for Western deal makers, then boarded an ancient Aeroflot aircraft for the onward
flight to Siberia. When he touched down in Noril'sk in the half-light of a
bleak November day, he could make out the carcasses of wrecked aircraft
that littered the airport; evidently they had been plundered for spare parts
to keep the rest of the fleet going. Anderson gritted his teeth and tried not
to think about the safety of the flight he would take home. But when he
visited Noril'sk's mine the next day, he was surprised at how well it was
working.[4]

Anderson had seen many mines before, but this one was different. It was nothing like the Appalachian coal mines, where men crouch as they go underground; it was nothing like the open-pit mines in the western United States or the spectacularly deep shafts in southern Africa. The Siberian approach to mining was truly Soviet in scale: You could drive underground in a vast truck and tour a bewildering warren of caverns. The scale of the excavation exceeded anything that could possibly have been needed to extract the ore, but this excess was a blessing. If one tunnel or one trolley system developed a problem, there would be several alternative ways of getting the ore out; if a mechanical drill broke, there would be two defunct ones near to hand, and their carcasses could be plundered for spare parts like the abandoned planes at the airport. Noril'sk's redundant scale allowed it to keep going, and Anderson soon concluded that the stories of a collapse in production had been deliberately exaggerated. Local officials understood that rumors of a collapse were bullish for palladium prices. Since they all had stakes in the mine's sales, they seized every chance to tell visiting foreigners about an imminent production breakdown.

Anderson could see that something else might collapse, however. As he built his contacts in Russia, he confirmed that the Russians were selling more palladium than they mined: They were ripping the stuff out of disused Soviet military equipment and selling it. Sooner or later, this plundering would have to stop: Somewhere around the year 2000, Anderson calculated, there would be no more missiles to be scrapped, and the price of palladium would skyrocket. And so, following Anderson's investigations, Tiger held on to its palladium position, even though the logic for owning it had changed. The position lost money for the next three years; but then, as we shall see, things started to get interesting.

TIGER'S SIBERIAN FORAY WAS PART OF A LARGER PHE-nomenon. In the early 1990s the closed parts of the world economy opened up to Western capital, and hedge funds seized the opportunity. Before 1990, westerners were barred from the Kola Peninsula, whether to fish or to inspect mines; before 1990, likewise, the countries of East Asia and Eastern Europe allowed only a trickle of foreign money into their equity and bond markets, which were in any case too small to hold much opportunity. But around the turn of the decade, when Thorpe McKenzie led his first group of anglers to Siberia, emerging markets came into their own. The outstanding stock of developing-country bonds shot up from around $40 billion to $100 billion in the space of a year, and blistering growth continued through the rest of the decade. Traditional asset managers warmed to peripheral economies only gradually, but hedge funds moved fast. By the early 1990s, they were filling their coffers with the debt of countries such as Peru and reaping healthy profits.[5] In 1992 Soros and Druckenmiller launched a new fund called Quantum Emerging Growth to take advantage of this new frontier. The following year Louis Bacon's Moore Capital followed suit with a specialized emerging-market vehicle.

From the point of view of developing countries, there was much to like in this new order. Hedge funds were willing to provide capital when others were not; once hedge funds led the way, other Western asset managers would eventually follow; and because foreigners were generally sophisticated in their choice of which companies to finance, their presence frequently boosted the quality of capital in an economy as well as the mere quantity.[6] But the global spread of hedge funds also entailed risks. Hedge funds could provide capital to an emerging economy and juice its growth for a few years, but they could also yank their money out and cause growth to crater. As Britain's government had discovered in 1992, and as Alan Greenspan had discovered two years later, deep and fast-moving capital markets could force wrenching movements in currencies and interest rates, shattering the illusion that economic statesmen were the masters of their nations' destinies. If this was true in the rich world, it was even truer in frail emerging economies. At the end of 1994, Mexico succumbed to a full-blown currency crisis. And Mexico's troubles turned out to be a dress rehearsal for a far bigger drama—one that was in large part conceived at Soros Fund Management.

In the years after the sterling trade, Stan Druckenmiller had led the Quantum Fund to yet more profits. In 1993, the golden period for the bond market, Quantum was up 63 percent; the following year, despite the bond crash, it still battled to a gain of 4 percent; in 1995 it was back in stride again with a return of 39 percent.[7] But during these years, Druck-enmiller began a long-running debate with Soros about the proper size of their hedge fund. The sterling trade had shown that bulk could be a weapon in facing down a government, but it had also shown that Quantum was unnecessarily large. Soros and Druckenmiller had believed that given their fund's size, they should sell $15 billion worth of sterling, but they had only been able to sell $10 billion; it followed that if their fund had been one third smaller, they would have aimed to sell $10 billion and actually sold that amount, yielding a percentage gain on their capital that would have been a third higher. For Druckenmiller, a stellar performance number was the main goal: His earnings were tied to it and his ego was invested in it. For Soros, on the other hand, the calculation was different. His ego was invested as much in the size of his empire as in the scale of his returns: Owning a global firm made him a global player, raising the profile of his writings and philanthropy. Soros was known as the only private citizen to have his own foreign policy, and he reveled in the fact that eminent statesmen beat a path to his office. One day a Soros employee overheard the boss tell Druckenmiller that Henry Kissinger was visiting.

"Would you like a word with him?" Soros asked Druckenmiller.

"Does he know anything?" Druckenmiller countered dismissively.

"Oh, yes," Soros answered, finding a way to vaunt his political connections while not seeming in awe of Kissinger's star power. "I don't like him, but he does know things."

Soros and Druckenmiller reached a compromise on the size of their hedge fund. Soros Fund Management would continue to accumulate assets, but they would not all go to Quantum. By 1996, just over half the $10 billion at Soros Fund Management was housed in three other funds: Quantum Emerging Growth, Quasar (which invested with outside hedge-fund managers), and Quota (which was managed by Nick Roditi, a secretive London-based macro trader). To run these new start-ups, Soros recruited new talent, including a Princeton-trained economist named Arminio Fraga. When the two men met in early 1993, Fraga, a Brazilian, had just left a position as a deputy governor at his country's central bank. Within a few days, Soros had offered him a partnership.

"Here, Stan, I hired this guy," he told Druckenmiller breezily.

Druckenmiller eyed Fraga, a slight, polite man with an academic demeanor. It was one of those moments when he might have been thinking, "How am I supposed to run this place when I can't choose who works for me?" But his big frame gave nothing away.

"Fine," he said. "Let's see if he's any good."[8]

For the next four years at Soros, Fraga performed the benign function of hedge funds: to finance emerging economies that were shunned by traditional investors. He bought the bonds of big Latin countries such as Brazil and Venezuela; he branched out into exotica such as Moroccan loans; he bought shares in Brazilian utilities, which were absurdly cheap by international standards. Then in late 1996 Fraga attended a talk by Stan Fischer, the number two at the International Monetary Fund. The mood was mostly upbeat: Mexico's currency had recovered from its crisis, and emerging markets were booming. Still, somebody asked Fischer the question "Who do you think is the next Mexico?"

"I'm not sure there's another one out there at the moment," Fischer answered. "But I do see some imbalances in Asia. That might be interesting to look at."[9]

That comment, Fraga recalled later, "put a little light in my mind."[10] A few weeks afterward, Fraga read a joint IMF–Federal Reserve paper titled "The Twin Crises," which laid out in terrifying detail how a currency collapse could interact with the collapse of a banking system.[11] Casting his mind back to Fischer's remarks, Fraga approached Druckenmiller.

"Do you mind if I go and take a look at what is going on in Asia?" he asked him.

"Sure," came the answer. "Go."[12]

IN JANUARY 1997, FRAGA LANDED IN THAILAND. AS HE made the rounds of local officials, company executives, and economists, it quickly became clear that the country fitted the double-crisis model laid out in the IMF-Fed paper. Thailand's exports had been hammered by the rise of China as a low-cost rival, and to make matters worse, Thailand's currency was linked to a basket of currencies dominated by a strong dollar, further eroding its ability to compete in world markets. As a result, Thailand was running a large trade deficit, but it was refusing to adjust: Rather than abandon its link to the dollar and allow a falling currency to restore its competitiveness, the country was consuming more than it produced, paying for the difference with loans from foreigners. This arrangement left the Thais exposed. If the foreigners tired of lending to Thailand, the country would have to export enough not only to cover its import bill but also to repay outsiders. To boost exports and cut imports, the Thai baht would have to fall—sharply.

At the time of Fraga's fact-finding visit, the willingness of foreigners to finance Thailand was already crumbling. In 1996 a major Thai bank had collapsed, raising doubts about the wisdom of lending to the country. Thailand's central bank had cut interest rates to stave off further bank trouble, but this had dampened returns for foreign creditors and given them another reason to go elsewhere. Fragile banks and a reliance on foreign capital were coming together in the way that the IMF-Fed paper had described, and it was clear to Fraga that this interaction could turn toxic. If a withdrawal of foreign money drove Thailand to devalue, the banks would be tipped from fragility into outright ruin. Much of the foreign lending to Thailand was denominated in dollars, and it had been channeled into real estate and other projects that generated revenue in baht. If the dollar jumped against the baht, these debts would become impossible to service.

The tipping point for Fraga came during a visit to the Bank of Thailand. Together with David Kowitz, Soros's expert on Asian equities, and Rodney Jones, an economist who worked for Soros in Hong Kong, Fraga was granted an audience with a high-ranking official at the central bank. Invoking his own experience as the deputy governor of Brazil's central bank, Fraga offered some thoughts on the dilemma that Thailand confronted: On the one hand, the government was committed to defending its exchange rate, which would involve keeping interest rates high enough to attract capital; on the other hand, Thailand had a trade deficit and wobbly banks, which made devaluation and lower interest rates attractive. Fraga had a mild manner, and his Brazilian background helped; he seemed more like a benign emerging-market peer than a menacing Wall Street predator. So the official looked at Fraga and gave him an answer that was at once honest and naive. Until now, he said simply, Thailand had accepted whatever interest rates proved necessary to maintain the exchange rate within its designated band. But now priorities might have to shift. Given the growing troubles at the banks, getting interest rates down might matter more than defending the level of the currency.[13]

The official might as well have offered up a suitcase full of money. He had conceded that Thailand's currency peg was unsustainable, meaning that shorting the baht was a no-brainer. Fraga and his colleagues could practically visualize the suitcase, cash spilling from its seams; but in order to reel in their prize, they had to pretend they hadn't noticed it. If their host realized the full power of his comment, he could snatch the suitcase back: The central bank could hike interest rates, raising the cost of borrowing the baht in order to sell it short; or it might resort to some administrative crackdown on foreign speculators. Ever polite and self-effacing, Fraga nodded pleasantly at the Thai official and allowed the discussion to move on. After a little while, David Kowitz gently led the conversation backward.

"Excuse me. I'm out of my depth here," he said humbly. "Can you just repeat what you said a few minutes ago, just to make sure I got it right?"

The official repeated his statement, and the Soros team got what it was looking for. Their host had told them that he knew the game was up: He had confessed and reconfessed his nakedness. Whatever the official pronouncements on Thailand's commitment to its exchange-rate peg, it was only a matter of time before the baht was devalued.

After a stop in South Korea, Fraga returned to New York and reported back to Druckenmiller. The big man listened to Fraga's story and quickly approved a trade, and over the space of a few days in late January, the Soros team sold short about $2 billion worth of the Thai currency.[14] The selling was both a prediction of a crisis and a trigger that could bring it on: To defend the baht against the pressure from Druckenmiller and Fraga, the government sold a chunk of its dwindling foreign-currency reserves and raised interest rates by 3 percentage points—a punishing hike given that Thai banks were tottering.[15] But the rate hike came too late to scare the predators away. The Soros team had taken out baht loans of six months' duration and had locked in the low interest rates that had existed before the government hiked them. Secure in their positions, Druckenmiller and Fraga could afford to wait until the end of July for the inevitable to happen.[16]

In the months and years to come, a spirited argument would break out as to whether hedge funds precipitated Asia's financial crisis. We will get to that question, but for now the opposite one stands out: Why didn't Druckenmiller and Fraga do *more* to force a Thai devaluation? Back in 1992, the Soros team had sold $10 billion worth of sterling, around two and a half times the firm's capital. But the $2 billion Thai trade represented just a fifth of capital—a fraction of the selling of which Druckenmiller was capable. By repeating the leverage of his earlier exploit, Druckenmiller could have sold an additional $23 billion or so of baht, multiplying the Soros funds' returns and wiping out most of the foreign-currency reserves held at the Bank of Thailand. Its reserves thus depleted, Thailand would probably have capitulated within days, so a quick and magnificent profit apparently lay within Druckenmiller's grasp. Why didn't he seize it?[17]

In the popular imagination, the Soros team's ruthlessness is unbounded. But the truth was that it had only a limited appetite for speculating aggressively in emerging markets. Soros himself was of two minds about speculation—he liked to say that markets, instead of swinging like a pendulum, could swing like a wrecking ball, laying waste to economies.[18] Druckenmiller was clearer in his purpose, but he was not focused on Thailand: He was taking advice from Fraga and his team, so lacked the intense conviction that he felt when a trade was his entirely. Further down the hierarchy at the Soros funds, there were complex emotions. Rodney Jones, the Hong Kong–based economist, had challenged Fraga and Kowitz about the morality of speculation in developing countries: If currencies crashed, millions of innocents would be forced into desperate poverty.[19] Back in 1992, Soros had famously urged Druckenmiller to "go for the jugular." But when it came to Thailand in 1997, some members of the Soros team felt squeamish.

In the aftermath of the discussions in Thailand, Jones settled on his own way of living with what he was doing; and in a book published after the Thai crash, Soros offered an identical defense of his funds' actions.[20] The defense boiled down to a simple idea: Speculation could benefit poor societies if it served as a signal, not a sledgehammer. The function of the virtuous speculator was to alert governments to the need for change—in Thailand's case, that the baht had to devalue. This signaling could avoid hardship for ordinary people, since the more a government procrastinated about devaluation, the more brutal the eventual currency collapse would be. Reserves would dwindle to zero, so that when the crisis came there would be nothing left to cushion the shock as capital flooded out of the country. This case for speculation was potentially correct, but it could only justify speculation of a mild sort. An all-out attack on the Thai baht would have precipitated a crisis rather than prodded the government to avoid one.

In the weeks following Druckenmiller's first baht sale, Thailand's behavior revealed a flaw in the Jones-Soros rationalization. Speculative signals would only be helpful if governments were wise enough to respond to them. But rather than prompting the Thais to devalue sensibly and early, Druckenmiller's short position provoked disastrous defiance: The government threw away its foreign-currency reserves, buying baht from Druckenmiller at a rate that was sure to leave it with a loss once devaluation happened. Meanwhile, the Thai economy continued to weaken. When Rodney Jones next visited in the last days of April, the country was visibly grinding to a halt: Jones counted a hundred cranes on the Bangkok skyline, but almost none were working. Overextended real-estate companies had stopped servicing their loans; eighty-seven out of ninety finance companies in Thailand were said to be insolvent. Thailand had experienced a financial crisis at the end of the 1970s, but Jones could see, to his horror, that the next one would be worse. Back then, the total stock of loans was worth 40 percent of GDP; now, thanks to the globalization of capital flows, the ratio was 140 percent, rendering the consequences of a banking bust more serious for the real economy. The only silver lining, Jones concluded, was that the authorities still had a little time. They could come to their senses and devalue before a panic forced them into it.

As it turned out, Jones's presence in Thailand helped to precipitate the crisis that he dreaded. The Thai press got wind of his visit, and the news that a foreign hedge fund was circling spooked jittery local investors. Thai financiers and companies began to dump baht and buy dollars, forcing another round of central-bank intervention to defend the currency's level. On the evening of Sunday, May 11, Prime Minister Chavalit Yongchai-yudh reinforced the sense of crisis by appearing on television and vowing to support the baht, then adding the self-defeating message that he could not promise to succeed in doing so. Just as in the case of Britain, which continued to defend sterling even as it knew the game was up, so the Thai leadership lacked the courage to accept the logic of their untenable position. And just as in the British case, the reaction from the Soros team was predictable.

Three days after Chavalit's televised statement, Druckenmiller increased his bet against the baht from $2 billion to $3.5 billion. The new position still represented only a third of the Soros funds' capital, a fraction of what Druckenmiller could have sold if he had leveraged up aggressively. But now Druckenmiller was no longer the only player in the game; Thai investors were leading the charge out of the baht, and other hedge funds were following. Paul Tudor Jones, who spoke with Druckenmiller several times each day, was quick to put on a trade, as did several of the other macro funds from the tight-knit group around him. The biggest player after Druckenmiller was probably Julian Robertson's Tiger, which built a short position in the baht that eventually came to $2 billion.[21]

The day that Druckenmiller increased his position, the Bank of Thailand was forced to use at least $6 billion of its reserves to maintain the baht's level; and over the next week, the onslaught continued.[22] But

Thailand's government still refused to embrace devaluation; and a visit from the IMF's Stan Fischer, the man who had set Fraga on his path, failed to persuade it to accept the inevitable. Rather than bow to the markets, the Thai government counterattacked.

This gets to a second reason why Druckenmiller had not gone for the jugular. Financial traders must contend with market risks, but they also face political ones.[23] On May 15, the day after Druckenmiller upped the ante, the Thai authorities forbade all banks from lending baht to anyone outside the country. This put short sellers in a bind: They could no longer borrow baht in order to sell them unless they secured the loans offshore at punitive interest rates. Tiger, for example, had financed some of its positions by borrowing baht on a short-term basis, figuring that it could roll over the loans as they came due; now it was forced to renew them at vastly higher interest rates: At one point in early June, the cost of holding Tiger's position hit $10 million *per day*.[24] The clampdown on lending to foreigners, combined with the central bank's aggressive intervention, succeeded in reversing the baht's fall: In the three weeks after Druckenmiller's second strike, the Thai currency gained 10 percent against the dollar and hedge funds booked perhaps $500 million in losses. The region's English-language newspapers were reporting gleefully that hedge funds were losing the "battle of the baht," and the prime minister called the central bank to promise its staff a victory party. The Bank of Thailand was said to be gunning personally for Soros. According to one newspaper account, it was bent on inflicting losses on his funds of as much as $4 billion.[25]

Faced with this onslaught, Druckenmiller cut his short position from $3.5 billion to $3 billion. Had he leveraged up and sold baht to the max, he might have precipitated devaluation; but that was more than the political system seemed likely to tolerate. Yet although Druckenmiller was not going to stick his neck out, he was not going to walk away; he knew that the Thais were closer to collapse than they admitted publicly. The central bank's position was ostensibly robust: Even in late June, it reported reserves of more than $30 billion. But it had effectively sold a vast quantity of reserves by taking positions in the forward market, which did not show up on its balance sheet. This maneuver had fooled almost all outsiders, including inspectors from the International Monetary Fund and members of the Thai government itself. But by doggedly calling the banks that executed the government's sell orders in the forward markets, Jones had pieced together the alarming rate at which real reserves were dwindling. By his reckoning, the Bank of Thailand had used up $21 billion worth of reserves in May alone, a stunning two thirds of its war chest.[26]

Jones took little pleasure in this finding. His moral justification for speculation had been battered: Far from reacting to speculators by adjusting their policies quickly, Thailand's leaders were digging in their heels and condemning their people to a calamity. The combination of high interest rates and uncertainty about the Thai currency had pushed the financial system to a breaking point. Banks were charging exorbitant rates to lend to other banks, not knowing which among them would survive, and money was ceasing to flow through the economy. On June 25 Jones worked out his anguish in a memo entitled "The Economics of Deflation: What Keynes Would Say to Thailand." For a country to choose sky-high interest rates in preference to devaluation was "sheer lunacy," Jones wrote, and he invoked Keynes's reflections on this folly going back to Roman times. In A.D. 274, Emperor Aurelian's zeal to protect the integrity of the coinage caused deflationary misery and provoked a rebellion. The fighting that ensued resulted in the deaths of seven thousand soldiers and doubtless many more civilians.

Jones's anguish could not save the Thai people. Clamping down on baht loans to foreigners turned out to be about as effective as blocking up one hole in a showerhead: It only accelerated the pace at which capital whooshed out through other openings. Harassing short sellers encouraged foreigners who had lent dollars to Thai businesses to demand repayment, and the businesses dumped baht as they scrambled to meet their obligations. Besides, the attack on short sellers made it expensive to borrow baht but by no means impossible; if you were convinced that the currency was about to collapse, it paid to borrow it at sky-high interest rates in the offshore market just for a short period. As more capital fled Thailand, the odds of a collapse increased. On Tuesday, July 1, according to at least one account, Julian Robertson's Tiger unleashed a barrage of baht selling, adding $1 billion to its short position until the Bank of Thailand finally ran out of reserves and it became impossible to find buyers for the currency.[27] Thailand had finally been pushed over the edge. Robertson had played a role analogous to Druckenmiller's in the sterling crisis.[28]

On the other side of the world, at around 4:30 A.M. Bangkok time, Bank of Thailand officials conceded that they had no more ammunition with which to defend the currency. After months of resistance, the baht peg had snapped: Over the next three months, it fell by 32 percent against the dollar. The Soros funds gained about $750 million from the devaluation, and Julian Robertson gained perhaps $300 million;[29] meanwhile, Thailand's output collapsed by 17 percent from its peak, destroying businesses and jobs and plunging millions into poverty. By an uncanny coincidence, July 1, 1997, was the day when Britain ceded control over Hong Kong. It also was the day when a new kind of imperialism put its stamp on Southeast Asia.

In the wake of the devaluation, hedge funds were inevitably vilified. There was some fairness to these complaints, since the Soros team had indeed led the selling in January, forcing the government to raise interest rates and throttle its weak economy. There was an additional element of fairness, given Tiger's role on the last day—though at the time almost nobody knew about this. But in a larger sense, the complaints missed the point. The roots of the crisis stretched back to 1995 and 1996, when the Thais had refused to devalue their exchange rate gradually in the face of China's rise; speculators had merely forced an adjustment that was ultimately inevitable. Besides, although Soros and Tiger were part of the trigger for the crisis, they were not quite the villains that critics imagined. In particular, Druckenmiller had refused to leverage to the max, rightly fearing a political backlash. As the endgame played out in June, he had actually *reduced* his position.

As it turned out, Druckenmiller's caution contained a prophecy. As Thailand's crisis spread across East Asia and beyond, the image of the hedge fund as superpredator proved less and less accurate.

IN LATE SEPTEMBER 1997, GEORGE SOROS FLEW TO HONG Kong. He went for the annual meetings of the World Bank and International Monetary Fund, and the reception he received mirrored his dual persona. Soros the speculator was predictably reviled: Having earlier called him a "criminal" and a "moron," Prime Minister Mahathir Mohamad of Malaysia called for a ban on "unnecessary, unproductive and immoral" currency trading. But Soros the statesman-philanthropist was the toast of the meetings. He addressed a packed auditorium on how to stabilize the world economy and was lionized by the press, not least because he could rail against speculation as fiercely as the best of them. "The main enemy of the open society, I believe, is no longer the communist but the capitalist threat," he declared, despite his own capitalist fortune. "The laissez-faire idea that markets should be left to their own devices remains very influential," he went on. "I consider it a dangerous idea."

By the late 1990s, Soros had no doubt as to which side of his persona should dominate. He wanted to be a thinker, a statesman, a great public figure; he did not want to be a neoimperialist and smasher of small currencies.[30] Inevitably, there was a risk that this preference might color his investment views: In a discussion with David Kowitz and Rodney Jones during the Hong Kong meetings, Soros declared confidently that the time for shorting Asian currencies had passed, even though Mahathir's outburst against markets had triggered a new sell-off in the region. The lieutenants had doubts about the boss's rosy prognosis, but Soros was not in the mood to listen. Although he would not micromanage the funds' decisions—he would leave these to Druckenmiller and the team—his optimistic bias was evident.

The bias played out first in Indonesia. In the run-up to the Hong Kong meetings, the Soros team bought about $300 million worth of Indonesian rupiah, believing that the turmoil in Thailand had spilled over to neighbors without justification.[31] Rather than repeat the Thai error of defending an unsustainable exchange-rate peg, the Indonesians had let their currency fall 11 percent in August; now a rebound might be in the offing. Following a visit to Indonesia by Arminio Fraga and Rodney Jones in October, the Soros funds increased the rupiah bet to about $1 billion.

Not all hedge funds thought this was sensible. Julian Robertson's Tiger, which had bet on the rupiah too, dumped its holdings at the end of October. But the Soros team followed the technocratic consensus, which held that the decline in the rupiah would prove temporary. The IMF seemed confident that Indonesia would pull through, and on November 2 it announced a $33 billion credit line for the country, designed to give the central bank the foreign reserves it needed to bolster confidence in its money. The next day the rupiah rallied healthily, and Soros's position was showing a small profit.

Up until this point, Soros's optimism at the Hong Kong meetings had achieved a shaky vindication. Yet by mid-November, the Soros team and its IMF allies were losing their moorings. The IMF's $33 billion credit line had been extended in exchange for two key commitments: Indonesia would close down sixteen corrupt banks, and it would run a responsible monetary policy. But the cronies around the ailing President Suharto were determined to frustrate this plan. The corrupt banks belonged to the cronies so were impossible to close down; and the cronies were also hammering on the central bank for loans, which inflated the money supply and destroyed confidence in the rupiah. By late November, the currency was in free fall; and in early December things got worse. Suharto was rumored to be seriously ill, and the prospect of a power vacuum panicked the country. By December 15 the rupiah was down 44 percent from its high in early November, and the trade had cost Soros $400 million.

The strange thing was that the Soros team continued to stick with the currency. In the aftermath of the Wall Street crash ten years earlier, Soros had dumped his positions as soon as they went wrong, capping out his losses. But this time the Soros team seemed paralyzed, despite the clear signs that Indonesia had turned into a disaster. On December 10 Rodney Jones got his hands on data from the Bank of Indonesia, which confirmed that the central bank had been printing money that found its way to the lenders run by Suharto's cronies. Jones fired off a note to Soros headquarters in New York, laying out the details of the monetary binge. But the funds still stuck with the rupiah position.

Around the same time the Indonesian finance minister, Mar'ie Muham-mad, was dispatched by his government to reassure foreign investors. Muhammad had spent years building up a reputation as a respected tech-nocrat; now his task was to defend a recovery program in which money was being printed to pay off the undeserving friends of the Suharto fam-ily. On a stop in New York, Muhammad met Soros and his lieutenants at the Plaza Hotel; but although he was going through the motions of talking up Indonesia's prospects, his heart was not in it. Soros, Fraga, and Druckenmiller posed question after question, but, placed in an impos-sible position, Muhammad refused to meet their gaze, mumbling his way through a series of evasive answers.

"Oh my God," Druckenmiller said as he strode back to the office. "I can't believe that we are long.

"I don't believe anything that guy said," he continued. "I don't even believe he's from Indonesia."[32]

The group made its way across midtown Manhattan, back to the Soros offices by Columbus Circle. They knew that they were trapped in an appalling trade, but there were so few willing buyers for rupiah that it was not obvious how to get out of it.[33] Casting around for some kind of exit, David Kowitz suggested using the rupiah to buy a physical commodity such as iron, which could eventually be bartered.

"That's an interesting idea," Soros said gravely, in his thick central European voice. But nobody followed up on Kowitz's proposal—not even when Indonesia's government, unable to print money fast enough, released plastic souvenir banknotes as legal currency. The Soros team followed the rupiah down to the bottom, eventually losing about $800 million. The profits from the Thai baht trade had been wiped out in their entirety.[34]

The Indonesian fiasco dented the image of the Soros funds as relentless superpredators. But it was compounded at the same time by an extraordi-nary missed opportunity.

IN MID-NOVEMBER 1997, RODNEY JONES VISITED SOUTH Korea. Calling on a local bank, he found its boardroom festooned with triumphant notices of financings it had done for Thai companies. Jones knew these companies, and he knew that they had since gone bust; inquiring as to how many of the bank's Thai borrowers were behind on their payments, he learned that the total came to more than fifty. As he made the rounds of other offices, Jones realized that this was just the tip of the iceberg. Thailand's bust had clobbered South Korea's financial firms, leaving them short dollars that they were likely never to recover. With a bit more digging, Jones found that South Korea's central bank was scrambling to cover up the mess by depositing dollars in Korean banks, using its reserves of foreign currency. And this discovery led to the bombshell: Like the central bank of Thailand five months previously, South Korea's central bank was misleading the markets. Officially, its foreign-currency war chest contained $57 billion. But if you subtracted the amounts promised to wounded banks or committed on the forward markets, the real number was closer to $20 billion.[35]

Jones had uncovered the equivalent of that Thai suitcase full of prize money. In the fortnight prior to his visit, the South Korean won had dipped by 4 percent against the dollar, and the stock market had weakened. But nobody imagined that the central bank had already chewed through two thirds of its reserves, or that Korea was in the midst of a full-blown banking-cum-currency crisis of the sort that Fraga had anticipated in Thailand. Only a month earlier, the IMF had completed its annual assessment of South Korea's economic health and concluded that the country was immune from the turmoil elsewhere in the region. But in a memo to Soros headquarters dated November 17, Jones was able to explain why the IMF was flat wrong. Korea was "in the late stage of the crisis," he warned. The official and widely believed numbers on the dollar debts of South Korean companies understated their real liabilities by a whopping $60 billion; and much of this debt would mature within weeks. A catastrophic collapse was in the offing.

Over the course of the next month, the Jones memo proved prescient. Nine days after it landed in New York, the IMF's top Asia hand flew into Seoul on an emergency mission; ushered into a meeting at the central bank, he discovered that its reserves were falling at a rate of $1 billion per day and were now down to $9 billion.[36] Just as Jones had reported, much of the dollar debt held by Korean borrowers was of short maturity, so money was flying out of the country at a rate that would exhaust the reserves imminently. On December 3, the IMF announced a hastily assembled $55 billion package of loans to South Korea—a record number for an IMF bailout—but given that the dollar obligations of the private sector were more than twice that size, the package was inadequate. By the end of December, the won had fallen 60 percent from its level at the time of Jones's November 17 memo.

Yet Jones's spectacular call earned the Soros team precisely nothing. Despite the strong language in the November 17 memo, and despite a follow-up message from Jones the next day, no action was taken to sell the won short and repeat the gains in Thailand. It is not certain why this was. At the time of Jones's memo, top IMF officials believed that South Korea would escape trouble; this may have persuaded the Soros team to focus on other challenges.[37] But it is hard to escape the suspicion that Soros's dual persona contributed to the missed opportunity as well. The boss wanted to be a statesman, not a wrecker of nations. If he was going to get involved in South Korea, it would be not as a scourge but as a savior.[38]

In the first days of January 1998, Soros traveled to Korea. He went as the guest of Kim Dae-jung, the country's president-elect, and there were camera crews waiting at the airport. The great man dined with Kim at his home and affectionately called him "DJ"; he visited the top industrialists and breakfasted with Michael Jackson, who was plotting to take over a theme park from a bust South Korean underwear maker.[39] Addressing the local media, Soros was not shy about laying out what Korea should do. He criticized the IMF prescriptions for the country, which involved saddling it with more debt, and called for a "radical restructuring of industry and of the financial sector," comprising a cleanup of accounting practices and flexibility for managers in firing workers.[40] If Korea did these things, he said, his Quantum Fund would be willing to invest substantial sums in the economy, and other Western investors would flood in. Investors responded to Soros's pronouncements by rushing into South Korean stocks, and Seoul's KOSPI index jumped by a quarter in the ten days following his visit.[41]

Soros's mission to South Korea did his own fortune few favors. Not only had he missed the chance to short the won on the way down; his funds did not take a stake in Korea's rebound until the following October. But the South Korea trip had a different payoff. The press coverage of his visit inevitably emphasized the comparison with the atmosphere in Hong Kong: Back in September, one Asian leader had vilified Soros as a criminal and moron; now another Asian leader was giving him the red-carpet treatment. Asked about the contrast between Mahathir and Kim, Soros allowed himself a smile.

"One of them must be wrong," he answered.[42]

THE STRUGGLE BETWEEN SOROS'S TWO PERSONAS WAS most acute in Russia. As far back as 1987, before the Soviet Union crumbled, Soros had set up a branch of his Open Society Institute in Moscow. In the 1990s the institute supported educational reform, the printing of textbooks free of Marxist ideology, and provided millions of dollars' worth of grants to support scientists. István Rév, a Hungarian historian who served on Soros's philanthropic boards, thought that Soros was drawn to Russia by the same forces that fascinated Napoleon: "Its vastness, its historical challenge, its backwardness, its perpetually unfulfilled promise."[43] Not wanting his philanthropy to be seen as a Trojan horse for his financial interests, Soros made it a principle not to get involved in Russian investments, though he allowed Druckenmiller and the team to take positions. But in the spring of 1997 he cracked. He took an astonishing financial gamble in Russia, one that mirrored his errors in Indonesia and South Korea.

Soros was not the only Western financier to fall for Russia. At the end of 1996, when President Boris Yeltsin reenergized his economic reform program, hedge-fund managers began jetting to Moscow, going out to the Bolshoi Opera and taking walks through the famous Novodevichy Convent gardens. A flood of foreign capital poured in. Portfolio investment increased from $8.9 billion in 1996 to $45.6 billion in 1997, equivalent to 10 percent of Russia's GDP; the Russian equity index almost tripled in the first nine months of the year, making it the hottest among a lot of hot emerging markets. There were risks in this euphoria, to be sure: Property rights and the rule of law were vague concepts in Russia. But from the point of view of portfolio investors, Russia seemed a good bet so long as the reformers had the upper hand in Yeltsin's government. If the reformers lost out, the foreigners could dump their shares and bonds and head for the exit.

As a creature of the markets, Soros understood the importance of an exit strategy. But in 1997, he staked $980 million on a venture that was almost totally illiquid. Going over the heads of Druckenmiller and his colleagues, he joined a consortium bidding for 25 percent of Svyazinvest, Russia's sprawling, state-owned telephone utility. It was an investment that might pay off over the long term: With nineteen phone lines per hundred people, compared with fifty-eight per hundred in the United States, telecoms in Russia had undeniable potential. But a $1 billion-odd stake in a state company was not something you could dump easily if Russian politics turned bad, and it entailed the sort of risk that seemed crazy to most foreigners. Even amid the torrent of portfolio investment into Russia, foreign direct investment into the country never amounted to more than a trickle.

If the Svyazinvest bet seemed reckless on its face, it was all the more crazy given what Soros knew about Russia.[44] In June 1997, shortly before the Svyazinvest auction was due to close, Soros received a secret request from the Russian government for emergency financing. President Yeltsin had sworn to start making good on the backlog of unpaid state wages and pensions by July 1, and he needed a temporary loan to meet the deadline. Unbeknownst to the markets or the International Monetary Fund, which was monitoring the parlous state of Russia's debt, Soros lent the government several hundred million dollars. Had he not done so, Yeltsin's brittle legitimacy might have cracked and unpaid workers might have rioted.

From the point of view of Soros the philanthropist-statesman, the secret loan raised questions. Soros was going behind the back of the International Monetary Fund even as he urged Russia to become a responsible member of the international monetary system.[45] But from the point of view of Soros the investor, the secret loan looked even more bizarre. Soros was about to plunk down a hard-to-exit bet of $1 billion on the theory that Russia was turning the corner to stability; but the desperation evidenced by the secret loan screamed out that stability was tenuous. In its triumph against sterling, and again in the Thai baht trade, the Soros team had used its insights into governments' financial and political frailties to stage profitable attacks. In Russia in 1997, Soros had a privileged window on these frailties, yet he invested as though he had never even thought about them.

Soros behaved this way because of his messiah complex. In his role as a philanthropist, he had tried to save Russia from its sins; now he convinced himself that he could save Russia even more if he risked his fortune in the country. As he put it himself:

> I deliberately chose to expose myself. To be a selfless benefactor was just a little too good to be true. It fed my self-image as a godlike creature, above the fray, doing good and fighting evil. I have talked about my messianic fantasies; I am not ashamed of them. . . . I could see, particularly in Russia, that people simply could not understand what I was all about. . . . It seemed to me that to appear as a robber capitalist who is concerned with cultural and political values was more credible than to be a disembodied intellect arguing for the merits of an open society. I could serve as a role model for the budding robber capitalists of Russia. And by entering the fray as an investor, I descended from Mount Olympus and became a flesh and blood human being.[46]

Soros's hope was that the Svyazinvest privatization would mark a turning point for Russia.[47] Until 1997, Russia's state assets had been transferred at knocked-down prices to the country's oligarchs, with foreign investors excluded; this time foreigners were allowed in, and the auction would be won by the highest bidder. Up to a point, Soros was right: When the bids were opened in July 1997, the consortium to which he contributed did indeed win out by offering the most money. But it was not remotely obvious that the messiah's participation was necessary for this victory;

and besides, the victory was Pyrrhic. The oligarchs who lost the auction owned newspapers and television stations, and these soon released a string of smear stories about the winning faction. For weeks the mudslinging dragged on, forcing three government officials to resign and distracting the Yeltsin administration from its reform agenda. Far from helping Russia to turn a corner to a cleaner kind of capitalism, the Svyazinvest episode plunged the government into chaos.

Meanwhile, shock waves started to arrive from Asia. Banks that had lent to Thailand, Indonesia, and South Korea began to register losses and were forced to pull some loans from Russia. Russian financiers could see that the war over Svyazinvest meant the end of economic reform, so they joined the scramble to get money out of the country. The economic collapse in Asia drove down the price of oil, which is Russia's primary export. Caught between collapsing export income and capital flight, Russia faced an excruciating crunch. In order to attract investors, the government was forced to offer ever higher interest rates on its bonds. By April 1998, the annualized interest rate on short-term ruble bonds hit 30 percent, even though their short maturity reduced the risks to purchasers. In May the yield on these so-called GKOs reached an astonishing 70 percent.

The chaos following the Svyazinvest auction made Soros's illiquid $1 billion bet look crazy. But the prospect of earning 70 percent from short-term government bonds was a different matter entirely, and soon half the hedge funds in New York were salivating. Three-month bonds with double-digit yields were surely the bargain of the decade; Russia's finances presented some risks, but these seemed acceptable on a short horizon. The West was not going to let a nuclear power like Russia default and descend into chaos, the argument went; if worse came to worst, the United States would force the IMF to increase its support for the country. In June, Goldman Sachs underwrote a $1.25 billion issue of Russian bonds, and the issue was so popular that it sold out within an hour. Every macro investor in Manhattan, from Soros to Tiger and on down, was hungry for Russian investments.[48]

But the most exotic Russia play of the moment had nothing to do with GKOs. It was about palladium.

———

SINCE HIS FIRST TRIP TO SIBERIA IN 1994, DWIGHT ANDER-
son had continued to build Tiger's palladium position. He learned to
navigate Russia's palladium bazaar: Each year the parliament and the
government export company would haggle over how much of the metal
should be sold, then the central bank, finance ministry, and officials in
Noril'sk would argue over who could sell how much of the allotment.
Anderson nurtured his relationship with the key selling officials over long
meals and whiskeys, buying the metal whenever he got the chance. And
then in the summer of 1998 he saw an opportunity to break out of this
pattern. The financial desperation of the Russian state could change the
game for palladium.

Anderson approached his Russian friends with a modest proposal. He
offered to buy the entire stock of nongold precious metals held by the
central bank and finance ministry. He would take the palladium, the rhodium, and the silver. All of it.

Anderson's audacious plan involved delicate logistics. Some of the metal
would have to be brought to Moscow from Siberia by armored train; the
entire consignment would then be flown to Switzerland and placed in
a bank vault with Tiger's name on it. Tiger would pay $4 billion once
the metal was in its hands, an amount that would relieve the immediate
pressure on the Russian budget. It would then sell the stockpile gradually
into the market, sharing the profits with the Russian government. The
eventual proceeds to Moscow would come in around $8 billion, or so
Anderson estimated.

Anderson flew to Moscow in July to meet a senior official at the central
bank. The climate seemed propitious for a deal: GKO yields had jumped
from 70 percent in May to more than 100 percent. Anderson and his
counterpart got along well; President Yeltsin apparently knew about the
deal and had approved it. Returning to the Tiger offices on Park Avenue
after a few days, Anderson felt that the deal of a lifetime was almost in the
bag: Soros and Napoleon could salivate over Russia's limitless romance,
but Anderson was about to show that a single hedge fund in New York

could buy the treasure of the country. Then a message reached Manhattan from Moscow. There would have to be a commission.

Anderson looked at the request and responded carefully. Tiger had no problem paying commissions on its trades, he said; after all, it paid them all the time to stockbrokers. But Tiger could not agree to the details of the Russian proposal. The Russians wanted two contracts for the metal sale: an official one that made no mention of the commission and a private one that laid down how it should be paid into a bank in Cyprus. Russia's parliament and people would only see the official version, so no questions would be asked about who kept the commission.

Anderson said he had a problem with that. "It's got to be one contract," he insisted.

For a while there was silence from Moscow. Then a response came back: Okay, understood—what about paying the commission into a bank in Gibraltar?

Anderson had to explain himself again. It didn't matter if the payment was to Cyprus, Gibraltar, or some other haven. But it had to be disclosed, and there had to be one contract. Tiger's lawyers and Russia's lawyers had to be looking at the same piece of paper, and it would have to stand up to public scrutiny, both in the West and in Russia.

The messages bounced back and forth between New York and Moscow until eventually it became clear that agreement was impossible. For the Russians, there was no earthly reason to sell without a private commission. For Anderson, there was no way to salvage the deal of the decade.[49]

BY THE TIME THE PALLADIUM NEGOTIATIONS BROKE down in late July, Russia's crisis was taking on a new intensity. A large IMF loan had been announced on July 13, but it had calmed the markets only briefly. The week after the IMF announcement, a second Goldman Sachs–backed bond issue, intended to raise a whopping $6.4 billion, only attracted bids for $4.4 billion. The Russian bond market tumbled, quickly followed by the stock market: Suddenly even risk-seeking hedge funds were leery of financing Russia. With their options running out, the Russians reopened secret talks with their old friend George Soros.

Yeltsin's economic team made Soros a proposal. The state would auction off another 25 percent of Svyazinvest; meanwhile, the winners of the first auction would provide an immediate bridge loan to the government, just as Soros had done a year earlier. But this time Soros was not ready to play ball: In the summer of 1997, he had furnished Russia with a few hundred million dollars, but now it would take billions to tide the country through its crisis. On Friday, August 7, Soros telephoned Anatoly Chubais and Yegor Gaidar, Yeltsin's top economic officials, and told them to get real. Foreign investors and Russian investors were tired of buying Russian debt, and it would be impossible to roll over the vast quantities of GKOs as they matured. To make it through this crunch, Russia needed billions, not millions.

After listening to Soros, Gaidar gave his estimate of Russia's funding need: He put it at $7 billion. Soros countered that Gaidar was still low-balling the challenge: He reckoned $10 billion was needed. The Svyazinvest consortium could kick in $500 million, Soros suggested. The rest would have to come from Western banks and governments.[50]

Soros's next call was to David Lipton, the top international man at the U.S. Treasury. Soros urged the Treasury to contribute to a bridge loan, using the same facility that it had used in its Mexico bailout three years previously. Lipton retorted that there was no support in Congress for this sort of rescue: The Russians had already been given their last chance in the form of the July IMF package. On Monday, August 10, Soros spoke briefly with Lipton again. He called Lawrence Summers, the number two at Treasury, and on Friday he spoke with Treasury secretary Robert Rubin. To galvanize the Treasury team, Soros urged Senator Mitch McConnell, an influential Republican, to call Rubin and offer his party's support for a last-ditch attempt to save Russia. In this flurry of telephone diplomacy, Soros was going beyond the role he had played in South Korea, when he had behaved like the International Monetary Fund, laying out the economic policies that would attract private capital. Now he aspired to broker a full-blown government rescue.

Not for the first time, Soros's dual personas caused trouble. His government interlocutors did not know how to interpret his views: Was Soros saying what would be good for the world, or was he saying what would be good for his portfolio? Sensing that his private discussions were not gaining traction, Soros went public with his Russia plan by publishing a long letter in the *Financial Times* on August 13; now it was investors' turn to feel uncertain. Soros proposed that, as part of a package that would include new Western financing, the Russians should reduce the burden of the ruble-denominated GKOs by devaluing the currency by 15 percent to 25 percent. It was a sensible policy prescription, but to everyone in the markets it read as a public announcement that Soros was shorting the ruble. On the reasonable assumption that Soros was getting ready to repeat the sterling trade of 1992, investors ran for the exit; the day after Soros's letter appeared, the yield on GKOs hit 165 percent. On Monday, August 17, facing an inexorable assault from the markets, Russia devalued the ruble and defaulted on its debts to foreigners.[51]

The truth, of course, was that Soros had not shorted the ruble. He had seen the inevitability of devaluation and even hastened the moment; but instead of selling the life out of the currency in the knowledge that politicians would do nothing to save it, he had attempted to make politicians behave differently. Indeed, far from being short the ruble, the Soros funds were vastly long—on top of the $1 billion exposure to Svyazinvest, they owned all kinds of Russian bonds and equities.[52] As a result of the default and devaluation, Quantum and its sister funds lost 15 percent of their capital, or between $1 billion and $2 billion.[53]

For Stan Druckenmiller, whose lifework was the performance of the Quantum Funds, it was a bitter moment. For anyone who knew the size and manner of the loss, it made nonsense of the idea that Soros was a superpredator. But Soros himself processed the failure on an entirely different level. Looking back on the experience, he wrote, "I have no regrets with regard to my attempts to help Russia move toward an open society: They did not succeed but at least I tried."[54]

Soros had come down from Mount Olympus like a messiah to save sinners. He had suffered crucifixion.

10

THE ENEMY IS US

For years the Bank of China building in Hong Kong was heavy and squat: It projected the granite solidity of the old-fashioned finance. Then the bank bought itself a face-lift from the Chinese-American wizard I. M. Pei, and in 1990 it emerged as a soaring, daring, giddy thing: a slim, stiletto-heeled goddess on the catwalk of Hong Kong's financial district. The architect explained that his triangular towers were intended to evoke bamboo, their sectioned shafts of aluminum and glass tapering as they rose into the sunlight. But the comparison could be pushed further than Pei knew. Through the miracles of modern leverage, financial institutions were indeed growing as quickly as bamboo, sucking money out of the world's burgeoning bond markets and pumping it back in again. But thanks to that same leverage, the new financial palaces were thin sided and hollow. An unexpected sideways blow could topple them.

For anyone who knew the two Bank of China buildings, the celebration that took place in September 1997 was ironically located. A confident young hedge fund called Long-Term Capital Management—the epitome of the new financial engineering that Pei's structure evoked—picked the art gallery at the squat old premises to throw a party. To the south and the west lay Indonesia and Thailand, which were struggling with currency crises; ensconced in a hotel suite not far away, Malaysia's prime minister was waging his campaign against speculators. But Long-Term Capital seemed to float above the region's storm. Its small team of economists had earned a stunning $2.1 billion in profits the previous year; and its magic formula appeared to work irrespective of the turmoil roiling Asia.[1] The fund's prestige and prominence were reflected in the party's guest list, which included an A team of private-sector bosses and financial officials who were in town for the IMF/World Bank annual meetings. After the champagne had stopped flowing, the economists returned to their hotel to find a fax of the front page of that morning's *Wall Street Journal*. There, above the fold, the *Journal* reported their decision to return two fifths of their fund's capital, $2.7 billion, to outside investors. In the new world of soaring leverage, Long-Term Capital had no need for so much client cash. By boosting its borrowing, it could maintain its towering portfolio on a thinner foundation. It could be ambitious and slender, like an I. M. Pei creation.[2]

Long-Term Capital Management's founder, John Meriwether, had been one of the first executives on Wall Street to see the potential in financial engineering. As a rising star at Salomon Brothers in the mid-1980s, he had set out to transform the small trading group he managed into "a quasi-university environment."[3] Meriwether's plan was to hire young stars from PhD programs and encourage them to stay in touch with cutting-edge research; they would visit finance faculties and go out on the academic conference circuit. He recruited Eric Rosenfeld, a Harvard Business School professor, then scooped up Larry Hilibrand, who had not one but two degrees from the Massachusetts Institute of Technology. By 1990 Meriwether's team included Robert Merton and Myron Scholes, who would later win the Nobel Prize for their pioneering work on options pricing.

In the mid-1980s, most Salomon partners had not gone to college, much less a PhD program.[4] The personification of the firm's trading culture was Craig Coats Jr., a tall, handsome, charismatic stud believed by many to be the model for the hero in Tom Wolfe's *The Bonfire of the Vanities*. Coats ran Salomon's government-bond trading the old-fashioned way: While Meriwether's professors debated whether the relationship between two bonds was out of its normal range, or whether the volatility of a bond price was likely to decelerate, Coats's main tool was a firm belief in his own instincts. But remarkably quickly, the superiority of Meriwether's professors became obvious. By the end of the 1980s, the small quasi faculty accounted for 90 percent of the profits at Salomon. Coats left Salomon Brothers after a big trading loss; Meriwether, for his part, was elevated to the position of vice chairman. Quantitative precision had triumphed. It was the end of anti-intellectualism on Wall Street.[5]

There was a problem with this victory, however. If Meriwether's hundred-strong department could generate tens of millions of dollars, what was the purpose of Salomon's six thousand other employees? Meriwether's lieutenants complained that the fruits of their brilliance were being spread to undeserving corners of the firm. Larry Hilibrand, the double-MIT lieutenant, campaigned to shutter the fancy internal catering service that Salomon maintained for the benefit of its investment bankers, even suggesting that the investment banking division should be closed entirely. Eventually this push bore fruit in a secret deal: To keep the rocket scientists happy, Salomon's overlords granted them a fixed 15 percent of their group's profits. By securing a guaranteed performance fee, Meriwether had created a hedge fund within a bank. Creating a hedge fund instead of a bank was merely a step away for him.

The event that forced that extra step was not of his own choosing. In 1991, the Treasury bond scandal that embarrassed Michael Steinhardt and Bruce Kovner triggered a full-blown crisis for Salomon Brothers. The firm's government-bond trader, Paul Mozer, had cheated repeatedly in the auctions; Meriwether, who was responsible for overseeing Mozer, resigned from the firm and paid a $50,000 fine imposed by the Securities and Exchange Commission.[6] After scouting about for opportunities, Meriwether resolved to set up on his own. He would reassemble his team of rocket scientists and would do it without the unnecessary trappings of a big bank: Functions like marketing, clearing, settling, and operations would be outsourced, so that there would be no need to spread the professors' trading profits through undeserving back-office departments. The way Meriwether saw it, he was inventing a new kind of financial institution for a new age. A world in which a small brotherhood of academics could earn more than a large bank required a fresh kind of setup. It required "Salomon without the bullshit."[7]

IN FEBRUARY 1994, MERIWETHER LAUNCHED LONG-TERM Capital Management. He brought along Eric Rosenfeld, Larry Hilibrand, Robert Merton, and Myron Scholes; in all, eight members of his Salomon brain trust joined in setting up the company. The professors leased space at 600 Steamboat Road in Greenwich, Connecticut, in the same four-story building overlooking the Long Island Sound to which Paul Tudor Jones had moved recently. Instead of New York suits and ties, they showed up for work in golf shirts and chinos. Sometimes in the lunch hour, bluefish could be spotted jumping out of the sound, and a team of eager quants would arm themselves with fishing rods and race out in hot pursuit of them.

Stripped down to its essentials, Long-Term Capital's approach to the bond market recalled A. W. Jones's innovation.[8] Just as a Jones manager might buy Ford shares and short Chrysler, believing Ford's management to be superior, so Meriwether's team would buy one bond and short a similar one, believing the first bond's cash flow to be more promising. The hedging out of market risk worked better with bonds than with stocks. A Jones manager—or for that matter, a long/short stock picker at Julian Robertson's Tiger—might think Ford's managers were better than Chrysler's, but it was only an opinion. It involved judging the characters of the managers, eying the designs of their new cars, collecting the gossip on the morale of their sales teams. But bond investing was a different game: There was just a loan, an interest rate, and a promise to repay on a date certain. A bond analyst could find you two securities that were almost indistinguishable: The issuer was the same, the principal would be repaid in the same year, the legal documents describing the investor's rights were word-for-word identical. If one of these bonds was trading for less than the other, you could buy the cheap one and short its overpriced pair. This was arbitrage, not simple investing, and it promised almost certain profits.

The quintessential LTCM trade started with the fact that newly issued Treasury bonds, known as "on-the-run" Treasuries, were bought and sold with great frequency. Traders who valued this liquidity were willing to pay a premium over marginally older, less frequently traded "off-the-run" Treasuries. But during the bond's lifetime, the premium disappeared; the payout on a 30-year bond and a 29½-year bond were bound to come together by the time they hit their repayment dates. Meriwether's team could simply sell the overpriced new bonds; buy the cheaper, older ones; and then wait patiently for the inevitable convergence. In ordinary times, admittedly, the profits from this strategy were barely enough to offset transaction costs. But when the market was panicky, the liquidity pre-mium could balloon: Skittish traders wanted to own bonds they could sell in a hurry, and they were prepared to pay for the privilege. Meriwether's lieutenants waited for these moments of panic, then put on the convergence trade. Larry Hilibrand, the LTCM partner who had campaigned against Salomon's fancy catering unit, compared markets to Slinkies. They would always spring back. You just had to wait until the panic subsided.

Another classic Meriwether trade involved the Italian bond market.[9] Italy's cumbersome tax rules deterred foreigners from investing in the country's bond market; as a result, demand was suppressed and the bonds were a bargain. A foreigner who figured out how to get around the tax obstacle could buy the bonds and collect a yield of, say, 10 percent. Then he could hedge the position by borrowing lire in the international money market at perhaps 9 percent, pocketing the 1-percentage-point difference. And the solution to the tax problem was hiding in plain sight. The trick was to go into partnership with a bank that was unencumbered by the tax issue because it was registered in Italy.[10] Starting when they were still at Salomon Brothers and continuing into their first years at LTCM, Meri-wether's team seized on the Italian trade with an enthusiasm unrivaled on Wall Street. During LTCM's first two years of trading, Italy contributed around $600 million of the firm's $1.6 billion profits.[11]

LTCM was not the only player to crowd into Italy. Other banks and hedge funds followed; meanwhile, the Italian government got rid of the tax obstacle. But as the original trade ceased to be profitable, LTCM had fun in other corners of the Italian market. Italy's retail investors were plunking their savings in a particular type of government bond that corner-shop banks sold to them, and because of this captive group of purchasers, the bond in question was clearly overvalued. Long-Term sold the bond short, then used the proceeds from those sales to buy lire bonds with higher interest rates, pocketing the spread as usual.[12] Moreover, Italian savers were gradually waking up to the attractions of mutual funds and were switching their money away from direct bond purchases. As a result, demand for the bonds that LTCM had shorted went down, adding to LTCM's profits.

Meriwether and his partners scoured the world for this sort of opportunity. They spotted probable convergences in all kinds of settings: between different bonds of the same maturity, between a bond and the futures contract that was based on it, between Treasury and mortgage-backed bonds or between bonds in different currencies.[13] The common theme was that market anomalies occur when the behavior of investors is distorted—whether by tax rules, government regulation, or the idiosyncratic needs of large financial institutions. French insurance companies, for example, needed to buy French government bonds of particular maturities—not because they thought those maturities represented a bargain, but because they needed assets that matched the maturities of their promises to insurance customers. Similarly, in October 1996 a Federal Reserve ruling induced U.S. banks to issue lots of bonds and swap the payments on them into a floating rate; this flood of issuance depressed the fixed rate available in the swaps market. In each of these cases, LTCM took the other side—effectively trading against people who were buying or selling because institutional requirements compelled them to do so. By being the flexible player with the freedom to mirror the quirks of the inflexible ones, Long-Term provided liquidity to the markets. French insurers and American banks fulfilled their institutional imperative at a better price than they would otherwise have done. Meanwhile LTCM itself reaped fabulous profits.

Long-Term Capital Management's success showed how lucrative this game was. Even after subtracting its 2 percent management fee and its hefty 25 percent performance fee, LTCM returned 19.9 percent in its ten months of trading in 1994, followed by 42.8 percent in 1995 and 40.8 percent the year after. It generated these returns, moreover, without riding the markets: The gains from its convergence trades were not correlated with any stock or bond index. Small wonder that LTCM had no difficulty raising capital. To its office in Greenwich it added bureaus in London and Tokyo; having launched with a slim staff of 41 people, Long-Term employed 165 by the time of the Bank of China party in the fall of 1997.[14] Eric Rosenfeld, whom Meriwether had plucked from Harvard just a decade earlier, built a ten-thousand-bottle wine cellar, stocked directly from France. An LTCM partner named Greg Hawkins kept thoroughbred horses.[15] Meriwether himself bought Waterville, an enchanting golf course in County Kerry, Ireland, to which he invited other Wall Street heavyweights to cement his business relationships. "Everybody was enamored with their intellect," a Merrill Lynch salesman remembered. "It was like Kennedy's inner circle—Camelot! They have the best and the brightest."[16]

Of course, within a year of the Bank of China party, LTCM had blown up. Not for the first time, the newfangled finance turned out to be fragile, with large and unappreciated risks for the entire world economy.

IN HIS BEST-SELLING ACCOUNT OF LONG-TERM CAPITAL Management's brief life, Roger Lowenstein portrays the fund's demise as a punishment for hubris. This is ultimately correct, but it is not as though the firm was crass about its risk taking. Meriwether and his partners were not gambling irresponsibly with OPM—Wall Street's contemptuous acronym for "other people's money." To the contrary, most of the partners invested nearly all their earnings in the business, year after year; and by ejecting $2.7 billion of outsiders' capital in the fall of 1997, they ensured that nearly a third of the remaining fund was their own savings. Unlike many financiers who reduce their institutions to ruin, Long-Term Capital's partners had every incentive to be prudent.

It is true that LTCM operated with extremely high leverage. Indeed, leverage was the very essence of the firm: The pricing anomalies it found were too small to be worth much without the multiplier of borrowed money. In 1995, for example, Long-Term's return on assets, at 2.45 percent, was modest; but leverage transformed an indifferent return on assets into a spectacular return on capital—2.45 percent became 42.8 percent. The leverage was safe, Meriwether reasoned, because LTCM hedged out nearly all the risks in its trades. Soon after it opened, for example, the firm created a $2 billion position in on-the-run and off-the-run Treasuries. The exposure might have sounded daunting for a $1 billion fund, but Meriwether's team calculated that betting on convergence was one twenty-fifth as risky as owning either bond on its own. The firm's $2 billion position was the equivalent of an $80 million position for an unhedged investor.

LTCM was one of the first hedge funds to quantify its risk mathematically.[17] Macro traders like Druckenmiller kept their exposures in their head; they had a feel for how much a market might swing and how much they could lose on any major position. Long-Term used a technique developed in the 1980s known as "value at risk," which was essentially a formalization of the macro traders' mental computations. LTCM worked out the volatility of each position, then translated that finding into a dollar amount that could be lost in normal circumstances. For example, Long-Term might buy one Italian bond and short another one, betting that the gap between them would converge; by studying the history of this trade, it might discover that, on ninety-nine days out of a hundred, the worst that was likely to happen was that the gap would widen by ten basis points.[18] If the trade was sized such that a one-basis-point widening cost LTCM $10 million, the fund's loss from a ten-basis-point move would be $100 million.

Meriwether and his partners performed value-at-risk calculations for every position in their fund, then combined each potential loss into a total for the whole portfolio. The trick was to estimate the correlations among the various trades. For example, two positions that were perfectly correlated would require a straightforward addition of exposures—if you risked $100 million in California state bonds and $100 million in New York state bonds and the two moved in lockstep, your total risk came to $200 million. But if two positions were uncorrelated, a fall in one would sometimes be cushioned by a rise in the other, and the combined risk would be smaller. For instance, if you risked $100 million on a convergence bet involving mortgage prepayment rates and another $100 million on something completely unrelated, such as Italian retail bonds, your total exposure would come to $100 million multiplied by the square root of the number of positions—in this case, $141 million. The more you introduced new uncorrelated trades to the portfolio, the more risk could be dampened. The third uncorrelated position would add only $32 million of risk to the portfolio, even if, taken by itself, it threatened a loss of $100 million.[19] The fifth uncorrelated position would add $24 million of risk; the tenth would add only $16 million; and so on. Through the magic of diversification, risk could almost disappear. Trades that seemed crazy to others on a risk/return basis could appear highly profitable to Meriwether and his partners.

Ten years later, when the credit bubble imploded in 2007–2009, value-at-risk calculations fell out of favor. Warren Buffett admonished fellow financiers to "beware of geeks bearing formulas." Nevertheless, Meriwether's metric represented an advance on the traditional leverage ratio as a way of gauging risk. The traditional ratio failed to account for swaps and options, even though these could be a huge source of risk to a portfolio. It failed to distinguish between hedged bets and unhedged ones, so that an outright bet on Italian bonds would be treated as no more risky than a long/short bet on two similar bonds' convergence. Most fundamentally, the traditional leverage ratio compared capital to assets, whereas value at-risk compared capital to potential losses. There was no doubt that LTCM had chosen the more relevant yardstick: The whole point of capital was to serve as a cushion against losses, so it was the size of potential losses that determined whether a fund's capital was adequate.[20] To exaggerate only slightly, the traditional approach of comparing capital to assets was like measuring the size of the U.S. armed forces relative to the number of foreigners on the planet. It was inconceivable that every foreigner would attack the United States at once, just as there seemed to be virtually no prospect of all LTCM's assets losing value simultaneously.

There were obvious objections to value-at-risk calculations, but LTCM's brain trust was quite aware of most of them. For example, it knew full well that the models forecast the biggest loss that could happen on ninety-nine out of a hundred days; by definition, some days would be worse than that. But a basic insight in financial economics is that markets tend to self-correct, so LTCM was confident that a period of unusual losses would be followed by compensating gains in the portfolio. If a normal price relationship broke down, hitting LTCM with a big loss, other arbitrageurs would see a profitable opportunity to invest; their buying would drive prices back into line, and LTCM's portfolio would bounce back again. In years to come, critics ridiculed value-at-risk calculations for ignoring the worst day in a hundred, likening them to car air bags that are designed to work all the time except during a collision. But because of the corrective power of arbitrage, ignoring the worst day in a hundred was less reckless than it appeared to be. A bad day for Long-Term would be followed by a better one. The market always tended to spring back. This was the Slinky effect to which Larry Hilibrand alluded.

Of course, the tendency to self-correct was only a tendency. An extreme event could force prices out of their habitual patterns, for a long time or even permanently. LTCM's models were unlikely to predict such shocks: Like all models, they were based on historical data so could not be expected to anticipate extraordinary events that would by definition be unprecedented. But LTCM's partners understood this Achilles' heel too. They sought to compensate for the imagination deficit in their models, brainstorming about potential surprises that could throw off their calculations. For example, they could see that their bond trades would go haywire if the planned European Monetary Union was derailed, and while derailment seemed highly improbable, LTCM was not going to rule out the possibility. So the partners repeatedly stress-tested their portfolio to see how it would perform if monetary union blew up. If they found that the resulting losses could threaten the survival of the fund, they cut back their positions.

LTCM also took pains to consider a related risk that was much discussed in later years—the risk to the fund's liquidity rather than its solvency. The fund's trades often involved buying an illiquid instrument and hedging it with a more liquid one. For example, off-the-run Treasury bonds were cheap precisely because they were less liquid than on-the-run ones. By buying illiquid securities in numerous markets, Long-Term was exposing itself to a particular risk: In a panic, the liquidity premium would rise everywhere, and apparently uncorrelated bets would simultaneously lose money. At precisely such a moment, brokers might withdraw credit from LTCM, forcing the fund to liquidate its positions in the worst possible circumstances. Investors might withdraw capital too, compelling further fire sales. The corrective power of arbitrage might turn out to be the equivalent of an ambulance that is located too far away. Even if markets swung back to equilibrium in the end, LTCM might not survive to reap the benefits.

Meriwether and his partners took this liquidity risk seriously. Their fund was called Long-Term Capital Management for a good reason: It was only over the long term that markets could be relied upon to spring back to their efficient level. It followed that LTCM needed a capital structure that would protect it from the calamity of fire sales. So rather than following the usual practice among hedge funds and borrowing short-term money from brokers, Meriwether made at least some effort to secure longer-term loans and special lines of credit that he could call on in a crisis.[21] Driven by the same logic, Long-Term broke with the usual hedge-fund practice of allowing investors to withdraw capital on a monthly or quarterly basis. Instead, it insisted on a three-year commitment, later shifting to a policy of allowing investors to withdraw up to one third of their stake annually.[22]

In the wake of LTCM's failure, it was easy to forget these multiple precautions. Meriwether and his partners came to be seen as the victims of a reckless faith in their models—which fueled the belief that some modest addition of caution could prevent similar disasters. But the truth was both more subtle and harder to live with. LTCM's risk management was more nuanced and sophisticated than critics imagined, and the lessons drawn from its failure included several prescriptions that LTCM itself had implemented. In the course of the ensuing decade, there were calls for value-at-risk calculations to be supplemented with stress tests; LTCM had done that. There were calls for financial institutions to pay attention to liquidity risks; LTCM had done that. And yet LTCM failed anyway, not because its approach to calculating risk was simplistic but because getting the calculations right is extraordinarily difficult. To stress-test your portfolio, you have to conceive of all the inconceivable shocks that could occur; to compute your fund's value-at-risk and liquidity risk, you have to estimate the correlations among your various positions and guess how these could change in extreme circumstances. The real lesson of LTCM's failure was not that its approach to risk was too simple. It was that all attempts to be precise about risk are unavoidably brittle.

SOON AFTER THE BANK OF CHINA PARTY, IN OCTOBER 1997, Merton and Scholes received the news that they had won the Nobel Prize for economics. The award was greeted as a vindication of the new finance: The inventors of the option-pricing model were being thanked for laying down a cornerstone of modern markets. By creating a formula to price risk, the winners had allowed it to be sliced, bundled, and traded in a thousand ways. The fear of financial losses, which for centuries had acted as a brake on human endeavor, had been tamed by an equation. The Merton-Scholes hedge fund, Long-Term Capital Management, was celebrated as a stunning fulfillment of the professors' vision. By calculating the risk of losses, Long-Term could hold the capital it needed and no more, turning minuscule price anomalies into fabulous profits.

Yet as the scholars savored their glory, Long-Term reached a fateful crossroads. Back in the 1980s, Meriwether and his professors had been the upstarts on Wall Street; one decade on, nearly all investment banks had fixed-income arbitrage desks that competed with them directly.[23] In the first half of 1997, LTCM's profits had started to slow down, and the partners began to do some soul-searching. One response to shrunken opportunity was to shrink the fund, returning money to investors. But LTCM was not ready to shrink to the point of giving up. To keep the money machine going, Meriwether and his team began to venture into equities.

Though primarily a bond fund, LTCM had dabbled in equities before 1997, and in principle the firm could make a case that its skills matched the challenge. The fund was not going to pick stocks or judge companies: That was for Julian Robertson and his Tigers. But it was going to find trades with the mathematical clarity of bonds—trades involving two almost identical securities that were valued differently or trades in which the normal relationship among various prices had broken down, presumably temporarily. The simplest examples involved stocks that traded in two markets at once. Long-Term's favorite was Royal Dutch/Shell, which was owned by two listed companies, Royal Dutch Petroleum of the Netherlands and Shell Transport of Britain. The Dutch shares and the British shares represented claims on the same flow of profits, but the British ones traded at a discount to the Dutch ones. Like the gap between on-the-run and off-the-run bond prices, this gap seemed irrational. By buying the cheap British shares and shorting the expensive Dutch ones, Long-Term could collect more dividends than it paid out as a result of being short; and because it was hedged, it could be indifferent as to whether Royal Dutch/Shell's share price rose or plummeted. Meriwether and his partners seized upon this opportunity and played it in vast size. To many traders on Wall Street, the professors in Greenwich were starting to overreach themselves.[24]

LTCM's biggest equity venture was a bet on markets' steadiness—a strategy that caused Morgan Stanley to dub the firm "the central bank of volatility."[25] It was typical of Meriwether's faculty: Rather than take a view on which way a market might move, the professors bet on *how far* it would move, never mind the direction. In the fall of 1997, LTCM noticed that jittery investors were paying a fat premium to insure themselves against sharp moves in stocks: Some were buying call options, thinking that the market might spike up; others were buying put options, seeking to offset the risk of an abrupt crash in prices. As a result, five-year options on the S&P 500 were selling at a price that implied the index would fluctuate by 19 percent per year, way higher than the 10 percent to 13 percent that had been typical in the 1990s. True to their usual pattern, Meriwether and his partners saw a chance to act as the balancers of irrational panic. They sold call options and put options, collecting the premiums in the belief that they would not have to pay out to buyers. So long as volatility remained within its usual range, the bet could not go against them.

Even as they stacked up these wagers, the partners remained focused on their prudential guidelines. Their value-at-risk calculations told them that the most they were likely to lose on ninety-nine out of a hundred trading days was $116 million and the most they could lose over the span of twenty-one trading days was $532 million. The odds of losing everything were vanishingly low; the fund had only lost 2.9 percent in its worst-ever month, and the calculations indicated it would take a ten-sigma event, an event that occurs one in every 10^{24} times, to put them out of business. To be sure, these projections were based on historical prices, and history could be a false friend. But at the twice-weekly risk meetings in Greenwich, the partners imagined all the shocks that could ambush them. They gamed out the consequences of a crash on Wall Street or a Japanese earthquake. "We thought we were being conservative," Rosenfeld said later.[26]

The first sign that they were not conservative enough came in May 1998. The IMF's bailout of Indonesia faltered and the Suharto regime collapsed. The troubles in East Asia spilled into Japan, which suffered a recession—two consecutive quarters of declining output—for the first time since 1974. Russia's authorities were forced to triple interest rates to halt an exodus of capital, and the volatility of equity indices all over the world shot upward. Investors reacted to these ructions as they generally do. They piled into the safest investment they could find, U.S. government bonds, sending the yield on thirty-year Treasuries down to its lowest point since they were first issued in 1977. In other words, they panicked.

None of this was good for LTCM. If the fund's trades had one premise in common, it was that cool heads would prevail: Irrational panic would be corrected by the rational calm of arbitrage. Before the May–June turmoil, LTCM had been short Treasuries and long the "swap rate" paid to money-market investors, believing that the abnormally wide gap between risk-free Treasuries and riskier market instruments reflected temporary risk aversion. But the world's intensifying economic crisis created risk aversion of an extreme form, causing the spread between Treasuries and riskier instruments to widen and wounding LTCM severely. Equally, LTCM had been betting against equity volatility so aggressively that a single-percentage-point rise cost it $40 million, and now the expected volatility of the S&P 500 index shot up from 19 percent on May 1 to 26 percent by mid-June. As all these bets went wrong, the fund lost 6 percent in May and another 10 percent in June, way more than its value-at-risk calculations had anticipated.[27] Long-Term's partners canceled their vacations and debated whether something fundamental had gone wrong. But then the fund recovered in July. The partners trimmed their positions and relaxed, dismissing the spring shock as a freak misfortune.[28]

ON MONDAY, AUGUST 17, RUSSIA STUNNED THE WORLD BY defaulting on its debt payments to foreigners. Unlike Soros and Druckenmiller, LTCM had little direct exposure to Russia, but it soon became clear that the indirect effects would be appalling. Russia's default led to the bankruptcy of an aptly named hedge fund, High-Risk Opportunities, which in turn threatened a handful of financial firms to which High-Risk owed money. By Friday, August 21, there were rumors that Lehman Brothers might go under, and the panic set off another round of flight to quality. Even more viciously than in May and June, safe government securities rose in value and everything remotely risky fell; and Long-Term's bets on a calm world blew up disastrously. Long-Term had been betting that U.S. Treasury rates and swap rates would converge; but the gap, which typically moved less than a basis point each day, widened by a stunning eight basis points.[29] Long-Term had a similar bet in Britain; again, the spread between British government bonds and market rates widened sharply. In emerging markets, LTCM had constructed essentially the same trade: It shorted relatively stable bonds and owned risky ones, and again it lost badly. By the end of that Friday, Long-Term had lost a total of $550 million, 15 percent of its capital.[30]

It was the middle of August, and most of Long-Term's senior partners were enjoying the vacation they had deferred earlier in the summer. John Meriwether was in China. Eric Rosenfeld was in Idaho. LTCM's counsel, Jim Rickards, was with his family in North Carolina. The skeleton crew in Greenwich stared at the trading screens in wonder. It was not just money that was going up in smoke. Long-Term's confident assumptions were burning too; it was a bonfire of the fund's own vanities. LTCM had thought its portfolio was safe because relationships in credit markets were generally stable; now they were stormy. LTCM had thought its portfolio was safe because the correlation between its different strategies was low; with panic driving every market the same way, its positions fell in lockstep. LTCM had thought its portfolio was safe because its value-at-risk estimates suggested it could lose no more than $116 million in a trading day. But now its estimate was off by more than $400 million. Most fundamentally, LTCM had believed in the corrective power of arbitrage. Markets could be irrational, but a run of bad returns practically ensured that profit-seeking traders would dive in and order would be reestablished. As they watched their portfolio burning, the traders waited in vain for the market to spring back. The Slinky effect had been suspended.

At midday on the East Coast, Eric Rosenfeld called in from a golf course in Idaho. His 9:00 A.M. tee time had been a little delayed, and he just wanted to be sure that everything was fine in Greenwich. When he heard what was happening, he knew his vacation was over, and pretty soon all the partners were hurrying back home.[31] Before Meriwether boarded his flight home from China, he took care to call Jon Corzine, the boss of Goldman Sachs, warning him that LTCM had suffered a bad day but promising that there was no cause to worry.

That Sunday evening, the partners discussed how they could stem the losses. They would have to liquidate some positions, but selling on the open market would not be easy in a panic. Rosenfeld phoned Warren Buffett in Omaha to see if he would buy Long-Term's $5 billion portfolio of bets on stocks of companies involved in mergers. Buffett refused graciously. The next morning Meriwether breakfasted with Soros and Druckenmiller at Soros's Fifth Avenue apartment: Perhaps Quantum might like to invest in LTCM on special concessionary terms, since Long-Term had hit a rocky patch just lately? Meriwether explained that his positions were a bargain for anyone with the financial muscle to hold on through the turmoil, and Soros and Druckenmiller seemed intrigued.[32] But the most that Meriwether could extract from the breakfast was a conditional offer. Soros would put up $500 million at the end of August if Meriwether was able to raise another $500 million from other investors.

Armed with Soros's pledge, Meriwether scrambled to find the other

$500 million. He explored the possibility of a deal with his old colleagues at Salomon Brothers. He dispatched Larry Hilibrand to Omaha to make Buffett a new and better offer. He made overtures to Prince Alwaleed of Saudi Arabia and to the computer magnate Michael Dell. He called up Herb Allison, the boss of Merrill Lynch, but even the relationship forged on the golf links in Ireland was not enough to save him. "John, I'm not sure it's in your interest to raise money," Allison counseled. "It might look like you're having a problem."[33] The advice was infuriating but true.[34] While rebuffing Hilibrand, Buffett was reacting to Long-Term's evident distress by ordering his lieutenants to monitor Berkshire Hathaway's exposure to hedge funds. The bosses at Salomon Brothers were issuing similar edicts, demanding that its brokerage unit cease extending loans to almost all the hedge funds that it dealt with.[35] The more Long-Term scrambled to raise money, the more the panic spread—and the more Long-Term's bets on a calm world declined in value. The partners were running on a moving carpet that was pulling them away from home. Far from boosting the fund's capital, their sales efforts were destroying it.

It was not just that the Slinky effect had been suspended. Arbitrageurs were experiencing a kind of *Pogo* moment: "We have met the enemy and he is us!" said the character in Walt Kelly's comic strip. The Russian blowup, coming on the heels of the East Asian turmoil, had caused all the main arbitrage players to lose money; like LTCM, they were scrambling for fresh capital. In these stressed circumstances, the arbitrageurs lacked the muscle to correct pricing anomalies; indeed, they faced margin calls from their brokers that forced them to dump positions, driving prices away from their efficient equilibrium. The partners' faith in arbitrage, exaggerated at the best of times, was now 180 degrees off target—arbitrage had been replaced by a kind of *reverse* arbitrage. The unwinding of each arbitrage portfolio damaged all the other ones: The cycle was self-reinforcing. Meriwether's own legacy, the Arbitrage Group at Salomon Brothers, had performed so badly earlier in the year that its bosses had resolved to close it down; the selling hammered other arbitrage outfits, LTCM included. Every trade in Long-Term's portfolio went wrong in a correlated way, not necessarily because they were similar in an economic sense but because they were similar in terms of the types of fund that held them. Looking back on LTCM's history, Eric Rosenfeld considers the failure to anticipate this trader-driven correlation to be the fund's central error. If LTCM had foreseen this possibility, its risk calculations would have come out differently. No longer would diversification have appeared to magic risk away. Every LTCM trade would have been sized more cautiously.[36]

Meanwhile, Long-Term was discovering another risk that it had underestimated. It had not fathomed that its own success could create a special vulnerability. Even though Long-Term shrouded itself in secrecy, routing its trades through multiple brokers so that none of them could understand its bets, an army of imitators had pieced together much of its strategy. The upshot was that LTCM's large portfolio was mirrored by an even larger superportfolio created by its disciples, meaning that LTCM's trades were monstrously crowded.[37] By the spring of 1998, every bank or hedge fund that might buy LTCM's positions had already followed Meriwether's example and bought them; if a trade went wrong and Meriwether needed to retreat, there would be nobody to sell to. Moreover, the canny players on Wall Street could see what was going on. On the one hand, there was nobody left to buy LTCM's positions, so there was no way they were going up. On the other hand, a shock that forced the arbitrageurs to sell would cause LTCM's portfolio to collapse precipitously. The "central bank of volatility" was indeed like a central bank. Its trading presented predators with a one-way bet, and as soon as the predators woke up to this fact, the game would be over.

There was a painful irony in LTCM's predicament. For the first four years of its short life, it had earned billions by trading against adversaries whose behavior was driven by institutional imperatives as opposed to market judgments. But now, with the arbitrage army suddenly bereft of capital, Long-Term had become the victim of just such an institutional imperative—banks and brokerages were pulling loans, so arbitrageurs had become forced sellers. To a predatory trader, the biggest prize in this environment was to short anything Long-Term might own. Meriwether noticed grimly that the LTCM trades that were unknown to Wall Street bounced back after the post-Russia Friday shock; it was the known trades that kept bleeding money. Spreads between risky bonds and risk-free Treasuries grew wider and wider, and the premium between the shares of Royal Dutch and Shell Transport leaped from 8 percent to 17 percent despite there being no fundamental reason why they should do so. "It ceased to feel like people were liquidating positions similar to ours," one of Meriwether's team recalled. "All of a sudden they were liquidating our positions."[38]

That month, August 1998, turned out to be one of the most brutal in the history of hedge funds. By the time Labor Day arrived, three out of four funds had lost money. Meriwether and his partners lost 44 percent of their capital, or $1.9 billion.[39] They calculated that this loss should have occurred less than once in the lifetime of the universe. But it had happened anyway.

At the end of the month, Meriwether put a call in to Vinny Mattone, an old friend from Bear Stearns.

"Where are you?" Mattone asked brusquely.

"We're down by half," Meriwether replied.

"You're finished," Mattone said matter-of-factly.

"What are you talking about?" Meriwether protested. "We still have two billion. We have half—we have Soros."

"When you're down by half, people figure you can go down all the way," Mattone said. "They're going to push the market against you."[40]

Meriwether called Merrill Lynch, UBS, and Deutsche Bank, seeking a capital infusion. Nobody would cough up $500 million, and the Soros opportunity vanished.

MERIWETHER REPORTED LTCM'S LOSSES IN AN INVES-tor letter on September 2. He reaffirmed his faith in arbitrage, writing optimistically of "this unusually attractive environment." But nobody was fooled. The letter was leaked even before the last copy was faxed out, and the *Wall Street Journal* ran a front-page story the next day detailing Meriwether's losses. Now the whole world knew that Long-Term was on deathwatch, and every player on Wall Street started to trade against it.[41] Most junk bonds rallied in early September, but the particular bonds that

LTCM owned remained dead in the water. Long-Term had a small position in hurricane bonds, securities that permit insurers to sell the risk of a hurricane; the day Meriwether's letter leaked, the bonds plummeted 20 percent, even though the probability and cost of hurricanes was utterly unaltered.[42] In Europe, the gap between government bonds and market interest rates widened in Britain and narrowed in Germany, for no fundamental reason other than that Long-Term was betting that the opposite would happen. "It's not about the market anymore; it's about you," the general counsel, Jim Rickards, told Meriwether. "If you're long, they're short. If you're short, they're long."[43]

On September 13 Meriwether appealed to Jon Corzine of Goldman Sachs. He needed help in raising $2 billion, the amount that Long-Term now needed to stave off bankruptcy. Corzine said yes, but at an extraordinary price. In exchange for $1 billion from Goldman plus a promise to raise an additional billion elsewhere, Goldman demanded half of the LTCM management company, full access to the fund's strategies, and the right to impose limits on the fund's positions; what's more, the deal would only go through if Goldman raised the money and Long-Term passed a detailed inspection of its portfolio. These terms meant that Goldman would win either way. Either it would get half of Long-Term at a bargain price or it would get the right to inspect Long-Term's trading books, paying nothing at all for information that might be worth millions. The predeal due diligence would allow Goldman's experts to see precisely what Long-Term owned and therefore precisely which trades would crater if Long-Term's demise forced it to dump holdings.

Long-Term sensed it might be setting itself up for abuse, but it had no alternative. Jim Rickards tried to get Goldman's inspection team to sign a nondisclosure agreement; he was brusquely informed that Goldman would sign nothing.[44] According to Rickards, Goldman's inspectors plugged an oversized laptop into LTCM's network and downloaded the details on its positions. Goldman denied that this occurred, but pretty soon the bank's proprietary trading desk was selling positions that resembled LTCM's, feeding on Long-Term like a hyena feeding on a trapped but living antelope. The firm made only a qualified effort to defend what it was up to. A Goldman trader in London was quoted as saying: "If you think a gorilla has to sell, then you sure want to sell first. We are very clear on where the line is; that's not illegal." Corzine himself conceded the possibility that Goldman "did things in markets that might have ended up hurting LTCM. We had to protect our own positions. That part I'm not apologetic for."[45] Goldman's defense was that its selling was not influenced by its privileged knowledge of LTCM's books and that a Chinese wall separated the inspectors who visited Long-Term from the traders who managed Goldman's proprietary capital. There was no proof to the contrary, but some Wall Streeters suspected that the Chinese wall might be porous.

Meriwether and his partners decided it was time to inform the Federal Reserve that failure was a possibility. William McDonough, the head of the New York Fed, was on his way out of town. It fell to Peter Fisher, the number two, to wade into the crisis.

On Sunday, September 20, Fisher hitched a ride in an assistant's Jeep from his home in New Jersey to Greenwich. If anyone could figure out a way to fix this mess, Fisher was the man; an expert financial plumber and unflappable nice guy, he had a way of cutting through complexity with simple propositions. But as Fisher listened to the details of Long-Term's positions, no neat solutions came to mind. Because it was so leveraged, LTCM held a sprawling portfolio worth $120 billion, but that was only the beginning of the challenge. What really rattled Fisher was that Long-Term's portfolio included a few extraordinarily concentrated bets: He figured that Long-Term's position in futures on British government bonds, or "gilts," might represent as much as half of the open interest in that market. LTCM owned a similarly outlandish position in Danish mortgages, and its portfolio of equity options was enormous. The issue was not simply that LTCM's collapse would cause a broad fall in markets around the world. Fisher was worried that some particular markets might cease trading altogether.[46]

According to Long-Term's calculations, its seventeen biggest counterparties stood to lose something in the range of $3 billion among them if the fund was wound up immediately. But if LTCM's holdings had to be liquidated in a rush, the losses would be considerably bigger. Moreover,

Fisher presumed that the big players on Wall Street had similar trades on their own books, so if Long-Term was liquidated at speed, the damage would be magnified by a huge hit to the shadow portfolio. A speedy and costly liquidation seemed horribly likely. In past financial collapses involving a failed bank or brokerage, regulators had been able to take charge of the remaining assets and avoid a fire sale. But Long-Term was a different case. Because it was a hedge fund, it had no assets for regulators to seize; rather, its assets were held by its brokers, as collateral against borrowing. If Long-Term defaulted on just one loan agreement, the cross-default clauses in all the other ones would be automatically triggered. Closeout agreements would flutter from a thousand fax machines, and ownership of Long-Term's positions would be transferred to its brokers—which would dump them, rapidly. Sitting among the unmanned workstations in Long-Term's quiet offices, conferring with a colleague from the Treasury, Fisher confronted a problem that had bedeviled the failure of Askin Capital Management and would haunt regulators in the next decade.[47] Firms that entangle themselves with dozens of partners can be too complex and intertwined to be buried easily.

Fisher got back into his assistant's Jeep, still worrying about the consequences of a sudden liquidation. East Asia was in a recession, Russia was fast heading for one, and the resulting market turmoil had already inflicted sharp losses on Wall Street.[48] The prospect of a $3 billion-plus hit to Wall Street's capital would have been unlovely at the best of times, but it was especially nasty given the Street's compromised immune system.[49] There were already rumors that Lehman Brothers was teetering on the brink of bankruptcy; if LTCM's collapse pushed Lehman over, Lehman's collapse would certainly have further consequences. Moreover, the precarious state of Wall Street's balance sheets reduced the odds of the best sort of solution—a private-sector takeover of Long-Term that would save it from chaotic fire sales. Later that evening, Jon Corzine called Fisher to warn him that Goldman's efforts to find a buyer were not making progress. Meanwhile, Long-Term was losing hundreds of millions of dollars per day. It would be lucky to make it to another weekend.

When Fisher arrived at work on Monday, he felt his fears were coming

true even faster than expected. Markets in Asia and Europe were tumbling, and Wall Street looked set to follow. Television commentators were
speculating that the release of President Clinton's videotaped deposition
on the Monica Lewinsky sex scandal, scheduled for later that morning,
was rattling investors—a theory that Fisher found grimly amusing.[50] But
the truth was that the word was out: Each attempt to arrange LTCM's
rescue had spread the knowledge of its trouble to another predator, and
now every bank, brokerage, and hedge fund was feeding on the bloodied torso. Salomon executives reported that Goldman's Tokyo desk was
"banging the shit" out of Long-Term; Goldman executives reported that
Salomon was doing the same thing in Europe. Around midday, attacks
on Long-Term's positions in equity options grew so extreme that options
prices implied a crash every month. By the end of that Monday, LTCM
had lost $550 million, one third of its equity. For the first time its capital
had sunk below $1 billion.[51]

Fisher stayed in touch with the bosses of the big three banks—
Goldman, Merrill Lynch, and J.P. Morgan. He kept hoping for signs of a
private-sector rescue, but it was clear that a lone bank would be unable to
perform that role safely. If a lone purchaser bought LTCM's entire portfolio, it would have to sell some of the holdings; knowing this, others would
continue to sell positions to get in front of the inevitable liquidation. The
solution to this problem was for a consortium to purchase the portfolio:
That way, each would get a piece that was small enough to hold, and the
hyenas would stop feeding. The hitch was that traditional rivalries among
the main banks seemed to preclude such an alliance—unless the Fed bro-
kered one.

Toward the end of Monday, Fisher invited the heads of the big three
banks to breakfast at the Fed the next morning. Once gathered around
the table, all three said they favored joint action; it would protect the markets from chaos and be less painful for everyone. The question was how
to structure a rescue. LTCM's creditors could each buy bits of the portfolio, lifting them out of the fund. Alternatively, a consortium could inject
capital into the fund to stabilize it. After two hours of discussions, Fisher
asked the bankers to go away and develop a rescue plan that all three of

them could back. Then Fisher would convene a larger meeting at the Fed involving a wider group of the fund's creditors.

By the end of the day, the bankers had converged on the view that money would have to be injected into Long-Term. Lifting bits of the portfolio out was not going to work; LTCM's cat's cradle of trades was too complicated. But if new capital was to be injected, who should bear the cost? The price tag was rising: Back in August, when Meriwether had breakfasted with Soros and Druckenmiller, LTCM had needed a lifeline of $1 billion; three weeks later Meriwether had asked Corzine to raise $2 billion; now it would take a $4 billion injection to stabilize the portfolio. Collectively, the bankers knew that coughing up the $4 billion was their least bad option; if they let LTCM go down, its massive portfolio would crash on the markets, costing every major Wall Street player a fortune. But each bank had an incentive to free ride—to let rivals shoulder the cost of the recapitalization.

When Fisher convened LTCM's sixteen main counterparties at the Fed on Tuesday evening, it was impossible to conclude a deal. The big three banks had come up with a blueprint that involved the sixteen top creditors kicking in $250 million each; inevitably, the smaller banks complained that their burden should be lighter. Around 11:00 P.M., with no resolution in sight, Fisher suggested that the group break until ten the next morning.

When the bankers' negotiations resumed, they were no easier than they had been the previous evening. Lehman Brothers pleaded, with some reason, that its balance sheet was so fragile that it could not put up the $250 million. Two French banks refused to share their part of the burden, each offering only $125 million. The biggest shock came from Bear Stearns, Long-Term's lead broker. Despite having earned millions in fees from Long-Term in the good times, Jimmy Cayne, the CEO of Bear, adamantly refused to put up a single dollar. Philip Purcell, the chairman of Morgan Stanley, protested that Bear's free riding was "not *acceptable*," and David Komansky of Merrill Lynch exploded in Cayne's face. The discussions grew so ugly that Peter Fisher began gaming out the consequences of an impasse. "I remember thinking, 'If this thing isn't going to work, I'm going to have to stand on the table and say, 'Don't touch your cell phones. Close the door. We're now going to draft a statement that says there's no deal,'" Fisher recalled later. The lack of a rescue would tip global markets into a free fall. The bankers that had been party to the failure should not be allowed to sell ahead of ordinary investors.[52]

In the end, Fisher did not have to jump on the table. Eleven banks agreed to increase their contributions to $300 million each, while smaller amounts from Lehman and the French brought the total to $3.625 billion. The money was just about sufficient to declare a rescue. Long-Term would be bought and global markets would be saved, though Meriwether and his partners, who had kept so much of their own money in the fund, would see their personal fortunes reduced to almost nothing. "We believed in ourselves," LTCM's counsel, Jim Rickards, said later. "There was no hypocrisy there. I like to say we lost money the old-fashioned way: through honesty and hard work."[53]

AS SOON AS LTCM HAD BEEN SAVED, THE ARGUMENTS began about the meaning of the rescue. During congressional hearings on October 1, members of the House Financial Services Committee vented about the threat to economic stability posed by a handful of secretive traders. Representative Paul Kanjorski, a Democrat of Pennsylvania, suggested that the nation's foreign enemies had no further need to develop weapons of mass destruction: They could harm the United States more easily by partnering with hedge funds. And yet, for all the outrage, the debate following LTCM's failure was mostly just an echo of the one following the bond-market collapse in 1994. The nation's top regulators were forced to recognize that hedge funds do pose risks. But they did little to reduce them.

It is tempting to be harsh about the failure to respond vigorously. Back in 1994, regulators had argued that banks and brokerages were too savvy to allow their hedge-fund clients to take wild bets with their money. Now this argument had been destroyed: Wall Street's finest had exposed themselves to LTCM in such an extreme way that it took the intervention of the Fed to save them. And yet, in the face of this experience, the nation's top regulators continued to resist a crackdown on hedge funds. "Individuals who lend money to others have a very important interest in getting that money back," Alan Greenspan reminded the House hearings, falling back on the idea that private creditors would check hedge fund excesses.[54] It was not until 2009 that Greenspan conceded that risk monitoring by lenders was a flimsy defense against financial excesses. Even then, he presented the concession as though the crisis of 2007–2009 had come out of the blue—as though LTCM had never happened.[55]

Yet before delivering a harsh verdict, it is important to acknowledge that there were good reasons for Greenspan's diffidence. They began with the fact that a clampdown on hedge funds would not have ended dangerous trading, since recklessness was not restricted to the hedge-fund industry. Long-Term had been too leveraged. It had overlooked the danger that its trades could implode spectacularly if other arbitrageurs were forced to dump copycat positions suddenly; it had misjudged the precision with which financial risk can be measured. But there was no reason to suppose that Long-Term's errors were possible only at hedge funds. Indeed, Long-Term's collapse had rattled the authorities because it had coincided with frightening losses at investment banks such as Lehman Brothers. In the wake of LTCM's failure, Greenspan and his fellow regulators could see that the real challenge was the leverage in the financial system writ large. Ironically, this was what Soros had tried to explain to Congress in his testimony four years earlier. Sure enough, the culprits in the crisis of 2007–2009 were leveraged off-balance-sheet vehicles owned by banks (known as conduits or structured investment vehicles, SIVs), leveraged broker-dealers, and a leveraged insurer. Hedge funds were not the villains.

If hedge funds were only part of the challenge, why didn't regulators clamp down on the wider universe of leveraged investors? Again, the answer echoes 1994: The regulators believed they lacked a good way of doing so. They could not simply announce a cap on leverage: The ratio of borrowing to capital was an almost meaningless number, since it failed to capture whether a portfolio was hedged and whether it was exposed to risks via derivatives positions. Regulators could not simply cap hedge funds' value at risk, either: LTCM's collapse had shown that this measure could be misleading. The frustrating truth was that the risks in a portfolio depended on constantly changing conditions: whether other players were mimicking its trades, how liquid markets were, whether banks and brokerages were suffering from compromised immune systems. The Fed's Peter Fisher, who was at the center of the regulatory brainstorming following LTCM, could see the theoretical case for government controls on hedge funds and other leveraged players. But it seemed so unlikely that the government would get the details right that he never pushed for action.

In the next few years, moreover, a parallel experiment in regulation proved Fisher's hesitation well founded. Starting in 1998, a committee of global regulators set out to design a modern set of risk controls, eventually promulgating the so-called Basel II capital requirements. Even though this exercise excluded insurers, broker-dealers, and hedge funds, concentrating exclusively on banks, it still chewed up six years and ended in abject failure. In an attempt to write rules that would capture the subtle risks in banks' portfolios, the Basel II framework deferred to banks' own models of how much risk they were taking: In other words, the regulators' bottom line was that banks should self-regulate. When the crisis hit in 2007, European banks that had adopted Basel II proved hopelessly fragile. If regulators had tried to control the leverage of hedge funds and other shadowbanks, they might have done no better than the Basel standards.

Just as in 1994, regulators' unwillingness to impose direct controls on investment banks and hedge funds forced them back to plan B—express concern about financial risk but reassure the nation that the dangers are tolerable. Greenspan mused publicly about the dangers of financial modeling, which could get too far ahead of human judgment. He urged creditors to remember that hedge funds might perform well in the good times and then suddenly blow up when markets hit unexpected volatility. But while acknowledging the flaws in modern finance, Greenspan emphasized the cost of returning to the premodern age. If banks were required to hold capital worth 40 percent of their assets, as they had done after the Civil War, there would be far fewer episodes of market turbulence, the Fed chairman conceded. But capital would be more costly and living standards would be lower. "We do not have the choice of accepting the benefits of the current system without its costs," he concluded.[56]

In the context of 1998, this was a fair verdict. The benefits of modern finance outweighed its risks, and attempts to reduce risks via government regulation appeared uncertain to succeed—as the Basel experiment suggested. Still, with the unfair luxury of hindsight, the decision to leave risk control to the market was wrong. Banks learned one lesson from the LTCM episode—they reined in the leverage extended to hedge funds, as they should have done in the wake of Askin's failure in 1994. But other lessons went unheeded. LTCM's failure had shown the craziness of insuring the whole world against volatility without holding capital in reserve; but over the next decade, the giant insurer AIG repeated the same error. LTCM's failure had exposed the fallacy that diversification could reduce risk to virtually zero; but over the next decade investors repeated this miscalculation by buying bundles of supposedly diversified mortgage securities. Most fundamental, LTCM's failure had provided an object lesson in the dangers of leveraged finance. And yet the world's response was not only to let leveraged trading continue. It was to tolerate a vast expansion.[57]

11

THE DOT-COM
DOUBLE

In the opening riff of *The Right Stuff*, Tom Wolfe describes the way that military pilots rationalize the deaths of comrades. One airman lets his speed fall before he extends his aircraft's flaps; he crashes and is burned beyond all recognition. His friends gather after dinner and shake their heads and say it is a damned shame, but they would never make that error. A short while later, another aviator corkscrews to his death because his controls malfunction. His friends agree that he was a good man, but sadly inexperienced. Yet a third airman passes out in the cockpit because a hose is disconnected in his oxygen system, and his jet noses over and screams into the Chesapeake Bay. His comrades are incredulous: How could anybody fail to check his hose connections?[1]

The week after LTCM's crash, Julian Robertson delivered his verdict on the dramas of September. In a letter to his investors, he reported that Tiger had lost almost 10 percent in the course of that tumultuous month, but he refused to concede that Long-Term's fate was relevant to Tiger's prospects. Long-Term had caught ablaze because of recklessness and inexperience, whereas Robertson had a proud eighteen-year record. Long-Term's mathematical models were designed to harvest minuscule arbitrage returns with billions in borrowed money, whereas Tiger sought out opportunities that might pay off big time without the need for dangerous leverage. Indeed, just one year earlier, Tiger's investment commandos had been up an eye-popping 70 percent before subtracting fees, reflecting the success of its long/short equity selections and its currency trading in Asia. "Our business is no more like theirs than it is like a high volume, low margin supermarket," Robertson sniffed. "The question might be asked as to what Tiger is going to change in light of the hue and cry over leverage," he wrote. "The answer is nothing."[2]

Within a few days, Robertson had trouble with his own oxygen hoses. Tiger's 10 percent loss in September 1998 was followed by a shocking 17 percent drop in October, and the manner of Tiger's humiliation bore an embarrassing resemblance to the LTCM experience. Just as Long-Term had made reasonable bets in unreasonable sizes, so Robertson's October losses reflected an almost suicidally large wager that the yen would fall against the dollar.

The origin of Tiger's losses went back to the summer, when a confident Julian Robertson had written an upbeat investor letter. His fund was up 29 percent in the first half of 1998, and he had recently returned from a powwow in Europe with Tiger's external advisers. Margaret Thatcher and Senator Bob Dole had been in attendance, with financial rainmakers from Japan and Mexico. Robertson had been particularly impressed by the discussion of the yen. Japan was deregulating its financial markets, allowing investors to shift money abroad; and with yen interest rates at just over 1 percent, it seemed obvious that Japanese savers would seize the chance to earn more on their investments. As Japanese capital flooded abroad, the yen would head down. Robertson left his investors in no doubt that he would short Japan's currency.

Robertson's July letter soon proved doubly incautious. Just as Long-Term Capital Management had underestimated its exposure to a generalized "deleveraging"—a pulling in of bets by sophisticated traders that would cause the forces of arbitrage to reverse—so Robertson had underestimated the extent to which deleveraging would hit his yen trade. Precisely because yen interest rates were low, traders borrowed the Japanese currency to finance their positions around the world; if they dumped those positions and paid their yen back, the currency would be pushed upward—the opposite of what Robertson was expecting. When Russia's default inflicted losses on leveraged traders, driving them to sell holdings, both Long-Term and Tiger got hit. Indeed, Friday, August 21 was not only the day when Long-Term lost more than half a billion dollars, causing the professors to rush back from their vacations. It was the day that Tiger's yen bet started to go wrong. Japan's currency rose 7 percent against the dollar over the next month, and Tiger saw over $1 billion of its capital evaporate.

That was only the start of Tiger's troubles, however. Just as Long-Term was hammered by rivals who knew too much about its positions, so Robertson found himself in a similar predicament. His spectacular investment record and booming personality attracted plenty of attention, and his monthly letters to partners were eagerly faxed around Wall Street. The moment that Robertson sent out his July letter, every trader knew he was short Japan's currency; and the more the yen rose, the more they expected him to be forced to staunch his losses by buying back yen and closing his position. On October 7 the yen jumped especially sharply, and traders sensed that Robertson would crack. They drove the yen up still more, calculating that Tiger's compelled exit from its trade would deliver yen holders a handsome profit.

By around 10:00 A.M. on October 8, 1998, Japan's currency had appreciated by an astonishing 12 percent since the previous morning. More than $2 billion of Tiger's equity had gone up in smoke; in the space of just over a day, the firm had lost *two hundred times* more capital than the $8.8 million with which it had been founded. Years later, in April 2009, the news that Morgan Stanley had lost $578 million in the space of three months was shocking enough to make the front page of the *Financial Times*. But in just over twenty-four hours, Robertson had watched four times more than that vanish.

Robertson convened a crisis council of his top lieutenants. They gathered in his splendid corner office, with its panoramic views of Manhattan; but the spectacle that mattered was flashing and blinking in the windowless core of their building, where the trading desk monitored the yen's surge upward. The currency had been trading at 130 to the dollar the previous morning; it was now trading at 114; by the end of this meeting, who knew where it might be? By an irony that was no doubt lost on the participants, the man who dominated the crisis council was none other than Michael Bills, the son of the military aviator who had joined Tiger after Tom Wolfe called him and talked about the fighter-pilot culture. Bills argued to his colleagues that the market had gone crazy because it thought Tiger was on its knees; if Tiger could show that it still had the right stuff, it could restore Wall Street to its senses. Bills proposed that Tiger should attack rather than retreat. Rather than closing out its yen short, as the market expected, it should demonstrate its fearlessness by *adding* to its bet against Japan's currency. One brave gesture would prove to predatory traders that it was not easy meat. The yen would stop speeding upward.

The meeting broke up after about thirty minutes. The yen had risen from 114 to 112 during this time, vaporizing another half billion dollars. Dan Morehead, Tiger's currency trader, hurried to his cockpit to execute the Bills plan. He would add $50 million to Tiger's bet against the yen, gambling that this signal would break the currency's momentum.

Morehead called a dealer at one of the big banks. He asked for a two-way price on dollar-yen, not wanting to give away whether he was buying or selling. Normally it took a couple of seconds for the bank to quote a price. This time there was a lengthy silence. The expectation that Tiger would soon be forced to buy yen by the billion had scared potential sellers to the sidelines; who wanted to shed yen when Tiger was about to force their price up? Because of the dearth of sellers, the market had dried up; there were no trades and no prices. Morehead's bank dealer would have to name a price in a vacuum. He was clearly terrified to do so.

After fully half a minute, the answer came back. The bank would sell Tiger dollars using an exchange rate of 113.5 yen to the dollar; it would buy dollars back using an exchange rate of 111.5 yen to the dollar. The two-yen gap between the quotes was astronomical—maybe forty times the spread that Morehead saw in a normal market. Like LTCM before it, Tiger was discovering that liquidity can dry up when it's most needed.

"I buy," Morehead said.

In that instant, the bank that took his order knew that Tiger was not going to be squeezed out of its trade. Julian Robertson and his Tigers still had the will to fight! Only a fool would trade against them! Seconds later the dearth of sellers came to an abrupt end: The bank's proprietary traders began dumping yen, and the dumps communicated the sea change to every currency desk on Wall Street. The yen started falling as quickly as it had risen earlier in the day. The aviator's son had won. Tiger had been in a tailspin, but disaster had been averted.[3]

In one respect at least, Robertson had been vindicated. His contention that Tiger was different from superleveraged LTCM was right; Tiger's debt-to-equity ratio was around five to one, which gave it the muscle to hold on to its yen short rather than getting squeezed out of the position.[4] But this vindication was scant comfort to Tiger's partners. During the course of October, Robertson managed to lose $3.1 billion in currencies, primarily from his bet against the yen; and his excuses were not persuasive. "The yen, which was as liquid as water, suddenly dried up like the Sahara," he pleaded to his investors, failing to add that liquidity had evaporated not least because of Tiger's recklessness.[5] Tiger had been short an astonishing $18 billion worth of the currency—a position almost twice as large as Druckenmiller's famous bet against sterling.[6] By trading currencies even more ambitiously than his rivals at Quantum, Robertson had baked his own Sahara.[7]

In the aftermath of this disaster, Robertson promised his investors that he would scale back his currency trading. But Tiger's yen losses were just a foretaste of the troubles in store—troubles that came in the surprising guise of a technology bull market.

THE TECHNOLOGY BUBBLE OF THE LATE 1990S SERVES AS a test for two views of hedge funds.[8] On the one hand there is the optimistic view—that sophisticated traders will analyze prices and move them to their efficient level. On the other hand there is a darker view—that sophisticated traders lack the muscle to enforce price efficiency and that, knowing the limits of their power, they will prefer to ride trends rather than fight them. Among the hedge funds we have encountered, there are examples of both schools. Long/short investors, from A. W. Jones in equities to John Meriwether in bonds, aim to buy underpriced securities and sell expensive ones, pushing prices to their efficient level. Meanwhile, trend followers such as Paul Tudor Jones make no claim to understand the fundamental value of anything they trade. They buy securities as they go up and dump them as they go down. They are not interested in forcing prices toward some sort of equilibrium.

If ever irrational markets cried out for efficiency-enforcing arbitrage, the dot-com bubble surely was a clear example. Equity analysts usually value companies by looking at their earnings and their likely growth—these give a measure of the cash that will ultimately flow to investors. But the technology start-ups that flooded the market in the late 1990s had no earnings at all; by traditional yardsticks, their intrinsic worth was *zero*. Nevertheless, investors fell over themselves to buy tech stocks, or even stocks that in some way seemed connected to the Internet. In November 1998, for example, a plodding bookseller named Books-A-Million announced it was improving its Web site; within three days of this unremarkable news, its share price jumped tenfold. The following March a start-up called Priceline.com gained 425 percent on its first day of trading, which meant that this untested Web site for selling airline tickets was deemed to be worth more than United Airlines, Continental Airlines, and Northwest Airlines combined. The airlines own terminals, landing slots, and fleets of passenger aircraft, but never mind. Priceline.com owned some software, a couple of computers, and a chunk of William Shatner, the *Star Trek* actor who appeared in its commercials.[9]

How would hedge funds respond to this insanity? If they were the efficiency-enforcing actors that optimists imagine, they would sell the Internet stocks short until they brought their prices down to a more rational level. If they were trend followers, on the other hand, they would buy into the bubble and reinforce it. For believers in markets, it is hard to accept that intelligent investors would miss the opportunity to short something that is evidently overpriced—indeed, this is what investors need to do in order to justify their existence. The case for tolerating highly paid investment managers, after all, is that they contribute something useful to society: By enforcing efficient pricing, they allocate scarce capital to the companies that will use it best—not to bubbly start-ups with underwhelming ideas that will take scarce capital and waste it. Bubbles channel money to managers who don't know how to manage. They finance business plans that nobody wants. And when they eventually burst, they leave ordinary savers with losses.

But there are limits to arbitrage, as we have seen. No one investor can deflate a bubble by himself. Even the biggest hedge funds of the late 1990s, Tiger and Quantum, had just over $20 billion under management at their peaks; they could hardly challenge the momentum of the technology-heavy NASDAQ stock index, whose total capitalization topped $5 trillion. Because hedge funds remained small relative to the market, a bet against the bubble would come good only if others bet the same way, and a hedge fund could sustain heavy losses in the meantime. If those losses spooked investors into yanking their money out of the hedge fund, the fund would have to unwind its bet against the bubble before it paid off. "The market can stay irrational longer than you can stay solvent," Keynes famously declared. Being early and right is the same as being wrong, as investors have repeatedly discovered.

As the bubble inflated in 1999, Julian Robertson declined to fight it. He had no doubt that technology stocks were way too high, but he had lost money on technology shorts the previous year and had concluded that there was no safe way to bet against the bubble. He was comfortable shorting individual companies, because he could hedge out the risk of a general rise in the market by going long similar stocks. But when the entire technology sector was overvalued, hedging became hard: Robertson couldn't short all tech stocks while going long an equivalent bucket of assets, since there was no such equivalent. Besides, the momentum in the tech bubble seemed almost unstoppable. Robertson likened the NASDAQ to a locomotive hurtling down the tracks. It was certain to come off the rails, but there was no telling when. Only a fool would stand in front of it.[10]

Rather than fight a bubble he viewed as absurd, Robertson decided to ignore it. Having resolved to scale back his macro bets after his losses on the yen, he resolved to stay clear of the tech sector also. But this strategy brought fresh problems of its own. Tiger had grown so big that it was hard to deploy its capital at the best of times; now, with two investment frontiers considered off limits, Tiger's size problem grew critical. Robertson concentrated his bets on traditional value stocks such as Federal-Mogul Corporation, an auto parts supplier, and Niagara Mohawk, a power company—the very essence of the old economy. But it was hard to find appealing companies in which Tiger could take meaningful stakes.

Robertson's difficulties were summed up by his investment in US Airways. In early 1996, the airline's board had appointed a cost-cutting turnaround artist as chief executive, and Robertson had wisely bought a large stake in the company. By the summer of 1998, the bet had paid off: US Airways stock had quintupled. But rather than declaring victory and selling, Robertson had held on—despite the fact that the stock's appreciation meant that his stake was now worth an astronomical $1.5 billion and represented about one fifth of the company.[11] Recognizing the dangers, Tiger's airline analyst had counseled Robertson to sell part of the position when US Airways organized a share buyback in early 1998, but Robertson had refused: "It's one of my best ideas," he had countered.[12] Given the finite number of opportunities available to a supersized value investor, Robertson was prepared to hold on to a position long after his original investment thesis had paid off, never mind the fact that it had grown too big to be liquid.

The risks in this behavior soon became apparent. At the start of 1999, US Airways reported disappointing profits and the stock dropped like a stone, shedding 29 percent in three weeks of trading. Robertson wrote to his investors, defiantly predicting that the stock could triple by the end of the year as the market regained its respect for old-economy companies. But the news failed to get better. In July the airline's machinists voted to reject a pay contract, and a strike seemed on the cards; in August work stoppages forced some flight cancellations. As the stock continued to head down, there was no way that Robertson could sell his vast position on the open market without sending its price into free fall; he had become an

owner rather than an investor. Tiger was reduced to rooting around for
a strategic buyer of the airline that might take a large block off its hands,
and meanwhile, Robertson's other value bets were souring. Federal-
Mogul, the auto parts maker, fell 30 percent in the first half of the year,
while Niagara Mohawk was flat. The investing public was losing interest
in old-fashioned value stocks. "We are going through a most unusual market where in many instances fundamentals are being ignored," Robertson
wrote to his investors in April.[13]

By the summer of 1999, Robertson's decision to ignore the tech boom
was causing a crisis on Park Avenue. Tiger had lost 7.3 percent in the
first half of the year; meanwhile, technology-heavy mutual funds were
up by a quarter or more, and day traders operating from kitchen tables
were outperforming Robertson's special-forces unit. Coming on top of the
losses on the yen in the fall of 1998, the latest setbacks strained investors'
patience: Having withdrawn a net $3 billion from Tiger in the six months
to March, Robertson's partners withdrew another $760 million at the end
of the second quarter. The more investors pulled out, the more Robertson
was forced to liquidate holdings.[14] And once Wall Street understood that
Tiger had become a forced seller, the old predatory instincts returned.
Each month in his letter to investors, Robertson reported Tiger's top ten
stock positions, so there was no secret as to what he held; naturally his
rivals did their best to sell ahead of him. On one hair-raising day in June,
a rumor that Tiger would face $3 billion in withdrawals at the end of the
month triggered a spasm of predatory sales: Tiger's portfolio lost $72 mil-
lion in fifteen minutes, at a time when the broad market was steady.[15] The
rumor turned out to be wrong, but that was only modest consolation.

In 1998, LTCM had gone into its death spiral as its brokers began to
call in loans, leading Robertson to write to his investors about the dangers
of excessive leverage. In 1999, Tiger was in danger of unraveling too—
not because brokers were calling in their loans but because investors were
calling in their equity. In both cases, moreover, widespread knowledge of
the hedge funds' holdings contributed to their troubles. Commentators
who insist that hedge-fund transparency would stabilize markets might
usefully ponder this lesson.[16]

ONE MILE NORTH OF TIGER'S OFFICE, A SHORT WALK FROM
Central Park, Robertson's friends and rivals at Quantum were fighting
a parallel battle. At the start of 1999, Stan Druckenmiller, Quantum's
supremo, had shared Robertson's conviction that tech stocks were too
high; but he had acted differently. Undeterred by the market's momentum, Druckenmiller had placed an unhedged, outright bet against the
tech bubble, picking a dozen particularly overvalued start-ups and shorting $200 million worth of them. Immediately, all of them shot up with
a violence that made it impossible to escape: "They'd close one day at a
hundred and open at one forty," Druckenmiller remembered with a shud-
der.[17] Within a few weeks the position had cost Quantum $600 million.
By May 1999, Druckenmiller found himself 18 percent down. For the
first time in his long career, he faced the prospect of a year with significant
negative performance.[18]

Druckenmiller confronted an acute form of the danger that men-
aced Robertson. The previous year Quantum had been up 21 percent
up while Tiger was down 4 percent, but now that he had stood in front
of the technology locomotive, Druckenmiller's losses were twice as bad
as Robertson's. Inevitably, investors chafed. In May a big feeder fund
called Haussmann Holdings announced that it had cut its investments
in Soros Fund Management by more than half, and the press reported on
a stream of Quantum analysts who were leaving for better opportunities.
Commentators started to ask whether the Druckenmiller legend was over.
There were rumors that the big man might take a three-month medical
leave. When these were vigorously denied, a fresh round of rumors inti-
mated that Soros might be tiring of his alter ego.

And yet in an important way, Druckenmiller was better equipped
for the technology boom than Robertson. Tiger's value-investing tradition made it almost unthinkable for Robertson to buy into the bubble.[19]
Druckenmiller's blend of traditional analysis and charts made him altogether less predictable. Whereas Robertson had no patience for investing
on the basis of momentum, Druckenmiller was fully capable of following

the fundamentals in one period and surfing the trend in the next one. In May 1999 Druckenmiller allocated some of Quantum's capital to a new hire named Carson Levit, who loaded up on dot-com stocks. The skeptic who had shorted the bubble now climbed aboard the bandwagon.

Two months later, Druckenmiller attended the annual technology and media conference in Sun Valley, Idaho. It was a festival of new-economy bullishness and buzz: Everyone from Hollywood moguls to presidential contenders to Silicon Valley whiz kids got together in the shadow of breathtaking mountains; and even Warren Buffett, whose value-investing style had been hammered by the bubble, could be seen pottering about in a polo shirt and baseball cap, chatting with Bill Gates and Michael Bloomberg.[20] When Druckenmiller returned from Sun Valley that summer, he had the zeal of the convert.[21] He allocated more of Quantum's capital to Carson Levit and hired a second technology enthusiast named Diane Hakala, whose hobby was to perform dizzying spins as an aerobatic pilot. Levit and Hakala piled into the same sorts of stock that Druckenmiller had shorted in the first part of the year. They were "in all this radioactive shit that I don't know how to spell," Druckenmiller said later.[22]

The radioactivity did wonders for Quantum's performance. Tech stocks took off like a rocket: Names like VeriSign, Qualcomm, and Gemstar were hailed as the heroes of the new era. Whereas in the first half of the year Quantum had trailed Tiger, now Quantum actually benefited from its rival's misfortune. As withdrawals by Tiger's investors forced Robertson to sell stocks, he dumped a vast stake in South Korea Telecom that he had bought before the bubble. The pressure of Robertson's selling caused South Korea Telecom to drop by a third in July and August. Carson Levit bought into this liquidation on the cheap. The stock promptly tripled.[23]

In the last months of 1999, Druckenmiller made more from surfing tech stocks than he had made from shorting sterling eight years earlier. Quantum went from down 18 percent in the first five months of the year to up 35 percent by the end of it. Druckenmiller had pulled off one of the great comebacks in the story of hedge funds, and it had nothing whatever to do with pushing markets to their efficient level.

MEANWHILE, OTHER HEDGE FUNDS WERE GRAPPLING
with the tech bubble. In early 1999, an army of short sellers picked a fight
with the Internet service provider America Online, which had embraced
a bubbly new way of accounting for its marketing expenditures. If the
company spent $1 million on attracting new subscribers, it did not recog-
nize that cost immediately; it treated its advertising as an *investment*, to
be counted against revenues bit by bit, like the cost of buying plant and
machinery. The short sellers were correct that this was a low trick, and
eventually America Online abandoned it.[24] But the company's share price
refused to break its upward stride: The short sellers won the accounting
argument, but they still lost their shirts in the investment. Mary Meeker,
the Morgan Stanley analyst who had been dubbed the "Queen of the Net"
by *Barron's*, conceded that old-school value investors, brought up on the
classic teachings of Ben Graham and David Dodd, might have trouble
seeing the value in a company that would report losses if it respected the
accounting rules.[25] But that was the old timers' problem. At one new-
economy gathering, a banker was overheard saying, "No traditional
Graham and Dodd investor invested in AOL. They shorted it. And got
fucked. They're learning the new model."[26]

A few months later, a hedge fund called Greenlight Capital took
another shot at a puffed-up Internet outfit. Its target was Chemdex, a
business-to-business network for companies to sell chemicals to one
another. Chemdex earned a commission on every trade that the companies made through its network, but it booked the entire value of the goods
exchanged as revenue. This stratagem seemed so outrageous that Greenlight's founder, David Einhorn, could not resist having a go: He took a
large short position in Chemdex in September 1999, when the company's
stock was trading at $26. But in the unhinged atmosphere of the bubble,
even the most questionable accounting failed to faze other investors. In
December, Queen Mary of Morgan Stanley declared, "We think Chemdex has got what it takes," and by February the stock had risen more than

sixfold, to a mind-bending $164. Needless to say, by late 2000 Chemdex had collapsed to $2 per share. But that was too late to help Einhorn, who was forced out of his Chemdex short before the bubble burst, nursing enormous losses.[27]

Despite periodic suspicions that short sellers at hedge funds can manipulate markets, the tech market of 1999 swatted away hedge-fund skeptics like flies on the rump of an elephant. The manipulation took place elsewhere: Companies were cooking their accounts, auditors were turning a blind eye, and investment banks engaged in shameless hype about the tech companies they brought to market. Seeing that they had no hope of bucking the mania, hedge funds mostly chose to jump on for the ride. Some bought into the bubble because they believed the hype or because their style was to milk trends. Some reasoned that the Fed's monetary policy was extraordinarily loose, so the hot asset of the moment would attain stratospheric valuations.[28] And some bought initial public offerings of tech stocks because they were insiders in a dubious game: As part of the hype that fueled the bubble, investment banks created a scramble for tech stocks by parceling out new issues cheaply, virtually printing money for the lucky funds with access to initial offerings. In sum, hedge funds were no more prone to ride the bubble than other types of money managers; but they were not more contrarian, either.[29] While the bubble was building, only the bravest value investors were foolhardy enough to fight it.

The bravest and the foolhardiest of all was Julian Robertson. Tiger lost 17 percent in the third quarter, even as momentum surfers were reaping extraordinary profits. The hemorrhaging of investors continued: When the window for redemptions opened at the end of September, a net $1.3 billion was yanked away from Robertson. Tiger had gone from a peak of $21 billion in assets in August 1998 to $9.5 billion just over a year on, and some $5 billion of the decline was due to clients voting with their wallets. For Robertson, it was not just money that he was losing. He had made Tiger his family, his personal network of power brokers and friends; he had run a special-forces unit and led team-building excursions out west; he was not used to defeat, still less the ignominious rout he was experiencing. Sometimes in his lowest moments, he would call his old lieutenant, John Griffin, who was now running a hedge fund of his own. "John, can you believe that I got a letter from so-and-so who has been in Tiger since 1982?" Robertson would say. "He says he's buying a house. He needs his money back. He's just lost faith in me."[30]

In an attempt to slow the race for the exit, Robertson announced that he would allow investors to redeem capital from his funds on two occasions per year rather than four. But although this was a mild restriction compared with the lockups that hedge funds imposed on clients in the next decade, Robertson backed down from his new policy. His investors protested that they had proved their loyalty by keeping their money in his funds through the past, terrible year, so why should they now be chained to the *Titanic*? Robertson conceded that they had a point, but the next generation of hedge-fund managers learned from his defeat. To reduce the mismatch between yankable capital and potentially illiquid investments, they permitted investors to withdraw their cash at ever less frequent intervals.

Unable to lock in money, Robertson was forced to sell positions whether or not they were liquid. This made him a sitting duck. His rivals knew what he had to unload, and they went short in anticipation. Between August and October, as rumors of Tiger's unraveling mounted, the number of US Airways shares sold short rose from 1.6 million to 3.8 million, driving the already battered stock down by another tenth; between September and October, short sales of Federal-Mogul leaped from 3.7 million shares to 6.5 million, forcing the stock down by 80 percent. Reflecting on Tiger's gargantuan liquidations—Robertson had sold some $40 billion of stocks and $60 billion of other positions over the past year—some considered it a miracle that Tiger was still standing at all. "How many financial institutions could have a $100 billion downsizing of their balance sheet?" asked Philip Duff, Tiger's chief operating officer. "Few of those would probably survive," he added.[31]

At the end of 1999, Robertson's tone began to telegraph that the end was indeed coming. He pleaded with his investors that a great technology can change people's lives without necessarily generating profits for investors. He pointed out that the managers of the companies in Tiger's portfolio were buying their stock back, suggesting that they regarded their own equity as cheap, whereas managers of tech firms were eagerly selling stakes in their own enterprises. "We are in wild runaway technology frenzy: meantime most other stocks are in a state of collapse," he wrote in December. "I have never seen such a dichotomy. There will be a correction."[32] The next month Robertson uncorked his frustration at the behavior of an "irrational public." "This is the public that in the month of December drove the unprofitable companies in the NASDAQ up some 38 percent. There has to be a day of reckoning."[33]

The day of reckoning did come, shortly after Robertson predicted it. On March 10, 2000, the NASDAQ crested, and over the next weeks the air whooshed out of one of history's great bubbles. But the turn had come too late. By the time the NASDAQ began to fall, Robertson had made his decision to get out, and he was too beaten up to change it. On March 30, with the NASDAQ already 15 percent off its peak, Robertson broke the news to his investors. After months of assuring them that there would be light at the end of the tunnel, he confessed that he was sick of waiting for it. Rational measures of valuation had taken a backseat to "mouse clicks and momentum," as Robertson put it, and he had no stomach for more punishment. Because of capital withdrawals by his investors, the market had stayed irrational longer than he had stayed solvent, just as Keynes had warned. It was time to bring the curtain down on Tiger.[34]

WHILE TIGER SUFFERED THROUGH THE LAST PHASE OF the bubble, Quantum had enjoyed a nervous sort of victory. The terrific technology profits of late 1999 had rescued Druckenmiller from the humiliation of a down year, but anyone could see that the run would end eventually. At Quantum's weekly research meetings, Druckenmiller would worry that the bubble could burst any time; and the discussion would revolve around how the bust might be anticipated. As if to reinforce his nervousness, the tech-heavy NASDAQ index fell sharply at the start of January, then turned around and vaulted to new heights; the volatility was hair raising. At one point in February, while watching a biotech firm called Celera Genomics skyrocket, Druckenmiller told a Quantum trader that the market was insane. He needed to get out quickly.[35]

"I just want you to know, I'm selling everything out," Druckenmiller told Soros. "This is fucking nuts."

"I'm really glad you're doing it," Soros replied. "I haven't been comfortable with this."[36]

Druckenmiller duly dumped his tech holdings and focused on currencies. It was a potential moment of triumph: Quantum's supremo had gotten out before the bubble burst, and he was back to focusing on his strong suit as a macro trader. But the markets conspired to taunt Druckenmiller almost as cruelly as they had tormented Robertson. First, Druckenmiller got stuck on the wrong side of Europe's fledgling currency, the euro. Next, the NASDAQ stocks that he had sold continued to rush upward. Carson Levit and Diane Hakala, Quantum's in-house new-economy enthusiasts, were still running technology subportfolios, surfing the bubble, and all of a sudden the big man's anxieties shifted. Having earlier worried that the bubble might blow up in his face, he now worried about losing face: He had doubted the new economy and misjudged the euro, and now these kids and their radioactive stocks were making a fool of him. Not for the first time, Druckenmiller turned on a dime. He bought all his tech stocks back and gave Levit and Hakala room to run. For a while the good times rolled again.

Then on March 10 the NASDAQ turned, and many of the stocks that Quantum held fell faster even than the market. Druckenmiller himself had been a huge buyer of a firm called VeriSign, which lost almost half its value in a month, plummeting so hard that it was difficult to sell out of it. "I knew I was dead," Druckenmiller said later; and by the end of March Quantum had lost about one tenth of its capital.[37] By pivoting aggressively one too many times, Druckenmiller had failed to escape before the party ended.

Druckenmiller left the office for a vacation in Florida. One year earlier, he had led Quantum back from behind; now he lacked the will to do it. Like his friend Julian Robertson, he was too drained to go on; and although Robertson's decision to pull the curtain down on Tiger seemed exquisitely mistimed, Druckenmiller realized that he envied Robertson's new freedom. "Money is supposed to be enjoyed," he told his wife, "but if I can't enjoy two weeks with my kids, what's the point of it all?"[38] He had carried Quantum on his shoulders for twelve years, and that was enough for him.

"I'm tired, exhausted. I fought out of the hole last year; I just can't do it," Druckenmiller told Soros.[39]

Soros looked at Druckenmiller and recognized the desperation he had once felt himself. Years earlier, when he had run Quantum almost alone, Soros had come to hate the all-consuming nature of the task; he had compared himself to a sick person with a parasitic fund swelling inexorably inside his body. Druckenmiller had been saying for some time now that he wished Quantum were not so large, that he needed some kind of exit, that he could not go on forever. In the end, Soros reflected, Druckenmiller had only been able to free himself by blowing up the fund. It was an expensive method of escape, but it was certainly effective.[40]

On April 28, Soros convened a press conference. He announced that Quantum was down 21 percent for the year and that assets at Soros Fund Management had fallen by $7.6 billion since August 1998, when they had reached their high-water mark of $22 billion. He explained that Stan Druckenmiller was leaving after a dozen years; Quantum would henceforth be managed as a sedate, low-risk endowment. Within the space of just one month, the two largest and most storied hedge funds had pulled down the shutters. "We have come to realize that a large hedge fund like Quantum Fund is no longer the best way to manage money," Soros said sadly. "Markets have become extremely unstable."[41]

With that, Soros appeared to draw a line under an industry that he had helped to invent. But he could not have been more wrong. It was too early to write an epitaph for hedge funds.

12

THE YALE MEN

On June 1, 2001, 2,920 people showed up for dinner at the Jacob Javits Convention Center on the western edge of Manhattan. They had come to participate in what had become one of the great rites of the summer: the annual gala of the Robin Hood Foundation, the charity conceived by Paul Tudor Jones in the wake of the crash of 1987. After thirteen years in operation, Robin Hood had distributed over $90 million to organizations that fought poverty, teen pregnancy, and illiteracy in New York City, and the gathering in 2001 promised to take the crusade to the next level. The guests filed into a cocktail area that mixed the vibe of a disco with a sort of rain-forest aesthetic: Hundreds of green poles rose nearly twenty feet into the air; an image of green treetops was projected onto the wall; a constantly shifting green light scanned the room for celebrities. There was the actress Meg Ryan, the baseball personality Keith Hernandez, and the newsman Tom Brokaw—and there were many, many hedge-fund managers. The caterers went about their business with paramilitary intensity. Traffic cops armed with fluorescent batons directed servers around the kitchen.[1]

The Robin Hood dinner was proof that Soros's epitaph for hedge funds had been delivered prematurely. Stan Druckenmiller himself was a sponsor of the event, having returned to the markets almost immediately after leaving Quantum—he was now running his own firm, Duquesne Capital Management. A who's who of the titans turned out at the gala, paying $5,000 per ticket and bidding lustily in the auction. One guest forked over $540,000 for the privilege of lunch with a leading financial mogul. Another shelled out $260,000 for the "Be a Star" package, which included a part as an extra in Russell Crowe's *A Beautiful Mind*, a walk-on in Drew Barrymore's *The Duplex*, and dinner with the Hollywood power couple Catherine Zeta-Jones and Michael Douglas. Paul Tudor Jones's wife, Sonia, bid $420,000 to attend a yoga lesson taught by Madonna and Gwyneth Paltrow—"Come on, people, you can't stretch by yourselves!" the comedian Jerry Seinfeld urged as he auctioned off this item. Once the selling was over, a slice of the wall around the dining room dropped away. Cannons spewed confetti on the guests. Robert Plant, known to not-so-young members of the audience as Led Zeppelin's lead singer, strutted onto the dance floor.

By the end of that evening in 2001, Jones's foundation had pulled in $13.5 million, demonstrating that hedge-fund wealth had become a social force of some significance. Meanwhile, George Soros's Open Society Institute, the oldest and largest of the hedge-fund philanthropies, was disbursing $450 million per year; and in 2002 Arki Busson, who fed capital to Paul Jones and others from investors in Europe, created ARK—Absolute Return for Kids—which became the Robin Hood equivalent in London. And yet the greatest philanthropic impact of hedge funds lay elsewhere— not so much in the charities that they bankrolled as in the profits that accrued to the endowments that invested with them. By the early 2000s, *billions* of dollars of hedge-fund earnings had flowed into the coffers of universities, boosting their ability to finance everything from scientific research to scholarships for students from poor families. And just as this bonanza changed the outlook for learning, so it changed the character of hedge funds too. As they took in institutional money, hedge funds grew larger, slicker, and more methodical in style. They were emerging as a real industry.

The pioneer of this alliance between endowments and hedge funds was David Swensen of Yale University. He was tall, angular, ascetic, and cerebral—a "stiff-backed midwesterner," one friend called him—and he was possessed above all by a fierce sense of moral purpose. Growing up in River Falls, Wisconsin, he founded a recycling club through a church group; his mother and sister were Lutheran ministers; and his ambition was to follow in the state's progressive political tradition and be elected to the Senate. But after enrolling in Yale's economics PhD program, Swensen took a different turn. He befriended the future Nobel laureate James Tobin. He got to know Wall Street's preeminent bond firm, Salomon Brothers, which provided market data for his dissertation. He developed a passion for finance and for the Yale environment.

When Swensen completed his doctorate in 1980, Salomon immediately hired him, and he thrived on the competitive culture of Wall Street. He helped to make financial history the following year by playing a role in the creation of the first currency swap, a deal between IBM and the World Bank that allowed the technology company to hedge its exposure to Swiss francs and German marks; and in 1982 he was lured away by Lehman Brothers to run the bank's fledgling swaps desk.[2] But in 1985, when his former professors lobbied him to take over Yale's troubled endowment, Swensen accepted happily. He gave up investment-banking bonuses for a book-lined office on the university campus, taking a pay cut of 80 percent. Years later, a Wall Street admirer remarked that Swensen could have been a billionaire if he had applied his talents to running a hedge fund. "What's the matter with you?" the admirer asked. "A genetic defect," Swensen responded.[3]

When Swensen took over the endowment at Yale, more than four fifths of its assets were invested in U.S. stocks, bonds, and cash, with only a tenth in so-called alternative investments—in short, it resembled most other college endowments. For a young man returning from the innovative world of Wall Street, this seemed a little tame; besides, it was an affront to the research of Swensen's mentor, James Tobin, who had helped to advance the idea that portfolio diversification is the one free lunch in economics. In a modern financial system, Swensen reasoned, diversification should mean more than simply holding a broad mix of U.S. bonds and equities: Assets such as foreign equities, real estate, private equity, oil, gas, and timber all offered ways to add equity-type returns while diversifying risk substantially. Then there was another kind of asset that took Swensen's fancy. He called it "absolute return," and over the next years the term entered the investment lexicon. It was a synonym for hedge funds.

The moralist in Swensen had no desire to help hedge-fund managers earn fortunes. But the economist in Swensen was impressed by the design of hedge-fund incentives. He knew that the larger an investment fund, the harder it was for a fund manager to generate returns, so he disliked fees that were tied to the volume of capital a manager amassed, preferring the performance fees that accounted for most hedge-fund revenues. He recognized that performance fees alone can encourage too much risk—hedge-fund managers get a fifth of the upside but pay no equivalent penalty if they blow up—so he sought out hedge-fund managers who had their own savings in their funds and was encouraged to discover many of them. But what really interested Swensen was the scale and source of hedge-fund profits. Hedge funds promised equity-sized returns that were uncorrelated with the market index, offering the free lunch of diversification.

It took a little while for Swensen to recognize the potential in hedge funds. In 1987, two years after he assumed the helm at the endowment, he received a visit from a Yale alumnus who had heard of his appointment at a homecoming football game. The visitor said he had a small fund out on the West Coast; perhaps Yale might want to invest with him? Swensen and his deputy, Dean Takahashi, listened to the pitch.

"We're not interested," they told the supplicant. "We'll never be interested."

THE SUPPLICANT WAS TOM STEYER, AND HIS HEDGE fund was called Farallon. Steyer sported a sweeping red-blond parting, jaunty sideburns, and faded woven wristbands; though he had grown up in New York, he exuded the vibe of his adopted home of San Francisco. He was ebullient, funny, and comfortable in his own skin; he could fill a conversation with mental and athletic juice, running with ideas like the soccer star that he had been in college. Steyer came equipped with another quality that would appeal to Swensen later on: He had an acute sense of right and wrong, which colored everything from his lifestyle to his approach to business. Long after Steyer built Farallon into one of the world's biggest hedge funds, he was renowned for his beat-up car, his habit of flying commercial, and his utter indifference to fashion.[4] His office consisted of a desk in the middle of an open-plan hallway. Behind him was a breathtaking panorama of San Francisco, except that Steyer kept the blinds down.[5]

Steyer founded Farallon in 1985, the same year that Swensen took over the Yale endowment. He was motivated partly by a desire to escape Wall Street for a life on the West Coast and partly by that sense of justice. As a young analyst at Morgan Stanley, he had been upset to discover that investment-bank advisers can be paid for being wrong; sounding convincing mattered more than actually being right, since the objective was simply to extract fees from the clients. After a stint at Stanford's business school, Steyer had worked at Goldman Sachs for the merger-arbitrage unit run by Robert Rubin, the future Treasury secretary. This suited him better: Goldman got paid in this business only when Goldman was right, though the distribution of the profits among employees sometimes generated arguments. The way Steyer saw things, setting up an independent fund was the logical next step. He had begun at a firm that took no responsibility for bad investment calls. He had moved to a firm that took responsibility collectively but that did not always recognize an individual's contribution. Now, by starting a freestanding fund, Steyer would be out there on his own, with no buffer between the quality of his investment calls and the rewards he got from them.

Steyer rented some cheap space in downtown San Francisco with a couple of desks, one for himself and one for a partner.[6] He would ride the elevator up to his office at 5:30 in the morning, clutching his coffee and doughnut, ready to analyze the merger action at the start of the New York trading day. The investment style he practiced was the same one he had learned at Goldman Sachs. When a takeover bid was announced, the stock in the target company would move most of the way to the bid price: For example, if it had been trading at $30 and the bid was for $40, it might shoot up to $38. This presented Steyer with a choice. If he bought the stock and the merger was consummated, he would pocket another $2 per share; but if the merger was called off and the stock fell back to its old price, he would forfeit $8. Knowing whether to risk $8 to make $2 required a special skill. You had to judge whether antitrust regulators would block the merger, or whether shareholders would revolt. You had to estimate the odds that another suitor might emerge stage left, perhaps pushing the stock above $40.

Steyer pursued his work with a competitive passion that sometimes seemed overboard. When he took some losses in the crash of 1987, he started to show up at three in the morning, accompanied by his wife, who feared for his stability.[7] But despite the hit in 1987, Steyer did extremely well: An arbitrageur who analyzes mergers from a desk at Goldman Sachs can analyze them pretty much as well from a desk in San Francisco, especially when his body and soul are tied up in his performance. By buying target companies in deals that would be consummated, Steyer eked out profits, month by month. And by shorting the acquiring firms, he hedged out the risk from general market movements.

Toward the end of the 1980s, Steyer expanded his horizons. This was partly a survival strategy, since the takeover boom skidded to a halt when the junk-bond market collapsed in 1989, leaving merger arbitrageurs with few mergers to analyze. But Steyer was playing offense too: The junk-bond collapse created an opportunity to apply his analytical skills in a different context.[8] The companies at the center of the junk-bond market filed for bankruptcy one by one; and an investor who could figure out which piece of busted debt to buy was likely to profit handsomely. To make matters even better, pension funds, mutual funds, and other institutional investors were forced sellers of junk: Their rules forbade them to hold the bonds of companies in default, so they were compelled to concede bargains to nimble players such as Farallon.[9] When Drexel Burnham Lambert, the kingpin of the junk-bond market, filed for bankruptcy in 1990, Steyer bought a large slice of its debt at cents on the dollar; and when he sold his stake in 1993, Farallon's portfolio chalked up a 35 percent profit.[10] With the Drexel transaction Steyer had scored a dazzling double. He had profited from the mergers made possible by Drexel's bonds, and he had profited again from Drexel's implosion.

Steyer had created what would later be known as an "event-driven" hedge fund. He specialized in events that caused existing prices to be wrong—moments when a disruption suddenly rendered the market's settled view inoperative. The moment before a takeover bid, a company's share price embodies the verdict of investors who have projected future earnings: The price is efficient in the sense that it has been analyzed to death already. The moment after the takeover bid, the old calculations are scrambled: Now the analysts have to look at the size of the takeover premium, the time until it is likely to be realized, the rate at which it should be discounted, and so on. In similar fashion, an event such as a bankruptcy scrambles yesterday's consensus on the value of a company's bonds. Again, the challenge is to look afresh at the cash flows that each busted bond seems likely to generate.

Even before the Drexel coup, the news of Steyer's performance had reached the ears of David Swensen. Steyer was making excellent money irrespective of whether the stock market was up or down—he offered diversification. Steyer was generating profits by focusing on occasions in which settled prices were scrambled; to a financial economist attuned to the limits of the efficient-market hypothesis, the success did not look merely lucky.[11] These two factors were enough to make Swensen reconsider his initial refusal to invest in Farallon. But before he went further, Swensen had to take the measure of Steyer the man. He wanted partners with integrity, and he wanted something more as well. Beating the market was only possible for people with a sort of obsessive passion. "Great investors tend to have a 'screw loose,' pursuing the game not for profit, but for sport," Swensen wrote later.[12]

As Yale did its due diligence, it found that Steyer had all the qualities that the endowment could hope for. This guy was not running a hedge fund because he craved luxury: You just had to look at his office to see that. This guy shared Swensen's passion for pure compensation incentives: He insisted that Farallon employees keep their liquid savings in the fund so that they would feel the pain if they lost money.[13] Steyer also embraced the convention of a "high-water mark," meaning that if his fund was down he would take no further fees until he earned the money back for his investors.[14]

In the fall of 1989, Swensen flew to San Francisco. He visited Farallon's scruffy office and approved of what he saw; but over a cheap lunch with Steyer and another Farallon partner, Fleur Fairman, Swensen repeated his earlier verdict that Yale would not invest with them. Hedge funds, he said bluntly, would stiff their clients if their strategies went wrong. Rather than working without compensation to earn the capital back, as the "high-water mark" promise suggested, hedge funds would simply close up shop, reopening under a new name with a fresh set of investors.

"Look, the reason we don't want to do this honestly is in this format, if you lose money, you won't want to earn it back. You'll close down and start a new fund. That's the problem with the whole format."

Steyer might have argued back, but Fairman beat him to it. "That's a bunch of bullshit!" she exclaimed, and Swensen could see that she was furious. "If you think that's who we are then we don't want your money anyway!" Fairman carried on. "You have no idea who we are! It's just ridiculous that you'd say that!"[15]

This was a better response than Swensen could possibly have wished for. He had found the integrity he sought: Fairman took her decency so seriously that she flew off the handle when you questioned it.

In January 1990, Yale invested with Farallon. The university injected $300 million into Steyer's fund, boosting his capital to a total of $900 million and kick-starting a gradual change in the social impact of hedge funds.

SWENSEN'S PARTNERSHIP WITH STEYER BEGAN THE RE-positioning of Yale, ultimately affecting the investment style of nearly all endowments. Until the Farallon deal, Yale had a smattering of holdings in private equity and "real assets" such as real estate, but nothing in hedge funds. Half a decade later, in 1995, the allocation to hedge funds had jumped to 21 percent, with another 31 percent in private equity and real assets.[16] Other universities followed, with a lag: For a typical university endowment, the allocation to hedge funds rose from nothing in 1990 to 7 percent in 2000.[17] In the years after the dot-com crash, endowments that experimented with hedge funds were rewarded particularly well: From July 2000 through June 2003, the S&P 500 lost 33 percent of its value while the HFR index of hedge funds gained 10 percent. Yale itself was up 20 percent over this period, and a couple of years later, when the university celebrated the twentieth anniversary of Swensen's arrival, his investment decisions were celebrated for generating $7.8 billion of the $14 billion in the Yale endowment—that was the amount by which he had outperformed the average university fund during his tenure. Fully $7.8 billion: It was a staggering number! With Swensen eclipsing storied education philanthropists such as Harkness and Mellon, hedge funds became more than just vehicles for the rich to get richer. By 2009 roughly half the capital in hedge funds came not from individuals but from institutions.

The rush of endowment money into hedge funds ensured that there was no need at all to write an epitaph for the industry. At the start of 2000, when Soros proclaimed that the hedge-fund era was over, hedge-fund assets had stood at $490 billion. By the end of 2005, they stood at $1.1 trillion. Soros's epitaph was at least partially apt for his own type of trader: The first years of the new century were a relatively lean time for macro hedge funds. But event-driven funds such as Farallon made up for that.[18] Farallon's assets ballooned from $8 billion in 2002 to $16 billion in 2006, and imitators crowded in. Och-Ziff, created by another veteran of the Robert Rubin arbitrage group at Goldman Sachs, grew from $6 billion to $14 billion over the same period. Perry Capital, another Rubin offshoot, grew from $4 billion to $11 billion. This "Rubin three" soon exceeded the Commodities Corporation three in terms of asset size. By 2006, Caxton, Tudor, and Moore marshaled a combined total of $35 billion, $6 billion less than the total for Farallon, Perry, and Och-Ziff; and a host of other products of the Rubin arbitrage group, including Frank Brosens of Taconic Capital, Eric Mindich of Eton Park, and Edward Lampert of ESL Investments, were flourishing. In the hedge-fund family tree, perhaps only Julian Robertson had more offspring.

It was not just that returns earned by event-driven funds were impressive. From the point of view of endowment managers, who reported to oversight committees that asked skeptical questions, the returns were pleasingly explicable. Macro traders like Paul Tudor Jones might talk about Kondratiev waves and breakout points: To the average investment committee, this was hocus-pocus. But event-driven funds like Farallon involved no mystery at all. These guys studied legal labyrinths. They understood the odds that a given merger would go through. They could judge how a particular slice of subordinated debt was likely to be treated by a particular bankruptcy judge in a particular court. With this sort of edge, of course they would make money! Besides, the endowment oversight committees could grasp that event-driven funds succeeded because others were hobbled. Institutional investors had rules that forced them to sell the bonds of companies in default, so they were required to cede profits to Steyer and his imitators. The more endowments displaced rich individuals as the chief investors in hedge funds, the more it mattered that hedge-fund strategies could be understood. A rich investor can bet his personal fortune on a mysterious genius if he so chooses. Endowment committees must protect their backs with PowerPoint presentations.

Along with profits and transparency, the event-driven merchants promised consistency. They used very little leverage, which in the wake of Long-Term's blowup was a selling point in itself; partly as a result, their returns were almost miraculously steady.[19] Farallon's consistency was legendary: Between 1990 and 1997, there was not a single month in which the fund lost money. As a result, Farallon's Sharpe ratio, a measure of returns adjusted for risk, was roughly three times higher than that of the broad stock market, making it an overwhelmingly attractive place for endowments to park savings.[20] Even during the height of the dot-com madness, Steyer sailed along serenely. He did not ride the bubble like Stan Druckenmiller. He did not get run over by it like Julian Robertson. Instead, he applied his methods to analyzing the epic takeover battles of the era, hedging out the market risk as he did so. Naturally, this strategy looked good when the market collapse sank both Druckenmiller and Robertson.

In sum, the event-driven hedge funds were producing understandable, unvolatile returns—returns, moreover, that reflected pure investment skill and were uncorrelated with the market index. This was the holy grail, the elixir that endowment consultants called alpha, and institutional capital flooded into their coffers. And yet the triumph of the event-driven hedge funds was not bereft of risk. Even the stars like Farallon had vulnerabilities that few suspected.

BY THE LATE 1990S, FARALLON WAS OPERATING OUT OF a fashionable skyscraper in yuppie downtown San Francisco. The commander's work space was modest as always, but there was a Henry Moore sculpture outside and a lawn where beautiful people ate organic sandwiches. From this bastion of serenity, Steyer's small operation was venturing to ever farther-flung frontiers. In 1998 it launched a merger-arb operation in London, arriving within a few months of its rivals, Och-Ziff and Perry Capital. It bought a stake in Alpargatas, a bankrupt Argentine textile and shoe maker. It installed new managers at Alpargatas and restructured the firm's debt; soon some two thousand idled workers found themselves employed again, and Farallon had proved that it could do well by doing good in a frontier economy.[21] But nothing could match what was about to follow. In November 2001, Farallon set out to buy the biggest bank in Indonesia.

Farallon's target, Bank Central Asia, had been founded by Liem Sioe Liong, who had been Indonesia's richest man and a firm friend of the country's modernizing dictator, Suharto. Liem's empire was said to account for 5 percent of Indonesia's output, and the secret of his success was best illustrated by the flour business. Playing on his connections to Suharto, Liem arranged for Indonesia's government to sell him imported wheat at a subsidized price and then to buy it back from his flour mills at a markup—nice work if you can get it.[22] Untroubled by competitive pressure, Liem's flour mill in Jakarta grew to be the largest in the world; the second-largest, in Surabaya, belonged to Liem also. And although the mills were supposed to sell their flour back to the government, an impressive quantity found its way to another Liem enterprise, Indofood, which consequently controlled 90 percent of Indonesia's instant-noodles market. In similar fashion, Liem prospered mightily in coffee, sugar, rubber, cement, rice, and cloves. Naturally, a man of his standing needed his own bank. Naturally, the bank was the nation's largest.

By the time Farallon came on the scene, Liem's empire had imploded. The patriarch had hedged his political risk by awarding Suharto relatives large stakes in his firms.[23] But the currency crisis that cost Soros and Druckenmiller a fortune triggered a slow-motion revolution in Indonesia, culminating in the fall of the Suharto government. From that moment on, Liem's political insurance policy became a target painted on his chest— friends of the fallen president were now enemies of the people. Rioters broke into Liem's compound, set his cars ablaze, and smashed his Chinese vases. Shorn of their political protection, Liem's businesses went bust, and since many of their loans had come from Bank Central Asia, they threatened to bring the bank down with them. To stem depositors' understandable panic, the government rescued it.

Farallon was used to event-driven investing, but the collapse of the Suharto regime was a more extreme event than the average takeover announcement. Millions of people were driven into poverty; thousands of demonstrators died in clashes with the police; hundreds of businesses were looted. Many Indonesians blamed the calamity on Western hedge funds, and American financiers in the country had been known to receive death threats. But the more Farallon studied Indonesia, the more the opportunities in the country seemed too good to pass up. Indonesia's government was the classic noneconomic seller. The International Monetary Fund was goading it to off-load the chunks of the private sector that it had been forced to rescue, and to do so at almost any price; precisely because most financial players would not set foot in the country, Farallon could expect limited competition in bidding for distressed assets. During the crises of 1997, hedge funds had profited by betting against governments that set illogically high prices for their currencies. In the hangover from those crises, hedge funds would profit by betting against governments that set illogically low prices for the broken jewels of their economies.

By the fall of 2001, Farallon had amassed $1 billion worth of holdings in Indonesia.[24] It had bought stakes in PT Semen Cibinong, Indonesia's third-largest cement company, and PT Astra International, the largest automaker; it bought the Jakarta Container Port Terminal and sold it on to Hong Kong–based Hutchison. Then one day Ray Zage, Farallon's point man in Indonesia, got an unusual message from a government contact. Bank Central Asia would be reprivatized soon. Perhaps Farallon would like to bid for it?

It was an astonishing proposal: A small San Francisco fund would take over the commanding heights of the world's largest Muslim country. Farallon boasted no more than a few dozen employees; Bank Central Asia had eight million accounts and eight hundred branches. Farallon was the product of the Goldman arb culture plus a dollop of California cool; Bank Central Asia had been the embodiment of Indonesia's crony capitalism. Andrew Spokes, a dapper English banker whom Steyer had recruited from the Goldman Sachs office in Hong Kong, later conceded that the deal was a stretch. "We were a little off piste," he conceded, coolly inspecting his cuffs.[25] He sounded like a vintage James Bond who skis an avalanche in a tuxedo.[26]

By the time the Bank Central Asia opportunity arose, the September 11 terrorist attacks had made Indonesia dicier than ever. A country torn by economic disaster and political revolution seemed vulnerable to Islamist extremism. The huge California state retirement fund, CalPERS, was getting ready to announce that it would not invest in Indonesia, period; even the intrepid Goldman Sachs tightened the limits on the Indonesian exposure that it would tolerate.[27] The Farallon team began to behave differently on its periodic visits to the country, especially when it found itself in concentrated clumps of foreigners. Ray Zage viewed the area between the customs checkpoint and the taxi rank at the airport as a natural kill zone. "I remember Ray observing it would be great not to be mowed down there," Spokes recalled matter-of-factly.[28]

Farallon proceeded to weigh up the case for buying Bank Central Asia. The discipline of event-driven investors is to zone out the chatter and the panic and focus on value—when market prices cease to be a guide, you decide what to pay for an asset based on the cash flows it will generate.

Spokes pushed past Bank Central Asia's reputation as the center of Liem's crony-capitalist empire and focused on three facts. Since nationalization, the bank's rotten loans to Liem's enterprises had been replaced with special recapitalization bonds, so that instead of depending on repayments from busted crony companies, BCA depended on repayments from the Indonesian state: BCA was really less a bank than a government bond fund. Moreover, BCA enjoyed access to cheap capital from retail depositors: Unlike most other bond funds, BCA came bundled with bargain-basement leverage.[29] Finally, if the local economy picked up, the bank could start making profitable loans to businesses: BCA was a bond fund, plus bargain-basement leverage, plus a free option on Indonesia's recovery. As to the political risk, Spokes had an answer to that too. Precisely because the world viewed Indonesia as scary, the post-Suharto leadership could not afford to treat Farallon capriciously. If they cheated a foreign investor in a high-profile deal, their reputation would be mud indefinitely.

After some spirited debate, the Spokes argument for off-piste investing convinced Steyer and the other partners. Only a year or so earlier, Farallon had had no track record in Indonesia; now it would be bidding for Bank Central Asia—and going up against a consortium led by Standard Chartered, a venerable lender with deep roots in the region. In late 2001, Farallon duly submitted an offer of $531 million, and in March 2002 the government announced that it had won: A hedge fund from latte land had bought control of the top bank in the nation. The outcome was so improbable that conspiracy theories blossomed. Was Farallon a front for the U.S. government? Was it a Trojan horse for Liem, who dreamed of reviving his old empire?

Despite the fervid whispers, Farallon's investment was a blessing for Indonesia. Farallon installed a new chairman, brought in some consultants, and patiently coaxed the bank out of the Suharto era. By 2006, when Farallon sold most of its stake to an Indonesian partner, BCA's share price had risen 550 percent since the purchase; just as with the Argentine shoe company, Farallon had shown it could do well by doing good in a tough country. But Farallon's investment had another effect too. The spectacle of a swashbuckling hedge fund dashing into Indonesia turned heads in New York and London, and institutional investors began to give the country a sympathetic second look. In the year leading up to the BCA purchase, a mere $286 million of net portfolio investment had trickled into Indonesia; but the following year almost $1 billion of foreign capital came in, and the year after that brought more than $4 billion.[30] Farallon had scrambled the market's settled view on all Indonesian assets, setting the stage for a rebound. An event-driven fund had created an event, helping to turn the economic tide for a nation of 240 million people.[31]

AS FARALLON WAS BIDDING FOR BANK CENTRAL ASIA, another adventure half a world away was proceeding less smoothly. Steyer had gone into business with a Colorado rancher named Gary Boyce, a flamboyant horse trainer and dreamer of wild dreams about the wealth in the valley of his childhood. Boyce had approached Farallon with a plan to buy land in the valley and pump water from the aquifer beneath—the water could supply Boulder, Colorado Springs, and even Denver. Farallon's alliance with the Yale endowment made it alert to the potential of "real assets" like water. Steyer and his team invested.

Southern Colorado's valleys were as remote in their own way as Jakarta's back alleys. To get to Gary Boyce's homestead, the Farallon people had to fly to Denver, then drive south for four hours to Alamosa, a small town with a True Grits Steakhouse, a TropArctic Lube Center, and a store plastered with posters announcing Tecate Imported Beer, Extra Gold Lager, and new Bud Light Lime—lattes had some competition in this neighborhood. After Alamosa, the visitor pressed on into the San Luis Valley, past lonely trailer homes, over pancake-flat land covered in harsh scrub, under cotton-candy clouds that sat motionless on distant mountains. At the far edge of the valley lay Gary Boyce's ranch house: a handsome adobe structure with hollow walls to keep out the heat. Boyce wore shirts with mother-of-pearl studs on the pockets. On the desk in his study lay a pair of ornate pistols.

You could see why Steyer and his team took this man for the perfect local partner. Boyce grew up poor in the San Luis Valley, then became the three-time winner of the Colorado dirt-biking championship. He was a veteran of the politics of water: During a fight over an earlier venture to tap the San Luis aquifer, he had founded a newspaper called the *Needle* to pierce the developer's bubble.[32] And while Boyce was a true local, he was also worldly: He had grown wealthy training horses for upper-crust Virginians, and wealthier still by marrying an MGM heiress. Confident that Boyce had the moxie to get a new version of the water project launched, Steyer created a partnership to finance his ambitions. Half the capital came from Farallon and the other half came from Yale, though Yale played no role in managing the project.

Backed by Farallon's money, Boyce duly bought a ranch in the San Luis Valley in 1994, outbidding the Nature Conservancy, which wanted to turn the land into a national park. He spent $3 million on an environmental study that showed water could be extracted without damaging the local soils. He hired lobbyists to plead for the project in the Colorado legislature. Meanwhile, Boyce spent half a million dollars on collecting signatures to get two referenda in front of Colorado's voters. The first measure required valley farmers and ranchers to place consumption meters on their wells; the second forced farmers to pay user fees for some types of water. Both measures were essential to Boyce's scheme, since they would establish a fair price for the resource he would be selling. Boyce spent another $400,000 on advertisements to build support for his ballot initiatives, assuring his partners at Yale and in San Francisco that they would be voted through. Steyer went out to the valley to visit, bringing his mother along for a vacation. She bonded happily with Boyce and tried her hand at elk hunting.[33]

Not everyone was happy, however. The farmers in the valley revolted against Boyce's proposals: They were outraged at the prospect of a user fee, and they claimed that the valley's sandy soils would clog the meters. As the arguments grew heated, Steyer began to wonder if he had chosen the right local partner after all.[34] Being born locally was not the same as being respected locally; perhaps the mother-of-pearl shirt studs and decorative pistols marked Boyce out as a poseur, not a regular local with Colorado credibility. When it came time to vote, in November 1998, Boyce's water initiatives were defeated by a large margin. Steyer and his Yale partners had spent four years and more than $20 million on the project, but now they had no choice but to recognize its failure.[35] Casting about for an exit, Farallon invited the Nature Conservancy to revive its old plan for a national park, and the two sides signed a deal at the end of 2001. But then an obstacle cropped up. Boyce blocked the path to the exit by filing a suit against Farallon.

Boyce's argument in court was that the water scheme was still viable. By bailing out prematurely, Farallon was damaging the value of Boyce's stake in the project. The lawsuit delayed the sale to the Nature Conservancy, and soon various onlookers saw an opportunity to make mischief. Colorado senator Wayne Allard accused Yale of profiting at the expense of Colorado's taxpayers, who would bankroll the Nature Conservancy's purchase, and demanded that Yale lower its asking price of $31.3 million—even though Yale's role was merely that of a passive investor.[36] Allard suggested Farallon had misled Yale about the environmental costs of the project, even though Boyce's referenda had failed because of the proposed user fees and meters, not because anyone had shown that his environmental study was faulty. For nearly all of its history, Farallon had tried to stay out of the headlines, and it was certainly not accustomed to public abuse from a senator. The involvement with Boyce was growing ever more uncomfortable.

At the start of 2004, Farallon emerged victorious in its legal struggle against Boyce, and pressed to conclude the sale to the Nature Conservancy. To buy peace from the critics, Yale announced it would donate $1.5 million to subsidize the cost to Colorado's taxpayers. But Farallon was soon ambushed by another surprise: A bizarre coalition of protesters announced itself on several college campuses. Its leaders declared that they were part of an "unFarallon campaign" aimed at forcing college endowments to withdraw their capital from Farallon. A protest soccer game at the University of Texas featured players dressed up as crony capitalists. A "transparency fairy" in a feathered mask waved her wand outside Swensen's office at Yale, willing the endowment to be more open and accountable.[37]

The street theater drew attention to a new unFarallon Web site, which listed all manner of supposedly nefarious activities. It cited Farallon's investment in a coal-fired power project in Indonesia: Coal was evil. It invoked Farallon's investment in Argentina: The workers had suffered. It paraded the plight of the tiger salamander on a California golf course in which Farallon had invested: Unless the golf lords dug some ponds, the salamanders would be threatened.[38] Indeed, Farallon was complicit in no less a crime than the Iraq war: It owned a $3 million stake in Halliburton, the oil-services firm once headed by Vice President Cheney. The activists demanded that Farallon's secretive mastermind meet them to discuss "the ethics of Farallon's investment practices." "We are stakeholders in the investments you make with university money," they lectured Steyer, apparently imagining an adversary with a monocle and top hat. "We do not want our universities to profit from investors that harm other communities."[39]

Steyer did his best to stand up for himself. He wrote to the unFarallon campaign, pleading that he cared as much as anyone about strong business values. He wrote to Farallon's investors, stating the obvious truth that the Web site was "factually inaccurate." But the demonstrations continued. In April students held a rally in front of the office of Yale's president. They staged a mock attempt to extract water from an aquifer under the campus, and they broke ground for a new coal-fired power plant. When the students showed up at a meeting of Yale's Advisory Committee on Investment Responsibility, David Swensen's patience was stretched even further.[40] After sitting through a recital of complaints about the endowment's failure to disclose the details of its investments, he decided it was time to engage his tormentors, and he approached them after the meeting: A tall, wiry figure in a fleece vest, towering over a group of grungy students, arguing intensely. The students' demand for more transparency was simply impractical, he explained; in order to compete successfully in markets, investors must protect proprietary secrets. If Yale wanted to reap the benefits of hedge funds, it had to promise not to leak information about their dealings: It needed to ensure that it was "the highest-quality limited partner possible." The students were unmoved. "I think it's more important to look at Yale as the highest-quality global citizen," one of them retorted.[41]

In picking on Swensen and Steyer, the students had chosen two of the least appropriate targets in the hedge-fund universe. Far from being a Cheney acolyte, Steyer was an open-fisted backer of the Democratic presidential candidate, John Kerry. Far from being a money-obsessed monster, Swensen had missed a chance to be a billionaire because of his "genetic defect." But none of this mattered. Hedge funds had grown with the help of college endowments. They could not expect immunity from the vagaries of college politics.

FARALLON CLOSED THE SALE TO THE NATURE CONSER-vancy in September 2004. The water project had been a failure, but the land had gained value, so Steyer and his partners came out with a small profit. But the Colorado episode exposed a vulnerability—both in Farallon and in ambitious bargain-hunting funds more generally. Bargains often lurk in quirky places: in the details of the junk-bond market's debris, in postcrisis Indonesia, in tangled feuds between ranchers and farmers in a remote Colorado valley. To invest successfully in these sorts of situations, you need to understand the traps in the terrain, and young hedge funds sometimes lack the manpower to survey it adequately. If Farallon's people had spent more time in the San Luis Valley, they might have realized that Gary Boyce was an unsatisfactory partner.[42] But in a fund that doubles its assets every four or five years, it can be hard to grow in-house expertise as fast as incoming capital.

But the vulnerability in Farallon-style funds goes deeper than that. Their returns partly reflect a willingness to buy illiquid investments. If busted junk bonds represent value, it is probably because most investors are frightened to buy them—so if you decide you want to sell later, such assets will be hard to exit. If you buy a bank in Indonesia, the same argument applies; if you make a mistake, you can't expect to get out easily. In ordinary liquid markets, prices are fairly efficient and second-guessing them is hard. In illiquid markets, by contrast, there are bargains aplenty—but mistakes can be extremely costly.[43]

Hedge funds that buy illiquid assets benefit from an accounting quirk that can flatter their performance. By definition, it is hard to know what an illiquid asset is worth—you lack the continually updated price discovery that comes with constant trading. As a result, hedge funds with illiquid assets don't so much report their profits as *estimate* them—there is no objective price for much of what they hold, so they have to come up with a subjective value. In a few cases, hedge funds may take advantage of this murkiness to exaggerate their returns, though this game is not sustainable. But even if funds make every effort to report their results honestly, they cannot help but "smooth" them. A hedge fund may estimate the value of an illiquid asset every few weeks; if it rises 5 percent and then falls back within that period, it will be recorded simply as flat—with the result that some sharp volatility along the way is not acknowledged. As a result, hedge funds with illiquid assets are not as stable as their numbers suggest. Their risk-adjusted returns look wonderful because some of the risk goes unreported.

But the biggest danger for buyers of illiquid assets is that, in a crisis, these assets will collapse the hardest. In moments of panic, investors crave securities that can be easily sold, and the rest are shunned ruthlessly. Long-Term Capital's apparently diverse portfolio concealed a single bet that the world would be stable: When this proved wrong, apparently unrelated positions collapsed simultaneously because many of them boiled down to an attempt to harvest a premium for holding illiquid assets. Likewise, apparently diversified event-driven funds may be taking a concentrated bet on illiquid investments. In 1998, Long-Term Capital paid the ultimate price for taking too much of this sort of risk. In 2008, buyers of illiquid assets paid heavily again, as we shall see presently.

13

THE CODE BREAKERS

Not so many hedge funders have been to East Setauket. It is an hour's drive from Manhattan, along the Long Island Expressway; it is separated from the hedge-fund cluster in Greenwich by a wedge of the Atlantic Ocean. But this sleepy Long Island township is home to what is perhaps the most successful hedge fund ever: Renaissance Technologies. Starting around the time that David Swensen invested in Farallon, Renaissance positively coined money; between the end of 1989 and 2006, its flagship fund, Medallion, returned 39 percent per year on average.[1] By the mid-2000s, Renaissance's founder, James Simons, had emerged as the highest hedge-fund earner of them all. He was not the world's most famous billionaire, but he was probably its cleverest.

Simons was a mathematician and code breaker, a lifelong speculator and entrepreneur, and his extraordinary success derived from the combination of these passions. As a speculator, he had dabbled in commodities since his student days, acquiring the trading bug that set him up for future stardom. As an entrepreneur, he had launched a string of businesses; the name of his company, Renaissance Technologies, reflected its origins in high-tech venture capital. As a code cracker, Simons had worked at the Pentagon's secretive Institute for Defense Analyses, where he learned how to build a research organization that was closed toward outsiders but collaborative on the inside. As a mathematician, he had affixed his name to a breakthrough known as the Chern-Simons theory and won the American Mathematical Society's Oswald Veblen Prize, the highest honor in geometry. In an expression of his diverse passions, Simons used a wedding gift to speculate successfully on soybeans, got fired from the Institute for Defense Analyses for opposing the Vietnam War, and drove from Boston to Bogotá on a Lambretta motor scooter—all while still in his twenties. Having grown to know Colombia at the end of that road trip, he teamed up with some local friends to launch a tile factory in the country.

Simons's early adventures in markets had little to do with mathematics. He traded commodity futures on the basis of hunches about demand and supply, riding the wild booms and busts of the 1970s. But the mathematician inside him yearned to substitute models for seat-of-the-pants judgment, and he loved the idea of a machine that would do his trading for him. Starting in the late 1970s, Simons recruited a string of outstanding mathematical minds to help create such a machine. There was Leonard Baum, a cryptographer who had worked with Simons at the Institute for Defense Analyses. There was James Ax, a winner of the American Mathematical Society's foremost prize in number theory. And there was Elwyn Berlekamp, a Berkeley mathematician who was yet another veteran of the Institute for Defense Analyses. The names and ownership structures of Simons's various ventures changed along with the collaborators he drew into his net. He had an investment fund in Bermuda and a company on the West Coast, as well as the operation on Long Island, where he had chaired the math department of Stony Brook University before quitting in 1977 to focus on his businesses.

It was not just that Simons's recruits were intellectually formidable. Their experiences in cryptography and other aspects of military communications were relevant to finance. For example, Berlekamp had worked on systems that send signals resembling "ghosts"—faint traces of code in seas of statistical noise, not unlike the faint patterns that hide in broadly random and efficient markets. Soldiers on a battlefield need to send messages to air cover that are so wispy and translucent that they won't betray their positions: Not only must the enemy not decode the messages; it must not even suspect that someone is transmitting. To Berlekamp, the battlefield adversaries fooled by such systems bore a striking resemblance to economists who declared markets' movements to be random. They had stared at the ghosts. They had seen and suspected nothing.[2] The Simons team took their experience with code-breaking algorithms and used it to look for ghostly patterns in market data. Economists could not compete in the same league, because they lacked the specialized math needed to do so.

The early efforts of the Simons team were only moderately successful. Despite his preeminence as a mathematical modeler, Leonard Baum quickly tired of the quest for golden algorithms; he read the business papers and took a huge bet on the British pound, which paid off handsomely. James Ax stuck with the computer-trading project; but he was a volatile personality and his system's returns could be volatile also. Still, by 1988 Simons had built the platform for his later success. Together with Ax he launched the Medallion Fund, named in honor of the medals the two men had won for geometry and number theory. Medallion traded commodity and financial futures on the basis of computer-generated signals; and although the heart of the system was unremarkable—it was a trend-following model not unlike the one built at Commodities Corporation more than a decade before—a small portion of the money was deployed according to a different set of rules. This was the kernel of the future Simons fortune.

The kernel was the brainchild of Henry Laufer, a member of the mathematics faculty at Stony Brook University.[3] Laufer was a self-contained figure. Once, following an argument, Ax had tried to punish him by refusing to speak to him for months; Laufer had failed to notice. But Laufer's eccentricity was matched by his talent. In a triumph of ghost hunting in the mid-1980s, he had spotted patterns in the way that markets move right after an event perturbs them. In the period after a new data release, a commodity or currency would spike upward and downward as different investors reacted, and although the jiggering appeared random to the naked eye, a scientist with high-resolution statistical goggles could make out patterns in the movements. It was not that a commodity would jigger in the same way following every piece of news: That would have been too obvious. But if you scrutinized thousands of reactions to thousands of events, certain sequences emerged in slightly more than half of all the observations. By betting on those sequences repeatedly, the Simons team would win more often than it lost. And by betting enough times and in great enough size, it could be assured of handsome profits.[4]

The algorithms that describe Medallion's lucrative patterns were and have remained a secret. But the reason for their discovery, and for the phenomenal profits that they brought, can be understood, at least roughly. Part of the success lay in the choice of the short term. By examining a commodity's behavior over brief periods, Laufer could collect thousands of observations, boosting his chances of finding repetitive patterns that were statistically significant. Moreover, short-term signals were likely to be more valuable as well as easier to find. If you can predict which way a commodity will move over the next few days, it takes only that long to place your wager and collect your reward; a Tiger investor aspires to buy a company that will double its value in two years, but a statistical trader who makes a quarter of a percent in twenty-four hours will end up considerably richer. Finally, predictions over the short term tend to inspire more confidence than the long-term sort. There's less time for unforeseen factors to knock the forecast off target. Because it was dealing in short-term predictions that were relatively robust, the Simons team could leverage its bets and magnify its profits.

When Simons and Ax launched the Medallion Fund in 1988, about 15 percent of its capital was driven by the short-term signals, with the rest allotted to traditional trend-following models.[5] The fund began promisingly, then dipped into a terrifying nosedive; by May 1989 it was down almost a quarter from its peak, and Simons decided to suspend trading. James Ax insisted passionately that the model would soon resume its profitable run, but Simons was so convinced that Ax was wrong that he ended the partnership. Enlisting the help of Berlekamp and Laufer, he embarked on a "study period" to decide Medallion's future.

The trouble, Simons and his team decided, was that the trend-following mainstay of Medallion's system had run out of juice. Too many Commodities Corporation wannabes had crowded in; brokers such as Dean Witter were marketing dozens of commodity funds to their clients; trend following had grown trendy.[6] After some months of deliberation, Simons and his colleagues resolved to make Laufer's short-term signals the new heart of the system. In 1990, the first full year of trading after the relaunch, Medallion notched up 56 percent after subtracting fees. It was a good beginning.

Elwyn Berlekamp reacted to this bonanza by cashing out. He sold his share of the management company that ran Medallion and returned to his research interests at Berkeley. But Simons responded with the entrepreneurial conviction that distinguished him. For more than a decade, he had charmed a shifting cast of mathematicians into collaborating on his ventures, believing that the cryptographer's methods could crack the market's code eventually. Now he felt he had been proven right, and he was determined to press his advantage. Having bought Berlekamp's share of the management company, he rolled what was left of it into his operations at Renaissance Technologies. Armed with the profits that Medallion was now generating, he redoubled his efforts to hire mathematicians onto his team, installing his brain trust in the Long Island High Technology Incubator building near the Stony Brook hospital. Pretty soon, the investment paid off. The expanding research team discovered that the patterns that worked in American commodities markets often worked in foreign markets too. And, after some setbacks, the Simons team's ghost-hunting methods discovered patterns in equity markets.

As the Long Island brain trust expanded, Simons added computer scientists, physicists, and astronomers to his roster, though he never hired economists. He wanted people who would approach the markets as a mathematical puzzle, unconnected to the flesh and blood and bricks and mortar of a real economy. Of course, the scientists' abstraction could sometimes lead to strange results. On one occasion, a member of the faculty gave a presentation on how Medallion had performed over the past week; he presented Friday's results first, followed by Monday's, Thursday's, Tuesday's, and then Wednesday's, assuming that his colleagues would find this bizarre sequencing natural, since computers sort days alphabetically. Another time Renaissance hosted a dinner for five hundred investors. A scientist volunteered to help Simons write a program to figure out the seating plan; he would assign probabilities to which sorts of people would get along best with which others, then let the computer optimize the table settings. For a while the blackboard in Simons's office was covered with estimates for the likelihood that a single female algebraic geometer would get along with a married male judo instructor, and so on. When the big night arrived, the program seated one of Renaissance's long-time investors next to a woman he may have liked too much. She had sued him for sexual harassment.

Most of the time, though, the mathematical approach to the world proved gloriously successful. Simons invested heavily in computers, which were fed with every conceivable form of data: prices from financial markets, economic releases, information from newswires, even time series on weather. The deeper the team went with its ghost hunting, the more it succeeded in discovering profitable patterns. In one simple example, the brain trust discovered that fine morning weather in a city tended to predict an upward movement in its stock exchange. By buying on bright days at breakfast time and selling a bit later, Medallion could come out ahead— except that the effect was too small to overcome transaction costs, which is why Renaissance allowed this signal to be public.

Many of the patterns that Renaissance discovered were individually modest; to a first approximation, after all, markets are efficient. But by discovering a large number of minor inefficiencies and blending them into a single trading program, Renaissance built a system that racked up profits year after year, especially during periods of turbulence. In 1994, the year Michael Steinhardt lost billions in the bond-market meltdown, Medallion returned 71 percent after subtracting fees. In the crash of 2008, it was up 80 percent after fees—and almost 160 percent before them.

By the time Simons retired, in 2009, he had become a billionaire many times over. In 2006 alone, his personal earnings reportedly came to $1.5 billion, as much as the corporate profits generated by the 115,000 employees of Starbucks and the 118,000 employees of Costco put together. The secretive code cracker found his photograph on magazine covers: a comb-over of white hair and a grizzled white beard framing the lined face of an inveterate smoker. And to the astonishment of others in the hedge-fund universe, Medallion's magic proved resilient to competitive pressure throughout the 1990s and 2000s. As of this writing, in early 2010, it shows no sign of diminishing.

———

THE FIRST COMPETITIVE CHALLENGE TO RENAISSANCE
came from David Shaw, a computer scientist from Columbia University.
Shaw launched his eponymous company, D. E. Shaw, in 1988—the same
year that Medallion began trading. Much like the Simons team, Shaw
focused on fairly short time scales, and he hired mathematicians and scientists rather than traders and economists. Much like the Simons team,
he pursued numerical precision with a zealous intensity: His staff soon
discovered that it was no good telling him that a programming task might
take three to eight weeks; you had to say that it would take 5.25, but with
an error of two weeks.[7] Yet for all these similarities, there were differences
between Shaw and Simons too. These proved to be significant.

Shaw got into finance via Morgan Stanley's proprietary trading desk,
which hired him to create a computer system to support its quantitative
trading. It was 1986, and big things were stirring at Morgan. The firm's
secretive Analytical Proprietary Trading unit ran a computerized effort
to profit from short-run liquidity effects in stock markets. As Michael
Steinhardt had discovered in the 1970s, a big sell order from a pension
fund could push a stock's price out of line; provided that there was no
information behind the sale—that is, provided that the pension fund was
selling because it needed cash rather than because it was reacting to bad
news—Steinhardt could profit by buying and holding the stock until it
rose back to its previous level. Morgan Stanley's Analytical Proprietary
Trading unit aimed to beat Steinhardt at this game. To identify price
moves that were not based on information, a team of quants sorted stocks
into pairs: Ford's movements tended to track those of GM, American Airlines tracked United Airlines, International Paper tracked Georgia-Pacific,
and so on. If one of these stocks fell while the paired one stayed put, it
was probably being pushed by an institutional block trader that needed to
raise cash—in which case the price would soon revert, creating an opportunity to profit.[8] Of course, Morgan Stanley's method was not infallible,
but it did not need to be. The firm just had to be right more than half the
time in order to generate profits.

After a couple of years at Morgan, Shaw wanted to do more than build a bank unit's computer system. He had been struck by the limits to Morgan's approach. Having figured out how to profit from simple pairs trading, the Analytical Proprietary Trading group had invested in all manner of research: It brought in physicists who sought to apply chaos theory to the markets, mathematicians who tried to develop complex differential equations to model stock movements, and even, according to one veteran's account, systems that used 3-D glasses to hunt for patterns in prices.[9] But to a person with Shaw's computer-science training, Morgan was ignoring some potentially interesting avenues. The way Morgan's team tried to find anomalies in financial data was nothing like the way that a university computer-science team would have approached the challenge, and the techniques used to combine the anomalies into trading models were also different. Not knowing exactly where his hunch would lead, Shaw quit Morgan, rented an office above a communist bookshop in Greenwich Village, and launched his own company.

Within six months of opening his doors, Shaw's distinctive approach began to yield progress. Whereas Morgan had searched for complex nonlinear patterns and found little of interest, Shaw quickly identified promising anomalies. Much as with the Simons team, the ghosts that Shaw discovered were hard to explain: When he found recurring patterns and printed them out, there were no familiar terms that could be used to make sense of the squiggles on the paper. The effects were so far from being intuitive that Shaw had no need for high-speed trading systems: He did not need to get orders to market faster than rivals because he was confident that he would have none.[10] Pretty soon, the profits started to roll in, and Shaw outgrew the premises in Greenwich Village. He moved to a loft in the Flatiron District in 1989 and then to a futuristic tower on West Forty-fifth Street two years later; meanwhile, Morgan Stanley's frustrated bosses closed down the Analytical Proprietary Trading unit. A magazine writer who visited Shaw's outfit in 1994 was struck by what he saw: By now the firm employed 135 people and accounted for as much as 5 percent of the daily turnover on the New York Stock Exchange. The dress code was casual and the firm had a faintly Bohemian feel. Staffers rolled out sleeping bags to stay over at night. "It is easier to focus if you don't go home," explained a young employee named Jeffrey Bezos, who went on to found the Internet retailing giant Amazon.[11]

Like other quantitative traders, Shaw's approach to markets differed fundamentally from that of economists. The economists generally started from the assumption of perfect arbitrage: If two bonds or two equities were theoretically the same, then they should be worth the same; if they were not, the economists tended to presume that they ought to converge eventually. But the scientists were not looking for relationships between prices that *ought* to exist. They were looking at the data and asking what relationships *did* exist.[12] Moreover, the data that they looked at had been painstakingly swept for typing glitches and errors—it was cleaner than anything available to most finance professors. Time and again, an eager academic would contact D. E. Shaw, claiming to have discovered a profitable anomaly in the markets. Time and again, Shaw's faculty would find that the anomaly consisted merely of misreported numbers. The academic's strategy might consist, for example, of buying stocks whose price had cratered suddenly. But if a price series shows IBM trading at $60, then at $61, and then at $16, that last number is not a buy signal. It is a typo.

Once Shaw had created his quantitative team, he reached beyond the modeling of stock prices. Options proved to be a fertile field. The early options models, created among others by the two LTCM Nobel laureates, Robert Merton and Myron Scholes, assumed that stock-price changes were distributed normally. The 1987 crash had demonstrated that this assumption was not merely shaky; it was dangerously wrong—the truth was that extreme price moves happened far more frequently than the normal distribution anticipated. The challenge was to come up with a better pricing model, and Shaw saw his chance: His mathematicians were better at modeling than other market players; but as market participants themselves, they had better access to price data than mathematicians at universities. Sure enough, Shaw's team came up with an options-pricing model that gave him an edge in multiple markets. The firm milked misalignments in various kinds of equity derivatives, notably in Japan.[13] It branched into "convertibles"—bonds with stock options attached. It opened an options market-making operation and soon came to account for half the trades in some parts of this business.

By 1995 Shaw's outfit had swelled to more than two hundred employees, and there was no doubting his achievement. Yet it was not the same sort of achievement as the Medallion fund. Shaw had created a machine to discover anomalies in stock prices, much as Renaissance had done for futures and then later also for equities, and Shaw's firm claims that some of its strategies produced Medallion-sized returns of 40 percent plus.[14] But although the Shaw team is secretive about the details, it cannot have harnessed as much capital to those golden algorithms, since otherwise its total returns would have been higher. Meanwhile, Shaw has been more willing to branch out. In 1995 the firm launched the Internet service provider Juno Online, as well as FarSight, an early venture in online banking and brokerage. Alongside its efforts in options market making, Shaw waded into the so-called third market, in which listed equities were traded away from the stock exchange. This business was dominated by a genial networker named Bernie Madoff, and so Shaw's team jumped in, figuring that its quantitative edge would allow it to make decent money. But Madoff had ways of making up for his lack of cutting-edge analysis, and Shaw's quants failed to turn a profit.

Shaw's willingness to experiment was both a strength and a weakness. By launching multiple ventures, he diversified his risks, and some of the new ventures paid off handsomely. But Shaw was sometimes moving into fields that were already popular, running the risk of getting stuck in crowded trades when markets turned turbulent. In 1997, his firm formed an alliance with Bank of America, which aimed among other things to mine anomalies in bonds. Unfortunately, its strategies turned out to overlap with the sorts of arbitrage practiced by LTCM and its imitators. The result was that D. E. Shaw got hurt in the bond-market turbulence that accompanied Long-Term Capital's collapse in 1998—"It could have been the end of the game for Shaw at that point," one of the firm's traders said later. The company sold part of its trading book, taking a loss that wiped out that year's gains in all its other strategies combined. Having learned how highly leveraged fixed-income strategies could get hit in a liquidity crunch, Shaw abandoned bond arbitrage for a few years, though by 2002 it had tiptoed back into it.

WHILE SHAW WAS BUILDING HIS MACHINE, ANOTHER effort was under way in a surprising corner of the industry. Paul Tudor Jones, rock-and-roll trader and Robin Hood founder, was investing the fruits of his winnings in a computer-trading project. The early phases of this effort were in keeping with Jones's exuberant youth. The trading systems had names like Madonna and Material Girl; they were statistically crude and their results were less exciting than their namesakes. But in the early 1990s Jones's style changed. Having been cockily public, he lowered his profile. Having been a hot Manhattan bachelor, he married and settled down in Greenwich. His company became more grown-up, too. The Bruce Willis sneakers were put away, and Tudor changed from a single-trader outfit to a sleek institutional platform that supported multiple portfolio managers. Jones brought in James Pallotta, a Boston-based stock picker who would complement his macro trading; he brought in a London-based wizard named Mark Heffernan, who had once been described as the greatest discretionary trader in the Goldman Sachs empire. Tudor's expanding ambitions affected its computer-trading aspirations too, particularly after the arrival in 1995 of Sushil Wadhwani.

Wadhwani was at once an accomplished economist and a creature of the markets. He had taught economics and statistics at the London School of Economics, and he went on to serve on the monetary policy committee of the Bank of England. But he came to Tudor via Goldman Sachs, where he had worked as an investment strategist. His work at Goldman involved advising the bank's proprietary traders and its external clients, not least Paul Tudor Jones; and by rubbing shoulders with these players he had learned the limits of pure economic thinking.[15] Contrary to what a team of modern-portfolio theorists might imagine, identifying an illogical price anomaly was only the start of a trader's thought process; the next step was to identify a trigger—a reason why the anomaly might correct—since otherwise it might persist indefinitely. The trigger could be an upcoming election, a psychological tipping point identified in the charts, or some factor that would change the behavior of large institutional investors. Whether consciously or otherwise, the great discretionary traders were acting on signals from this blend of inputs. Wadhwani's mission at Tudor was to build a machine that mimicked their eclectic thinking.

Wadhwani's system drew on careful observation of Paul Jones and his ex-Goldman colleague, Mark Heffernan. He began by creating a naive model: For example, the system might buy the stock-market index if economic indicators were positive, if institutions were sitting on large pools of uninvested cash, and if signals from the options market suggested that sentiment was ready to turn upward. Then he would watch Jones and Heffernan trading and probe them on the reasons for their moves. Why had one of them put a certain position on at ten o'clock? Why had he increased it three hours later? The traders were generally considering the same factors that were already in Wadhwani's program, but they were combining them in different ways. The more Wadhwani listened, the more he refined his model.[16]

Deciding when to buy the stock-market index—or a currency or oil future—was only part of the challenge. The next question was how much to bet on each position. Short-term trading systems like the one that powered Jim Simons's Medallion Fund also confronted this problem, but in a different way: Because they were operating on short time frames, they risked moving the price against them if they traded suddenly and hard, so they calculated how much they could bet without destroying their own profits. But Wadhwani was creating a system to trade liquid markets over a longer horizon; he had time to build a position to whatever size he liked without moving the price adversely. The limiting factor was the risk he was prepared to take. If he bet too little, he would leave money on the table; if he bet too much, he would risk insolvency. To all great human traders, knowing when to go for the jugular and when to be patient is a large part of the skill; spotting the best opportunities and betting big could make a greater contribution to the bottom line than increasing the share of bets that you were right on. Wadhwani's models tackled this problem by assigning particular trades a "z score": The greater the confidence of winning, and the higher the likely payoff from a win, the more the system would bet on a position.

As Wadhwani progressed with his modeling, he could see that it was not just the sizing of trades that needed to be determined flexibly. The *type* of trades needed to change in different environments. In moments of turbulence, animal spirits mattered more than in calm times, so the computer system needed to weight measures of sentiment from the options market more heavily.[17] Equally, when the economy entered a recession, each negative data point was likely to have a larger impact on financial markets than the previous one. A bad employment number might hurt stocks slightly in good times but a lot more in a downturn. Most fundamentally, a serious effort at computerized investing needed to be based on more than one program. In stable times, LTCM-style arbitrage could pay off well: You needed a program that bet on price anomalies disappearing. In unstable times, arbitrage was dangerous: You needed a trend-following program. The ideal, Wadhwani realized, was to devise ways of shifting between these strategies automatically.

Wadhwani left Tudor for the Bank of England in 1999, before he had had time to build out his vision. A first version of his program, a trend-following system called Techno-Fundamentals, ran money successfully from the end of 1997, but the job of creating a system that would shift according to the market environment remained uncompleted. Wadhwani returned to the task when he set up his own hedge fund, Wadhwani Asset Management, in London in 2002, and meanwhile, Tudor's program trading continued to develop. By 2008 Paul Jones's firm had more than fifty people working on its computerized trading, and their algorithms were driving more than $3 billion of Tudor's $17 billion capital.[18] The rock-and-roller with the Bruce Willis sneakers had accomplished quite a transformation.

And yet, just as with D. E. Shaw, there were limits to this achievement. The systems that Tudor created were not as original as those developed by James Simons's team at Renaissance Technologies. The fact that Tudor's system was built by an economist from Goldman Sachs and based partly on the instincts of a trader from Goldman Sachs was revealing: No matter how brilliant Wadhwani and Heffernan might be, they came from the heart of the financial establishment, and other parts of that establishment were likely to hatch strategies that were at least somewhat similar. A handful of prized experts moved among a handful of firms. Each move reduced the odds that any single firm would build a unique system.

Meanwhile, Simons plowed his own road. He hired established scientists and mathematicians, not the young quants that Shaw favored and certainly not Wall Street veterans.[19] He limited cross-fertilization with rivals by locating his operation in Long Island, away from the hedge-fund heartlands of New York, Greenwich, and London. He had no use for ideas that came from academic finance: For a while the faculty in East Setauket plowed through the academic finance journals and met weekly to discuss the latest articles, but then it abandoned this as fruitless. The Renaissance researchers built systems that were in a class of their own. "I can only look at them and realize that you have the gods of the business and then you have mere mortals like me," Wadhwani said, echoing the view of the entire industry.[20]

IN 1993 SIMONS MADE TWO IMPORTANT ADDITIONS TO HIS brain trust: Peter Brown and Robert Mercer. They came from IBM's research center, and they drove much of the success of Medallion over the next years, eventually taking the reins when Simons opted for retirement. The two men complemented each other well. Brown was a magnesium flare of energy: He slept five hours per night, riffed passionately on every topic of the day, and for a while got around the office on a unicycle. Mercer was the calm half of the duo: He was an icy cold poker player; he never recalled having a nightmare; his IBM boss jokingly called him an automaton. Before arriving at Renaissance, Brown and Mercer had worked a little on cryptography, but their real achievement lay elsewhere. They had upended a related field—that of computerized translation.

Until Brown and Mercer decided to take on translation, the subject was dominated by programmers who actually spoke some foreign languages. The approach was to understand the language from the inside, to know its grammar and its syntax, and to teach the computer that "la fille" means "the girl" and "les filles" is the plural form, much as you might teach a middle schooler. But Brown and Mercer had a different method. They did not speak French, and they were not about to wade into its syntax or grammar. Instead, they got hold of Canada's parliamentary records, which contain thousands of pages of paired passages in French and English. Then they fed the material into an IBM workstation and told it to figure out the correlations.

Unlike the work that Brown and Mercer later did at Renaissance, their experiment at IBM was written up and published.[21] It began with some scrubbing of data: Just as financial-market price histories must be checked for "bad tics"—places where a sale is reported at $16 instead of $61—so the Canadian Hansard contained misprinted words that might confuse a translation program. Next, the computer began to search the data for patterns. For all it knew at the outset, a given English word was equally likely to be translatable into any of the fifty-eight thousand French words in the sample, but once the computer had checked through the twinned passages, it found that most English words appeared in only some: Immediately, nearly 99 percent of the uncertainty was eliminated. Then the computer proceeded with a series of more subtle tests; for example, it assumed that an English word was most likely to correspond to a French word that came in the same position in the sentence. By now some word pairs were starting to appear: Couplings such as *lait*/milk and *pourquoi*/why shouted from the data. But other correlations spoke in a softer voice. To hear them clearly, you had to comb the data multiple times, using slightly different algorithms at each turn. "Only in this way can one hope to hear the quiet call of *marqué d'un asterisque*/starred or the whisper of *qui s'est fait bousculer*/embattled," Brown and Mercer reported.

To the code crackers at the Institute for Defense Analyses, this method would not have seemed surprising.[22] Indeed, Brown and Mercer used a tool called the "expectations maximization algorithm," and they cited its inventor, Leonard Baum—this was the same Leonard Baum who had worked for IDA and then later for Simons.[23] But although the idea of "statistical machine translation" seemed natural to the code breakers, it was greeted with outrage by traditional translation programmers. A reviewer of the Brown-Mercer paper scolded that "the crude force of computers is not science," and when the paper was presented at a meeting of translation experts, a listener recalled, "We were all flabbergasted. . . . People were shaking their heads and spurting grunts of disbelief or even of hostility." "Where's the linguistic intuition?" the audience wanted to know—to which the answer seemed to be, "Yes that's the point; there isn't any." Fred Jelinek, the IBM manager who oversaw Brown and Mercer, poured salt into the wounds. "Every time I fire a linguist, my system's performance improves," he told the naysayers.[24]

By the time Brown and Mercer joined Renaissance in 1993, the skeptics were capitulating. Once the IBM team's program had figured out the sample passages from the Canadian Hansard, it could translate other material too: If you presented it with an article in a French newspaper, it would zip through its database of parliamentary speeches, matching the article's phrases with the decoded material. The results outclassed competing translation systems by a wide margin, and within a few years the advent of statistical machine translation was celebrated among computer scientists as something of an intellectual revolution.[25] Canadian political rhetoric had proved more useful than suspected hitherto. And Brown and Mercer had reminded the world of a lesson about artificial intelligence.

The lesson concerned the difference between human beings and computers. The early translation programs had tried to teach computers vocabulary and grammar because that's how people learn things. But computers are better suited to a different approach: They can learn to translate between English and French without paying much attention to the rules of either language. Computers don't need to understand verb declensions or adjectival inflections before they approach a pile of political speeches; they prefer to get the speeches first, then penetrate their code by combing through them algorithmically. Likewise, computers have no trouble committing millions of sentences to memory; they can learn languages in chunks, without the crutch of grammatical rules that human students use to prompt their memories. For example, a computer can remember the English translations for phrases such as "la fille est intelligente, les filles sont intelligentes," and a dozen other variations besides; they do not necessarily need to understand that "fille" is the singular form of "filles," that "est" and "sont" are different forms of the verb "être," and so on.[26] Contrary to the harrumphing of the IBM team's critics, the crude force of a computer's memory can actually substitute for human notions of intelligence and science. And computers are likely to work best when they don't attempt to reach results in the way that humans would do.

What clues might this hold about Medallion's performance? Quite possibly, none: Again, the reasons for the fund's spectacular success are secret. But it's clear that the way Brown and Mercer approached programming was fundamentally different from the way other hedge-fund programmers thought about it. At Tudor, for example, Sushil Wadhwani trained a machine to approach markets in a manner that made sense for human traders. By contrast, Brown and Mercer trained themselves to approach problems in a manner that made sense for a computer. At D. E. Shaw, the approach was frequently to start with theories about the market and to test them against the data. By contrast, Brown and Mercer fed the data into the computer first and let it come up with the answers. D. E. Shaw's approach recalls the programmers who taught computers French grammar. The Brown-Mercer approach resembles that of code crackers, who don't have the option of starting with a grammar book. Presented with apparently random data and no further clues, they sift it repeatedly for patterns, exploiting the power of computers to hunt for ghosts that to the human eye would be invisible.

Renaissance's quantitative rivals have reason to avoid ghost hunting. The computer may find fake ghosts—patterns that exist for no reason beyond chance, and that consequently have no predictive value. Eric Wepsic, who runs statistical arbitrage at D. E. Shaw, gives the example of the Super Bowl: It used to be said that if a team from the original National Football League won, the market would head upward. As a matter of statistics, this relationship might hold; but as a matter of common sense, it is a meaningless coincidence. Because of the threat from coincidental correlations masquerading as predictive signals, Wepsic suggests that it is often dangerous to trade on statistical evidence unless it can be intuitively explained. In the 1990s, for example, D. E. Shaw's systems began to detect curious correlations between previously unrelated stocks—cable companies, media companies, and consumer electronics firms all seemed to be responding to a strange new force field. On the basis of this evidence alone, Shaw's team would have been inclined to dismiss the correlations as a statistical fluke. But once the firm realized that the correlations made intuitive sense—they reflected the technology euphoria that had pushed into all these industries—they seemed more likely to be tradable.[27] Moreover, signals based on intuition have a further advantage: If you understand why they work, you probably understand why they might cease to work, so you are less likely to keep trading them beyond their point of usefulness. In short, Wepsic is saying that pure pattern recognition is a small part of what Shaw does, even if the firm does some of it.

Again, this presents a contrast with Renaissance. Whereas D. E. Shaw grew out of statistical arbitrage in equities, with strong roots in fundamental intuitions about stocks, Renaissance grew out of technical trading in commodities, a tradition that treats price data as paramount.[28] Whereas D. E. Shaw hired quants of all varieties, usually recruiting them in their twenties, the crucial early years at Renaissance were largely shaped by established cryptographers and translation programmers—experts who specialized in distinguishing fake ghosts from real ones. Robert Mercer echoes some of Wepsic's wariness about false correlations: "If somebody came with a theory about how the phases of Venus influence markets, we would want a lot of evidence." But he adds that "some signals that make no intuitive sense do indeed work." Indeed, it is the nonintuitive signals that often prove the most lucrative for Renaissance. "The signals that we have been trading without interruption for fifteen years make no sense," Mercer explains. "Otherwise someone else would have found them."[29]

BY THE LATE 2000S THE RENAISSANCE RESEARCH EFFORT had long since outgrown the rented premises in the Long Island High Technology Incubator building. Simons had moved the faculty to a campus with a gym and lighted tennis courts, a pond with bulbous gold-fish, and a big skylight in the entrance hall that splashed sun onto a slate staircase. The place felt like an upmarket science facility—comfortable, low-key, eerily clean—and on the door of one office along an antiseptic corridor, somebody had stuck an article with the title "Why Most Published Research Findings Are False." The windowless rooms that housed racks of computer servers were guarded with elaborate key systems, but the facility's most striking feature was its openness. Whereas other quantitative hedge funds enforced fierce internal Chinese walls, doling out information to employees on a need-to-know basis in an effort to protect secrets, the atmosphere at Renaissance was altogether different. The scientists roamed the corridors freely, constrained only by the danger that Peter Brown would crash into them on his unicycle. Mirrors had been positioned at critical corners so you could see if Brown was coming.

Simons believed passionately in this open atmosphere. Like the Institute for Defense Analyses, his operation was closed to outsiders in order to protect secrets, yet open on the inside so as to promote teamwork. On Tuesday mornings on the Renaissance campus, the entire faculty of ninety or so PhDs would gather for what they called the Big Meeting. Every refinement to Medallion's trading program began with a presentation at one of these sessions: A researcher would explain his idea, complete with simulations showing how it would blend in with the other signals already in the system; then he would answer questions. A colleague might ask how the proposed signal would have fared during the LTCM crisis; another might wonder how it would have performed during a period of low volatility. In the days after the Big Meeting, the scientists were free to wander into the proponent's room and ask follow-up questions. At the end of this peer-review period, a Small Meeting would take place: This time only those scientists who still had questions would show up, and Brown and Mercer would decide whether to give the green light. Then there was one final check. Henry Laufer, the veteran ghost hunter from the 1980s, retained the title of chief scientist and the right of veto.

Simons had devised a compensation system to reinforce this culture of teamwork. The researchers' pay was linked to the profits of the firm, not to the narrower results of some subunit. Collaboration was written into the firm's technology infrastructure as well. At IBM, Brown and Mercer had created a system on which multiple programmers could work simultaneously, and they repeated this trick at Renaissance; a researcher could even

adapt the in-house programming language in order to express a new idea—
in computing, as in everyday speech, neologisms can be useful.[30] Into this
collaborative architecture the faculty fed the reams of data that modern
society generates. The more finance went global, the more statistics from
foreign markets were fed into the system. The more business went digital,
the more new data became available—e-commerce sales, Web-surfing habits, and so on. The computerization of finance created a vast information
windfall. In the old days, it had been possible to track a stock price trade by
trade. Now it was possible to see each bid and offer for each stock—including those that never got consummated. The more the possibilities expanded,
the more they exceeded the reach of a few minds. But the collaborative
faculty at Renaissance could manage this complexity and thrive on it.

The firm's culture of teamwork involved a risk, however. It presumed
that no member of the team would leave with the trading secrets and set
up a rival. Like "The Firm" in John Grisham's novel, Renaissance thought
carefully about the matter of employee loyalty. It instructed job appli-
cants that, if they joined Renaissance, they could never work elsewhere
in the financial industry; it generally did not hire from Wall Street partly
because anyone who left one team of traders might later choose to leave
a second one. To enforce the noncompete and nondisclosure agreements
that researchers were made to sign, they were required to invest a fifth of
their pay in the Medallion Fund, and the money was locked up as a sort
of bail payment for four years after they departed. And of course it helped
that the firm was based in the quaint town of East Setauket, miles from its
competitors. Once a researcher installed his kids in local schools, he didn't
want to go anywhere.

In 2003, however, this formula sprang a leak. In its drive to hire the
best brains on the planet, Renaissance had discovered one of the achievements of the old Soviet Union: The country recruited the brightest kids
from its fifteen republics and transported them to the Institute of Physics
and Technology in Moscow. There, separated from their families, these
prodigies underwent intensive training, and the ones who survived this
assault course found themselves internationally marketable after the Soviet
system disintegrated. Renaissance recruited one of these Russians, and he

recommended another one, and pretty soon the faculty in East Setauket had a sizable Russian caucus. But Renaissance's leaders had never paused to ponder the behavioral consequences of a Soviet upbringing. Kids raised in that failing political system were likely to assume that authority is corrupt and that a person's only obligation is to look out for himself; and kids who had been separated from their parents were all the more likely to mature as hardened individualists. Sure enough, after spending long enough on the Renaissance faculty to master its secrets, two of the Russian researchers presented Simons with an ultimatum. They refused to sign the firm's noncompete agreement and demanded higher pay. If Simons refused, they would quit and join a rival.[31]

Simons refused to be blackmailed, and the Russians left to join another hedge fund. On the face of it, this looked like a catastrophic blow. Because of the open structure at Renaissance, the Russians understood a lot about how the system worked. If they started trading on Renaissance's signals, they would siphon off part of its profits; it would be as though pirates were making generic copies of a pharmaceutical company's blockbuster therapy. Patents do not protect financial innovations in the way that they protect medical ones, so Simons's legal remedies were uncertain. And yet the remarkable thing was that Medallion's performance continued to leave rivals in the dust. Like the magician who drinks poison and survives, Simons emerged looking more mysterious than ever.

How could this survival act be possible? Part of the answer may lie with Renaissance's lawyers: By suing the Russians and their new employer, Simons may have deterred them from rolling out a rival system at full speed; and in 2006 a settlement laid down that the Russians would cease trading.[32] But lawyers are not the whole answer, since the Russians did operate a rival system for two or three years, and during those years Medallion did extremely well—even if its profits would probably have been higher still without the alleged theft of intellectual property. The lesson seems to be that the infrastructure of Renaissance is as important as its research, and that the research itself advances constantly. It takes enormous amounts of time and money to set up systems that absorb a trillion bytes of data daily, that make these data accessible and malleable to researchers, and that turn the research findings into hundreds of thousands of automated trades that go off without a glitch in markets from Spain to Singapore.[33] And while the Russians were struggling to create a halfway comparable platform, the faculty at Renaissance was moving on. Each Tuesday in East Setauket brought another Big Meeting and another set of fresh ideas. The Russians were running to catch up with a fast moving target.

JAMES SIMONS HAD A PARADOXICAL EFFECT ON THE REST of the hedge-fund industry. The Medallion Fund was like the Formula One race car that an auto firm might build: Most customers never got the chance to climb inside, but the existence of this mouth-watering machine encouraged them to buy ordinary vehicles. A fund that trades short-term signals cannot afford to get too large, since liquidity and time constraints prevent it from putting too much on each trade. Medallion therefore closed to new outside investors in 1993, and by the 2000s the $6 billion or so in the fund consisted almost entirely of employees' money.[34] But the very existence of Medallion had a halo effect on the rest of the industry, offsetting the blow to the reputation of black-box trading administered by the collapse of Long-Term Capital.

Each time Simons's picture appeared on the cover of a financial magazine, more eager institutional money flooded into quantitative trading systems. Simons himself capitalized on this phenomenon. In 2005 he launched a new venture, the Renaissance Institutional Equities Fund, which was designed to absorb an eye-popping $100 billion in institutional savings. The only way this huge amount could be manageable was to branch out from short-term trading into more liquid longer-term strategies—and since pure pattern recognition works best for short-term trades, it followed that Simons was offering a fund that would rely on different sorts of signal—ones that might already have been mined by D. E. Shaw and other rivals. By the summer of 2007, the new Simons venture had raked in more than $25 billion, making it one of the largest hedge funds in the world. But then the financial crisis hit. Like almost everybody else, Simons felt the consequences.

14

PREMONITIONS
OF A CRISIS

B y the middle of the 2000s, the scale and persistence of hedge
funds' success was transforming the structure of the industry.
The first generation of hedge-fund titans had been seen as freak-
ish geniuses, whose eye-popping returns were possibly lucky and certainly
not reproducible. But by 2005 nobody could argue that hedge funds
were exceptional in any way: More than eight thousand had sprouted,
and the long track records of the established funds made it hard to dismiss their enviable returns as the products of good fortune. Bit by bit, the
old talk of luck and genius faded and the new lingo took its place—at
hedge-fund conferences from Phoenix to Monaco, a host of consultants
and gurus held forth about the scientific product they called alpha. The
great thing about alpha was that it could be explained: Strategies such as
Tom Steyer's merger arbitrage or D. E. Shaw's statistical arbitrage delivered uncorrelated, market-beating profits in a way that could be understood, replicated, and manufactured by professionals. And so the era of
the manufacturer arrived. Innovation and inspiration gave way to a new
sort of alpha factory.

You could see this transformation all over the hedge-fund industry. By
the early 2000s, there was no longer much doubt that long/short equity
stock picking, as practiced by Julian Robertson's Tiger, could deliver

market-beating returns. The challenge was not so much to invent the strategy; it was to implement it successfully. Dozens of Tiger look-alikes sprang up to do the job, many of them run by men who had themselves worked for Tiger; and an eager industry of hedge-fund consultants and funds of funds emerged to allocate capital to the most promising among them. The biggest sponsor of Robertson clones was none other than Robertson himself. After shuttering Tiger in 2000, he turned his offices into an incubator for "Tiger seeds," which managed his money, benefited from his coaching, and used the prestige of association with the great man to raise more capital from outsiders. Under the old Tiger model, Robertson had maintained personal control of all the big investment calls, but now he let his protégés run their own shows: He had switched from inventing an investment technique to franchising it. The switch provided Robertson with a lucrative final chapter to his illustrious career. By 2006 the reinvented Tiger complex was managing $16 billion. The premises on Park Avenue grew bigger than ever.

The purest expression of the new factory chic was the so-called multistrategy hedge fund. Rather than claiming an edge in a particular investment style, the multistrategy funds began from the principle that you could develop an edge in whatever style you liked: You just had to hire the people. Like a pharmaceutical giant that vacuums up ideas from university researchers and biotech start-ups, the multistrategy factories collected multiple alpha-generating strategies under one roof, blending them together so as to diversify away risk, then shifting capital among the various styles according to market conditions. The factories talked little about invention and a lot about process; they viewed hedge funds less as vehicles for financial creativity than as financial products. A Chicago-based hedge fund called Citadel emerged as a prime exponent of the multistrategy mind-set; its goal, an executive explained, was "to see if we can turn the investment process into widget making."[1] Ken Griffin, Citadel's thirtysomething boss, was a keen consumer of management texts. His staff sneaked glances at the tomes on his desk so that they could brace themselves for the next six-step plan, and he pushed people out of his company with a mechanical determination. Griffin liked to compare hedge funds to buses. People get on. People get off. The bus keeps rolling forward.

The new multistrategy funds grew from babies to behemoths in the blink of an eye. Again, Citadel was a case in point. Griffin had started out trading convertible bonds from his dorm room at Harvard, and at the start of 2000, when he was still just thirty-one, he was running about $2 billion. Then the age of the manufacturer arrived and Citadel took off, so that its assets swelled to $13 billion by 2007. The firm found it could charge clients almost anything it pleased: It billed them for expenses amounting to more than 5 percent of their capital before slapping on the 20 percent performance fee.[2] Griffin's personal earnings were said to be the second-highest in the industry, just behind James Simons, and he let it be known that Citadel would one day compete with Goldman Sachs and Morgan Stanley.[3] Meanwhile, Eton Park Capital Management, launched in 2004 by an ex-Goldman merger arbitrageur named Eric Mindich, offered another example of multistrategy growth. Mindich raised $3 billion in assets before even opening his doors; four years on, he was managing $11 billion. During the 1990s, all the top hedge funds had struggled with the burden of bigness, and many had returned capital to investors. But by 2007 alpha factories managing $5 billion plus accounted for 60 percent of the assets in the industry.[4] A magazine published a list of all the hedge funds in the "Billion-Dollar Club." If you were not on the list you were a nobody.

There was a powerful logic in this rush to bigness. Small companies may excel at generating ideas, but big companies excel at implementation. Once the hedge-fund industry had progressed through its garage-workshop phase, it took sleek professional outfits to bring its inventions to market. The successful alpha factories boasted state-of-the-art computers that executed lightning trades, legal departments that understood the rules in multiple countries, treasury departments that negotiated the best terms from brokers, and marketing departments that churned out glossy monthly reports to satisfy high-maintenance institutional investors. Since their edge lay in the efficiency of their platforms rather than the originality of their ideas, it was natural to use the platforms to support multiple alpha-generating strategies—and multiple strategies meant that the new funds could manage huge amounts of money. The multistrategy format responded to customer pressure too. The fund-of-funds industry, which collected money from endowments and pension funds and allocated it to hedge funds, had amassed almost $400 billion in assets by 2005, partly by promising to shift capital nimbly among different hedge-fund strategies as market conditions altered. The way MBA-minded hedge funds saw it, they could cut out the middleman. If endowments were looking for a product that would shift flexibly among strategies, multistrategy hedge funds would build the widget that the clients wanted.

And yet, for all its logic, the sudden growth of alpha factories made wise observers feel uneasy. Too many people were making too much money too fast. Opportunistic consultants staged workshops on how to open a hedge fund; a book called *Hedge Funds for Dummies* appeared in the stores; and grandees with no known background in asset management, such as Madeleine Albright, the former secretary of state, jumped into the industry. The frenzy recalled the extremes of the leveraged-buyout boom in the 1980s or the dot-com mania in the 1990s. Surely this bubble could not last? Wasn't it bound to end painfully?

IN THE MID-2000S, AS THE HEDGE-FUND BUBBLE WAS growing, an outfit named Amaranth emerged as the very model of the modern alpha factory. Its founder, Nick Maounis, was a convertible-arbitrage specialist by background, but he had hired experts in merger arbitrage, long/short equity investing, credit arbitrage, and statistical arbitrage; and in 2002, following the collapse of the corrupt energy company Enron, Maounis had snapped up several stranded employees to open an energy-trading operation. Maounis made the standard arguments for this mission creep: A blend of alpha-generating strategies would diversify away risk, and Amaranth would move capital aggressively among strategies as market conditions shifted. The fund's energetic shape-shifting was a point of pride. In the first months after Amaranth's launch in September 2000, nearly half of its capital had been focused on merger arbitrage. A year later, that strategy had been cut to practically zero, and more than half of Amaranth's capital was focused on convertible arbitrage. Scroll forward another year, and the portfolio began to shift into bond trades, and then into statistical arbitrage and energy. There seemed no good reason for a pension plan to hire a fund of funds when it could go directly to Amaranth, bypassing the middleman's fees, particularly since Amaranth's results were excellent. In its first three full years of operation, Amaranth returned 22 percent, 11 percent, and 17 percent—this at a time when the S&P 500 was mostly heading downward.

Yet for all Amaranth's glittering appearance, there was a certain hollowness about it. Contrary to his marketing patter, Maounis had no clear edge in deciding which strategy to shift into. He upped his allocation to investment styles that had worked well recently and cut back on those that fared poorly; but there was no sure way to identify which strategies would succeed in the near future.[5] Moreover, precisely because alpha had become a commodity, dozens of rival factories were driving down returns by manufacturing the same thing: Amaranth's shape-shifting was less about cleverly timing market cycles than about desperately searching for the next trick to keep profits from tanking.[6] And because Maounis was allocating capital to specialist traders whose books were difficult to understand, his decisions were necessarily affected by instinct. Gut feelings about the various traders on his team could sway decisions dangerously.

These dangers came together in the shape of a young Canadian named Brian Hunter. Standing six feet five inches tall, occasionally donning a jersey of the National Hockey League's Calgary Flames, and equipped with a graduate degree in math, Hunter was imposing physically as well as intellectually. He was earnest, soft-spoken, and unfailingly calm, and from the moment he landed at Amaranth in 2004, his returns from trading natural gas stood out conspicuously.[7] He had spotted an anomaly in winter gas prices. Unlike oil, which is shipped around in tankers, natural gas is delivered mainly in pipelines; supply routes cannot easily be changed to fill unexpected local shortages. As a result, gas prices are volatile: Time and again, a blast of cold weather would cause demand for household heating to spike, and in the face of rigid supply, prices would leap upward. Hunter's discovery was that options whose value would shoot up in a shortage were strangely cheap—they represented bargain weather insurance. Hunter loaded up on these options, figuring he had found a classic asymmetrical trade: The most he could lose was the small cost of buying the options, but if a shock hit the market and the gas price spiked, he could earn many times more than that. Another way of cashing in on the same insight was to buy a pair of futures contracts: Hunter would go short a summer contract and long a winter contract, betting that the narrow spread between the two would widen if winter prices leaped upward. The strategy had worked in recent winters, and in November 2004 it came good again. The price of natural gas jumped to around 80 percent above its low point in the summer, and Amaranth cashed in handsomely.

In the spring of 2005, Maounis confronted an unpleasant dilemma. Many of Amaranth's strategies were faring poorly. Convertible arbitrage had hit a wall and showed no sign of recovering. Maounis had invested heavily in statistical arbitrage, telling colleagues he wanted a piece of James Simons's action, but he had little to show for it. The one star act in the Amaranth lineup was Brian Hunter and his winter gas; but in April, Maounis learned that Hunter had been offered a $1 million bonus to sign on with a rival firm, SAC Capital. Feeling his back against the wall, Maounis took a chance. Rather than lose his star player, he promoted him. Hunter became cohead of Amaranth's energy desk, gaining the authority to place his own trades; meanwhile, Maounis pumped up the share of his firm's capital allocated to the energy desk from 2 percent the previous spring to around 30 percent. With these two decisions, Maounis effectively bet his company on a thirty-two-year-old trader who had been with him for barely one year. In the go-go atmosphere of the mid-2000s, this was the sort of thing that happened.

Hunter's promotion was all the more remarkable given his background. He had come to Amaranth from Deutsche Bank, where he had supervised gas trading. In December 2003, his trading group had lost $51 million in a single week, but Hunter's response was nothing if not brazen. In a suit he later brought in New York state court, Hunter ascribed the loss to "an unprecedented and unforeseeable run-up in gas prices," as though his failure to foresee the market's behavior rendered him blameless. He pointed to the "well-documented and widely known problems" with Deutsche Bank's trading and risk-management software, which made it hard to exit losing trades—as though his taking of excessive risks could be laid at the door of Deutsche's managers. Hunter also argued that even though his group had registered a loss, he himself had earned $40 million for the bank during 2003: Therefore, he deserved a bonus. By February 2004, Deutsche Bank's managers had concluded that there was no place for Hunter on their trading team. This was the man whom Amaranth was now promoting.[8]

Four months after that promotion, Maounis had cause to celebrate. Hunter had continued to bet that winter gas prices might spike, and suddenly the mother of all weather shocks arrived: In August Hurricane Katrina slammed into the Louisiana coastline, flooding New Orleans and ravaging gas-production rigs in the Gulf of Mexico. The next month Hurricane Rita followed, and the nation's gas supply was hit again. By the end of September, natural gas prices had hit a record, and the effect on Amaranth's returns was dramatic. Having been down 1 percent in the first half of 2005 because of the sluggish performance of most of its strategies, Amaranth was up 21 percent by the end of the year, while the average hedge fund mustered a return of just 9 percent. Hunter and his gas trades earned $1.26 billion, accounting for just about all of Amaranth's profits, and Hunter reportedly pocketed a tenth of that.[9] Thanks to his performance, Amaranth's assets swelled to about $8 billion, making it the world's thirty-ninth-largest hedge fund. In its annual Christmas mailing, Amaranth sent clients toy gasoline pumps and a card that quoted Benjamin Franklin. "Energy and persistence alter all things," the card proclaimed. Seldom had one of the Founders been taken so out of context.

On any reasonable reckoning, Hurricanes Katrina and Rita constituted freak events. But whereas Hunter had been ready to blame unforeseeable extremes for his Deutsche Bank losses, he was happy to take credit when unforeseeable extremes made him a hero. Maounis grew increasingly enamored of his young star. He seemed to view Hunter as a convertible

arbitrage trader transported to a different space. He was generating profits while taking little risk: There was no way that winter gas would fall
below the price of summer gas, so his potential losses appeared limited.[10]
Amaranth's risk department only reinforced Maounis's conviction; at one
point, a member of the risk team responsible for natural gas assured Maounis that Hunter was the greatest commodity trader he had ever witnessed.
Hunter had no difficulty persuading Maounis to allow him to move his
family and trading team to his native Calgary. He commuted to his Canadian office in a Ferrari, though sometimes snowy conditions forced him
to use a Bentley.

During the first months of 2006, Hunter's successful run continued.
His trades earned profits of roughly $2 billion between January and the
end of April, again driving nearly all of Amaranth's performance. At a time
when the average multistrategy hedge fund was up just 5 percent since the
year's start, Amaranth was up roughly six times more; Maounis began to
say that, although he had failed to strike gold in statistical arbitrage, he
had discovered another secret weapon that was just as potent.[11] And yet to
some savvy observers, Hunter's extraordinary profits were cause for alarm.
There was no way that Hunter could be generating this sort of money
without taking outlandish risks; and besides, there was a darker worry.
With the rise of the new alpha factories, hedge-fund capital devoted to
energy trading had soared from around $5 billion in 2001 to more than
$100 billion in 2006: The trades were growing crowded. Thanks to this
flood of capital, any strategy that made sense to energy specialists at hedge
funds was almost bound to come good as others piled in. But it could also
blow up if the stampede reversed itself.

In the case of Brian Hunter, an extreme version of this phenomenon
seemed to be occurring. The weight of his *own* money might be driving
his profits. Amaranth had allowed him to ramp up his positions in a niche
market: By the end of February, Hunter held an astonishing 70 percent
of the natural-gas futures contracts for November 2006 delivery on the
New York Mercantile Exchange and about 60 percent of the contracts
for January 2007. By means of this enormous position, Hunter was betting that November gas would fall in value and that January would rise;

and so long as he added aggressively to his wager, his view was likely to be self-fulfilling. After all, it was not clear that his strategy was making money because market fundamentals were on his side. By early 2006, gas output had recovered from the devastation of the hurricanes, and mild winter weather was reducing gas demand, so that by April the quantity of gas held in storage was nearly 40 percent above the previous five-year average. Under these circumstances, the success of Hunter's bet on summer/winter spreads seemed hard to explain—except when you looked at the astonishing growth in his positions. By around the end of April, Amaranth owned upward of one hundred thousand NYMEX contracts, or more than 40 percent of the total outstanding for all months on the exchange. Hunter was a momentum trader who traded on his own momentum.[12]

In May 2006, a team from the private-equity giant Blackstone visited Hunter in Calgary. Blackstone ran one of the longest-standing funds of funds, and it had invested $125 million in Amaranth. But now it was having second thoughts. Amaranth might be up a whacking 13 percent in April alone, but the size of Hunter's profits showed he was taking dangerously large bets in a volatile market. Amaranth's risk control department had calculated that because winter gas prices would never fall below summer prices, the most Hunter could lose in a single month was $300 million, a tolerable 3 percent or so of equity. But Hunter's own trading had rendered this assessment obsolete: The spread between summer and winter gas had widened from $1.40 in mid-February to $2.20 in late April as Hunter had built his positions, meaning that there was plenty of room for the spread to shrink disastrously. Besides, the small size of the gas market—and the fact that the main buyer of Hunter's positions was none other than Hunter himself—created a liquidity risk: Hunter would have nobody to sell to if he needed to get out of a position. Blackstone informed Amaranth that it would withdraw its capital at the next opportunity. There was a penalty fee for short-notice redemptions, but Blackstone was happy to pay it.[13]

Meanwhile, Maounis was finally reckoning with the fact that his star trader had overreached himself. He told Hunter to cut back on his risk, but this was easier said than done: Nobody wanted to buy Amaranth's contracts, just as the Blackstone team had worried. The moment Hunter tried to unload some of his positions, the market turned, and the glorious results of April were followed by horrifying losses. By the end of May, Amaranth was down by more than $1 billion—nearly four times more than the risk department had deemed possible.

Maounis and his lieutenants scrambled to stabilize their operation. Traders in other strategies were told to cut back positions in order to free up capital, and Amaranth paid Morgan Stanley a large fee to shoulder some of Hunter's exposure.[14] But it was too little, too late. Hunter's wild profits and losses had come to the notice of other gas traders, and it was clear that his positions were too big to hold on to. What's more, there was no particular mystery about what these positions were: You just had to check which pairs of contracts had widened during March and April to figure out which ones Hunter had been piling into.[15] Like Long-Term Capital caught in its bond trades, or like Julian Robertson caught in US Airways, Amaranth was trapped. "It was naïve to think that they could get out of the market with a size of 100,000 positions," one rival trader later said. "I knew Amaranth would eventually implode. It was just a question of when."[16]

Amaranth managed to hang on through the summer. Hunter was under instructions to reduce his positions, but since he could not do that without incurring crippling losses, he played a waiting game, hoping that something would let him out of his predicament.[17] At the end of July, the rumor of another late-summer hurricane brought the old bravado back. Hunter jacked up his bets sharply, causing the summer/winter spreads to widen and triggering the implosion of a rival hedge fund named MotherRock that had the opposite bet on.[18] In August, Maounis granted an interview to the *Wall Street Journal*, bravely declaring, "What Brian is really, really good at is taking controlled and measured risk"; looking back on that extraordinary comment, one Amaranth veteran compared Maounis's enduring faith in the young man to that of a jilted lover.[19] But the moment of truth was approaching. Amaranth suffered losses at the end of August and faced a margin call from its brokers.

The hurricane season ended uneventfully. Predatory rivals began to target Amaranth's positions.[20]

ON A RAINY MID-SEPTEMBER DAY, MAOUNIS TOOK A LIM-ousine ride from his office in Greenwich to the Pierre Hotel in Manhattan. The traffic was bad; he should have taken the train; but managers of multibillion-dollar hedge funds are seldom at home on public transport. Maounis was on his way to a Goldman Sachs hedge-fund conference that was emblematic of the times. A ballroom was set up with dozens of tables, each manned by a team of hedge-fund chieftains; groups of institutional investors moved from stall to stall, listening to a pitch and then hurrying off to hear the next one. Maounis speed-dated his way through a couple of investor groups, repeating the patter that he knew by heart—Amaranth had a world-class fundamental equity team, a world-class credit team, a world-class quantitative team, a world-class commodities team, and all of this was wrapped up in a world-class infrastructure. Then an unwelcome e-mail arrived. There was trouble back at the office.

That Thursday, September 14, was effectively the end for Amaranth. The fund lost $560 million in a single day, as the spread on one of its key summer/winter positions collapsed to a third of its size at the start of September. At a tense meeting at Maounis's home that evening, Amaranth's top brass agreed they needed to raise capital immediately to meet margin calls. Maounis called Goldman Sachs to see if it would buy his energy portfolio. Other Amaranth officials reached out to other banks, desperately hoping for a bid from somewhere.

By Saturday morning, squadrons of investment bankers were descending upon the Amaranth office in Greenwich, jamming its parking lot with fancy cars and devouring the Pop-Tarts in its pantry. Teams of intense analysts conferred anxiously with bosses at country homes in the Hamptons; meanwhile, Amaranth's positions hemorrhaged money in after-hours trading. Goldman made an offer, then Merrill Lynch made an offer, and early on Monday morning Amaranth thought it had a deal to stabilize the firm by selling a chunk of its assets to Goldman. It looked as though the

Long-Term Capital plotline would repeat itself. A risk-loving hedge fund had blown up. The Wall Street establishment would pick up the pieces.

Maounis knew he had to get the news of Goldman's offer out fast. The New York Mercantile Exchange would open soon. By now every commodity trader in the world had heard of Amaranth's distress, and it would be open season on Hunter's gas positions. Maounis sent out a letter to his investors, reporting that Amaranth had lost half the capital it had managed at its peak, but assuring them that a deal to raise fresh capital was "near completion."

That Monday morning in Chicago, Ken Griffin, the boss of the multistrategy fund Citadel, was working out at home on an elliptical trainer. The contraption was rigged up with monitors so he could keep track of the news at the same time as his e-mail, and a message from Scott Rafferty, Citadel's head of investor relations, popped up in Griffin's in-box. The e-mail reported that Amaranth was down 50 percent. For a second or two, the number didn't fully register; Griffin continued to pump the pedals up and down, thinking, *It can't say that.* Then he stopped and hurried to the phone. He needed to speak to Rafferty.

"Fifty?" Griffin demanded. "Over what period?"

"A month," Rafferty responded.

Griffin thought about what Vinny Mattone had told Meriwether when Long-Term Capital was failing. If you are down by half, you are not going to recover.

Meanwhile in Greenwich, Maounis organized a conference call to clinch the deal with Goldman. But when the two firms began talking, along with officials from the NYMEX, Amaranth's clearing broker, J.P. Morgan, torpedoed the project. J.P. Morgan's brokerage department had lent the firm money to finance its gas trades, holding the futures contracts as collateral; now that the value of this collateral was doubtful, the bank was uncertain of repayment. The law gave J.P. Morgan the right to pursue Amaranth's assets through the bankruptcy courts, and even to claw back assets from other firms that bought them as Amaranth was going under. From Goldman's perspective, the threat of a clawback created an impossible hurdle: It was hard enough to value Hunter's gas book amid all the market turmoil, but legal uncertainty made the deal unthinkable. Goldman wanted Morgan to promise not to come after it through the bankruptcy courts. Morgan balked and the deal faltered.

As Wall Street's banking titans wrestled one another to a stalemate, Amaranth's chief operating officer, Charles Winkler, got a note from his assistant. He had received a call from Ken Griffin, and he hurried to his office to return it.

Winkler had worked for Griffin at Citadel, and the two men had been friends. But when Winkler got Griffin on the line, he found he was not in the mood for pleasantries. "Charlie, what can we do and how can we help?" Griffin demanded.

This was an audacious question. Amaranth's gas positions had already bled $4 billion or $5 billion by Monday morning; how could a $13 billion hedge fund digest this radioactive portfolio? If the likes of Goldman had worked through the weekend without nailing a deal, what made Griffin think he could do better?

Winkler knew Griffin too well to write him off, so he answered his question forthrightly. "It's real simple," he said. "We need a bridge loan and a couple hundred million to stay in business."[21]

Griffin began marshaling the resources of the firm that he had built around him. Buying a book that constituted a large chunk of the entire gas market would involve multiple risks: He needed to get his mind around the logic of the trades, how they were financed, who the counterparties were, whether Citadel's computer systems were capable of handling them. The whole premise of a multistrategy hedge fund—that the edge lay in the efficiency of the platform—would now be tested to the full. If Griffin thought his firm was a potential rival to Morgan Stanley and Goldman Sachs, this was his chance to prove it.

Griffin arranged some forty Citadel staffers into groups to work on the transaction. He put two lieutenants on a plane to Greenwich, and the pair of them showed up looking half the age of their investment-banking rivals. Meanwhile, he got on a conference call with Maounis and his top advisers. By lunchtime the discussion had gone way beyond a bridge loan; Amaranth was losing money so fast that it needed to off-load all its energy

positions, not just its gas positions. The more Amaranth's positions unraveled, the greater Griffin's advantage over his investment-banking rivals:
For the banks, every movement of the goalposts required consultation up
and down a chain; Griffin, chief executive and chief deal maker rolled
into one, was free to react instantly. The same speed advantage applied
at lower levels of the firm. Citadel's technology chief knew how to get
trade data transferred from Amaranth's computers, loaded into Citadel's
system, and synced up with Citadel's accounting and risk-management
software: A larger bureaucracy might have required a committee or two
to do that.[22] In the Long-Term Capital crisis eight years earlier, Goldman
Sachs had announced an interest in buying the distressed portfolio but
had not pulled off a deal. This time a hedge fund had grown large enough
to play in the big league, and it was proving relentlessly effective.[23]

By the evening, the talks between Amaranth and Citadel had eclipsed
the talks with all the various investment-bank suitors. But one obstacle
remained. Amaranth's sale of its energy book might lead to bankruptcy,
in which case the transaction might be subject to review by a court. Like
Goldman Sachs earlier that day, Citadel could not value Amaranth's book
in the face of this uncertainty.

Griffin and his team worked through the night, looking for a way
around this legal obstacle. Then, in a lucky break, a solution arrived on
Tuesday morning. An executive from J.P. Morgan called to propose a deal:
Morgan would waive its right to claw back assets in bankruptcy provided
it could be the 50 percent purchaser of Amaranth's positions. Griffin
accepted, but then a new challenge arose: What if some other creditor
pressed a claim on Amaranth that undermined Citadel's calculations?
Assessing this risk required understanding the nonenergy parts of Amaranth's portfolio: Was there another broker that had financed trades that
were now insufficiently backed by collateral? Griffin did not know the
answer, and for a moment the deal seemed set to slip away. But then Bob
Polachek, one of the two Citadel staffers who had camped out in Greenwich, came up with the missing information. He had taken it upon himself
to check all of Amaranth's brokerage statements by working through the

previous night. He assured Griffin that there were no undiscovered holes, and at 5:30 the next morning, the sale of Amaranth went forward.[24]

The sale was a triumph for Griffin and his investors. Partly thanks to J.P. Morgan's offer, but also because Citadel's execution platform had proved at least as good as those of the top banks, a hedge fund had stolen a deal that Wall Street had regarded as its own. The moment Citadel and J.P. Morgan took ownership of Amaranth's portfolio, its value started to come back; predatory traders could see that the gas contracts were no longer about to be dumped, so they cut their bets and prices recovered. Citadel eventually earned a profit of about $1 billion from the transaction. Griffin's plan to build the next Goldman Sachs had taken a significant step forward.

AMARANTH'S COLLAPSE CONFIRMED THAT HEDGE FUNDS had entered bubble territory. They had grown too fast for the available talent; under pressure to perform, they were capable of granting inexperienced traders the leeway to blow up spectacularly. The multistrategy format made this danger especially acute. Veterans such as Stan Druckenmiller or Louis Bacon understood risk because they traded every day, and they were determined to avoid a major loss because their own savings and reputation were bound up in their companies. But the new alpha factories were structured in a different way: They believed in delegation. The boss of a large multistrategy fund could not hope to be an expert in every risk his traders took, particularly when fast asset accumulation compelled equally fast adaptation to new styles. And once risk decisions were delegated down the chain, the multistrategy funds had to contend with a mild version of the problematic incentives that plague large banks and brokerages. Traders want bonuses; bonuses are won by betting big; and a firm's central risk department seldom controls wizards who acquire an aura of invincibility. By the time Amaranth folded, $6 billion of its investors' equity had gone up in smoke, a larger quantity than Long-Term Capital had incinerated.

Yet Amaranth's collapse could not fully explain the calls for regulation that followed. Charles Grassley, the chairman of the Senate Finance Committee, complained in a letter to Treasury secretary Henry Paulson that ordinary Americans were increasingly exposed to hedge funds via their pension plans; he demanded to know why the funds were allowed to get away with secrecy. But Amaranth had disclosed its strategies to its investors in monthly reports; indeed, it was the *lack* of secrecy that had made it a target once the market turned against it. Likewise, a survey of private economists conducted by the *Wall Street Journal* found that a majority favored tougher oversight for hedge funds, and one popular regulatory measure was compulsory registration with the Securities and Exchange Commission. But it was not at all clear what registration would achieve. As a result of Amaranth's failure, American taxpayers suffered no harm; there was no round-the-clock crisis meeting at the New York Fed and no apparent damage to the financial system. The pension funds that lost money were angry, but Amaranth had represented a tiny share of their assets. The effect of the fund's collapse was no greater than the effect of a bad day for the S&P 500. In sum, the market had disciplined Amaranth for its errors while inflicting minimal damage on the wider economy. No regulatory clamp could have done better.[25]

Ever since Long-Term Capital's demise, Wall Street had worried about the next hedge-fund blowup. Now the event had taken place, and the scars were barely visible. The critics of hedge funds continued to worry that these leveraged monsters could ignite systemic fires—after all, Long-Term Capital had done so. But Citadel's lightning purchase of Amaranth's portfolio had proved that there was another side to this story. Perhaps hedge funds might occasionally ignite fires. But they could also be the firefighters.

15

RIDING THE STORM

aniel Sadek did not have an easy childhood. Born in Lebanon in 1968, his schooling was interrupted by the country's civil war, and his body was scarred by a gunshot wound and a flying piece of metal. He left Lebanon for France, then fetched up in California at eighteen, landing jobs as a gas-station attendant and then later as a car salesman. But around 2000, the scales fell from his eyes. He was selling Mercedes cars—lots of them, one after the next—to customers who were in the mortgage business. Discovering that he could get a license to sell home loans without taking classes, Sadek embarked upon a fresh career. If he had wanted to become a professional barber, he would have needed 1,500 hours of training to qualify for a state license.

By 2005, Sadek's company, Quick Loan, had seven hundred employees. It was one of the top fifty "subprime" lenders in the nation, meaning that it specialized in customers who were too risky to qualify for normal mortgages. Its marketing campaign was not subtle. "No income verification. Instant qualification!!" promised one ad. "You can't wait. We won't let you," proclaimed the company slogan. The California Department of Corporations recorded a string of complaints against Quick Loan, including allegations of fraud and underwriting errors.[1] But Sadek did not let that cramp his style. He bought a mansion on the coast and an apartment in Vegas; he sported a necklace, flip-flops, and long hair; he acquired a collection of fast cars, some restaurant investments, and a movie company. When his actress girlfriend needed a film part, he bankrolled a production called *Redline*. It was "an action flick loaded with cars, chrome, and silicone," the *Boston Globe*'s reviewer wrote, "everything you'd expect it to be, and yet so much less." During the course of filming and promoting the movie, the cast demolished more than $2 million worth of Sadek's sports cars. "Fear nothing; risk everything," ran the movie's tagline.

In 2006, Kyle Bass, a hedge-fund manager in Dallas, heard about Sadek and his filmmaking. The story confirmed what Bass was starting to suspect: The American mortgage market was in the grips of something truly wild—a bubble that exceeded anything that might exist within the hedge-fund industry. Between 2000 and 2005, the volume of risky subprime loans had quadrupled, and a growing share of these loans was flowing to people who could not repay. "Prior bankruptcy. Tax Liens. Foreclosures. Collections and Credit Problems. OK!" proclaimed another Quick Loan ad, as though the firm was actively seeking out deadbeats. Sadek's attitude toward this seeming suicide was summed up by his movie. As Kyle Bass put it later, "When they started catapulting Porsche Carrera GTs and he says, 'What the hell, what are a couple of cars being thrown around?' I'm thinking, 'That's the guy you want to bet against.'"[2] Around the time that Amaranth was blowing up, Bass and his company, Hayman Capital, figured out how Sadek's mortgages were being packaged together and sold off in the form of mortgage bonds. Bass shorted a large quantity of those bonds, then settled back and waited.

Other hedge-fund managers had similar epiphanies. For Michael Litt, the cohead of a large alpha factory called FrontPoint Partners, the light went on when he visited the mortgage desk at Lehman Brothers. The mortgage team had recently relocated to a gigantic new trading floor; and while Litt was touring the premises, he heard a group of traders teasing one of their buddies. A tailor had come to measure the men for some new $6,000 suits, and this guy had ordered *only one*—to any self-respecting mortgage jock, he was positively wussy! A little while later, Litt was on a plane home from London, reading a report from the Bank for International

Settlements that explained how sophisticated finance had suppressed market volatility. Litt remembers thinking that something was wrong; looking out the window he could see the outline of Greenland, which had
once been hospitable to human settlement and then had frozen over. At
forty thousand feet it suddenly hit him. Volatility was low because the
world was awash with wild money; but abundant liquidity was giving the
false sense that stability was due to some magical structural improvement
in the financial system. Investors from Asia to Arabia were wiring billions
of dollars to fund managers in New York, buying every piece of paper that
Lehman's mortgage desk could sell, and yet the smart folks at the Bank
for International Settlements appeared to be missing the freeze that would
follow. Litt rebalanced FrontPoint's portfolio to get ready for a shock. In
the fall of 2006, the firm bet against the subprime mortgage sector and
took a bearish stance in several other trading strategies.[3]

Over the course of the next year, Hayman Capital and FrontPoint
both profited handsomely.[4] But the man who made the mother of all
killings on this mother of all bubbles was an unassuming figure called
John Paulson. Neither tall nor short, neither handsome nor plain, neither glad-handingly eager nor offensively standoffish, he came across as
Mr. Average. After graduating from Harvard Business School in 1980, he
had progressed from a management consultancy to an early hedge fund
named Odyssey Partners and thence to Bear Stearns, where he worked on
mergers and acquisitions. In 1994 he had launched a tiny hedge fund of
his own, setting himself up in a Park Avenue building that incubated several other hedge-fund start-ups. Over the next decade, Paulson and Company succeeded steadily, growing its capital from $2 million at inception
to $600 million in 2003; then the great hedge-fund asset boom carried
it away, so that by 2005 it was managing $4 billion. Even then, Paulson
kept his profile low. He had only seven analysts on his staff; and although
he had amassed a personal fortune, he had done so in the quietest way
possible.[5]

Paulson was a loner and a contrarian. He had no doubt of his own
ability and no need for affirmation. Plowing his own road as a boutique-
hedge-fund manager, he had honed the art of the unconventional long

shot. He specialized, for example, in a form of merger arbitrage that focused on long odds: As well as investing in mergers that were expected to be consummated and collecting a modest premium, Paulson sometimes bet against the ones that might blow up, or in favor of ones where the market might be shocked by a surprise bid from a rival acquirer. Paulson also made money by calling turns in the cycle. When the economy was booming, he looked for the moment to go short, and vice versa. Some of the people who worked for him had the same maverick vibe. Paolo Pellegrini, a tall, elegant Italian with heavy-framed glasses and a permanently amused twinkle in his eyes, had spent years chasing fruitlessly offbeat ideas; "I'm a romantic type," he said later.[6] When Pellegrini signed on as Paulson's analyst for financial companies in 2004, he realized that for the first time in his life, his unconventional style was welcomed.

Much of Paulson's skill lay in the detail of his positions. He expressed his skepticism about booms via a strategy known as capital-structure arbitrage, which started from the fact that the various bonds issued by a given company might be treated differently in bankruptcy. So-called senior bonds had the first claim on the company's remaining assets and so would get paid back first; junior bonds made do with whatever was left over. So long as the company was healthy, investors didn't focus on this dull legal nuance, so the senior and the junior bonds traded at similar prices. But if the economy was weakening, an opportunity arose. Paulson could assess which companies were heading for bankruptcy—they might be in a cyclical industry, for example, or they might have too much debt. Then he could short the junior bonds that would get hit the most if the company went down, sometimes hedging his position by going long the senior bonds.

In early 2005, Paulson started to feel that the economic cycle was getting ready to turn downward. Bonds that he had bought at a discount during the previous recession were now trading at silly heights; financial markets were frothy thanks to a long period of low interest rates. Paulson began to hunt for the best way to bet against this bubble. He wanted to find American capitalism's weakest spot—the thing that would blow up the loudest and fastest if the economy slowed even a little. The dream target would combine all the standard vulnerabilities: It would be in a cyclical industry, it would be loaded up with too much debt, and the debt would be sliced into senior and junior bonds, so that Paulson could short the junior ones, where all the risk was concentrated. Paulson experimented with shorts on car-company bonds, on the theory that consumers were taking out car loans that they could not afford. He shorted an insurance company and a couple of home lenders. But there was a risk in all these trades. The car companies, insurers, and home lenders all had value as franchises—they had buildings, brands, customer relationships—so even if they collapsed under the weight of their debts, they would probably still be worth something. If Paulson was going to be contrarian, he wanted to short something that could be totally wiped out. In the spring of 2005, he hit on the right target.

The target was mortgage securities, which combined every imaginable charm that a short seller could wish for. Home prices, and therefore mortgages, were certainly cyclical, even though the great American public had convinced itself that home prices could only go upward. Equally, home prices were built on huge mountains of household debt, and the moment that families hit hard times, they would be unable to make their payments. As to the division of junior from senior debt, Paulson had never seen anything quite like the feast that the mortgage industry served up. Lenders like Daniel Sadek generated mortgages that were sold to Wall Street banks; the banks turned these into mortgage bonds; then other banks bought the bonds, rebundled them, and sliced the resulting "collateralized debt obligation" into layers, the most senior ones rated a rock-solid AAA, the next ones rated AA, and so on down the line to BBB and lower—there might be eighteen tranches in the pyramid. If the mortgages in the collateralized debt obligation paid back 95 percent or more of what they owed, the BBB bonds would be fine, since the first 5 percent of the losses would be absorbed by even more junior tranches. But once nonpayments surpassed the 5 percent hurdle, the BBB securities would start suffering losses; and since the BBB tranche was only 1 percent thick, a nonpayment rate of 6 percent would take the whole lot of them to zero. In contrast to auto-company bonds, there was no franchise value to worry about, either. A bankrupt company might be worth something to someone. A pile of loans with zero payout is worth, simply, zero.

In April 2005, Paulson placed his first bet against these mortgage securities. He bought a credit default swap—an insurance policy on a bond's default—on $100 million worth of BBB-rated subprime debt. There was a huge asymmetry in the risk and the reward: He paid $1.4 million for a year's worth of insurance, but if the securities were wiped out, he stood to pocket the full $100 million. The question was whether the odds of default were good: You can get a juicy payout by betting on a single number in roulette, but that's because your chances of winning are abysmal. To figure out the odds, Paulson turned to Paolo Pellegrini, the offbeat Italian. Armed with a $2 million research budget, Pellegrini bought the largest mortgage database in the country, hired an outside firm to warehouse the numbers, and brought in extra analysts to figure out the past behavior of default rates.

Pellegrini's first discovery was not encouraging. He and Paulson had begun by thinking that families with unpayable mortgages were bound to default. But now Pellegrini saw there was a catch: so long as house prices continued to head up, homeowners would be bailed out by the option of refinancing.[7] But Pellegrini made a second discovery as well. The mortgage-industrial complex argued that house prices, which in the summer of 2005 were appreciating at a rate of 15 percent annually, would never fall across the country in a synchronized way; it had never happened before, so bonds backed by bundles of mortgages drawn from different states were regarded as relatively riskless. Because Pellegrini was a newcomer to the mortgage game, he was unburdened by this article of faith, and his number crunching showed that its basis was shaky. If you adjusted house prices for inflation, there had been national slumps in both the 1980s and 1990s, so there was every reason to suppose that the extraordinary run-up of the early 2000s would be followed by another downturn. Moreover, to block the option of refinancing, it was not actually necessary for house prices to fall; if prices merely went flat, home owners would lack the collateral to take out new and larger mortgages. Pellegrini's analysis suggested that zero house-price appreciation would eventually lead to a mortgage default rate of at least 7 percent, wiping out the value of all BBB bonds. The verdict could be summed up in a phrase: *Zero would mean zero.*

By early 2006, Paulson's initial mortgage bets had failed to make money, and some of his investors were muttering that he had strayed beyond his competence. But the more Paulson contemplated the results of Pellegrini's research, the more he was convinced that he had found the opportunity of a lifetime. House-price appreciation was slowing as the Fed's interest rate hikes pushed up the cost of mortgages, so the odds of flat house prices had to be at least even: This was like betting on red in a roulette game. But the potential reward was seventy or eighty times the stake, double the payout from betting on a single roulette number. Paulson drew up a simple table to describe what he could do. If he set up a fund with $600 million of capital and spent 7 percent of that taking out insurance on BBB mortgage bonds, the worst that could happen was a loss of $42 million. The rewards, on the other hand, were almost limitless. If the BBB bonds suffered a relatively mild default rate of 30 percent, the fund would gain 341 percent, or $2 billion. If they suffered a default rate of 50 percent, it would gain 568 percent, or $3.4 billion. And if the bonds suffered a default rate of 80 percent, which Paulson considered highly likely, the fund would gain 909 percent—an astonishing $5.5 billion. When Paulson explained this to investors, a few thought he had gone crazy. A gain of 909 percent? When did that ever happen? But Paulson was not a man to be deterred. In the summer of 2006, he set up a new hedge fund to do exactly what his table said, seeding it partly with his own money and enlisting Pellegrini as the comanager.

The challenge was how to do the trades in the size that he now wanted. Paulson could bet against mortgage bonds by borrowing them and selling them short, a cumbersome operation. Or he could buy an insurance policy—a credit default swap from a bank—but that depended upon finding a bank that was interested in selling. To Paulson's great good fortune, in July 2006 Wall Street's top investment banks created an easier option: Hoping to earn themselves a stream of trading commissions, they launched a subprime mortgage index, known as the ABX. Paulson now found that, on any given day, it was easy to buy insurance on, say,

$10 million of subprime paper. Then, a week or two later, he took a call from one of the big banks. The man on the line was an ABX trader.

"What's your picture?" the trader demanded. He was willing to deal with Paulson in size. How many millions' worth of subprime bonds did he want to buy insurance on?

Paulson considered. He didn't want to scare the trader off. If the guy knew how much insurance Paulson really wanted, he surely would not be stupid enough to sell without first moving the price against him.

"Five hundred million," Paulson ventured.

"Done," the trader responded.

"Another five hundred million," Paulson said.

"Done," the man repeated. He wasn't flinching in the least. Then he said again, "Tell us your total picture."

"Call me again tomorrow," Paulson said, and the next day he bought insurance on another $1 billion of subprime bonds. In the first half of the year, he had hustled to lay his hands on $500 million of this stuff. Now, in just two days, he had bought four times that quantity.

"Tell us your picture," the trader said again.

Paulson thought to himself, this is the holy grail. He remembered Soros's words: Go for the jugular.

"I'll do another three billion," he said.[8] At this, there was a silence on the line. The trader agreed to another billion, then balked at doing any more. But by calling around the other banks, Paulson established positions totaling $7.2 billion for his credit fund.[9] At the end of 2006, he launched a second fund with the same strategy.

A few weeks after that, the tide turned for Paulson. On the afternoon of February 7, 2007, New Century Financial Corp., the country's second largest subprime lender, made a startling announcement. Its fourth quarter earnings, due out the next day, would have to be postponed because the firm was still calculating losses—a shock given that it had been expected to report a healthy profit. It turned out that New Century's subprime loans were blowing up still faster than the skeptics feared; some of its borrowers were unable to make their first payments. That same day, the

British bank HSBC, which was the third-largest subprime lender in the United States, announced that it would have to set aside $10.6 billion in loan-loss reserves because of busted mortgages.

The following morning, as the share prices of New Century and HSBC tumbled, Paulson was sitting at his desk when his head trader informed him that the ABX index had slid five points. Because of his massive positions, a 1 percent decline in the ABX handed Paulson a profit of $250 million; in a single morning he had netted $1.25 billion, about as much as Soros had earned from his wager against sterling. At the end of that month, when Paulson reported his February results, his office received a phone call from an incredulous client.

"Is this a misprint? It's 6.6 percent, right, not 66 percent?"[10]

The results were not a misprint. Once house prices stopped appreciating, overindebted families began turning in their keys, so that BBB-rated mortgage securities were worth practically nothing. Within months New Century had declared bankruptcy and HSBC had sacked its U.S. executives; but every blow to the mortgage industry was a bonus for Paulson. On a hot day in the summer, Paulson was in the middle of a meeting with a pair of potential clients when a colleague came in and whispered something in his ear. Paulson abruptly excused himself, leaving his guests in the stuffy conference room. When he returned after a few minutes, he could not wipe a wide smile off his face. His visitors eventually asked him if there was somewhere else he needed to be. Unable to contain himself, Paulson divulged his secret.

"We just got our marks for the day," he blurted out. "We made a billion dollars."[11]

PAULSON'S MEMORY OF SOROS'S INJUCTION TO GO FOR THE jugular was more fitting than he realized. The subprime bubble was a twenty-first-century version of the policy errors that earlier hedge funds had exploited. In the 1970s, incompetent central banks had stoked inflation, allowing commodities traders to ride glorious trends. In the 1990s, central banks had committed themselves to untenable exchange-rate pegs that macro traders like Soros attacked gleefully. By the 2000s, inflation and unsustainable currency pegs were gone; but the passing of these follies made way for a new one. Because inflation had been vanquished, central banks felt free to stimulate economies with low interest rates, rendering money cheap and creating the conditions for an asset bubble. Because exchange rates were now stable, Wall Street was emboldened to take other sorts of risk, leveraging itself up and further adding to the bubble. Each new era brought a fresh kind of blunder, creating a fresh opportunity for traders too. The heyday of macro hedge funds might be over, but a new heyday of credit hedge funds had arrived. John Paulson was the new George Soros.

There was another sense in which the Soros memory was relevant. The famous macro trades had yielded extraordinary profits because there were willing suckers on the other side—in 1992, it was the British government. Equally, Paulson's subprime mortgage trade required a sucker: He could only build vast short positions on mortgages if somebody else was buying them. Of course, the mystery was who these buyers were—and why they were so eager to throw away their money.

When the mortgage bubble burst in 2007 and 2008, extraordinary losses cropped up all over the financial system. Daniel Sadek's handiwork, and millions of other loans that smelled equally putrid, had been packaged and sold to investors from Japanese insurers to Norwegian pension funds. Inevitably, some hedge funds were caught holding subprime garbage too; a couple of medium-sized outfits called Peloton Partners and Sailfish Capital sank under the weight of mortgages. Peloton, in particular, was hardly a model of financial prudence: Its London-based managers became famous when their secretary stole £4.3 million from their accounts without their realizing that anything might be amiss, though they told the jury at her trial that their bank account felt "one or two million light." Still, by any reasonable reckoning, the hedge-fund sector as a whole survived the bubble extraordinarily well: By and large, it avoided buying toxic mortgage securities and often made money by shorting them. In 2007, hedge funds specializing in asset-backed securities, a category including mortgages, were up 1 percent on average, according to Hedge Fund Research, a data provider in Chicago—in other words, they completely dodged the subprime bullet. Meanwhile, hedge funds as a whole gained 10 percent during the year—not bad for a crisis.[12]

If hedge funds mostly recognized subprime assets for the garbage that they were, who did lead the buying? The answer, to a large extent, was banks and investment banks—firms such as Citibank, UBS, and Merrill Lynch. On first inspection, this seems strange. These firms were proud of the trading desks that managed their proprietary capital. And yet, unlike hedge funds, the banks and investment banks bought subprime mortgages by the bucketful. Citibank's losses were so astronomical that the U.S. government was forced to rescue it, buying more than a third of its shares. UBS ended up needing a lifeline from the Swiss government. Merrill sold itself to Bank of America to avoid going down. And whereas the failure of hedge funds such as Peloton and Sailfish—like the earlier failure of Amaranth—cost taxpayers nothing, the failure of Citi and its peers imposed enormous burdens on government budgets and the world economy.

Why this stark contrast with hedge funds? There are four principal reasons, and they begin with regulation. Banks that take deposits, such as Citi and UBS, are required by regulators to hold a minimum amount of capital in order to shore up their solvency. This should have made the banks more resilient than hedge funds when the mortgage bubble imploded. But capital requirements, while necessary, can become a crutch: Rather than running their books in a way that rigorous analysis suggests will be safe, banks sometimes run their books in a way that the capital requirements deem to be safe, even when it isn't. Subprime mortgages presented a classic example of this problem. Bonds backed by toxic mortgages were given the top (AAA) rating, partly because the rating agencies were paid by the bond issuers, which dulled the incentive to be critical. Once the AAA seal of approval was affixed to subprime assets, banks were happy to hold them because capital requirements allowed them to do so without putting aside much capital. Regulation and ratings agencies thus became a substitute for analysis of the real risks in mortgage bonds.[13] Because hedge funds are in the habit of making their own risk decisions, undistracted by regulation and ratings, they frequently fared better.

If capital standards turned out to be a mixed blessing, the second problem hinged on incentives. Hedge-fund incentives are not perfect. The
managers keep a fifth of the profit in a good year but don't give back a
fifth of their losses in a bad year; therefore they may be tempted to gamble
recklessly. But hedge funds have a powerful advantage. Their managers
generally have their own wealth in their funds, which gives them a strong
reason to control risks effectively. By contrast, bank proprietary traders do
not risk their personal savings in the pools of money that they manage.
Instead, bank traders often own company stock. But the value of that
stock is driven by a variety of different profit centers within the bank. If
the prop desk loses money, its errors will be diluted by the other business
lines. The stock may react marginally or not at all. The effect is too weak
to change prop traders' incentives.

This contrast points to a third reason why the banks fared poorly in
the credit bubble: Those multiple profit centers distracted executives. The
banks' proprietary trading desks coexisted alongside departments that
advised on mergers, underwrote securities, and managed clients' funds;
sometimes the scramble for fees from these advisory businesses blurred
the banks' investment choices. Again, the subprime story illustrated this
problem. Merrill Lynch is said to have sold $70 billion worth of subprime
collateralized debt obligations, or CDOs, earning a fee of 1.25 percent
each time, or $875 million. Merrill's bosses obsessed about their stand-
ing in the mortgage league tables: The chief executive, Stan O'Neal, was
prepared to finance home lenders at no profit in order to be first in line
to buy their mortgages.[14] To feed their CDO production lines, Merrill
and its rivals kept plenty of mortgage bonds on hand; so when demand
for CDOs collapsed in early 2007, the banks were stuck with billions of
unsold inventory that they had to take onto their balance sheets. The
banks therefore became major investors in mortgages as an unintended
by-product of their mortgage-packaging business. When the scramble for
commissions distorts investment choices in this way, it is hardly surprising
that the investment choices are horrendous.

The final explanation for the banks' fate hinges on their culture.
Hedge funds are paranoid outfits, constantly in fear that margin calls

from brokers or redemptions from clients could put them out of business. They live and die by their investment returns, so they focus on them obsessively. They are generally run by a charismatic founder, not by a committee of executives: If they see a threat to their portfolio, they can flip their positions aggressively. Banks are complacent by comparison. They have multiple streams of revenue and their funding seems secure: Deposit-taking banks have sticky capital that enjoys a government guarantee, while investment banks felt (wrongly, as it turned out) that their access to funding from the equity and bond markets made them all but impregnable. The contrast between hedge-fund paranoia and bank complacency emerged most clearly in the years after Russia's default and the Long-Term Capital crisis in 1998. For the most part, hedge funds responded to that shock by locking up investors for longer periods and negotiating guarantees from brokers to stabilize their capital. Meanwhile, banks trended in the opposite direction: Their buffers of equity capital fell by about a third between the mid-1990s and the mid-2000s. Even in 2006 and 2007, when the mortgage bubble was bursting, many banks were too sluggish to adjust. They sold John Paulson billions of dollars of mortgage insurance via the new ABX index, but they did not stop to ask themselves what Paulson's buying might tell them.

The contrast between banks and hedge funds was summed up by the story of Bear Stearns, even though there was a twist to it. Bear Stearns had a reputation as a vigilant manager of its trading risks; it was exactly the kind of institution that would not be expected to buy poisonous mortgage securities. But by the mid-2000s, Bear had emerged as the number one packager of mortgage-backed securities on Wall Street, up from the third slot in 2000; and to keep the sausage factory going, Bear had bought up subsidiaries that made subprime loans directly to home buyers, both in the United States and in Britain. Inevitably, this expansion shifted managers' attention: They were less focused on what mortgages might be worth than on how to create lots of them. Meanwhile, in 2003, Bear devised an ambitious "10 in 10" strategy for its asset-management division: Revenues and profits from this unit would rise to 10 percent of Bear's total by the year 2010, never mind the fact that Bear's asset-management subsidiary was starting down this road from a position of insignificance. Again, this pursuit of fee income helped to seal Bear's fate. The bank hurriedly assigned unqualified executives to build out its asset-management business by launching internal hedge funds, and some of these funds loaded up on subprime debt. That misjudgment set Bear on the path that led to its collapse the following year—and to the Federal Reserve being forced to absorb $29 billion of Bear's toxic securities.

The failure of Bear's internal hedge funds could be seen as evidence of hedge funds' riskiness. But the truth is that the Bear funds were a product of bank culture, not hedge-fund culture. Like other hedge funds launched under the umbrella of large banks, the Bear funds were managed by people who were seeded within a large firm, not by entrepreneurs who launched independent ventures. They raised capital with the help of the parent bank's network and brand, which lowered the barriers to entry that freestanding hedge funds must reckon with. They knew that if they failed, the parent bank might bail them out, softening their vigilance. The investment thesis of the Bear funds underlined their close ties to the mother ship. Two of the funds were run by Ralph Cioffi, who had previously worked on Bear's sales desk, peddling mortgage-backed securities to institutional clients. His plan for his hedge funds was to buy those same mortgage-backed securities and leverage them up by an astonishing thirty-five to one. This was the sort of risky bet that made sense to a deep-pocketed, fee-hungry parent. It would have been less likely to fly with a real hedge fund.

Ralph Cioffi himself was not the sort of figure who could have launched his own hedge fund easily. As a salesman, he had virtually no experience in controlling portfolio risk—indeed, some Bear executives argued that he should not be allowed to do so. Paul Friedman, the COO of Bear's fixed-income desk, said afterward, "There were a fair number of skeptics internally who couldn't figure out how this guy—who was bright but had never managed money—was now going to be running money. He knew nothing about risk management, had never written a ticket in his life that wasn't someone else's money."[15] Likewise, Cioffi was short on managerial ability: In a brief stint as a supervisor, he had performed disappointingly. Even with Bear smoothing the way, Cioffi had trouble handling the administrative challenge of running a hedge fund. He failed to secure the approval of his fund's independent directors before buying securities from other divisions of Bear Stearns. The paperwork was in such a disastrous state that a law firm had to be brought in to investigate. In a complaint that summed up the trouble with hedge-fund subsidiaries within banks, an investor protested that it had put money in Bear's funds because of the parent firm's reputation for managing its own risks and claimed that Bear treated outside clients differently.[16] The truth was that Bear and other banks that jumped onto the hedge-fund bandwagon were less intent on risk management than on leveraging their brands. If you wanted a reason why John Paulson made billions from the mortgage bubble and his former employer went out of business, the non-hedge-fund character of Bear's internal hedge funds came close to supplying it.[17]

In June 2007, Cioffi's leveraged subprime mortgage funds blew up. They had been marketed on the strength of the Bear Stearns brand, so now Bear felt obliged to rescue them with an emergency loan—vindicating the view that deep-pocketed parents dull the incentive to be vigilant. Meanwhile, Paulson's mortgage wager generated the biggest-ever killing in the history of hedge funds. By the end of 2007, his flagship mortgage fund was up a cumulative 700 percent, net of fees.[18] His company generated an estimated $15 billion in profits, and Paulson himself pocketed between $3 billion and $4 billion—he was "the man who made too much," according to one magazine profile. The following year, when Paulson recommended changes to Treasury secretary Hank Paulson's bank bailout plan, his reception in Congress recalled the deference that Soros frequently enjoyed. "I was thinking we probably had the wrong Paulson" in charge, remarked Representative John Tierney of Massachusetts.

Yet if Bear's failure and Paulson's triumph constituted a victory for hedge funds, it was too early to be sure that they would survive the shocks that followed.

THE MONTH AFTER THE BEAR FUNDS FAILED, KEN GRIFFIN of Citadel headed off to France on vacation. He was a man in his prime.

His formidable firm occupied a landmark tower in Chicago's downtown business district. He had paid $80 million for a painting by Jasper Johns. He had recently married his French bride at the Hameau de la Reine in Versailles, the eighteenth-century mock village where the young Queen Marie Antoinette had once played peasant. But in the summer of 2007, Griffin found his vacation impossible to enjoy. Every day began with phone calls back to Chicago and ended the same way, and by Friday morning, Griffin had had enough. "Don't take this the wrong way," he told his wife. "You can come or you can stay. I'm going."[19]

That Friday, July 27, was the day when the subprime troubles morphed into a larger credit crisis. Loans from guys who catapulted Porsches, byzantine collateralized debt obligations with eighteen layers, the whole pyramid of side bets on the ABX index—until just recently, all could be dismissed as a mania confined to one corner of the markets. But that Friday a Boston-based hedge fund named Sowood Capital Management began to catch fire. Its $3 billion portfolio was down sharply, and it was starting to receive margin calls from brokers.[20]

The remarkable thing about this development was that Sowood had avoided subprime securities. Its boss, Jeffrey Larson, had made his reputation working for the Harvard endowment, which had matched Yale's enthusiasm for absolute return by creating its own stable of in-house hedge-fund managers. By the end of his twelve-year stint with Harvard, Larson had been running $3 billion of the $20 billion endowment. Then in 2004 he had persuaded Harvard to seed an independent multistrategy fund. The new firm, Sowood, had acquired about seventy employees. It had notched up gains of 10 percent annually in its first three years, largely by focusing on credit markets.

At the start of 2007, Larson had rightly sensed that default rates might be heading upward. In a version of the capital-structure arbitrage that John Paulson favored, he bought relatively safe "senior" bonds and shorted riskier paper, positioning himself to do well in a downturn. The subprime losses that buffeted Bear Stearns did not appear to threaten him and might even be good news. In early July, Larson injected another $5.7 million of his personal savings into Sowood.[21]

Soon after that, Larson was forced to reckon with his error. Other leveraged players that had lost money in mortgages were raising capital by dumping nonmortgage positions; and in the third week of July, Sowood's holdings of corporate bonds began to suffer serious losses. High-quality bonds that were supposed to be fine in a downturn were often the easiest to sell, so they were dumped first; when traders deleveraged indiscriminately, the logic of capital-structure arbitrage went out the window. Larson turned to his old mentors at Harvard, hoping for an emergency injection of capital; Harvard decided that would be too risky. By the morning of Friday, July 27, the news of Sowood's troubles had spread around Wall Street, and traders began to position themselves for a contagious spiral. Margin calls might force Sowood to dump its corporate-bond portfolio in a fire sale, hitting other bond funds, triggering more sales and driving the market downward. Of course, these fears were self-fulfilling, and the bonds fell hard that afternoon. Sowood was hemorrhaging money, and even when the market closed for the weekend, the fund continued to get hit in after-hours trading.

Around lunchtime on Sunday, Jeff Larson placed a call to Ken Griffin.[22] Larson recalled how Citadel had bought Amaranth's trading book the previous year. He asked whether Griffin might want to do the same for Sowood's portfolio. The sooner Sowood could find a buyer, the sooner it could stop predators from targeting its positions. Larson needed a deal before the markets opened the next morning.

Griffin got on the phone to his lieutenants. Gerald Beeson, one of the two executives who had parachuted into Amaranth, had just started his own vacation on a beach near Chicago. He drove back at top speed, dialing several colleagues on the way; he stopped off at home to throw on some long pants and raced to the airport. By around seven o'clock that evening, half a dozen Citadel officials had taken over a conference room at Sowood's offices in Boston, where they discovered that Sowood had also summoned Morgan Stanley. As the two teams examined Sowood's portfolio, it quickly became clear that many of the positions were difficult to value; they consisted of derivatives that were traded "over the counter" between companies, rather than on a transparent, centralized exchange, so only a firm that traded all these instruments itself had a hope of figuring out the going rate for them. Sowood's tangle of legal arrangements with brokers and trading partners had to be assessed. The data that described its trades had to be uploaded into the buyer's systems.

At around 9:00 P.M., the head of the Morgan team called Griffin in Chicago.

"Ken, we'll pick this up in the morning."

"We'll get this done by then," Griffin answered. He heard a noise on the line. He wasn't sure if the other guy was laughing at him.

By 7:00 A.M. on Monday, Griffin had done what he had promised. He and his team had worked through the night and bought Sowood's entire trading book. Jeff Larson explained to his investors that "Citadel offered the only immediate and comprehensive solution." Sowood's two funds were down 57 percent and 53 percent for the month; Harvard's endowment had taken a $350 million hit; but at least the nightmare had now ended.[23] The deal was announced publicly, calming the fear that Sowood might dump its positions. The bond market recovered more than 4 percent that day, and the panic was over. One hedge fund had imploded, threatening to start a systemic fire. Another hedge fund had swooped in, acting as the fireman.

Almost immediately, a new fire started.

THE NEXT FRIDAY, AUGUST 3, A RATINGS AGENCY AN-nounced that Bear Stearns's debt might be downgraded. It was the first time a Wall Street firm's financial health had been questioned in the crisis, and Bear Stearns's stock fell so hard that its bosses convened a conference call in an attempt to calm investors. More than two thousand people dialed in, but there was no calming effect at all. Bear's chief financial officer blurted out that the credit markets were behaving in the most extreme manner he had witnessed in his long career; "he fucking blew the market up," Bear's treasurer said sweetly.[24] On CNBC a few hours afterward, the financial pundit Jim Cramer fanned the flames. "It is time to get on the Bear Stearns call!" he ranted, excoriating the Fed for sitting on its hands. "We have Armageddon."[25]

Cramer could not guess where the next fire would come from. But away on the sidelines of the subprime drama, quantitative hedge funds were starting to sense trouble. In the second half of July, computerized systems that traded equities were no longer performing well, and some were even losing money. As the quants analyzed the problem, they discovered something disturbing. It was not that a new risk was swamping the buy and sell signals that had been profitable for years; the signals themselves were no longer working. The quants had programs that bet on momentum in stock prices; programs that bet that momentum would reverse; and programs that bet that cheap stocks with low price-to-earnings ratios would outperform expensive ones.[26] All these bets were fizzling at once. Somewhere out there in the trading universe, one or maybe several quants were liquidating their holdings, perhaps because they had lost money on their mortgage bets and needed to raise cash. Their forced selling was driving prices against anyone who had a comparable portfolio.[27]

At the end of July, Mike Mendelson, a hard-charging ex-Goldman quant, decided it was time to cut the risk in his trading book. Mendelson now worked for AQR, an investment company set up in 1998 that managed $10 billion of capital in hedge funds and another $28 billion in traditional ones. AQR's chief founder, Cliff Asness, had contributed to the academic literature on pricing anomalies in stocks; having programmed his computers to milk these effects, he delivered steady, uncorrelated returns while also sleeping soundly. Although AQR's losses in late July had been too modest to disturb anybody's rest, Mendelson had heard that another big quantitative fund had suffered a bad loss. Erring on the side of prudence, he trimmed leverage. Then, in the first days of August, AQR's models started to work again. Whoever had been liquidating quant positions must now have stopped. The trouble seemed to be over.

On Monday, August 6, Mendelson sat through some routine meetings at AQR's office, a utilitarian suite in a featureless building just by Greenwich station. Around midmorning, he strolled out to the local Subway sandwich store, and as he waited in line he checked his funds' performance on his BlackBerry. He peered for a few seconds at the screen. The numbers were all red, and they were not small, either. In the past three hours, AQR had lost tens of millions of dollars.[28]

"Oh, God, this is ridiculous," Mendelson thought to himself. Some quant somewhere must be deleveraging, but on a monstrous scale. Or maybe several quants were bailing all at once? How long could this go on?

The one thing Mendelson knew was that he would have to cut leverage quickly. If a fund has $100 of capital to support $800 of positions, a 5 percent loss will leave it with $60 in capital and $760 worth of positions: Its leverage rockets up from eight to one to more than twelve to one.[29] If there is another 5 percent loss the next day, the leverage will not merely rise another 50 percent; it will practically triple, from twelve to one to thirty-three to one. A third 5 percent setback will drive leverage to infinity and beyond, since the fund's capital will be negative. Back in AQR's offices, Mendelson and his colleagues sketched a hyperbolic curve on a notepad, showing how leverage could accelerate upward. The only way to survive was to keep leverage on the flattish, left-hand portion of the curve. If AQR's funds were down 5 percent, they might have to sell almost two fifths of their positions to keep leverage stable. Otherwise they would begin a death spiral.

Meanwhile, versions of this drama were playing out at other quantitative hedge funds. Most were not like Jim Simons's Medallion: They were trading well-known price anomalies, not esoteric secrets; "there is no $E=MC^2$ under the hood," as Asness put it.[30] Even Simons confessed that his large fund for institutional investors traded on signals that were understood by others; everyone had read the same academic papers, had looked at the same data, and was making the same types of bets, especially on stocks with momentum and value.[31] In normal times, this didn't matter: Even if an army of funds was chasing "value," there were dozens of ways to measure this phenomenon, so crowding was limited. But as with all investment strategies, crowding did turn out to matter during a panic: Selling by one big fund caused losses at other ones, especially since quantitative strategies had grown large enough to shove prices around.[32] Once rival funds started to incur losses, the logic of the hyperbolic curve would force them to sell too. By Monday afternoon, Mendelson began to see how bad things could get. Not only would AQR have to sell a huge chunk of its positions to keep its leverage stable in the face of initial losses. As its competitors sold too, it would have to sprint to stay still, racing other quants to cut the size of its portfolio.

The next day was even more brutal than Mendelson had expected. AQR's models lost money twice as quickly as on Monday, and the firm instructed its computers to dump billions of dollars' worth of positions. The good news was that technology made it possible to liquidate a portfolio much faster than in earlier years; the bad news was that AQR's rivals could liquidate just as quickly. Every quant was firing off torpedoes at every other quant; there were rumors of funds that were down 10 percent or worse. At the Renaissance campus in Long Island, Jim Simons huddled with his top lieutenants in front of the computer screens, tweaking the parameters on his models like a pilot navigating a hurricane. Cliff Asness, AQR's founder, blew up in the office and smashed computer screens.[33] He took a call from Ken Griffin, who by now had a reputation for buying the corpses out of car wrecks. "I looked up and saw the Valkyries coming and heard the grim reaper's scythe knocking on my door. I did my best to run to the light," Asness said later.[34]

While this chaos unfolded, policy makers appeared to occupy a parallel universe. On Tuesday, August 7, the second day of the quant quake, the Fed's interest-rate committee issued a warning about the risks of inflation. The next day President Bush visited the Treasury to meet with his economic advisers. "[I]f the market functions normally, it will lead to a soft landing," he said hopefully. On Thursday the tone from Washington began to change, but less because of the carnage at quantitative funds than because of trouble from Europe: The giant French bank BNP Paribas had suspended redemptions from three internal money-market funds, citing "the complete evaporation of liquidity." Subprime losses were clearly scaring the markets, and the European Central Bank responded with $131 billion in emergency liquidity. By Thursday afternoon, the

Fed's chairman, Ben Bernanke, had turned his office into a makeshift war room, and his chief lieutenants dialed in from various vacation locations. Early the next morning, the Fed reversed its earlier emphasis on inflation, pledging to provide enough cash "to facilitate the orderly functioning of financial markets."

Meanwhile in Greenwich, Mendelson was starting to see light at the end of the tunnel. It had nothing to do with the Fed's U-turn and everything to do with other hedge funds. Starting on Tuesday, Mendelson had begun to call brokers and friends in the markets—anybody who might know anything about how other leveraged quant funds were positioned. The business was dominated by a handful of firms. There was Jim Simons's new fund, which ran more than $25 billion of institutional money. There was Highbridge Capital, a subsidiary of J.P. Morgan. There were D. E. Shaw, Barclays Global Investors, and Goldman Sachs Asset Management. Mendelson wanted to know how much the big players had cut leverage so far: If they got themselves down into the flat part of the hyperbolic curve, the selling pressure would end and the storm would be over. After working the phones all day Tuesday, Mendelson reached a buddy just after midnight. The guy had rushed back early from vacation and was falling apart: He was exhausted, blabbering, at the end of his tether. Mendelson could tell he was about to liquidate his whole book. He ticked one firm off his list and hit the phones again the next morning.

By Thursday evening, Mendelson had figured out that only one big player had yet to cut leverage. He guessed it might be one of the hedge-fund subsidiaries of his old firm, Goldman Sachs: the $5 billion Global Equity Opportunities Fund. Goldman's executives had decided that the fund's positions were too big to sell, so its leverage had rocketed up as its bets got hammered. When the market opened on Friday, one of two things would happen. Either the fund would liquidate, hitting other quant funds for a fifth straight day. Or it would be recapitalized by its parent company.[35]

When Friday morning came, Mendelson could not care less about the Fed's stance on inflation. He was looking at his own trading model. Within a few minutes, it was generating profits—its performance practically

screamed out that the Goldman subsidiary had been rescued and that
the quant liquidations had ended. Acting on that signal, AQR began to
releverage as quickly as possible; the more it could catch the upswing as
money flooded back, the more it could make up for the past four days
of carnage. The following Monday, Goldman Sachs announced publicly
what Mendelson had already guessed. It had recapitalized the Global
Equity fund with $3 billion in fresh money.[36]

The quant quake of August 2007 ended as abruptly as it had started.
Friday and Monday were great days for the models, and most of the
quants recouped at least part of their losses. But the drama prompted a
new round of debate about hedge funds, and the agonizing outlasted the
disruption in the markets. Granted, Amaranth and Sowood had been rescued by a fellow hedge fund, making it hard to argue that the sector was
destabilizing. Granted, hedge funds—or at least, nearly all freestanding
hedge funds—had dodged the mortgage bullet, suggesting that they were
better money managers than their banking rivals. But the storm in the
equity market was surely a warning. The most sophisticated hedge funds
had lost control of their models. The rocket scientists had blown up their
rockets.

The most persuasive critics came from within the hedge-fund establishment. Andrew Lo, an MIT professor who ran his own hedge fund,
published a widely cited postmortem on the quant quake; and Richard
Bookstaber, an MIT alumnus who had worked at several major funds,
pressed the warnings he had recently published in a pessimistic book on
finance.[37] Lo and Bookstaber contended that the rise of leveraged hedge
funds created a new threat: Trouble in the mortgage or credit markets
could saddle a multistrategy fund with losses, forcing it to liquidate equity
holdings; distress could leap from one sector to the next; the financial
system as a whole was riskier. Lo and Bookstaber linked this warning
to a gloomy view of hedge funds' investment performance. There were
too many quant funds chasing small market anomalies. This crowding
diminished investment returns, which in turn drove hedge funds to use
dangerous amounts of leverage to maintain profits.

There was some truth in all this pessimism. During the LTCM crisis, credit markets had been in turmoil but quantitative equity funds had been fine; the rise of leveraged traders helped to explain why the fire had jumped the fire wall this time.[38] But it was one thing to say that crowding was a problem in moments of turmoil, quite another to assert that it was forcing down returns in the good times and making dangerous leverage inevitable. Lo's paper presented the returns from one quantitative strategy—buy stocks that are doing badly and sell ones that are doing well—and made much of the fact that profits from this simple contrarian model had deteriorated since 1995, apparently substantiating the case that hedge funds had no choice but to employ more scary leverage. But basic contrarian strategies were not central to the quant quake, because the quants themselves could see that there were limited profits in them. The big money in quant funds was in other strategies—for example, sell expensive growth stocks with high price-to-earnings ratios and buy cheap, dowdy ones with low ratios. The price gap between growth stocks and value stocks had shown little sign of narrowing in the years leading up to 2007; as Asness put it, "We are fond of saying that if these strategies are truly horribly overcrowded, then someone has apparently forgotten to tell the prices."[39] Other quants made versions of the same point. Marek Fludzinski, the head of a hedge-fund company called Thales, tested virtually identical trading strategies to see if the presence of one of them would erode the other one's returns; remarkably, it did not, suggesting that crowding was not actually a problem.[40] It was true that uncrowded bets could suddenly feel intensely crowded in a moment of turmoil; but this held for virtually all trading strategies, not just quantitative ones. "Of course, 'good investing gets clocked as some investors rush for exits' is not as catchy a story as 'quant brainiacs follow their computers to a well-deserved doom,' so I'm probably not going to win this battle in the media," Asness lamented.[41]

If quant strategies were not as crowded as the critics suggested, and if scary amounts of leverage were therefore not inevitable, what of the charge that hedge funds increased the risk of broad systemic blowups? Here too the Lo-Bookstaber critique needed to be qualified. During the first three days of the quant quake, the signals in the traders' models performed abysmally, but the broader market remained calm—the average American household with its nest egg in an index fund would have noticed nothing, undermining the notion that this was a crisis for the whole financial system. On the fourth day of the quant quake, the market did suffer a hard fall, but this reflected the crisis in the credit markets more than the tremors in quant land. The great thing about liquidating so-called market-neutral strategies was that the effect on the overall market was neutral: For every stock the quants sold, they covered a short position. It was true that if Goldman Sachs had not rescued its subsidiary, the deleveraging would have lasted longer, potentially forcing multistrategy funds to dump positions in other markets and spreading the trouble. But the way things actually turned out, the market punished overleveraged traders while the broader system suffered little harm. This was how capitalism was meant to discipline its children. No regulator could have done better.

In the final analysis, it was hard to disagree with Mike Mendelson's verdict on the quant quake: "A bunch of us lost a bunch of money and had a really tiring week, which sucked, believe me. But I don't think it was a big public policy issue."[42]

16

"HOW COULD THEY DO THIS?"

O n a Thursday evening in March 2008, James Chanos walked
out of his office in midtown Manhattan and set off to meet Carl
Bernstein, one of the journalists famous for breaking the Water-
gate scandal. Chanos felt some professional affinity with investigative
reporters: He ran a hedge fund, Kynikos Associates, that specialized in
digging up financial dirt at companies, shorting their stock, and profiting
when the bad news surfaced and the stock cratered. In the bull market of
the 1980s and 1990s, short selling had been an unrewarding niche, and
Chanos had resembled the investigative newsman who toils in obscurity
and seldom lands on the front pages. But the sluggish market of the 2000s
had been glorious. Chanos had been among the first to see through the
fraudulent energy company Enron. He had shocked the world in 2005
by claiming that the giant insurer AIG had "Enron-like" characteristics.
And in 2007 he had returned over 30 percent, largely by shorting financial institutions that were slow to admit losses from the mortgage bubble.[1]
By March 2008, behemoths such as Citigroup and Merrill Lynch were
fessing up to billions of dollars' worth of trouble, but Chanos had much
to celebrate.

That Thursday evening, as he threaded his way through the evening
crowds in Manhattan, Chanos took a call on his cell phone. The caller

ID announced that the call was from someone at Bear Stearns—a bank whose relations with hedge funds had turned testy. Concerned about Bear's stability following its enormous mortgage losses, a string of famous funds had closed the "margin accounts" they held at Bear to leverage their trades; and because Bear borrowed against the assets in those accounts, Bear's access to funding was collapsing. Bear executives suspected that hedge funds were ganging up to short their stock, deviously reinforcing these raids by closing their margin accounts.

Chanos took the call on his cell phone and kept walking along Madison Avenue.

"Jim, hi, it's Alan Schwartz."

Chanos realized he was speaking to Bear's chief executive. "Hi, Alan," he responded.

"Jim, we really appreciate your business and your staying with us. I'd like you to think about going on CNBC tomorrow morning, on *Squawk Box*, and telling everybody you still are a client, you have money on deposit, you have faith in us, and everything's fine."

Chanos thought for a moment. Bear had wailed loudly and publicly about short sellers; now it was coming to a short seller for help. The rabbit was pleading with the python.

"Alan, how do I know everything's fine? Is everything fine?"

"Jim, we're going to report record earnings on Monday morning."

"Alan, you just made me an insider," said Chanos, annoyed. "I didn't ask for that information, and I don't think that's going to be relevant anyway. Based on what I understand, people are reducing their margin balances with you, and that's resulting in a funding squeeze."

"Well, yes, to some extent, but we should be fine."

Chanos refused to do what Schwartz asked of him. As the most visible short seller on Wall Street, his testimony could have buoyed confidence in Bear, but Chanos was not going to risk his own credibility by vouching for a bank that might be imploding. Besides, he was leaving at seven o'clock the next morning for a vacation in the Bahamas. He proceeded on his way to the Post House restaurant, just off Madison Avenue, where he dined on steaks with Bernstein and his five Kynikos partners.

If Chanos had resented Schwartz's suggestion when he first heard it, his mood morphed into unrestrained outrage over the next day or so. At six-thirty on Friday morning, when *Squawk Box* was on the air, word began to spread that the Fed was brokering a rescue for Bear Stearns; the closing of its hedge funds' margin accounts had been followed by a collapse of confidence and a classic bank run. Schwartz had known the previous evening that his bank was going down, and yet he had tried to inveigle Chanos onto television anyway. "That fucker was going to throw me under the bus," Chanos recalled later.[2]

Chanos's exchange with Schwartz captured the transformed relationship between banks and hedge funds. Back in 1994, Bear Stearns had sunk the wayward hedge fund Askin Capital, forcing it into default and seizing a good portion of its assets. In 1998, Bear had informed Long-Term Capital Management that it was toast, refusing to clear its trades and slamming its door on the Fed-brokered rescue. But in 2008, the tables had turned: Bear Stearns was toast, hedge funds had the power, and Wall Street buzzed with sinister stories about how hedge funds had abused it. A vivid *Vanity Fair* account of Bear's failure gave credence to the notion that Bear had been the victim of a hedge-fund conspiracy, even citing a "vague tale" that at a breakfast the following Sunday, the ring-leaders had celebrated Bear's demise and plotted a follow-up assault on Lehman Brothers. One of Lehman's top executives heard that the breakfast had taken place at the Four Seasons Hotel and that the short sellers had ordered mimosas made with $350 bottles of Cristal to toast their achievement.[3] But even as the story grew in the telling, the Securities and Exchange Commission investigated the allegations and prosecuted no one, and the very image of the breakfast strained credulity.[4] If hedge-fund chiefs had conspired to bring Bear down, they would have been breaking the law. They would not have incriminated themselves by gathering right after the event to chest-bump in public.[5]

Even if the talk of a criminal conspiracy was overwrought, there was no doubt that hedge funds were shorting the banks—and that Lehman was their next target. The short interest in Lehman's stock rose to more than 9 percent of its shares, meaning that almost one in ten had been borrowed and sold by a short seller. Lehman's share price was down more than 40 percent since the start of the year, and the firm's worried leaders felt obliged to counterattack. They accused hedge funds of a reckless policy of "short and distort," and Lehman's combative chief executive, Richard Fuld, virtually declared war. "I will hurt the shorts, and that is my goal," he vowed at the firm's annual meeting.[6]

Fuld did his best to persuade the authorities in Washington to solve his problem. They should restrict short selling of Lehman shares, for instance by reinstating the defunct uptick rule, which prevented speculators from shorting a stock while it was falling. In April, Erik Sirri, a top Securities and Exchange Commission official, pressed Fuld for evidence that hedge-fund behavior justified this sort of treatment. What evidence did Fuld have that the funds were colluding to push Lehman under?

"Just give me something, a name, anything," Sirri challenged.

Fuld would not answer. His lieutenants had provided the SEC with leads, largely consisting of rumors that traders were gunning for Lehman. But you couldn't prove a conspiracy without the power of subpoena. The way Fuld saw it, it was the SEC that had that power, so there was something upside-down about the SEC turning to Lehman for the evidence.

Frustrated in Washington, Fuld turned next to Jim Cramer, the well-connected TV pundit. He invited him over to breakfast and pumped him for information about the supposed conspiracy of short sellers.

"Why don't you just give me the names of people telling you negative things about us?" Fuld growled.

"Look, there isn't anybody," Cramer protested.[7]

Toward the end of May, at a high-profile investment conference at the Time Warner Center in New York, an infuriatingly boyish-looking hedge-fund manager named David Einhorn stood up in front of a large crowd and took the pressure on Lehman to the next level. This was the same David Einhorn whose firm, Greenlight Capital, had shorted Chemdex and other frothy dot-com stocks, and now the wind was at his back as he explained why Lehman was in trouble. The bank was underplaying problems on its balance sheet, Einhorn maintained: It held $6.5 billion worth of dicey collateralized debt obligations but had marked down their value by only

$200 million at the end of the first quarter—a suspiciously small shift given the sharp slide in credit markets. Meanhile the bank had informed investors on a conference call that it would book a loss on its hard-to-value "Level Three" assets, but then had turned around and reported a profit; again, Einhorn demanded an explanation. If Lehman was covering up the full extent of its troubles, the consequences would be terrible not only for Lehman's shareholders but also for the financial system. Like a prosecutor intent on putting away a villain, Einhorn called upon regulators to guide Lehman to own up to its losses before taxpayers had to pay for them.

"For the last several weeks, Lehman has been complaining about short sellers," Einhorn concluded pointedly. "When management teams do that, it is a sign that management is attempting to distract investors from serious problems."

The day after Einhorn's speech, Lehman's shares dipped by almost 3 percent, and they continued to slide thereafter. Lehman executives did their best to discredit Einhorn's attack, but the markets were against them. In June, Lehman reported a loss of $2.8 billion for the second quarter, and commentators credited Einhorn for forcing the bank to come clean about its true position.[8] More than a few people wondered whether this was altogether a good thing. "There's truth to his argument, but now is not the time," one Wall Streeter said of Einhorn's crusade. "Two years ago would've been heroic. If he brings down Lehman, the guarantors are going to be me and you the taxpayer."

IT WAS NOT JUST THE SHORT SELLERS WHO WERE FEEL-ing their oats. One year earlier, in the week after the quant quake, George Soros had invited Julian Robertson, Jim Chanos, and a handful of other heavyweights to lunch at his estate on Long Island. Over a lunch of striped bass, fruit salad, and cookies, the group debated the economic outlook. The consensus among the guests was that a full-blown recession was unlikely, but Soros disagreed so strongly with this view that he returned to active investing.[9] Since the departure of Stan Druckenmiller, Soros had farmed out most of his fortune to external managers. But now, at the age of seventy-seven, he retook the reins; by the end of 2007, his fund was up a remarkable 32 percent, and Soros himself emerged as the second-highest earner in the industry. It was just like old times, and other macro traders fared well too, riding an imploding credit bubble in the rich world and continuing growth in the emerging economies. Macro funds were short rich-world markets and short the dollar. They were long emerging markets, long oil, and frequently long other commodities. In the eighteen months to June 2008, the average macro fund was up about 17 percent, according to Hedge Fund Research—not a bad return in a period of financial crisis.

The bubbling confidence of hedge funds was expressed in their new "activism"—the practice of buying large stakes in firms and demanding changes in their strategy. In the first weeks of 2008, a former ice-hockey player named Phil Falcone, whose Harbinger Capital had made a killing shorting subprime mortgages the previous year, muscled into the newspaper business. He bought 4.9 percent of the *New York Times*, then called upon the *Times* board to accept four of his allies as directors. The way Falcone saw it, the *Times* had a piece of the Boston Red Sox, a NASCAR squad, some regional newspapers and television channels; it was time to dump this peripheral nonsense and build out the core newspaper brand on the Internet. In March, the Sulzberger family, which owned the bulk of the *Times*'s voting shares, conceded two of the board seats that Falcone wanted; and Falcone responded by increasing his stake to 19 percent. In April, Arthur Ochs Sulzberger Jr., the Times Company chairman, backhandedly acknowledged the gravity of the challenge. At the annual shareholders' meeting, he stood up on the stage and protested that "this company is not for sale." Contrary to rumor, there were some things in New York that hedge funds did not control yet.

Hedge fund activism flourished in London too, most notably in the person of Chris Hohn, who ran a hedge-fund-cum-charity styled the Children's Investment Fund. A slice of Hohn's profits flowed through to his philanthropic arm, which supported child-survival projects and AIDS programs. But Hohn was quite capable of mixing high-mindedness with hardball: In 2005, he bought a chunk of Deutsche Börse, the entity that owned the German stock exchange, and forced its chief executive to resign, telling him at one point, "My position is so strong that we can bring Mickey Mouse and Donald Duck onto the supervisory board."[10] Two years later, Hohn cajoled the Dutch bank ABN AMRO into selling itself to a trio of suitors; and in the summer of 2008 he followed up by buying 8.7 percent of the American railroad company CSX and demanding board representation. CSX fought back as best it could. It arranged for its friends in Congress to haul Hohn's people before a committee. It sued him in New York court, alleging violations of the SEC's disclosure rules. It appealed to rank-and-file shareholders to reject this evil British lunge for strategic American rail infrastructure. Finally, in an attempt to foil the agents from the temperate isle, CSX staged its annual meeting in June 2008 in a steamy Louisiana rail yard. "We saved you from the Huns twice," a shareholder declared at that meeting, which took place in an enormous tent.[11] But Hohn was not to be denied. Even though CSX's managers tried to delay and fudge the vote, his candidates won four seats on CSX's board by the middle of September.

The sheer reach of the hedge funds was illustrated by their forays into emerging markets. A classic example came from Kazakhstan, a sprawling expanse of Eurasia that most Wall Streeters had only heard of via *Borat*. Thanks to its enormous oil reserves, Kazakhstan was growing at 8 percent or 9 percent a year, and the country was running an export surplus; it was a pretty sure bet that the currency would appreciate against the dollar. The question was how to cash in on this rise. Because of its oil revenues, the government had no need to issue debt, so there were no sovereign bonds for foreigners to purchase. Starting around 2003, hedge funds found a way around this obstacle. Rather than buying sovereign bonds, they lent directly to Kazakh banks, getting exposure to the Kazakh currency plus a higher interest rate on their money. They repeated versions of this trick all over the world, so that by 2008 hedge funds had lent to everyone from Brazilian coffee exporters to Ukrainian dairy farms. Ukraine's capital, Kiev, became such a hot destination for hedge funds that its top hotel charged eight hundred euros nightly.

Of course, there were awkward questions about this emerging-market lending. In order to ride an appreciating currency, the hedge funds were exposing themselves to the default risks posed by coffee exporters, dairy farms, and so on. They were behaving like traditional commercial lenders—they were pretending to be banks!—and yet they lacked the capacity of real banks to do due diligence on borrowers. A second-tier company in Russia could now borrow directly from hedge funds without anybody spending time at its offices, inspecting its books, or figuring out how a loan could be recovered in the event of bankruptcy. The hedge funds might be lending against collateral that consisted of dairy herds on the other side of the world; the notion that they could show up in the Ukrainian countryside and take delivery of live cows was farcical. But in the heady atmosphere of the mid-2000s, nobody much cared. Hedge funds were the rising force in finance, and they could do no wrong; traditional banking and persnickety loan officers were too dull to bother with. The subprime credit crisis, which revealed the shockingly poor risk management at banks, did nothing to shake this verdict.

Early in the crisis, in April 2007, Jim Chanos had attended a meeting in Washington. A team of German regulators had asked him, "So what are your views about hedge funds and financial stability?" Chanos had responded that the Germans were looking the wrong way: "It's not us you should be worrying about—it's the banks!" he had told them.[12] A bit more than a year later, in mid-2008, Chanos was proved abundantly correct. Bear Stearns had failed; Lehman was under fire; and the two government-chartered home lenders, Fannie Mae and Freddie Mac, were leaking money at an alarming rate. Fannie and Freddie had a whole government agency dedicated to their oversight, and they were about to collapse into the arms of taxpayers. Meanwhile unregulated hedge funds were stalking targets from the *New York Times* to Kazakhstan, and dancing in between the land mines.

But over the horizon, new threats were forming. The world was about to get more complicated.

BY THE SUMMER OF 2008, PAUL TUDOR JONES HAD IN-stalled his growing firm in a large mansion on a broad lawn, a few miles outside of Greenwich. The place combined gentility with in-your-face exuberance; it was at once courtly and brash, not unlike its master. Two curving staircases ascended gracefully from a hushed entrance hall; there were marble floors and antique rugs and finely sculpted table legs; and Jones's office was decorated with deer antlers and a glorious stuffed bear— "What else do you give a big bear at 50?" an inscribed plaque demanded. But the path to Jones's office was guarded by a vast aquamarine mural of a killer shark, its teeth glinting with murder; and on one wall of his quarters, six enormous screens had been set into the wood panels, each gleaming with a market chart or cable-news feed. Pinned up by a window, a page torn from a yellow legal pad bore a scrawled message from Jones to himself: "Always look for a trending market."

In late June of that year, Jones got himself convinced that the trend was downward. The S&P 500 index had jumped sharply in April and kept rising in May, but Jones thought this was a sucker's rally. The United States was in the grip of the greatest credit bubble of all time, and Jones studied every precedent there was—Japan in 1989, the United States in the late 1920s, Sweden in the 1990s. He pored over the price patterns in these historical analogues, hunting for hints about how the market might behave. Then on Saturday, June 28, at 3:05 A.M., he fired off a eureka e-mail to colleagues. "I hate being an alarmist, really," began the subject line. "But the current WEEKLY S&P against the DAILY DJIA back in 1987 is really alarming to me."[13]

Jones's thinking would have seemed a touch obscure to some investors. It started from the fact that, in 1987, declines in the bond market had spooked stocks, since higher interest rates meant that less money would slosh into the equity market. In the first half of 2008, Jones reckoned, rising oil prices had had the same effect: The inflationary pressure from dear oil was driving the Fed to keep interest rates up, draining liquidity from asset markets. Hitting upon this sort of parallel gave Jones an adrenaline-soaked high; the markets of 1987 and 2008 were "eerily similar," he whooped in the e-mail—"same plot just different characters." Next, Jones ventured an argument that inverted Franklin Roosevelt: "I am also really bothered by the absence of fear in the options market," he wrote;

investors should fear the lack of fear itself, since optimism left plenty of room for sentiment to deteriorate. Finally, Jones pointed to the fact that the Dow Jones Industrial Average had closed at its lowest level in 250 days, and this at a time when investor sentiment was bullish; "that has NEVER happened in the 21 year history of this indicator including '87," Jones reported in his e-mail. To cap it all off, the chart of the weekly S&P 500 index looked exactly like that of the daily Dow Jones average back in 1987; you could map one onto the other and see a perfect fit—that had to mean something! The suggestive power of two different indices plotted on two different time intervals tipped Jones over the edge. "I realized, oh my God, this is going to be the ugliest third quarter in history," Jones said later.[14]

For the next two months, Jones continued to play the historical detective. Sometimes he thought that the S&P chart resembled the recession of 2001; sometimes it looked like 1987. But no matter which analogue appealed, Jones remained negative on the market outlook, and in the end his reading of the charts mattered less than the instinct behind it. What really counted was that Jones was looking at an asymmetrical bet, and he understood this intuitively. A leveraged financial system in a credit crisis is like a high-wire artist in a storm. The wire is going to wobble, and the artist may lose his balance and tumble a long way. But he is definitely not going to levitate upward.

Over the course of his long career, Jones had been working up to this moment. He had watched leverage grow exponentially since the 1980s and had frequently expressed misgivings. During the dot-com mania of the late 1990s, he had written to Alan Greenspan, the Fed chairman, urging him to raise margin requirements on stock traders so as to slow the flood of cash that was inflating the tech bubble. A few years later, in the mid-2000s, he had received regular phone calls from a senior official at the Fed, asking him what risks he sensed in the markets. He had answered repeatedly that debt was building upon debt: Nobody could know which part of the pyramid might crack; but the higher it grew, the greater the risk of a catastrophe. Clearly Tudor itself was part of this alarming edifice. At the end of each year, Jones would stay late at the office with Tudor's president, Mark Dalton, reviewing the compensation of Tudor employees. At some point in these sessions, Jones would look at Dalton and say, "Can you imagine if the financial system ever had to liquidate? What if this enormous contraption that we've been part and parcel of building had to be unwound?"

"I don't even want to think about it," Dalton would answer.[15]

ON FRIDAY, SEPTEMBER 12, 2008, AT AROUND SIX O'CLOCK in the evening, a column of sleek, dark cars approached the New York Federal Reserve building. The cars disgorged the chief executives of Wall Street's leading banks, who were greeted by Treasury secretary Hank Paulson, New York Fed president Timothy Geithner, and SEC chairman Christopher Cox—it was the government personified. The subject of the meeting was Lehman Brothers, whose fortunes had continued to slide disastrously since David Einhorn's speech in May; and the government delegation was intent on delivering a clear message—there would be no public money for a Lehman bailout. As the politician at the meeting, Paulson felt he had already risked taxpayers' money enough. He had approved government support for the rescue of Bear Stearns and for the rescue of the giant mortgage lenders Fannie Mae and Freddie Mac; he had been denounced by Senator Jim Bunning, Republican of Kentucky, for "acting like the minister of finance in China." The way Paulson saw things, Lehman presented an opportunity to draw a line: to teach bankers a salutary lesson that they must face the consequences of their own errors. Of course, the markets might react badly if Lehman went under. But the Treasury secretary and his colleagues believed that the risk was worth running. After all, Lehman had been in the emergency wing for months, and its trading partners had presumably prepared for its collapse. The government team would try to find a private buyer for Lehman; but if it could not do so, it would step aside, betting that Lehman's failure would not cause chaos.[16]

If Paulson and his colleagues had seen the world as hedge funds do, they would not have made this fateful call, which led to the worst freeze-up in the financial system since the 1930s. The Paulson team was walking into a version of the trap that had snared the Bank of England in 1992: It looked at the odds of various outcomes in the way that policy makers do, but it failed to ask the trader's question—what is the *payout* in each instance? From a policy maker's perspective, Lehman's failure might engender chaos or it might not; if you thought there was a fifty-fifty chance of calm, you might choose to take the risk, especially if you were anxious to teach banks a lesson in responsibility. But from a trader's perspective, this calculation was naive; a fifty-fifty chance of calm meant that chaos was virtually certain in practice. Hedge funds from London to Wall Street would conduct a thought experiment: In the calm world, markets would be flat; in the chaotic world, markets would crater; if traders shorted everything in sight, they would lose nothing in the first instance but make a killing in the second one. Faced with this asymmetrical payout, every rational hedge fund would bet aggressively on a collapse. And because they were going to make those bets, collapse would be inevitable.

Paul Tudor Jones had no trouble reaching that conclusion. There was no need to parse the details of how many institutions had readied themselves for the possibility of Lehman's demise; as Jones put it later, "You knew Lehman Brothers would be the kickoff for a big down move. You knew that."[17] Everybody understood that Lehman was part of a bewildering daisy chain of interlocking transactions. Everybody understood that the financial system was leveraged up to its eyes. And the sheer symbolism of Lehman's implosion would be an awe-inspiring thing. Lehman Brothers was a venerable institution that had survived the Depression and world wars; its failure would scream out that nothing was safe—"it would make everybody say, 'Oh my God, is my son good for the loan I lent him?'" Jones exclaimed. "The optics of that would be so bad that everyone was going to shoot first and ask questions later," he carried on. "The *question mark* would completely totally create financial panic and chaos."[18]

The news of Lehman's bankruptcy started to leak out around lunchtime on Sunday. Even if many hedge funds had positioned their portfolios for bad news, it soon became clear that they were not fully inoculated. American funds belatedly realized that Lehman's London operation would declare bankruptcy under British law, which meant that hedge fund accounts that might have been "segregated," or safe, under American rules would now instead be frozen. Hedge-fund lawyers rushed into their offices from weekend homes in the Hamptons, frantic to determine whether their assets with Lehman were subject to the British rules or the American ones. They put their outside counsels on speed dial and peppered them with questions. Investors called in a panic, demanding to know the size of their exposures. Nobody had clear answers, which only compounded the hysteria. By the evening, the size of the impending tsunami had begun to sink in. Eric Rosenfeld, the Long-Term Capital partner who had lived through the traumatic failure of his own firm, recalls hearing the news of Lehman's bankruptcy on his car radio. "I couldn't believe it. I was shocked. I was almost hyperventilating. How could they do this?"[19]

When the markets opened on Monday, Paul Tudor Jones experienced the extreme highs and lows that only he was capable of. On the one hand, he was perfectly positioned in his own trading book; he had seen the wave coming, and he rode it down, as the S&P 500 fell 4.7 percent by the close of trading that evening. On the other hand, it was the worst day of his professional life. Tudor had tried to withdraw the remainder of its assets from Lehman Brothers the previous week, but the request had arrived a day late, so the firm had $100 million frozen in Lehman's London operation.[20] Tudor wrote off the entire sum as a loss, but that turned out to be the least of its problems.

Tudor had made a mistake that was as egregious in its own way as Paulson's miscalculation on Lehman. It had allowed the firm's emerging-market credit team to build a giant portfolio of loans to firms in emerging markets. Banks in Kazakhstan, banks in Russia, Ukrainian dairy farms—Tudor had them all, and they accounted for a significant portion of the assets in the firm's flagship BVI fund. Like Brian Hunter at Amaranth, Tudor had spotted a genuine opportunity at the outset: Loans to emerging markets could give the fund exposure to strong currencies; the loans paid high interest rates that more than compensated for the default risk; and as other hedge funds piled into the same trade, they drove up the currency and loan market, boosting returns and encouraging the bosses at Tudor to allocate extra capital to the strategy. But once Lehman collapsed, the true risks in emerging markets were revealed. Suddenly, storied banks in the United States could not raise money anymore, and banks in Kazakhstan or Russia seemed certain to face trouble. The loans in the emerging-market portfolio immediately lost around two thirds of their value, costing Tudor over $1 billion.[21]

For a trader like Paul Jones, the worst thing was that he was trapped in these positions. When he speculated in futures, he always knew he could turn on a dime; indeed, he never created a position without putting in a "stop" that would take him out if he began to suffer losses. But the emerging-market loans were utterly illiquid: After Lehman declared bankruptcy, nobody wanted to hold any loans at any price, so there was no way to get rid of them. "I realized that our emerging-market trading book was going to get absolutely hammered and there was nothing I could do about it. . . . That was the worst moment of my whole life," Jones said later.[22] In his anguish and his helplessness, he thought back to what he had read about the only disaster that approached this one in scale. "I used to always think, 'Holy cow, how'd these guys in 1929 lose it all? How could anybody be so boneheaded? You'd have to be a complete moron!' And then that day, I thought, 'Oh my God. I see how these guys in '29 got hurt now. They were not just sitting there long the market. They had things that they couldn't get out of.'"[23]

Jones's losses from emerging-market loans dwarfed the gains from his own trading book. Tudor had been up 6 percent or 7 percent for the year on the eve of Lehman's failure, an impressive performance given that the stock market was down substantially. But by the end of the year, Tudor was down 4 percent, even though Jones himself had seen the storm coming.[24] Tudor was forced to impose "gates" on its funds, suspending investors' access to their capital. A chastened Paul Jones promised to narrow Tudor's focus and stick to the liquid markets he knew best. The age of the diversified alpha factory was perhaps receding.

THE FAILURE OF LEHMAN BROTHERS SPELLED THE END
of the modern investment-bank model. Lehman and its rivals had borrowed billions in the short-term money markets, then used the money to buy assets that were hard to sell in a hurry. When the crisis hit, short-term lending dried up instantly; everyone could see that the investment banks might face a crunch, and of course the fear was self-fulfilling. To stave off this sort of bank run, commercial banks have government insurance to reassure depositors and access to emergency lending from the Federal Reserve. But investment banks have no such safety net. Believing that they were somehow invincible, they had behaved as though they did have one.

The next domino to fall was Merrill Lynch, the investment bank famous for its "thundering herd" of nearly seventeen thousand stockbrokers. On the weekend that Lehman's fate was decided, Merrill Lynch's chief executive, John Thain, shuttled between the New York Fed and meetings with Ken Lewis, his counterpart at the Bank of America. Over a series of negotiations that culminated at 1:00 A.M. on Monday morning, Thain agreed to sell Merrill for a song. Almost a year earlier, Merrill had rebuffed an offer from Bank of America that was worth $90 a share. Now, with the investment-bank model in tatters, Merrill was willing to do a deal for $29 a share without hesitation. One of Wall Street's oldest names was collapsing into the arms of a Main Street commercial bank. As one newspaper wrote, it was as if Wal-Mart were buying Tiffany's.

Now that Bear, Lehman, and Merrill were gone, the two remaining investment banks, Morgan Stanley and Goldman Sachs, came under pressure. All of Wall Street knew that their reliance on short-term funding, coupled with extremely high leverage, made them vulnerable to a bank run; and the Morgan and Goldman stock prices began to show up permanently at the top of the CNBC screen, in what traders called the "death watch."[25] The trouble at the giant insurer AIG only made things worse. By writing credit default swaps, AIG had sold protection against the danger that all manner of bonds might go into default—it was the kind of crazy risk taking you got when you located an ambitious trading operation inside the bosom of a well-capitalized firm, imbuing the traders with a heady sense of invulnerability. Inevitably, AIG's credit default swaps lost billions when the likelihood of default spiked up amid the crisis following Lehman. On Tuesday, September 16, the government was forced to rescue the firm, lending it an astonishing $85 billion.

The day after that, rumors that Morgan Stanley was exposed to AIG's mess helped to drive Morgan's stock down 42 percent by the middle of the afternoon. Hedge funds clamored to get their assets out of Morgan, desperate to avoid being caught in another Lehman-type trap. Morgan's chief executive, John Mack, raged against short-selling conspirators who were supposedly driving him under. It was a repeat of the battles that Bear Stearns and Lehman had waged against hedge funds in their own moments of crisis.

Around the same time, Ken Griffin of Citadel calculated the odds that his hedge fund might fail also. He had aspired to build a firm like Morgan Stanley or Goldman Sachs, and he had some of the same vulnerabilities. He had leveraged his capital by more than ten to one—a far less aggressive ratio than the thirty-to-one that was typical of investment banks but well over the single-digit multiple that was normal for hedge funds.[26] And because Citadel had issued a small quantity of five-year bonds, there was a market for credit default swaps on its debt, so traders could telegraph anxieties about its liquidity.[27]

Griffin constructed a quick probability tree. He put Morgan Stanley's chances of survival at 50 percent. If Morgan went down, the odds of Goldman following were 95 percent. If Goldman failed, the odds of Citadel collapsing were almost 100 percent, since the forced selling by Morgan and Goldman would destroy the value of Citadel's holdings. If you put that sequence together, Citadel's chances of survival clocked in at only around 55 percent. "That's a pretty bad day—when you realize twenty years of your work now comes down to whether or not some firm that you have no influence over fails," Griffin said later.[28]

Yet if Citadel shared some of the vulnerabilities of the investment banks, the way it dealt with the crisis was different. Following the path that Lehman had traveled back in the summer, Morgan and Goldman lobbied regulators to clamp down on short sales of their stock. It was an awkward demand for the two firms to make: Morgan and Goldman were short sellers themselves, since their own proprietary traders were happy to take both sides of any position; and both had built up a flourishing prime-brokerage business, financing and executing short sales by hedge funds. But in the frenzied days after Lehman, neither Morgan nor Goldman was going to stand on principle. As their stock prices cratered on Wednesday, the two firms worked the phones; and by the end of the day, both New York senators, Chuck Schumer and Hillary Clinton, were calling on the Securities and Exchange Commission to give Morgan and Goldman the short-selling ban that they demanded.

On Thursday SEC chairman Christopher Cox expressed doubts about helping the bankers, but he found himself alone. "You have to save them now or they'll be gone while you're still thinking about it," insisted the Treasury secretary Hank Paulson.[29] At around 1:00 P.M., the Financial Services Authority in London announced a thirty-day ban on short selling of twenty-nine financial firms, signaling that the authorities would now do whatever it might take to save flagship companies. On Goldman's trading floor, some three dozen traders greeted the news like infantrymen who have been rescued by air power: They stood up, placed their hands over their hearts, and sang along to "The Star-Spangled Banner," which someone was playing over the loudspeaker system.[30] Later that evening, the SEC went one better than London, banning the short selling of shares in about eight hundred financial companies.

The ban brought Morgan and Goldman some brief breathing room, but it amounted to a frontal government assault on hedge funds' viability. Stock-picking funds lost hundreds of millions of dollars as a result of the rule change: "We went from playing chess to rugby at halftime," one Tiger cub complained; and the claim that the ban protected the financial system was a stretch, since corporations ranging from Internet incubators to retailers were included.[31] But even as they tried to pull the hedge funds down with them, the investment banks were not out of the woods; and they immediately resumed their lobbying. During the good times,

Morgan and Goldman had reveled in the fact that they were not deposit-taking banks, subject to the Fed's regulatory oversight. But now they performed a swift U-turn: They demanded to be swept under the Fed's purview because they wanted guaranteed access to its emergency lending. On the evening of Sunday, September 21, Morgan and Goldman got what they desired. The Fed extended its protection to them, and their vulnerability ended.

Because it was classified as a hedge fund, Citadel did not get the same access to emergency Fed lending. On the contrary, the government had kicked it in the teeth, since the ban on short selling cost it dearly. Citadel had built up a giant portfolio of convertible bonds, which it hedged by shorting stocks: The idea was that the options embedded in the bonds were underpriced relative to the underlying equity. The ban on short selling made it impossible to hedge new convertible positions, so demand for convertible bonds cratered and Citadel was left with shocking losses.[32] By the end of September, its main funds were down 20 percent for the month; and the more Citadel's equity base shriveled, the more its leverage ratio went up. Since its creation in 1990, Citadel had grown from nothing to $15 billion in assets and 1,400 employees. Now its survival was in question.

Griffin assembled his lieutenants to consider the firm's options. If he cut leverage by selling convertible holdings, rivals would see he was desperate and would start squeezing his portfolio. If he did nothing, on the other hand, he would soon run out of cash and be unable to meet margin calls. Meanwhile, Griffin and his team were focused on an additional danger. If trading partners started to worry about Citadel's survival, they would mark down the estimated value of its derivatives contracts, forcing Citadel to cough up cash until its coffers were empty. That was what brokers had done to Askin Capital, Long-Term Capital, and pretty much every failing institution since then.

In the first weeks of October, Citadel fought a two-front war against these enemies. It jettisoned assets that were not part of its main strategies, thus raising capital without telegraphing its distress too obviously. It closed derivatives contracts with other firms, replacing them in some cases with contracts on an exchange—unlike brokerages and banks, the exchange was not going to squeeze them.[33] Where it was not possible to close out derivatives contracts, Citadel took comfort in what was arguably one of its greatest strengths: a state-of-the-art back office. Unlike many hedge funds, Citadel maintained the computer infrastructure, data feeds, and financial models to track the daily value of every derivative contract purchased from a bank; the better it understood what these things were worth, the harder it would be for counterparts to push the daily marks against it. This sort of plumbing was Citadel's pride and joy. Recalling Long-Term Capital's promise to do without a back office—to create "Salomon without the bullshit"—a Citadel staffer joked that Long-Term had things upside down. Salomon's back office had constituted the firm's true edge. The LTCM partners were the bullshit.

Citadel's computer infrastructure increased Griffin's chances of saving his company. But his key advantage lay in the terms of his funding. Unlike investment banks, which were willing to do the lion's share of their borrowing on extremely short terms, Citadel's treasury department had been more careful. It had analyzed the mix of assets in its portfolio, calculating how long it would take to sell each kind; then it had lined up a blend of loans with the same mix of maturities. The idea was that Citadel should only rely on overnight funding to the extent that it had assets that could be sold overnight; harder-to-sell investments were backed by harder-to-yank borrowing. Citadel's five-year bond issuance, unusual for a hedge fund, was part of this focus on borrowing longer term, and Griffin's team had also negotiated bank loans that were locked in for as long as a year. Even a crisis was not going to push Citadel into a death spiral of fire sales—or at least that was the theory.

In practice, of course, it was hard to feel so confident. Citadel had planned for a crisis, but not a crisis on this scale, and nothing could insulate it from what was going on around it. Other hedge funds, which had done less to lock in their financing securely, faced margin calls that forced them to dump convertible bonds and other positions; the weight of their selling caused Citadel to suffer yet more losses. Rumors that Citadel might be about to go under seemed to surface at dizzying speed. Citadel had been hit with margin calls! The Fed was calling Citadel's trading partners, asking the size of their exposures! The truth was that the Fed was indeed calling around Wall Street, telling banks not to pull loans; but whether this saved Citadel or served to fuel the rumor mill could be debated. On some days in October, CNBC parked a truck outside the Citadel Center. A new deathwatch was beginning.

On the morning of Friday, October 24, a young Griffin lieutenant named Dan Dufresne set off to catch a train to the office. Soon after he left home, he took a call on his cell phone from the New York office of a European bank. As head of Citadel's treasury department, Dufresne stayed in touch with all the banks that financed Citadel's positions.

"Hey, Dan," the voice said. "Just so you know, there are rumors that are picking up momentum in Europe that the Fed is in your office in Chicago, organizing a liquidation of your assets."

Dufresne decided he would get a cab. He was not going to discuss Citadel's alleged demise in a crowded commuter train.

"I'm hearing from our guys in London that this is happening," the voice pressed. "Is it? I'm sure it's not, but you need to know that it's picking up speed."

Dufresne assured his contact that it was just another rumor. He talked to him for maybe ten minutes, but as soon as he hung up he got another phone call. It was the same rumor again. By the time Dufresne had reached his desk at the Citadel Center, there had been a third call and a fourth one. Dufresne's colleague Gerald Beeson had been in the office early. He had been peppered with questions from European trading desks since five o'clock that morning.

Dufresne and Beeson suspected that financial journalists had gotten hold of this rumor and were bouncing it off everyone they knew. They must have called every bank in London. The rumor was spreading faster than Citadel could douse it.

A little while later, James Forese, Citigroup's head of capital markets, placed a call to Ken Griffin. According to the rumors Forese was hearing, Griffin was visiting the Fed in Washington, looking for a bailout. Credit default swaps on Citadel's bonds were trading at distressed levels.

They were signaling more trouble even than Lehman's had on the eve of bankruptcy.

After dialing Citadel's number, Forese was put on hold for a minute. Then Griffin picked up and started talking.

"You're calling me for one of three reasons. One, to see if I'm alive. Two, to see if we have any money . . ."

Forese cut him off. "The reason I'm calling is to offer you help. If you need to liquidate portfolios and need someone to discreetly handle that, you know we would do that for you."

"We're losing a lot of money," Griffin conceded. "But we've got a lot of liquidity." Because Citadel had locked up long-term funding with its counterparts, it was not facing margin calls. Because it had the back-office systems to track the precise value of everything it owned, the banks were less aggressive than they might have been in moving the marks against it. Besides, Citadel had sold plenty of assets to raise cash. It had been more proactive than Bear or Lehman in preventing its leverage from spiraling upward.

Forese wondered whether all this would be enough. "You guys are getting killed in the rumor mill," he ventured.

"I know. I can't get rid of the rumors," Griffin conceded. The rumors were making people think that Citadel was about to dump its portfolio of convertible bonds. The threat of a fire sale was driving down prices, compounding Citadel's difficulties. Every time a Citadel executive got a panicky phone call from a trading counterpart, he explained why the rumors were false. But no matter how many panicky callers Griffin's team assuaged, the rumors were growing more hysterical.

"You need a good window to get your story out," Forese said.

"I don't know what the forum for that is," Griffin answered. The last thing he wanted to do was stage a conference call that appeared to confirm the market's worst suspicions. Bear and Lehman had done calls. A fat lot of good it had done them.

Forese remembered that Citadel had issued some five-year bonds. Without signaling panic or anything out of the ordinary, the firm could convene a phone call for the bondholders. What's more, doing the call in that format would give the message extra weight. Griffin could get in trouble with the regulators if he gave his bondholders anything other than the truth. That would make Griffin's assurances believable.

"That's a pretty good idea," Griffin allowed. He hung up and summoned his lieutenants.[34]

Around ten-thirty in the morning, Griffin's inner circle convened around a whiteboard. Somebody jotted down the half dozen points that Citadel needed to get across. Griffin wanted Gerald Beeson, the supercharged chief operating officer, to do most of the talking. Another note was added to the whiteboard: "Speak slowly."

"How many call-in lines?" somebody asked. When a big company such as Coca-Cola held its quarterly investor call, it usually arranged about 250 lines. But Citadel had only a handful of bondholders.

"Five hundred," somebody ventured.

"A thousand," Beeson countered.

The call was scheduled for 3:30 P.M., but there was no way it could begin on time. Well over a thousand callers attempted to dial in—traders, investors, financial reporters. This was to be the culmination of the Citadel deathwatch, the biggest financial drama since Lehman's failure; on some Wall Street trading floors, the call was played over loudspeakers. There was a twenty-five-minute delay as more phone lines were arranged. Those who managed to get in on the call were treated to some grating techno music.

Eventually, Beeson began to give his pitch. Yes, it was true that Citadel's two flagship hedge funds were down 35 percent. But the firm was a long way from running out of cash. Its financing was secured. It had an untapped $8 billion credit line. There was no way it would go under. Adam Cooper, Citadel's general counsel, held up a sign in front of Beeson to remind him not to speak too fast. "To call this a dislocation doesn't go anywhere near the enormity of what we've seen," said Beeson, emphasizing that Citadel would still survive. "We will prosper in the new era of finance," Griffin added, mustering all the confidence that he could manage. After twelve minutes, the call was over.

Griffin got off the phone and went to answer questions from his staff in a town-hall meeting. Beeson spent the afternoon on a series of calls with reporters. He hammered home the same message. Citadel had moved aggressively to raise cash. Its credit lines were all secured. Even though the government had rescued Morgan Stanley and Goldman Sachs while leaving hedge funds in the cold, Citadel was not going under.

The next day the CNBC truck was gone from its usual position outside the Citadel Center. For the time being at least, the fires had been doused.[35]

FOR THE NEXT SEVERAL WEEKS, CITADEL'S LOSSES CONtinued. By the end of the year its two flagship funds were down a stunning 55 percent; the $9 billion that evaporated was the equivalent of at least two Long-Term Capitals. But although nobody said so, Citadel's humiliation was a model of how the financial sector should work. Investors who had risked their capital with Griffin, and been rewarded for years, were forced to take extraordinary losses—exactly as should happen. But the financial system was not destabilized, and taxpayers were not called upon to throw Citadel a lifeline. The episode showed that leveraged trading firms with billions under management do not necessarily need government rescues when markets go berserk; careful liquidity management can substitute for the Fed's safety net. The old-line investment banks had built castles of leverage on foundations of short-term loans; when the crisis came, the whole edifice toppled. But because he shared the paranoid culture of hedge funds, Griffin had leveraged himself a bit more cautiously and relied less on short-term loans; when the moment of truth came, Citadel survived it. And so it turned out that an upstart Goldman imitator could be better for the financial system than the real Goldman—not to mention incomparably better than Bear Stearns or Lehman Brothers.

Citadel's experience dramatized the wider experience in the hedge-fund industry. Hedge funds had danced through the minefields until Lehman's collapse in September, but they were whipsawed in the panic that followed. They based their strategies on short selling, and the government banned that. They based their portfolios on leverage, and leverage dried up as brokers hoarded capital. By the end of 2008, most funds had lost money; almost 1,500 had gone bust; many a titan found his reputation justly deflated. And yet, even in the worst period of their history, hedge funds proved their worth. The industry as a whole was down 19 percent in 2008, but the S&P 500 fell twice that much. And unlike the banks, investment banks, home lenders, and others, hedge funds imposed no costs on taxpayers or society.

This point was largely lost amid the crisis. The bursting of the hedge-fund bubble left no room to think about the policy meaning; the titans had flown so high that the spectacle of their fall was mesmerizing. Back in the first half of 2008, Phil Falcone of Harbinger Capital had returned 43 percent and stalked the *New York Times*; in September he lost more than $1 billion in a week thanks to Lehman's collapse and the SEC ban on short selling. In February 2007, an alpha factory called Fortress had gone public amid great fanfare, creating paper wealth of $10.7 billion for its helicopter-riding chiefs; by December 2008, Fortress's assets had collapsed by almost a third, and the firm was forced to fire two dozen portfolio managers. John Meriwether and Myron Scholes, veterans of the Long-Term Capital saga, had each set up new hedge funds in 1999 that did well for several years; by the end of 2008, both were near the precipice. Chris Hohn of the Children's Investment Fund finished 2008 down 42 percent and seemed to lose his intellectual moorings too. "Quite frankly activism is hard," he said, as though surprised by his discovery.[36]

Stunned by these reversals, investors scrambled to get their money out. Hedge funds might have fallen far less than the S&P 500, but customers expected them to be up in any sort of market, as though the magicians who ran them had abolished risk rather than merely managing it. Even the macro hedge funds, which gave up only a small sliver of their earlier gains in the months after Lehman, were not exempt from this storm: They had to contend with $31 billion of net redemptions because everybody was withdrawing cash from everybody. Hedge funds responded with the tool to which Tudor had resorted—they locked investors in by suspending quarterly redemptions and "gating" their money. Sometimes investors were lucky to be taken prisoner: The gates averted the need for disastrous fire sales of assets and were accompanied by a suspension of management fees. But other times the gates were an outrage. One prominent hedge fund was said to have charged a departing investor a fee for early redemption; then it blocked the redemption, refused to return the fee, and carried on charging a management fee on top of that.

The larger the hedge fund, the more peremptory and arrogant the managers tended to be—and frequently it was the bigger funds that had the worst performance. The big alpha factories were stuck in losing positions when liquidity dried up: Tom Steyer's Farallon, which had been managing $36 billion at the start of 2008, shriveled to $20 billion in 2009. Meanwhile, nimbler boutiques—closer in spirit to the Steyer of the previous decade—frequently escaped with minor scratches. Rock Creek Capital, a savvy fund-of-funds, calculated that hedge funds with assets under $1 billion were down a relatively modest 12 percent in 2008. Meanwhile the funds that Rock Creek tracked with $1 billion to $10 billion in assets were down 16 percent, and those with more than $10 billion were down 27 percent.

And yet, for all the losses, hedge funds' mystique survived the crisis. They were repellent and attractive, objects of envy and yearning; they remained the wizards of modern capitalism's favorite pastime, the unabashed pursuit of money. In November 2008, after two months of market pandemonium, five hedge-fund barons were called to testify in Congress, in what promised to be a show trial: The billionaires would be scolded for upending the economy. But some way through the proceedings, an unexpected tone emerged. Peering down from his dais, Representative Elijah Cummings, Democrat of Maryland, recounted his neighbor's reaction to the day's hearing. It was not a reproach, an accusation, nor even an expression of pity. It was a simple question, tinged with awe. "How does it feel to be going before five folks that have gotten more money than God?"[37]

CONCLUSION:
SCARIER THAN WHAT?

Early in the first hedge-fund boom, in 1966, bankers at Merrill Lynch, Pierce, Fenner & Smith agreed to underwrite a convertible debt offering for Douglas Aircraft. As they worked with their client, they learned that Douglas was cutting its earnings forecast to $3.50 per share, about a quarter lower than projected. A little while later they heard that Douglas's earnings might come in at under $3; and then they were informed that earnings would be, ahem, zero. This was a bombshell. The news would send Douglas's share price into a free fall; and Merrill's bankers, who were privy to the information by virtue of their role as insider advisers, were strictly forbidden to leak it to Merrill's brokerage customers. But not for the last time at an investment bank, internal controls failed. On June 21 the facts about Douglas Aircraft's collapsing prospects made their way to Lawrence Zicklin, a Merrill Lynch broker who handled the firm's hedge-fund clients.[1]

Zicklin had a direct wire from his desk to Banks Adams, a segment manager who ran money for A. W. Jones. The wire had been installed a year earlier, and its presence signified that Zicklin was expected to tell Adams everything he knew the moment he knew it. The Jones men were paying Merrill generous commissions, and they expected service in return; Zicklin was not about to make the stunning Douglas Aircraft news some kind of holy exception. According to an administrative proceeding filed by the Securities and Exchange Commission, Zicklin called Adams, who immediately placed orders to sell 4,000 shares of Douglas short. Then Zicklin also phoned Richard Radcliffe, the ex-Jones man who had set up a new hedge fund with Barton Biggs, and Radcliffe shorted 900 Douglas. John Hartwell, a mutual-fund star who was running a model portfolio for Jones, got the call too. He dumped 1,600 Douglas shares instantly.

The next morning the *Wall Street Journal* ran a bullish story on the aircraft industry. As far as the average investor was concerned, nothing was amiss with Douglas, and its stock actually advanced a dollar. But that day some of the best-connected money managers attended one of the regular lunches hosted by Bob Brimberg, a legendary broker. Brimberg combined a formidable intellect with a formidable physique: He was as wide as a truck, and the scale that his partners had installed by his desk failed to stop him from becoming wider. At a typical lunch at Brimberg's, the host would ply his guests with meatballs and corned-beef sandwiches and cocktails. Then he would demand to know what they were buying and selling; and no money manager would risk an outright lie, because he would not be invited back again.[2] On June 22, Brimberg pumped his guests as usual. Somebody said something about Merrill Lynch and Douglas, and that afternoon the guests were jumping on the phones, calling the Merrill desk to demand confirmation. By the end of the next day, thirteen Merrill clients had dumped 175,800 shares in Douglas. Six of the thirteen were hedge funds, an impressive tally for an industry that was still little known outside Wall Street. The sales became the subject of a drawn-out inquiry by the Securities and Exchange Commission, which forced several of the funds into expensive settlements.

Almost half a century later, hedge funds were still getting privileged information and still getting into trouble. This time the center of the scandal was Raj Rajaratnam, a voluble Sri Lankan-born investor with a Bob Brimberg physique, who ran a hedge-fund company called the Galleon Group. He was less a master of the universe than a master of the Rolodex, as the SEC's enforcement chief remarked; he had no amazing special sauce, but he had a lot of special sources. According to a criminal complaint brought by the Manhattan district attorney's office in 2009, Rajaratnam's contacts gave him advance warning that a technology manufacturer called Polycom would announce unexpectedly good earnings; Galleon allegedly turned that tip into a quick half-million-dollar profit. The contacts whispered that the private-equity group Blackstone was about to bid for Hilton Hotels; Galleon allegedly pocketed $4 million. The contacts knew for certain that Google's earnings would disappoint; this time the supposed windfall weighed in at $9 million. Rajaratnam's Rolodex extended to a senior executive at Intel and a director at McKinsey, both of whom were apparently prepared to leak secrets in return for a share of the takings. According to the prosecutors, the conspirators sought to cover up their trail by frequently discarding mobile phones, a technique reminiscent of drug gangs. After an illegal trade, one of the accused allegedly destroyed his phone by tearing the SIM card in half with his teeth. In the face of all these allegations, Rajaratnam pleaded innocent.

Clearly, hedge-fund managers are not angels. Their history is full of blemishes, from Michael Steinhardt's collusive block trading to David Askin's nonexistent mortgage-prepayment model. The very structure of a hedge fund has worried regulators since the early days. At the time of the Douglas Aircraft case, regulators fretted that hedge-fund patrons included rainmakers and senior executives at public firms—what if these well-placed folk leaked privileged facts to the men who looked after their money? Two generations later, these suspicions seem to have been vindicated in the Galleon affair, and it would be naive to suppose that other 1960s misgivings have lost their relevance. The Douglas case showed that the enormous commissions that hedge funds generate for brokers create a potential for abuse, and it's a pretty fair bet that such abuses continue. There are criminals and charlatans in every industry. Hedge funds are no different.

And yet, equally clearly, hedge funds should not be judged against some benchmark of perfection. The case for believing in the industry is not that it is populated with saints but that its incentives and culture are ultimately less flawed than those of other financial companies. There is no evidence, for example, that hedge funds engage in fraud or other abuses more often than rivals. In 2003 an SEC inquiry looked for such evidence and found none; and indeed a freestanding hedge fund is arguably less likely to receive illegal tips than an asset manager housed within a major bank, which is privy to all manner of profitable information flows from corporate clients and trading partners. For sensitive news to reach the wrong ears inside a modern financial conglomerate, it merely has to pierce the Chinese walls dividing equity underwriters or merger advisers from proprietary traders. For the news to reach a hedge fund, it has to take the additional step of exiting the building.

What is true for fraud and insider trading is also true for most other accusations leveled at hedge funds: The charges might be better directed against other financial players, as we shall see presently. But the heart of the case for hedge funds can be summed up in a single phrase. Whereas large parts of the financial system have proved too big to fail, hedge funds are generally *small enough to fail*. When they blow up, they cost taxpayers nothing.

AFTER THE BUST OF 2007–2009—AND AFTER THE CIRCU-itous regulatory debate that has followed—it is hard to overstate this small-enough-to-fail advantage. The implosion of behemoths such as Lehman Brothers and AIG caused a freeze-up in the global credit system, creating the steepest recession since the 1930s. The cost of the bailouts compounded the crisis of public finances in the rich world, accelerating the shift of economic power to the emerging economies. The U.S. national debt jumped from 43 percent of GDP before the crisis to a projected 70 percent in 2010, while public debt in China, India, Russia, and Brazil remained roughly constant; meanwhile in Europe, countries such as Greece and Ireland teetered on the brink of bankruptcy. According to the International Monetary Fund, the cash infusions, debt guarantees, and other assistance provided to too-big-to-fail institutions in the big advanced economies came to a staggering $10 trillion, or $13,000 per citizen of those countries.[3] The sums spent on rescuing well-heeled financiers damaged the legitimacy of the capitalist system. In December 2009, President Barack Obama said plaintively that he "did not run for office to be helping out a bunch of fat cat bankers."[4] But help them out is what he did, and populist anger at his openhanded policies is hardly surprising. Even more worryingly, neither Obama nor any other leader knows how to prevent too-big-to-fail institutions from fleecing the public all over again. The worst thing about the crisis is that it is likely to be repeated.

To see why this is so, start with the catch-22 that bedevils government support for the financial sector. On the one hand, many financial institutions are indeed too big to fail; if governments refuse to rescue them, seeking to protect taxpayers' money, they open the door to a meltdown that will cost taxpayers even more—as the post-Lehman crisis demonstrated. On the other hand, each time the government pays the bills for the risk taken by financiers, it reduces the cost of that risk to market players, dampening their incentive to reduce it. If there were no deposit insurance, for example, depositors would face losses when banks went under; they might refuse to entrust their savings to risk-hungry banks, or might demand higher interest rates as compensation. Equally, if governments did not backstop banks (and now investment banks) by acting as lenders-of-last-resort, investors who buy bonds issued by banks might do more to monitor their soundness. The point is not that there should be no deposit insurance or lender-of-last-resort liquidity insurance, since letting big institutions fail is simply too costly. But the unpleasant truth is that government insurance encourages financiers to take larger risks; and larger risks force governments to increase the insurance. It is a vicious cycle.

You can observe this cycle at work in the history of banking. Over the past century, governments have repeatedly broadened the scope of last-resort lending, loosened its terms, and extended deposit insurance to a larger share of banks' customers. As governments have underwritten more risks, risk taking has grown. Since 1900, U.S. banks have tripled their leverage from around four to twelve; they have taken more liquidity risk by using short-term borrowing to purchase long-term assets; and they have focused more of their resources on high-risk proprietary trading.[5] The 2007–2009 crisis, in which governments extended the reach of deposit insurance, guaranteed savings held in supposedly uninsured money-market funds, and bent over backward to pump emergency liquidity into all corners of the markets, is likely to induce even more recklessness in the future. Put simply, government actions have decreased the cost of risk for too-big-to-fail players; the result will be more risk taking. The vicious cycle will go on until governments are bankrupt.

There are two standard responses to this scary prospect. The first is to argue that governments should not bail out insurers, investment banks, money-market funds, and all the rest: If financiers were made to pay for their own risks, they would behave more prudently. For example, if investors had been forced to absorb the cost of the Bear Stearns bankruptcy in early 2008, rather than having the blow softened by a Fed-subsidized rescue, they might have prepared themselves better to absorb the costs of Lehman's failure some months later. But this purported solution to the too-big-to-fail problem denies its existence: Precisely because some institutions are indeed too big to fail, they cannot be left to go under. What's more, the behemoths and those who lend to them understand their inviolability all too well; the government may claim that it won't rescue them, but everybody understands that it will have no choice when the time comes. Even the soft version of this laissez-faire prescription is unconvincing. One can speculate about a world in which regulators save really large institutions but allow medium-sized ones such as Bear to go under. But this is not the world we inhabit. Regulators will usually lean toward intervention because they don't want a disaster on their watch. That is human nature, and there is no way to change it.

The second standard response to the vicious cycle is to devise regulations that break it. Safety nets for banks may encourage risk taking, and risk taking may force the growth of safety nets; but this arms race can be stopped by imposing capital requirements on banks, monitoring their liquidity, restricting their proprietary trading—and generally by curbing their risk appetites. Up to a point, tougher regulation holds out hope; as I finished writing this book, governments across the rich economies were getting ready to try it. But the world has experimented with multiple regulatory efforts by multiple agencies in multiple countries, and it has learned to its cost that no regulatory system is foolproof. The firms that went wrong in 2008, for example, were overseen by a broad array of agencies applying a broad array of rules. American deposit-taking banks were overseen by the Federal Reserve, the Federal Deposit Insurance Corporation, and two smaller bodies, and they were required to abide by the Basel I capital-adequacy standards: They did miserably. American investment banks were overseen by the Securities and Exchange Commission and required to abide by a different set of risk limits: Two failed, one sold itself to avoid failure, and two were rescued by the government. The government-chartered housing finance companies, Fannie Mae and Freddie Mac, had a special government department devoted to their oversight: They had to be nationalized. The giant insurer AIG crashed through the regulatory net; money-market funds, supposedly overseen by the Securities and Exchange Commission, required an emergency guarantee from the government. Meanwhile in Europe, the chaos was equally awful. London's Financial Services Authority was thought to be a model regulator; Britain was nonetheless beset by a string of costly disasters. In continental Europe, banks were subject to an updated version of the Basel capital requirements. It did not make any difference.

When so many regulators fail at once, it is hard to be confident that regulation will work if only some key agency is differently managed, better staffed, or cleansed of alleged laissez-faire ideology. Rather, the record suggests that financial regulation is genuinely difficult, and success cannot always be expected. Again, there are reasons why this should not come as a surprise. Determining what it takes to make a financial institution robust involves a series of slippery judgments. The amount of capital needed should not be measured relative to assets, since assets could mean anything from a scary portfolio of mortgage bonds to a safely hedged book of government bonds. Instead, capital should be measured against risk-weighted assets, but then you have to define risk—and be prepared to argue about the definition. Further, it is not just the amount of capital that determines how resilient an institution is. Borrowing short-term makes you more vulnerable to a sudden loss of confidence than borrowing long-term, so the structure of an institution's funding must be reckoned with. Trading illiquid instruments that cannot be sold quickly, whether they are complex mortgage securities or loans to Kazakh banks, is riskier than trading on a well-organized exchange, creating another dimension on which regulators are obliged to make a judgment. Competent officials can navigate such tricky challenges and sometimes do—regulators are like air-traffic controllers, who are ignored when things go well and excoriated after a disaster. But at each step of the way, the regulators' desire for safety will bump up against financial institutions' appetite for risk. Given the brainpower and political influence of large financial firms, they are bound to win some of the arguments over judgment calls. Regulation will be softer than it should be.

If financial behemoths cannot be left to go under, and if regulation is both essential and fallible, policy makers should pay more attention to a third option. They should make a concerted effort to drive financial risk into institutions that impose fewer costs on taxpayers. That means encouraging the proliferation of firms that are not too big to fail, so reducing the share of risk taking in the financial system that must be backstopped by the government. It also means favoring institutions where the incentives to control risk are relatively strong and therefore where regulatory scrutiny assumes less of the burden. How can governments promote small-enough-to-fail institutions that manage risk well? This is the key question about the future of finance; and one part of the answer is hiding in plain sight. Governments must encourage hedge funds.

Hedge funds are clearly not the answer to all of the financial system's problems. They will not collect deposits, underwrite securities, or make loans to small companies. But when it comes to managing money without jeopardizing the financial system, hedge funds have proved their mettle. They are nearly always small enough to fail: Between 2000 and 2009, a total of about five thousand hedge funds went out of business, and not a single one required a taxpayer bailout. Because they mark all their assets to market and live in constant fear of margin calls from their brokers, hedge funds generally monitor risk better and recognize setbacks faster than rivals: If they take a severe hit, they tend to liquidate and close shop before there are secondary effects for the financial system. So rather than reining in risk taking by hedge funds, governments should encourage them to thrive and multiply and absorb more risk, shifting the job of high-stakes asset management from too-big-to-fail rivals. And since the goal is to have more hedge funds, burdening them with oversight is counterproductive. The chief policy prescription suggested by the history of the industry can be boiled down to two words: Don't regulate.

THIS VERDICT IS OPEN TO SEVERAL OBJECTIONS, AND THE first concerns the way that hedge funds treat their customers. Ever since the 1960s, the 20 percent performance fee has excited envy and alarm—surely this heads-I-win-tails-you-lose format promotes wild punts with clients' capital? More recently, academics have advanced a subtle version of this criticism: The incentive fee may induce hedge funds to generate pleasingly smooth returns that conceal a risk of blowup. A fund can take in $100, stick it in the S&P 500 index, then earn, say, $5 by selling options to people who want to insure themselves against a market collapse. If the collapse occurs, the hedge fund gets wiped out. But, over a five- or even ten-year time frame, the odds are good that a collapse won't happen, so each year the fund manager will beat the S&P 500 index by 5 percentage points—and be hailed as a genius. When this sort of trickery is rewarded with hedge-fund performance fees, the argument continues, rogues are bound to try it out.[6] The upshot is that investors who ought to have the benefit of consumer-protection regulation will be left to get hurt. And when options-selling hedge funds blow up, markets will be destabilized.

These complaints about hedge-fund incentives seem plausible—until you take a look at the alternatives. Investing in a hedge fund is safer than other behaviors that do not excite controversy—buying stock in an investment bank, for example. Hedge funds have a powerful reason to control risk better than banks, as we have seen: The majority of them have the managers' own wealth in the fund, alongside that of their clients. Moreover, if hedge funds' 20 percent performance fees seem to invite excessive risk taking, bank performance fees are far larger. In recent years, investment banks have distributed fully *50 percent* of their net revenues as salary and bonuses; even though this comparison is not perfect, it puts the criticism of hedge-fund fees in perspective. Investment-bank compensation creates a larger incentive for managers to shoot for the moon, damaging financial stability when they miss it. And whereas the formula for fees at hedge funds is fixed ahead of time, banks reserve the right to decree the appropriate level each year. The payout can change on the managers' say-so, and rank-and-file shareholders have no right to be consulted.

How do hedge funds compare with mutual funds? On the face of it, hedge funds are scandalously expensive: Whereas mutual funds tend to charge a management fee of about 1 percent, hedge funds tend to demand a management fee of 1 percent to 2 percent plus the performance fee of around 20 percent. But to understand which vehicle is the rip-off, you have to distinguish between alpha (returns due to the fund manager's skill) and beta (returns due to exposure to a market index). An investor can buy exposure to a simple index such as the S&P 500 for a mere ten basis points (tenths of a percent), so the actively managed mutual fund with a 1 percent fee is effectively charging ninety basis points for delivering alpha. Unfortunately, study after study has found that active mutual-fund managers, as a group, do not beat the market.[7] They are charging ninety basis points and delivering nothing. Their fee per unit of alpha turns out to be *infinite*.

Even if the average actively managed mutual fund is a rip-off, there is still a fair question as to whether hedge funds are better. This book has described the many ways hedge funds make money: by trading against central banks that aren't in the markets for a profit; by buying from price-insensitive forced sellers; by taking the other side when big institutions need liquidity; by sensing all kinds of asymmetrical opportunities. It stands to reason that talented investors, free of the institutional impediments that constrain rivals, and powerfully motivated by performance fees, can rack up impressive profits—even when they pursue conceptually simple stock-picking strategies like those of the Tiger cubs, discussed in the appendix. But in its focus on the pioneers who shaped the industry, a history of hedge funds is necessarily biased toward winners. Perhaps the average hedge fund that attempts these strategies loses money? Or perhaps whatever alpha it makes is gobbled up by those performance fees?

The answer to these reasonable questions will continue to be debated.

Hedge funds generate returns partly by taking exotic types of risk; because these are difficult to measure, a precise verdict on the size of hedge funds' risk-adjusted returns is bound to be elusive. As a group, funds-of-funds report returns that are lower than the returns reported by the hedge funds in which they invest; the gap is larger than can be explained by fees, suggesting that reported hedge-fund returns are frequently exaggerated. Nevertheless, the tentative bottom line on hedge-fund performance is surprisingly positive.

The best evidence comes in the form of a paper by Roger Ibbotson of the Yale School of Management, Peng Chen of Ibbotson Associates, and Kevin Zhu of the Hong Kong Polytechnic University.[8] The authors start with performance statistics for 8,400 hedge funds between January 1995 and December 2009. Then they correct for "survivorship bias": If you just measure the funds that exist at the end of the period, you exclude ones that blew up in the meantime—and so overestimate average performance. Next, the authors tackle "backfill bias": Hedge funds tend to begin reporting results after a year of excellent profits, so including those atypical bonanzas makes hedge funds appear unduly brilliant. Having made these adjustments, the authors report that the average hedge fund returned 11.4 percent per year on average, or 7.7 percent after fees—and, crucially, that the 7.7 percent net return included 3 percentage points of alpha. So hedge funds do seem to generate profits beyond what they get from exposure to the market benchmarks. And despite much griping about excessive hedge-fund fees, there is alpha left over for clients.

One final comparison seems worthwhile: How do hedge funds stack up against their rivals in private equity? The two vehicles are both loosely described as "alternatives" by the investment industry, and they have some things in common: They are structured as private partnerships; they use leverage; they charge performance fees. Increasingly, private-equity companies have started hedge funds, and vice versa, further blurring the distinction. And yet the promise to investors is fundamentally different. Hedge funds aim to buy securities or currencies that the market has mispriced: They play a game of numbers and psychology. Private-equity funds promise to improve the performance of individual firms. They install new chief executives and get their hands on the controls, revamping everything from advertising budgets to middle-management incentives. Their claim is not that securities are mispriced but that management can be improved by an intelligent owner.

So can it? Much as with hedge funds, you have to separate beta and alpha. By owning a portfolio of unlisted companies, private-equity funds deliver exposure to corporate profits that resembles the exposure from a stock-market index: This is the beta in their performance. The hope is that the funds can justify their fees by doing better than that—by beating the index and generating alpha. As it turns out, the academic verdict is positive for private-equity funds that specialize in venture capital, but ambiguous for buyout funds that take public companies private. Using various methodologies, three influential studies have found that venture capitalists generate alpha of around 4 to 5 percent per year, whereas buyout funds appear to generate returns that are little different from the S&P 500 benchmark.[9] Moreover, private-equity funds have a clear disadvantage relative to hedge funds. They demand that investors commit capital for as much as a decade.

Of course, hedge funds are not a substitute for other investment vehicles. For ordinary savers, mutual funds that cheaply mimic an index remain the best option. But from the point of view of large investors, hedge funds compare well with most of their rivals. They are not more prone to insider trading or fraud, and they deliver real value for their clients. "Where are the customers' yachts?" the author Fred Schwed demanded in his classic account of Wall Street. To which the response is: Ask Harvard! Ask Yale! Their endowments returned, respectively, 8.9 percent and 11.8 percent annually between 1999 and 2009—and this despite the losses in the credit crisis. Hedge funds are a major reason why universities can afford more science facilities and merit scholarships, and why philanthropies from the Open Society Institute to Robin Hood have more money to give out. And if hedge funds also serve rich clients well, thereby contributing to the troubling gap in modern society between the superwealthy and the rest, the answer is not to smother their trading. It is progressive taxation.

————

IF HEDGE FUNDS ARE GOOD FOR THEIR CLIENTS, WHAT
other arguments point in favor of regulating them? A long-standing line
of criticism focuses on trend-following hedge funds, which allegedly drive
prices to illogical extremes, destabilizing economies. What merit might
there be in this objection?

The first thing to be said is that most hedge funds make money by
driving prices *away* from extremes and toward their rational level. This
is what arbitrage funds do, including the fast-trading statistical arbitrage
funds that are frequently excoriated. Equally, when a Julian Robertson–
style stock picker buys underpriced companies and shorts overpriced ones,
he is moving stocks closer to the level that reflects the best estimate of
their value, helping to allocate capital to the firms that will use it most
productively. Likewise, commodity traders who respond quickly to news
of gluts and shortages tend to stabilize markets, not deepen the panic,
because their responses generate price signals that force healthy adjustment. When a commodity trader bids up the oil price on the news of a
coup in Africa, he is telling the world's motorists to economize before
unsustainable consumption pushes prices up even more sharply.

Still, it clearly is true that markets sometimes overshoot, and that
trend-following hedge funds can contribute to this problem. Warning
motorists to ease up on the gas pedal is a good thing when there is a
real oil shortage, but if hundreds of traders jump on the bandwagon and
push oil prices needlessly far, they are merely hurting consumers and
companies and setting up the market for a destabilizing correction. In
2007, for example, investors pushed the price of a barrel of crude up from
$61 to $96, which was probably a fair response to booming demand in
emerging markets. But in the first half of 2008, oil rose to $145—a level
that probably exceeded anything that was justified by the fundamentals.
In the same way, currency traders are sometimes sending rational signals and sometimes driving currencies to irrational extremes. The Soros-
Druckenmiller sterling trade fits into the rational category: Germany's
postunification commitment to high interest rates made the sterling peg

untenable. So does Thailand's 1997 devaluation: The country's growing trade deficit was incompatible with its pegged exchange rate. But clearly there are also times when the currency market overshoots. In 1997, Indonesia was running a small trade deficit and a flexible exchange rate, yet it suffered a far bigger devaluation than Thailand because political instability sent the markets into a panic.

If trend-following can be destructive, could hedge-fund regulation dampen it? Of course, restrictions on hedge funds would limit contrarian trend-bucking as well as trend-following trading, and there are no data to prove what the effect would be on balance. But despite the proud tradition of trend-following hedge funds from Commodities Corporation to Paul Tudor Jones, hedge-fund regulation would probably exacerbate the markets' tendency to overshoot. Because of the way they are structured, hedge funds are more likely to be trend bucking than other types of investors.

Hedge funds combine three features that equip them to be contrarian. First, they are free to go short as well as long, unlike some other institutional investors. Second, they are judged in terms of absolute returns; by contrast, mutual-fund managers must be cautious about bucking the conventional wisdom, because their performance is measured against market indices that reflect the consensus. Third, hedge funds have performance fees. To muster the self-confidence to be a trend bucker, you have to invest heavily in research, and performance fees generate the resources and incentives to do that. John Paulson did not develop the conviction to face off against the mortgage-industrial complex without spending serious money on homework. He purchased the best database on house-price statistics, commissioned a technology company to help him warehouse it, and hired extra analysts to interpret the numbers.

Even a self-described trend follower such as Paul Jones underlines the contrarian potential of hedge funds. Jones is a trend follower because he knows that contrary to the efficient-market view, investors frequently react to information gradually. Pension funds, insurance funds, mutual funds, and individuals all absorb developments on their own timescales, so prices respond incrementally rather than in one jump. But precisely because he understands the markets' momentum, Jones has a knack for sensing when it has gone too far. He is the last person to exacerbate a trend, because once a move becomes overextended, he is looking to profit from its reversal. That is why he bet against the trend on Wall Street by shorting the market on the eve of the 1987 crash. That is why he did the same in Tokyo in 1990. And in the summer of 2008, as it happens, Jones saw that the oil market was overheated too. "Oil is a huge mania," he declared in a magazine interview a few weeks before the bubble burst. "It is going to end badly."[10] When a trend begins to distort the economy because it has lost touch with fundamentals, the most famous hedge-fund trend follower of them all is likely to become a trend breaker.

The same can be said for hedge funds in general. In Europe's exchange-rate crisis, Soros and Druckenmiller did not simply lead an attack pack of trend followers against every currency indiscriminately. On the contrary, they actually made money betting that the French franc would resist pressure for devaluation. Equally, during the crisis in East Asia, hedge funds helped to precipitate devaluation in Thailand, because the trade deficit made the peg illogical. The crazy crash of the rupiah was driven not by hedge funds but by Indonesians who were rushing to expatriate their money. Far from jumping on that bandwagon, the Soros team pushed back against it unsuccessfully. Ultimately, another hedge fund, Tom Steyer's Farallon, helped to begin Indonesia's turnaround with its contrarian purchase of Bank Central Asia.

The point is not that hedge funds are never guilty of herding—clearly there are times when they are. In 1993 Michael Steinhardt rode a red-hot bond market into bubble territory; the next year he paid heavily. But the point is that, because of their structure and incentives, hedge funds are more likely to be contrarian than other types of investors. The regulatory lesson is contrarian too. The best way to dampen trend following is not to constrain hedge funds. It is to let them go about their business.

IN SUM, HEDGE FUNDS DO NOT APPEAR TO BE ESPECIALLY prone to insider trading or fraud. They offer a partial answer to the too-big-to-fail problem. They deliver value to investors. And they are more likely to blunt trends than other types of investment vehicle. For all these reasons, regulators should want to encourage hedge funds, not rein them in. And yet there is one persuasive argument for regulating hedge funds—or rather, regulating some of them.

The persuasive argument is that hedge funds are growing. The case in favor of hedge funds is a case for entrepreneurial boutiques; when hedge funds cease to be small enough to fail, regulation is warranted. Equally, when hedge funds become public companies, they give up the private-partnership structure that has proved so effective in controlling risk: Again, the case for regulation becomes stronger. Even though some five thousand hedge funds failed between 2000 and 2009, and even though none of them triggered a taxpayer bailout, the Long-Term Capital experience serves as a warning. No public money subsidized Long-Term's burial. But the Fed was sufficiently concerned to convene the undertakers.

How large does a hedge fund have to be to warrant regulation? Unfortunately, there is no simple answer. The systemic consequences of a hedge fund's failure depend on when it occurs. Part of the reason why LTCM triggered the intervention of the Fed was that it happened at a time when markets were already running scared in the wake of Russia's default. By contrast, part of the reason why Amaranth's failure had no systemic consequences was that it came at a time when Wall Street was comfortably awash in easy money. Still, even though it's impossible to know in advance whether the failure of a given hedge fund would trigger government intervention, there are three major clues to the answer: the size of its capital, the extent of its leverage, and the types of markets that it trades in.

Consider the case of LTCM. On the first test—size of capital—it looked unthreatening: At a bit under $5 billion, its capital was half the size of Amaranth's. The second test, however, raised a forest of red flags: LTCM was leveraged twenty-five times, meaning that its sudden collapse would cause $120 billion worth of positions to be unloaded on the markets; and the fund's derivative positions created another $1.2 trillion of exposure. Finally, some of the markets in which LTCM traded were esoteric and illiquid, so that a fire sale by LTCM could cause them to freeze up completely. The combination of these considerations caused the Fed's Peter

Fisher to get involved in LTCM's burial. The lesson is that, as of 1998, a $120 billion portfolio attached to an enormous derivatives book was large enough to trigger regulatory concern, given the additional conditions of post-Russia panic and the fund's participation in illiquid markets.

Now consider the precedents from 2006–2008. In the case of Amaranth, the three tests would have correctly predicted that the fund's collapse would not cause a problem. With capital of $9 billion, Amaranth was a large but not enormous hedge fund. Its leverage was normal, so its total portfolio was smaller than LTCM's. And its disastrous natural-gas trades were nearly all conducted on exchanges, meaning that they could be liquidated easily. In sum, there were no red flags in any of the three categories, so it is not surprising that Amaranth's failure generated more newspaper headlines than shocks to the financial system. Similarly, the three tests would have predicted the systemic insignificance of Sowood's collapse the following year: A $3 billion fund with leverage in the normal range is plenty small enough to fail, particularly when its troubles are concentrated in the relatively liquid corporate bond market.

The two most revealing lessons of this period come from the quant quake of 2007 and Citadel's near failure a year later. In both cases, the first two tests would have raised a red flag. As a group, the quant funds deployed at least $100 billion of capital in the strategies that went wrong, and were leveraged about eight times, producing a combined superportfolio of at least $800 billion. Likewise, Citadel had $13 billion in capital and was leveraged eleven times, producing a portfolio of $145 billion, not counting derivatives positions. Yet although their total exposure was worrisomely large, neither the quant funds nor Citadel proved systemically important, because they passed the third test with flying colors. The quant funds traded exclusively in superliquid equity markets, so when the crisis came they could cut leverage rapidly. Citadel, for its part, had a big book of over-the-counter transactions with other firms that could potentially be difficult to exit. But to the extent that Citadel held these illiquid positions, it took pains to lock up medium- and long-term borrowing to back that portion of its portfolio—it managed its liquidity as LTCM had tried to do, but more successfully. By backing investments that could not be sold instantly with loans that could not be yanked instantly either, Citadel avoided tumbling into a death spiral of forced selling in illiquid markets. The lesson is that portfolios above a certain threshold may prompt regulatory concern; but if regulators are satisfied that the firm's liquidity is well managed, they should leave it to go about its business.

These experiences suggest a tiered series of regulatory responses. When a hedge-fund company builds up total leveraged assets of more than, say, $120 billion, it should undergo regulatory cross-examination about the size of its derivatives positions and its liquidity management. Obviously the choice of threshold will be somewhat arbitrary, but given that markets have grown considerably since LTCM caused trouble with its $120 billion portfolio, setting the bar at that level seems appropriately cautious. Next, when a hedge fund acquires total assets of more than, say, $200 billion, it should face the second level of oversight, which would include scrutiny of its leverage—and, if those tricky calculations of risk-weighted assets suggest that its capital buffer is too thin, the fund would be required to add some extra padding. Again, this seems a cautious bar: At $200 billion, a hedge fund would still be considerably smaller than a small investment bank such as Bear Stearns, which held assets of $350 billion as of 2006. Finally, if a hedge fund goes public, the presumption of competent risk management should be softened, and the firm should attract more frequent and insistent attention from regulatory examiners.

This three-tiered oversight regime would deliberately leave nearly all hedge funds outside the net. As of January 2009, *Institutional Investor* magazine listed only thirty-nine hedge funds worldwide with capital over $10 billion. The other nine thousand or so funds, accounting for a bit over half the capital in the sector, would be left alone unless unusually high leverage got them over the $120 billion threshold. There would be no need to make the nine thousand register with government agencies and no need to saddle them with time-consuming oversight—unless they were suspected of insider trading or other violations. Unburdened by compliance costs, the vast majority of hedge funds would be free to grow and thrive, hopefully taking over some of the risk that is currently managed by too-big-to-fail behemoths. Meanwhile, the small number of hedge funds that pose genuine risks to the financial system would be handled in a different way. They would be treated as though they were investment banks, since that is roughly what they would be.

In 1949, when Alfred Winslow Jones set up his hedged fund, the old-line merchant banks that ultimately emerged as modern investment banks were neither global nor public. Firms such as Goldman Sachs, Morgan Stanley, and Lehman Brothers began as private operations that deployed the partners' capital in a flexible way, much like today's hedge funds. They managed risk ferociously—they were speculating not with other people's money but rather with their own—and they were largely unregulated. Over the next half century, however, the investment banks sold shares in themselves to the public and opened offices around the world, not so much because sprawling public enterprises are superior platforms from which to manage risk but because the rewards to the leaders of these firms were irresistible. Every investment bank that went public unlocked millions of dollars of instant wealth for the partners, who swapped illiquid ownership stakes for liquid stock. Every expansion into a new market created a fresh opportunity to risk shareholders' capital and to collect the 50 percent quasi performance fee if the risks turned out to be lucrative. The incentives that are baked into a public company pushed the investment banks to take ever greater risk, until eventually they paid the price. When Goldman Sachs and Morgan Stanley became bank holding companies at the end of 2008, they were admitting that they could survive the consequences of their public-company status only if the Fed backstopped them.

Today, hedge funds are the new merchant banks—the Goldmans and Morgans of half a century ago. Their focus on risk is equally ferocious, and they are equally lightly regulated. But the same logic that tempted the old merchant banks to go public will seduce some hedge funds too; already a handful have sold shares in themselves, and doubtless more will follow. When that happens, hedge funds will pose the threat to the financial system that they have wrongly been accused of posing in the past. The wheel of Wall Street turns. Greed and risk are always with us.

ACKNOWLEDGMENTS

My first debt is to my sources. Over the course of three years, I conducted hundreds of interviews, including perhaps 150 face-to-face recorded encounters lasting anywhere up to four hours. Many of my subjects responded to multiple requests for additional detail, patiently helping me to reconstruct events as accurately as possible. I am especially grateful to those who shared old letters, e-mails, and memoranda that captured the protagonists' reasoning at key moments. Robert Burch IV provided me with the founding manifesto of hedge funds, the "Basic Report" written in 1961 by his grandfather, A. W. Jones. Julian Robertson allowed me to read all his monthly letters to investors, spanning the twenty-year life of his Tiger fund; spiced with observations about fur-wearing men in Aspen and the difficulty of lowering one's body temperature after a tennis match in Hong Kong, the two fat binders of Roberston's letters were a book in themselves. Rodney Jones kept almost daily notes of the Asian financial crisis, allowing me to reconstruct the Soros funds' role in Thailand, Indonesia, and South Korea in more detail than would have been possible based on interviews alone. Paul Tudor Jones wrote nocturnal e-mails that illustrated his thought process brilliantly. John Paulson's memo to his investors laid out the logic of betting against the credit bubble so clearly that it makes you wonder how anyone could have been on the other side. For all these gems, and for the hours of conversation, I am deeply grateful. Where possible, I name sources in my endnotes, sometimes also quoting their memories and views at greater length than could be worked into my narrative. Inevitably, some of those to whom I am indebted cannot be thanked publicly. They know who they are.

Throughout this project, I have had the good fortune to work at the Council on Foreign Relations, where I direct the Maurice R. Greenberg Center for Geoeconomic Studies. Richard Haass, the council's president, has succeeded in building the study of international finance and economics into the council's traditional focus on international relations. This book is one consequence of his view that "the last time I checked, the world is not stovepiped." Gary Samore and James Lindsay, the two directors of studies for whom I have worked, were generous in allowing me the time needed to complete a project of this scale. Richard and Jim provided useful comments on the manuscript; I am pleased that Gary did not do so, since by the time I finished, he was responsible for the U.S. government's efforts to control weapons proliferation, a task from which he must not be distracted. My CFR colleagues Benn Steil and Brad Setser (until he followed Gary to the White House) have been terrific debating partners on questions of international finance. Leigh Gusts, Marcia Sprules, and Nicholaos Fokas of the CFR library tracked down microfilm of key articles that predated the online era. My loudest and most emphatic thank you goes to the CFR researchers who helped me assimilate vast quantities of material from primary and secondary sources. They mined financial history books, assembled news accounts, and transcribed those endless hours of interviews. Peter Rudegeair in particular immersed himself in this project for almost two years, and his talent for ferreting out colorful detail made him an invaluable collaborator. Chad Waryas, Peter Tillman, Jaclyn Berfond, and James Bergman all made extensive contributions. Paul Swartz, the data guru at the council, downloaded and analyzed the numbers I needed to anchor my story. I once asked Paul to check the performance of Italian bonds in the spring of 1994. He reported that no convenient Italian-bond index exists—and therefore he had constructed one.

The Council on Foreign Relations draws strength from its members, and this book is no exception. In New York, Robert Rubin, the council's cochairman, convened a series of dinners with investment experts to discuss portions of my manuscript; his comments on several chapters helped me to sharpen my message. In Washington, D.C., Peter Ackerman led a similar series of meetings with financial policy makers, and was himself a terrifically enthusiastic reader. The council arranged for John Y. Campbell of Harvard and Richard Sylla of New York University to review the manuscript; since both waived their anonymity, I can thank them for their flattering and helpful comments. Several friends read all or portions of the book and provided their feedback. I should like to thank in particular Morris Goldstein and Ted Truman, both of the Peterson Institute for International Economics, as well as Craig Drill of Craig Drill Capital, Steve Freidheim of Cyrus Capital Partners, Tom Hill of the Blackstone Group, Douglas Elliott of the Brookings Institution, and my father, Christopher Mallaby. Throughout the three years of this project, my wife, Zanny Minton Beddoes of *The Economist,* has been my intellectual soul mate and much more besides.

This book would never have gotten off the ground without the enthusiasm of Scott Moyers, who was my editor at the Penguin Press and is now my agent at the Wylie Agency. Scott's encouragement was seconded by Andrew Wylie, who rightly insisted that I rethink my original proposal and grapple harder with the rich variety of thought that explains the success of hedge funds. When Scott left Penguin, I was extremely fortunate to be adopted by Ann Godoff, the publisher at the Penguin Press. Ann's flair for narrative, and her gut sense for the right balance between analysis and storytelling, make her the perfect editor. The team she has built around her at Penguin has been helpful throughout. I should particularly like to thank Karen Mayer for her careful and good-humored legal vetting, and Lindsay Whalen for keeping track of photos, copy edits, and cover designs. In London, Michael Fishwick and his team at Bloomsbury have been a joy to work with.

When I began this project, my youngest daughter, Molly, was three. Now she is six; the book has taken half her lifetime. The rest of my family may sometimes have felt that way too. For their love and patience, I am hugely grateful.

APPENDIX I:
DO THE TIGER FUNDS
GENERATE ALPHA?

Between its inception in May 1980 and its peak in August 1998, Julian Robertson's Tiger fund earned an average of 31.7 percent per year after subtracting fees, trouncing the 12.7 percent annual return on the S&P 500 index.[1] Counting in the collapse in 1999 and 2000, average performance was around 26 percent per year, still an impressive number. Over the twenty-one calendar years in which Tiger's investment decisions were controlled by Robertson, the fund was up in seventeen of them. This is particularly striking given that Tiger's staple business was stock selection, the discipline at which consistent outperformance has been found by academic studies to be nonexistent.

Could it be that Robertson was merely lucky? The laws of probability lay down that if one thousand people flip twenty-one coins, four of them will come up with heads seventeen or more times, mimicking Robertson's performance. That still means that there are 996 in 1,000 chances that Robertson's performance reflected skill. But, following the argument of Warren Buffett described in chapter five, there is a way to test the four-in-one-thousand possibility that Robertson's record was a fluke. If fund managers who worked for Robertson went on to do well, it would suggest that they learned something from him. Robertson's results could then be ascribed to skill with almost complete confidence.

To conduct this test, I sought the help of the Hennessee Group, which has been collecting data on hedge funds since 1987. No hedge-fund database is perfect, since all rely on voluntary self-reporting. Hennessee turned out to have monthly results for half of the thirty-six "Tiger cub" funds run by managers who had worked for Robertson at some point before 2000. (Tiger cubs are separate from "Tiger seeds," which are funds that have received capital from Robertson since 2000.) The Hennessee data included two funds that blew up, so it was not subject to the "survivorship bias" that bedevils hedge-fund performance statistics. And because Tiger cubs tend to invest in equities rather than in less liquid loans or derivatives that are not traded on an exchange, their results are likely to be adjusted to reflect price moves promptly and cleanly. Every up and down wiggle is captured, minimizing the "smoothing bias" that occurs when hedge funds mark their portfolios to market infrequently.

Hennessee had never examined Robertson's protégés as a group, but Hennessee's senior vice president, Samuel Norvell, agreed to construct a Tiger Index for me. The results are presented at the end of this appendix, and the first striking finding is that the Tiger Index rose a lot. Between 2000 and 2008, it gained 11.9 percent per year, and that was despite the fact that performance was dragged down by a fall of almost 20 percent in 2008. The Tiger cub returns beat the pants off the S&P 500 index, which fell by an average of 5.3 percent per year during this period. It also beat Hennessee's general hedge-fund index (up just 4.8 percent per year) and Hennessee's index of hedge funds that practice the same long/short equity style as the Tiger group (up an average of 4.4 percent per year).

The strong performance of the Tiger Index suggests that Robertson transferred some kind of advantage to his offshoots—meaning that skill, not coin-flipping luck, would be likely to explain his own returns between 1980 and 2000. But the argument does not end there. Conceivably, the Tiger cubs might have achieved higher returns by taking extra risk, in which case there would be nothing to brag about. Thanks to the Nobel laureate William Sharpe, we have a way of testing whether this was so: If you divide the Tiger cubs' returns by their volatility, you get a Sharpe ratio of 1.42—that is, a risk-adjusted return that is superior by far to any of the benchmarks. For instance, Hennessee's general hedge-fund index had a Sharpe ratio of just 0.59. The comparison makes it difficult to resist the conclusion that the Tiger cubs learned something from Robertson.

Let's try to resist a little longer. There are ways for hedge funds to game the Sharpe ratio by behaving like undercapitalized insurance companies.[2] For example, a fund can sell options that insure against extreme swings in the market. For months and maybe years, the insurer will collect a steady stream of premiums from these options, delivering consistent, market-beating returns; but one day the extreme market swing will occur, at which point the fund will go bankrupt. Theoretically, unscrupulous hedge-fund managers may deliberately take this sort of hidden risk, calculating that the extreme swings may not arrive for years, allowing them to grow rich in the meantime. But the odds that the Tiger results reflect this sort of strategy are vanishingly small. For one thing, option writing is not a big part of the Tiger culture; nor do Tiger funds specialize in the sort of trades that can be equivalent to insurance selling. For another, the period covered by the Hennessee data includes the end of 2008, a period of extreme volatility in which undercapitalized quasi-insurance funds would have gone out of business.[3] (Indeed, some did.) So the Tiger cubs' superior Sharpe ratio looks like real evidence of skill, not the product of sly insurance selling.

Just for fun, let's throw in one final thought experiment. Think of the Tiger Index as a contestant in Buffett's coin-flipping contest. Between 2000 and 2008, the Tigers had positive returns in 79 months out of 108 and beat the S&P 500 index in 62 months out of 108. The chance of beating the market index that frequently by luck is only 7.43 percent. So the coin-toss test suggests that there are twelve chances out of thirteen that the funds in the Tiger Index had real skill, or alpha.

Pinpointing alpha is a slippery game, and imperfect data can only yield imperfect conclusions. But the weight of the evidence is overwhelmingly that both Robertson and his protégés had real skill, even though they practiced a branch of investing in which alpha generation is sometimes said to be impossible.

Hennessee Tiger Index

Selected Statistics, 2000–2008

	Annualized Compound Return	Annualized Standard Deviation
Hennessee Tiger Index	11.89%	7.42%
Hennessee Hedge Fund Index	4.78%	6.66%
Hennessee Long/Short Equity Index	4.44%	7.76%
Hennessee International Index	7.63%	7.83%
S&P 500 Index	-5.26%	15.20%

	Number of Months		% of Months
	Positive	Negative	Positive
Hennessee Tiger Index	79	29	73%
Hennessee Hedge Fund Index	70	38	65%
Hennessee Long/Short Equity Index	67	41	62%
Hennessee International Index	75	33	69%
S&P 500 Index	59	49	55%

Historical Performance

	Jan	Feb	Mar	Apr	May	Jun	Jul
2008	-4.81%	2.81%	-2.70%	1.89%	2.17%	-2.15%	-1.62%
2007	1.21%	0.74%	2.31%	1.84%	3.48%	0.81%	2.61%
2006	4.17%	0.33%	2.56%	1.01%	-3.45%	-0.49%	-0.77%
2005	1.91%	2.01%	-0.47%	-0.63%	1.69%	2.16%	1.54%
2004	2.15%	1.10%	1.15%	-0.33%	-1.30%	-1.11%	-1.47%
2003	-0.08%	0.54%	0.24%	1.42%	1.08%	1.78%	1.00%
2002	1.59%	0.90%	-0.31%	1.28%	1.43%	-1.19%	-1.21%
2001	-0.50%	4.32%	2.44%	-0.18%	2.36%	3.18%	0.39%
2000	0.92%	0.61%	2.58%	1.54%	2.20%	1.97%	1.73%

Sharpe Ratio	Annualized Tiger Alpha (versus Benchmark)	Correlation (versus Benchmark)
1.42	N/A	N/A
0.59	8.95%	0.54
0.47	9.95%	0.46
0.85	6.55%	0.72
-0.34	12.79%	0.26

Largest Consecutive Loss				Value of $1000
%	Months	Peak	Valley	(Invested at Inception)
-19.85%	12	Dec-07	Dec-08	$2,749
-20.87%	13	Oct-07	Nov-08	$1,523
-19.74%	13	Oct-07	Nov-08	$1,478
-24.48%	13	Oct-07	Nov-08	$1,938
-46.28%	25	Aug-00	Sep-02	$615

Aug	Sep	Oct	Nov	Dec	Year
-1.40%	-11.51%	-2.55%	-0.79%	-0.42%	-19.85%
-0.35%	3.75%	6.86%	0.36%	1.91%	28.47%
0.85%	0.06%	2.50%	3.10%	0.77%	10.92%
-0.58%	2.23%	-0.41%	2.77%	3.54%	16.84%
-0.02%	2.13%	1.84%	1.34%	1.59%	7.20%
1.67%	0.40%	2.64%	0.49%	0.65%	12.46%
1.24%	0.73%	0.40%	-0.79%	1.81%	5.96%
2.73%	2.04%	0.38%	0.13%	2.26%	21.26%
2.49%	3.38%	3.79%	4.51%	3.21%	33.00%

APPENDIX II:
PERFORMANCE OF
THE PIONEERS

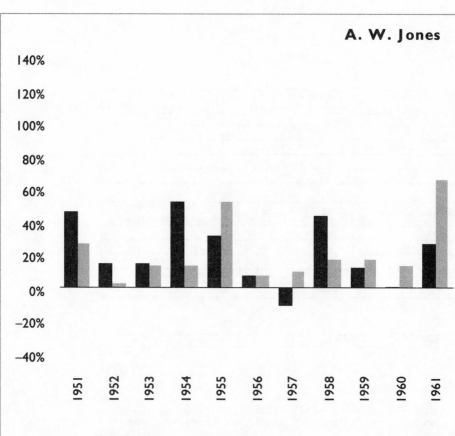

A. W. Jones

Notes: Returns are net of fees.
Results not reported for calendar year are compared with S&P 500 data for the same period.

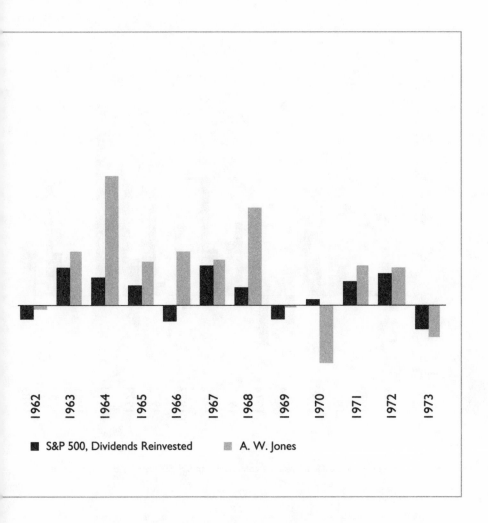

1962 1963 1964 1965 1966 1967 1968 1969 1970 1971 1972 1973

■ S&P 500, Dividends Reinvested   ■ A. W. Jones

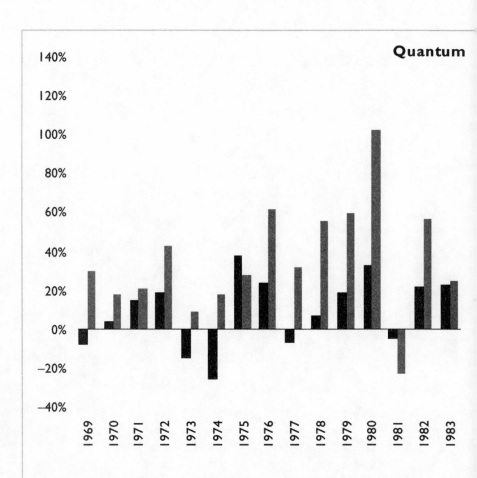

Quantum

Notes: Returns are net of fees.
Results not reported for calendar year are compared with S&P 500 data for the same period.

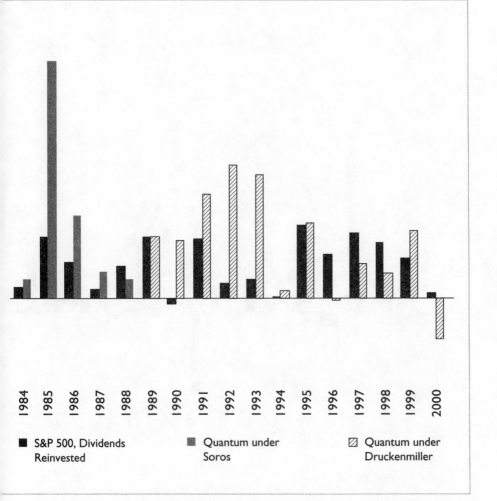

1984 1985 1986 1987 1988 1989 1990 1991 1992 1993 1994 1995 1996 1997 1998 1999 2000

■ S&P 500, Dividends
Reinvested

■ Quantum under
Soros

▨ Quantum under
Druckenmiller

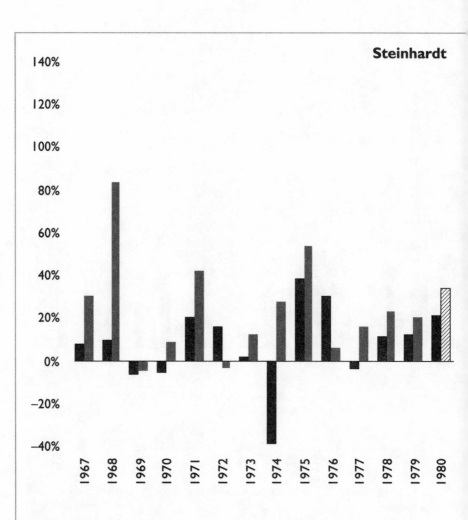

Steinhardt

Notes: Returns are net of fees.
Results not reported for calendar year are compared with S&P 500 data for the same period.

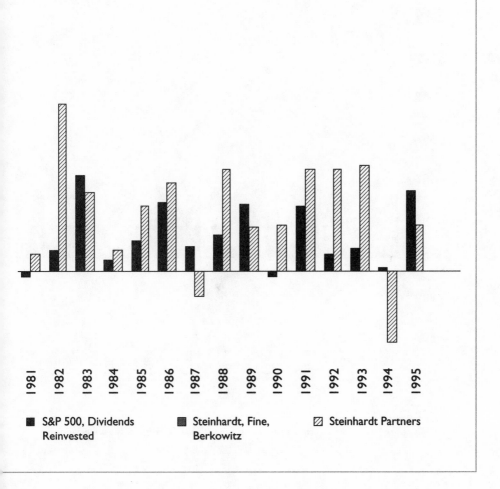

1981 1982 1983 1984 1985 1986 1987 1988 1989 1990 1991 1992 1993 1994 1995

■ S&P 500, Dividends   ■ Steinhardt, Fine,   ▨ Steinhardt Partners
  Reinvested   Berkowitz

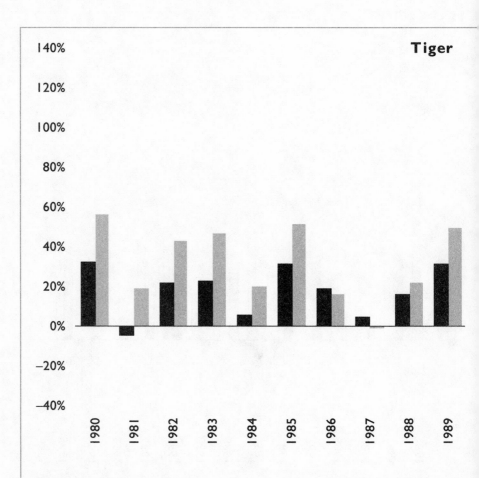

Notes: Returns are net of fees.
Results not reported for calendar year are compared with S&P 500 data for the same period.

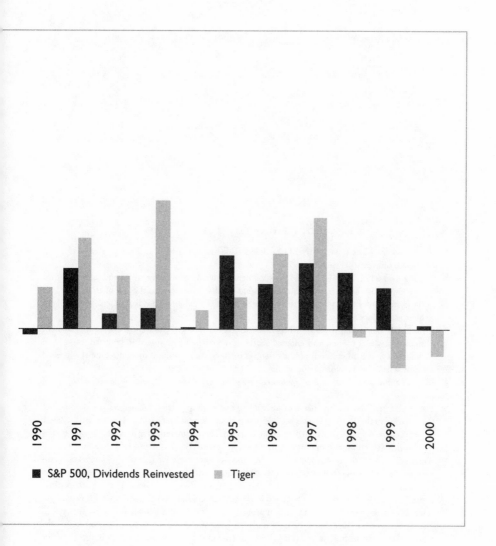

1990　1991　1992　1993　1994　1995　1996　1997　1998　1999　2000

■ S&P 500, Dividends Reinvested　　■ Tiger

NOTES

INTRODUCTION: THE ALPHA GAME

1. Joseph Nocera, "The Quantitative, Data-Based, Risk-Massaging Road to Riches," *New York Times Magazine*, June 5, 2005, p. 44.
2. Visiting Asness in July 2009, I found the superheroes piled up on a coffee table pending their return to their usual positions on a recently cleaned windowsill. Asness regarded the task of arranging them in the correct order as too delicate to delegate to an assistant and had not had time to restore them to their usual glory.
3. It should be noted that in 2007, when Blackstone went public, Schwarzman got a cash payment of more than $600 million and retained shares in the company estimated to be worth more than $7 billion. On the other hand, public offerings by hedge funds around the same time also created enormous paper wealth for the founders.
4. Michael Steinhardt, *No Bull: My Life In and Out of Markets* (New York: John Wiley & Sons, 2001), p. 179.
5. Elaine Crocker, who was in charge of identifying and seeding portfolio managers at Commodities Corporation in the 1980s and who became president of Moore Capital in 1994, comments, "Rarely do portfolio managers articulate why they are successful. Sometimes they try to do so but are wrong. I have worked with hundreds of portfolio managers and found that articulating why they are successful is quite difficult for them—although often they are not aware that it is." (Elaine Crocker, e-mail communication with the author, September 8, 2009.) Similarly, Roy Lennox, a longtime macro trader at Caxton, says, "Trading can be intuitive. We are looking at so many factors in the markets [that] a lot of our analysis operates on a subconscious level. All of a sudden you just know this is the right trade. If somebody really quizzed you, you probably couldn't clearly articulate your views and would just say, no no no, I *know* this is the right trade. It's because all these things have been taken in—the market action, the technicals, the things that you read in the newspapers or on Bloomberg and the conversations you have with other traders, analysts and policy makers. It just comes together." (Roy Lennox, interview with the author, June 24, 2009.)
6. Jonathan R. Laing. "Trader With a Hot Hand—That's Paul Tudor Jones II," *Barron's*, June 15, 1987.
7. Malcolm Gladwell, *Blink: The Power of Thinking Without Thinking* (New York: Penguin Books, 2005), p. 67. I am grateful to Chad Waryas for pointing out the parallel between trading and tennis.

8. Andrei Shleifer and Lawrence H. Summers, "The Noise Trader Approach to Finance," *Journal of Economic Perspectives* 4, no. 2 (Spring 1990). In the wake of the financial crisis of 2007–2009, it was said that financial economists had finally been forced to wake up to market inefficiencies. But their existence had already been widely accepted among economists for at least two decades.

9. There are many more examples. Richard Thaler, the leading light in behavioral finance, is involved in the investment-management firm Fuller & Thaler. At Long-Term Capital Management, Eric Rosenfeld, a former finance professor at Harvard Business School, was more important but less famous than Merton and Scholes, the Nobel laureates. Kenneth French is a director of Dimensional Fund Advisors. Asness set up AQR with John Liew, whom he had known at Chicago's PhD program.

10. Gwynne Dyer, "The Money Pit and the Pendulum," *The Globe and Mail*, January 17, 1998.

11. For a description of this trade-off, see Jeremy C. Stein, "Sophisticated Investors and Market Efficiency" (working paper downloaded from Stein's Web site at Harvard).

12. See Benn Steil, "Lessons of the Financial Crisis," Council Special Report No. 45 (Council on Foreign Relations, March 2009).

13. Near the end of 2008, the ratio of Citigroup's total assets to its tangible net worth was fifty-six to one. At the end of 2007 the total assets of the Swiss bank UBS exceeded its equity by fifty-three times.

14. It is true that hedge funds do not always mark their assets to market in a perfect way: There is evidence that they fudge them to make their returns appear less volatile. But hedge funds are nonetheless much closer to marking assets to market than are other financial institutions, notably banks.

CHAPTER ONE: BIG DADDY

1. Britt Erica Tunick, "Capital Gains: The Firms in Our Sixth Annual Ranking of the World's 100 Biggest Hedge Funds Manage an Altogether Staggering $1 Trillion," *Alpha*, May 2007.

2. Steve Fishman, "Get Richest Quickest: In the Precarious Hedge-Fund Bubble, It's Either Clean Up—Or Flame Out," *New York*, vol. 37, no. 41, November 22, 2004.

3. Peter Landau, "The Hedge Funds: Wall Street's New Way to Make Money," *New York* vol 1, no. 29 (October 21, 1968): pp. 20–24.

4. Adam Smith, *The Money Game* (New York: Vintage Books, 1976), p. 41.

5. John Brooks, *The Go-Go Years* (New York: Weybright and Talley, 1973), p. 128.

6. The account of Jones's early life comes principally from the author's interviews with Jones's children, Anthony Jones and Dale Burch, conducted sequentially on May 22, 2007. State Department files and entries about Jones in the Harvard yearbooks confirm the narrative.

7. According to State Department records, Jones worked as a clerk and export buyer from 1924 to 1926. He was hired as a statistician and analyst for an investment counselor and held this job from 1926 to 1928. State Department Historian's Office, e-mail communication with the author, June 5, 2007.

8. Charles Kindleberger, *The World in Depression* (Berkeley: University of California Press, 1986), p. 132.

9. According to State Department files, the marriage took place on January 17, 1932. The circumstances of Anna's previous marriage and associated custody battle are described in detail in a letter from Jones to the American consul general in Berlin, George S. Messersmith, dated March 22, 1932, held on file in the National Archives. This episode in Jones's life was discovered by Harold Hurwitz, a leading historian of Germany's anti-Nazi Left, who generously provided me with copies of documents and letters relating to Jones's life in the 1930s. (Harold Hurwitz, interview with the author, June 7, 2007.) I am also indebted to Peter Lowe, the nephew of one of the leaders of the Leninist Organization, who confirmed several details, and to Mark Hove at the Office of the Historian in the State Department. (Peter Lowe and Mark Hove, e-mail communications with the author, June 6 and 7, 2007.) The name of Jones's wife is confused by her multiple marriages and her use of pseudonyms: She also went by "Hannah Koehler" and by "Nelly."

10. The group was often known simply as the "Org" and later changed its name to Neu Beginnen.

11. Confidential State Department memorandum, February 20, 1933.

12. Mary was illustrating a medical book at the time she met Jones. "I was doing this illustrating when I met my husband, and he said, 'How can you draw those things when you can marry me?' So we were married." Mary Carter Jones, taped interview for Henry Street Oral History Project, 1993, box T2:23, Henry Street Settlement Records Series 8, Social Welfare History Archives, University of Minnesota, Minneapolis. My thanks to the Henry Street Settlement for permitting access.

13. According to Hurwitz, in the mid-1930s Jones was working for the Leninist Organization, now renamed Neu Beginnen, in New York. Moreover, Hurwitz speculates that Jones was involved in U.S. intelligence operations. According to records in the U.S. embassy in Paris, Jones maintained contact with the State Department in 1937 and as late as 1939 and received payments for a "rent allowance"; he may have been funded by the State Department to stay in touch with the German underground. Further, State Department files indicate that in April 1944 the department considered arranging a military deferment for Jones, suggesting a continuing connection between the government and Jones more than a decade after no official one existed. State Department files and Hurwitz interview.

14. The story of the Joneses' visit to Spain is told in their joint report: Alfred W. Jones and Mary Carter Jones, "War Relief in Spain: Report to the American Unitarian Association." (American Friends Service Committee and the American Unitarian Association, 1938).

15. Adam Smith, introduction to *The Money Managers*, ed. Gilbert Edmund Kaplan and Chris Welles (New York: Institutional Investor Systems, 1969), p. xiii.

16. In his contribution to the twenty-fifth yearbook for the Harvard class of 1923, Jones explains his interest in sociology as a reaction to his experiences in Germany: "I came home in the midst of the Depression to try to find out if anything like that could happen here." *25th Anniversary Yearbook of the Harvard Class of 1923* (Cambridge, MA), p. 450.

17. Alfred Winslow Jones, *Life, Liberty and Property: A Story of Conflict and a Measurement of Conflicting Rights* (Philadelphia: J.B. Lippincott Company, 1941), p. 23.

18. Alfred Winslow Jones, "The Free Market and the Future," *Fortune* 25, April 1942, pp. 98–99, 126, 128.

19. Smith, *The Money Game*, p. 11. I also owe to Smith the paradox that money is at once an abstraction and a medium for emotional expression. Smith entertainingly quotes Edward Crosby Johnson II, who in the 1950s established Fidelity as a dominant investment firm and made the same point in his own way: "The market is like a beautiful woman—endlessly fascinating, endlessly complex, always changing, always mystifying. I have been absorbed and immersed since 1924 and I know this is no science. It is an art. . . . It is personal intuition."

20. Alfred Cowles III and Herbert E. Jones, "Some A Posteriori Probabilities in Stock Market Action," *Econometrica* 5(3) (July 1937): 280–94.

21. In his contribution to the twenty-fifth-anniversary edition of his Harvard yearbook, Jones wrote extensively about his interests as of early 1948: There was a whole paragraph about his political views and a paean to gardening; finance wasn't mentioned.

22. "With a wife and two children, I needed something more lucrative, and turned to Wall Street." Alfred Winslow Jones contribution to the *Fiftieth Anniversary Report of the Harvard Class of 1923* (Cambridge, MA).

23. Data on Jones's returns up to 1961 come from the unpublished "Basic Report to the Partners," May 31, 1961, provided to me by Robert Burch IV, Jones's grandson. Data on returns from 1964 on come from the files of Clark Drasher, a fund manager for A. W. Jones. Data on the years 1962 and 1963 come from press accounts, notably Carol J. Loomis, "The Jones Nobody Keeps Up With," *Fortune*, April 1966, pp. 237–47.

24. Loomis, "The Jones Nobody Keeps Up With."

25. In his excellent biography of Warren Buffett, Roger Lowenstein reports that investors who entrusted their money to the future sage of Omaha in 1957 enjoyed a sixteenfold return over the next thirteen years. Jones was up just under fifteenfold in this period, but there were other thirteen-year periods in which he was up seventeenfold. See Roger Lowenstein, *Buffett: The Making of an American Capitalist* (New York: Broadway Books, 2001), p. 118.

26. This description comes from Richard Radcliffe, Clark Drasher, and Banks Adams, who worked for Jones as fund managers, and from Richard Gilder, who visited the office regularly in the late 1950s

and early 1960s as one of the fund's brokers. Richard Radcliffe, interviews with the author, April 6 and 16, 2007; Clark Drasher, interview with the author, April 10, 2007; Banks Adams, interview with the author, April 16, 2007; Richard Gilder, interview with the author, April 3, 2007.

27. How Jones came up with this idea is not clear. He may have known of the investment partnership operated by Ben Graham, the father of value investing and mentor to Warren Buffett. Graham's partnership in many respects resembled a hedge fund: It went both long and short, charged performance fees, and used leverage. Another potential source of inspiration, according to Richard Radcliffe, who joined A. W. Jones in 1954, is a legendary broker named Roy Neuberger. An unpublished profile of Neuberger by the writer "Adam Smith" reports that Neuberger arrived on Wall Street in the 1920s without having finished college and that he balanced long and short investments. When the 1929 crash came, Neuberger's portfolio emerged unscathed while most investors were ruined. Neuberger later met Jones through a neighbor near his country home. "He was starting a real hedge fund, and I became his broker," Neuberger told Smith. On Ben Graham's partnership, see Jim Grant, "My Hero, Benjamin Grossbaum," remarks delivered on November 15, 2007, at the Center for Jewish History (available at http://www.grantspub.com/articles/bengraham/). On Neuberger, see Adam Smith, "Roy Neuberger: Where the Money Is," unpublished article dated December 5, 2003. The article was circulated by Craig Drill of Drill Capital, whose advice to me has been tireless.

28. Kaplan and Welles, *The Money Managers*, pp. 112–13.

29. "A Basic Report to the Partners."

30. Ibid. For further evidence of how short selling was often seen as unworthy of respect, see Martin T. Sosnoff, "Hedge Fund Management: A New Respectability for Short Selling," *Financial Analysts Journal*, July–August 1966, p. 105.

31. Until 2007, shorting was only permitted on an uptick; one could not short a stock that was already moving downward. In addition, all profits from short sales, like profits from short-term investments on the long side, are taxed like ordinary income, which in Jones's era could mean at rates up to 90 percent. Meanwhile, long-term gains on stocks, which at the time meant gains on stocks that the firm had held for at least six months, were taxed at lower rates, usually 25 percent.

32. Richard Radcliffe recalls the velocity calculation as being a bit rough-and-ready. "We took the last five market highs and the last five lows and we looked up what the stocks had done in those highs and lows. . . . Sometimes there weren't five really good moves, so it was very crude. . . . I did it myself for my hedge fund after I left, but then I figured what the hell, it wasn't worth it." Radcliffe interview, April 16, 2007.

33. Jones's prescience in separating alpha from beta was first pointed out to me by Robert Burch IV. Robert Burch IV, interview with the author, April 18, 2007.

34. Dale Burch interview.

35. This is a slightly simplified version of a table given in Jones's 1961 "Basic Report."

36. For a flavor of how Jones's innovations are underappreciated, consider the following passage from *Capital Ideas Evolving*, by the late Peter L. Bernstein, the most widely read (and readable) historian of investment theory: "Markowitz's famous comment that 'you have to think about risk as well as return' sounds like a homey slogan today. Yet it was a total novelty in 1952 to give risk at least equal weight with the search for reward." Bernstein appeared unaware that Jones managed money based on this insight. Peter L. Bernstein, *Capital Ideas Evolving* (Hoboken, NJ: John Wiley & Sons, 2007), p. xiii.

37. Mark Rubenstein, *A History of the Theory of Investments* (Hoboken, NJ: John Wiley & Sons 2006), p. 122.

38. On Jones's propensity for secrecy, it is striking that he never told his children anything about his first marriage, which they only discovered by accident when Jones's son Anthony married an Austrian, causing the authorities to look up his family records. (Anthony Jones interview.) Moreover, Jones never mentioned his time in Berlin to Richard Radcliffe, who worked for him for a decade, even though the Berlin period must have remained vivid in Jones's memory. (Radcliffe interview, April 16, 2007.) Concerning Jones's business secrecy, a broker who later founded a hedge fund said, "We knew that Jones was making a fortune and that people who were associated with him were doing extremely well. But we didn't know how he was doing it." See Kaplan and Welles, *The Money*

Managers, pp. 115–16. It was not until 1966, seventeen years after the launch of the fund, that Jones's techniques were described in the financial media.

39. John Tavss, a tax lawyer who began his career working for Valentine, recalls that on another occasion Valentine's wife came to meet him at his office. He asked her to wait while he had a word with a colleague; then he disappeared down a corridor, got locked in conversation for an hour, and proceeded home, forgetting that his wife was waiting for him. John Tavss, interview with the author, April 18, 2007.

40. The top rate on regular income was 91 percent between 1951 and 1964; the top rate on capital gains was 25 percent during that time. In 1965, the top rate on regular income was lowered to 70 percent, where it stayed until 1968. Valentine of Seward & Kissel also figured out that a departing partner could be paid out with shares that carried with them unrealized investment gains, thereby ridding the hedge fund of tax liabilities; he continued to come up with ingenious tax designs for the successor generation of hedge funds, notably Tiger. John Tavss recalls, "He could take almost any problem and start spouting out potential solutions. He would come up with five ideas immediately." (John Tavss interview.) Craig Drill recalls: "Everyone in the hedge fund business who knew about this was very quiet about it for ten, or twenty, or thirty years." (Craig Drill, interview with the author, March 20, 2007.)

41. "If a partner dropped out or he had a slot, he'd just mention it at dinner and say, 'Are you happy?' That's what he said to Pauline Plimpton—widow of the founder of the law firm Debevoise & Plimpton—and she said, 'Yeah, I'm getting terrible results,' and she became a partner." (Dale Burch interview.)

42. The Securities Act of 1933 contains an exemption for "transactions by an issuer not involving any public offering." To avoid being deemed to be making a public offering, an investment partnership had to limit the number of partners. Likewise, the Investment Company Act of 1940, which imposes limits on the use of leverage, short selling, and high fees, contains an exemption for partnerships with fewer than one hundred partners that do not offer themselves publicly. Hedge funds were also anxious to avoid entanglement with the Investment Advisors Act, which prohibits "compensation to the investment advisor on the basis of a share of capital gains." To avoid registration under this act, hedge-fund managers argued that they were advising fewer than fifteen clients, an assertion that hinged on the claim that the "client" was the investment partnership rather than the more numerous partners. If the SEC had rejected that assertion and forced hedge funds to register, it would probably have crushed them. Richard Radcliffe, the first fund manager hired by A. W. Jones, recalls: "We always were afraid of getting regulated, and the way we would have been regulated would have been if we had too many partners there. . . . We got up close to a hundred, and we decided that we should have another fund. And we even separated out the investment strategies to make it look as if we were not just trying to get around the rules." (Radcliffe interview, April 16, 2007.) Clark Drasher, another A. W. Jones alumnus, offers a similar account. (Drasher interview.)

43. Brooks, *The Go-Go Years*, p. 144.

44. Alfred Cowles, "A Revision of Previous Conclusions Regarding Stock Price Behavior," *Econometrica* 28, no. 4 (October 1960).

45. By 1965, Jones's earlier faith in charts was coming under attack even from the chartists themselves. In his 1949 essay in *Fortune*, Jones had singled out a Russian immigrant named Nicholas Molodovsky as "the most scientific and experimental of technical students," reporting that with the exception of two episodes in which he had called the market wrong, "his predictions have been nearly perfect." But in 1965 Molodovsky, by then the editor of the influential *Financial Analysts Journal*, commissioned a paper from a rising academic star named Eugene Fama, which appeared under the title "Random Walks in Stock Market Prices." Fama compared chart following to astrology. By popularizing Fama's random-walk theory, Molodovsky was burning the ground under Jones's feet; the premise of Jones's fund was under attack from one of its progenitors. The blow must have felt especially heavy since Jones and Molodovsky were close; Molodovsky introduced Jones to Richard Radcliffe, whom Jones hired subsequently, and Radcliffe recalls Molodovsky as an intellectual influence on the Jones fund during his period there between 1954 and 1965. Radcliffe interviews.

46. By 1968, Donald Woodward, Jones's chief operating officer, was willing to say categorically that stock selection, not market timing, was the key to success. "Our judgment about the prevailing market trend has not been our strong point," he said. See "Heyday of the Hedge Funds," *Dun's Review*, January 1968, p. 76.

47. The description of the Jones stock-picking style is based on interviews with seven of the firm's employees: Richard Radcliffe, Carlisle Jones, Clark Drasher, Banks Adams, Alex Porter, Alan Dresher, and Walter Harrison. Radcliffe interview; Carlisle Jones, interview with the author, June 9, 2007; Drasher interview; Adams interview; Alex Porter, interview with the author, April 4, 2007; Alan Dresher, interview with the author, May 30, 2007; Walter Harrison, interview with the author, April 17, 2007. See also the entertaining but somewhat jaundiced description of Jones in Barton Biggs, *Hedgehogging* (Hoboken, NJ: John Wiley & Sons, 2006), pp. 81–85. Biggs, who ran a model portfolio for Jones, recalls, "Alfred Jones understood the performance game and the value of getting an edge from research before anyone else did." *Hedgehogging*, p. 83.

48. Jones's distaste for committee meetings extended to charitable obligations. Recalling her work on multiple civic committees during World War II, Mary Jones remarked: "My husband hated going on committees in wars—he just loathed it—he'd say, 'Make Mary do it,' or something like that." Mary Jones interview with Henry Street Oral History Project.

49. "At the time, nobody else ran a fund with these sorts of measurements. The brokers were eager to work for Jones because they could see how well their model portfolios were doing. And if they did well they got commissions. So we got good service. We got their best ideas. If the ideas went to the mutual funds, you did not know how they reached their decision." Radcliffe interview, April 16, 2007.

50. Biggs, *Hedgehogging*, p. 83.

51. Clark Drasher, who worked for A. W. Jones between 1963 and 1973, recalls: "The culture was not big on meetings. Everyone agreed that meetings were a waste of time. If you had a hot idea you didn't want the other guys to know because you wanted your segment to outperform the other guys' segments. Every May we would sit down and argue about who should get how much of the total general managers' fee." (Drasher interview.) Alex Porter, who started at A. W. Jones in 1967, recalls: "The practice was that they hired three or four people, and at the end of the year, one or two left and others came in. To a great extent it was performance driven." (Porter interview.)

52. Biggs, *Hedgehogging*, p. 84.

53. Kaplan and Welles, *The Money Managers*, p. 113.

54. The Russian-Yugoslav connection dominated a dinner mentioned in Kaplan and Welles, *The Money Managers*. On Jones's social contacts at the United Nations, Mary Jones recalls, "I knew most of the secretary generals and their staff. A lot of the ambassadors too." Mary Jones interview with Henry Street Oral History Project.

55. The first segment manager to defect from A. W. Jones was Carlisle Jones (no relation). He says of his former boss: "I don't think he knew the difference between a stock and a bond. . . . I was very jealous. He would nap for an hour. Then he would read the books or papers. The books probably didn't have to do with investment. . . . A lot of times I didn't feel as though I was properly compensated." Carlisle Jones interview.

56. The defector was Richard Radcliffe. (Radcliffe interview.) See also Biggs, *Hedgehogging*.

57. The estimate for 1968 comes from "Heyday of the Hedge Funds." The range for 1969 reflects estimates given at the Practicing Law Institute's forum on Investment Partnerships, held on March 7, 1969, and quoted in Joseph P. P. Hildebrandt, "Hedge Fund Operation and Regulation" (unpublished J.D. thesis, Harvard University) April 15, 1969. I am grateful to Craig Drill, an indefatigable collector of historical gems, for giving me a copy.

58. "Hedge Funds: Prickly," *Economist*, May 25, 1968, p. 91. Other estimates from the time put the number lower.

59. Jones considered the popular term for his style of investing a grammatical outrage. "My original expression, and the proper one, was 'hedged fund,'" he told friends in the late 1960s, when the expression in its corrupted form entered the language. "I still regard 'hedge fund,' which makes a noun serve for an adjective, with distaste." Brooks, *The Go-Go Years*, p. 142.

60. Loomis, "The Jones Nobody Keeps Up With."

61. Alex Porter recalls: "I read Carol Loomis's article in *Fortune*, and I called up Mr. Jones and didn't get him but got Don Woodward, who was the chief operating officer, and told him I wanted to come and work for him." Porter first ran a model portfolio, then went to work for Jones in 1967, remaining until the early 1970s. Porter interview.

62. This partner was Dean Milosis. The guess about Jones's personal income comes from "Heyday of the Hedge Funds." p. 76.

63. A comprehensive description of the regulatory questions asked about hedge funds in 1969 is given in Hildebrandt, "Hedge Fund Operation and Regulation." See also Carol Loomis, "Hard Times Come to Hedge Funds," *Fortune*, January 1970.

64. By contrast, the S&P 500 average gained 1 percent in the year to June 1, 1966, 7 percent the year after that, and 10 percent in the following one. The Jones funds were run on a financial year ending May 31; hence the comparison with S&P 500 returns ending June 1.

65. Clark Drasher recalls: "I don't think I really took this volatility thing seriously. Maybe I didn't give a hoot about it. I told Jones it was not a real measure of risk. I didn't like it because often something I wanted to do in bulk was restricted because of the volatility factor. A lot of mathematical baloney went on. All this attempt to be scientifically precise makes you feel good, but at the end of the day you made money if your selections were good or not. . . . Most of the time we were not balanced. We would get carried away in rising markets. You'd hate to be short much of anything in the 1960s. So when the bad times came in 1969 we got hit." (Drasher interview.) Similarly, Banks Adams recalls: "When the 1960s came and the markets were going straight up, those [volatility] numbers were just useless. Let's take Texas Instruments: It didn't fluctuate, it was going straight up. Telephones proved to be more volatile than Texas Instruments, which was doubling and tripling every year. A. W. Jones's thinking came out of the 1940s and 1950s." (Adams interview.)

66. Bernstein, *Capital Ideas Evolving*, p. 9. See also Edwin Burk Cox, *Trends in the Distribution of Stock Ownership* (Philadelphia: University of Pennsylvania Press, 1963), pp. xiii, 211.

67. Smith, *The Money Game*, p. 209.

68. The S&P 500 fell 23.4 percent over the same period. Jones's larger losses reflected the fact that he was more than 100 percent long.

69. Dale Burch interview.

CHAPTER TWO: THE BLOCK TRADER

1. This number comes from the Securities and Exchange Commission's "Institutional Investor Study Report," published in March 1971. See Wyndham Robertson, "Hedge Fund Miseries," *Fortune*, May 1971, p. 269.

2. The estimate of 150 hedge funds as of January 1970 comes from the painstaking census conducted by Carol Loomis. See Carol Loomis, "Hard Times Come to Hedge Funds," *Fortune*, January 1970. In 1969, the annual report of the Securities and Exchange Commission stated that the number of hedge funds was "approaching 200"; but as noted in the previous chapter, estimates ranged up to 500.

3. In the spring of 1971, the Securities and Exchange Commission released its long-awaited report on institutional investors. It reiterated the doubts about performance fees and called for hedge funds to register under federal law. But the fire had gone out of the campaign. In particular, the SEC had found no evidence to support the idea that hedge-fund trading was disruptive to markets. See Wayne E. Green, "SEC Finds No Link of Institutions to Price Swings: Doubts Needs for Curbs," *Wall Street Journal*, March 11, 1971, p. 6.

4. In an article published in January 1968, Donald Woodward put the size of the Jones funds at "well past" $100 million. According to notes kept by Clark Drasher, assets in 1969 came to $107 million and assets in 1973 came to $35 million. According to Jones's grandson, Robert L. Burch, internal records kept by the Jones partnership show that the capital had shrunk to $25 million by 1984. See "The Heyday of the Hedge Funds," *Dun's Review*, January 1968, p. 78; Clark Drasher, interview with the author, April 10, 2007. Robert L. Burch, e-mail communication with the author, May 18, 2007.

5. Michael Steinhardt, *No Bull: My Life In and Out of Markets* (New York: John Wiley & Sons, 2001), p. 81.

6. The lawyer was Paul Roth. He recalls: "They wanted to have their names in the firm and pulled straws to see the order. I was there that day in Howard Berkowitz's Manhattan apartment. I told them that 'Steinhardt, Fine, Berkowitz' sounded like a Jewish delicatessen. I was somewhat concerned—how do you go out with a name like that?" Paul Roth, interview with the author, October 3, 2007.

7. Jerrold Fine, interview with the author, August 29, 2007.

8. Steinhardt, Fine, Berkowitz & Company reported results for years to the end of September. To facilitate comparison, the S&P 500 numbers given here are also for the years to September.

9. See Robertson, "Hedge Fund Miseries," p. 270.

10. Howard Berkowitz interview, August 28, 2007. Jerry Fine interview, August 29, 2007. For the Spacek quote, see John Bogle's forward to Adam Smith, *Supermoney* (New York: John Wiley & Sons, 1972), p. xiii.

11. David Rocker, an analyst with Steinhardt, Fine, Berkowitz, recalls: "To make money on the short side you have to be a scrapper. The government is against you. The media was against you; it was un-American to be short. The company management was against you. Advances in stock prices tend to be long and gentle, whereas falls are sharp and short. And so most days when you go in the office, the short seller is taking it in the nose. There were not a lot of people at the time who were willing to take it in the nose." David Rocker, interview with the author, July 31, 2007.

12. Steinhardt, *No Bull*, p. 127. Elaborating on this point in an interview with the author, Steinhardt says, "We did seem like gunslingers and wise guys. I was concerned that they'd pass legislation to outlaw short selling because there was talk about that. But to the specific answer to your question [on how he responded to being resented], I felt very good that I had the wisdom, judgment, and courage to put myself in that position." Michael Steinhardt, interview with the author, October 4, 2007.

13. Steinhardt interview.

14. John LeFrere, interview with the author, August 28, 2007. The LeFrere story is not an isolated incident. When an analyst named Oscar Schafer joined the firm, Steinhardt called him the first day and asked what he was up to. Schafer replied that a friend of a friend fancied Commonwealth Oil, so he might take a look at it. Steinhardt immediately bought a huge block of the stock. Schafer was terrified. Oscar Schafer, interview with the author, August 29, 2007.

15. Michael Steinhardt recalls: "Tony was, as you've heard, very unusual because of his ability to express himself unequivocally. In such a way that he was vulnerable . . . It was that vulnerability that made you respect him when he was right and when he was wrong, and made you think he was a man of courage and conviction." Asked about the sources of Cilluffo's conviction, Steinhardt says: "It could be a mystery because we were dealing with a person who had lots of street smarts and who was intelligent, but wasn't intelligent in the way that the rest of us were in having taken economics 101 and 102 and finance and that good stuff; he didn't have that. His intelligence came from a different source and his judgments came from a different source. To talk about Kondratiev waves and put overwhelming emphasis on it, that was something only he could do. With conviction and a little bit of naïveté. I don't think he knew too much. But he knew what he had to know. Why he felt as he did was a mystery because he couldn't articulate it." Michael Steinhardt, interview with the author, September 10, 2007.

16. Tony Cilluffo, interview with the author, September 25, 2007. See also Steinhardt, *No Bull*, p. 122.

17. Steinhardt, *No Bull*, p. 128. Steinhardt adds: "I especially was influenced by him. I was prepared to give him his head." Steinhardt interview, October 4, 2007.

18. Steinhardt, *No Bull*, p. 186.

19. Steinhardt interview, October 4, 2007. See also Steinhardt, *No Bull*, p. 187. In an interview with Jack D. Schwager, Steinhardt approvingly cites a fellow investor who says, "All I bring to the party is twenty-eight years of mistakes." See Jack D. Schwager, *Market Wizards: Interviews with Top Traders* (New York: New York Institute of Finance, 1989), p. 211. It should also be noted that when Steinhardt tries to give examples of his feel for the markets, he can sound underwhelming. "Often

listening to an idea led me to an entirely different conclusion than the proponent of that same idea," he writes, as though the experience of realizing what you think by listening to someone who thinks otherwise were remotely unusual. Steinhardt, *No Bull*, p. 187.

20. Ibid., pp. 189–90.

21. One former Steinhardt colleague says: "There was no upside to Michael's aggression. In the end it drove me away. I would not treat a dog that way."

22. Howard Berkowitz says, "We were all research analysts, we were all very intense in our management process, we knew about the companies we visited, we understood what was going on. Markets were less efficient back then." (Berkowitz interview.) Jerry Fine insists, "We were, in my opinion, 100 percent research driven." (Fine interview.)

23. Other examples of hedge-fund success based primarily on stock picking include Julian Robertson's Tiger fund and its offshoots. See chapter five and the appendix.

24. One of the few money-supply watchers in the 1960s was Henry Kaufman of Salomon Brothers. He describes his profession in the 1960s as having "a handful" of members in the entire country. These tended to advise bond investors, not equity investors. Henry Kaufman, interview with the author, September 10, 2007. Another exception was James Harpel, a hedge-fund manager who ran Century Capital. Harpel recalls that his focus on the bearish implications of high interest rates was considered unusual in the early 1970s. James Harpel, interview with the author, October 2, 2007.

25. Cilluffo was watching the data on net free and borrowed reserves. Tony Cilluffo, interviews with the author, July 23 and September 25, 2007.

26. Interviews with six of Cilluffo's colleagues produced this picture of a man whose opinions were followed but whose reasoning could be mysterious. For example, Oscar Schafer recalls, "Tony, for a long time, had an amazing ability to say, 'Tuesday the market will go down.' And on Tuesday the market would go down." (Schafer interview.) David Rocker says of Cilluffo, "He did his own thing. Nobody else could figure it out." (Rocker interview.) Michael Steinhardt says of Cilluffo's monetary analysis, "I think it was an edge. The question was, was it blind luck or something different?" A bit later, he adds: "Maybe he could have been talking moonbeams or something else, but the fact is that he was right. When anyone questioned him deeply about these things, you immediately got the sense that his knowledge was superficial and that he was totally uneducated in these areas." (Steinhardt interview, October 4, 2007.)

27. William J. Casey (chairman of the Securities and Exchange Commission), "The Changing Environment for Pension Plans" (address to the American Pension Conference, October 7, 1971).

28. In 1960 the big savings institutions had accounted for just a quarter of the turnover on the New York Stock Exchange. By 1969 they accounted for more than half of it. The share rose steadily from then on. By the mid 1980s institutions were reckoned to account for 80 to 90 percent of stock-exchange turnover. See Charles J. Ella, "Modern Moneyman: A Hedge Fund Manager Mixes Research, Risks to 'Perform' in Market," *Wall Street Journal*, October 31, 1969, p. 1.

29. Block trading was to reach 30 percent of total turnover by 1980 and 50 percent by 1984. New York Stock Exchange data presented graphically in Randall Smith, "Street Hazard," *Wall Street Journal*, February 20, 1985, p. 1.

30. "It was rare for someone who was running the firm, like me, to be sitting on the desk, getting block indications and speaking to senior block traders, in contrast to most other firms, which had people who were nothing but clerks doing the same thing. So if you are a senior guy at a brokerage firm, who would you rather speak to? Me or some clerk? You would rather speak to me, open up to me, have me on your side. By being there, I got a better call than most others." Steinhardt interview, October 4, 2007. See similar remarks in Schwager, *Market Wizards*, p. 213.

31. Steinhardt interview, September 10, 2007.

32. Steinhardt, *No Bull*, p. 97.

33. Steinhardt recalls: "There were opportunities created by dealing with [Salomon's] Jay Perry. There were times he was eager to get his print on the tape. When you knew that, you offered him the wrong price. The wrong price on 300,000 shares is three eighths of a point. That's a lot of money in your pocket. That's what I did really well." Steinhardt interview, October 4, 2007.

34. Steinhardt interview, October 4, 2007.

35. Explaining their assumptions in a seminal article in 1961, Franco Modigliani and Merton Miller included the condition whose real-world absence Steinhardt exploited: "No buyer or seller (or issuer) of securities is large enough for his transactions to have an appreciable impact on the then ruling price." Merton H. Miller and Franco Modigliani, "Dividend Policy, Growth, and the Valuation of Shares," *Journal of Business* 34 (1961), p. 412. Meanwhile, Eugene Fama acknowledged that stock-market specialists, armed with privileged knowledge of unfulfilled buy and sell orders, could outperform the market. But he failed to see that this apparently minor qualification had become more significant with the rise of block trading. Now it was no longer just the specialists who knew what trades were coming down the pike; block traders like Steinhardt also had access to market-moving information. And the value of this information had gone up, because the big block trades were likely to move the price more than the small orders handled by the specialists. Eugene F. Fama, "Efficient Capital Markets: A Review of Theory and Empirical Work," *Journal of Finance* 25 (1970): 409–10.

36. For an elegant exposition of this point, see Richard Bookstaber, *A Demon of Our Own Design* (New York: John Wiley & Sons, 2007), pp. 183–84.

37. "I used to generate vast amounts of commissions relative to my capital because I did all sorts of things that generated huge commissions for my own purposes that I felt had some circular benefit: You generate commissions, you get good ideas, you have the ability to be more liquid than the next guy because the broker will buy your stuff when he needs to and not the next guy's stuff; and you get a better call on new issues and research." (Steinhardt interview, September 10, 2007.)

38. In another example of preferential treatment in 1986, a Goldman Sachs analyst recommended Southwest Airlines Co.'s stock to Steinhardt's traders the night before he gave the recommendation to the rest of Goldman's clients. George Anders, "Investors' Investor: Powerful Trader Relies on Information Net, Timing and a Hot Pace—Michael Steinhardt in Action; One Eye on His Screens, One Ear to Rumor Mills—Fees Alone Cost $22 Million." *Wall Street Journal,* March 3, 1986.

39. Steinhardt describes one instance in which he demanded to know the identity of the seller and even canceled his buy order after the fact. "Usually the seller doesn't know his ass from his elbow. Are there occasions when he does? You bet. We once bought a block of Equity Funding, a big dislocated block, and we sensed right away that something was wrong. And we went to Goldman and they had bought some stock too. And we asked and we found out who the seller was, and it was clear to us that the seller knew something. . . . It was an insider thing. Who am I to stop payment on that trade? I'm not supposed to know the seller, and even if I do, I'm not supposed to have proof that he knew anything. But I did." Steinhardt continues: "At one point, in the early eighties, we were Goldman Sachs's largest account. To be Goldman's biggest account, a mere hedge fund. Can you imagine the turnover we must have been doing? It required me having intimate relationships with the people at the trading desks at the major firms where I could trust them and they could trust me. Where they could give me information that was almost always to my benefit. And to their benefit as well. It was another source of income for us." Steinhardt interview, October 4, 2007.

40. John Lattanzio joined Steinhardt in 1979. John Lattanzio, interview with the author, October 4, 2007.

41. Cary Reich, "Will Weinstein, Former Head Trader, Oppenheimer & Co.," *Institutional Investor,* Vol. 21, no. 6, June 1987, pp. 38–42. Weinstein as much as admits in the interview that he colluded with the chief traders at Salomon Brothers and Goldman Sachs. Conversations with Steinhardt confirm that, as the biggest block trader on the buy side, he was part of the same circle.

42. "If he [the broker] had something coming, if he knew he had a huge seller, he would say to me, 'You know, it wouldn't be a bad thing for you to get short on blah blah blah.' Why would he want me to get short on blah blah? Because he had a huge seller and he knew, at some point, he was going to trade that stock down. And if he had me as a buyer covering my short, it would be good for him; it would be, almost certainly, good for me because I would be buying it lower." Steinhardt interview, October 4, 2007.

43. Ibid.

44. Ibid.

45. This calculation assumes that the odds of making a positive return in any given year are one in two. For a normal mutual fund, this assumption would be false: The stock market moves up in more years than it falls, so the odds of making a positive return are higher than that. But for a hedge fund that was both long and short, and that invested heavily in bonds, the assumption of one in two seems roughly fair.

46. "Steinhardt Fine Firm Agrees to Court Order in Seaboard Case," *Wall Street Journal*, April 23, 1976, p. 3.

47. To be sure, none of these reforms succeeded in eliminating the insider advantage. "It's impossible to disseminate information exactly homogeneously," Steinhardt says of the regulators' efforts. Steinhardt interview, September 10, 2007.

48. Anise C. Wallace, "Pullback at Block Trading Desks," *New York Times*, December 24, 1987, p. D1.

49. Dan Dorfman, "Sabbatical for a Superstar," *Esquire*, August 29, 1978, p. 12.

CHAPTER THREE: PAUL SAMUELSON'S SECRET

1. Justin Fox, *The Myth of the Rational Market: A History of Risk, Reward, and Delusion on Wall Street*, (New York: HarperCollins, 2009), p. 124.

2. Peter L. Bernstein, *Capital Ideas Evolving* (Hoboken, NJ: John Wiley & Sons, 2007), p. 113.

3. Samuelson explains, "Fama's theory of the random walk and mine are not the same. Mine is that there are no easy pickings. . . . If you read the numerous papers I have written on the efficient-market hypothesis, you will realize it is not a dogma. If you can get information early, before it is widespread, you can't help but get very rich." Paul Samuelson, interview with the author, February 5, 2008.

4. Bernstein, *Capital Ideas Evolving*, p. 143.

5. Explaining his investment with Buffett, Samuelson wrote, "Experience has persuaded me that there are a few Warren Buffetts out there with high rent-earning ability because they are good at figuring out which fundamentals are fundamental and which new data are worth paying high costs to get. Such super-stars don't come cheap: by the time you spot them their fee has been bid sky high!" See Paul A. Samuelson, foreword to Marshall E. Blume and Jeremy J. Siegel, "The Theory of Security Pricing and Market Structure," *Journal of Financial Markets, Institutions and Instruments* 1, no. 3 (1992): 1–2. For more on Samuelson's investment with Buffett, see Roger Lowenstein, *Buffett: The Making of an American Capitalist* (New York: Broadway Books, 2001), pp. 308–11.

6. The other outstanding example of an early quantitative firm is Princeton-Newport, created in 1969. For an entertaining account of Princeton-Newport, see William Poundstone, *Fortune's Formula: The Untold Story of the Scientific Betting System That Beat the Casinos and Wall Street* (New York: Hill and Wang, 2005).

7. My thanks to Jan Kunz, who worked for Commodities Corporation from its start and who provided me with a copy of the launch prospectus.

8. In 1964 Cootner published an influential book titled *The Random Character of Stock Market Prices*, which was a compilation of all the efficient-market papers published up until then.

9. The Apollo graduate was Morris Markovitz.

10. Many hedge funds that are marketed to investors that don't pay U.S. tax are legally structured as offshore corporations. Commodities Corporation was unusual in being an onshore corporation.

11. In a lecture delivered at Princeton University in May 1999, Weymar recalled, "I was particularly taken by the theme and role of the hero in the western canon. If one is contemplating heroism, it helps to be driven by existential angst, and mine was palpable during my 20's and 30's." F. Helmut Weymar, "Orange Juice, Cocoa, Speculation and Entrepreneurship" (Beckwith lecture at Princeton University, May 1999). I am grateful to Helmut Weymar for providing me with the text of the lecture. A former Commodities Corporation employee says bluntly: "Helmut wanted to be king of the world, basically. He got interested in art and then he stopped doing it because he thought, 'I'll never really make a splash in the art world.' So he did it because he needs and wants to be superior to others and be seen as superior to others."

12. F. Helmut Weymar, interview with the author, April 19, 2007.

13. Weymar interview; Weymar, "Orange Juice, Cocoa, Speculation and Entrepreneurship."

14. Weymar, "Orange Juice, Cocoa, Speculation and Entrepreneurship."

15. These descriptions of Weymar and Vannerson come from Jan Kunz, one of the start-up employees at Commodities Corporation (Jan Kunz, e-mail to the author, February 5, 2008), and from Irwin Rosenblum, the author of the autobiographical account *Up, Down, Up, Down, Up: My Career at Commodities Corporation* (Bloomington: Xlibris, 2003). I am grateful to Irwin Rosenblum and his book for this vignette and several other points in this chapter.

16. Weymar interview.

17. Commodities Corporation survived because Nabisco was keen to keep it in business in order to retain access to Weymar's cocoa forecasts and Vannerson's wheat forecasts. Nabisco was able to over-rule the other shareholders, which wanted to close the firm, because it held a senior claim on the remaining assets. In case of liquidation, Nabisco would have reclaimed its $500,000, leaving the other investors with only $400,000 of their original $2 million. Having been virtually wiped out, the other shareholders decided that there was little to be lost by allowing Commodities Corporation to continue trading. Weymar interview.

18. Ibid.

19. This quip is attributed to Frank Vannerson. Morris Markovitz, interview with the author, November 1, 2007.

20. Weymar recalls: "Valuable as market analysis and data generation may be, money management discipline is even more important to successful speculation. . . . Most successful speculative derivatives traders generate more losing trades than profitable trades. They are successful only because their gains on positive trades are substantially larger than their tightly controlled losses on negative trades." Weymar, "Orange Juice, Cocoa, Speculation and Entrepreneurship."

21. For example, Paul Tudor Jones began his hedge fund, Tudor, with the help of seed capital from Commodities Corporation. An official at Tudor recalls: "When we incubated young traders, when they came close to kickouts he [Paul Jones] would bring them into the office and say, 'You've got to write an analysis on why this happened and how it's not going to happen again.' He took that away from Commodities Corporation."

22. Weymar interview; Irwin Rosenblum, interview with the author, April 19, 2007. Rosenblum was responsible for implementing the new risk controls and describes them in his autobiography. See also Tully, "Princeton's Rich Commodity Scholars."

23. Elaine Crocker, who rose to become a senior manager at Commodities Corporation and later president of Moore Capital, recalls, "The kickout forced you to liquidate your positions and get out of the market for thirty days. During this period you would plot the history of your trades in the period leading up to your losses and see whether you had violated your own trading philosophy. Most of the time, the answer would be yes. The whole system allowed traders to develop an approach to markets that would work for them, but at the same time held them accountable for sticking to it." Elaine Crocker, interview with the author, July 30, 2008.

24. In the mid-1980s MIT information theorist Robert Fano wrote a paper questioning the random walk in stock prices. Colleagues warned him that submitting the article for publication in a peer-reviewed journal would get him branded a crackpot. See Poundstone, *Fortune's Formula*, pp. 127–28. Similarly, Scott Irwin, who published one of the first articles to affirm the existence of trends, vividly recalls the difficulty of getting such views published. Scott Irwin, interview with the author, February 14, 2008.

25. As Weymar put it, "Happily blessed by an inquiring and open mind, Frank overcame the bias of his Princeton economics training." Weymar, "Orange Juice, Cocoa, Speculation and Entrepreneurship." Vannerson himself notes, "The academics were slow to come around. I think currencies did it, where trends were so obvious a child could see them." Frank Vannerson, e-mail communication with the author, February 11, 2008.

26. Vannerson believes he was the first to create an automated trend-following system: "I am pretty sure I was the first to put the whole thing together." A similar system was developed a little later by Ed Seykota, a legendary trader at the brokerage Hayden Stone whom Vannerson remembers as a "friendly rival." (Frank Vannerson, e-mail communication with the author, October 28, 2007.) But

the truth may be that Vannerson created the second automated system. Dennis Dunn of Dunn & Hargitt recalls creating such a system in the late 1960s. (Dennis Dunn, e-mail communication with the author, February 25, 2008.) It's worth noting that *Fortune*'s excellent profile of Commodities Corporation, cited above, wrongly reported that TCS was invented after 1971.

27. Because of Weymar's mixed feelings, the company's launch prospectus mentioned the firm's research into price trends only in passing. Commodities Corporation aimed to market its superior knowledge of fundamentals, not its computerized trend following.

28. Recalling his status as the first non-PhD trader, Marcus says: "It created a certain amount of controversy. The whole idea was that this would be the best and brightest. I wouldn't have been hired if it wasn't for Amos pushing. Once I was hired, I wouldn't say that I faced considerable opposition. Some of their PhDs hadn't done as well as they had hoped." Michael Marcus, interview with the author, November 21, 2007.

29. Markovitz recalls, "Mike got a private jet. He wanted to have his wedding in Hawaii so [he] flew everyone out and put them up. He was a businessman, he would be cautious, he wouldn't waste it, but when it was for his own pleasure, his own enjoyment, life is short, you've got the money, spend it. It was pocket change to him, he might as well." Markovitz interview, February 5, 2008; Jack D. Schwager, *Market Wizards: Interviews with Top Traders* (New York: New York Institute of Finance, 1989), pp. 10 and 36.

30. Helmut Weymar, who commented on a draft of this chapter, objects that Marcus paid great attention to fundamentals, so that the shift away from Commodities Corporation's initial faith in fundamental analysis was less stark than I suggest here. (Helmut Weymar, personal communication with the author, August 1, 2008.) But there seems little doubt that in Weymar's initial trading the fundamentals dominated the chart following while in Marcus's trading the opposite was true. Marcus recalls: "The trend followers used to say that the fundamentals were embedded in the trend and that you could make more money if you waited until the fundamentals were being acted upon and causing a trend in one direction." (Marcus interview.) Note also Kovner's remark, later in this chapter, that the most profitable opportunities exist when there is no fundamental information. The contrast with the firm's founding prospectus, which emphasized econometric modeling and made no mention of trends, is fairly conclusive.

31. "You had advantages on the floor. Your advantage was that you knew a lot about the technical insides of one market. You could see who was buying, who was selling, how the orders were getting filled, where the stops were. The drawback was that you were pinned down to that market. If you were trading cotton, and soybeans were having a fabulous move, you would miss out. I later decided that you were better off giving up that technical advantage and having the opportunity to pick and choose among a number of markets." Marcus interview.

32. Ibid.

33. There were several libertarians at Commodities Corporation. Markovitz recalls: "There was a lot of the antiauthoritarian, libertarian sentiment. I think a lot of people in the business who weren't that way when they started became that way. I think it accelerates your awareness when you study the markets, analyze them, you see when the government interferes with the markets, ninety-nine times out of a hundred there is no benefit and it just creates problems." Markovitz interview, February 5, 2008.

34. Schwager, *Market Wizards*, pp. 19–20. On price controls and lumber, see also Barry Bosworth, "The Inflation Problem during Phase III," *American Economic Review* 64, no. 2, Papers and Proceedings of the Eighty-sixth Annual Meeting of the American Economic Association (May 1974): pp. 93–99; and William Poole, "Wage-Price Controls: Where Do We Go from Here?" *Brookings Papers on Economic Activity* 1973, no. 1 (1973), p. 292.

35. Jeffry A. Frieden, *Global Capitalism: Its Fall and Rise in the Twentieth Century* (New York: W. W. Norton & Co., 2006), p. 364.

36. Xue-Zhong He and Frank H. Westerhoff, "Commodity Markets, Price Limiters, and Speculative Price Dynamics," *Journal of Economic Dynamics & Control,* 29(9) (September 2005): 1,578.

37. Meanwhile, investors sought safety in gold, driving the price above $300 an ounce in the summer of 1979 and above $800 in the winter—a far cry from the $35 mandated by the Bretton Woods system.

38. Marcus interview, November 21, 2007.
39. Marcus recalls, "I remember being in Bermuda and trying to curtail the growth of big government. That fitted in with my libertarianism." (Marcus interview.) Markovitz also recalls clashing with Weymar at the Bermuda conference. The following years brought even more forceful efforts to get Weymar to curtail overhead. (Markovitz interviews.)
40. For example, a company that contracted with school systems to provide lunches reckoned it had no need to insure itself against a spike in food prices until 1973, when it suddenly lost money as its input costs skyrocketed; from that time on, it insured itself by locking in its costs via the futures market. See Roger W. Gray, "Risk Management in Commodity and Financial Markets," *American Journal of Agricultural Economics* 58, no. 2 (May 1976): pp. 280–85. The article also notes that after 1973, commodities markets experienced "unprecedented high hedging levels relative to speculation."
41. Commodities Corporation arranged this loophole with a grain wholesaler. Markovitz interview, November 1, 2007; Marcus interview.
42. Commodities Corporation traders studied the "White Book," a summary of the trading ideas of Amos Hostetter, a revered elder statesman at the company. Burton Rothberg, a trader who recalls the influence of the White Book, also emphasizes Vannerson's influence. "Commodities Corporation really learned that trends always go further than you think. There was a lot of mathematical work on this by Frank Vannerson, and we found that over the short term trends tended to continue at every level. The theory was that unless you had a really good reason, you want to stay with the trend." Burton Rothberg, interview with the author, February 5, 2008.
43. Richard J. Sweeney, "Beating the Foreign Exchange Market," *Journal of Finance* 41(1) (March1986), pp. 163–82; Louis P. Lukac, B. Wade Brorsen, and Scott H. Irwin, "A Test of Futures Market Disequilibrium Using Twelve Different Technical Trading Systems," *Applied Economics* 20, no. 5 (May 1988): pp. 623–39. These publications were followed by B. Wade Brorsen and Louis P. Lukac, "A Comprehensive Test of Futures Market Disequilibrium," *Financial Review* 25 (4) (November 1990): 593–622. Belief in the existence of momentum effects became mainstream with the publication of Narasimhan Jegadeesh and Sheridan Titman, "Returns to Buying Winners and Selling Losers: Implications for Stock Market Efficiency," *Journal of Finance,* vol. 48, no. 1, March 1993, pp. 65–91.
44. Irwin interview.
45. Marcus interview.
46. Philip Weiss, "George Soros's Right-Wing Twin," *New York,* July 24, 2005.
47. Marcus recalls: "At the time I met Bruce, he was driving a taxi part-time and trading part-time. I was astounded by the depth and breadth of his knowledge. I would try to come up with something esoteric and arcane that would impress him, and he was right there and knew about it and could talk about it. Here was a guy working part-time and driving a taxi, but he was a colleague already." Marcus interview.
48. Rosenblum, *Up, Down, Up, Down, Up,* p. 98.
49. Markovitz interviews.
50. Rosenblum, *Up, Down, Up, Down, Up,* p. 98. Recalling Marcus's prediction that Kovner would become the president of Commodities Corporation, Paul Samuelson says, "My comment was, 'Bruce Kovner couldn't afford to be president of Commodities Corporation.'" (Samuelson interview.) Rosenblum also remembers Kovner as follows: "He was extremely ambitious and had all the requisite skills needed to fulfill those ambitions. He was brilliant, verbal, and confident and possessed of a great deal of personal charm. Helmut was totally taken by him and like most people in the company, would go out of his way to please Bruce. Bruce became very close to Michael [Marcus] who took him under his wing and taught him a great deal about trading." (Rosenblum, *Up, Down, Up, Down, Up,* p. 52.) Meanwhile, Kovner himself says of Samuelson, "He was always delightful. He was rather bemused by the fact that there are people who make money in these markets." (Bruce Kovner, interview with the author, October 14, 2009.)
51. Kovner emphasizes that he regarded Weymar's original efforts to estimate the "efficient" price for a commodity as less fruitful than Marcus's efforts to judge the market's direction. Trying to come up with a point estimate for the right price of cocoa or anything else was difficult and potentially

dangerous, since it could lead to obstinacy in trading. "As a trader of a leveraged fund you had to be centrally concerned with path rather than end points." Kovner interview.

52. Roy Lennox, who was hired by Kovner as a trading associate in 1980, recalls, "When I got the job with Bruce, I called up his assistant for some reading suggestions before I started. One of the books he had her send me was about reading charts. I thought, 'Oh my god, I was taught in business school that charts don't work, that markets are efficient.' But then Bruce told me that charts are just representations of market psychology and therefore extremely valuable, and indeed indispensable, for trading." Roy Lennox, interview with the author, June 24, 2009.

53. Schwager, *Market Wizards,* p. 32.

54. Kovner interview; Lennox interview.

55. Burton Rothberg recalls, "There was an infusion of outside money in the late seventies, early eighties. Helmut was opposed to managing outside money, but guys like Bruce wanted to take the money. There was a little a revolt." (Rothberg interview.) Markovitz recalls, "We had been arguing for at least a year, a couple of years, about trading outside money. Helmut was nervous that once he let traders out of his control, they might leave." (Markovitz interview, February 5, 2008.)

56. Elaine Crocker recalls, "We tried to hire Paul but he didn't want that. When he came down to Princeton to meet Helmut, Helmut told him, 'Remember, you will lose money at some point.' Afterwards Paul wrote a thank you letter, claiming that he had paid for dinner and been told he would lose money." Crocker interview.

57. Commodities Corporation continued for many years, eventually being absorbed into Goldman Sachs in 1997. But its heyday ended in the early 1980s. The firm lost money on trading in 1981, but Weymar allowed administrative expenses to grow unsustainably, from $15 million in 1981 to $23 million in 1982 to $27 million in 1983. See Rosenblum, *Up, Down, Up, Down, Up,* pp. 102 and 106–7.

CHAPTER FOUR: THE ALCHEMIST

1. The historian was Ralf Dahrendorf, director of the LSE between 1974 and 1984. This description of the climate at LSE and Soros's early life is taken from the excellent Michael T. Kaufman, *Soros: The Life and Times of a Messianic Billionaire* (New York: Knopf, 2002).

2. Soros reckoned he needed $500,000. Ibid., p. 83.

3. Soros also knew Steinhardt, Fine, and Berkowitz, who had set up their hedge fund two years earlier, in 1967. But A. W. Jones was the chief role model: "Double Eagle was modeled after AW Jones," Soros recalls. Soros's exposure to A. W. Jones was reinforced by the fact that his junior partner, Jim Rogers, had worked for Neuberger & Berman, A. W. Jones's main broker. George Soros, interview with the author, January 16, 2008; Jim Rogers, interview with the author, November 20, 2007. See also John Train, *The New Money Masters* (New York: Harper & Row, 1989), p. 17.

4. Soros comments, "The key to reflexivity is a misconception of reality, and this is where the fundamental misconception of economic theory comes in. The theory is that people act in their self-interest, but the fact is that they act in what they perceive to be their self-interest, and their best interest is not necessarily what they believe is in their best interest." Soros interview.

5. Soros's investment note, "The Case for Mortgage Trusts," is reprinted in *The Alchemy of Finance* and explains the reflexive logic of the investment trusts, as follows: Suppose a trust starts with 10 shares worth $10 each and earns $12 of income on total capital of $100. Seeing that high yield, five new investors pay $20 each for a share in the trust, so that the investment fund now has capital of $200. Assuming that the trust puts the new capital to work as efficiently as the first tranche, the trust will now have $24 in earnings to split among fifteen shareholders. Per share earnings will have gone up from $1.20 initially to $1.60 after the new capital injection. See George Soros, *The Alchemy of Finance* (Hoboken, NJ: John Wiley & Sons 1987), pp. 64–67. In another example of the application of reflexive thinking to markets, Soros observed that acquisitive conglomerates that knew how to talk up their stock price would soon be on a roll: The strong stock price would empower them to pay for acquisitions using their newly valuable equity; the acquisitions would mean higher earnings and an even stronger stock price; the cycle would repeat itself. (Ibid., p. 59.)

6. Rogers recalled that when he attended Oxford he was surrounded by Americans who wanted to become president. He wanted instead to invest all over the world—to be a "gnome of Zurich." (Rogers interview.) After leaving Soros in 1980, Rogers became known as a commodities guru and as the author of the book *Investment Biker*.

7. George Soros, interview with the author, June 10, 2008. See also Robert Slater, *Soros: The Unauthorized Biography, the Life, Times and Trading Secrets of the World's Greatest Investor* (New York: McGraw-Hill, 1996), p. 78.

8. Soros interview, January 16, 2008.

9. George Soros, *Soros on Soros: Staying Ahead of the Curve* (New York: John Wiley & Sons, 1995), p. 49. Soros adds, "If a story is interesting enough, one can probably make money buying it even if further investigation would reveal flaws. Then later, if you discern the flaw, you feel good, because you are ahead of the game. So I used to say, 'Jump in with both feet; take one out later.'" Soros interview, June 10, 2008.

10. Anise Wallace, "The World's Greatest Money Manager," *Institutional Investor*, June 1981, pp. 39–45.

11. Soros, *The Alchemy of Finance*, p. 42.

12. Ibid., p. 372.

13. Ibid., pp. 39, 42, and 372.

14. There is some dispute about the responsibility for the deterioration in the relationship between Soros and Rogers. In his unauthorized biography of Soros, cited above, Robert Slater suggests that Soros was a poor judge of character and incapable of recognizing the achievements of subordinates. There may be some truth to this, particularly since Soros's break with Rogers came at a time when Soros was undergoing a broader emotional reorientation, which involved divorce and visits to a psychotherapist. But Henry Arnhold, head of the firm for which Soros and Rogers launched the Double Eagle Fund, remembers Rogers as by far the more difficult member of the duo. (Henry Arnhold, interview with the author, February 27, 2008.) Having encountered both Rogers and Soros, the author is inclined to go with Arnhold's version.

15. The performance of the Quantum Fund in the years to 1985 is given in Soros, *The Alchemy of Finance*, p. 150.

16. Soros, *Soros on Soros*, pp. 56–57.

17. Not all economists believed that currencies tended toward equilibrium. The most influential paper to argue for exchange-rate overshooting was "Expectations and Exchange Rate Dynamics," by Rudiger Dornbusch of MIT, published in 1976 in the *Journal of Political Economy*. Dornbusch's argument did not hinge on the trend following by speculators that Soros emphasized; instead, he explained that currencies overshoot in response to monetary shocks because of the interplay between sticky prices for goods and fast-adjusting capital markets. However, Dornbusch's sticky-price assumption was a minority view within academic macroeconomics through the 1980s. On this point, see Kenneth Rogoff, "Dornbusch's Overshooting Model After Twenty-Five Years," IMF Working Paper No. 02/39. Presented at the Second Annual Research Conference, International Monetary Fund (Mundell-Fleming Lecture), November 30, 2001, revised January 22, 2002. Given that Dornbusch represented a minority view, Soros was not attacking a straw man. On the other hand, other hedge-fund managers were won over to Soros's view. As described in chapter seven, Stanley Druckenmiller found Soros's view of currencies valuable after the fall of the Berlin wall. See Jack D. Schwager, *The New Market Wizards: Conversations with America's Top Traders* (New York: HarperCollins, 1992), p. 203.

18. Soros also argued that economists tended to exaggerate the extent to which shifts in interest rates would help to drive currencies to equilibrium. If the United States ran a trade deficit, this implied a relatively low demand for investment capital and hence low interest rates; speculators would shift money out of dollars to currencies that yielded more, so weakening the dollar and helping to reduce the trade deficit. But in practice speculators cared less about the interest they could earn on dollars than about the dollar's trend. Thus, in November 1984, a fall in U.S. interest rates had been followed after a short pause by a jump in the dollar. The market's logic was that if the dollar did not drop in response to falling interest rates, the upward trend must be robust and it was time to buy the life out of the currency.

19. In this conclusion, Soros anticipated the views of the economics profession. Writing in 2002, Kenneth Rogoff, a Harvard professor then serving as the International Monetary Fund's chief economist, commented, "If there is a consensus result in the empirical literature, it has to be that nothing, but nothing, can systematically explain exchange rates between major currencies with flexible exchange rates." See Rogoff, "Dornbusch's Overshooting Model."

20. Soros noted the stock market's weakness as a reason to short the dollar and noted that other currencies were testing the upper limits of their trading ranges, suggesting that a breakout might be coming. Soros, *The Alchemy of Finance*, pp. 155–56.

21. Ibid., p. 149. Soros loosely observed a rule that enforced some risk control: He took more risk with his recent profits than with his capital. This might sound peculiar: Capital merely represents previous years' profits, so why protect it more cautiously than profits earned recently? But Soros's rule encouraged big risk taking in years when he had performed well, while forcing a cooler approach at times when he was weaker. If the performance of traders exhibits trends, the Soros rule had the effect of encouraging risk taking in periods when he was in sync with the markets. Likewise, the risk-control system at Commodities Corporation reined traders in once they lost a certain percentage of their capital.

22. "We had someone in for lunch in George's private dining room, upstairs on thirty-three, and something connected and he immediately just went over and picked up the phone and told the trader to put on a position. . . . He could completely reverse himself." (Gary Gladstein, interview with the author, March 18, 2008.) Gladstein joined Soros Fund Management in 1985 and was managing director from 1989 until 1999.

23. Soros confesses that he hung on to his dollar shorts by the skin of his teeth. Soros, *The Alchemy of Finance*, p. 163.

24. Some critics wonder whether Soros was tipped off about Plaza, perhaps by banking sources in Europe. But the fact that Soros bought yen massively after the announcement proves that he did not see the Plaza accord coming.

25. "This was like the biggest move they had ever seen in their entire life. So they were obviously all taking a profit, selling the yen. And this was a man who I worked for for twelve years, I never heard him raise his voice, never heard him swear. You'd only have to be in a room with me about an hour to see either of those events occur. And apparently he raised his voice, he was just furious that these guys were selling the yen and he just had them transfer all the yen over to his account rather than sell them." (Stanley Druckenmiller, interview with the author, March 13, 2008.) Druckenmiller got the story from Steve Okin, a trader who worked for Soros at the time and later worked for Druckenmiller. Druckenmiller also tells the story in Schwager, *The New Market Wizards*, p. 208.

26. Druckenmiller comments, "People want to feel good about themselves and feel they have a win. But this is when you really, really want to pile on. You can't have enough." Druckenmiller interview.

27. These yen and German mark accumulations are over the baseline established on September 6, 1985, the date of the previous diary entry. However, the buying seems to have occurred in the five days after Plaza. See Soros, *The Alchemy of Finance*, p. 164.

28. Soros suggests that his political antennae were an important part of his edge. "It's easier, in a way, to understand the mentality of the authorities than it is to understand the market, because the market is more anonymous. . . . So I would say, perhaps, that my application of boom-bust thinking has been in understanding how the authorities are acting more than the market itself." (Soros interview, January 16, 2008.) Moreover, Soros knew political leaders as well as economic officials. Richard Medley, who later worked for Soros, organized a conference featuring top policy makers from the Plaza-accord countries in Washington in November 1985. Medley recalls getting a call from Senator Bradley, who insisted that Soros be allowed to attend, even though the conference was oversubscribed. (Richard Medley, interview with the author, January 14, 2008.) Gary Gladstein emphasizes the usefulness of Soros's contacts with Quantum backers in Europe: "The board of Quantum was primarily European private bankers. They were very well connected, very well respected, and from time to time I know George would call them and ask them their thoughts." (Gladstein interview.)

29. The additional buying took place between September 27 and December 6. Soros, *The Alchemy of Finance*, pp. 164 and 177.

30. Ibid., p. 176. Indeed, Gary Gladstein, who joined Soros's firm in October to serve as chief administrative officer, was astonished by the leverage in his new firm's portfolio. Gladstein interview.
31. Soros, *The Alchemy of Finance*, p. 309.
32. Soros, *Soros on Soros*, p. 59. Soros pointed out that Quantum's return over the full fifteen months of the experiment, which included a "control period" in 1986, came to 114 percent.
33. Anatole Kaletsky, "Thursday Book Review: The Alchemy of Finance," *Financial Times*, July 16, 1987, p. 20.
34. Paul Tudor Jones recalls that the range of factors that Soros blended together was a revelation. "George Soros is one of the most profound thinkers in the markets. The book was a highly intricate piece of analytics. Looking at the interlocking relationships. He knitted things together; it was an education." (Paul Jones, interview with the author, April 23, 2009.) Jim Chanos, a celebrated short seller, is another money manager who believes *Alchemy* was a milestone. The book "really went into the whole feedback loop on perceptions and how they are important in the marketplace. For the first time he put in what traders knew to be true, but in a framework that you could think about; that you could debate and test." (Jim Chanos, interview with the author, February 6, 2008.) Equally, Scott Bessent, who later worked for Soros, recalls his reaction to the book: "I remember, I'm twenty-five and I read this and couldn't believe someone would invest this way. You would have some of these and these, short some of those. His risk management was in his head. No fund-of-funds person would have given him any money." (Scott Bessent, interview with the author, January 18, 2008.)
35. Paul Tudor Jones II, foreword to the first edition of *The Alchemy of Finance*, p. xvi.
36. Jim Chanos, who operated out of Soros's offices in the late 1980s, recalls, "It was the quietest place you've ever heard. The most raucous you heard was during lunch, when people yelled at the cook for making jerk chicken for the second time that week. . . . Steinhardt was much different. People screaming. Michael firing people. It was truly a different atmosphere." Jim Chanos interview.
37. John J. Curran, "Are Stocks Too High?" *Fortune*, September 28, 1987, p. 28.
38. James B. Stewart and Daniel Hertzberg, "Before the Fall," *Wall Street Journal*, December 11, 1987, p. 1.
39. Druckenmiller interview.
40. The Ways and Means Committee of the U.S. House of Representatives was considering legislation to eliminate the tax deductions for some interest expenses and to tax "greenmail"—payments made by companies to corporate raiders to buy back their stock at above-market prices to prevent the raider from taking over the company. See Mark Carlson, "A Brief History of the 1987 Stock Market Crash with a Discussion of the Federal Reserve Response" (Federal Reserve discussion paper, November 2006).
41. Soros, *Soros on Soros*, p. 60. In conversation with the author, Soros reaffirmed, "I came out and the market had fallen, and I said to myself that I should have been following the market. Had I done that I would have lightened up." Soros interview, January 16, 2008.
42. Druckenmiller interview.
43. Schwager, *The New Market Wizards*, p. 199.
44. Druckenmiller interview.
45. The Wall Streeter was Muriel Siebert of Siebert Financial. Quoted in Corey Hajim and Jia Lynn Yang, "Remembering Black Monday," *Fortune*, September 17, 2007, p.134.
46. Medley interview.
47. Druckenmiller interview.
48. This interchange is presented as told by Druckenmiller, who describes it as "a very clear recollection." Druckenmiller interview.
49. This is Druckenmiller's own expression. Druckenmiller interview.
50. This is the conversation as recounted by Druckenmiller.
51. Druckenmiller recalls, "To my horror, I picked up the *Barron's* Sunday morning and it turns out he was the guy who was selling his position." Druckenmiller interview.
52. One London lender, which held stocks belonging to Quantum as security against a loan, came close to triggering a crisis by refusing to release any of them even though it was sitting on more collateral than the loan covenant demanded. (Robert Miller, interview with the author, March 7, 2008.) It was Miller's job to manage Quantum's relationships with its bankers.

53. Soros interview, January 16, 2008.

54. "A Bad Two Weeks—A Wall Street Star Loses $840 Million," *Barron's*, November 2, 1987.

55. Gary Gladstein, interview with the author, March 18, 2008.

56. Michael Steinhardt, *No Bull: My Life In and Out of Markets* (New York: John Wiley & Sons, 2001), p. 176.

57. Ivan Fallon, "Quantum Loss," *Times* (London), November 15, 1987.

58. Howard Banks, "Cover Boy," ed. Gretchen Morgenson, *Forbes*, November 30, 1987, p. 12.

59. In 1981 Steinhardt announced his arrival in the bond market by borrowing nearly three times the value of his fund and betting that interest rates would soon come down; when the bet came good the following year, the result was a spectacular 78 percent return for Steinhardt and his partners.

60. Paul Tudor Jones, who came out of the commodity tradition, described *Alchemy* as "a revolutionary book. Remember, this was the period when trend following . . . [was] the vogue in investing. It was the time when technical analysis . . . reached its zenith. . . . [But] an intellectual framework for understanding the course of social, political, and economic events was noticeably forgotten." (Jones, foreword to Soros, *The Alchemy of Finance*, p. xv.) Meanwhile, Stanley Druckenmiller, who came out of the equity tradition, was struck by *Alchemy* for the opposite reasons: Soros broke with the nostrums of fundamental analysis and was ready to buy and sell on technical signals. (Druckenmiller interview.) Soros himself noted that "the Quantum Fund combines some of the features of a stock market fund with those of a commodity fund." (Soros, *The Alchemy of Finance*, p. 149.)

61. There was also a fusion between macro investing and micro investing. Hedge-fund investors who looked at the overall economy and those who looked at specific stocks borrowed each other's tricks, with varying success. For example, Mark Dalton, the president of Paul Tudor Jones's firm, recalls conversations between Tudor and Julian Robertson's Tiger in the late 1980s and early 1990s. "We had a series of conversations probably over three or four years. . . . I think it probably influenced both of us. . . . Clearly we recognized that the complementary analytical capabilities and information flow of long-short equity to macro could be very helpful." Mark Dalton, interview with the author, September 29, 2008.

62. Donald MacKenzie, *An Engine, Not a Camera: How Financial Models Shape Markets* (Cambridge, MA: The MIT Press, 2006), p. 206.

63. Ibid., p. 193.

64. Moreover, much of the market's trouble came from the breakdown of its back-office systems, which caused markets to seize up and exacerbated the panic. Portfolio insurance was far from being the sole culprit.

65. Soros, *The Alchemy of Finance*, p. 5.

66. MacKenzie, *An Engine, Not a Camera*, p. 114.

67. Ibid., p. 115.

68. In the mid-1970s, the stocks of small firms had been found to outperform those of big firms; and later researchers discovered that outperformance was concentrated in the first two weeks of January. Both findings appeared to damage the efficient-market theory, since returns were not supposed to reflect firm size or the vagaries of the calendar. But once the small-firm effect and the January effect became known, speculators pounced and they were arbitraged away. Just as the theorists predicted, a handful of well-informed investors had pushed prices to their efficient level. In 2002, G. William Schwert found that the small-firm effect had disappeared and that the January effect had halved since its identification. See G. William Schwert, "Anomalies and Market Efficiency" (working paper 9277, National Bureau of Economic Research, 2002).

CHAPTER FIVE: TOP CAT

1. This account of the Jensen-Buffett debate comes from Roger Lowenstein, *Buffett: The Making of an American Capitalist* (New York: Broadway Books, 2001), p. 316–18, and from the text of Buffett's speech, reprinted as "The Superinvestors of Graham-and-Doddsville," in *Hermes*, the Columbia Business School Magazine.

2. Buffett emphasized the point that the Grahamites had built their records independently. If they had just been copying one another, their similar returns would not have proved anything.

3. The account of Julian Robertson in this chapter and later in the book is based primarily on some twenty-five hours of conversation with twelve former or current employees, most of whom do not want to be identified. In addition, it is based on the voluminous and colorful letters that Robertson wrote to his investors between 1980 and 2000. I am grateful to Julian Robertson for allowing me to read the full set of these letters and for granting me an extensive interview.

4. George Soros (not the source of the Louis Bacon anecdotes) reflected on the loneliness and objectivity of the trader: "My philanthropy rescued me from the isolation to which my pursuit of profit consigned me. . . . In most social situations—in politics and in personal and business relations—it is possible to deceive oneself and others. In the financial markets, the actual results do not leave much room for illusions." George Soros, *The Alchemy of Finance* (Hoboken, NJ: John Wiley & Sons, 1987), p. 43.

5. Robert L. Burch, e-mail communication with the author, May 18, 2007.

6. Thorpe McKenzie, interview with the author, August 15, 2008; Thorpe McKenzie, e-mail communication with the author, October 8, 2009.

7. Robertson made gestures toward delegation, but these were hollow. Dwight Anderson, a former analyst, says publicly what his ex-colleagues confirm privately: "Everyone at Tiger was really just an analyst—Julian was the only portfolio manager." Quoted in Steven Drobny, *Inside the House of Money* (Hoboken, NJ: John Wiley & Sons, 2006), p. 253.

8. Thorpe McKenzie, Robertson's colleague at Kidder Peabody in the 1970s and his junior partner in setting up Tiger, recalls Robertson's invoking A. W. Jones. "Julian always said that if you did not know whether the market was going to go up or down, A. W. Jones had said that you could still get out and pick stocks to go long and short. That was one of the first things Julian ever said to me." McKenzie interview.

9. Julian H. Robertson, letter to the limited partners, March 8, 1983.

10. For example, Robertson bought puts on the S&P 500 in 1985. In a letter to his limited partners, he explained: "Most banks and investment advisory concerns would throw up their hands at the use of such 'speculative' options. In reality though, what could be more conservative?" Julian H. Robertson, letter to the limited partners, July 1, 1985. It's interesting to note that around the same time, Warren Buffett was ridiculing derivatives and proposing a 100 percent tax on profits from them.

11. Julian H. Robertson, letter to the limited partners, March 30, 2000.

12. Julian H. Robertson, letter to Robert A. Karr, February 17, 1995.

13. Daniel A. Strachman, *Julian Robertson: A Tiger in a Land of Bulls and Bears* (Hoboken, NJ: John Wiley & Sons, 2004), p. 62.

14. Between 1980 and 1997, Tiger beat the S&P 500 index in fourteen out of eighteen years. In this period his balance of short and long positions varied. But in late 1987, for example, Robertson's portfolio was less than 70 percent net long, meaning that it would capture only about two thirds of the rise of the market index. No matter: The S&P 500 rose 16.6 percent the following year, while Tiger rose 21.6 percent. Some time later, in April 1994, Robertson informed his investors that Tiger was 50 percent net long, adding that this was about average for Tiger over the previous several years. Julian H. Robertson, letter to the limited partners, April 8, 1994.

15. It can be argued that stock in small companies is relatively likely to be owned by founders or directors, who may sell in order to realize wealth—providing buyers such as Tiger with an easy bargain. On the other hand, insiders who sell stock sometimes have an informational advantage over buyers.

16. Maggie Mahar. *Bull!: A History of the Boom and Bust, 1982–2004* (New York: HarperBusiness, 2004), p. 56.

17. Julian Robertson, interview with the author, December 12, 2007.

18. Julian H. Robertson, letter to the limited partners, January 17, 1985.

19. Katherine Burton, *Hedge Hunters: Hedge Fund Masters on the Rewards, the Risks, and the Reckoning* (New York: Bloomberg Press, 2007), p. 4.

20. Julie Dalla-Costa, "Tigers . . . Together?" *Absolute Return*, July/August 2008, p. 29.

21. A former Tiger employee recalls, "The thing that was special about him was that he was extremely symmetrical. If he thought you hadn't done your homework, or that your analysis was flawed, he

would be very aggressive, very confrontational. Symmetrically, though, if he thought you had done exceptional work or were generating exceptional outcomes he would lavish you with praise, and publicly. You were his big tiger." Robertson's habit of calling ideas either the best ever or the worst ever is described by several former Tiger analysts.

22. A Tiger alum recalls, "Julian sat in the center of the L. It was just a blast. We were all close to one another, and Julian was right there. We all overheard each other's conversations. It was just a constant flow of information and ideas. And you had one of the greatest investors ever right there. It was just fun every day." Another Tiger recalls, "There was no notion of privacy. You expected to get in early, seven A.M., and leave at five P.M. During that time, you were on. No personal phone calls. You were talking about companies, ideas, industries, news. Julian was loud. You could hear every conversation."

23. One former Tiger employee recalls, "I came in with a short idea and he said, 'Well, you know, my friend so-and-so is the biggest bull on that stock.' We'd have a bull-bear debate. He'd get the guy on the phone. I'd say what I thought; he would say what he thought. Julian made the decision."

24. The White-House-to-shit-house recruit was Lou Ricciardelli.

25. "The first time I met Paul I don't think he had much money at all. We had a friend, a mutual accountant. I'm convinced the reason he invested with me was because we were both baseball nuts." Robertson interview.

26. Asked about getting ideas from the partners, Robertson says, "We really encouraged that. . . . We called on them a lot." (Robertson interview.) A former Tiger employee recalls that in 1986 Tiger created a new fund called Puma partly in order to be able to take money from chief executives and other well-connected businesspeople. "People like that we really wanted in the fund," this source says. Regulators had raised questions about hedge funds' access to information from well-placed investors during the flurry of inquiries in the late 1960s, but no rule was ever promulgated to obstruct this channel. Company executives and directors are free to recommend their stock to hedge funds or anyone else so long as they do not disclose inside information.

27. A Tiger alum recalls, "He could come into a meeting where you kind of thought, 'I'm glad the boss is coming so the management team gets to see the guy who runs the place, but it's not like we've talked about this sector lately. I wonder what he's going to know.' And it was uncanny what he would know."

28. Jim Chanos, interview with the author, May 29, 2007; Jim Chanos, e-mail communication with the author, August 6, 2008.

29. Julie Rohrer, "The Red-Hot World of Julian Robertson," *Institutional Investor*, May 1986, p. 134.

30. Robertson wrote to his investors in 1985 that the generic stocks were a sure win, despite what they had cost him in the past few months. "I feel so confident that mentally, I am almost accruing future profits from our past losses." Julian H. Robertson, letter to the limited partners, May 25, 1985.

31. John Griffin, speech to 100 Women in Hedge Funds on behalf of iMentor, November 14, 2007.

32. Strachman, *Julian Robertson*, p. 200.

33. A Tiger veteran sums up the sense of separation between Tiger and traditional fund managers. "It was us and them. They were the mutual funds, the dumb money, the indexed money, the money that didn't care. We looked at what we were doing as so different. It was paid for performance. It was going short and long. It was using leverage. And the returns were there. We went at it each year thinking we could make thirty or forty percent. We would go for it."

34. Julian H. Robertson, letter to the limited partners, February 4, 1991.

35. "John and I, we used to compete viciously on the tennis court all over the world." Robertson interview.

36. Julian H. Robertson, letter to the limited partners, February 4, 1991.

37. Gary Weiss, "The World's Best Money Manager—What You Can Learn from Julian Robertson," *Business Week Assets*, November/December 1990.

38. Julian H. Robertson, letter to the limited partners, February 4, 1991.

39. This is the conversation as recalled by John Griffin and Julian Robertson.

40. Julian H. Robertson, letter to the limited partners, November 10, 1994.

41. Rohrer, "The Red-Hot World of Julian Robertson," p. 134. In another interview in 1996 Robertson lamented that Soros could get an appointment with Hans Tietmeyer, the president of the Bundesbank,

at a moment's notice, whereas Robertson had to hustle for an audience. (Gary Weiss, "Fall of the Wizard," *BusinessWeek*, April 1, 1996.) A hedge-fund manager who knows Robertson comments, "To my mind Julian always had this inferiority complex that he wanted to be Soros. It was kind of like Morgan Stanley versus Goldman Sachs. He would run around being Macro Man so he could be like George."

42. The difficulty of finding stocks in which Tiger could take financially meaningful positions frustrated some Tiger analysts and contributed to defections. See, for example, Dwight Anderson's complaint: "The entire universe of stocks that I could invest in had collapsed to about 20 names." (Quoted in Drobny, *Inside the House of Money*, pp. 251–52.) It is notable that most Tiger cubs have tried to control the growth of their funds, though the manageable ceiling for long/short equity funds has risen as markets have grown deeper and more liquid.

43. "Japan remains a fertile hunting ground for both longs and shorts, opportunities resulting from a lack of real analysis, and a market psychology that ignores fundamental valuations." Julian H. Robertson, letter to the limited partners, September 9, 1992.

44. Tim Schilt, internal memo to Tiger staff, August 21, 1995.

45. The day after the Plaza accord, Robertson's dollar-related bets netted $8.3 million, his best haul in a single day, though still less than the $30 million that Soros pocketed that Monday. Rohrer, "The Red-Hot World of Julian Robertson," p. 134.

46. Robertson himself wrote to his partners, "Druckenmiller's, Jones's, and Soros's grasp of macro economics is in another league from mine." (Julian H. Robertson, letter to the limited partners, April 5, 1991.) Speaking somewhat tactfully, the former Tiger commodity analyst Dwight Anderson has said: "In stocks, Julian had enough experience to have a great filter, but in commodities and macro, because he didn't have 40 years of experience, he relied more on his analysts to guide him." (Drobny, *Inside the House of Money*, p. 250.)

47. Arnold Snider, Tiger's drug-stock analyst, went out on his own in late 1993. The next three years were marked by a series of high-profile departures.

48. This episode is reconstructed from conversations with three eyewitnesses.

CHAPTER SIX: ROCK-AND-ROLL COWBOY

1. In 1984 a survey carried out by Sandra Manske of Tremont Partners identified only sixty-eight hedge funds, leading to the estimate that the number of funds extant at any one time in the 1973–87 period was under one hundred. The numbers quoted for 1990 and 1992 come from Hedge Fund Research.

2. A table published in *Forbes* identified ten hedge funds with assets of more than $1 billion—there were the Big Three, the Commodities Corporation trio, and four others: Odyssey Partners, managed by Leon Levy and Jack Nash; Omega Partners, managed by Leon Cooperman; Ardsley Partners, managed by Philip Hempleman; and John W. Henry, managed by the eponymous John Henry. See Dyan Machan and Riva Atlas, "George Soros, meet A. W. Jones," *Forbes*, January 17, 1994.

3. The story comes from John Porter, who worked at Louis Bacon's Moore Capital. See Steven Drobny, *Inside the House of Money: Top Hedge Fund Traders on Profiting in the Global Markets* (Hoboken, NJ: John Wiley & Sons, 2006), p. 145. Equally, in an interview in 1987 with *Barron's*, Jones said: "News is overrated in markets. . . . Futures markets react to new developments too quickly for news to matter, and one must remember the truism that price makes news and not vice versa." See Jonathan R. Laing, "Trader with a Hot Hand—That's Paul Tudor Jones II," *Barron's*, June 15, 1987.

4. A longtime colleague of Jones says, "What Paul will tell you is that he makes his money, for thirty years without a losing year, assessing human reaction. There's a body of information and he assesses human reaction with respect to this information. Fear and hope . . . that's the whole business." Another former Jones colleague says, "There's a skill set which I think he has in abundance, which is to have a feel for the market. By looking at prices and talking to people, he would know how prices would behave, how many people are in the same position. He would know, for example, if a lot of people own the same position, in which case if things reverse they could suddenly get very ugly very quickly."

5. A former pit trader describes the Jones technique as follows. "Say you notice that one of the traders is long two thousand contracts. He is an individual and he is speculating. If the market starts falling

hard, he is going to have to get out, because you understand his risk psychology. So if you have a big order, you wait for a quiet time in the pit, then you go into the middle of the pit and start screaming as loud as you can that you are ready to sell in huge quantity. It is like yelling fire in a movie theater. You start a panic. You get the market going down, everyone is starting to sell, and then when this crescendos, you buy back whatever you sold at the start and more, thereby completing your order."

6. Scott McMurray, "Quotron Man: Paul Tudor Jones II Swaggers and Profits Through Futures Pits," *Wall Street Journal*, May 10, 1988. See also Stephen Taub, David Carey, Amy Barrett, Richard J. Coletti, and Jackie Gold, "The Wall Street 100," *Financial World*, July 10, 1990, p. 56.

7. *Trader: The Documentary*, 1987, Glyn/Net Inc.

8. In one example of Jones's loose grip on the causes of his own success, analysis by Commodities Corporation, which had seeded Jones, determined that he tended to lose money on cotton, the market he believed he knew best. When the Commodities Corporation analysis was presented to Jones, he had difficulty accepting it.

9. A 1987 profile in *Barron's* reports: "And a year ago in April, Jones's research chief, 27-year-old Peter Borish, decided to start tracking daily the bull market of the twenties against the post-1982 bull market. He admits to fudging the exercise somewhat by juggling the starting periods. As a Monday-morning quarterback, he could see that starting the twenties countdown in February 1925 and the eighties market in October of 1982, he got a particularly snug fit. 'It wasn't totally unfair,' Borish observes, 'because the starting points had some historic parallels as both occurred four years after serious sentiment lows—the 1921 recession and the 1979 Carter financial crisis.'" Jonathan R. Laing, "Trader with a Hot Hand—That's Paul Tudor Jones II," *Barron's*, June 15, 1987.

10. In June 1987, *Barron's* reported that Borish expected the crash to come in February 1988. (See Laing, "Trader with a Hot Hand.") In the *Trader* documentary, filmed in 1986 and 1987, Borish had predicted that the crash would occur in March 1988. Jones's own predictions of the aftermath of the crash were even further off the mark. In the *Trader* documentary, he forecasts that it will take six to eight years after the crash for the economy to recover.

11. Jack D. Schwager, *Market Wizards: Interviews with Top Traders* (New York: New York Institute of Finance, 1989), p. 130.

12. In 1987 Jones told *Barron's*, "Prechter has become such a powerful market force because of his incredible track record that we decided to fade him. For the same reason, he'll probably be long at the all-time top." Laing, "Trader with a Hot Hand."

13. The quote comes from the *Trader* documentary. Jones also said, "I consider myself a premier market opportunist. That means I develop an idea on the market and pursue it from a very low risk standpoint until I have repeatedly been proven wrong, or until I change my viewpoint." See Schwager, *Market Wizards*, p. 129. Putting Jones's theorizing about Elliott waves further into perspective, Jones says, "The whole concept of the investment manager sitting up there and making all these incredible intellectual decisions about which way the market's going to go. I don't want that guy running my money because he doesn't have the competitive nature that's necessary to be a winner in this game."

14. Elaborating on how he would write a script for the market, Jones says, "I put myself in the mental position of being short the market, and I think how I would react emotionally to different events and see what it would take to get me to take my position off. And I write that down and that will be the high for the day. Because the high for the day will be the point at which the shorts capitulate. I close my eyes and imagine myself long. I say, 'Okay, where is the point I get nervous? Where would I say, "Oh my God, I have to get out?"' And that would be my projected low for the day. That preparation is important to try to determine great entry points to buy and to sell. You know every single high and low is going to be made in the context of these emotional extremes being hit. Execution is fifty percent of the game." Paul Tudor Jones, interview with the author, April 23, 2009.

15. A former Tiger recalls, "Paul Tudor Jones is a trader. In 1987 we were very aware of the risks in the market, both of us. When the crash came, Jones made a lot of money. He came in to breakfast at Tiger in the summer of 1987. Talked about momentum and technicals and trading. Julian had no

space in his mental map for that. We were saying, 'Japan and U.S. are overvalued.' Paul was saying, 'Technically, it looks like there is a fall coming.' He talked to us about us potentially managing a short-only book for him. We passed on it. But we shared the same sense of risk from very different origins."

16. Sushil Wadhwani, who worked for Jones in the 1990s, emphasizes his flexibility as a trader. "You'd talk to Paul in the morning his time and he'd be long something. The next day, that market would have gone down and you would fear he had lost money, but when you spoke to him again you would find that he had changed his mind and had gone from long to short. That's tremendous flexibility. It's very important in this game that one doesn't get hung up and anchored to a view." (Drobny, *Inside the House of Money*, p. 171.) Equally, Louis Bacon emphasizes the distinction between commodity traders and equity traders. In one investor letter, Bacon wrote: "Those traders with a futures background are more 'sensitive' to market action, whereas value-based equity traders are trained to react less to the market and focus much more on their assessment of a company's or situation's viability." (Riva Atlas, "Macro, Macro Man," *Institutional Investor*, vol. 34, no. 7, July 2000, pp. 44–56.)

17. Speaking of the crash of 1987, Jones says: "There was a tremendous embedded derivatives accident waiting to happen in the crash of '87 because there was something in the market at that time called portfolio insurance that essentially meant that when stocks started to go down it was going to create more selling because the people who had written these derivatives would be forced to sell on every down-tick. So it was a situation where you knew that if you ever got to a point where the market started to go down that the selling would actually cascade instead of dry up because of the measure of these derivative instruments that had been written." Paul Tudor Jones II, interview by Joel Ramin, January 13, 2000, available at http://chinese-school.netfirms.com/Paul-Tudor-Jones-interview.html.

18. Louis Bacon, interview with the author, July 21, 2009.

19. Jack D. Schwager, *Market Wizards: Interviews with Top Traders* (New York: CollinsBusiness, 1993), p. 134.

20. Louis Bacon, who was up about 40 percent in 1987, made most of his profits by going long the bond market the same way that Jones did. (Bacon interview.) Bruce Kovner recalls making more money on his bond position after the 1987 crash than he had from shorting the stock market. (Bruce Kovner, interview with the author, October 14, 2009.)

21. Discussing his Japan trade with *Barron's* in May 1990, Jones said, "Under- or overvaluation is only part of the battle. The key thing is to be able to time one's entry into a position at the precise moment when the market is about to move in your favor. Markets can stay undervalued, say, for months and years at a time. You don't want to waste your resources in that kind of position. In fact, if you put a gun to my head and ask me to choose between fundamental and technical analysis, I would take the technicals every time." See Jonathan R. Laing. "Past the Peak—Super Trader Paul Tudor Jones Bearish on Most Markets," *Barron's*, May 7, 1990.

22. Jones describes his view of Japan extensively in interviews with *Barron's* in February and May 1990. These provide something close to Soros's "real time experiment" during the Plaza Accord trade of 1985. See Laing, "Past the Peak—Super Trader Paul Tudor Jones Bearish on Most Markets." Also see "Barron's Roundtable 1990: Bargains and Bubbles—Part I—Baron, Lynch, Jones, and Rogers Pinpoint Plenty of Both," *Barron's*, February 5, 1990.

23. In an interview in 2000, Jones emphasized the importance of understanding how other players are positioned. "The secret to being successful from a trading perspective is to have an indefatigable and an undying and unquenchable thirst for information and knowledge. Because I think there are certain situations where you can absolutely understand what motivates every buyer and seller and have a pretty good picture of what's going to happen. And it just requires an enormous amount of grunt work and dedication to finding all possible bits of information." Paul Tudor Jones II, interview by Joel Ramin.

24. In January 1990, short-term interest rates in Japan stood at 7.25 percent and longer bonds yielded considerably more than that.

25. In the *Barron's* Roundtable interview in February 1990, Jones correctly predicted that the Nikkei would rebound after falling to around 36,500, since that had been the point from which the Nikkei

had broken out for the last stage of its bull rally the previous November. Jones also said that if the rebound proved weak, the market would fall again. This proved accurate.

26. In May 1990, with almost uncanny accuracy, Jones said to *Barron's*, "Japan has a long way to go yet on the downside. The slide won't resume, however, until late summer, I suspect. . . . I am lightly long Japan right now." Jones also predicted that the fall would have severe consequences for Japan's economy. The stocks in the Tokyo market were worth an enormous $4 trillion—160 percent of the annual output of Japan's economy. A 20 percent fall in the Nikkei would wipe out $800 billion of wealth, something equivalent to 35 percent of Japan's GDP. Jones predicted that the destruction of so much wealth would trigger "an enormous economic contraction." Sure enough, Japan's economy remained stagnant for much of the decade. See Laing. "Past the Peak—Super Trader Paul Tudor Jones Bearish on Most Markets."

27. Jones remembers the clocklike arrival of hedge-selling pressure by cotton farmers at year-end, no matter what was occurring fundamentally in the market. "The farmers clung emotionally to the hope that prices would some how improve if they could just wait," he recalls. "Of course, those hopes were usually dashed, but the phenomenon gave us something to exploit." Laing, "Trader with a Hot Hand."

28. Jones seems to have learned the value of visibility from Eli Tullis, the cotton trader under whom he served an apprenticeship in New Orleans. Jones recalls of Tullis, "Everyone always knew what his position was. He was very easy to tag. Eli's attitude was, 'The hell with it, I'm going to take them head on.'" Schwager, *Market Wizards*, p. 121.

29. *Trader: The Documentary.*

30. This description is taken from Laing, "Trader with a Hot Hand."

31. Schwager, *Market Wizards*, p. 129.

32. A 1988 *Wall Street Journal* profile captures Jones's trading style. "Charles Christensen, a futures analyst with Refco, says that's what happened on February 25 in the Chicago Board of Trade's Treasury bond futures pit, the most active futures market in the U.S. The futures were near their highs late in the day when Tudor Investment's trader suddenly appeared on the edge of the bond pit, both arms raised above his head, gesturing frantically to sell all at once 1,000 contracts—with a face value of about $95 million. Even big brokerage firms rarely offer to sell that many at a crack. 'The local traders looked at each other and said, "Who's buying?"' Mr. Christensen says. 'The answer was, "Nobody," so they all tried to sell ahead of him.' But many couldn't, they drove the price even lower, and Mr. Jones's trader apparently bought back the contracts cheaply. The estimated profit: $3 million. 'It's phenomenal: The man is such a good psychological trader,' Mr. Christensen gushed. 'He knows exactly when the market is acting exhausted so he can move in.'" McMurray, "Quotron Man."

33. James Elkins, interview with the author, April 23, 2008. Elkins was the president of Elkins/McSherry.

CHAPTER SEVEN: WHITE WEDNESDAY

1. Druckenmiller recalls, "When I went over there, I did expect to get fired in a year, but I didn't really care because I thought I would get some kind of postgraduate education." Stanley Druckenmiller, interview with the author, March 13, 2008.

2. Druckenmiller interview. Gary Gladstein recalls Druckenmiller's arrival: "George did think that he was going to be a superstar, but no one really knew that for sure. There were a number of people previously that George had been very enthusiastic about." Gary Gladstein, interview with the author, March 18, 2008.

3. Druckenmiller recalls, "I never learned enough about fundamental analysis, not having been to business school, not having a CFA. By necessity and also because my first boss, my mentor, used technical analysis, I had to rely quite heavily on charts." Druckenmiller interview.

4. Jack D. Schwager, *The New Market Wizards: Conversations with America's Top Traders* (New York: CollinsBusiness, 2005), p. 193.

5. Druckenmiller recalls, "I started there as an S&P trader; he didn't know that I traded bonds and currencies and all this other stuff before I got there. Even then he was running around insulting

everyone, telling everyone that his successor was coming in, which must not have been a good thing to hear for the others. I didn't really have a defined role the first three to six months. I almost quit it. . . . I still had my Pittsburgh firm, and I flew to Pittsburgh one day, and when I landed I found out that George had sold my bond position out. You have to understand, I had been in charge of a portfolio my entire career basically. I had the number one mutual fund out of twenty-two hundred mutual funds and basically had one lucky period after another. And no one had ever done anything like that to me. I basically blew a gasket over the phone when I found out. He was fine about it. He was apologetic. I was, by far, the rude one, but with reason." Druckenmiller interview.

6. This is the exchange as recalled by Soros. (George Soros, interview with the author, June 10, 2008.) Druckenmiller confirms his feelings at the time, adding the last line of the exchange reported here. "He wasn't the boss of the trading, and I wasn't the boss of the trading, and it was awful. I believe I was screwing up his trading and I believe he was screwing up mine. You just can't have two cooks in the kitchen." (Druckenmiller interview.)

7. The colleague was Robert Johnson, who moved from Bankers Trust to become a partner at Soros Fund Management in September 1992. Robert Johnson, interview with the author, July 29, 2008.

8. Performance data for Quantum here and elsewhere in the book, including in the chart given in the appendix, describe the return an investor would have received if he had reinvested distributions back into the fund. In practice, not all investors were permitted to do this because Quantum had more money than it could manage. I am grateful to Gary Gladstein, the former chief administrative officer and managing director of Soros Fund Management, for providing me with a complete set of performance data for Quantum, and to Michael Vachon, George Soros's spokesman, for the data on Soros Fund Management.

9. Soros describes Druckenmiller's authority from 1989: "He really ran the thing, and our relationship was good enough so we could discuss things and I could express views, but it didn't stop him from doing his thing." (George Soros, interview with the author, January 16, 2008.) And again: "If we had a difference of opinion, his opinion prevailed. I had the right to give him advice, so I was the coach, like a football player or tennis player." (Soros interview, June 10, 2008.) Equally, Druckenmiller recalls, "There were many times where he would question my positions and therefore want me to reduce them, but I rarely listened. He may have just been testing me." (Druckenmiller interview.)

10. Druckenmiller recalls, "I did not like the publicity we had at Soros. I tolerated it because I thought it was for a noble purpose. He needed it as a platform for his philanthropy. I didn't read it as he was doing it for his ego. He was trying to meet with heads of state, and he needed a platform, which it surely gave him. So the idea of me staying in the background and him doing the publicity was fine." Druckenmiller interview.

11. Druckenmiller recalls: "The way I figure out the economy is literally from the bottom up and from company anecdotal information, knowing that housing leads retail and retail leads capital spending. From listening to the guys on the ground. When you talk to companies and to guys who run companies, you get a whole additional perspective on the economy. . . . I learned a lot at Soros, but not what I thought I would learn. I did not learn what makes the yen go up or down, or what makes the stock market go up or down. Soros's great gift was how to use leverage, and how much money to have down based on the risk/reward and your sense of conviction. His view on the yen or the euro was better than random, but not much. And yet he was still one of the great money managers ever because he knew how to bet his convictions." Ibid.

12. Speaking about *Alchemy*, Druckenmiller says, "I found the first chapter basically unreadable. I found the currency chapter interesting and actually quite useful. . . . A budget deficit of huge proportions could actually be bullish for a currency because it drove up rates and sucked in capital. That, at the time, was very unique thinking which, to some extent, became conventional thinking in the next fifteen to twenty years." Ibid.

13. Druckenmiller recalls, "Everybody forgets that the deutsche mark went down hard after the first two or three days. Everyone thought it would be polluted by this horrible East German money. I saw it differently." Ibid.

14. "It was one of those situations that I could see as clear as day," Druckenmiller said later. His $2 billion bet was equivalent to almost 100 percent of the capital in Quantum. It was even bigger than

Soros's bet at the time of the Plaza accord in 1985—though, as a proportion of the assets in Quantum, it was smaller. Schwager, *The New Market Wizards*, p. 203.

15. Druckenmiller recalls, "If you had a floating currency, this is one of the situations where the deutsche mark would have just been screaming against the pound. The fact that they were linked, and all that pressure able to build and build, created an explosive situation. Now I think I only did, like, a billion and a half in August. It was a bit of a flyer; I put it on for six months. I didn't see the immediate catalysts, but I knew there were potential tremors growing there. And sometimes that's what you'll do; you'll put on a position, partly because you think it's going to work eventually, but also because it makes you watch it." Druckenmiller was so confident about the asymmetry of this bet that he did not regard $1.5 billion as a big position. "A billion and a half, I don't want to talk about it cavalierly, but it was like an intellectual position for me to put on. . . . If it had been something where we could have lost fifteen percent, it would have been very big. But I just couldn't see that happening." Stanley Druckenmiller, interview with the author, June 4, 2008.

16. Craig R. Whitney, "Bundesbank Chief is at Eye of Currency Storm," *New York Times*, October 8, 1992.

17. "I got the message," Soros said later. See George Soros, *Soros on Soros: Staying Ahead of the Curve* (New York: John Wiley & Sons, 1995), p. 81. The date and place of this encounter with Schlesinger is not given by Soros, who refers simply to a Schlesinger speech "at a prestigious gathering." However, it seems highly likely that the speech Soros attended was the Basel speech on September 8. Druckenmiller confirms that Soros called him with the tip on the lira's likely devaluation around this time, shortly before the weekend during which Italy devalued. (Druckenmiller interview, March 13, 2008.)

18. Soros's intuition was right. In his memoir, Norman Lamont, the British finance minister of the time, recounts a conversation between Eddie George, deputy governor of the Bank of England, and Hans Tietmeyer, his opposite number at the Bundesbank. Tietmeyer had noted pointedly that many Germans would welcome the end of plans to create a single currency. See Norman Lamont, *In Office* (London: Little, Brown, 1999), p. 227.

19. "I'm sure the lira idea came from him and not me. I'm also sure that the pound idea came from me and not him." Druckenmiller interview, March 13, 2008.

20. Johnson recalls, "I could just feel the energy of the two men just picking up . . . There's a funny kind of body language when you say something to people, and their eyes kind of start to go to each other. Like they're looking at each other like 'Whoa, yeah.' It was visceral." Johnson interview.

21. Scott Bessent recalls that Quantum wanted to limit its risk in the sterling trade to the investment gains it had made so far that year. Hence Quantum worked out what it would lose if sterling moved to the far side of the band permissible within the exchange-rate mechanism and capped the capital it risked accordingly. (Scott Bessent, interview with the author, January 18, 2008. See also Steven Drobny, *Inside the House of Money: Top Hedge Fund Traders on Profiting in the Global Market* (Hoboken, NJ: John Wiley & Sons, 2006), p. 275.) But Johnson and Druckenmiller have a different memory. Druckenmiller says, "I didn't think that [sterling moving to the other end of the band] was remotely possible. I felt very strongly that just couldn't happen because these economies were so ass-backwards. So yeah, theoretically it could have gone to the other side of the band. I didn't even consider it, to tell you the truth." (Druckenmiller interview, June 4, 2008.)

22. This exchange is recalled by Robert Johnson. Johnson interview; Robert Johnson, e-mail communication with the author, November 10, 2008.

23. "It was almost like you could feel a big inhale. You know, like you've seen when Michael Jordan goes to dunk. You can just see his eyes get big. It was fascinating. I walked out of there with absolutely no question that we were going to go after this thing. I knew other people in the banks and counterparties would imitate us." Johnson interview.

24. On an average day in 1986, for example, $58 billion worth of currencies were traded on the world's markets; but by 1992 the daily turnover had almost tripled to $167 billion. These data come from the U.S. Federal Reserve. They include spot trading, forward trading, and swaps and are adjusted for double reporting by participating dealers. Interestingly, before 1986 the foreign-exchange markets were so insignificant that the Fed did not collect data on them. See http://www.newyorkfed .org/markets/triennial/fx_survey.pdf.

25. The intervention came on August 21, 1992. At the end of Europe's trading day, the dollar's value had scarcely budged from its preintervention level, and four days later the dollar hit a record low against the deutsche mark. Contemporary news accounts show that the authorities' failure was not regarded as inevitable; the triumph of market muscle over government intervention was not fully understood until after sterling's debacle a month later. For example, a Reuters story on the August intervention quotes Klaus Weiland, a trader at Deutsche Girozentrale-Deutsche Kommunalbank, as saying: "Today's intervention restores some of the central banks' credibility." (Erik Kirschbaum, "Central Banks Battle to Support Flagging Dollar," Reuters, August 21, 1992.) Commentators in the *Economist* and the *Financial Times* noted that the central banks' failure raised doubts about the efficacy of intervention, but they presented these doubts as a novel factor in global finance. "Yesterday's action raises questions about the credibility of internationally co-ordinated exchange rate policy," the FT's Lex Column noted ("D-Day for the Dollar," Lex Column, *Financial Times*, August 22, 1992); the failed intervention "has reinforced the lesson that currency intervention works only if it is allowed to affect domestic monetary policy; it cannot do the job on its own," the *Economist* noted ("Forever Falling?" *Economist*, August 29, 1992, p. 65). Writing with the benefit of hindsight, Norman Lamont, the British finance minister, was more definitive in describing the August failure as a telling portent of a changed world. (Lamont, *In Office*, p. 222.)
26. Italy had devalued the lira previously, most recently in 1987. But those earlier devaluations had been smaller and had been initiated by the Italian government in order to boost exports. In 1985, for example, the Italian government was widely thought to have instructed ENI, the Italian energy giant, to initiate a deliberate run on the lira in order to force Italy's European partners to accept devaluation. In 1992, by contrast, the Italians fought devaluation tooth and nail, with the support of the Bundesbank.
27. By any previous standards, the Bundesbank's intervention was colossal. The largest ever intervention by the Federal Reserve, which had taken place in 1989, had involved the selling of just $1.25 billion.
28. The passage that follows draws extensively on Lamont, *In Office*, pp. 220–26.
29. Ibid., p. 231.
30. Soros recalled: "When Norman Lamont said just before the devaluation that he would borrow nearly fifteen billion dollars to defend sterling, we were amused because that was about how much we wanted to sell." Anatole Kaletsky, "How Mr. Soros Made a Billion by Betting Against the Pound," *Times* (London), October 26, 1992.
31. Will Hutton, "Inside the ERM Crisis: Black Wednesday Massacre," *Guardian*, December 1, 1992, p. 15.
32. "I did not in any way foresee the scale of what was to happen, let alone that the next day would see the end of our membership of the ERM. It simply did not cross my mind." Lamont, *In Office*, p. 245.
33. "Basically, it was the German central bank just trashing Britain. . . . It was so obvious what was going on." Druckenmiller interview, March 13, 2008.
34. Speaking of Soros's advice to go for the jugular, Druckenmiller says, "This gets back to the genius we were talking about. I can do all my fancy analysis. I can have the concepts, I can do the economics, and I can even have the timing, but one simple statement like that in terms of size . . . We probably got twice the profit I would have had without that snide comment he made about 'Well, if you love it so much . . . .' " (Druckenmiller interview, March 13, 2008.) Gerry Manolovici, an equity specialist at Soros Fund Management, recalls, "Schlesinger was asked after the lira devaluation whether now everything was stable. And Schlesinger said, 'No, other countries missed the opportunity to devalue.' At this Soros went nuts. He scoured the world for credit to put on short positions." (Gerry Manolovici, interview with the author, March 31, 2008.)
35. Soros recalls, "Basically, I said, 'This is the moment, they are capitulating, go for the jugular.' And he went, and even I went. I don't normally make phone calls, but I was also calling looking for counterparties." Soros interview, January 16, 2008.
36. Druckenmiller recalls, "We really went after this thing and kept going and going and going like the Energizer bunny. . . . So anybody with a brain is going to ask his dealer, 'What the hell is going on?' And I know people talk. It's Quantum." Druckenmiller interview, June 4, 2008.

37. Soros recalls, "I remember we called everyone who was willing to put on an additional position to sell sterling. . . . It wasn't possible to find counterparties who were willing because they had limits to how much they could do." Soros interview, January 16, 2008.

38. Louis Bacon recalls, "I don't think I'd ever talked to George before. Having George talk was like having a demigod coming down from on high to talk to you." Louis Bacon, interview with the author, July 21, 2009.

39. Bessent interview.

40. Scott Bessent recalls, "We could push the bank against the wall. They would have to buy an unlimited amount of sterling from us." Bessent interview.

41. David M. Smick, *The World Is Curved* (New York: Portfolio, 2008), pp. 183–84.

42. Lamont, *In Office*, p. 249.

43. The minister was Kenneth Clarke. See Philip Johnston, "Ministers Caught in a Maelstrom as the Pound Plunged Through the Floor," *Daily Telegraph*, September 13, 2002.

44. Soros interview, January 16, 2008; Scott Bessent, e-mail communication with the author, November 8, 2008.

45. The $27 billion includes $4.1 billion worth of sterling purchases by other central banks. Under the rules of the exchange-rate mechanism, these would have to have been repaid by the Bank of England. See Lamont, *In Office*, p. 259.

46. The magnitude of sterling's fall depends on the period chosen. At its trough, reached in March 1993, sterling was 16 percent down, implying a cost to British taxpayers of over $4 billion. But the immediate fall was 14 percent, and sterling fluctuated around that level through December.

47. There are various estimates of the total sterling selling by Soros Fund Management. Druckenmiller recalls that he sold about $7.5 billion on behalf of Quantum, a figure that would have excluded selling by Soros in his side account. (Druckenmiller interview, March 13, 2008.) Soros, in an interview one month after the trade, put the total sterling sales at almost $10 billion. Meanwhile, two former Soros employees give substantially higher estimates. Kaletsky, "How Mr. Soros Made a Billion."

48. According to news reports, these banks were Citicorp, J.P. Morgan, Chemical Banking, Bankers Trust, Chase Manhattan, First Chicago, and Bank America. (See Thomas Jaffe and Dyan Machan, "How the Market Overwhelmed the Central Banks," *Forbes*, November 9, 1992, pp. 40–42.) It is notable that hedge funds made larger profits on the sterling trade than banks, even though banks managed far more capital. Further, hedge funds were the leaders in the currency trades, with banks that executed their trades then copying them on their own books. The IMF's Capital Markets report, commissioned after the collapse of the European exchange-rate mechanism, noted that the determination of hedge funds "to position themselves favorably for possible exchange rate realignments in the ERM apparently served as a signal for other institutional fund managers to re-examine their own positions. . . . Thus, although hedge funds have less than $10 billion in capital, their potential influence on forex markets [was] larger." (International Monetary Fund, "International Capital Markets," 1993, p. 11.) Given the size of Soros's profits relative to those of the banks, the IMF was understating the point by a wide margin.

49. As of late October, Soros's profits on his sterling position stood at $950 million. But at that time Soros was correctly expecting that sterling would ultimately fall further, so the eventual profit was probably larger. If Soros Fund Management exited its estimated $10 billion position with a profit averaging 14 percent, a reasonable estimate of the truth, it would ultimately have made $1.4 billion. Kaletsky, "How Mr. Soros Made a Billion."

50. Stephen Taub, Nanette Byrnes, and David Carey, "The $650 Million Man," *Financial World* 162, no. 14 (July 6, 1993): pp. 38–61.

51. The Swedish trade was conceived by Robert Johnson. On the secrecy of the Swedish trade, Druckenmiller recalls, "By then at least we learned to keep our mouth shut." Druckenmiller interview, June 4, 2008; Johnson interview.

52. David Israelson, "France Tries to Halt Speculation on Franc," *Toronto Star*, September 23, 1992.

53. Larry Elliott, Mark Milner, Ruth Kelly, and David Gow, "After Black Wednesday: The Currency Puzzle Remains Unsolved," *Guardian*, September 17, 1993, p. 17.

54. Robert Johnson recalls, "One of the reasons I left Banker's Trust and joined Soros is I didn't know if Banker's Trust had the courage to go after something so threatening to government structures when they have to have a banking license. I knew George did." Johnson interview.

55. Soros recalls, "I warned him [Trichet] that he's liable to be attacked, and I said, 'I'd like to be helpful and therefore I will not take a position.'" (Soros interview, June 10, 2008.) Elsewhere Soros has said, "When the French franc came under attack, I really believed I could have toppled it if I joined the fray. This led me to behave rather foolishly. I chose to abstain from speculating against the franc in order to be able to express what I thought were constructive suggestions. This had doubly unfortunate results: I lost what was a profit opportunity, *and* I annoyed the French authorities even more with my comments than I would have done by speculating against the franc. It taught me a lesson: Speculators ought to keep quiet and speculate." (Soros, *Soros on Soros*, pp. 85–86.) This passage gives a sense of Soros's split personality but should be treated with a grain of salt. For one thing, Quantum made money by not betting against the franc. For another, Soros failed to keep quiet and speculate during the emerging-market crisis, as described in chapter nine.

56. "I fight for many causes in my life, but I don't particularly feel like defending currency speculation." Soros, *Soros on Soros*, p. 83.

57. Kaletsky, "How Mr. Soros Made a Billion."

CHAPTER EIGHT: HURRICANE GREENSPAN

1. I am grateful to Michael Steinhardt and Tricia Fitzgerald for providing full historical performance data, which are also presented in Appendix II.

2. Shadowbanks later made loans to companies and home buyers, whereas Steinhardt's early version focused on the government bond market.

3. Steinhardt recalls that his main broker, Goldman Sachs, was providing leverage "overjoyedly." Michael Steinhardt, interview with the author, December 15, 2008.

4. Steinhardt recalls that his leverage on U.S. government bonds was exceptionally high. His leverage on European bonds was more like twenty to one, and the leverage for his funds as a whole might have been less than ten to one. Steinhardt interview. See also Steinhardt, *No Bull*, p. 224.

5. The Goldman partner was Leon Cooperman, formerly the boss of the asset management division of Goldman. The Salomon partner was Stanley Shopkorn, the head of equity trading. In 1993 John Meriwether left Salomon Brothers and raised $1.2 billion for a fund called Long-Term Capital Management.

6. The estimate of three thousand hedge funds comes from the International Advisory Group in Nashville. Even this excluded offshore funds. See Gary Weiss, "Fall Guys?" *BusinessWeek*, April 25, 1994.

7. Dyan Machan and Riva Atlas, "George Soros, Meet A. W. Jones," *Forbes*, January 17, 1994, pp. 42–44.

8. Laurie P. Cohen and Michael Siconolfi, "The Cruelest Month: Before May's Squeeze, One in April Wounded Investors in Treasurys," *Wall Street Journal*, October 7, 1991.

9. Laurence Zuckerman, "$76 Million to Settle Treasury Note Charges," *New York Times,* December 17, 1994.

10. Michael Siconolfi. "Salomon, Two Funds Set to Settle Claims," *Wall Street Journal*, March 31, 1994.

11. Bob Woodward, *Maestro* (New York: Simon & Schuster, 2000), p. 116.

12. Further illustrating his concern about a potential Wall Street backlash, Greenspan had used the occasion of his January 31 testimony before Congress to deliver a warning to equity investors: "Short-term interest rates are abnormally low in real terms," he declared, signaling that a rate hike was coming. (See Hearing of the Joint Economic Committee, "1994 Economic Outlook," 103rd Congress, Second Session, January 31, 1994.) In his autobiography, Greenspan recalls that his message was unusually explicit in that testimony: "It was like banging a pot." (Alan Greenspan, *The Age of Turbulence: Adventures in a New World* (New York: Penguin Press, 2007), p. 154.) Vincent Reinhart, a senior Fed economist at the time, recalls that Greenspan's effective anticipation

of equity-market reactions was matched by the surprise he experienced at the hands of the bond market. (Vincent Reinhart, interview with the author, September 11, 2008.)

13. Federal Open Market Committee transcript, February 3–4, 1994.
14. By February 8, the ten-year bond yield was 5.98 percent, twenty-four basis points up from the yield at the start of the month.
15. During 1993, Quantum made big profits on the yen-dollar rate and was acutely sensitive to the links between the exchange rate and trade talks. By January 1994, Druckenmiller's bet against the yen was worth an astonishing $25 billion, demonstrating not only his confidence in the trade but also the rapid growth of Quantum since the sterling coup less than two years earlier. Although this trade blew up in February, Druckenmiller was fortunate to have sold his large portfolio of European bonds in January 1994. Combined with a successful trade in copper, this allowed him to get through the turbulent year of 1994 without losses. Stanley Druckenmiller, interview with the author, June 4, 2008. See also David Wessel, Laura Jereski, and Randall Smith, "Stormy Spring," *Wall Street Journal*, May 20, 1994.
16. Between February 11 and February 15, the ten-year Treasury yield moved from 5.88 percent to 6.20 percent.
17. Data for Japan come from Bloomberg Generics, a time series of active debt issues. No such series exists for Italy and Spain; data for these countries come from analysis of expired bond issuance by Paul Swartz of the Center for Geoeconomic Studies at the Council on Foreign Relations.
18. "Where It Hurts: Bets on Foreign Debt Go Bad and Punish Big Players in U.S.—Bankers Trust and Others Feel Pain From Europe and 'Emerging Markets'—Steinhardt Takes a Big Hit," *Wall Street Journal*, March 3, 1994.
19. Randall Smith, Tom Herman, and Earl C. Gottschalk Jr., "Mean Street," *Wall Street Journal*, April 7, 1994.
20. Steinhardt, *No Bull*, p. 224. Various news accounts put Steinhardt's European risk at $7 million per basis point or lower, but I have taken Steinhardt's estimate in his autobiography as the most authoritative.
21. Steinhardt recalls, "We were losing money and I couldn't quite catch my breath; things were happening and we had positions and it was as if I just didn't quite have the ability to understand where we were and why we were where we were. It was as if we were playing yesterday's or last year's game." Steinhardt interview.
22. "I remember Michael being very upset. I just want to sell them. I just want out. It's over, just sell them. And the guy not being able to execute it and sell them." John Lattanzio, interview with the author, December 15, 2008.
23. "Where It Hurts."
24. Steinhardt, *No Bull*, pp. 225 and 227. Steinhardt elaborates: "My great problem, as humbly acknowledged, was I didn't know what I was talking about. I didn't know the names of the securities, the names of the French ten-years, whatever they call them. . . . I didn't know who made the markets and all this other stuff. . . . I didn't know that there could be substantial differences between the French bonds and the Germans and the gilts and the Americans. . . . I mean, I didn't know. And that's when I got killed. . . . Was I ever dumb and cocky." Steinhardt interview.
25. Askin told one magazine that "most managers are not as comfortable as we are with prepayment risk, nor the structural risk inherent in this market. We understand it, we can measure it, and we can hedge it." Final Report of Harrison J. Goldin, Trustee, to the Honorable Stuart M. Bernstein, United States Bankruptcy Judge, Southern District of New York. In re Granite Partners, L.P., Granite Corporation, and Quartz Hedge Fund. Case Nos. 94 B 41683 (SMB) through 94 B 41685 (SMB) inclusive. New York, NY, April 18, 1996, 27.
26. See Saul Hansel, "Markets in Turmoil: Investors Undone: How $600 Million Evaporated," *New York Times*, April 5, 1994. The success of Askin's marketing was not surprising given his reputation at Drexel, where he was considered one of the foremost experts on prepayment risk.
27. The bankruptcy trustee would later find that Askin lacked the analytical models necessary to determine whether his portfolio was market neutral. See Final Report of Harrison J. Goldin, 27–28.

28. The bankruptcy trustee found no evidence of the proprietary prepayment model on Askin's computer, and no employee of his firm was able to verify its existence. See Final Report of Harrison J. Goldin, 28.

29. Final Report of Harrison J. Goldin, 84–85.

30. Even when Askin tried to accept some of these low prices, it proved impossible to do so. The instruments were held by other brokers as collateral, and the brokers had hedged the risk in the instruments with offsetting trades. Because the offsets were too complex to unwind, the brokers refused to release the collateral. See Final Report of Harrison J. Goldin, 95.

31. Woodward, *Maestro*, p. 126.

32. *The Late Edition*, CNN, April 3, 1994 (transcript retrieved from Nexis).

33. Al Ehrbar, "The Great Bond Market Massacre," *Fortune*, October 17, 1994.

34. "We had a far greater impact than anticipated," Greenspan said bluntly. Federal Open Market Committee conference call, February 28, 1994.

35. Blinder's protest against yellow suspenders is recalled by Vincent Reinhart, a former Fed economist. Reinhart interview.

36. See President's Working Group on Financial Markets, "An Assessment of Developments with Potential Implications for Market Price Dynamics and Systemic Risk," September 27, 1994.

37. Lynn Stevens Hume, "Gonzalez Derivatives Legislation, Hedge Fund Hearing Due in April," *Bond Buyer*, March 28, 1994.

38. The paper was by Don R. Hays of Wheat First Securities. It was circulated on April 5, 1994.

39. Brett D. Fromson, "Hearings on 'Hedge Funds' Planned," *Washington Post*, March 25, 1994, p. G7.

40. Robert Johnson, interview with the author, July 29, 2008.

41. "Hedge Funds." Hearing of the House Banking, Finance, and Urban Affairs Committee. April 13, 1994. 103rd Congress, Second Session.

42. Steinhardt recalls: "I was really miserable. And I was miserable, I would say, in the second quarter and into the third quarter. I couldn't get out of it, even when I was pretty much out of the bonds, I couldn't ever quite mount a successful offensive. Every time I started something, it just didn't work." Steinhardt interview.

43. A Steinhardt employee recalls of the last year: "He would intellectually hedge himself. If you had a view on something and put a trade on, he would come in and say, 'I was just talking to'—pick your famous guy—'and he thinks it's the dumbest idea he's ever heard ever, and he has no idea why you're doing this.' Then he'd say, 'But I don't know anything about this, so do whatever you want . . .' And he'd leave. So now you're screwed because if it goes badly he can say, 'I told you this was a bad idea.' If it worked, he could say, 'Why wasn't it bigger? I told you that you could do whatever you want. . .'' He would do this consistently."

44. Contemporary press accounts put the earnings for 1995 at $500 million. See Stephanie Strom, "Top Manager to Close Shop on Hedge Funds," *New York Times*, October 12, 1995, p. D1. However, Steinhardt's records show that returns were 26.8 percent (before fees) on assets of $2.7 billion, suggesting profits of just over $700 million.

45. Some commentators have suggested that Steinhardt's dollar losses in 1994 were so large as to outweigh the gains over the rest of his career, since the earlier gains, though impressive in percentage terms, were on a relatively small asset base. This claim is not borne out by an examination of Steinhardt's internal records.

46. Stephen Taub, "The Hedge Rows of Wall Street," *Financial World*, September 13, 1994, p. 38.

47. Riva Atlas and Dyan Machan. "To be or not to be: Nothing personal, mind you, but Alan Greenspan pushed Michael Steinhardt—and a lot of other hedge fund operators into a corner. Many of them will not survive. Will Steinhardt?" *Forbes*, September 26, 1994.

48. In a June 1995 letter to investors, Kovner announced that he would be returning $1.3 billion of Caxton's $1.8 billion in assets under management after closing one of his two foreign funds, the $800 million GAM fund, and his $450 million U.S. fund. According to press accounts of the announcement, Kovner stated, "The lower liquidity in currency, fixed-income, and commodity markets hurt our performance." (See Peter Truell, "A Big Hedge Fund Returns $1.3 Billion to Its

Investors," *New York Times*, June 9, 1995.) Louis Bacon's Moore Capital also suffered withdrawals around this time; his poor performance was compounded by an acrimonious split with a senior lieutenant. The same went for Quantum: "We find that our size is hindering us," Soros wrote to his clients. (Peter Truell, "Some Big Funds, Like Soros's, Have Difficulty Despite Trend," *New York Times*, July 27, 1995.) Those who returned capital to investors almost certainly did boost their performance over the ensuing years, since later research was to find an inverse correlation between size and investment returns. For example, in 2009 the software firm PerTrac Financial Solutions reported that between 1996 and 2008 hedge funds managing less than $100 million made 13 percent a year, compared with 10 percent for those running more than $500 million. (Stephen Taub, "The Hedge Rows of Wall Street," p. 38.) Likewise, data from Rock Creek Capital, reported in chapter sixteen, reinforce the view that size is an impediment.

49. The survey was conducted by Republic New York Securities and based on a modest sample of 130 hedge funds.

50. The five-year performance data come from International Advisory Group, a Nashville-based consulting firm. A few years later, a paper from the Yale School of Management found that offshore hedge funds returned a bit less than the S&P 500 index: 13.3 percent from 1989 through 1995, compared with the benchmark return of 16.5 percent. But hedge funds appeared much less risky: The annual standard deviation of their returns was 9.1 percent, versus 16.3 percent for the S&P 500. Meanwhile, swings in the S&P 500 stock index explained only 36 percent of swings at hedge funds. See Stephen J. Brown, William N. Goetzmann, and Robert G. Ibbotson, "Off-Shore Hedge Funds: Survival and Performance 1989–1995" (Yale School of Management working paper no. F-52B, January 2, 1998.) Another paper, based on different data and looking at an overlapping period (1989 to 1998), confirmed that hedge-fund volatility was low. The annualized standard deviations of monthly returns for equally weighted and value weighted portfolios of all hedge funds were, respectively, 5.75 percent and 8.94 percent, much less than the standard deviation of the S&P 500, which was 13.2 percent. See Franklin R. Edwards, "Hedge Funds and the Collapse of Long-Term Capital Management," *Journal of Economic Perspectives* 13, no. 2 (Spring 1999), p. 196. See also the positive finding for hedge-fund alpha reported in the conclusion.

CHAPTER NINE: SOROS VERSUS SOROS

1. See Andrew Meier, "Cursed Cornucopia," *Time*, December 29, 1997; Paul Klebnikov, "A Company Built on Bones," *Forbes*, November 6, 1995; Michael R. Gordon, "Siberia Tests Russia's Ability to Profit from Privatization," *New York Times*, December 9, 1997; Robert G. Kaiser, "Norilsk, Stalin's Siberian Hell, Thrives in Spite of Hideous Legacy," *Washington Post*, August 29, 2001.

2. Paul Tudor Jones recalls, "I cross myself every time I think about that helicopter ride." Paul Jones, interview with the author, April 23, 2009.

3. Thorpe McKenzie, interview with the author, August 15, 2008.

4. Dwight Anderson, interviews with the author, August 26, 2008, and October 2, 2008.

5. Arturo Porzecanski, an economist at Kidder Peabody in 1993, remembers trying to persuade his bank's clients of the merits of buying Peru's debt. Only hedge funds were prepared to set aside Peru's record of default and act on Porzecanski's argument. Arturo Porzecanski, interview with the author, June 24, 2008.

6. Between the late 1990s and the mid-2000s, the benefits of these cross-border capital flows were underestimated by economists, whose empirical tests found little relationship between the openness of a country's capital market and its growth rate. But in an article published in 2007, Peter Henry of Stanford punched a hole in this pessimistic consensus. By searching the data for a relationship between capital-account openness and the growth rate, economists had been setting the wrong test, Henry argued. The act of letting in foreign capital should be expected to create a one-off lowering of the cost of borrowing, and hence a few years in which dozens of new ventures could be financed; but once an economy had milked this advantage, it was likely to return to its original growth rate. Opening up to foreign capital, in other words, should be expected to create a permanent increase in the level of family incomes, since even if the economy returned to its original growth rate it would be growing from a higher base; but it should not be expected to lead to permanent acceleration in

growth. Sure enough, when Henry looked for temporary growth effects, he found that they were powerful: In the three years after the stock market in a typical emerging economy opened up to foreign capital, the average annual growth of real wages in the manufacturing sector increased by a factor of seven. Henry checked his results against a control group of economies that had not opened up their stock markets. These experienced no such wage acceleration. See the introduction to Peter Blair Henry, "Capital Account Liberalization: Theory, Evidence and Speculation," *Journal of Economic Literature* 45 (December 2007), pp. 887–935. For the sevenfold increase in manufacturing wages, see Peter Blair Henry and Diego Sasson, "Capital Account Liberalization, Real Wages and Productivity" (working paper, March 2008). Also relevant is Ross Levine, Norman Loayza, and Thorsten Beck, "Financial Intermediation and Growth: Causality and Causes," *Journal of Monetary Economics* 46, no. 1 (2000). This paper finds that a doubling in the size of private credit in an average developing country is associated with a 2 percentage point rise in annual economic growth, meaning that after thirty-five years the economy would be twice as large as it would have been without ample opportunities to borrow.

7. I am grateful to Gary Gladstein, the former chief administrative officer and managing director of Soros Fund Management, for these data.

8. Arminio Fraga, interview with the author, June 6, 2008.

9. Ibid.

10. Ibid.

11. The paper was by Graciela Kaminsky of the Federal Reserve and Carmen Reinhart of the International Monetary Fund. It was later published in the *American Economic Review.*

12. Fraga interview.

13. A participant at the meeting recalls, "It was really kind of a bombshell statement to make. Talk about being pathetically ignorant when you say that to the three guys from Soros."

14. Rodney Jones, interview with the author, June 18, 2008. Sources differ as to whether the Soros team established the initial position in late January or early February, but Jones, who kept real-time notes of the crisis and was focused exclusively on the region, is confident that the sales occurred in the last ten days of January.

15. According to data subsequently released by the Bank of Thailand, the full measure of reserves, which includes forward-market operations, registered a fall of $4.4 billion in February. No forward data are reported for the change in January, but the $2 billion sale by Soros Fund Management appears to have driven a substantial proportion of the decline in Thai reserves in this period.

16. Druckenmiller recalls, "When I shorted it, it cost nothing. Like the British pound the first time, like half a percent." Stan Druckenmiller, interview with the author, June 4, 2008.

17. On February 12, Rodney Jones, the Hong Kong–based Soros economist, wrote a memo to Druckenmiller and Soros, laying out Thailand's acute vulnerability. The Thai central bank held only $36 billion in reserves. Moreover, the private sector owed $85 billion to foreigners who would want their money out in a panic. This implied that a determined attack on the baht by Druckenmiller would have quickly forced devaluation.

18. It is also the case that Soros was not paying sufficient attention to Thailand to repeat the trick of 1992, when he had urged Druckenmiller to "go for the jugular." Robert Johnson, the economist who had advised Soros and Druckenmiller on the sterling trade, ran into Soros at Davos at the end of January 1997. Soros appeared unsure whether the Thai trade was worth bothering with. Robert Johnson, interview with the author, July 29, 2008.

19. Rodney Jones interview, June 18, 2008.

20. "By selling the Thai baht short in January 1997, the Quantum Funds managed by my investment company sent a signal that it may be overvalued. Had the authorities responded, the adjustment would have occurred sooner and it would have been less painful. As it is, the authorities resisted and when the break came it was catastrophic." George Soros, *The Crisis of Global Capitalism* (New York: PublicAffairs, 1998), pp. 142–43.

21. The extent of contact between Druckenmiller and Paul Jones is confirmed by people who worked at both funds. The size of Tiger's position is recalled by Dan Morehead, who executed Tiger's macro trades during this period. On the other hand, Rob Citrone, who was Tiger's macro analyst, thinks

the position was considerably larger—as big as $5 billion. Because of the way that Tiger worked, however, a trader is more likely to have known the real position than an analyst. Rob Citrone interview, September 30, 2009. Morehead interview, September 2, 2008.

22. Rodney Jones, who tracked the reserves closely, put the leakage on May 14 at $6.5 billion. On the other hand, Paul Blustein, another careful observer, puts it at $10 billion. According to Thai central bank data, total loss of reserves in all of May came to $18.3 billion. See Paul Blustein, *The Chastening: Inside the Crisis that Rocked the Global Financial System and Humbled the IMF* (New York: PublicAffairs, 2001), p. 71.

23. Rodney Jones recalls, "Soros did not go even bigger because of fear of crazy reaction. One did not know how that would play out. This was why the baht short could not be sized as aggressively as the sterling short in 1992. You were dealing with a developing country, and it was much harder to understand the reaction function." (Rodney Jones, interview with the author, July 21, 2008.) In addition, David Kowitz recalls that he was worried in February about possible government countermeasures. "They were shooting bullets at us, making the thing strengthen, so we looked like we were losing a lot of money. It was a bit stressful, and I probably would've folded, but Stan Druckenmiller, he doubled down. It was a famous call." (David Kowitz, interview with the author, August 26, 2008.)

24. Morehead calculated this amount for a memo he wrote to his Tiger colleagues on June 3, 2007. Dan Morehead, interview with the author, September 2, 2008.

25. Barry Porter, "BOT Out to Make Soros Pay for Attack; BOT and Soros Do Battle," *South China Morning Post*, June 24, 1997, p. 1.

26. Rodney Jones's calculations were not far off. Data released later by the Bank of Thailand show that reserves fell by $18.3 billion in May, slightly less than the $21 billion that Jones estimated. As a share of total reserves, the fall in May was even larger than Jones thought, since total reserves at the end of the month, net of forward sales, came to only $5.3 billion.

27. Morehead interview. Morehead was Robertson's currency trader. His account fits with the memory of another currency trader at a different hedge fund who was deeply involved in Thailand. On the other hand, Rob Citrone, Tiger's macro analyst, says he does not recall the episode; but Robertson did not always inform analysts of his actions. In any event, Tiger documents record that the fund was up an impressive 13.1 percent in July 1997, the month of the Thai devaluation. In a letter to investors at the end of the quarter, Robertson reported that the 29.3 percent gain in July to September mainly reflected two factors: profits in equities and in Asian currency trading. Julian H. Robertson, letter to the limited partners, October 7, 1997.

28. According to data on central-bank reserves kept by Rodney Jones, the $1 billion of selling by Tiger would have accounted for two thirds of the decline in the reserves on the last day before the peg broke, implying that Tiger played a role akin to Quantum's in sterling's 1992 devaluation. Rodney Jones, interview with the author, February 9, 2009.

29. The Soros team sold $500 million of its baht position in June 1997, some $2.5 billion in August and September, and another $500 million toward the end of the year. The positions had been created around January 20–24 ($2 billion) and around May 14–15 ($1.5 billion). Using average exchange rates for the six-month forward market, Paul Swartz of the Council on Foreign Relations calculates that Soros's total earnings from the baht trade would have come to about $750 million. The estimate of Tiger's profit comes from Dan Morehead, though again, Rob Citrone has a different memory: He believes the profits exceeded $1 billion. Morehead interview; Rob Citrone, interview with the author, September 30, 2009.

30. David Kowitz recalls, "I don't think he liked to be the bad guy. He wants to be remembered as a great statesman. Being blamed for the destruction of pathetic third-world countries wasn't helpful for that." Kowitz interview.

31. Speaking in Hong Kong on September 21, Soros revealed that Quantum was long the rupiah, explaining that markets had overshot in the case of the Indonesian currency and that the Indonesian government's consistent approach to reform gave him confidence. See Thomas Wagner, "Rubin Sees Promise in Southeast Asia, But Markets Fall Again," *Associated Press*, September 22, 1997; AFX News, "Soros Says Mahathir 'Menace' to His Own Country," September 22, 1997.

32. Kowitz interview.

33. Reflecting on the rupiah trade, Arminio Fraga recalls: "We often heard 'These big speculators can go into these small markets and manipulate them for their profit,' but we never saw it that way. For us it was always extremely dangerous. If you had made the wrong fundamental call and you went into something and you were caught wrong, usually you paid dearly to get out." Arminio Fraga, interview with the author, June 6, 2008.

34. Because Druckenmiller and Fraga had earned between $200 million and $300 million on smaller Asian currency trades during 1997, their Asian calls made money even though Thailand and Indonesia roughly canceled each other out. Among the smaller Asian trades, the most important was a short position on the Malaysian ringgit. Druckenmiller recalls that the short position was worth $1.5 billion but that he took profits early, when the ringgit started to fall, limiting the profit from the trade but also rendering false the inflated Malaysian rhetoric about the Soros funds' hostility. Druckenmiller interview.

35. Rodney Jones, memo to Stanley Druckenmiller, Arminio Fraga, and David Kowitz, November 17, 1997.

36. Blustein, *The Chastening*, p. 4.

37. Rodney Jones recalls, "Arminio [Fraga] called Stan Fisher [the number two at the IMF] after I had been there in Korea in November. Stan said the IMF staff had been there and they don't think this is a problem." Rodney Jones interview, July 21, 2008. On the other hand, Edwin Truman of the Federal Reserve recalls being in Seoul with Stan Fisher shortly after Jones's visit. By this time, Fisher knew that South Korea was in trouble, making it less likely that his influence accounts for the Quantum team's reluctance to short South Korea. Edwin Truman, correspondence with the author, December 22, 2009.

38. Robert Johnson recalls, "George's purpose for years was production, and it moved to distribution. He was intuitively a speculator, but his heart was all tied up in his philanthropy." Likewise, Rodney Jones recalls, "Mahathir had done psychological damage. Soros no longer wanted to be the bad speculator." Robert Johnson, interview with the author, July 29, 2008. Rodney Jones, interview with the author, July 21, 2008.

39. Robert Johnson recalls, "George was accused of being the Trojan horse. People said his philanthropy in eastern Europe was really a Trojan horse for pecuniary gain. He was very sensitive about that. If the president invited him to Korea and then he bounced Korea, it would create a scar that might be permanent. He never went to Malaysia until well after the argument with Mahathir. Once he showed up somewhere in an official capacity, he started blanking out that part of the grid for those who were taking positions." Robert Johnson, interview with the author, July 29, 2008.

40. Kevin Sullivan, "Soros Buoys Korean Stocks; Market Climbs After Financier Calls Crisis Fixable," *Washington Post*, January 6, 1998, p. D1.

41. Between January 5 and January 15, the KOSPI index rose from 396 to 506.

42. Sullivan, "Soros Buoys Korean Stocks."

43. Michael T. Kaufman, *Soros: The Life and Times of a Messianic Billionaire*. New York: (Knopf, 2002), p. 230.

44. Commenting on the financial logic of Soros's Svyazinvest stake, Gary Gladstein, managing director of Soros Fund Management at the time, says, "That was a terrible investment. We didn't do much due diligence on it. George decided he wanted to take a position, because George operates from his gut and he felt good about it at the time." Gary Gladstein, interview with the author, March 18, 2008.

45. Looking back on the secret loan to Russia, Soros calls it "a somewhat questionable maneuver." George Soros, interview with the author, June 10, 2008.

46. George Soros, *Soros on Soros: Staying Ahead of the Curve* (New York: John Wiley & Sons, 1995), p. 143.

47. Soros recalls, "I got involved because I was, in effect, betting the government was making the transition from robber capitalism to legitimate capitalism. . . . I was combining two considerations—a political one, which was to help to transform the economy into legitimate capitalism, and a financial one, which was to make a profit. Obviously, they didn't combine well." (George Soros, interview with *New York Review of Books*, January 14, 1999.) Equally, Robert Johnson comments, "He felt

that if he was a beacon of investment in Russia, others would follow and the capital inflows would transform the society and integrate them into the G7. There's a philanthropic side of George that started to interfere with the speculative one." (Johnson interview.)

48. On July 7, 1998, Julian Robertson wrote to his investors, "With yields at 102 percent, we are being well paid to take the risks of owning sovereign Russian debt."

49. Anderson interviews.

50. Soros's actions starting August 7 are described in his diary and reprinted in Soros, *The Crisis of Global Capitalism*, pp. 156–67.

51. Soros recalls, "I called Larry Summers and said, 'If they devalue and you give them a bridge loan, they could really put their house in order.' And Larry said, 'You are the only one advocating us getting in; everybody else tells us to pull the plug and get out.' That's when I wrote an article in the *FT* advocating my plan publicly. And then I was blamed for provoking the collapse." George Soros, interview with the author, June 10, 2008.

52. Gladstein marvels, "George went around saying that Russia was going to collapse. Meanwhile, we have this huge position in Russia that we can't sell. We had Russian equities, bonds; we had Russian exposures all over." Gladstein interview.

53. The main victim of Soros's Russia escapade was Stan Druckenmiller, who recalls: "Even though it was his trade, it became my position. You know, he always put his philanthropy and his statesmanship ahead of his money management. So 1998 was the first year when Soros Fund Management had a huge separation with Duquesne [Druckenmiller's old hedge fund, which he still managed]. Duquesne was in the fifties and Quantum was only up twelve. That's how devastating it was." Druckenmiller interview.

54. Soros, *The Crisis of Global Capitalism*, p. 168.

CHAPTER TEN: THE ENEMY IS US

1. By way of comparison, Morgan Stanley, a far larger institution, had earned just $1.0 billion in 1996. Eric Rosenfeld, presentation at Harvard Business School, April 22, 2009. Rosenfeld was a senior founding partner at LTCM.

2. James Rickards, interview with the author, February 12, 2009; James Rickards, e-mail communication with the author, March 30, 2009. Rickards was LTCM's chief counsel.

3. Donald MacKenzie, *An Engine, Not a Camera: How Financial Models Shape Markets* (Cambridge, MA: The MIT Press, 2006) pp. 215–16.

4. Other Wall Street houses hired quants around this time. For example, Fischer Black, the third inventor of the options-pricing formula, moved to Goldman Sachs in 1984. But Black and most other quants were kept off the trading floor. The difference at Salomon was that Meriwether brought Rosenfeld and the others into the heart of the action.

5. Roger Lowenstein writes of Coats, "Tall, likable, handsome, bound to get along with clients. Sure, he had been a goof-off in college, but he had played forward on the basketball team, and he had trading in his heart." (Roger Lowenstein, *When Genius Failed: The Rise and Fall of Long-Term Capital Management*, New York: Random House, 2000, p. 11.) For the juxtaposition of Coats and the Arbitrage Group, I am indebted to Michael Lewis, "How the Eggheads Cracked," *New York Times*, January 24, 1999.

6. Lowenstein, *When Genius Failed*, pp. 20, 21n.

7. The phrase was coined by an LTCM employee. See Kevin Muehring, "John Meriwether by the numbers," *Institutional Investor*, November 1, 1996.

8. Like many hedge funds, Long-Term did not like to acknowledge that it was a hedge fund. "We had moved on from thinking of ourselves as a mere 'hedge fund' and had started to think of ourselves as a new kind of 'financial technology company.'" (Rickards e-mail.) Lowenstein also reports that Merton saw Long-Term Capital not as a "hedge fund," a term that he and the other partners sneered at, but as a state-of-the-art financial intermediary that provided capital to markets just as banks did. (Lowenstein, *When Genius Failed*, p. 30.)

9. What follows on Italy is drawn partly from "Portfolio Outline," an internal LTCM document that describes many of the firm's positions at the time of liquidation, and partly from discussion with Eric Rosenfeld and an e-mail exchange with James Rickards, the former LTCM general counsel, and other sources.

10. The foreign investor could get around the Italian tax obstacle by borrowing money from a local bank and using it to buy government bonds; the bank would hold on to the bonds as collateral. For the purposes of Italian tax law, the bank was deemed to be the owner of the bonds, so the tax problem was solved and the foreigner was left to collect high interest payments from the Italian government. Admittedly, the foreigner's receipts from these bonds were set with a fixed interest rate, whereas its payments on its offsetting lira loan floated: If the floating rate rose, the trade would become a loser. But this mismatch was solved by converting the floating payment into a fixed one via the international swaps market. The final messiness was the risk that the Italian government might default, but there were opportunities to hedge that in the fledgling market for credit default swaps.

11. Lowenstein, *When Genius Failed*, p. 77.

12. The Italian government issued floating-rate bonds with a seven-year maturity, called Certificati di Credito del Tesoro (CCTs). These CCTs were off-limits to retail investors, who instead bought short-term Italian treasury bills called Buoni Ordinari del Tesoro (BOT). LTCM bought CCTs and shorted BOTs, betting on their convergence. See LTCM, "Portfolio Outline."

13. Ibid.

14. Andre Perold, "Long-Term Capital Management, L.P. (A)" (Harvard Business School case study 9-200-007, November 5, 1999).

15. Lowenstein, *When Genius Failed*, p. 90.

16. Ibid., p. 84.

17. What follows on risk management is drawn partly from Eric Rosenfeld's draft article for the *Encyclopedia of Quantitative Finance*, ed. Rama Cont (Hoboken, NJ: John Wiley & Sons, 2010).

18. To work out the worst loss on ninety-nine out of a hundred days, LTCM would take the standard deviation of a position, meaning the amount of variation from the mean that occurred in 68 percent of cases, and multiply by 2.58 to get the variation from the mean that occurred in 99 percent of cases. Thus, a position with a standard deviation of six basis points would not fall by more than about fifteen basis points in 99 percent of cases, or on ninety-nine days out of a hundred.

19. Rosenfeld, Harvard Business School presentation. See also Perold, "Long-Term Capital Management."

20. For example, at the time of the Bank of China party, LTCM's leverage was about nineteen to one— extraordinarily high relative to most other hedge funds. But, according to the firm's calculations, LTCM's value at risk was $720 million, and its $6.7 billion in capital was more than enough to absorb that. See Perold, "Long-Term Capital Management."

21. Many hedge funds borrowed cheaply by financing positions in the repo market with overnight money. Long-Term was willing to pay more in order to lock the money up for six to twelve months. It also arranged a three-year loan and a standby credit. Rosenfeld presentation; Perold, "Long-Term Capital Management."

22. Having done its best to lock up capital in these ways, LTCM calculated the residual liquidity risk, gaming out scenarios in which its brokers changed the terms of their lending. For example, rather than lending LTCM 100 percent of the money it needed to buy Italian government bonds, the brokers might demand that Long-Term put up "margin," or capital, equivalent to 5 percent of the value of its positions. To withstand that sort of shock, LTCM made sure to hold emergency reserves of capital. Thus, in September 1997 the firm was using less than $1.7 billion in working capital to meet margin requirements imposed by its brokers, while its total working capital came to $7.6 billion.

23. Rosenfeld observed, "Everyone else started catching up to us. We'd go to put on a trade, but when we started to nibble, the opportunity would vanish." Lewis, "How the Eggheads Cracked."

24. It is not in fact clear that LTCM's Royal Dutch/Shell trade really was a case of overreach. It is true that arbitrage in stocks was different from arbitrage in fixed income. Whereas convergence in bond prices must happen by the time the bonds mature, there is no such forcing event in stocks: The gap

between Royal Dutch Petroleum and Shell Transport had existed for years and might exist forever. It is also true that LTCM staked a huge $2.3 billion on its position, a size that even aggressive trading desks viewed as outlandish. For example, the Goldman Sachs proprietary trading desk bet one tenth as much as LTCM on the Royal Dutch/Shell convergence. But LTCM felt able to make such a large bet because it could finance it more cheaply than its rivals. This allowed it to hold the trade with a view to capturing the "carry" resulting from the gap in dividend yield, rather than holding it in the hope that the two stocks would converge. Its rationale for putting on the trade was different from that of other trading desks, which is why it did it on a larger scale. Even with the benefit of hindsight, and even while acknowledging errors in LTCM's risk management, Eric Rosenfeld views the Royal Dutch/Shell trade as sound. (Eric Rosenfeld, interview with the author, April 16, 2009.) For a critical view of LTCM's position, see Lowenstein, *When Genius Failed*, p. 100.

25. Lowenstein, *When Genius Failed*, p. 126.

26. Rosenfeld interview. Relatedly, Rosenfeld explains that Long-Term's partners debated the question of whether they should reduce the size of their trades in light of the fact that profit opportunities were smaller than in 1994–96. They concluded that this was not their job: Investors expected them to incur risk of a specified and constant size, not to exercise discretion in taking risk on and off. If investors had wanted to reduce risk, they could have withdrawn funds from LTCM.

27. Rosenfeld, Harvard Business School presentation.

28. Rosenfeld interview.

29. LTCM made money on swap spreads in 1997 by going long Treasuries and betting on the spread broadening. In 1998 it was short Treasuries and betting on the spread narrowing. See Perold, "Long-Term Capital Management."

30. Rosenfeld, Harvard Business School presentation.

31. Rosenfeld interview. Similarly, Rickards recalls, "I was on vacation in North Carolina with my family and it was a Friday. Then I got a call from Jim McEntee, and he said, 'Jim, there's a partners' meeting on Sunday. I think you ought to be here.' So we got in the car and drove home. This was a group that liked to play golf. There was nothing normal about a Sunday meeting. And then we just worked for seven weeks almost nonstop after that." Rickards interview.

32. Gary Gladstein, managing director of Soros Fund Management, recalls, "Meriwether came in offering us a very attractive deal with reduced fees and certain percentage of the firm." (Gary Gladstein, interview with the author, March 18, 2008.) Druckenmiller recalls, "We were out of our own pond, and we really didn't know what we were doing, so we didn't do it." (Stanley Druckenmiller, interview with the author, June 4, 2008.)

33. Lowenstein, *When Genius Failed*, p. 153.

34. Rickards recalls, "What you realize [when you suddenly need to raise capital] is that everybody will see you. They might not have any intention of investing with you, but to them it's information. You're the desperate ones, so you're like, 'What do you want to know?' We had had high-quality operational security for four years, and all of the sudden we're pouring our hearts out." Rickards interview.

35. Gary Gladstein, managing director of Soros Fund Management, recalls of this period, "The major bank we dealt with was Kleinwort Benson. Kleinwort had been acquired by Dresdner. The CEO of Dresdner made this comment in Europe that he didn't have any exposure to hedge funds. Then he finds out that he has major exposure to hedge funds because Kleinwort Benson is doing most of the financing for us. So immediately he said that Kleinwort had to close down the account." Gladstein interview.

36. Rosenfeld interview.

37. The imitators were legion. One upstart named Convergence Asset Management launched in January 1998 and raised $700 million in a single month from investors who had been shut out of LTCM, and by the summer of that year, LTCM-style funds were said to account for a quarter of all swaps trading in London. The hedge-fund manager (and future TV celebrity) James Cramer recalled, "I can't believe how many times I was told to do a trade because the boys at Long-Term deemed it a winner." MacKenzie, *An Engine, Not a Camera*, p. 228.

38. The quote comes from Richard Leahy, a Long-Term partner. See Lewis, "How the Eggheads Cracked."

39. Rosenfeld, Harvard Business School presentation.

40. Lowenstein, *When Genius Failed*, pp. 156–57.

41. Rickards recalls, "The whole world knew. So now you could start to trade against us, whereas before if you were on the other side of a trade from LTCM, you might not like it. Now, it's like, 'Okay, these guys are going to die. Figure out what they have and trade against it.'" Rickards interview.

42. MacKenzie, *An Engine, Not a Camera*, p. 234.

43. Meriwether observed: "I like the way Victor [Haghani] put it: The hurricane is not more or less likely to hit because more hurricane insurance has been written. In the financial markets this is not true. The more people write financial insurance, the more likely it is that a disaster will happen, because the people who know you have sold the insurance can make it happen. So you have to monitor what other people are doing." See Lewis, "How the Eggheads Cracked."

44. "When we engaged Goldman, a couple of things happened. I'm the lawyer, so I said, 'I need you guys to sign a nondisclosure agreement.' They're like, 'No way. You're desperate; we'll help you, but we're not signing anything.' Typical Goldman. So I say okay. I didn't have a lot of leverage. So they came in and they literally, in front of our eyes, downloaded our positions and took them back to their headquarters." Rickards interview, February 12, 2009.

45. The quotations from the Goldman trader in London and from Corzine are taken from Lowenstein, *When Genius Failed*, pp. 174–75.

46. Peter Fisher, interview with the author, March 6, 2009.

47. Fisher recalls thinking, "It's not going to be like Drexel Burnham. We're not going to be at the command center trying to decide what we're going to do with the collateral, and we can kind of work it out because we've actually got the assets. This is a hedge fund and there are no assets here. So in the event of default, all that risk is now transferred to these seventeen brokers, who are going to be duty-bound to liquidate. Their lawyers are going to tell their trading desks, 'We gotta close this out as fast as you can because we have a duty—we can't just sit on these positions.'" Fisher interview. See also Lowenstein, *When Genius Failed*, pp. 188–89.

48. The stock prices of banks such as Merrill Lynch and J.P. Morgan had fallen by almost half over the summer.

49. In later congressional testimony, both William McDonough, the head of the New York Fed, and Greenspan emphasized that the Fed's willingness to broker a rescue of LTCM was heightened by the already febrile state of the markets. In light of the later collapse of the hedge fund Amaranth, this is important. Amaranth looked in 2006 like proof that hedge funds could blow up without destabilizing the financial system. But the world could absorb shocks in 2006 in a way that it could not in 1998—or, for that matter, in 2008. This is why it is impossible to say categorically whether hedge funds, or even some subset of hedge funds, do or do not pose systemic risk. The answer depends on market conditions, as argued in the conclusion.

50. Fisher recalls, "All the talking heads are saying that it's because the video of Bill Clinton's Monica Lewinsky deposition is going to be aired at nine o'clock New York time. I remember very clearly as the week progressed that Dave Komansky [Merrill Lynch's boss] and I just thought that was the funniest thing ever." Fisher interview.

51. Rosenfeld, Harvard Business School presentation.

52. By Wednesday Bill McDonough had returned from London and was chairing the meetings, but Fisher was participating as a backbencher. Fisher interview.

53. Rickards interview.

54. Alan Greenspan, "Private-sector refinancing of the large hedge fund, Long-Term Capital Management." Statement before the Committee on Banking and Financial Services, U.S. House of Representatives, 105th Congress, Session 2, October 1, 1998.

55. "In August 2007, the risk-management structure cracked. All the sophisticated mathematics and computer wizardry essentially rested on one central premise: that the enlightened self-interest of owners and managers of financial institutions would lead them to maintain a sufficient buffer against insolvency by actively managing their firms' capital and risk positions. For generations, that premise appeared incontestable [sic] but, in the summer of 2007, it failed." Alan Greenspan, "We Need a Better Cushion Against Risk," *Financial Times*, March 27, 2009, p. 9.

56. Alan Greenspan, "Private-sector refinancing of the large hedge fund, Long-Term Capital Management." Statement before the Committee on Banking and Financial Services, U.S. House of Representatives, 105th Congress, Session 2, October 1, 1998.

57. Reflecting on the evolution of his thinking, Peter Fisher comments, "I was reluctant to say then, 'Therefore we should regulate leverage.' I guess I got myself halfway there. I was saying, 'The problem was leverage, but how do we regulate that?' Ten years on the problem is leverage and we just got to regulate it; we got to find a way. So that's the policy change for me in ten years." (Fisher interview.) Equally, Vincent Reinhart, a senior Fed economist at the time of the LTCM failure, reflects, "Extraordinarily, 1998 was followed not by a reining in of leverage but by an acceleration. The opposite of the logical lesson was drawn." (Vincent Reinhart, interview with the author, September 11, 2008.)

CHAPTER ELEVEN: THE DOT-COM DOUBLE

1. See Tom Wolfe, *The Right Stuff* (New York: Picador, 1979), p. 9.
2. Julian H. Robertson, letter to the limited partners, October 2, 1998. Emphasis in the original.
3. The account of the yen loss is based mainly on an interview with Dan Morehead, Tiger's currency trader. (Dan Morehead, interview with the author, September 2, 2008.) Robertson himself wrote that "the dollar/yen trading market, which is typically quoted in $100 million increments with a 5 basis point bid/offer spread, collapsed in the early part of October to a $50 million increment and 50 basis point spread. Given this thinness, volatility reached unprecedented levels with the price moving 17 percent in one 48-hour period." (Julian H. Robertson, letter to the limited partners, November 4, 1998.)
4. Tiger's "Quarterly Review," circulated to investors in July 1999, reports that total leverage for Tiger Management stood at just over 500 percent as of January 1, 1999. This ratio factored in the use of futures and took account of both equity and macro positions.
5. Robertson letter, November 4, 1998.
6. Discussing the vast size of Tiger's yen short, a former Tiger analyst explains, "You had to be willing to fight with Julian to make things bigger or smaller. Because when Julian fell in love with an idea, at times he would just keep taking it up. There were no risk limits, size limits, position limits, whatever else. So you had to have the personal fortitude to go through a very unpleasant process, to have him be pissed at you, to fight him not to be bigger. And as the population of Tiger changed at that time period, fewer people were willing to fight him, confront him. . . . Julian would be like, 'I like this idea. Let's be bigger.' And the analyst was like, 'Yes, yes, yes.' So they just let Julian get bigger and bigger without letting him know that he was becoming the market."
7. Michael Derchin, Tiger's airline analyst, says Robertson "saw Soros make a lot of money on the macro side, and I think he got attracted to it. And so he made some very big macro bets that blew up on him." Michael Derchin, interview with the author, March 18, 2008.
8. For an excellent scholarly treatment of this dilemma, see Markus K. Brunnermeier and Stefan Nagel, "Hedge Funds and the Technology Bubble," *Journal of Finance* 59, no. 5 (October 2004).
9. John Cassidy, *Dot.con: The Greatest Story Ever Sold* (New York: HarperCollins, 2002), pp. 3–8.
10. Julian H. Robertson, letter to the limited partners, August 7, 1998.
11. Tiger's share of US Airways fluctuated around the 20 percent level. In June 1998 it was just about exactly 20 percent, judging from SEC filings. On March 5, 1999, Bloomberg reported that Tiger owned about 19 percent of US Airways. At the end of 1999, Tiger owned about 22 percent of the airline, according to Tiger's SEC 13F filing for the last quarter of 1999.
12. Derchin interview. Derchin was Tiger's airlines analyst.
13. Julian H. Robertson, letter to the limited partners, April 7, 1999.
14. "Most important in impacting our negative performance has been that Tiger has bought and sold some thirty-one billion dollars worth of securities over the last ten months. These sales of longs and purchases of shorts have been done primarily to reduce leverage in line with our smaller size. The cost of liquidating these positions has been high. . . . Tiger's success has been as a long-term investor. Quarterly withdrawals are incompatible with long-term investment." Julian H. Robertson, letter to the limited partners, August 6, 1999.

15. Richard A. Oppel Jr., "A Tiger Fights to Reclaim His Old Roar," *New York Times*, December 19, 1999.

16. Other prominent hedge-fund managers observing Tiger's plight explicitly drew the lesson that secrecy was essential to stability. For example, Louis Bacon of Moore Capital delivered a speech in London in April 2000 drawing this lesson. See Alexander Ineichen, "The Myth of Hedge Funds," *Journal of Global Financial Markets* 2, no. 4 (Winter 2001), pp. 34–46.

17. Stanley Druckenmiller, interview with the author, June 4, 2008.

18. Druckenmiller recalls, "I had never had a big drawdown from the day I arrived at Quantum until then. Even in '94, when everyone got smoked, I was up 4 percent. I had never known any period of tension. . . . Anyway, in 1999 I find myself down 18 percent in the month of May, and oh, by the way, the market is sharply up. You're talking about a very proud guy who has never had a down year, essentially, and I'm getting killed. Obviously this is in the newspaper." Stanley Druckenmiller, interview with the author, March 13, 2008.

19. Robertson's refusal to buy into the bubble was not quite absolute. In March 1999 he created a $200 million subportfolio to invest in technology, and by late 1999 Robertson claimed that the sub-portfolio was up 62 percent. But a $200 million subfund was too small to affect Tiger's prospects. According to Tiger's reports to investors, total exposure to the technology and communications sector (longs minus shorts) equaled 7 percent of Tiger's capital as of September 30, 1999. By contrast, exposure to the transportation sector came to 9 percent of capital. See also Oppel, "A Tiger Fights."

20. Jane Martinson, "Cyber Stars Corraled at the Ranch," *Guardian*, July 10, 1999, p. 27. Warren Buffett's Berkshire Hathaway fell 23 percent in 1999 against a 20 percent return for the S&P 500 (including dividends), marking Berkshire's first annual decline since 1990.

21. Gary Gladstein, the veteran managing director of Soros Fund Management, recalls Druckenmiller's visit to Sun Valley as a turning point. Equally, Carson Levit recalls, "Stan went out and got religion in Sun Valley on the new economy thing." Carson Levit, interview with the author, June 17, 2008.

22. Druckenmiller interview, March 13, 2008.

23. Levit interview. Robertson confirms that Tiger's sale of South Korea Telecom helped to drive the price down in the summer. See Julian H. Robertson, letter to limited partners, September 10, 1999.

24. David Einhorn. *Fooling Some of the People All of the Time: A Long Short Story* (Hoboken, NJ: John Wiley & Sons, 2008), pp. 33–34.

25. Cassidy, *Dot.con*, pp. 95–96.

26. Michael Lewis, *The New New Thing: A Silicon Valley Story* (New York: W. W. Norton, 1999), p. 165.

27. Einhorn, *Fooling Some of the People All of the Time: A Long Short Story*, p. 37. It should be noted that Einhorn's other short positions generated a large profit in 1999, a rare case of a hedge fund successfully bucking the bubble.

28. The Fed's monetary looseness featured in Druckenmiller's thinking. Druckenmiller interview.

29. An academic study of hedge funds in this period confirmed that their portfolios were heavy with tech stocks, especially in the third quarter of 1999. Technology stocks went from 16 percent of their equity portfolios to 29 percent in just three months, even though the tech sector accounted for just 17 percent of all U.S. stocks at the end of September. See Brunnermeier and Nagel, "Hedge Funds and the Technology Bubble."

30. John Griffin, interview with the author, November 29, 2007.

31. Oppel, "A Tiger Fights."

32. Julian H. Robertson, letter to the limited partners, December 8, 1999.

33. Julian H. Robertson, letter to the limited partners, January 7, 2000.

34. Julian H. Robertson, letter to the limited partners, March 30, 2000.

35. Druckenmiller interview. The role of Celera Genomics as a trigger is suggested in a detailed recon-struction of Quantum's last weeks, which quotes Druckenmiller as saying to a trader, "This is insane. I've never owned a stock that goes from $40 to $250 in a few months." See Gregory Zucker-man, "Hedged Out: How the Soros Funds Lost Game of Chicken Against Tech Stocks," *Wall Street Journal*, May 22, 2000.

36. Druckenmiller interview.
37. Ibid.
38. Zuckerman, "How the Soros Funds Lost."
39. Druckenmiller interview.
40. Thinking back on Druckenmiller's mood, Soros says, "He was torn because he felt loyal; he was engaged. And on the other hand, he felt it was too much. He couldn't bring himself to actually follow through and leave, so because of the inattention he created a situation where he blew up and then he could leave. An expensive way . . . " George Soros, interview with the author, June 10, 2008.
41. Steven Drobny, *Inside the House of Money: Top Hedge Fund Traders on Profiting in the Global Markets,* (Hoboken, NJ: John Wiley & Sons, 2006), p. 28.

CHAPTER TWELVE: THE YALE MEN

1. Sean Driscoll, interview with the author, October 27, 2009. Driscoll is the manager of Glorious Food, the caterer.
2. Roger Lowenstein, *When Genius Failed: The Rise and Fall of Long-Term Capital Management* (New York: Random House, 2000), pp. 103–104. See also Chrystia Freeland, "I Love Competition . . . I Love Winning," *Financial Times,* October 10, 2009.
3. Marcia Vickers, "The Money Game," *Fortune,* October 3, 2005.
4. Day after day during one five-year period, Steyer wore the same vibrant plaid tie to the office, desisting only when an assistant seized it, stains and all, and mounted it in a display box as though it were a deal trophy. See Loch Adamson, "Steyer Power," *Alpha,* January 2005.
5. Robert Rubin says flatly of Steyer, "He doesn't care what he can buy." Steyer and his wife used some of their wealth to support a community bank, One California, which they founded in 2004. Robert Rubin, interview with the author, June 10, 2008. See also Francine Brevetti, "New Bank Welcomes Clients That Others Shun," *Inside Bay Area,* October 4, 2007.
6. The partner was Katie Hall, who had known Steyer at Morgan Stanley and at Stanford.
7. Steyer recalls, "I got no full night of sleep for six months after the crash. I would go to sleep and wake up and then lie there. After the crash, my wife and I would come in at like three and just walk around. No market was open. We'd just hang around the halls, waiting for the market to open. . . . I have a nice wife. I think she thought I might open the window." (Tom Steyer, interview with the author, July 25, 2008.) Steyer's colleague Katie Hall recalls, "Tom is a very, very, very, very focused guy, and if he can't sleep he goes into the office." (Katie Hall, interview with the author, August 28, 2008.) Likewise, Meridee Moore recalls, "Sometimes you'd be right there with Tom trying to talk to him and he would pick up the phone. I used to go into a conference room and call him on the phone sometimes because it would be easier to get his attention. He would always take the phone call. I think that's an arbitrage thing. What if the phone call is from somebody saying the deal's about to break?" (Meridee Moore, interview with the author, July 24, 2008.)
8. Meridee Moore emphasizes the similarity in approach between merger arbitrage and distressed-debt investments. In bankruptcy, distressed debt is often converted into equity, and the payoff from that conversion is akin to the payoff from the deal premium in a merger: In both cases there is an expected return in a fixed time frame. Moore interview.
9. Meridee Moore recalls distressed debt investing in the early 1990s: "There were really three buyers, and all the regulators were putting pressure on the banks to sell their debt. So we have this wonderful supply-demand imbalance." Moore interview.
10. Steyer recalls that the conventional wisdom after Drexel's bankruptcy was that "everything Drexel's ever done was fraudulent, nothing they own is worth anything, these companies are all a joke. Everybody knew that, but it just didn't happen to be true. So if you could bid—which is what we were doing too—against that underlying absolutely accepted lie, then you can make a phenomenal amount of money." Steyer interview.
11. Swensen explains why event-driven funds have a systematic edge in David Swensen, *Pioneering Portfolio Management: An Unconventional Approach to Institutional Investment* (New York: Free Press, 2009), p. 183.

12. Swensen, *Pioneering Portfolio Management*, p. 252. Reflecting on what motivated Steyer, Meridee Moore says, "You get to research different things every day. You get to work on whatever you want. You're predicting outcomes. And if you're right, there's nothing more rewarding. It's the ultimate challenge. That's what keeps people going; it's not the money." Moore interview.

13. Steyer also wanted Farallon employees to have their liquid savings in the firm because otherwise they would expend precious energy on managing their personal portfolios elsewhere, and Steyer could not abide such a distraction. Steyer interview.

14. When Swensen started negotiating seriously with Steyer, he demanded a further refinement on the standard performance fee—Yale preferred to pay a slightly higher than usual rate, but the fee would kick in only after Farallon's returns exceeded the risk-free yield on Treasuries. Steyer could see the purity of this model. But he warned Swensen, correctly, as it turned out, that Farallon would end up earning more from Yale under the Swensen formula. Steyer interview.

15. Steyer interview.

16. The Yale Endowment Web site reports that its first allocation to "absolute return" was in July 1990. Data for 1995 allocations come from Josh Lerner, "Yale University Investments Office: August 2006" (Harvard Business School case study 9-807-073, May 8, 2007).

17. Lerner, "Yale University Investments Office."

18. In 2000, event-driven funds accounted for $71 billion in assets, or 14 percent of the industry total, according to Hedge Fund Research. In 2005, they accounted for $213 billion, or 19 percent. In 2007 they accounted for 436 billion, or 23 percent.

19. For example, Mark Wehrly, Farallon's general counsel, reports that Farallon borrows about $25 for every $100 in equity. Mark Wehrly, interview with the author, July 25, 2008.

20. Robert Howard and Andre F. Perold, "Farallon Capital Management: Risk Arbitrage" (Harvard Business School case study 9-299-020, November 17, 1999). According to this HBS study, the Sharpe ratios for two Farallon funds between 1990 and 1997 were 1.38 and 1.75. The S&P 500 had a Sharpe ratio of 0.50.

21. Enrique Boilini, who led Farallon's investment in Alpargatas, recalls that Gabic, a similar textile company, did not attract the interest of a foreign hedge fund, with the result that its factories were liquidated and all its workers lost their jobs. In turning Alpargatas around, Farallon worked with Texas Pacific Group, another U.S. investor. Enrique Boilini, interview with the author, August 8, 2008.

22. Mark Landler, "Year of Living Dangerously for a Tycoon in Indonesia," *New York Times,* May 16, 1999.

23. Dorinda Elliott, "The Fall of Uncle Liem," *Newsweek,* June 15, 1998.

24. Shoeb Kagda, "Stanchart, M'sian Plantations Among Shortlisted to Buy BCA," *Business Times* (Singapore), November 29, 2001.

25. Andrew Spokes, interview with the author, July 25, 2008.

26. Meridee Moore recalls of Spokes, "He sat in our office in San Francisco for eight months. The women here were just falling all over themselves. He was the most desirable bachelor in town." Moore interview.

27. CalPERS announced it would stay out of Indonesia in February 2002. Craig Karmin and Sarah McBride, "Calpers Pulls Out of 4 Countries, Dealing Blow to Southeast Asia," *Wall Street Journal,* February 22, 2002.

28. Spokes interview.

29. In a further pleasing detail, the government bonds paid a floating rate, so that BCA's owners would be hedged against changes in interest rates on bank deposits. Spokes interview.

30. Data are from Bank Indonesia's Web site, for years ending March 31, 2002, 2003, and 2004.

31. As Indonesia sought to reduce its debt burden with the Western donors of the Paris Club in April 2002, many, including U.S. executive director of the IMF Randal Quarles, cited the BCA deal as evidence that Indonesia was worthy of fresh IMF support. Andrew Spokes recalls: "We were really our own catalyst. It was event driven, and we were our own event, because that transaction pretty much turned around that entire market." Spokes interview.

32. Deborah Frazier, "Underground Water Plan Has a Friend in an Old Foe," *Rocky Mountain News,* October 4, 1996.

33. Gary Boyce, interview with the author, July 23, 2008.

34. Steyer interview.

35. Mark Wehrly recalls, "We were successful in basically polarizing every single constituency against us. So we got the politics wrong. I think we got the science right, but the world wasn't ready for it, and we were doing a horrible job persuading them that this was a good idea. So we retrenched." Wehrly interview.

36. "[Yale president Richard Levin] was misled, and I think that the school was misled by Farallon." Joe Light, "Ranch Deal Prompts Donation, Reevaluation," *Yale Herald*, February 1, 2002.

37. Andrea Johnson, who acted the role of the transparency fairy, recalls, "Obviously it was goofy, but you do these things for the photo op." Andrea Johnson, interview with the author, June 30, 2008.

38. Steve Bruce, Farallon's public-relations adviser, emphasizes the efforts to protect the salamanders. "They hired an environmental engineering firm to come in and do a study on salamanders: where they hatch their eggs, where they move them, how do they get to the beach, what sort of pesticides do you have to use, how do you keep the course in place without screwing up their breeding facilities. So by the time the critics brought it up, this was a red herring disguised as a salamander." Steve Bruce, interview with the author, June 25, 2008.

39. "Farallon Founder Hits Back at Critics," *Financial News* (Daily), March 28, 2004.

40. "I just remember David Swensen being really angry. It was very clear to me that he found our campaign extremely upsetting. It was personal to him, because he had received so many accolades even then, and it has only gotten more since then for his incredible management of the investment of the endowment. And I think more than that, there is a sense of pride in that endowment office that they are managing a nonprofit institution's money and that they have standards. I got the sense that he didn't feel like he invests in just whatever." Johnson interview.

41. Swensen's altercation with the students is recalled by Andrea Johnson and is captured in a news photograph and story. See Tom Sullivan, "Yale Defends Record Privacy," *Yale Daily News*, April 5, 2004; Johnson interview.

42. Meridee Moore recalls, "You have to get out there and figure out what the potato farmers are going to do. We weren't on the ground that much. That turned out to be much more important than we expected." (Moore interview.) Mark Wehrly, the Farallon general counsel, says, "Once in a while you end up with the wrong partner, and we did there, and it cost us." (Wehrly interview.)

43. Swensen himself argued that illiquid markets offered bargains. "Success matters, not liquidity. If private, illiquid investments succeed, liquidity follows as investors clamor for shares of the hot initial public offering. In public markets, as once-illiquid stocks produce strong results, liquidity increases as Wall Street recognizes progress. In contrast, if public, liquid investments fail, illiquidity follows as investor interest wanes. Portfolio managers should fear failure, not illiquidity." Swensen, *Pioneering Portfolio Management*, p. 89.

CHAPTER THIRTEEN: THE CODE BREAKERS

1. This figure is net of fees, which were considerable. Rather than charging clients a management fee of 1 percent or 2 percent and keeping 20 percent of the investment gains, Medallion charged a management fee of 5 percent. Sandor Straus, a mathematician who was a partner at Renaissance Technologies and its antecedents between 1980 and 1996, recalls that the 5 percent fee was chosen in 1988 because that was what was needed to cover technology expenses. In addition, the Medallion Fund charges a performance fee that has increased over the years from 20 percent to 44 percent. Sandor Straus, interview with the author, July 25, 2008.

2. Elwyn Berlekamp, interview with the author, July 24, 2008.

3. Sandor Straus regards Henry Laufer as the most important contributor to Medallion's success, notably because of the work he did starting in 1989. Laufer did his breakthrough work on short-term patterns between 1983 and 1985, according to Straus. Laufer then went back to academia for a while before reengaging with Medallion in 1989. Some public accounts erroneously state that Laufer's involvement began in the 1990s. Straus interview.

4. Robert Frey, a Renaissance alumnus, describes the firm's pattern recognition as neither mean reverting nor trend following. Rather, in response to a shock, the market moves around in multiple ways: "If I

think of an electrical circuit or any sort of physical system, if I put an input in, the initial output may be negatively correlated to the input, and then it may become positively correlated. It depends on how the thing resonates through the system." Robert Frey, interview with the author, July 28, 2008.

5. Straus interview.

6. Mark Silber, interview with the author, July 30, 2008. Silber is the chief financial officer of Renaissance Technologies.

7. Eric Wepsic, interview with the author, January 28, 2009. Wepsic is a member of D. E. Shaw's six-person Executive Committee.

8. Richard Bookstaber, *A Demon of Our Own Design: Markets, Hedge Funds, and the Perils of Financial Innovation* (Hoboken, NJ: John Wiley & Sons, 2007), p. 187.

9. Ibid., p. 189.

10. Trey Beck notes, "At Morgan Stanley, they had a whole bank of IBM mainframes. When we started we had one Sun workstation. We did not need NASA technology because we did not expect other people to be making the same trades." Trey Beck, interview with the author, August 31, 2009. Beck is a managing director at D. E. Shaw.

11. Michael Peltz, "Computational Finance with David Shaw," *Institutional Investor* 28, no. 3 (March 1994): pp. 92–94.

12. The economists' idealized models created different versions of this vulnerability in different parts of the world. Trey Beck of D. E. Shaw cites an example from emerging markets: Two apparently equivalent bonds issued by the same government might trade at different levels, tempting an arbitrage-minded economist to bet on convergence. But the difference might reflect a factor omitted from the economist's model: Perhaps the more expensive bond was substantially owned by a well-connected oligarch, with the result that its default risk was far lower because the government would not wish to alienate him. Beck interview.

13. Wepsic interview.

14. Trey Beck, interview with the author, September 2, 2009.

15. Wadhwani recalls, "Like a lot of ex-academic economists, I was very driven by value. And I guess the key thing I learned from observing great traders was actually that value is a great medium-term factor, but tactical trading is about many, many, many more things other than value. On average, be in the direction of value, but you want to pay attention to all these other things too." Sushil Wadhwani, interview with the author, July 28, 2009. See also Steven Drobny, *Inside the House of Money: Top Hedge Fund Traders on Profiting in the Global Markets*, (Hoboken, NJ: John Wiley & Sons, 2006), p. 174.

16. Wadhwani recalls, "Often it was the case that you were already using the input variables these guys were talking about, but you were perhaps using these input variables in a more naive way in your statistical model than the way they were actually using it." Wadhwani interview.

17. Mahmood Pradhan, who worked with Wadhwani at Tudor, elaborates: "There are times when particular variables explain certain asset prices, and there are times when other things determine the price. So you need to understand when your model is working and when it isn't. For example, sometimes current account deficits have a strong bearing on exchange rates. But other times people are quite willing to tolerate very large current account deficits because of some new preoccupation that is not in your model. Sovereign wealth funds may have emerged. Or the Asians have more capital. Or something else is going on that you may not be capturing." Mahmood Pradhan, interview with the author, April 29, 2008.

18. Mark Dalton, interview with the author, September 29, 2008. Dalton is the president of Tudor.

19. Eric Wepsic of D. E. Shaw confirms, "Our staff started on average a little younger, a little more right out of school, a lot of people who had just got their PhDs, or people like me who didn't even have a PhD." (Wepsic interview.) One of the few exceptions to the Renaissance rule of not hiring from Wall Street was Robert Frey, a mathematician who had been at Morgan Stanley.

20. Wadhwani interview.

21. See, for example, Peter F. Brown, Stephen A. Della Pietra, Vincent J. Della Pietra, and Robert L. Mercer, "The Mathematics of Statistical Machine Translation: Parameter Estimation," *Computational Linguistics* 19, no. 2 (1993). As noted below, the Della Pietra brothers followed Brown and Mercer from IBM to Renaissance Technologies.

22. As far back as 1949, code breakers had wondered about the application of their technique to translation. But they lacked computing power; statistical translation depended on feeding a vast number of pairs of sentences into a computer, so that the computer had enough data from which to extract meaningful patterns. But by around 1990, statistical translation was possible on a well-equipped workstation.

23. Mercer had spent a couple of summers at IDA working with Nick Patterson, a British mathematician who went on to join Simons. Simons's connection to Baum also helped him persuade Brown and Mercer to join up. Peter Brown recalls: "When Bob and I were contacted by Jim Simons we hadn't heard of him. But when we heard he had worked with Lenny Baum we started to take the offer seriously." Peter Brown, interview with the author, July 28, 2008.

24. An account of the reaction to the Brown-Mercer work is given in Andy Way "A Critique of Statistical Machine Translation." In W. Daelemans and V. Hoste (eds.), *Journal of Translation and Interpreting Studies: Special Issue on Evaluation of Translation Technology*, Linguistica Antverpiensia, 2009, pp. 17–41.

25. See, for example, Pius Ten Hacken, "Has There Been a Revolution in Machine Translation?" *Machine Translation* 16, no. 1 (March 2001): pp. 1–19. This source erroneously attributes the quote on firing linguists to Peter Brown.

26. The initial versions of the IBM program included no linguistic rules at all. Later versions did use some, but they played a far smaller role than in traditional translation programs.

27. Wepsic interview.

28. John Magee, a leading technician of the 1950s, made a point of reading the newspapers two weeks late in order to be sure that knowledge of the economy would not cloud his judgment.

29. Mercer says, "We will contemplate any proposed signal. But if somebody comes with a theory that does not make intuitive sense, we would examine it especially carefully." (Robert Mercer, interview with the author, July 28, 2008.) The same willingness to trade on statistical evidence was shared by earlier contributors to Medallion's success. For example, Elwyn Berlekamp recalls, "Mostly we looked at statistics at Medallion. We found that attempts to look at fundamentals did not get us very far." Elwyn Berlekamp, interview with the author, July 24, 2008. It is also interesting that Brown and Mercer's coauthors who followed them to Renaissance, Stephen and Vincent Della Pietra, explicitly presented their experience with statistical machine translation as relevant to finding order in other types of data, including financial data. See Adam L. Berger, Stephen A. Della Pietra, and Vincent J. Della Pietra, "A Maximum Entropy Approach to Natural Language Processing," *Computational Linguistics* 22, no. 1 (March 1996): pp. 39–71.

30. To manage the potential linguistic chaos resulting from this permissiveness, neologisms had to be submitted to a review. Mercer interview.

31. The Russian employees were Pavel Volfbeyn and Alexander Belopolsky. The firm that they defected to was Millennium. They argued through their lawyer that their new system was not based on proprietary secrets from Renaissance. See Thomas Maier, "Long Island's Richest Man from Math to Money," *Newsday*, July 5, 2006, p. A04.

32. Silber interview.

33. Robert Frey explains, "Those researchers were sort of like hothouse flowers. They sit there. If they need data, the data are provided. They have no clue of the hoops you have to jump through to make sure that the data are available and clean and ready. There are tens of terabytes of data available at the touch of a button. Someone going out, who left the greenhouse, so to speak, and went out into the cold, cruel world, I think would quickly find out that even if you could produce these simulations and do all of this stuff, which isn't trivial, you wouldn't have access to the historical data. You wouldn't really know how to call up somebody and execute a trade. If you said to me, Robert you don't have a noncompete agreement and we want you to recreate Renaissance, it would probably be four or five years before you could get to a point where you could actually trade." (Frey interview.) It should be said, however, that Medallion defectors who join a rival hedge fund that has research and trading infrastructure already in place could damage Medallion in well under five years.

34. The $6 billion number is for 2007 and is given in Richard Teitelbaum, "Simons at Renaissance Cracks Code, Doubling Assets," Bloomberg.com, November 27, 2007.

CHAPTER FOURTEEN: PREMONITIONS OF A CRISIS

1. Hal Lux, "Boy Wonder," *Institutional Investor*, January 2001.
2. The expense ratio for Citadel investors averaged just under 9 percent in the three years 2005 to 2007. Expenses covered costs such as brokerage, legal fees, tax and audit fees, and the building out of Citadel's computer infrastructure, which partially supported trading businesses whose profits flowed entirely to Citadel, not to outside investors. Meanwhile, other hedge funds found they could raise fees too. In November 2002, Bruce Kovner's Caxton announced that it would be hiking its fees to 3 percent of the principal plus 30 percent of the performance. Caxton said it needed to raise fees because of the competitive atmosphere in luring trading talent. See "Caxton to Hike Fees, Merge Funds," *Private Asset Management*, November 24, 2002.
3. Marcia Vickers, "Ken the Conqueror," *Fortune*, April 16, 2007, p. 80.
4. Gregory Zuckerman, "Shake-Out Roils Hedge Fund World," *Wall Street Journal*, June 17, 2008.
5. An Amaranth veteran recalls, "Typically at Amaranth when traders made money, they were allowed to keep that money in their portfolio, rather than saying, 'Oh, great, you just made a billion dollars for the firm, now we're going to take that and give it to the guys in converts.' That would not have been the way to motivate people."
6. A senior Amaranth executive recalls, "In 2003, 2004, 2005, multistrategy arbitrage returns were getting smaller. The business was getting saturated; the trades were getting crowded."
7. An Amaranth veteran recalls of Hunter: "He was incredibly intelligent. Just incredibly intelligent. Brilliant in terms of his analysis of, 'Okay, we think this is going to happen, and here's how we can use the various instruments out there to take advantage of that.' And just finding very interesting little market movements, submarket movements, and things going on and how to profit from those. And also how to construct what people like to describe as asymmetrical risk profiles. And people had a tremendous amount of respect for him because he could sort of make those arguments, and then when he implemented them, they were actually incredibly profitable."
8. One newspaper account reported, "Mr. Maounis says the firm knew of Mr. Hunter's history at Deutsche Bank but did extensive checks and found 'nothing that made us uncomfortable.'" See Ann Davis, "Private Money: The New Financial Order—Blue Flameout: How Giant Bets on Natural Gas Sank Brash Hedge-Fund Trader," *Wall Street Journal*, September 19, 2006.
9. According to one insider, Hunter's compensation for 2005 consisted of $75 million in cash and $50 million in deferred compensation.
10. An Amaranth veteran recalls Maounis saying of Hunter, "Don't you think he is a genius?" Another Amaranth veteran says of Maounis, "What I believe is, he must have said, 'Brian's book is like a zero-premium convertible book.' So even though notionally it looked large, it's really not that risky. So with hindsight everyone's saying, 'What in the fuck, are you crazy? Look at the size of this thing!' But the risk guys must have convinced Nick that even though notionally it was very, very large, from a risk perspective it was very, very small. Because that was Nick's upbringing. That was how a convertible bond portfolio could be."
11. A senior Amaranth executive recalls, "Nick was always very jealous of, envious, as we all are, of Jim Simons's ability to manufacture money with the Medallion fund. We spent a lot of money building stat-arb systems, hiring stat-arb people. Didn't even get in the same universe as that, but he kept trying and trying, looking for the holy grail. Nick had the true belief that there were certain people who were truly special at what they did. And he thought that Brian Hunter was truly special."
12. These details on Amaranth's positions, and many others that follow, are drawn from a lengthy report by the U.S. Senate Permanent Subcommittee on Investigations, which reports to the Committee on Homeland Security and Government Affairs. See U.S. Senate Permanent Subcommittee on Investigations, "Excessive Speculation in the Natural Gas Market," June 25, 2007. The report is not flawless. It draws the conclusion that Amaranth's failure makes the case for additional hedge-fund regulation, whereas the failure is better seen as an example of the market disciplining a rogue trader.

Further, the report makes much of the total exposure accumulated by Amaranth in various futures contracts, not explaining that the net exposure matters more and that natural-gas futures are traded over the counter, making it impossible to know how much of the total market Amaranth accounted for. Nevertheless, the Senate investigators did collect a vast amount of valuable data and testimony on Amaranth's natural-gas trading. In the judgment of the Senate report, "Amaranth's large-scale trading was a major driver behind the rise of the January/November price spread from $1.40 in mid-February to $2.20 in late April, an increase of more than 50 percent." The Senate report states, "On every trading day in May, Amaranth accounted for at least 55 percent of the open interest in the November 2006 contract . . . Put simply, Amaranth was too big for the market it had created." Even allowing for the caveat that NYMEX is not the whole of the gas-futures market, Amaranth's share of NYMEX trading is striking.

13. At the time, Blackstone kept its withdrawal secret. A Blackstone official explains that publicity might have caused other investors to flee Amaranth, creating a run on the fund that might have provoked a freeze on withdrawals, trapping Blackstone's money.

14. Amaranth's willingness to pay Morgan Stanley a large fee to get out of certain gas positions confirms the verdict that it had grown too big for the market. If it had been able to trade out of its positions easily, it would have done so. The Morgan Stanley evidence matters because Amaranth representatives have sometimes suggested that the fund was brought down not by its excessive size, but rather by conspiracies against the fund, ranging from predatory trading on the NYMEX in late August to J.P. Morgan's opposition to the Goldman Sachs deal in September.

15. Amaranth's broad exposures were well known because the fund provided investors with monthly reports detailing returns and outlining how these had been generated. Hedge-fund transparency is generally considered a good thing, but there is a risk to it.

16. U.S. Senate Permanent Subcommittee on Investigations, "Excessive Speculation in the Natural Gas Market."

17. A former trader at Amaranth comments, "They counseled Brian to get out. He needed to be ordered." Another Amaranth official says, a bit uncertainly, "I don't want to believe that Brian Hunter didn't try to reduce his positions. Because we were told that he was trying, but there just wasn't enough liquidity." Yet a third Amaranth veteran describes extensive debates within the firm as to how quickly to cut the natural-gas exposure; these concluded in the view that it was unwise to pay a high price in order to exit precipitously. It is not clear that Amaranth could have saved itself by opting to exit quickly at all costs. If Hunter had cut his positions aggressively any time after April, he might well have taken losses so large as to put Amaranth out of business.

18. Looking back on this period, one trader describes Hunter as "a menace." Equally, the Senate report quotes numerous traders to this effect. For instance, one says, "Everyone in the market knew Amaranth killed MotherRock." Amaranth denies it.

19. The Amaranth veteran comments, "Remember, I said the guy fell in love. Maybe that's what we're talking about. Maybe it's just another manifestation of the love. . . . I told you he thought this guy could do no wrong. And when he made that statement [to the *Wall Street Journal*] I'm sure he believed it."

20. An Amaranth official recalls that some of Hunter's summer/winter positions were designed to hedge others, but that by September supposedly offsetting positions were going wrong simultaneously, suggesting that Amaranth was being targeted by rival traders.

21. This dialogue comes from interviews with Winkler and Griffin and from a complaint filed by Amaranth against J.P. Morgan in the New York State Supreme Court on November 13, 2007.

22. Many big banks run multiple computer systems, which would have made it hard to sync Amaranth data into all the relevant divisions.

23. J. Tomilson Hill, vice chairman of the Blackstone Group, comments, "If Citadel had been big enough in 1998 to buy LTCM, the odds would have been much better that a deal would have gotten done." J. Tomilson Hill, interview with the author, September 9, 2009.

24. This account is based on interviews with Ken Griffin and other Citadel staff members, as well as with Karl Wachter and Charles Winkler of Amaranth.

25. One popular regulatory response to the growth of leveraged trading is to push over-the-counter derivatives such as swaps onto exchanges. Although this response is generally reasonable, it should

be noted that most of Hunter's gas exposure was on an exchange, and further that the exchange authorities were ineffectual in limiting his excessive trading. By contrast, the discipline of the market proved brutally effective.

CHAPTER FIFTEEN: RIDING THE STORM

1. John Gittelsohn, "High Roller of Home Loans," *Orange County Register*, May 20, 2007.
2. Mark Pittman, "Bass Shorted 'God I Hope You're Wrong' Wall Street," *Bloomberg*, December 19, 2007.
3. Michael Litt, interview with the author, July 2, 2009. The BIS report was "The Recent Behavior of Financial Market Volatility" (BIS paper 29, August 2006). For an account of FrontPoint's portfolio manager, Steve Eisman, see Michael Lewis, "The End," *Portfolio*, December 2008. It should be noted that the BIS was actually among the few official institutions to warn of the risk of a financial crisis, even though this warning was not apparent to Litt.
4. From inception in December 2006 to mid-October 2007, Bass's dedicated mortgage fund was up 463 percent. FrontPoint ran multistrategy funds, so the mortgage bets were diluted. Nevertheless, in 2007 FrontPoint's low-volatility multistrategy fund was up 23 percent and its midvolatility version was up 44 percent.
5. The following account of Paulson's subprime trade is reconstructed from conversations with John Paulson and Paolo Pellegrini and from a report produced by Paulson and Company. John Paulson, interview with the author, July 15, 2009; Paolo Pellegrini, interview with the author, July 2, 2009; Paulson and Company, "Paulson Credit Opportunities, 2007 Year End Report."
6. Pellegrini interview.
7. Paulson and Pellegrini soon realized their error. Their research showed that the percentage of mortgage loans extended on the basis of limited documentation had risen from 27 percent in 2001 to 41 percent in 2005, but it also showed that refinancing was covering up the problem of poor loan quality. Between 1998 and 2006, at least half of subprime mortgages were refinanced within five years.
8. This is the conversation as remembered by John Paulson. Paulson interview.
9. Paulson's plan was to buy insurance on $12 of subprime mortgages for every $1 he had in his fund, so a $600 million fund involved buying insurance on $7.2 billion of mortgages. The cost of this insurance was about 1 percent of the value of the mortgages, so 12 percent of the value of the fund. But Paulson earned 5 percent from the interest on the free cash in the fund, so that the net cost of putting on the bet was 7 percent of the fund's assets.
10. Gregory Zuckerman, *The Greatest Trade Ever: The Behind-the-Scenes Story of How John Paulson Defied Wall Street and Made Financial History* (New York: Broadway Books, 2009), p. 197.
11. Zuckerman, *The Greatest Trade Ever*, p. 208.
12. In 2008, according to Hedge Fund Research, asset-backed hedge funds were down 3 percent, a respectable showing given the carnage that surrounded them. Although the rest of the hedge-fund industry suffered a hard year in 2008, it was not because it fell for subprime mortgages.
13. In perhaps the clearest example of this folly, UBS vacuumed up $50 billion worth of AAA mortgage bonds, confident that AAA paper would always pay back; in 2007 alone, this decision accounted for $12.5 billion of losses.
14. Paul Muolo and Matthew Padilla, *Chain of Blame: How Wall Street Caused the Mortgage and Credit Crisis* (Hoboken, NJ: John Wiley & Sons, 2008), p. 190. Other accounts confirm O'Neal's determination to raise Merrill's ranking in mortgage securitization. See Bradley Keoun and Jody Shenn, "Merrill Loaded for Bear in Mortgage Market That Humiliated HSBC," *Bloomberg*, February 12, 2007.
15. William D. Cohan, *House of Cards: A Tale of Hubris and Wretched Excess on Wall Street* (New York: Doubleday, 2009), p. 281.
16. "Investors who sought to take advantage of the inimitable risk management reputation of Bear Stearns found themselves in a highly complex hedge fund investment program that relied on overworked junior personnel to manage a conflict reporting process required by federal law." Administrative complaint against Bear Stearns Asset Management filed by the Commonwealth of Massachusetts, quoted in Cohan, *House of Cards*, p. 302.

17. Hedge fund subsidiaries of other banks also fared poorly. UBS's Dillon Read Capital Management and Royal Bank of Scotland's Greenwich Capital were both wound down in 2007 following losses on subprime securities. Much as happened at Bear Stearns, UBS injected capital into its failed funds, took their losses onto its balance sheet, and then found itself in need of a government bailout. Of UBS's $19 billion in losses in 2007, Dillon Read accounted for $3 billion. Meanwhile, the Royal Bank of Scotland had to take RBS Greenwich's losses onto its balance sheet, contributing to the bank's later collapse into the arms of the UK government.

18. These figures come from Paulson and Company, "Paulson Credit Opportunities, 2007 Year End Report." The cumulative figure is reached by compounding the 20 percent return in 2006 with the 590 percent return in 2007.

19. This story and the ensuing account of the Sowood transaction is reconstructed from interviews with Ken Griffin, Gerald Beeson, and Adam Cooper of Citadel. Ken Griffin, interview with the author, July 9, 2009; Gerald Beeson, interview with the author, June 30, 2009; Adam Cooper, interview with the author, June 30, 2009.

20. Kyle Bass of Hayman Capital wrote in an investor letter dated July 31, 2007: "What is truly remarkable about this particular situation is the fact that Jeff Larson, the former manager of the $30 billion Harvard Endowment, is the principal Manager at this firm. Sowood was renowned as being a 'best-in-class' fund." Kyle Bass, letter to Hayman Capital investors, July 30, 2007. See also Jenny Strasburg and Katherine Burton, "Sowood Funds Lose More Than 50% as Debt Markets Fall (Update 4)," *Bloomberg,* July 31, 2007.

21. Gregory Zuckerman and Craig Karmin, "Sowood's Short, Hot Summer," *Wall Street Journal,* October 27, 2007.

22. Some press accounts note that Larson and Griffin spoke on Friday, July 27. But Griffin, Cooper, and Beeson separately recall that the key phone conversation was on Sunday.

23. Jeff Larson, letter to Sowood investors, July 30, 2007.

24. Cohan, *House of Cards,* p. 381.

25. Jim Cramer, "Street Signs," CNBC, August 3, 2007.

26. A quant firm could believe both in stock momentum and in momentum reversal. Both effects could exist, but on different time horizons.

27. For instance, Black Mesa, a small quantitative hedge fund based in New Mexico, reported in an investor letter that a pattern of liquidation started on July 25, 2007, and lasted through Friday. "The losses were found not to be attributable to common market risks," Black Mesa reported. "The losses were in our proprietary factors or, in other words, attributable to risks to which we deliberately expose ourselves."

28. Many in the quant industry suspect that the storm of deleveraging was started by Bruce Kovner's Caxton Associates. This is not quite right. It is true that Kovner assembled his portfolio managers on the evening of Sunday, August 5, and instructed them to cut risk. But the meeting did not include Aaron Sosnick, who managed the capital that Caxton committed to statistical arbitrage. Rather, Sosnick had cut his leverage substantially in the previous several days, so was not selling aggressively on Monday, August 6, the start of the quant quake. Bruce Kovner, interview with the author, October 14, 2009.

29. Quant equity hedge funds in the summer of 2007 seem to have been leveraged between six to one and eight to one. They sometimes described this as leverage of "three to four," meaning three to four times on the short side and the same amount on the long side, giving a total leverage of six to eight.

30. Clifford Asness, "The August of Our Discontent: Questions and Answers about the Crash and Subsequent Rebound of Quantitative Stock Selection Strategies," working paper, September 21, 2007.

31. Cliff Asness explains, "By and large much of quantitative investing is about common sense and discipline, rather than about esoteric math and computer algorithms. . . . The computers help us process the data and maintain a diversified and disciplined approach. . . . It's about good investing done broadly and without the often dangerous influence of tick-by-tick human emotion. Our strategies are not 'black boxes.'" (Clifford Asness, "The August of Our Discontent: Questions and Answers about the Crash and Subsequent Rebound of Quantitative Stock Selection Strategies,"

working paper, September 21, 2007.) In an e-mail to investors, Jim Simons wrote, "While we believe we have an excellent set of predictive signals, some of these are undoubtedly shared by a number of long/short hedge funds." (Jim Simons, e-mail to Renaissance Technologies investors, August 9, 2007.)

32. Satya Pradhuman, director of research at Cirrus Research, identified 148 companies with market capitalizations between $2 billion and $10 billion and 473 companies with market capitalizations between $250 million and $2 billion in which large quant funds had ownership stakes exceeding 5 percent. See Justin Lahart, "How the 'Quant' Playbook Failed," *Wall Street Journal*, August 24, 2007.

33. Scott Patterson, "A Hedge-Fund King Is Forced to Regroup," *Wall Street Journal*, May 26, 2009.

34. Asness, "The August of Our Discontent."

35. Cliff Asness comments, "Most of our lives are about automated quant trading. But when you have a conflagration of this size, having good intelligence, having good contacts on the Street, those things really matter." (Cliff Asness, interview with the author, July 9, 2009.) Similarly, Sushil Wadhwani, who was running his systematic funds in London, recalls, "I remember Friday morning. . . . It was a question of either someone came in with a bailout or they delevered." (Sushil Wadhwani, interview with the author, July 28, 2009.)

36. Here was yet another example of a hedge fund managed under the umbrella of an investment bank going wrong. The fact that the parent bank bailed out the hedge fund, as had happened at Bear Stearns, showed why the fund managers may have been less vigilant than their counterparts at independent funds with no deep-pocketed parents. J.P. Morgan analyst Stephen Wharton brought up this issue on Goldman's conference call, organized to announce the recapitalization. "I mean do you feel there is some moral hazard being introduced here in terms of how investment banks are reacting to problematic hedge funds managed by their asset management arms?" Naturally, Goldman rejected the comparison, pointing out that it was providing $2 billion of the $3 billion recapitalization, with the rest coming from outside investors. Goldman Sachs conference call, final transcript, *Thomson StreetEvents*, August 13, 2007.

37. See Amir E. Khandani and Andrew W. Lo, "What Happened to the Quants in August 2007?" working paper, November 4, 2007; Richard Bookstaber, *A Demon of Our Own Design* (Hoboken, NJ: JohnWiley & Sons, 2007). See also Richard Bookstaber, "What's Going On with Quant Hedge Funds?" (available at http://rick.bookstaber.com/2007/08/whats-going-on-with-quant-hedge-funds.html).

38. "I have said before that 'there is a new risk factor in our world,'" Cliff Asness wrote in the wake of the quant quake. "But it would have been more accurate if I had said 'there is a new risk factor in our world and it is us.'" See Asness, "The August of Our Discontent."

39. Cliff Asness and Adam Berger, "We're Not Dead Yet," *Alpha*, November 2008.

40. "It's hard to prove that if there are a lot of people in a space, returns get worse. You can look at the performance and conclude that, like Lo does. Increased assets in a space, performance goes down—it sounds reasonable. But if you try to actually demonstrate is by building a portfolio and saying, 'This is a portfolio I would like to get but can't because the market is slipping away from me,' you can't quite do that. At Thales we find we can trade the same model with a slight variation: one that sets trades on a two- to three-day time scale and one that trades on a five-day time scale. They don't even interfere with one another even though these are two models that are almost the same. The likelihood that our particular model is being interfered with by Shaw or Caxton or Citadel seems low." Marek Fludzinski, interview with the author, June 25, 2009.

41. Asness, "The August of Our Discontent."

42. Mike Mendelson, interview with the author, July 9, 2009.

CHAPTER SIXTEEN: "HOW COULD THEY DO THIS?"

1. In 2008, Kynikos was up more than 60 percent. Relative to the market's performance, however, the 2007 return of over 30 percent was even better. Kynikos takes a performance fee based on its returns relative to the market benchmark.

2. This remark and much of the telephone exchange between Chanos and Schwartz was reported by Gary Weiss and confirmed by the author in an interview with Chanos. See Gary Weiss, "The Man

Who Made Too Much," *Portfolio*, February 2009. Weiss also reports that Schwartz disputes the timing and detail of the call, saying it took place one day earlier, on Wednesday. However, Chanos remembers receiving the call on the way to see Bernstein, and Bernstein confirms that the dinner was on Thursday and that Chanos told him then about the phone call. James Chanos, interview with the author, September 23, 2009; Carl Bernstein, interview with the author, September 28, 2009.

3. Bryan Burrough, "Bringing Down Bear Stearns," *Vanity Fair*, August 2008; Andrew Ross Sorkin, *Too Big to Fail: The Inside Story of How Wall Street and Washington Fought to Save the Financial System—and Themselves* (New York: Viking, 2009), p. 15.

4. In an interview on September 21, 2009, an SEC spokesman confirmed that, eighteen months after Bear's failure, nobody had been prosecuted for conspiring to drive Bear Stearns down.

5. There is no evidence of a conspiracy to bring down Bear but plenty of evidence that Bear made mistakes that, coupled with high leverage and a reliance on short-term funding, sealed its own fate. The loss of confidence in Bear seems to have been brought on by the knowledge that it held huge mortgage positions and that other institutions holding similar positions were reporting major losses. On February 14, UBS had written down the value of its mortgage book, including "Alt-A" loans to wealthy borrowers. This had dire implications for Bear Stearns, which held a $6 billion portfolio of Alt-A mortgages and had used these as collateral to fund itself. On March 10, Moody's downgraded mortgage bonds that Bear had underwritten and hinted that further rating downgrades would be forthcoming. Given all this, the notion that Bear collapsed because of a short-selling conspiracy seems too simple. Moreover, when Bear was bought by J.P. Morgan, Morgan's analysis of Bear's mortgage book suggested that the bank's latent losses exceeded recognized ones by a wide margin, which is one reason why Morgan almost refused to buy Bear and eventually did so for a fraction of the $54 per share at which Bear had closed on Friday, March 14. Again, the point is that the shorts had good reason to be short. For the chest-bumping image, I am indebted to a hilarious post by Bess Levin on the Dealbreaker blog, July 1, 2008.

6. Hugo Lindgren, "The Confidence Man," *New York*, June 15, 2008.

7. Interviews with two ex-Lehman Brothers officials. See also Sorkin, *Too Big to Fail*, pp. 79 and 100.

8. In an e-mail analysis, value investor Whitney Tilson credited Einhorn with having made Lehman face facts: "The losses are the losses—Einhorn certainly isn't causing them. But thanks in large part to his questions, the company is selling assets, deleveraging and raising capital, all of which makes it more likely that the firm lives to fight another day rather than imploding and shaking the world financial system to its core." On his *New York Times* DealBook blog, Andrew Ross Sorkin put it more bluntly: "Few people had more reasonable claim to vindication on Monday than David Einhorn." See Hugo Lindgren, "The Confidence Man," *New York*, June 15, 2008.

9. Chrystia Freeland, "The Profit of Doom," *Financial Times*, January 31, 2009 (weekend supplement).

10. This threat is recalled by Werner Seifert, the Deutsche Börse chief executive, who tells his side of the story in his book, *Invasion of the Locusts: Intrigues, Power Struggles, and Market Manipulation* (Ullstein Taschenbuchvlg, 2007).

11. Michael J. de la Merced, "A Hedge Fund Struggle for CSX Is Left in Limbo," *New York Times*, June 26, 2008.

12. Gillian Tett, *Fool's Gold: How the Bold Dream of a Small Tribe at J.P. Morgan Was Corrupted by Wall Street Greed and Unleashed a Catastrophe* (New York: Free Press), 2009, pp. 160–62.

13. Paul Tudor Jones, internal Tudor e-mail, June 28, 2008.

14. "I just thought even though one was a weekly and one was a daily, the chart patterns were so similar and the backdrops were so similar—two huge credit bubbles with enormous overcommitment to a variety of asset markets, real estate and stock market bubbles happening simultaneously." Paul Tudor Jones, interview with the author, April 15, 2009.

15. Ibid.

16. After the fact, policy makers argued that they let Lehman fail because they lacked the legal authority to do otherwise. But policy makers had successfully stretched the legal bounds of their authority in

other cases, and they acted aggressively again in the following days with respect to AIG, and then with respect to Goldman Sachs and Morgan Stanley, which were hurriedly granted full access to the Fed's emergency loans. Moreover, the policy makers' claim that the Fed could not lend to Lehman because it lacked adequate collateral is weakened by the fact that in the three days after Lehman's bankruptcy, the Fed did actually lend Lehman's broker-dealer unit $160 billion to tide it over until its sale to the British bank Barclays. It seems overwhelmingly likely that the government would have found a legal way to save Lehman Brothers if it had guessed in advance the consequences of its failure.

17. Paul Tudor Jones, interview with the author, April 15, 2009.

18. Jones interview. Jones adds, "From a trading perspective, fear is a much stronger emotion than greed, which is why things go down twice as fast as they go up. And that's also just the law of nature. How long does it take for a tree to grow, and how quickly can you burn it down? It's much easier to destroy things than to build them up. So from a trading perspective, the short side is always a beautiful place to be because quite often when you get paid, you get paid in vertical no-pain type of moves."

19. Eric Rosenfeld, interview with the author, April 16, 2009. Echoing Rosenfeld, Louis Bacon recalls, "I grew my hedge fund within Lehman initially, and they were one of our closest counterparties, physically as well, since their headquarters was thirty paces from ours. Watching Lehman go under produced a foreboding nausea that was for me the financial equivalent of the horror of watching the World Trade Center go under, which I could also see clearly burning from my office. (I had worked for two years on the 102nd floor of Tower 2 for Shearson/Lehman, by the way.) It was not just the cold-sweat fear for the initial victims and your own safety, it was the instantaneous recognition that an entire American protective edifice had collapsed and that a longer-term downfall was inevitable." Louis Bacon, interview with the author, July 21, 2009.

20. Jones says of the $100 million trapped in Lehman, "We actually tried to get out on the Wednesday before. They were supposed to wire it out on Friday. They did not, so we were one day late on that." Jones interview.

21. The precise magnitude of Tudor's losses is unknown, but traders at other firms estimate that emerging-market loans fell by at least two thirds, and given that the portfolio was leveraged, Tudor's $2 billion presumably fell by more than that. Meanwhile, Paul Jones explains, "What I missed was the tail risk associated with something that for the prior eight years our manager had risk managed through in an excellent fashion. And also something that all of a sudden took on characteristics that heretofore it had never taken on, which was one hundred percent correlation with the U.S. stock market." Jones interview.

22. Jones interview. Jones adds, "What I was thinking was here's a guy who prides himself on being able to be liquid in relatively short order, and yet I had forty percent of our fund exposed to a strategy where liquidity had conveniently, totally disappeared."

23. Jones interview. Jones adds, "I guess it gets back to this old saying that my grandfather, who was a Depression baby, told me. He said, 'You're only as wealthy as what you can write a check for tomorrow morning.' I never understood it when he told that to me. I was really, really young—I was in my teens when he told that to me. I understood it for the first time last October when I saw the whole world crashing and when I saw within our BVI fund a variety of illiquid investments that we could not exit. I thought, 'Oh my God. I know exactly where that statement came from and what it means now.' And I will never ever violate that again."

24. Jones interview. The end-year losses would have been substantially larger without offsetting gains from macro trading.

25. James B. Stewart, "Eight Days: The Battle to Save the American Financial System," *New Yorker*, September 21, 2009, p. 74.

26. In 2006 Citadel reported in its bond-offering documents that its leverage was thirteen to one. By mid 2008, the ratio had fallen to eleven to one, according to Citadel officials.

27. Daniel Dufresne, Citadel's treasurer, affirms, "One reason why markets targeted us was we were the only hedge fund that had a credit-derivatives market active in our name because we had issued debt in 2006." Daniel Dufresne, interview with the author, June 30, 2009.

28. Ken Griffin, interview with the author, July 9, 2009.
29. Stewart, "Eight Days," p. 78.
30. Sorkin, *Too Big to Fail*, p. 438.
31. Steve Galbraith, "A September to Remember (Even if we would like to Forget)," Maverick Capital Management, letter to investors, October 9, 2008.
32. The convertible portfolio was losing money even before the short-selling ban. Lehman's failure triggered the fire sale of an estimated $2 billion of convertible bonds, which hit Citadel's holdings. But the short ban was an additional blow.
33. By way of illustration, Ken Griffin recalls, "We took all our energy derivatives and said, 'Guys, we don't want to face you. We want to face the clearinghouse instead, so let's transfer all the OTC positions we have to cleared positions. Let's reduce our bilateral exposure.'" Griffin interview.
34. This is the exchange as recalled by James Forese. James Forese, interview with the author, June 25, 2009. See also Marcia Vickers and Roddy Boyd, "Citadel Under Siege," *Fortune*, December 9, 2008.
35. This passage is based on interviews with Ken Griffin, Gerald Beeson, Adam Cooper, Dan Dufresne, and Katie Spring of Citadel.
36. Loch Adamson, "Rethinking Chris Hohn," *Alpha*, October 2008.
37. "Hedge Funds and the Financial Market." Hearing of House Oversight and Government Reform Committee, Panel II, 110th Congress, Session 2, November 13, 2008.

CONCLUSION: SCARIER THAN WHAT?

1. The account of the Douglas Aircraft episode is based primarily on research in the SEC archive by Chad Waryas of the Council on Foreign Relations. See "In the Matter of Investors' Management Co. Inc." Administrative Proceedings, file no. 3-1680. Securities Exchange Act Release no. 8947, Investment Advisers Act Release no. 268, July 30, 1970.
2. Brimberg appears as "Scarsdale Fats" in Adam Smith, *The Money Game* (New York: Vintage Books, 1976), pp. 190–91. Banks Adams, interview with the author, April 16, 2007.
3. "The State of Public Finances Cross-Country," IMF Staff Position Note, November 3, 2009. See in particular Tables 3 and 4. The numbers given for debt as a percentage of GDP come from the same publication.
4. Anna Fifield, "Obama in tough talk to 'fat cat' bankers," *The Financial Times*, December 15, 2009, p. 2.
5. Piergiorgio Alessandri and Andrew Haldane, "Banking on the State," paper based on a presentation to the Federal Reserve Bank of Chicago, November 2009.
6. See Dean P. Foster and H. Peyton Young, "Hedge Fund Wizards," The Berkeley Electronic Press, January 2008.
7. See for example Russ Wermers, "Mutual Fund Performance: An Empirical Decomposition into Stock-Picking Talent, Style, Transactions Costs, and Expenses," *Journal of Finance* 55, no.4, August 2000.
8. Roger G. Ibbotson, Peng Chen, and Kevin Zhu, "The A, B, Cs of Hedge Funds: Alphas, Betas, and Costs" (Yale working paper, 2010). An earlier version of this paper showing similar findings appeared in 2006.
9. The three studies finding these returns for private equity are: Steven N. Kaplan and Antoinette Schoar, "Private Equity Performance: Returns, Persistence, and Capital Flows," *Journal of Finance* 60, no. 4 (August 2005); Jones, Charles, and Matthew Rhodes-Kropf, "The Price of Diversifiable Risk in Venture Capital and Private Equity" (working paper, Columbia University, 2003); Alexander Ljungqvist and Matthew Richardson, "The Cash Flow, Return, and Risk Characteristics of Private Equity" (NYU Stern Working Paper Series, 2003). On the returns of buyout funds, Jones and Rhodes-Kropf estimate annual alpha of 0.72 percent per year, while Kaplan and Schoar are more negative. Ljungqvist and Richardson find stronger alpha for buyout funds, possibly because they focus on funds that were raised in the 1980s, when returns were higher.

10. Paul Tudor Jones II interview with Stephen Taub, "Alpha Hall of Fame," *Alpha,* June 2008, p. 66.

APPENDIX I: DO THE TIGER FUNDS GENERATE ALPHA?

1. This S&P 500 return excludes dividends. Including them would bring the return up to about 15 percent per year, not a material difference.
2. For this phrase and for many of the calculations in this appendix, I am indebted to my Council on Foreign Relations colleague Paul Swartz.
3. The Tiger Cub index fell 14.8 percent in the last four months of 2008. This was a lot less awful than the market index, which was down 29.6 percent.

INDEX

Page numbers in *italics* refer to tables.

Griffin, John, 120–24, 261
Griffin, Ken, 3, 4, 308–9, 318–21, 337–40, 342, 363, 366–70, 458*n*, 462*n*
Grisham, John, 304
gross domestic product (GDP), 11, 212, 376, 432*n*, 462*n*
growth stocks, 8–9, 42, 43, 346

Haghani, Victor, 447*n*
Hakala, Diane, 258, 263
Hall, Katie, 450*n*
Halliburton, 282
Harbinger Capital, 353, 371
Harrington, Michael, 35
Harvard University, 32, 79, 96, 339
endowment of, 338, 340, 384
Haussmann Holdings, 257
Hawkins, Greg, 226
Hayek, Friedrich, 83
Hayman Capital, 324, 325, 458*n*
hedged fund:
use of term, 36, 413*n*
see also A. W. Jones
hedge-fund managers, 4–5, 32, 87, 372
earnings of, 3
reasons for success of, 6, 408*n*
Hedge Fund Research, 332–33, 353, 451*n*, 457*n*
hedge funds:
activism of, 353–54, 371
banks compared with, 12–13, 333–37, 355, 381–82, 409*n*
client money returned by, 191, 439*n*–40*n*
dangerous and excessive power of, 171, 187–88, 206, 350
as edge funds, 5–6
encouraging of, 380–81
end of first era of, 40–41
Great Moderation and, 9, 11
as heroes vs. villains, 10, 25–26, 107–8, 322
independence of, 13
marking portfolios to market by, 13, 409*n*
in 1994, 9–10, 11, 191
number of, 36, 41, 130, 174, 307, 390, 413*n*, 414*n*, 429*n*, 437*n*
paranoia and focus of, 12–13
range of investment styles developed by, 192
regulation and, 187–92, 244–47, 322, 355, 381, 385–91, 453*n*
rich individuals vs. endowments as contributors to, 8, 274
secrecy of, 29–31, 256, 288, 291, 294, 303, 322, 449*n*, 454*n*
in skirmishes with academic views of the market, 5–8
as small enough to fail, 376, 380
social function of, 8–9, 25–26, 265–66
traditional investing compared with, 23–25
use of term, 36, 413*n*

as vehicles for loners and contrarians, 4, 44–47, 386, 387
volume of money in, 15
weakness in, 101
Heffernan, Mark, 295–98
Hemingway, Ernest, 1, 18
Hennessee Group, 396–97
Hennessee Tiger Index, 396–97, *398–99*
Henry, John W., 429*n*
Henry, Peter, 440*n*–41*n*
Herrlinger, P. David, 95
HFR index, 273
Highbridge Capital, 344
High-Risk Opportunities, 234
Hilibrand, Larry, 221–24, 229, 236
Hitler, Adolf, 18, 154
Hohn, Chris, 353–54, 371
home prices, 327, 328, 329, 331, 386
Homo economicus, 107
Hong Kong, 92, 98, 100, 122, 277
Bank of China building in, 220
British ceding of, 206
Soros at meetings in, 207, 208, 442*n*
Hostetter, Amos, 71, 420*n*, 421*n*
household debt, 11, 327
House of Representatives, U.S.:
Financial Services Committee of, 188–90, 244–47
Ways and Means Committee of, 425*n*
housing finance companies, 11, 355, 358, 379
HSBC, 331
Hungary, 83, 84, 102
Hunter, Brian, 311–16, 318, 360, 455*n*, 456*n*, 457*n*
Hurricane Andrew, 180
hurricane bonds, 239, 447*n*
"Hurricane Greenspan," 180
Hurricane Katrina, 313, 315
Hurricane Rita, 313, 315
Hurwitz, Harold, 409*n*, 410*n*

Ibbotson, Roger, 383
IBM, 45–46, 60–61, 106, 267, 303
translation and, 298–301
IMF, *see* International Monetary Fund
incentives, of banks vs. hedge funds, 334, 381–82
India, 376
Indofood, 276
Indonesia, 212, 215, 233
currency crisis in, 8, 207–9, 220, 276, 386, 387, 442*n*, 443*n*
Farallon in, 8, 275–79, 282, 283, 387, 451*n*
inefficient-markets theory, 6–8, 10, 54, 60, 107–8, 409*n*
inflation, 40, 43, 50, 51, 60, 76, 102, 179, 185, 187, 331, 332
budget deficits and, 151, 154
commodities markets and, 131

PHOTO CREDITS

ABOUT THE AUTHOR

Sebastian Mallaby is the Paul Volcker Senior Fellow in International Economics at the Council on Foreign Relations and a *Washington Post* columnist. He spent thirteen years at *The Economist* magazine, covering international finance in London and serving as the bureau chief in southern Africa, Japan, and Washington. He spent eight years on the editorial board of *The Washington Post*, focusing on globalization and political economy. His previous books are *The World's Banker* (2004), which was named as an editor's choice by *The New York Times*, and *After Apartheid* (1992), which was a *New York Times* notable book.